macromedia

Studio 8
STEP-BY-STEP

Projects for Macromedia Flash® 8,
Dreamweaver® 8, Fireworks® 8, and Contribute™ 3

THOMSON

COURSE TECHNOLOGY

Australia • Canada • Mexico • Singapore • Spain • United Kingdom • United States

Studio 8 Step-by-Step
Projects for Macromedia Flash® 8, Dreamweaver® 8,
Fireworks® 8, and Contribute™ 3

Executive Director, Learning Solutions
Nicole Jones Pinard

Senior Acquisitions Editor
Jane Mazares

Product Manager
Jodi Anderson

Editorial Assistant
Jeannine Lawless

Senior Marketing Manager
Kim Ryttel

Editor
Anuja Dharkar

Program Manager, Curriculum and Content Team
Maryann Amado

Development
Custom Editorial Productions, Inc.

Director of Production
Patty Stephan

Production Editor
GEX Publishing Services

Senior Manufacturing Coordinator
Justin Palmeiro

Cover Design
Steve Deschene

Compositor
GEX Publishing Services

TABLE OF CONTENTS

UNIT 1   MACROMEDIA DREAMWEAVER 8

UNIT 2   MACROMEDIA FIREWORKS 8

UNIT 3   MACROMEDIA FLASH 8

UNIT 4   MACROMEDIA CONTRIBUTE 3

Acknowledgments

EDITOR:

Anuja Dharkar

AUTHORS:

Dreamweaver 8: Skip Pickle

Fireworks 8: Anuja Dharkar and Dale Underwood

Flash 8: Scott Tapley

Contribute 3: Jay Heins

COPYEDITOR AND CONTENT CONTRIBUTORS:

Malinda McCain, Cathy DeHeer, and Judy Ziajka

TECHNICAL REVIEWER:

Jen DeHaan

PROJECT MANAGER:

Maryann Amado

Adobe, formerly Macromedia, would like to thank Rose Marie Kuebbing, and the rest of the team at Custom Editorial Productions, Inc. for managing the editing, development, and production of this book. Thanks also to the team at Course Technology, namely Jodi Anderson, and to the production house, GEX Publishing Services.

How to Use This Book

What makes a good text about Web authoring applications? Sound instruction and hands-on skill-building and reinforcement. That is what you will find in *Macromedia Studio Studio 8 Step-by-Step*. Not only will you find a colorful and inviting layout, but also many features to enhance learning.

Objectives— Objectives are listed at the beginning of each lesson. This allows you to look ahead to what you will be learning.

Step-by-Step Exercises— Preceded by a short topic discussion, these exercises are the "hands-on practice" part of the lesson. Simply follow the steps, either using a data file or creating a file from scratch. Each lesson is a series of these step-by-step exercises.

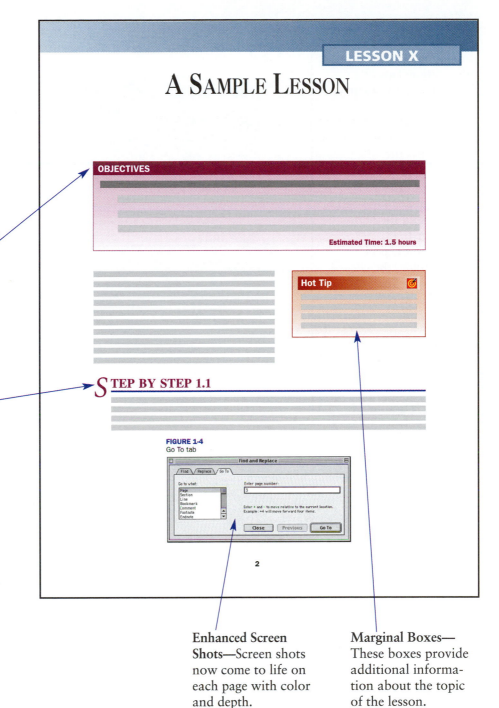

LESSON X

A SAMPLE LESSON

OBJECTIVES

Estimated Time: 1.5 hours

Hot Tip

STEP BY STEP 1.1

FIGURE 1-4
Go To tab

2

Enhanced Screen Shots— Screen shots now come to life on each page with color and depth.

Marginal Boxes— These boxes provide additional information about the topic of the lesson.

How to Use This Book

Special Feature Boxes—These boxes provide two types of information Tips & Techniques and Learn More. Tips & Techniques cover best practices or guidelines for specific techniques used for completing tasks. Learn More helps student build further knowledge that would help them in understanding the arena of web design/development, rich media design/development, or graphic design/development.

Summary—At the end of each lesson, you will find a summary to prepare you to complete the end-of-lesson activities.

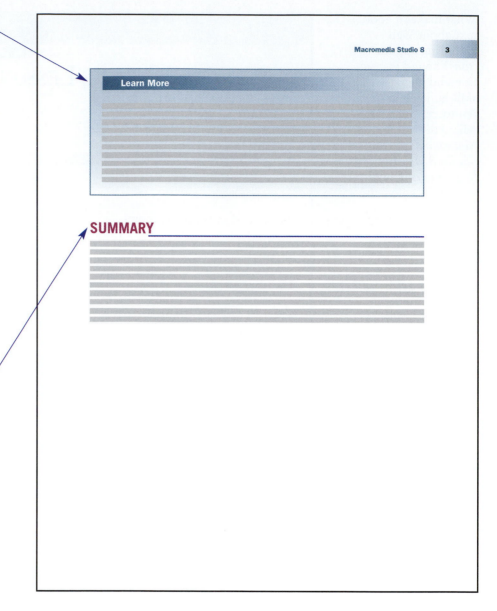

GUIDE FOR USING THIS BOOK

Please read this Guide before starting work. The time you spend now will save you much more time later and will make your learning faster, easier, and more pleasant.

Conventions

The different type styles used in this book have special meanings. They will save you time because you will soon automatically recognize from the type style the nature of the text you are reading and what you will do.

WHAT YOU WILL DO	TYPE STYLE	EXAMPLE
Text you will key	**Bold**	Key **Don't litter** rapidly.
Commands you will select	**Bold**	Click **File, Open**
Individual keys you will press	**Bold**	Press **Enter** to insert a blank line.
WHAT YOU WILL SEE	**TYPE STYLE**	**EXAMPLE**
Filenames in book	**Bold upper and lowercase**	Open **Diving.htm** from the data files.
Glossary terms in book	***Bold and italics***	The ***menu bar*** contains menu titles.
Words on screen	*Italics*	Highlight the word *pencil* on the screen.
Menus and commands	**Bold**	Choose **Open** from the **File** menu.
Options/features with long names	*Italics*	Select Normal from the *Style for following paragraph* text box.

Student Files

All data files necessary for this book are located on the *Review Pack* CD-ROM supplied with this text. These data files are also available on the Course Technology Web site; go to *www.course.com* and select Student Downloads.

Instructor Resources CD-ROM

The *Instructor Resources* CD-ROM contains a wealth of instructional material you can use to prepare for teaching this course. The CD-ROM stores the following information:

- Both the data and solution files for this course.

- ExamView® tests for each lesson. ExamView is a powerful testing software package that allows instructors to create and administer printed, computer (LAN-based), and Internet exams. ExamView includes hundreds of questions that correspond to the topics covered in this text, enabling learners to generate detailed study guides that include page references for further review. The computer-based and Internet testing components allow learners to take exams at their computers, and also save the instructor time by grading each exam automatically.

- Electronic *Instructor's Manual* that includes lecture notes for each project and references to the solutions for Step-by-Step exercises.

- Copies of the figures that appear in the student text, which can be used to prepare transparencies.

- PowerPoint presentations outlining features for each project in the text.

START-UP CHECKLIST

Macromedia Flash® 8 (Authoring)

Microsoft Windows

- ✓ 800 MHz Intel Pentium III processor or equivalent
- ✓ Microsoft Windows 2000, or XP
- ✓ 256 MB of free available system RAM (1GB recommended to run more than one Studio 8 product simultaneously)
- ✓ 710 MB of available disk space

Apple Macintosh

- ✓ 600 MHz Power PC G3 processor or better
- ✓ Apple Mac OS X 10.3, 10.4
- ✓ 256 MB of free available system RAM (1 GB recommended to run more than one Studio 8 product simultaneously)
- ✓ 360 MB of available disk space

Macromedia Flash® 8 (Playback)

Microsoft Windows

PLATFORM	BROWSER
Microsoft Windows 98	Internet Explorer 5.5, Netscape Navigator 4.7 or Netscape Navigator 7.x, Firefox 1.x, Mozilla 1.x, AOL 9, and Opera 7.11
Windows Me	Internet Explorer 5.5, Netscape Navigator 4.7, Netscape Navigator 7.x, Firefox 1.x, Mozilla 1.x, AOL 9, and Opera 7.11
Windows 2000	Internet Explorer 5.x, Netscape Navigator 4.7, Netscape Navigator 7.x, Firefox 1.x, Mozilla 1.x, CompuServe 7, AOL 9, and Opera 7.11
Microsoft Windows XP	Internet Explorer 6.0, Netscape Navigator 7.x, Firefox 1.x, Mozilla 1.x, CompuServe 7, AOL 9, and Opera 7.11

Apple Macintosh

PLATFORM	BROWSER
Mac OS X 10.1.x or Mac OS X 10.2.x	Internet Explorer 5.2, Netscape Navigator 7.x, Firefox 1.x, Mozilla 1.x, AOL for OS X, Opera 6, and Safari 1.0 (Mac OS X 10.2.x only)

Macromedia Dreamweaver® 8

Microsoft Windows

- ✓ 800 MHz Intel Pentium III processor or equivalent
- ✓ Microsoft Windows 2000, XP
- ✓ 256 MB of available RAM (1 GB recommended to run more than one Studio 8 product simultaneously)
- ✓ 650 MB of available disk space

Apple Macintosh

- ✓ 600 MHz Power PC G3 processor or better
- ✓ Apple Mac OS X 10.3, 10.4
- ✓ 256 MB of available RAM (1 GB recommended to run more than one Studio 8 product simultaneously)
- ✓ 300 MB of available disk space

Macromedia Fireworks® 8

Microsoft Windows

- ✓ 800 MHz Intel Pentium III processor or equivalent
- ✓ Microsoft Windows 2000 or XP
- ✓ 256 MB of free available system RAM (1 GB recommended to run more than one Studio 8 product simultaneously)
- ✓ 880 MB of available disk space

Apple Macintosh

- ✓ 600 MHz Power PC G3 processor or better
- ✓ Apple Mac OS X 10.3, 10.4
- ✓ 256 MB of available RAM (1 GB recommended to run more than one Studio 8 product simultaneously)
- ✓ 320 MB of available disk space

Macromedia Contribute™ 3

Microsoft Windows

- ✓ Intel Pentium II 300MHz+
- ✓ Microsoft Windows 98 SE, 2000, or XP
- ✓ 128 MB of free available system RAM
- ✓ 120 MB of available disk space
- ✓ Internet Explorer 5.0 or compatible

Apple Macintosh

- ✓ 500 MHz Apple Power Mac G3+
- ✓ Apple Mac OS 10.2.8 and later, or 10.3.4
- ✓ 128 MB of free available system RAM
- ✓ 120 MB of free hard disk space
- ✓ Internet Explorer 5.0 or compatible

PREFACE

Welcome to *Studio 8 Step-by-Step*. This course introduces you to the suite of Web, graphic, and rich media-authoring applications. It shows you how to use this suite to create appealing and cutting-edge digital communication. *Studio 8 Step-by-Step* is a project-based course in which you learn how to use the tools in Studio 8 while you build an understanding of the overall design and development process that is required for producing Web, graphic, and rich media communication. The overall process can be described as five stages: *Define, Structure, Design, Build and Test,* and *Launch*.

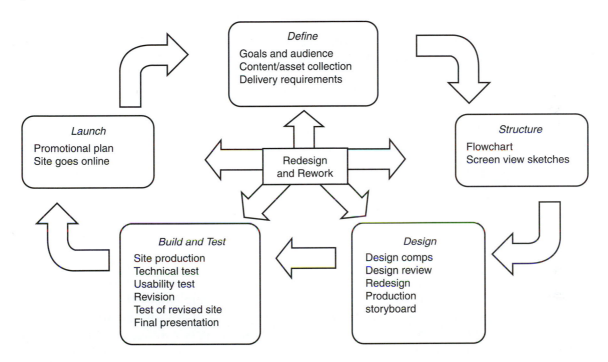

Define is the first stage of the process, in which you gather information from the client, including content, assets, and delivery requirements. Include these elements in a design document. *Structure* is the second stage, in which you construct a site flowchart and sketches of screen views; you may need to revisit the *Define* stage to build a complete flowchart. Next is the *Design* stage, in which you create compositions of a site, rich media elements, and storyboards. Building these elements further defines the site, graphic or rich media element and may involve returning to any of the previous stages when you need additional information. The fourth stage is *Build and Test*, in which you produce the Web site, graphic or rich media element and test it against the design and technical requirements. The final stage is *Launch*, in which you make the site, graphic, or rich media element public and advertise it to increase the number of site visitors.

The projects in this course focus on the *Build and Test* stage, but along the way provide you with the tools produced in the *Define*, *Structure*, and *Design* stages. These tools consist of the assets required to build the projects, such as design documents, storyboards, and flowcharts. Each of these tools strengthens your insight into the project background and provides you with the information you need to build the projects.

In each unit you build different types of digital communication projects—such as a Web site for a bank, logos for a Web site, or a video gallery—using a particular application in Studio 8. The skills needed to create digital communication are more than just knowing the technology to build these projects. Digital communication skills in the context of the design and development process, using Web tools include four key skill areas:

- Project management and collaboration

- Design

- Research and communication

- Professional web-authoring tools

Although you focus on the production stage (*Build and Test*), these different skill areas are emphasized through text that supports the production steps. Each unit includes multiple projects which culminate in the production of a graphic, Web site, or rich media element. At the end of each project is a set of On Your Own activities to further practice the skills you learn.

Unit 1: Macromedia Dreamweaver® 8

Macromedia Dreamweaver 8 is a professional visual editor for creating and managing Web sites and Web pages. You can incorporate text, images, video, animation, and other media into a Web site. You can use Dreamweaver to visually design your Web page in the convenient Layout view, or you can use the robust text-editing features when you want to hand-code a Web page.

In this unit you build different projects that help you develop the skills to understand Web design as well as the technical skills you need to implement designs. In the Dreamweaver 8 projects, you build a personal Web site, implement the design for a bank Web site by using cascading style sheets, and perform tests to make sure a catering Web site is accessible and complete. Through the completion of these projects you learn the following skills to build Web communications:

- Follow a design document to create a small personal Web site.

- Follow a design document to create pages in a large commercial Web site.

- Implement designs by assembling page elements in Dreamweaver.

- Review and test a Web site.

- Manage Web files.

Unit 2: Macromedia Fireworks® 8

Macromedia Fireworks 8 is a graphics program used to create and edit sophisticated images for the Web. With Fireworks, you can quickly create new images and manipulate existing images., You can create rollover buttons and navigation bars. You can use the optimization features in Fireworks to minimize the file size of your graphics without sacrificing quality. When you're ready, simply export the HTML code to your favorite editor, such as Macromedia Dreamweaver 8. The professional design tools in Fireworks even let you import digital camera files and scanned images, as well as files from popular image-editing programs and other graphics applications.

In this unit you build three projects that help you develop the skills to understand graphic design, as well as the technical skills to implement the designs. In the Fireworks 8 projects, you prepare photographs for use on a Web site, build a logo for a bank Web site, and build a page layout and navigation bar for a bank Web site. Through the completion of these projects you learn the following skills to build graphic communications:

- Follow a design document to prepare images for inclusion in a Web page.
- Run a batch process to prepare multiple images in one step.
- Use Web site specifications to draw logo images.
- Use Web site design criteria to define effects and blends.
- Integrate text and drawn images to generate a design described in Web site specifications.
- Use a Web site design document to generate a page comp and define elements of a navigation bar.
- Use a Web site design document to define colors and fonts of a page and a navigation bar.
- Generate and save a page comp.
- Build, optimize, and export a navigation bar for use in a Web site.

Unit 3: Macromedia Flash® 8 Professional

Macromedia Flash 8 is the professional-standard authoring tool for producing high-impact Web experiences. Although best known for its animated text and graphics, Macromedia Flash 8 is an excellent tool for producing advanced interactivity, rich content for mobile devices, and high quality video for Web sites.

In this unit you build three projects that help you understand rich media design, as well as develop the technical skills to implement the designs. In the Macromedia Flash 8 projects, you build an animated billboard to include on a film festival Web site, a digital narrative on the Paradise Beach Boardwalk, and a video gallery to include on a surf Web site. Through the completion of these projects you learn the following skills to build rich media communications:

- Follow a design document and storyboard to define the properties of an animated billboard.
- Draw and animate simple shapes and text to create an animated billboard for a Web site.
- Follow a design document and storyboard to produce an online documentary.

- Use Flash to simulate film-style techniques and effects that are used to tell a story.

- Create user-friendly navigation and features that provide ongoing feedback and put the audience in control of their online experience.

- Follow a design document and storyboard to produce an online gallery of video clips.

- Create Flash Video (FLV) files and prepare video for display on the Web.

- Implement methods for improving Flash performance by storing and accessing content outside the main FLA document.

- Ensure that your Flash documents are readable, usable, and accessible for the entire target audience.

Unit 4: Macromedia Contribute™ 3

Macromedia Contribute 3 makes Web publishing simple without in-depth knowledge of HTML. You can easily update content on Web sites, add images, and create links using familiar word-processing techniques. Many site designers use templates to design their Web sites, which allows you to focus on updating the content without having to worry about compromising the design or structure of a site.

In this unit, you complete two projects that help you build the skills you need to use Contribute for maintaining a Web site. You edit and update a course Web site and an electronic portfolio Web site. Both Web sites are based on templates and are designed to maintain a consistent look and feel. You learn to browse to the Web page you want to change, edit that page, and publish it. Through the completion of these projects you learn the following skills for Web maintenance and communication:

- Explore the Contribute interface and workflow process.

- Understand Web site connections.

- Edit existing content on a Web page.

- Add content and images to a Web page.

- Organize content on a Web page by using tables and lists.

- Link content to Web pages inside and outside a site.

- Build on a Web site by adding new pages and FlashPaper documents.

- Review and publish content on a Web page.

About Studio 8

People expect more from the Internet now—richer content and more dynamic applications. Whether you're a designer or developer, you need tools to work effortlessly and cost effectively while delivering the intuitive, effective experiences users demand. Studio 8 brings the power of Flash®, Dreamweaver®, Fireworks®, and Contribute™ together into one highly integrated and approachable solution—with everything you need to create the full spectrum of Internet solutions, from Web sites to Web applications and Rich Internet Applications.

MACROMEDIA DREAMWEAVER 8

MACROMEDIA DREAMWEAVER 8

IN THIS UNIT YOU WILL LEARN TO:

- Follow a design document to create a small personal Web site.

- Follow a design document to create pages in a large commercial Web site.

- Implement others' designs by assembling page elements in Dreamweaver.

- Learn collaboration techniques for working with others on a Web site.

- Verify that a Web site meets guidelines for best practices.

Summary

Macromedia Dreamweaver 8 is a visual editor used for creating Web pages. You can incorporate text, images, video, animation, and other media into a Web site.

In this unit you will build different projects that will help you develop the skills to understand Web design as well as the technical skills needed to implement the designs. To begin engaging in these projects you will first need to become familiar with Dreamweaver and planning Web sites.

Getting to Know Macromedia Dreamweaver 8

When you open Dreamweaver, you will notice a workspace area (where you can work in a Document window), the Insert bar above the workspace, the Property inspector below the workspace, and a group of panels to the right of the workspace, as shown in Figure 1. Use the Insert bar for adding objects such as images, tables, layers, or Macromedia Flash animations to the page. In the Property inspector, you can change the attributes of selected text or an object on the page. The panels enable you to modify elements of your page or to manage your site. You access the panels and the Property inspector from the Window menu.

FIGURE 1

The Dreamweaver workspace

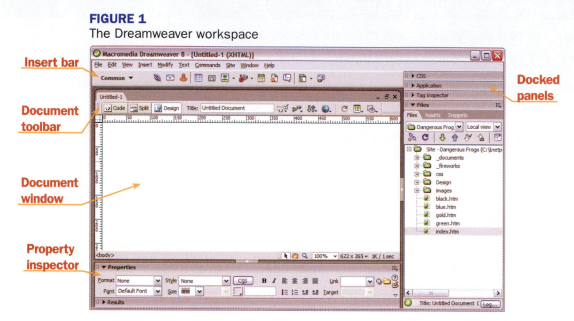

A check mark next to an item on the Window menu indicates the panel is open, but it could be hidden beneath another panel or the Document window. To display a hidden panel, select it again from the Window menu.

If a panel is selected but still does not appear, click the Window menu and then click Arrange Panels to reset all open panels to their default positions. The Insert bar moves to the upper left of the screen, the Property inspector moves to the bottom of the screen, and all other open panels move to the right of the screen, with no overlap.

The Document Window

You will do most of your work in the Document window. It gives you an approximate representation of your page as you add and delete elements. The title bar shows the document's title and filename. The Document toolbar lets you select the document view and enter the document title.

The Insert Bar

The Insert bar contains the objects or elements you want to add to your page, as shown in Figure 2. Among these are images, tables, special characters, forms, and frames. To insert an object, you can drag the object's icon from the Insert bar to its place in the Document window. Another method is to place the insertion point in your document where the object should appear and then click the object's icon on the bar. The object is then inserted into the document at the insertion point.

The Insert bar contains several categories, such as Common and Layout. The *Common category of the Insert bar* contains buttons for inserting the most commonly used objects. The Common category is shown in Figure 2 and described in Table 1.

FIGURE 2
The Common category of the Insert bar

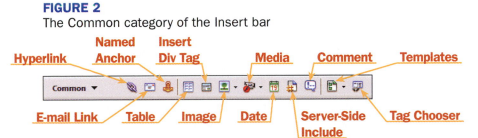

TABLE 1

Hyperlink	Insert a hypertext link.
Email Link	Insert a link to an e-mail address.
Named Anchor	Insert a link to a specific location on a page.
Table	Insert a table.
Images	Insert an image.
Media	Insert media objects, such as Flash, Shockwave, Applets, and ActiveX.
Date	Insert the current date, with an option for automatic updating when you save the document.
Comment	Insert a comment, which will not be displayed on your Web page.
Templates	Make a template based on the current document.
Tag Chooser	Insert an HTML tag.

The Layout Category of the Insert Bar

From the *Layout category of the Insert bar*, which is shown in Figure 3 and described in Table 2, you can insert tables and choose among three modes:

- *Standard mode* displays tables as a grid of lines.

- *Expanded Tables mode* adds cell padding and spacing to tables and increases table borders to make editing easier.

- *Layout mode* displays tables as boxes you can draw, drag, and resize.

FIGURE 3
The Layout category of the Insert bar

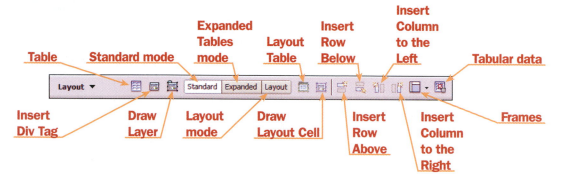

TABLE 2

Table	Insert a table.
Insert Div Tag	Insert a div tag to create a content block.
Draw Layer	Insert a layer to hold content at any location on a page.
Layout Table	Draw a whole table with cells to hold information or objects.
Draw Layout Cell	Draw individual cells in a table.
Insert Row Above	Insert a row above the current row in a table.
Insert Row Below	Insert a row below the current row.
Insert Column to the Left	Insert a column to the left of the current column.
Insert Column to the Right	Insert a column to the right of the current column.
Frames	Insert a frame.
Tabular Data	Insert tabular data, such as from a spreadsheet.

The Property Inspector

The Property inspector allows you to view and change the attributes of an object. The inspector is context sensitive—it relates to whatever you have selected in the Document window.

Depending on the selected object, there might be additional properties that are not visible. To view all of the properties, click the expander arrow in the lower-right corner of the inspector.

Figure 4 shows the expanded Property inspector as it appears when you are working with text.

FIGURE 4
The Property inspector

Dockable Panels

By default, Dreamweaver panels are docked in collapsible groups in the docking area on the right side of the workspace. This maximizes your screen area while giving you quick access to the panels you need.

You will also notice that the Document window and the panels snap to each other or to the sides of your screen. This helps you better manage your workspace.

To undock or move a panel group or individual panel, drag the gripper on the upper-left corner of the panel group as shown in Figure 5. Drag the panel group away from the panel docking area on the right side of the screen.

FIGURE 5
The Files panel group

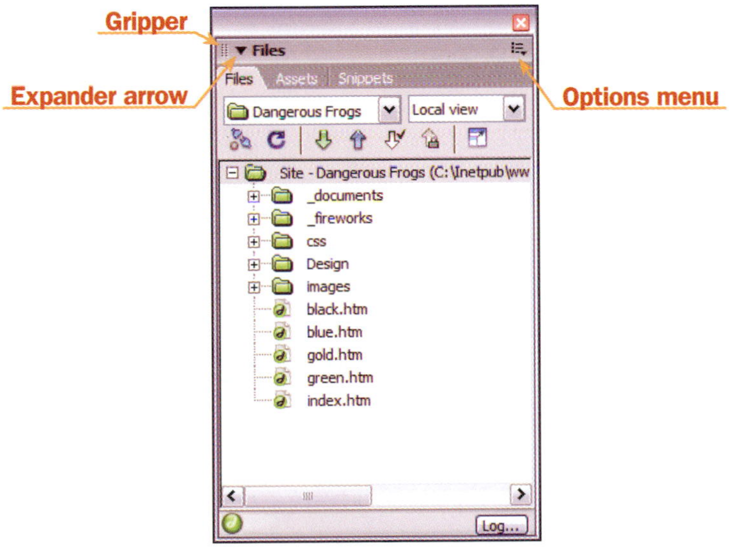

Gripper

Expander arrow   Options menu

To collapse or expand a panel group or panel, do one of the following:

- Click the title of the panel group or panel. (The title bar is visible even when the panel group or panel is collapsed.)

- Click the expander arrow in the upper-left corner of the panel group or panel.

Renaming a Panel Group

To change the name of a panel group, click the Options menu, the icon at the upper-right of the panel group, and choose Rename Panel Group. Enter the new name in the dialog box and then click OK. This is most useful if you decide to reorganize the panels or set up your own panel groups.

Hiding All Panels and the Property Inspector

If you find there are panels you do not use often or at all, you can close them so there is less clutter on your screen and so you can more easily see and access the panels you do use. To close an entire panel group, select Close Panel Group from the Options menu for that panel group. You can also choose to hide all the panels and the Property inspector by choosing Hide Panels from the View menu. This allows you a full-screen view of your document.

To view hidden panels, select Show Panels from the View menu. Panels that are closed when you choose Hide Panels remain closed when you show the panels again.

Specifying Preview Browsers

As you develop your Web pages, you will want to view your efforts in a browser—or in fact, in several browsers. In the Preferences dialog box, shown in Figure 6, you can specify which browsers you would like to use to preview your pages. Click the plus (+) button to add a browser to the list. When the dialog box opens, find the browser application.

FIGURE 6
The Preferences dialog box for Preview in Browser

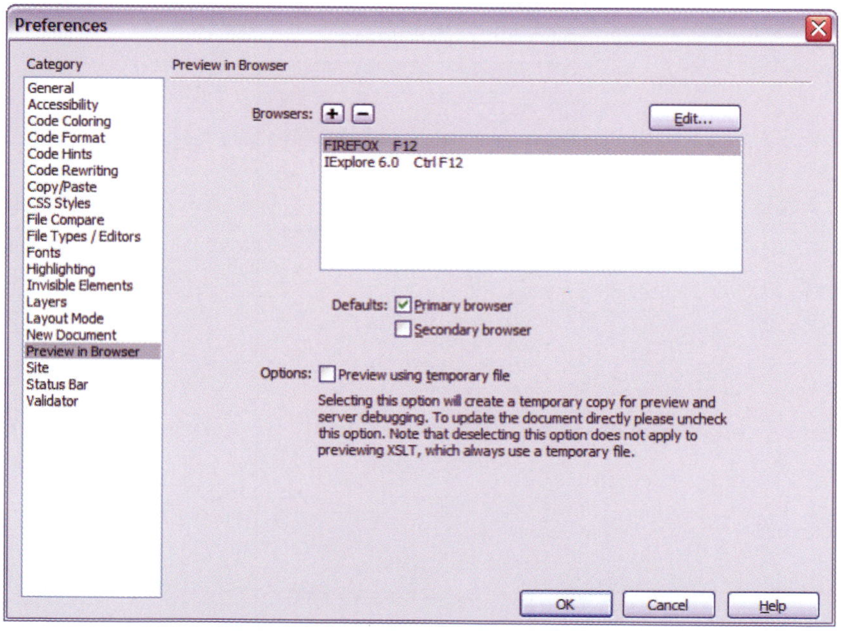

Select the primary browser by highlighting it in the list and then selecting the Primary Browser check box. You will select the secondary browser in the same fashion. These selections allow you to utilize the keyboard shortcuts Dreamweaver has made available to simplify the preview process. To view a page in the primary browser, press the F12 key on the keyboard (Windows) or

Option + F12 (Macintosh). To view a page in the secondary browser, press Ctrl + F12 (Windows) or Command + F12 (Macintosh). You'll be using these shortcuts often, so memorize them quickly. You can also access the preview through the Preview/Debug in Browser button on the toolbar and then selecting from the list the browser in which you want to view your work.

To remove a browser from the list, click the Preview/Debug in Browser button, click the Edit Browser List, select the browser name in the list and then click the minus (–) button. To change a browser choice, select the browser name in the list. Then click Edit and locate a different browser.

 ## Selecting Preview Browsers

1. Click **Edit** on the menu bar and then click **Preferences** (Windows), or click **Dreamweaver** on the menu bar and then click **Preferences** (Macintosh). Select **Preview in Browser** from the Category list on the left.

2. Click a browser name in the window on the right to identify whether it's a primary or secondary browser, or neither.

3. Follow the directions of your instructor or technical support personnel for adding any browsers and for setting the primary and secondary browsers.

4. Click **OK** when you finish adding or changing browsers.

> **Hot Tip**
>
> You can also access the Browser Preferences dialog box from the File menu: point to **Preview in Browser** and then click **Edit Browser List**. Or you can click the **Preview/Debug in Browser** button on the toolbar and then click **Edit Browser List**.

Setting Project Requirements

Every successful development project goes through a number of phases:

1. Planning and analyzing
2. Designing
3. Building
4. Testing
5. Implementing or launching

When designers plan a Web site, they consider a number of things:

- The information they want to share
- The various kinds of content they have
- The way information groups under headings

This information provides a number of ways to organize a site. When designing the site, designers make decisions about look and feel as well as usability. They consider:

- The fonts and colors they will use for page headings and for section headings

- The height and width they want as the dimensions for images

- The number of visitors they imagine will navigate the site

- The way visitors will know where they are in the site, and how visitors will return to the home page after they link to a page deep in the site—or to any page that is not the home page

Audience considerations are also integral to understanding the usability restrictions designers have. Some things they consider are the audience's:

- Age

- Gender

- Race

- Level of education

- Occupation

- Computer literacy

- Content expectations (that is, the type of information the audience will look for)

- Physical limitations, such as visual or motor impairments (for additional information, see the Tips & Techniques feature "Accessibility")

Designers also consider how the quality of the content will appear to people who come across the site but who are not the target audience.

Designers take into account the technical limitations visitors may encounter (for additional information, see the Tips & Techniques feature "Platform Considerations"). Large file sizes will make the site seem slow. Use of rich media such as Web applications, animations, or video may require plug-ins visitors have to download before they can view the site. Not all browsers display a Web page the same way. By planning ahead, designers reduce the difficulties visitors may encounter.

As designers and developers build each element of a site, they are deliberate in testing the element both in isolation and as a part of the whole site. As much as possible, they use different types of browsers and different connection speeds to test the site so they can duplicate the experience of as many different visitors as possible. They run these tests themselves, but it is even more important to have other people test the site. They then examine visitor feedback objectively. After all the hard work, it may be tempting to dismiss any comments that cause them to revisit earlier decisions, but such comments can lead to important improvements to the site.

You may want to jump right in and start creating Web pages. However, by taking the time to use pencil and paper to sketch out your layout and organize your content on mock Web pages, you will have a much clearer sense of the project and a much more predictable goal as a result.

Accessibility

In Web development, ***accessibility*** refers to a person's ability to use a Web site. Individuals with disabilities face a number of obstacles when accessing the Web. Designers can do much to avoid creating these obstacles. Some solutions are relatively simple to implement; others require a bit more thought and effort. When it comes to Web accessibility, think in terms of three types of impairments: visual, motor, and auditory.

People with visual impairment may not be able to see the computer screen at all, and they may rely on a screen reader to read the text to them. Or they may need to enlarge the text on the screen in order to read it. People with color blindness may have difficulty reading text when the color of the text does not contrast sufficiently with the color of the background behind it.

People with motor impairment may be unable to use a mouse. Instead, they may rely on some version of the Tab key to navigate their way through a page. (On most computers, pressing the Tab key moves the cursor or focus from one element on the page to the next. Pressing the spacebar activates elements such as links or buttons.)

Until recently, auditory impairment did not have much effect on a person's Web experience. However, in recent years, sound has become more common in video and rich media for communicating significant information. Providing a caption or other text equivalent is helpful when you use sound to communicate information on the Web.

Accessibility standards help Web designers identify and address these issues. Two such standards are Section 508 of the Federal Rehabilitations Act and the Web Content Accessibility Guidelines from the World Wide Web Consortium.

For many people with disabilities, the Web serves as an important access point to information and services, particularly from the government. Dreamweaver assists you in creating accessible pages that contain useful content for screen readers and comply with government guidelines. As you work in Dreamweaver, dialog boxes prompt you to enter accessibility attributes when you insert page elements. For example, the Accessibility dialog box for images reminds you to add text equivalents for graphics. Then, when the image appears on a page for a visitor with visual disabilities, the screen reader reads the description.

Remember that no authoring tool can automate the development process. Designing accessible Web sites requires you to understand accessibility requirements and make many subjective decisions about how visitors with disabilities interact with Web pages. The best way to ensure a Web site is accessible is through deliberate planning, development, testing, and evaluation.

Making a Web site accessible ultimately benefits a much larger number of people than just those in the target group. Making the Web easier to use overall makes it easier for everyone.

Macromedia Dreamweaver 8 Projects

This unit contains three projects that will help you build your skills in recognizing Web design decisions and building Web sites.

Project 1: Personal Web Site

You build a small Web site dedicated to Dangerous Frogs. The site shares scientific information and images. You learn how to define a Web site in Dreamweaver, how to structure a page, and how to add content and links to a page.

Project 2: Bank Web Site

This project finds you playing the role of a Web developer on a team responsible for the Experience Bank Web site. You work with HTML tables, Cascading Style Sheets, and Dreamweaver templates, learning to incorporate consistency on a large Web site.

Project 3: Local Caterer Web Site

Cafe Townsend has asked you to maintain and improve its Web site. Over the course of this project, you learn about ways to test a Web site, as well as how to manage the various files that make up a Web site.

Tips & Techniques

Platform Considerations

One of the goals professional Web developers strive for is consistency across the user experience. But that can be difficult to achieve. A visitor may come to your site by using a Windows computer, a Macintosh, or a Linux-based machine. The visitor may be using Internet Explorer, Safari, Firefox, Opera, or some other browser, and each of those browsers has several versions still in common use. And beyond that, the visitor may have a pop-up blocker or plug-in blocker installed, may have JavaScript turned off, may not be accepting cookies or may be behind a firewall—the number of possible configurations is overwhelming.

Fonts and colors are slightly different on a Macintosh than on a Windows machine. Internet Explorer does not display CSS div tags quite the way Mozilla Firefox does. From one browser to another, table borders and horizontal rules are displayed slightly differently.

The long and short of it is that you can not always tell what the visitor will see. Cascading Style Sheets can help with this, but not always, since not all browsers implement CSS the same way.

As you gain experience as a Web developer, you can do two things to minimize the impact of all these variations. The first is to test your site by using as many different configurations as possible. The more you see, the more you will be able to anticipate.

The second is to separate the content of your page from its design as much as possible. At first, this may be difficult. As you learn more about CSS, you'll discover new ways to do this. We'll touch on CSS only a little bit here—you need to learn other things first. For now, keep your page simple and keep your page layout loose.

PERSONAL WEB SITE

GOAL

- Follow a design document to create a small personal Web site.

TECHNICAL SKILLS

- Define a new Web site in Dreamweaver.
- Create a new Web page and set its document properties.
- Create and format text.
- Use heading styles and lists.
- Create a new style sheet.
- Add images to a Web page and set the image properties.
- Edit an image from within Dreamweaver.
- Create an image map.
- Use hyperlinks to connect documents.

Estimated time to complete this project: 4 hours, 20 minutes

Summary

A Web site is a collection of documents that display text, images, and other media elements. Web sites can range from personal and simple, conveying information about a specific topic, to huge, serving as virtual stores or marketing tools for businesses. The Web is a good medium for self-publication, allowing individuals to present their information at Web sites designed to suit their particular needs.

The Assignment

In this project, you use Macromedia Dreamweaver to produce a personal Web site describing frogs that use poison as a defense mechanism. The site consists of a home page, shown in Figure 1, that gives an overview of the topic, and four other pages that provide details about particular species of frogs. Although for a personal Web site you would need to start by creating a design document, flowchart, and storyboards, for the purposes of this project the design phase has already been completed, and the designer of this site has provided you with a design document, flowchart, and storyboards for a home page and content pages. You will use these documents to:

- Set up your Web site

- Add and modify text

- Add and modify images

- Create links

FIGURE 1
Dangerous Frogs Web site

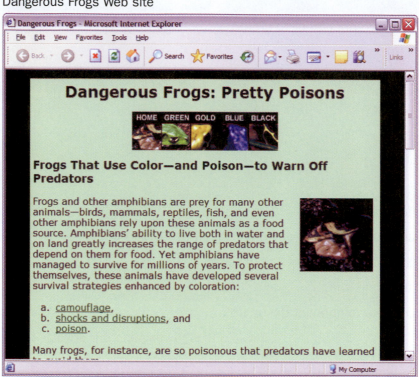

Web Site Design Document

Whenever you begin a Web site, you should first plan the site. Consider the information that the site will convey, what you want a visitor to do, and what technical limitations you may be up against. Because of the nature of Web site construction, the tasks will require a time commitment that is likely to extend over several days. Good planning (and good notes about your planning) will help you drive your project to completion.

During this planning, you will be thinking about your intended audience, discovering where more research is needed, determining what design decisions need to be made, and creating a checklist of assets (files such as images, movies, and text) you will use to build the site. The designer of the Dangerous Frogs Web site has already completed these planning steps and is providing you with the design document shown in Figure 2. You use the design document to:

- Determine the structure for your site

- Set document properties for your pages

- Import the necessary graphics and text
- Format the text using appropriate styles

FIGURE 2
Design document and flowchart for the Dangerous Frogs Web site

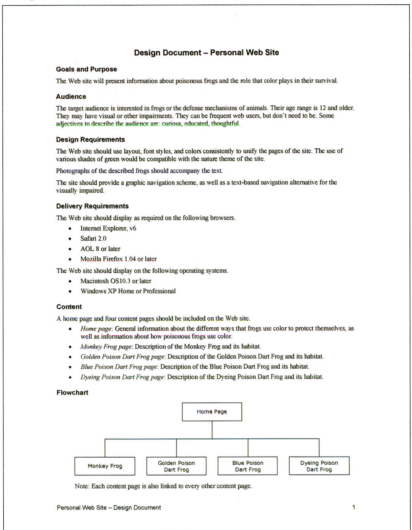

To print the design document for the Dangerous Frogs Web site, open the file named *DW_Project1_Design.pdf*. This file is located in the Design folder for this project.

Web Site Flowchart

You begin your planning by making notes or sketches. Drawing a site flowchart that shows each of your pages and their relationships to the others helps you make decisions about navigation and organization of content. You can quickly tell from the flowchart at the bottom of Figure 2 that the Dangerous Frogs Web site will consist of five pages: a home page and four pages dedicated to individual frogs.

Web Site Storyboards

Storyboards for a Web site lay out the information that the pages will contain. In your storyboards, you can sketch the layout for a typical page. You can write down colors you want to use, ideas about which content should go on which page, and thoughts about organization.

When you create a Web site, you likely will have common elements that appear on all the pages. For instance, the site navigation will probably be the same across the site, and you may have text at the bottom of each page, commonly known as a footer, including text-based navigation links, copyright information, or contact information. Instead of repeating all of these details on the specification sheet for each page, you can create a storyboard for the common elements of the content pages and describe these elements in detail on a single specification sheet.

Figure 3 shows the first page of the five-page storyboard for the Dangerous Frogs site.

Did You Know?

Once designers finish the design document, flowchart, and storyboards, they create a paper version of their site and have testers who fit the profile of the intended audience imagine that they are clicking through it to make sure that potential users can easily navigate the site.

FIGURE 3

First page of the storyboard for the Dangerous Frogs Web site

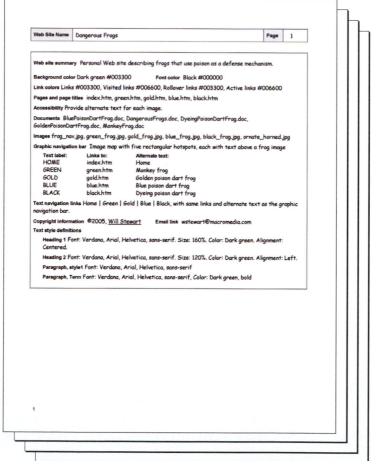

To print the storyboard for the Dangerous Frogs Web site, open the file named *DW_Project1_Storyboard.pdf*. This file is located in the Design folder for this project.

SETTING UP A WEB SITE

OBJECTIVES

Upon completion of this lesson, you will be able to:

- Create a site definition in Dreamweaver.

- Create a new Web page.

- Set document properties for a Web page.

Estimated time to complete this lesson: 30 minutes

Introduction

The requirements for the Dangerous Frogs Web site are defined in the design document, flowchart, and storyboards. Together, they will help you build the pages of the site. The best way to begin this project is to identify requirements from the design document that can be implemented as properties of the Dreamweaver document, such as page titles, background colors, overall text colors, and link colors.

Take a moment to review the design document and the flowchart. These documents are shown in Figure 2 and Figure 3. You may want to print them out before continuing.

Defining a Local Site

When you have created the Dangerous Frogs Web site, you will have a number of files that will need to be loaded to the Web server where the public can access them. It is good practice to keep all files relevant to a site in the same folder, using subfolders to organize the various types of content. After you define this main folder, it will be the root folder for your site, which is called your local site. This local site on your hard drive will mirror the actual pages on the Web server. The local site is where you do all your initial development and testing.

Note

Dreamweaver needs a properly defined site with a unique local root folder to maintain and update links between pages. When you upload a site, the relative links that worked within the local root will also work on the server. When you are ready to publish your site, all you have to do is copy that folder and all its files to the remote server. Assuming the images and links all work locally, they should work on the remote server as well.

If you connect a local site to a remote site, Dreamweaver maintains identical directory structures to ensure that links and references are not accidentally broken. If directories do not exist in the site where you are transferring files, Dreamweaver automatically creates them.

To set up a local site, create a folder on your hard drive. The name of the folder can be the name of the site or any name you choose. For example, in this project you have a folder called dangerous_frogs that contains all the files and folders you will use in this unit. All your files and subfolders are contained within this root folder.

Create a New Local Site

1. Using the file management tools on your system, copy the entire **dangerous_frogs** folder from the data files for this unit to the location where you will store your solution files (ask your instructor for specific directions).

2. Open Dreamweaver. Click **Site** on the menu bar and then click **Manage Sites**.

   If you have already defined at least one site in Dreamweaver (or a previous version of Dreamweaver), the Manage Sites dialog box opens, as shown in Figure 1-1. This dialog box lists all the sites you have previously defined and lets you create new ones. If you have not previously defined a site, the list will be empty, and many of the buttons will be inactive.

FIGURE 1-1
Manage Sites dialog box

3. Click the **New** button and then click **Site** to create a new site. The Site Definition dialog box opens. If the dialog box opens in Advanced mode, click the **Basic** tab to start the Site Definition Wizard, shown in Figure 1-2.

FIGURE 1-2
Site Definition Wizard

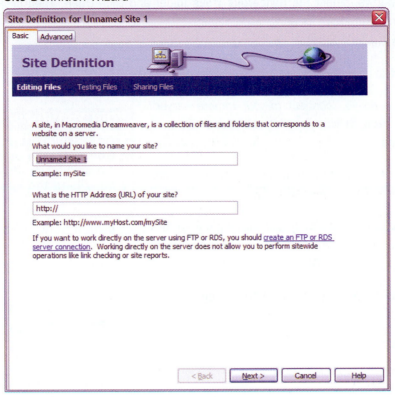

4. The wizard starts with *What would you like to name your site?* The name you assign to the site can be anything that identifies the site—this is for your reference only. Key **Dangerous Frogs**, followed by your initials, as the site name.

5. Click **Next** to move to the next step in the wizard.

6. Under *Do you want to work with a server technology such as ColdFusion, ASP.NET, ASP, JSP, or PHP?* click **No, I do not want to use a server technology**. Then click **Next**.

7. Under *How do you want to work with your files during development?* click **Edit local copies on my machine, then upload to server when ready (recommended)**. Later you will learn how to move your files to a remote Web server.

8. Under *Where on your computer do you want to store your files?* click the folder icon next to the text box.

The Local Root Folder text box specifies the folder on your hard drive where the files for this site are stored. It is the local equivalent of the site root folder at the remote site. Dreamweaver creates all site-root-relative links relative to the local root folder.

9. Locate your **dangerous_frogs** folder (the one you copied in step 1).

- For Windows, select the **dangerous_frogs** folder and click **Open**. Then click **Select** to use the dangerous_frogs folder as your root folder.
- For the Macintosh, select the **dangerous_frogs** folder and click **Choose**.

10. Click **Next** to move to the next step in the wizard.

11. Under *How do you connect to your remote server?* click the arrow to view the list of options and then select **None**.

12. Click **Next** to move to a summary of your site definition settings. Review your settings.

13. Click **Done** to finish defining your site. A message box may appear to notify you that the initial site cache will be created. If so, click **OK**.

14. Click **Done** to close the Manage Sites dialog box.

Creating Pages

Now that you have defined the Dangerous Frogs Web site in Dreamweaver, you need to create the pages for the site called for by the site flowchart, shown in Figure 1-3. The flowchart shows a home page and four content pages. You can generate these pages and then link them after they are created.

FIGURE 1-3
Site flowchart for the Dangerous Frogs Web site

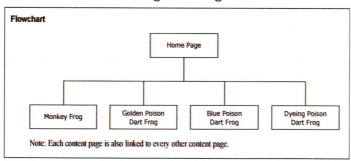

> ### Did You Know?
> Once you have defined a site, whenever you open Dreamweaver, it will automatically load the site information from the last site used. If you work in multiple sites, you can switch between them through the Files panel.

> ### Note
> Most Web sites are structured so that visitors first visit a home page for general information about the site or its contents. The home page then has links or navigation to allow easy access to other areas of the site. In some cases, the home page acts as a summary of the site. In other cases, it acts as a map, pointing visitors to one file or another, depending on what information they want to find. However a site is organized, visitors should be able to visit the home page to understand that organization quickly.

> ### Did You Know?
> From a technical standpoint, the home page typically is the page that visitors see if they simply type your site's domain into the address field of their browser, without knowing the addresses of specific pages (for additional information, see the Tips & Techniques feature "Default Pages").

Create a Home Page

1. In Dreamweaver, open the **Files** panel if necessary. Make sure that the Dangerous Frogs site you defined previously is selected.

2. Select the **Site** folder at the top of the Files panel.

3. Click the **Options** menu in the Files panel, point to **File,** and then click **New File.**
   A new file called "untitled.html" appears, located in the Site directory.

4. Rename the file **index.htm** (if necessary, click the name of the file to edit it). Then press **Enter** (Windows) or **Return** (Macintosh).

5. Following the site chart in Figure 1.3, create four other pages with the names **green.htm, gold.htm, blue.htm,** and **black.htm.**

   These five pages will encompass the entire Dangerous Frogs Web site.

Tips & Techniques

Default Pages

A Web address such as http://www.macromedia.com/ is called a Uniform Resource Locator, or URL. A URL is simply a means for identifying a file on a computer connected to the World Wide Web, called a Web server. If you know a file's URL, you can use it in your browser's address field. Your browser will then contact the other computer (in the example here, the computer located at www.macromedia.com) and request the file.

Of course, there are a lot of files on other computers, so the URL is often longer than just the name of the computer. For instance, the address http://www.macromedia.com/devnet/mx/dreamweaver/getting_started.html assumes that the computer hosting the Macromedia site has a directory (or folder) called "devnet" that contains a directory called "mx" that contains a directory called "dreamweaver" that contains a file called "getting_started.html."

Here is a question to consider: If all you type in the address field is the domain name of the site you are requesting (for instance, http://www.macromedia.com/), how does the Web server know which file to send you?

The answer is that most Web servers are configured to handle this situation. If a Web server receives a request for a directory that does not specify a filename, the typical Web server will look for any file named index.htm, index.html, default.htm, or default.html in the site root (the site root is the top-level directory of a domain). So when you type http://www.macromedia.com/ into the address field of your browser, what you see in the browser is actually http://www.macromedia.com/index.html.

Such a file is called a default page. It is always a good practice to create a default page whenever you create a new directory, and typically you will use this file as the main page of that directory.

Giving Your Page a Title

When users navigate to the Dangerous Frogs Web site, the title on the browser's title bar will identify what the page and site are about. Every HTML document should have a title. The title, used primarily for document identification, is displayed in a browser's title bar and as the bookmark name. Choose a short phrase that describes the document's purpose. The title can be of any length: you can crop it if it is too long to fit in the browser's title bar. On this site, the title "Dangerous Frogs" describes both the page and the site.

 ## Add a Page Title

1. Click **File** on the menu bar, and then click **Open**.

   Because you have already set the dangerous_frogs folder as the folder for this site, the Open dialog box will go to that folder automatically.

2. Open the **index.htm** file.

3. If you do not see the Title text box at the top of the Document window, just below the menu bar, click the **View** menu, point to **Toolbars**, and then click **Document**.

4. Key **Dangerous Frogs** in the Title text box, replacing the text "Untitled Document," and then press **Enter** (Windows) or **Return** (Macintosh), or click the document.

5. Save your document; click **File** on the menu bar and then click **Save**.

Specifying a Background Color

The Dangerous Frogs Web site has a dark green background color. In Dreamweaver, you can easily change the background color of a page by using a preset palette of colors known as the Web-safe color palette (for additional information, see the Tips & Techniques feature "About Web-Safe Colors"). You access that palette in the Page Properties dialog box. The specification sheet in Figure 1-4 shows the specific color of the background. It also shows other page properties that need to be set in the following sections.

FIGURE 1-4
Properties defined for the Dangerous Frogs home page

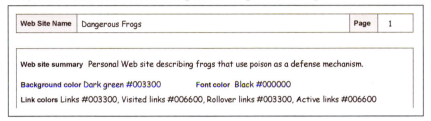

Web Site Name	Dangerous Frogs	Page	1

Web site summary Personal Web site describing frogs that use poison as a defense mechanism.

Background color Dark green #003300   Font color Black #000000

Link colors Links #003300, Visited links #006600, Rollover links #003300, Active links #006600

Tips & Techniques

About Web-Safe Colors

You can assign a color property to a number of elements on a Web page, such as the page background, text, and links. The tricky part is that colors are not displayed the same way on every computer monitor.

In HTML, you typically set the color by using hexadecimal values (you can also use names, but you are limited to the 16 color names that have been predefined). A hexadecimal value starts with a # symbol and is followed by three pairs of letters or numbers—for example, the hexadecimal value for blue is #0000FF.

A Web-safe color is one that appears the same in Netscape Navigator and Microsoft Internet Explorer on both Windows and Macintosh systems when running in 256-color (or 8-bit) mode. The conventional wisdom is that there are 216 common colors, and that any hexadecimal value that combines the pairs 00, 33, 66, 99, CC, and FF represents a Web-safe color.

When Web browsers first made their appearance, most computers were 8-bit and displayed only 256 colors. Today, the majority of computers are 16- and 32-bit systems and display thousands or millions of colors, so the justification for using the browser-safe palette is greatly diminished if you are developing your site for users with current computer systems.

Select a Background Color

1. With the **index.htm** page open, click **Modify** on the menu bar and then click **Page Properties**.

   The Page Properties dialog box opens.

2. Make sure **Appearance** is selected in the Category list.

3. Click the **Background Color** box.

   A color picker opens.

4. Move the eyedropper over a color swatch.

   The swatch's hexadecimal equivalent is displayed at the top of the color palette.

5. Click a dark green color to select it, or key **003300** in the Background Color text box, as shown in Figure 1-5.

FIGURE 1-5
Page Properties dialog box

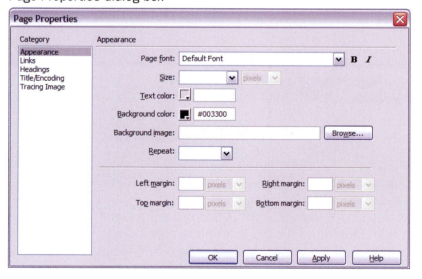

6. Click **Apply** to view the color change for your document without leaving the Page Properties dialog box.

Specifying the Default Font Color

When you change the background color of a page, you may also need to change the color of the text displayed on that page. Changing the background of the Dangerous Frogs Web site to dark green could present a problem—black text on dark green would be difficult to read. However, all of the site's text will appear on a separate colored background, so setting the text color to black is perfectly acceptable.

 ## Change the Default Font Color

1. With the **index.htm** page open, in the Page Properties dialog box, click the **Text Color** box.

   A color palette opens.

2. Select black, or key **000000**, for your text and click **Apply**.

Specifying Link Colors

The design for the Dangerous Frogs site also calls for you to change the color of text links used throughout the site. There are four link types that can be changed:

- Links: The initial color of a link—the color a user sees before clicking the link. The normal default browser color for a link is blue.

- Visited links: The color the link changes to when a user clicks the link. The normal default color for a visited link is purple.

- Rollover links: The color the link changes to when a user positions the pointer over the link. If you do not select a color, then the link color does not change when the pointer is over the link.

- Active links: The color the link changes to when a user holds down the mouse button after clicking the link. The normal default color for an active link is red.

Step by Step **Change Link Colors**

1. With the **index.htm** page open, in the Page Properties dialog box, click **Links** in the Category list.

2. Click the color box next to the link type you want to change, as shown in Figure 1-6.

FIGURE 1-6
Links color picker in the Page Properties dialog box

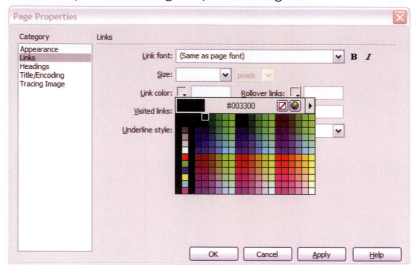

3. Set the colors for your links as follows:

   a. For Link Color, use **#003300**.

   b. For Rollover Links, use **#003300**.

   c. For Visited Links, use **#006600**.

   d. For Active Links, use **#006600**.

4. Click **OK** to close the Page Properties dialog box and return to your document.

5. Save the document.

ADDING AND MODIFYING TEXT ON A WEB SITE

OBJECTIVES

Upon completion of this lesson, you will be able to:

- Add content to a Web page.

- Understand Web page structure.

- Format text on a Web page.

- Create unordered and ordered lists.

- Insert special characters and other page elements.

- Use CSS external style sheets.

Estimated time to complete this lesson: 2 hours

Introduction

The purpose of the Dangerous Frogs Web site is to share information about poisonous frogs. In this lesson, you will learn about displaying text on a Web page to highlight and emphasize different kinds of information, to make your pages easier to read and scan. You will bring in text from outside documents, use preset headings, position text, make lists, add a date, insert special characters, format the font face and color, and learn to use cascading style sheets. More important, you will learn about *structuring* text on a page. The way you structure page content reveals the organization behind it.

Structuring and Adding Content to a Page

The content for the Dangerous Frogs Web site has already been prepared. Although this content was created in a different application, you can simply add it to a Web page, and then use Dreamweaver to format it to fit the structural organization planned for the site. For information on what considerations you should make in deciding what content to include in a site, see the Tips & Techniques feature "Basic Design Principles."

Basic Design Principles

When designing a site, it is important to keep the original goals of the site in mind. Keeping written records allows you to refer back to those notes. It is very easy to lose focus as you include more and more elements in your site, but the result is usually an incomplete site that has links that go nowhere.

For instance, the Dangerous Frogs site has these goals:

- Share information about how some frogs use poison as a defense mechanism
- Provide examples of frogs that use this mechanism

To meet these goals, the site has one page (the home page) that is dedicated to discussing why frogs are poisonous. In the course of sharing this information, describing other kinds of defense mechanisms briefly may be helpful, but this type of content should be limited. The other pages in the site are used to showcase species of frogs that use poison to protect themselves.

Also keep in mind three key design principles: consistency, usability, and readability.

Consistency makes the site predictable for your user. From one page to the next, the Home button (along with the rest of the navigation elements) should always be in the same place. The visitor's eye should not have to travel unnecessarily around the page to find where the content is, and it will not if you always put the content in the same place on the page. Use the same color and type style for section headings that are equivalent. Use templates and other Dreamweaver tools as aids as you implement this consistency.

Usability refers to the ease with which your visitor can perform tasks at your site. Is it easy to find the information that the site provides? How many clicks are required to discover answers to questions that your site addresses? Are links labeled clearly? Do you provide alternative text for images? Do pages load quickly? One way to evaluate the usability of your site is to ask yourself what task is the hardest to do at your site.

Readability refers to the ability to get meaning from the text on the screen. People typically do not read a Web page the same way that they do a book. Instead, they tend to scan the page for useful information. Scanning is difficult to do if a page has big blocks of text. It is a good idea to edit your text and remove anything that does not actually provide more information. Break up the text by using shorter paragraphs, ordered and unordered lists, and images. Use sections marked with appropriate subheadings. Use fonts that are easily readable, and use font colors that contrast with the background colors. Red text on a black background may provide the atmosphere you want, but it will be difficult for most people to read, and nearly impossible for someone who is color blind.

The best way to determine whether your design is good is to watch others use the site—a process called usability testing. When conducting a usability test, do the following:

- Write down three tasks that visitors to the site should be able to do.
- Give the list of tasks to your testers and ask them to do these things (for example, "Find information that tells how color is related to poison").
- Ask your testers to talk aloud about what they are doing as they try to accomplish the tasks.
- Take notes while watching testers complete the task, but refrain from speaking (within the bounds of courtesy).

If a tester struggles with the tasks, offer help only if absolutely necessary. Any help you give should result in a note to yourself about a problem that needs to be addressed.

Adding content to a Web page is simple. If the content is text, you can either type the text or copy and paste it from another source. For nontext elements, such as tables and images, use the Insert bar. To change the element, select it and use the Property inspector. The following activities walk you through a quick construction of the Dangerous Frogs home page.

Add a Table, Text, and an Image to the Page

1. With the **index.htm** page open, click **Insert** on the menu bar and then click **Table**, or click the **Table** button from the Layout category of the Insert bar.

   The Table dialog box opens.

2. Make the following changes in the Insert Table dialog box, as shown in Figure 2-1:

   a. Enter **3** in the Rows box and **1** in the Columns box.

   b. Change Table Width to **600 Pixels**.

   c. Set Border Thickness to **0**. This represents the width of the table border.

   d. Set Cell Padding to **5** and Cell Spacing to **0**.

> **Note** ✅
>
> You can add text to a page by typing it or by copying and pasting the text from an existing document you have previously prepared. If the text is from an application that supports drag-and-drop copying (for example, Microsoft Word on the Macintosh), you can open both Dreamweaver and the other application, and then either copy and paste or drag the text into Dreamweaver.

FIGURE 2-1
Properties for the Dangerous Frogs layout table

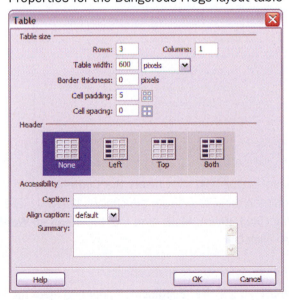

3. Click **OK** to close the dialog box.

   The table appears on the page.

4. Position the pointer anywhere along the top edge of the table. The pointer changes to a white arrow with a small table icon when you are close to the edge. Click when you see this pointer.

This selects the entire table.

5. In the Property inspector at the bottom of the screen, click the **Align** menu and then click **Center**. In the Bg Color text field, key **#CCFFD1** to set the background color for the table to light green.

6. Add the contents of Dangerous Frogs.doc to the middle cell of the table.

If you are using a Windows machine, follow these instructions:

a. In the Files panel, open the _documents folder in your site. Drag the file **DangerousFrogs.doc** to the middle cell of the table in the Document window.

The Insert Document dialog box appears, as shown in Figure 2-2.

FIGURE 2-2
Insert Document dialog box

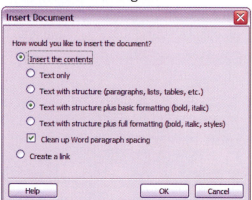

b. In the Insert Document dialog box, click **Insert the Contents** (even if this is selected, you may have to click this option in order to activate the choices below it). Then click **Text with structure plus basic formatting (bold, italic)**. Make sure that the **Clean up Word paragraph spacing** check box is checked. Then click **OK**.

If you are using a Macintosh, follow these instructions:

a. Launch **Microsoft Word**. Locate the **_documents** folder and open the file **DangerousFrogs.doc**.

b. Select all of the text in the document. Click the **Edit** menu and then click **Copy**.

c. Return to **Dreamweaver**. In index.htm, place the insertion point in the middle cell of the table. Then click the **Edit** menu and click **Paste**.

Dreamweaver imports the Word document you selected, leaving structural elements intact. Dreamweaver also cleans up any Word formatting that is not appropriate for a Web page.

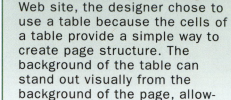

Inside the Design

Tables are used for organizing data, but they are also a simple way to organize content on a page. In the Dangerous Frogs Web site, the designer chose to use a table because the cells of a table provide a simple way to create page structure. The background of the table can stand out visually from the background of the page, allowing the designer some control over the page width. In addition, the table cells serve to divide the page into three main sections: header, body, and footer.

All of the new text should now be inside the table cell.

7. Click in the top cell of the table. Key **Dangerous Frogs: Pretty Poisons**. In the Property inspector, click the **Align Center** button, as shown in Figure 2-3.

FIGURE 2-3
Align Center button

8. Make sure the insertion point is at the end of the line and press **Enter** (Windows) or **Return** (Macintosh) to insert a new line.

9. In the Files panel, open the **images** folder. Drag the image **frog_nav.jpg** to the new line you created.

The Image Tag Accessibility Attributes dialog box appears, as shown in Figure 2-4.

FIGURE 2-4
Image Tag Accessibility Attributes dialog box

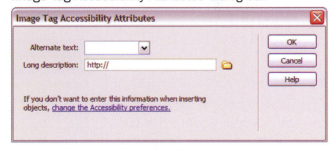

10. In the Alternate Text field, key **Frog navigation**. Then click **OK**.

The image appears on the page.

11. Save the file and preview it in your browser by pressing **F12** (Windows) or **Option + F12** (Macintosh).

12. Close the browser.

Applying Headings to Text

The phrase "Dangerous Frogs: Pretty Poisons" appears at the top of the home page. Since this is the title of the page, you will format this text using the Heading 1 style. The page also has several subsection titles, which you should format using the Heading 2 style. Use the design document to see the heading levels and set them on the home page, as shown in Figure 2-5.

FIGURE 2-5
Headings indicated on the design document for the Dangerous Frogs Web site

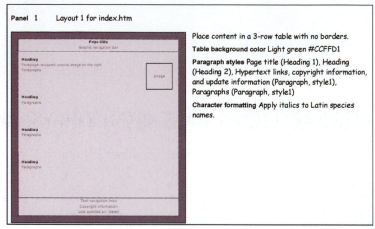

Format Text

1. With the **index.htm** page still open, at the top of the page, click anywhere within the text **Dangerous Frogs: Pretty Poisons**. In the Property inspector, click the **Format** menu and click **Heading 1**, as shown in Figure 2-6.

   You have now tagged the text with the Heading 1 style.

Inside the Design

Heading styles are preset styles in HTML that you can use to quickly set the hierarchy of the content on the page. Bigger and bolder text grabs the eye quickly and therefore is used to call attention to titles and important information. In the Dangerous Frogs site, the headings are used to set off the title and sections of text so that users can quickly scan the page and see the topics covered.

FIGURE 2-6
Format menu in the Property inspector

2. Each of the subsections of the page should be Heading 2 text. Select the text **Frogs That Use Color—and Poison—to Warn Off Predators**. In the Property inspector, click the **Format** menu and then click **Heading 2**.

3. Repeat step 2 for the text **Behavior: The First Clue** and **Coloration: The Second Clue**.

   The remainder of the text on the page should all be set to the Paragraph style. Dreamweaver did this automatically when you imported the text from Microsoft Word.

4. Save the file and preview it in your browser.

5. Close the browser.

Viewing Design View and Code View Simultaneously

So far, you have been working entirely in Design view. This view of your document is Dreamweaver's visual editing mode. Many Web developers also work in Code view, which allows you to see the HTML tags and other code that makes up your page.

Dreamweaver provides a third view that allows you to see Design view and Code view simultaneously. With this view, as you work you can see both your code and the effects of that code on your Web page. In these lessons, you will primarily use Design view, but you may want to use the Code and Design view as you work. Since this view allows you to see Dreamweaver write the code to carry out your design, this can help you learn HTML.

Switch Between Code View and Design View

1. With the **index.htm** page still open, on the Document toolbar, click the **Split** button.

   This splits the Document window so that it shows both the Code view and the Design view at the same time, as shown in Figure 2-7. Make sure that the position of the splitter bar—the separator between the two views—allows you to see enough of both. You can drag the border that separates the two views to adjust the height of the views.

FIGURE 2-7
Document window in split view

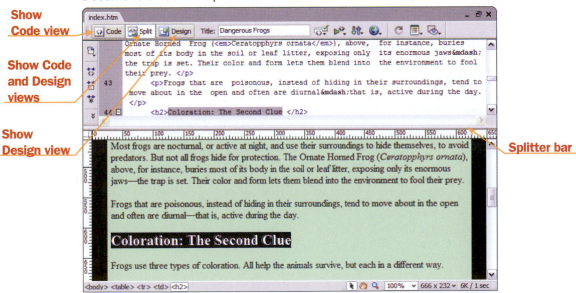

2. In Design view, look for the heading "Coloration: The Second Clue." In the second paragraph under that heading, in the third sentence, select the word **crypsis**.

The word is now selected in both Design view and Code view (you may have noticed the Code view jump to that part of the code that contains the word you selected).

3. In the Property inspector, click the **Italic** button (the dark capital **I**).

In Code view, you can see that the selected text is now surrounded by <em> and </em> tags.

4. Click the **Design** button to return to Design view.

5. Save the file and preview it in your browser.

6. Close your browser.

>
> **Note**
>
> You can edit the code in Code view, but changes you make to the code do not appear in Design view until you either click Refresh on the Document toolbar or click anywhere in Design view.

Understanding How Web Pages Are Structured

Throughout this project, you will do most of your work in the Dreamweaver visual editor, but it is helpful to understand that Dreamweaver is writing code for you as you work. Now that you have put some content on your page and you have seen how to switch between Design view and Code view, you will look more closely at how HTML structures a Web page. The Web is all about sharing information, and when it began, it consisted entirely of text.

Understanding Page Structure

When you create a new page in Dreamweaver, Dreamweaver automatically inserts several lines of HTML code into the page. This code structures the page and helps you get started. Previously, you created several new pages for the Dangerous Frogs Web site. Open green.htm and switch to Code view. You will see code that looks very similar to the code in Figure 2-8. This is code that every valid HTML file requires in order to be interpreted correctly by the widest number of browsers.

Again, Dreamweaver automatically wrote this code for you when you created the page.

FIGURE 2-8
Code that Dreamweaver creates in a new page

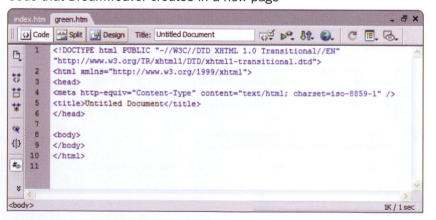

Here is what the code does:

- Line 1: The DOCTYPE declaration tells the browser which type of HTML your document complies with. Until you understand the different types of HTML and XHTML that you can work with, do not worry about this line. But do not remove it or change it, either.

- Line 2: The <html> tag tells the browser that this is an HTML document and should be displayed as one. Everything else on the page goes inside the <html> tag and its required closing tag </html>, on line 10.

Learn More

Understanding Basic HTML Tags

If you were coding a page by hand, you would start with the text and add tags to indicate how the text should be displayed and organized. The following table shows some of the more commonly used tags.

Common HTML Tags

TAG	DESCRIPTION
<h1></h1> <h2></h2> <h3></h3> <h4></h4> <h5></h5> <h6></h6>	HTML has six levels of headings—numbered 1 through 6—with Heading 1 having the largest font size. Headings are displayed in larger or bolder fonts than the normal body text. Tagging a paragraph as a heading automatically generates a space below the heading.
<p></p>	Used for body text. When working in the Dreamweaver visual editor, pressing Enter or Return at the end of a line of text automatically creates a new paragraph. In HTML, this creates space between the new paragraph and the paragraph above it.
<em></em>	Used to add emphasis. Browsers typically display text within this tag in *italics*.
<strong></strong>	Used to display text in **boldface**.
<u></u>	Used to display underlined text. This tag is typically not used. For one thing, it can be confused with hyperlinks, which most browsers display as underlined. For another, it is better to use CSS to "decorate" text in this way.
<a href=></a>	Used to create a link. The <a> tag requires an href attribute that indicates where the link should go to.
<table></table> <tr></tr> <td></td> <th></th>	Used to create a table. The attributes of the <table> tag set properties for the entire table. The <tr> tag is used to define a row in the table. The <td> tag is placed inside the <tr> tag to define the cells in that row. Replace <td> tags with <th> tags whenever you want to indicate that the contents of a cell should serve as a heading or label for a row or column.
<li></li> <ol></ol> <ul></ul>	Used to create lists. A <ol> or <ul> tag determines where the list starts and ends. Use <ol> tags for an ordered (or numbered) list, or use <ul> for an unordered (bulleted) list. Use one pair of <li> tags for each item in the list.

- Line 3: The <head> tag is the wrapper for the header tags that contain standard information about the page, such as the title of the page and keywords for the page. Any JavaScript or CSS would also typically be placed between the <head> tag and its </head> closer (on line 6).

- Line 4: The <meta> tag can be used in a number of ways to provide additional information about a page. It is commonly used to indicate the keywords that search engines should use to categorize the page. In Figure 2-8, Dreamweaver has added a <meta> tag that tells the browser what kind of content is on the page and what character set to use. The <meta> tag does not require a separate closing tag.

- Line 5: The <title> tag indicates the title of the page. This is the text that appears in the title bar of the browser window. It requires a closing </title> tag.

- Lines 8 and 9: All the content that should be displayed on the page is placed between <body> and </body>. When you use Design view in Dreamweaver to add content to a page, this is where the content will be placed.

For more information on the tags used in HTML, see the Learn More feature "Understanding Basic HTML Tags."

Formatting Text

Now you will continue formatting the text on the Dangerous Frogs home page. Once the text is on the page, you can use the Property inspector to format it as indicated in the design document as shown in Figure 2-9.

FIGURE 2-9
Text formatting indicated on the design document for the Dangerous Frogs Web site

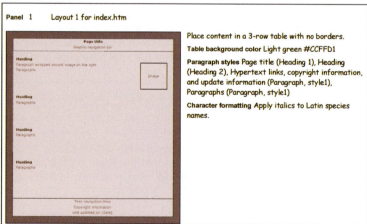

Indenting Text

The design calls for you to indent several paragraphs under the Coloration section. You can use the Text Indent and Text Outdent icons in the Property inspector, as shown in Figure 2-10, to do this. These options indent text at the left and right margins of the page.

FIGURE 2-10
Text Indent and Text Outdent icons

Text Outdent   Text Indent

 ## Indent and Outdent Paragraphs

1. With the **index.htm** page still open, find the heading "Coloration: The Second Clue." Select the four paragraphs that immediately follow this heading.

2. In the Property inspector, click **Text Indent**, or click **Text** on the menu bar and then click **Indent**.

   The four paragraphs are now indented.

3. Select the first paragraph under the heading "Coloration: The Second Clue." Then click **Text Outdent**, or click **Text** on the menu bar and then click **Outdent**.

   The first paragraph is now moved back to its original position.

4. Save the file and preview it in your browser.

5. Close the browser.

Hot Tip

Often you will find yourself repeating the most recent formatting you applied to another paragraph or to other selected text. The Redo command makes that task easier: just press a simple key combination. The first two items listed on the Edit menu are the Undo and Redo commands. You will want to remember their keyboard shortcuts:
- **Undo:** Ctrl + Z (Windows) and Command + Z (Macintosh)
- **Redo:** Ctrl + Y (Windows) and Command + Y (Macintosh)

Applying Character Formatting

Each of the indented paragraphs of the Coloration section defines a term. Occasionally you need a word or phrase to look different from the surrounding text to visually set it apart from other text. You will use boldface to make the terms stand out.

 ## Make Text Bold

1. On the **index.htm** page, find the section called **Coloration: The Second Clue**. In that section, at the beginning of the second paragraph, select the words **Protective Coloration.**

2. In the Property inspector, click the **Bold** button (the dark capital B), or click **Text** on the menu bar, point to Style, and then click **Bold**.

   The selected text now has bold formatting applied to it.

3. At the beginning of the next paragraph, select the words **Flash Coloration**.

4. Press **Ctrl + Y** (Windows) or **Command + Y** (Macintosh).

Because Bold was the last command used, it is applied to the selected text.

5. Repeat the bold formatting on the phrase **Warning Coloration** at the beginning of the last paragraph of this section.

6. Save the document.

Positioning Text

The design calls for a footer. The footer should not be too large or stand out too much, or it will distract from the rest of the text on the page and occupy too much space. Separating lines with a hard return begins a new paragraph and creates extra space between it and the paragraph above it. Using a line break, however, simply starts a new line of text without any extra spaces. This approach would be useful for an address line, for example, where you want a new line for each part of the address, but without the extra spacing of a paragraph. To keep the content of the footer from occupying a larger amount of page real estate than it deserves, you will separate each line of text with a line break.

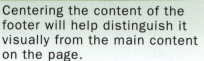

Inside the Design

Centering the content of the footer will help distinguish it visually from the main content on the page.

Hot Tip

You can create a line break by holding down the Shift key and then pressing Enter (Windows) or Return (Macintosh).

Create a Line Break and Center Text

1. With the **index.htm** page still open, position the insertion point in the bottom cell of the table.

2. Key **Home | Green | Gold | Blue | Black**.

3. Press **Shift + Enter** (Windows) or **Shift + Return** (Macintosh).

The text after the insertion point moves to the next line. A new paragraph has not been created, so there is no additional space between the two lines.

4. Key **Copyright 2005 by** and then your name.

5. In the Property inspector, click the **Align Center** button.

The text is now centered.

6. Save the file and preview it in your browser.

7. Close the browser.

Making Lists

Lists help organize information, and they make it easier for readers to scan the page for useful information. The Dangerous Frogs home page has two types of lists: one identifies survival strategies used by frogs and other amphibians, and the other provides a brief outline of the content on the other pages of the site. The first is an ordered list and the second is an unordered list. Dreamweaver gives you three kinds of preformatted lists: ordered (numbered), unordered (bulleted), and definition lists (a term and its definition).

Creating Ordered Lists

An ordered list consists of list items that are ordered numerically or alphabetically. You can use Arabic or Roman numerals or uppercase or lowercase letters.

 ### Create an Ordered (Numbered) List

1. With the **index.htm** page still open, position the insertion point in the fourth sentence of the first paragraph, just before the text "camouflage." Press **Enter** (Windows) or **Return** (Macintosh) to create a new paragraph.

2. In the same sentence, insert another new paragraph just before the text "shocks and disruptions," just before the text "poison," and again just before the final sentence of the paragraph. The page should look similar to that in Figure 2-11.

FIGURE 2-11
Dangerous Frogs home page

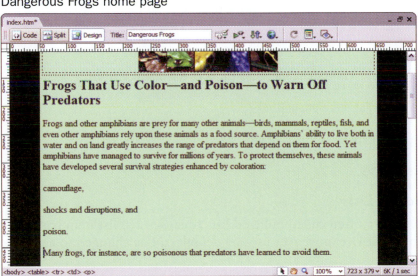

3. Select the three lines of text:

   camouflage,

   shocks and disruptions, and

   poison.

4. In the Property inspector, click the **Ordered List** button, shown in Figure 2-12, or click **Text** on the menu bar, point to **List**, and then click **Ordered List**.

The selected text is indented and numbered.

FIGURE 2-12
Ordered List and Unordered List icons

5. In the **index.htm** page, click in the line with the text "camouflage" or in any line in the list.

6. Click **Text** on the menu bar, point to **List**, and then click **Properties**.

The List Properties dialog box opens, as shown in Figure 2-13.

FIGURE 2-13
List Properties dialog box

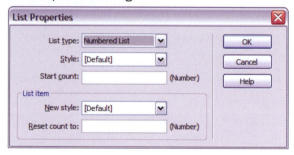

7. In the Style menu, click **Alphabet Small (a, b, c)** and then click **OK.**

All items in the list are alphabetized.

8. Save the file and preview it in your browser.

9. Close the browser.

Creating Unordered Lists

Unordered lists are often called bulleted lists because each list item has a bullet in front of it. The bullet symbol that Dreamweaver uses by default can be changed to a circle or a square.

 ## Create an Unordered (Bulleted) List

1. With the **index.htm** page still open, in the last paragraph, position the insertion point just before the text "the Monkey Frog." Press **Enter** (Windows) or **Return** (Macintosh) to create a new paragraph.

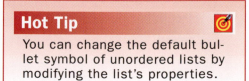
Hot Tip

You can change the default bullet symbol of unordered lists by modifying the list's properties.

2. Insert a new paragraph before "the Golden Poison Dart Frog," before "the Blue Poison Dart Frog, and" and before "the Dyeing Poison Dart Frog."

3. Select the four lines containing the names of the frogs.

4. In the Property inspector, click **Unordered List**, or click **Text** on the menu bar, point to **List**, and then click **Unordered List**.

The selected text is indented and bulleted.

5. Click any line in the list.

6. Click **Text** on the menu bar, point to **List**, and then click **Properties**.

The List Properties dialog box opens, as shown in Figure 2-14.

Hot Tip

When you are creating lists, keep these tips in mind:
- To change a bulleted list to a numbered list or a numbered list to a bulleted list, select the entire list and then apply the other list format.
- To convert a list to plain text, select the list and apply the list type again. This procedure works like a toggle to turn off the list formatting.
- If you selected extra text when you applied the formatting for the list, select just the extra text and apply the formatting again to remove the list formatting.
- If you are keying within an already formatted list and you want to end the list, press Enter (Windows) or Return (Macintosh) twice.
- List items are single-spaced by default. If you want additional spacing between the lines, select all the items in the list and then click Paragraph in the Format list in the Property inspector.

FIGURE 2-14
List Properties dialog box

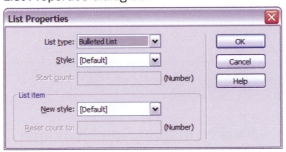

7. In the Style menu, click **Square** and click **OK**.

All items in the list now use the square bullet symbol.

8. Save the document.

Changing Font Properties

On the home page of the Dangerous Frogs Web site, you will notice that the type (or font) face, size, and color used for the text varies. These differences help show the relative importance of the various text elements on the page. Use the design document to make the changes to the font face and color, as shown in Figure 2-15.

Inside the Design

To make pages more interesting and easier to read, designers specify the typeface used to display the text. The Dangerous Frogs Web site has a lot of scientific information, so the design uses a san-serif font, with an eye toward making the site look more friendly than formal. The size of the body text is intended to be large enough to be readable by most visitors, and the sizes of all the other text (the headings and the footer) were selected to indicate their importance relative to the body text.

FIGURE 2-15
Font properties defined for the Dangerous Frogs home page

Text style definitions

    Heading 1 Font: Verdana, Arial, Helvetica, sans-serif. Size: 160%. Color: Dark green. Alignment: Centered.

    Heading 2 Font: Verdana, Arial, Helvetica, sans-serif. Size: 120%. Color: Dark green. Alignment: Left.

    Paragraph, style1 Font: Verdana, Arial, Helvetica, sans-serif

    Paragraph, Term Font: Verdana, Arial, Helvetica, sans-serif, Color: Dark green, bold

Changing the Font Face

The fonts used in the Dangerous Frogs Web site are standard fonts found on most machines. You can change the font for the entire page or for selected text on the page. However, for users to see your page as you designed it, the font you choose must be installed on the user's computer. Do not make the assumption that all fonts are loaded on everyone's computer. If your first choice is not

Learn More

Modifying Font Combinations

You can modify the choices that appear as font combinations and adjust the order in which the fonts will be used when a font on your site is not available on a visitor's computer. In the Property inspector's Font list, click Edit Font List, or click Text on the menu bar, point to Font, and then click Edit Font List. The Edit Font List dialog box opens. Select a font combination (such as Arial, Helvetica, sans serif) from the Font list at the top of the dialog box. The fonts in the selected combination appear in the Chosen Fonts list at the lower left of the dialog box. To its right is a list of all fonts installed on your system.

(Continued . . .)

Learn More

Modifying Font Combinations

You can choose from the following options:

- To add or remove fonts, select the font and then click the directional buttons between the Chosen Fonts list and the Available Fonts list.
- To add or remove a font combination, click the plus (+) or minus (–) button at the top left of the dialog box.
- To add a font not installed on your system, key the font name in the text box below the Available Fonts list and click the directional arrow to add it to the combination. Adding a font not installed on your system is useful; for example, if you are authoring on a Macintosh, you may want to specify a Windows-only font.
- To move a font combination up or down in the list, click the directional arrow buttons at the top right of the dialog box.

available, the browser will attempt to use the second choice and then the third (for additional information, see the Learn More feature "Modifying Font Combinations"). If none of the fonts are available on the user's computer, the text will be displayed in the browser's default font. In the following Step-by-Step, you will make some simple font changes to the text on the home page.

Note

Although a great deal of information is available concerning the use of type for print, not all of that information translates to the Web. You have to consider the fact that users are free to change the screen size or to change the font size and color of the text. The way type flows on a page can easily change from user to user. There is also a significant difference between font sizes on Windows and Macintosh computers. The same text appears smaller on a Macintosh computer than in Windows.

If you are accustomed to print work, you may be frustrated by the lack of typographic control in HTML, such as line and letter spacing. You are also unable to control widows (a single word on a line) in Web text, and line breaks in paragraphs. You can use Cascading Style Sheets to overcome most of these difficulties—more on that later.

Change the Font Face

1. With the **index.htm** page still open, at the top of the page, select the text **Dangerous Frogs: Pretty Poisons**.

2. In the Property inspector's Font list, click **Verdana, Arial, Helvetica, sans-serif**, as shown in Figure 2-16.

   The selected text changes to another font, depending on the fonts installed on your computer.

FIGURE 2-16
Property inspector's Font menu

3. Select all of the text in the middle cell on the page.

4. In the Property inspector's Font menu, click **Verdana, Arial, Helvetica, sans serif**.

5. In the footer, select all of the text and set the font to **Verdana, Arial, Helvetica, sans serif**.

   All the text on the page now has the same font face.

6. Save the file and preview it in your browser.

Note

In some cases, you may not want text to have a font setting but instead to use the user's default font. To make this change in the settings, select the text whose font you want to remove. Click Default Font in the Font list in the Property inspector, or click Text from the menu bar, point to Font, and then click Default.

Changing the Font Color

The design for the Dangerous Frogs site calls for the addition of color to certain text elements, using the same dark green color used in the background. This helps tie the elements together across the site, while at the same time helping your site stand out visually from other sites. You can easily change the color of your text in Dreamweaver. All colors used at your site are listed on the Assets panel in the Files panel group. To ensure that the colors you use are consistent across your site, you can save commonly used colors on the Assets panel as Favorites.

Add a Color to the Assets Favorites

1. With the **index.htm** page still open, click **Window** on the menu bar and then click **Assets** to display the Assets panel. If you have the Files panel group open, you can also click the **Assets** tab to open the panel.

Note

If your Site list has only black (#000000) and white (#FFFFFF), click the Options menu on the Files title bar and then click Refresh Site List.

2. Click the **Colors** icon at the left of the Assets panel and make sure that **Site** is selected at the top of the Assets panel.

3. Select **#003300**.

4. Click the **Options** menu and then click **Add to Favorites**, as shown in Figure 2-17.

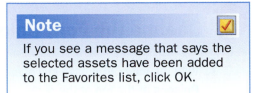

Note

If you see a message that says the selected assets have been added to the Favorites list, click OK.

FIGURE 2-17
Add to Favorites menu item

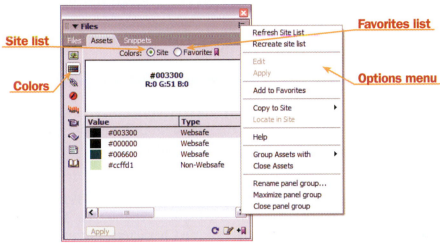

5. At the top of the Assets panel, click **Favorites**, as shown in Figure 2-18.

The color now appears in the Favorites list.

FIGURE 2-18
Color Favorites in the Assets panel

Note

Some colors have already been set up for you in the Favorites panel. These are stored in a folder named _notes in the data files supplied with this course and are automatically available when you choose dangerous_frogs as the folder for your site.

6. Select **#003300** and then click the **Options** menu and click **Edit Nickname**.

7. Key **dark green** as the nickname for this color and then press **Enter** (Windows) or **Return** (Macintosh).

Change the Font Color

1. With the **index.htm** page still open, in the Document window, select the text **Dangerous Frogs: Pretty Poisons** at the top of the page.

2. In the Assets panel, select **dark green**. Then click **Apply** at the bottom of the Assets panel.

3. Save the file and preview it in your browser.

4. Close the browser.

Inserting Special Characters and Elements

When working in Dreamweaver, you are generally typing at the keyboard. Sometimes you need characters and other information not directly accessible from the keyboard. On the Dangerous Frogs Web site (as on practically any site you work on), you will use a copyright symbol (©) to indicate who owns the material on the site. With Dreamweaver, you can use the Insert bar to easily insert special characters, e-mail links, and dates.

Adding Special Characters to Your Page

You will find the copyright symbol in the Characters menu in the Text category of the Insert bar. This menu contains the most commonly used special characters. To insert characters not found on this panel, click the arrow to the right of the Characters button in the Text category of the Insert bar, or click Insert on the menu bar, point to HTML, point to Special Characters, and then click Other. The Insert Other Character dialog box opens, as shown in Figure 2-19. You can select any needed characters from this dialog box.

FIGURE 2-19
Insert Other Character dialog box

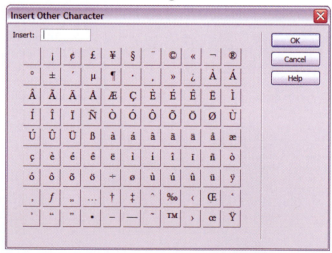

Enter Special Characters

1. With the **index.htm** page still open, at the bottom of the page, select the text **Copyright** and delete it. Leave the insertion point positioned at this location.

2. In the Text category on the Insert bar, click the **Characters** menu and click **Copyright**, as shown in Figure 2-20.

FIGURE 2-20
Choosing the copyright character

3. Save the file and preview it in your browser.

4. Close the browser.

Adding E-mail Links

You can link to an e-mail address to give your visitors an easy way to contact you from a Web page. The design for the Dangerous Frogs site specifies that this information be placed in the footer, as shown in Figure 2-21. You should always include some way for visitors to correspond or interact with you or someone in your organization. Fans of frogs may want to let you know about other resources, or people knowledgeable about the subject may have feedback for you that will improve your site.

Note

In addition to using the method described here to enter e-mail links, you can manually enter an e-mail link. First you select the text that you want to make into an e-mail link. Then, in the Link text box of the Property inspector, key **mailto:** and then the e-mail address. Make sure you key the colon and no spaces (for example, *mailto: education@macromedia.com*).

FIGURE 2-21
Footer specification for the Dangerous Frogs Web site

Text navigation links
Copyright information
Last updated on [date]

 **Enter an E-mail Link**

1. With the **index.htm** page still open, your name should be at the end of the copyright line you modified in the previous Step-by-Step. Delete your name and leave the insertion point positioned where your name was.

2. Click **Insert** on the menu bar and then click **Email Link**.

   The Email Link dialog box opens, as shown in Figure 2-22.

   FIGURE 2-22
   Email Link dialog box

   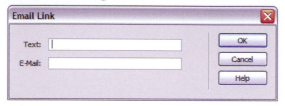

3. Make the following changes:

   a. For Text, key **Will Stewart**.

   b. For E-Mail, key **wstewart@macromedia.com**.

4. Click **OK**.

   The text appears as a link. The Property inspector shows the e-mail address in the Link text box.

5. Save the file and preview it in your browser.

6. Close the browser.

Adding a Date Automatically

The design document for the Dangerous Frogs Web site calls for a "last-modified" date on the home page, as shown in Figure 2-21. This helps you keep track of the date when you last made changes to the page. Dreamweaver lets you place the date and time on your pages to track this information. Dreamweaver can update the date and time automatically so you don't have to do it.

Once you have an automatically updated date in your document, you can change its formatting by selecting the date and then clicking *Edit date format* in the Property inspector. The Insert Date dialog box opens, as shown in Figure 2-23. Make appropriate changes to the options and then click OK.

 Insert the Date

1. With the **index.htm** page still open, make sure the insertion point is at the end of the line containing the e-mail link you created in the previous Step-by-Step. Press **Shift + Enter** (Windows) or **Shift + Return** (Macintosh) to create a new line just under the e-mail link.

2. In the new line, key **Last updated on**. Add one more space to the line and leave the insertion point in this position.

3. Click the **Date** button in the Common category of the Insert bar, or click **Insert** on the menu bar and then click **Date**.

   The Insert Date dialog box opens, as shown in Figure 2-23.

FIGURE 2-23
Insert Date dialog box

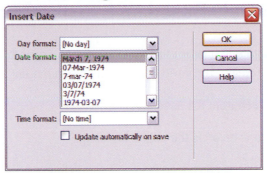

4. In the Insert Date dialog box, make the following changes to the date:
   a. In the Day Format menu, click **Thursday,** (with a comma).
   b. In the Date Format menu, click **March 7, 1974**.
   c. In the Time Format menu, click **10:18 PM**.

5. Check **Update automatically on save** to update the date on your page each time you save your document.

6. Click **OK**.

   The current day, date, and time appear below the e-mail link. This information will change every time you save your document.

7. Save the file and preview it in your browser.

8. Close the browser.

Using Cascading Style Sheets

Previously, you made some changes to the fonts on the Dangerous Frogs home page. For consistency in design, you will want to make the same font choices on the other pages in the site. However, the more design choices you implement, the more difficult it will be to remember your choices from one page the next.

Cascading Style Sheets (CSS) provide a way to save the formatting information from selected text and apply it to other text selections in your document or to any document in your site.

> **Note**
>
> The term *cascading* refers to the ability that CSS provides to have a single style (or *rule*) apply to many elements. In addition, it gives you the ability to apply multiple styles to the same element or Web page. For example, you can create one CSS rule to apply color and another rule to apply margins and apply them both to the same text on a page. The defined styles "cascade" to the elements on your Web page, ultimately creating the design you want.

On the Dangerous Frogs home page, there are several terms that should stand out from the rest of the text. However, instead of making these separate headings, you will set the style for one of the terms and then apply that style to the other terms as well.

Creating and Applying CSS Styles

To help simplify formatting text on the frog home page, you use CSS styles on the page. You will format some text, define a CSS style, and then apply that formatting style to other portions of the page.

 ### Create a CSS Rule Based on Existing Text

1. With the **index.htm** page still open, in the "Coloration: The Second Clue" section, select **Protective Coloration**, the term to which you previously applied bold formatting.

2. Apply the color **dark green** from the Assets panel.

   This phrase has the same color as the page's heading.

   The other two terms in this section need the same formatting, as do any other terms you want to call attention to in your site. You will use a CSS style to accomplish this.

3. In the Property inspector, click the **Style** menu and then click **Rename**.

   The Rename Style dialog box opens, as shown in Figure 2-24.

FIGURE 2-24
Rename Style dialog box

4. In the **Rename Style** menu, make sure **Style3** is selected. Name the style **Term** and click **OK**.

   The Results panel opens to show all occurrences of Style3 (in this case, there is only one occurrence). This happens because Dreamweaver uses the Find and Replace command to change all occurrences of Style3 to Term. It is showing you the results of that operation just as it would after any Find and Replace operation.

   > **Note** ☑️
   >
   > To apply a style to a selection, you must highlight all of the appropriate text before applying the style. To apply a style to an entire paragraph, you just need to place the insertion point anywhere within the paragraph—you do not need to select each word in the paragraph.

5. Collapse or close the Results panel by clicking the arrow next to the Results title.

6. Save the document.

Apply a CSS Style

1. With the **index.htm** page still open, select the text **Flash Coloration**.

2. In the Property inspector, click the **Style** menu and then click **Term**.

   The style is applied to the text.

3. Repeat steps 1 and 2 for the remaining text, **Warning Coloration**.

4. Save the document.

   You have created a new CSS style to use on your home page. You can also use CSS to specify how existing HTML tags are displayed. In the next Step-by-Step, you will redefine the Heading 2 tag.

 ## Redefine an HTML Tag

1. With the **index.htm** page still open, at the top of the page, click anywhere in the heading **Frogs That Use Color—and Poison—to Warn Off Predators**.

2. In the Property inspector, change the style to **None**.

   Even if the style is already set to None, set the selection to None again. This should set the font back to Default.

3. Repeat steps 1 and 2 for the headings **Behavior: The First Clue** and **Coloration: The Second Clue**.

4. Click the **CSS** button next to the Style menu.

   The CSS panel opens.

5. In the CSS panel, click the **Options** menu and then click **New**.

   The New CSS Rule dialog box opens, as shown in Figure 2-25.

FIGURE 2-25
New CSS Rule dialog box

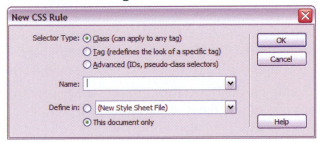

6. For Selector Type, select **Tag**. For Define in, select **This document only**. Then click the **Tag** menu and click **h2** (h2 is the HTML tag used to mark text as Heading 2). Then click **OK**.

    The CSS Rule Definition dialog box opens so you can create the new tag definition.

7. Start in the **Type** category. For Font, click **Verdana, Arial, Helvetica, sans-serif**. For Size, key **120%**. For Color, key **#003300**.

8. Switch to the **Block** category. For Text align, click **left**.

9. Click **OK** to close the CSS Rule Definition dialog box.

    The headings should now be set to a style similar to what it was when we started. So why go through all this?

    Here is why: Scroll down to the text **The Color of Poison** and click anywhere in the line. Set the Style to **None**. Then, in the Format menu in the Property inspector, click **Heading 2**. Now every time you set some text to Heading 2, it will have all of the characteristics of your first Heading 2. And if you ever decide to change the characteristics of the Heading 2 style, the change will be applied to all occurrences of that style throughout the page.

10. Now create a new rule for the Heading 1 format. Position the insertion point in the line containing the text **Dangerous Frogs: Pretty Poisons** at the top of the page. Set the Style to **None**; then repeat steps 5 and 6. When you repeat step 6, click h1 instead of h2.

11. In the CSS Rule Definition dialog box, set these attributes in the **Type** category:

    a. For Font, click **Verdana, Arial, Helvetica, sans-serif**.

    b. For Size, key **160%**.

    c. For Color, key **#003300**.

> **Note**
>
> If you want to delete a CSS style (one that you perhaps no longer need), click the Window menu and then click CSS Styles. On the CSS Styles panel, click All. Right-click the style you want to delete and choose Delete.

12. Switch to the **Block** category. For Text align, click **center**. Then click **OK**.

13. Save the document.

Applying Style Sheets

When you create a style, Dreamweaver places the code for the style inside the document you are working on. This is called an *embedded* style sheet. However, that does not allow you to use the styles on other pages. To do that, you must create an *external* style sheet. An external style sheet is a separate file that contains a list of styles and specifies their properties.

As you have been working on the Dangerous Frogs home page, Dreamweaver has been quietly writing CSS rules for you, adding them to the embedded style sheet for the page. Since you will use most of these rules on the other pages in the site, you will want to export the rules to an external style sheet.

Writing CSS by hand is beyond the scope of this book, but Dreamweaver provides some simple ways to create styles and style sheets.

Create and Use an External Style Sheet

1. Make sure that both the **index.htm** page and the **CSS** panel are open. If you do not see the CSS panel, click **Window** on the menu bar and then click **CSS Styles**.

2. In the CSS panel, click the **Options** menu and then click **Export**.

   The Export Styles as CSS File dialog box opens.

3. Navigate to and open the **css** folder in the site root. Save the new file in the css folder as **frogs.css**.

4. In the CSS panel, click the **All** button, shown in Figure 2-26.

   The CSS panel displays a list of the styles contained in the page.

FIGURE 2-26
CSS panel

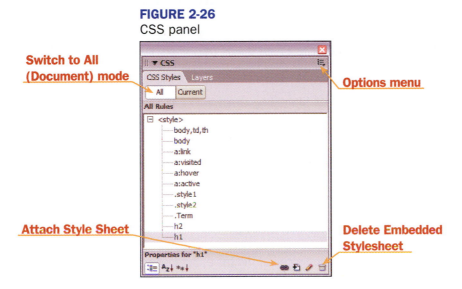

5. Select the **<style>** tag at the top of the All Rules list. Then click the **Delete Embedded Stylesheet** button (the trash icon) at the lower right of the panel.

   Much of the formatting you have created has now disappeared. Do not worry—it will be back soon.

6. At the bottom of the CSS panel, click the **Attach Style Sheet** button.

The Attach External Style Sheet dialog box appears, as shown in Figure 2-27.

FIGURE 2-27
Attach External Style Sheet dialog box

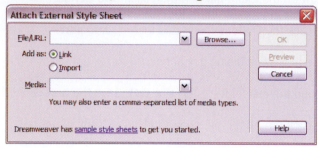

7. Click the **Browse** button. Navigate to and select the **frogs.css** file you saved earlier. Click **OK** (Windows) or **Choose** (Macintosh).

8. Back in the Attach External Style Sheet dialog box, make sure that **Add as Link** is selected. Then click **OK**.

The page is back with all of its formatting intact.

9. Save changes to the **index.htm** page.

10. Select the table that contains the page content. Click **Edit** from the menu bar and then click **Copy**.

11. In the Files panel, double-click the file **green.htm** to open it.

12. Click **Edit** on the menu bar and then click **Paste**.

13. Delete the contents of the middle cell of the table, but leave the top and bottom cells intact.

14. In the **_documents** folder, find the file **MonkeyFrog.doc**. Import the text from Microsoft Word, placing the text in the middle cell of the table in **green.htm**.

15. On the Document toolbar, change the title of the page to **Dangerous Frogs – The Monkey Frog**. In the top line of the page, change **Dangerous Frogs: Pretty Poisons** to **Dangerous Frogs: The Monkey Frog**.

16. Apply **frog.css** to the page, repeating steps 5 through 7.

17. Select the text **Phyllomedusa bicolor**. Italicize it and change its format to Heading 2.

18. Select the text **Habitat** and change its format to Heading 2. Do the same with the text **Description**.

19. Select each of the paragraphs on the page and use the **Style** menu on the Property inspector to change their style to **style1**.

20. Save the page and preview it in your browser.

21. Close the browser and close Dreamweaver.

WORKING WITH IMAGES

Introduction

The Dangerous Frogs Web site contains images that show the frogs described in the text. These images add information as well as break up the text so that it is easier to read. In this lesson, you will learn to insert images on a page, size and optimize the images, align the images, position the images on the page and with respect to text, and create image maps.

Note

When you publish images on the Web, it is important to know both the technical limitations and the legal limitations involved. See the Tips & Techniques features "Identifying Graphics Formats for the Web" and "Principles and Rules of Copyright."

Placing Graphics on the Page

The design for the Dangerous Frogs home page calls for an image of the Ornate Horned Frog to be displayed at the top of the page, as shown in Figure 3-1.

FIGURE 3-1
Image specified on the Dangerous Frogs specification sheet

Image in middle cell of the table
File ornate_horned.jpg
Alternate text
    Ornate horned frog
Format
    Right-justify at the top of first paragraph.
    Wrap text around image.
    Image size: 125 pixels by 125 pixels.
    Optimize image as a JPEG.
    Space around image: 7 pixels left and right, 2 pixels top and bottom.

Dreamweaver lets you choose how it references images: with document-relative or site-root-relative references. With document-relative referencing, Dreamweaver constructs the path to the image based on the location of your HTML document in relation to the graphics file. Site-root-relative referencing constructs the path to the image based on the location of that image in relation to your site root.

Generally, you should use document-relative links and paths. If you have an extremely large site, or if you plan to move pages frequently within the server, you might want to use site-root-relative referencing. Since the Dangerous Frogs site is relatively small, you will use document-relative references. For now, you are probably working only on your local computer, but if you want to move your site to the Web, document-relative links will make the migration much less troublesome.

Until you save your file, Dreamweaver has no way to create a reference. You should always save your document before you insert graphics. If you do not, Dreamweaver displays an alert box and then fixes the filename path when you do save the Dreamweaver file.

Insert a Graphic by Using the Insert Bar

1. Start Dreamweaver.

2. Open the page **index.htm**.

3. Click in the document to make sure the insertion point is at the beginning of the first full paragraph, before the text "Frogs and other amphibians are prey."

4. In the Common category on the Insert bar, click the small arrow next to the **Images** icon and then click **Image** (use the tooltips), or click **Insert** on the menu bar and then click **Image**, to insert a graphic on the page.

The Select Image Source dialog box opens.

> **Note**
>
> Dreamweaver will automatically load the last site definition used on the system. It should load your information if you were the last user. If it does not, use the list menu in the upper-left corner of the Files panel to locate and select your site's name (and, hence, your site definition) as it was created in Lesson 1.

5. Locate and open your **dangerous_frogs** folder, open the **images** folder, and select the file **ornate_horned.jpg**.

6. In the Relative to box, make sure **Document** is selected.

The document filename index.htm appears to the right of the menu.

7. Click **OK** (Windows) or **Choose** (Macintosh).

The Image Tag Accessibility Attributes dialog box opens.

8. In the Alternate Text box, key **Frog**. Then click **OK**.

Tips & Techniques

Identifying Graphics Formats for the Web

All current Web browsers support both the GIF and JPEG graphic formats. In general, use GIF if the artwork has large areas of solid color and no blending of colors, and use JPEG for photographic images or images with a large tonal range. For example, a picture of a blue sky with clouds looks "posterized" when saved as a GIF image. All the shades of blue are mapped to only a few colors and have a pronounced banded effect instead of a smooth blend from one blue shade to the next. GIF images are saved in 8-bit color mode, which means that only 256 colors can be represented. JPEG saves the image in 24-bit color mode, retaining many more colors and allowing more subtle blends.

Two other graphics formats are sometimes seen on the Web: BMP and PNG. BMP files, however, are usually much larger in size than comparable GIF or JPEG files. The PNG format is intended as a replacement for the GIF file format (the GIF file format was patented, while the PNG format is patent free), and it has more features than the GIF format does. However, older browsers typically do not support PNG files, so some visitors might not be able to view them.

If you are not sure which image format to use, check the file size. Whichever format gives you the smallest file size and still retains an acceptable level of quality for your image is the one you should select. Helping you optimize your images in this way is what Fireworks is good for. When you use Dreamweaver, you will want to make sure that Fireworks is at hand.

You can use transparency options to mask the background of a graphic. Transparency properties do not always work as you might expect, however, so be sure to test your pages on as many machines and browsers as possible.

Interlacing is a method of defining the way an image is displayed in the browser. Interlacing displays every other pixel on every other line and then goes back and repeats the process, filling in areas not already displayed. Without interlacing, the graphic is painted on the screen line by line, starting at the top of the image. Interlacing increases the file size slightly, but its advantage is that it provides a visual clue to the user that something is happening.

Principles and Rules of Copyright

Copyright is protection for intellectual property.

Intellectual property consists of anything an individual has written or created—music, text, pictures, photographs, sounds, and so on.

Fair use doctrine is part of the copyright laws. It states that "limited portions" of material may be used without written permission for certain purposes, such as reporting the news or schoolwork. It does not define "limited," though, so be sure you do not overuse material. The fair use doctrine requires you to give credit to the author or creator of any material you use.

Derivative works are copyrighted materials that have been altered or changed. Such material is protected by copyright laws. If you alter a copyrighted photograph by using computer software, that photograph is still protected, and you may not use it without written permission.

Academic standards for copyrighted material are higher than other standards. Because scholars and researchers study so many different ideas and are responsible for sharing those ideas with the world, they are required to satisfy higher standards of honesty. They must give credit not only when quoting the exact words of someone else but also for the ideas those words represent. As a researcher, you cannot paraphrase what someone else says and not give credit for it.

Bibliographies are lists of sources that have been used in research. When using the Internet for research or for design work, you need to give credit where it is due. Often, people who use graphics and images from the Internet for publication on their own Web page create a list of image credits rather than a bibliography.

Here are some guidelines to keep in mind:

- You cannot use copyrighted material without written permission from the creator of the material (or from its copyright holder).
- Material can be protected even if it does not display the © symbol. Even if no mention is made regarding copyright, you must assume that all material from another source is protected.
- Penalties for violating copyright laws can range from mild to severe. If you break the copyright law, you may simply receive an e-mail message from the author asking you to stop using the material. If you publish the material on a Web site, your Internet service provider may be obligated to shut down your site. In addition, you may be sued by the author or prosecuted by federal authorities.
- To make sure you are not violating any copyright law, it is important that you do the following:
  - Write or send e-mail to the author or creator and ask permission to use the material. Do not use it until you are given permission.
  - Follow the directions on the site regarding use of material. You may be asked to create a link on your page or to notify the author or creator.
  - Most important: *Do not* use any material if you do not have written permission.

9. In the Property inspector, in the image name text box (it is on the far left, under the word *Image*), key **ornate**, as shown in Figure 3-2. Then press **Tab**.

Although naming your images is not essential, it is a good practice. Nontext objects in a Web page must have names if you want to include user interactivity enhancements.

FIGURE 3-2
Property inspector for the Ornate Horned Frog image

10. Save your work.

Providing Alternative Text for Images

In the previous Step-by-Step, you were prompted to add alternative text to the Ornate Horned Frog image you inserted on the page, to make the image accessible. The Alt (short for Alternate) attribute lets you specify text to be displayed on browsers when graphics can not be displayed. This is a significant feature to add to any graphic, particularly graphics that are critical for navigation. If users have disabled graphic display or are using a text-only browser, at least they can see some of the information they are missing. People who are visually impaired may use a reader that speaks the alt text along with the text on a Web page. In some browsers, alt text is displayed briefly when the user moves the pointer over the graphic.

As you saw in the previous Step-by-Step, Dreamweaver prompts you to add accessibility attributes to images. (As you continue through these lessons, you will see similar prompts for other nontext page elements.) You can also use the Property inspector to control the alt text used for an image.

In the previous Step-by-Step, you added a photo to your page and labeled it with the simple alt text "Frog." But because this site is providing scientific information about frogs and the site will include photos of several species of frogs, that alt text is probably too generic. In this Step-by-Step, you will fix that problem.

> **Note**
>
> Adding alt text can be much easier than deciding what it should say. The alt text should reflect the general purpose of the image. If an image is largely decorative and does not convey content, keep the alt text fairly short. Too much information can be almost as bad as too little. Keep in mind that visitors using screen readers have to listen to this description before they can move on to the content of the page.

Work with Graphics and Add Alt Text

1. With the **index.htm** page still open, make sure the **ornate_horned.jpg** image is selected.

The Alt text field in the Properties inspector contains "Frog," the text you previously entered in the Image Tag Accessibility Attributes dialog box. Since there are several frog images in this site, it will be more helpful to make this alt text more specific.

2. In the Alt text box in the Property inspector, key **Ornate Horned Frog**. Then press **Tab**.

3. Save the document.

Editing Images from Within Dreamweaver

When you select the image of the Ornate Horned Frog on the Dangerous Frogs home page, you can check its width and height dimensions in the Property inspector. If you compare these to those specified in your design document, as shown in Figure 3-3, you will see that they do not match. You will need to crop the image.

FIGURE 3-3
Image dimensions on the Dangerous Frogs specification sheet

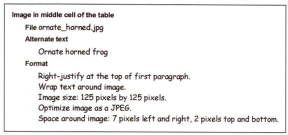

When you select an image, the Property inspector shows you several options for editing or modifying the image. From within Dreamweaver, you can quickly open an image in Fireworks to edit it in any number of ways. But Dreamweaver can also perform several quick modifications with even less effort. From the Property inspector, you can optimize an image to reduce its file size, adjust its brightness or contrast, sharpen it, or crop it.

 **Crop an Image**

1. With the **index.htm** page still open, select the Ornate Horned Frog image.

2. In the Property inspector, click the **Crop** button, shown in Figure 3-4. Dreamweaver will display a message to let you know that any change you make will permanently alter the image, but that you can use the Undo command to revert the image back to its original state. Click **OK**.

FIGURE 3-4
Property inspector for the Ornate Horned Frog image

3. Adjust the handle at the center top of the image so that the height of the photo is about **125** pixels. Adjust the handles on each side, pulling them out to each side, so that the image is **125** pixels wide. Watch the dimensions change in the Property inspector as you move a handle, so that you know where to reposition the handle. Then press **Enter** (Windows) or **Return** (Macintosh).

4. Save the file and preview it in your browser.

5. Close the browser.

Now is also a good time to make sure that the file size of the image is as small as it can be while maintaining good image quality.

 Optimize an Image

1. With the **index.htm** page still open, make sure the Ornate Horned Frog image is selected.

2. In the Property inspector, click the **Optimize in Fireworks** button.

The Find Source dialog box appears, as shown in Figure 3-5.

FIGURE 3-5
Find Source dialog box

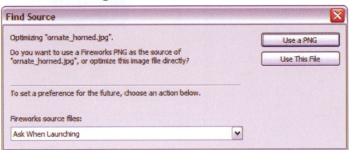

> **Note** ☑
>
> On the Macintosh, the Find Source dialog box is called the Find Source for Optimizing dialog box.

3. Click the **Use This File** button.

The Fireworks Optimize Images dialog box appears, as shown in Figure 3-6. Note that the file size of the image (displayed at the center top of the dialog box) is about 21K.

FIGURE 3-6
Fireworks Optimize Images dialog box

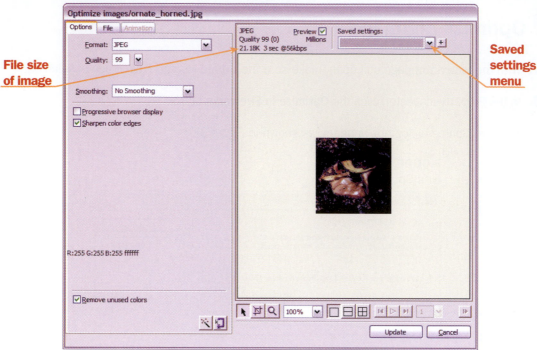

4. Click the **Saved Settings** menu and then click **JPEG Better Quality**.

The file size is now reduced to about 5K.

5. Click **Update**.

6. Save and preview the document.

Occasionally, you may find that an image would benefit from a slight color or quality alteration. Dreamweaver provides controls for this as well.

The page dedicated to the Monkey Frog needs an image. But when you import it, you will find that it is not quite the way you want it. To fix this image, you will need to make some adjustments using the image tools in Dreamweaver.

Adjust the Brightness and Contrast of an Image

1. Open the **green.htm** page and position the insertion point at the beginning of the line containing the heading **Habitat**.

2. Insert the **green_frog.jpg** image. When prompted for alt text, key **Monkey Frog**.

3. In the Property inspector, click the **Brightness and Contrast** button. If you see a dialog box warning you that this action will permanently alter the image, click **OK**.

4. Leave the Brightness set to **0**. Use the Contrast slider to set the Contrast to **25**.

You can toggle the Preview check box to compare the original image with the image as it will look when you click OK.

5. Click **OK**.

6. Save and preview the document.

Sizing Images

So far, you have created the home page for the site and one of the four pages dedicated to particular frogs. It is time to build a third page—the page for the Golden Poison Dart Frog. However, when you work on the page, you will find that the size of the frog image that you have does not match the dimensions specified on the design document, which calls for all of the images to be the same size: 125 × 125 pixels.

> **Note**
>
> Elements can be visually resized to a minimum of 8 × 8 pixels. To adjust the width and height of an element to a smaller size (for example, to 1 × 1 pixels), enter a numeric value in the Property inspector.

When you import a graphic, the width and height of the graphic are automatically displayed in the Property inspector. This gives the browser the information it needs to define the layout of the page.

In Dreamweaver, you can change the size of an image simply by selecting it and dragging the control handles. Visually resizing an image in this manner helps you to see how the image affects the layout at different dimensions. But this method does not scale the image file to the proportions that you specify—it just changes the way image is displayed. If you do visually resize an image in Dreamweaver but do not use an image-editing application (such as Fireworks) to scale the image file to the desired size, the user's browser has to scale the image when the page is loaded. This may cause both a delay in page download time and the improper display of the image in the user's browser.

Instead, you should adjust the image size in image-editing software (such as Fireworks). This will also ensure that you use the smallest file size possible.

> **Did You Know?**
>
> You can use the Width and Height attributes to create a special effect for a graphic without changing the file size of the graphic. For example, you can create a 1 × 1 pixel graphic of a color—a solid dot. Use the Width attribute to create a colored line across the page; use the Height attribute to change its height.

 ## Scale an Image in Fireworks

1. Open the **gold.htm** page. Copy the table from the **index.htm** page into the **gold.htm** page and attach the **frog.css** style sheet. Change the title of the page to **Dangerous Frogs – The Golden Poison Dart Frog** and the first line on the page to **Dangerous Frogs: The Golden Poison Dart Frog**. Replace the contents in the center table cell with the text from **GoldenPoisonDartFrog.doc**.

2. Change the lines containing the text **Phyllobates bicolor**, **Habitat**, and **Description** to Heading 2. Italicize **Phyllobates bicolor**. Set the remaining paragraphs to Style1.

3. In front of the text "Habitat" insert the **gold_frog.jpg** image. For alt text, key **Golden Poison Dart Frog**.

When the image is on the page, select it and examine its width and height in the Property inspector. Notice that its size is larger than called for in the storyboard for this page, as shown in Figure 3-7. For design purposes, it is better that the image dimensions all be consistent with the storyboard and with the other pages.

FIGURE 3-7
The Golden Poison Dart Frog is larger than it should be

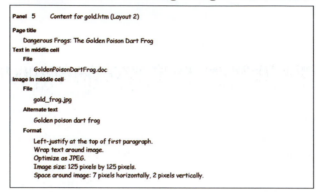

4. Select the image. In the Property inspector, click the **Optimize in Fireworks** button. When the File Source dialog box appears, click the **Use This File** button.

5. In the Fireworks Optimize Images dialog box, click the **File** tab.

You now see the file settings shown in Figure 3-8.

FIGURE 3-8
The Fireworks Optimize Images dialog box

6. Scale the image by setting the % menu to **75** (this is also called the *Scale image on export* field). You can also key the number into the % field and press **Tab** to see the change.

7. Click **Update**.

8. In Dreamweaver, you will see the Document window, but the image may still appear to be the same size. Select the image and click the circular arrow next to the H and W fields (this is the **Reset Image to Original Size** button).

9. Save and preview the document.

Wrapping Text Around Images

The storyboards for the Dangerous Frogs pages show the text wrapping around the images. The home page has the image on the right side of the page, and on green.htm and gold.htm, the images should be on the left.

Wrapping text around a graphic is a common formatting preference. You can achieve this easily by changing the Align attribute of the image. For text wrapping to work properly, make sure the image is inserted at the beginning of a paragraph. The text wraps to the bottom of the graphic and then returns to the left margin of the window.

Dreamweaver gives you several alignment options for images, including Top and Text Top. If you want your text to wrap or move to the top of the image, you might think that one of these options would work. However, multiline text can wrap only on either the left or the right side of an image, so the only options that will accomplish this are Left or Right (for more information about the image alignment options, see the Learn More feature "Image Alignment Options").

> **Inside the Design**
>
> Wrapping text around images makes the images seem a more integral part of the page. Switching the alignment of the image from one side of the page to the other helps the visitor quickly distinguish the home page from the other pages.

> **Note**
>
> If you want to place the image on the left and wrap the text on the right, select the image and choose Left in the Align field. If you want to place the image on the right and wrap the text on the left, select the image and choose Right in the Align field. The other alignment options on the menu are for the placement of a single line of text next to a graphic.

Wrap Text Around an Image

1. Open the **index.htm** page and select the **Ornate Horned Frog** image in the Document window. In the Property inspector, click **Right** on the Align menu, as shown in Figure 3-9.

   The image moves to the right of the paragraph and the text wraps around the frog image.

FIGURE 3-9
Property inspector, showing image properties

Align menu

2. Open **green.htm** and **gold.htm**, one after the other. In each file, select the image and set the Align property to **Left**.

Each of the pages about specific frogs will have frog images aligned on the left. The layout of the home page will be slightly different, with the frog image aligned on the right.

3. Save each file and preview the files in your browser.

4. Close the browser.

Modifying the Space Around Images

When you use an Align option to wrap text around the frog images, text will align close to the edge of the image. You will need to adjust the space around the image to add more of a margin and increase the readability of the page. You can do this in the Property inspector.

 ## Add Space Around an Image

1. With the **index.htm** page still open, select the **Ornate Horned Frog** image.

2. In the Property inspector, key **7** in the H Space text box.

This creates 7 pixels of space on the left and right sides of the image. You cannot add space on only one side with this method.

3. Key **2** in the V Space text box.

This creates 2 pixels of space at the top and the bottom of the image.

Learn More

Image Alignment Options

You need to understand how the alignment options work. The following seven options work well for aligning a single line of text near a graphic. However, they do not work for wrapping multiple lines around a graphic (use Left or Right instead). Here is what the Align menu options do:

- Baseline: Aligns the bottom of the image with the baseline of the text line.
- Top: Aligns the image with the top of the tallest item in the line.
- Middle: Aligns the baseline of the text line with the middle of the image.
- Bottom: Identical to Baseline.
- Text Top: Does what many people think Top should do, which is align the image with the top of the tallest text in the line (this is usually, but not always, the same as Top).
- Absolute Middle: Aligns the middle of the text line with the middle of the image.
- Absolute Bottom: Aligns the bottom of the image with the bottom of the text line.

4. In the **green.htm** and **gold.htm** pages, select the frog image in each page and repeat steps 2 and 3.

5. Save each file and preview it in your browser.

6. Close the browser.

Creating Image Maps

Previously, you added a navigation bar at the top of the page (the series of frog photos with labels). So far, however, this navigation bar does not do anything. It is time to change that.

The design document calls for each of the sections of this image to be linked to one of the pages in the site, as shown in Figure 3-10. For this, you will use an image map.

FIGURE 3-10
Navigation bar as specified for the Dangerous Frogs Web site

Graphic navigation bar	Image map with five rectangular hotspots, each with text above a frog image	
Text label:	**Links to:**	**Alternate text:**
HOME	index.htm	Home
GREEN	green.htm	Monkey frog
GOLD	gold.htm	Golden poison dart frog
BLUE	blue.htm	Blue poison dart frog
BLACK	black.htm	Dyeing poison dart frog

An image map is an image that has been divided into regions called *hotspots*. A hotspot can be clicked as a hyperlink. For instance, you could divide a single image of a world map by drawing a hotspot over each continent. Visitors to your site could then click a continent to go to a page on your site dedicated to that part of the world.

You can use Dreamweaver to insert an image map and to place individual hotspots on the map.

Create an Image Map

1. Open the **index.htm** page.

2. In the Document window, select the **frog_nav.jpg** image that you inserted previously in the top cell of the table.

3. In the Property inspector, key **frognav** in the Map text box, as shown in Figure 3-11. (If you do not see the Map text box, click the expander arrow at the bottom right of the inspector.)

> **Note**
>
> Do not use spaces or special characters in the name of an image map. You can have several image maps on a page, but each map name must be unique.

FIGURE 3-11
Property inspector's Map text box

Map text box

Pointer Hotspot Tool

Rectangular Hotspot Tool

Oval Hotspot Tool

Polygon Hotspot Tool

Hotspots can be in a variety of shapes. In the following Step-by-Step, you add several rectangular hotspots to the navigation image (Dreamweaver also lets you draw circular or polygonal hotspots, but since the frog images are all rectangular, the other shapes are not needed here). As you draw your hotspots, make sure that they are at least as big as the visible object so that users do not get frustrated trying to click something that they can see but that is not covered by the hotspot.

Create Hotspots

1. With the **index.htm** page still open, in the Property inspector, select the **Rectangular Hotspot** tool (refer to Figure 3-11).

2. Drag a rectangle around the word **Home** and the frog image beneath it.

   A translucent blue-green area with handles appears around the word and image. The Property inspector changes to show hotspot properties, as shown in Figure 3-12.

   FIGURE 3-12
   Hotspot Property inspector

   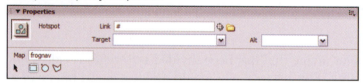

3. In the hotspot Property inspector, select the **Pointer Hotspot** tool (refer to Figure 3-11). If you need to resize the hotspot, drag a handle until the hotspot encompasses the appropriate area. If you need to move the hotspot, position the pointer inside the hotspot and drag. (The hotspot must be contained within the boundaries of the image.) The hotspot should look like that in Figure 3-13.

   FIGURE 3-13
   Home hotspot on the frognav image map

   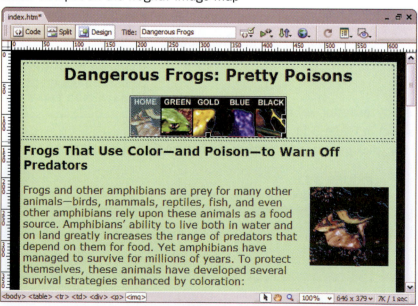

4. Make sure the rectangular hotspot is selected. In the hotspot Property inspector, key **Home** in the Alt text box.

This text serves the same purposes as alt text for an image.

5. Click the folder icon next to the Link text box, select **index.htm**, and click **OK**.

6. Save the file and preview it in your browser. Close the browser.

7. Select the frog navigation graphic.

8. In the Property inspector, select the **Rectangular Hotspot** tool again.

9. Drag a rectangle around the word **Green** and the frog picture beneath it.

The hotspot area appears, and the Property inspector changes to show hotspot properties.

10. Make the following changes:
   a. In the Alt text box, key **Monkey Frog.**
   b. In the Link text box, key **green.htm**. Make sure you delete the number sign (#) from this text box.

11. Do the same for the remaining sections of the navigation image, drawing rectangles around each one:
   a. For Gold, set the Alt text to **Golden Poison Dart Frog** and the link to **gold.htm**.
   b. For Blue, set the Alt text to **Blue Poison Dart Frog** and the link to **blue.htm**.
   c. For Black, set the Alt text to **Dyeing Poison Dart Frog** and the link to **black.htm**.

12. Save your file and preview it in your browser. Close the browser.

For consistency, this navigation bar should be placed on all pages of the site. You have already placed the navigation image on the other two pages you have worked on, so it is just a matter of copying the map.

Copy and Paste an Image Map

1. With the **index.htm** page still open, click one of the hotspots you created on the navigation bar. In the tag selector at the bottom of the Document window, click the **map#frognav** tag, as shown in Figure 3-14.

> **Note** ✅
>
> When you click a hotspot, be careful not to move it.

FIGURE 3-14
Tag selector with the <map#frognav> tag selected

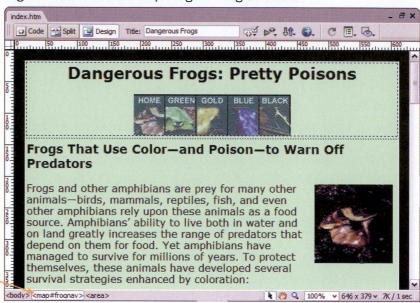

2. Click **Edit** on the menu bar and then click **Copy**.

3. Open **green.htm**. Select the frog navigation image. Click the **Edit** menu and then click **Paste**. Do the same in gold.htm.

4. Save the pages and preview them in your browser.

5. Close the browser and close Dreamweaver.

> **Note** ✅
>
> To delete a hotspot, select the graphic that contains the hotspot. Using the Pointer tool, select the hotspot. Click the Edit menu and then click Clear, or press Delete.

WORKING WITH LINKS

OBJECTIVES

Upon completion of this lesson, you will be able to:

■ Create a hyperlink to another page in your site.

■ Create a hyperlink to another site.

■ Use a hyperlink to open content in a new browser window.

■ Create a hyperlink to a named anchor.

Estimated time to complete this lesson: 35 minutes

Introduction

HTML's power comes from its capability to link regions of text and images to other documents. The browser highlights these regions (usually with color or underlining) to indicate that they are hypertext links—often called hyperlinks, or simply links. A link in HTML has two parts: the path to the file (or the URL of the file) to which you want to link, and the text or graphic that serves as the clickable link on the page. When the user clicks the link, the browser uses the path of the link to jump to the linked document. In some browsers, the path of the link is displayed in the status area of the browser window (the lower-left part of the window) when the pointer is positioned over the link.

In the Dangerous Frogs Web site, you have already created a navigation bar with the image map. Now you need to add links to help visitors quickly get to other pages of the site (or to a particular part of a page). This functionality makes your site easier to navigate, and it also helps visitors connect and organize ideas. In the previous lesson, you created links using an image map. In this lesson, you will learn additional methods for creating links in text.

Creating Hyperlinks

Hyperlinks can jump the user to another document within the current Web site or to a page at another Web site. For the link to work correctly, you have to provide the path to the target document in a format that the browser can follow. There are three types of paths that you can use: site-root-relative paths, absolute paths, and document-relative paths (for additional information, see the Tips & Techniques feature "Using Paths to Refer to Other Files").

For accessibility purposes, you should always provide redundant methods of navigation—that is, you should provide more than one method for navigating your site. It is good practice to create a way to navigate using only text links.

Previously, you added a footer to the bottom of the index.htm page. Now you will add functionality to this footer by linking it to the pages in the site.

Note

You must first save a document within a local site before site-root-relative or document-relative links will work. In all dialog boxes where you link a file to the current document, you can define the path as site-root relative, document relative, or absolute.

Tips & Techniques

Using Paths to Refer to Other Files

Site-root-relative paths provide the path from the site's root folder to a document. You may want to use a site-root-relative path if you are working on a large Web site that uses several servers or on one server that hosts several different sites.

If you move a document or folder out of a local site, site-root-relative links stop working. If you move folders containing linked files to a different defined local site, site-root-relative links continue to work as long as the folder structure branching from the root is the same as the original site's structure. A site-root-relative path begins with a leading forward slash, which stands for the site's root folder. For example, /images/ frog.jpg is a site-root-relative path to a file (frog.jpg) in the images subfolder of the site's root folder.

Absolute paths provide the complete URL of the linked document, including the protocol to use (usually HTTP for Web pages). For example, http://www.macromedia.com/ support/dreamweaver/getting_started.html is an absolute path. You must use an absolute path to link to a document on another server. You can also use absolute paths for local links (to documents in the same site). That approach is discouraged, however, because if you move the site to another domain, all your local absolute links will break.

Document-relative paths are the best choice for local links in most Web sites. Document-relative paths define the path to the linked file starting from the document. For example, a path to a file in the same folder would be expressed as myfile.htm. To link to a file in a subfolder of the current document, the path would be expressed as content/myfile.htm. To link to a file in the parent folder of the current file, the path would be expressed as ../myfile.htm (the ../ punctuation tells the browser to look for the file in the parent folder).

Create Links to Other Documents

1. Start Dreamweaver. In the Files panel, make sure your **Dangerous Frogs** site is selected. Then open the **index.htm** page.

2. In the Document window, scroll to the bottom of the page and find the text that says "Home | Green | Gold | Blue | Black." Select the text that says **Home**.

3. In the Property inspector, click the folder icon to the right of the Link text box.

   The Select File dialog box opens in the dangerous_frogs folder.

4. Select the **index.htm** file and click **OK** (Windows) or **Choose** (Macintosh).

   The filename index.htm appears in the Link text box.

5. Save the file and preview it in your browser. Close the browser.

6. Repeat steps 2 through 4 to link the word **Green** to the **green.htm** file, the word **Gold** to the **gold.htm** file, the word **Blue** to the **blue.htm** file, and the word **Black** to the **black.htm** file. Then save the file.

7. Copy the linked text **Home | Green | Gold | Blue | Black**. Open **gold.htm** and **green.htm**. In each page, replace the non-linked versions of this text in the footer by deleting them and pasting the linked version in their place.

8. Save the files and preview them in your browser. Close the browser.

Note

Dreamweaver will automatically load the last site definition used on the system. If you were the last user, it should load your information. If it does not, use the list menu at the upper left of the Files panel to locate and select your site's name (and, hence, your site definition).

Create a Link to an External Site

1. Open the **index.htm** page.

2. At the bottom of the page, select the text **Rainforest Conservation Fund**.

3. In the Property inspector, key **http://www.rainforestconservation.org/** in the Link text box, as shown in Figure 4-1. You must key the complete URL, including http://.

FIGURE 4-1
Property inspector, showing an URL link

Link text box

4. Save the file and preview it in your browser.

5. Close the browser.

Displaying Linked Content in a New Browser Window

When you link to a page, the linked page replaces the current browser page by default. Sometimes, however, you may want to display the browser page in a new location or window; for instance, you may want to do this for pages that are not part of your immediate site. If you link to a site outside your site, you lead your users out of your pages. If they have not bookmarked your URL, users may not remember how to return to your pages. If your outside links open a new browser window, your page remains in the original window. In the Dangerous Frogs Web site, you linked to an outside site, the Rainforest Conservation Fund, which you will now set to open in a new window.

 ## Target a Link

1. With the **index.htm** page still open, select the **Rainforest Conservation Fund** text. In the Property inspector, click the arrow on the Target box and choose **_blank**, as shown in Figure 4-2.

FIGURE 4-2
Property inspector's Target menu

2. Save the file and preview it in your browser.

When you click the linked text, the resulting page opens in a new browser window.

3. Close the browser, the **gold.htm** document, and the **green.htm** document. Leave Dreamweaver open for the next Step-by-Step.

Linking to Named Anchors

The Dangerous Frogs home page is fairly long. To help visitors quickly find information about the various types of coloration defenses, you can create links from the first paragraph to the content further down the page. These links will jump the user to specific places in the same Web page. This eliminates the tedium of scrolling through the document and helps the visitor find specific information quickly. To create this sort of link, you must create a jump-to point—a *named anchor*—that you can reference as the link.

Note

If the URL is long or complex, you can go to that site in your browser, select the URL in the browser's address field, and copy and paste the URL into the text box.

Note

The other choices available in the Target menu are for use with frames. Frames are beyond the scope of this book.

Note

Use caution when opening new browser windows. New windows impose extra RAM requirements on the user's computer as each window is opened. Most of the time, it is best to trust your visitors to find their way to and from your site. Opening new browser windows without a good reason can annoy your visitors.

In the following Step-by-Step, you will create named anchors for each of the coloration terms, as well as the links to jump to them.

Insert and Link to an Anchor

1. With the **index.htm** page still open, in the section titled "Coloration: The Second Clue," position the insertion point before the phrase "Protective Coloration."

2. In the Common category of the Insert bar, click **Named Anchor**, or click **Insert** on the menu bar and then click **Named Anchor** to insert a named anchor.

   The Named Anchor dialog box opens, as shown in Figure 4-3.

FIGURE 4-3
Named Anchor dialog box

3. In the Anchor Name text box, key **protective** and then click **OK**.

   A yellow anchor icon appears on the page to represent the anchor. (If you cannot see the icon, make sure Invisible Elements is turned on by clicking the **View** menu, pointing to **Visual Aids**, and then clicking **Invisible Elements**.)

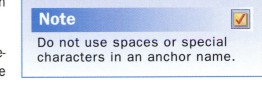

Note

Do not use spaces or special characters in an anchor name.

4. Add another named anchor called **flash** in front of the phrase "Flash Coloration."

5. Add a third named anchor called **warning** in front of "Warning Coloration."

6. Scroll to the top of the **index.htm** page. Find the ordered list in the first paragraph and select the text **camouflage**.

7. In the Link text box of the Property inspector, key **#protective**. Then press **Enter** (Windows) or **Return** (Macintosh). You must key the number sign (#) before the anchor name in the Link text box.

   Make sure the name you key is exactly the same as the anchor name. Anchor names are case-sensitive.

8. Save the file and preview it in your browser.

9. Close the browser.

One of many areas where HTML is case-sensitive is in the naming of anchors. If you name your anchor "top," for example, and then enter "#Top" in the Link text box, your link may not work consistently in all browsers. To avoid typing errors, you can use the Point to File icon in the Property inspector, as shown in Figure 4-4.

FIGURE 4-4
Point to File icon in the Property inspector

 Link by Using the Point to File Icon

1. With the **index.htm** page still open, add links to the other two items in the ordered list. Select the words **shocks** and **disruptions**.

2. Drag the **Point to File** icon and point to the **flash** anchor you created in the previous Step-by-Step (you may have to scroll the window to see the **flash** anchor). Release the mouse button when you are directly over the anchor.

    The link is created.

3. Using the **Point to File** icon or the **Link** field in the Property inspector, link **poison** to the **warning** anchor.

4. Save your file and preview it in your browser. Test the links.

5. When you finish, close the browser, close the document, and close Dreamweaver.

SUMMARY

You have successfully completed three of the five pages of the Dangerous Frogs Web site.

In this project, you learned to create a site definition in Dreamweaver, create new Web pages, add text and images to a Web page, and create links to other Web pages. You learned to format text and structure Web page content. These are the basic skills you need in order to create your own Web sites.

In the next project, you learn skills that will help you work on Web projects that are too big for one person alone. To this end, you find out more about how tables are used, what can be accomplished with CSS, and how to work with different kinds of media elements in Dreamweaver.

ON YOUR OWN – PERSONAL WEB SITE

ACTIVITY 1: FINISH THE DANGEROUS FROGS WEB SITE

You learned how to create Web pages in Dreamweaver, as well as how to format text, use images, and create links to these pages. Apply these same techniques to build the last two pages of the Dangerous Frogs personal Web site. You can use the storyboard that describes the site as a guide to build the blue.htm and black.htm pages for this site. You can find the storyboard in the Design folder from the data files for Project 1 of this unit.

You can review techniques for incorporating and formatting text on a Web page in Lesson 2. You can review techniques for using images on a Web page in Lesson 3. You can review techniques for using links in Lesson 4.

1. Follow the site summary in Figure 1 and the story-board for layout 2 in Figure 2 to build the common elements shared by **blue.htm** and **black.htm**, such as the table structure, the link to the external style sheet frogs.css, and the footer.

> **Note**
>
> Copy elements as necessary from other pages. Get table structure, navigation, and footer from one of the pages you have already completed. Remember to use the external style sheet.

FIGURE 1
Web site summary for Dangerous Frogs

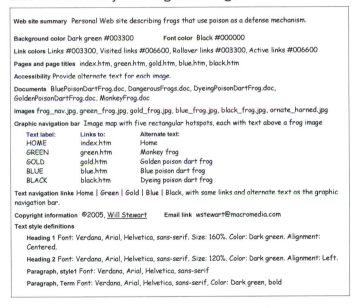

Web site summary Personal Web site describing frogs that use poison as a defense mechanism.

Background color Dark green #003300   Font color Black #000000

Link colors Links #003300, Visited links #006600, Rollover links #003300, Active links #006600

Pages and page titles index.htm, green.htm, gold.htm, blue.htm, black.htm

Accessibility Provide alternate text for each image.

Documents BluePoisonDartFrog.doc, DangerousFrogs.doc, DyeingPoisonDartFrog.doc, GoldenPoisonDartFrog.doc, MonkeyFrog.doc

Images frog_nav.jpg, green_frog.jpg, gold_frog.jpg, blue_frog.jpg, black_frog.jpg, ornate_horned.jpg

Graphic navigation bar Image map with five rectangular hotspots, each with text above a frog image

Text label:	Links to:	Alternate text:
HOME	index.htm	Home
GREEN	green.htm	Monkey frog
GOLD	gold.htm	Golden poison dart frog
BLUE	blue.htm	Blue poison dart frog
BLACK	black.htm	Dyeing poison dart frog

Text navigation links Home | Green | Gold | Blue | Black, with same links and alternate text as the graphic navigation bar.

Copyright information ©2005, Will Stewart   Email link wstewart@macromedia.com

Text style definitions

Heading 1 Font: Verdana, Arial, Helvetica, sans-serif. Size: 160%. Color: Dark green. Alignment: Centered.

Heading 2 Font: Verdana, Arial, Helvetica, sans-serif. Size: 120%. Color: Dark green. Alignment: Left.

Paragraph, style1 Font: Verdana, Arial, Helvetica, sans-serif

Paragraph, Term Font: Verdana, Arial, Helvetica, sans-serif, Color: Dark green, bold

FIGURE 2
Storyboard panel for layout 2

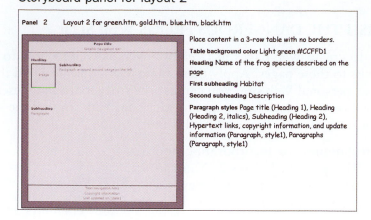

Panel 2   Layout 2 for green.htm, gold.htm, blue.htm, black.htm

Place content in a 3-row table with no borders.
Table background color Light green #CCFFD1
Heading Name of the frog species described on the page
First subheading Habitat
Second subheading Description
Paragraph styles Page title (Heading 1), Heading (Heading 2, italics), Subheading (Heading 2), Hypertext links, copyright information, and update information (Paragraph, style1), Paragraphs (Paragraph, style1)

2. Follow storyboard panel 6, shown in Figure 3, to build the content for the blue.htm page, such as text descriptions, images, and links.

FIGURE 3
Storyboard panel for blue.htm page

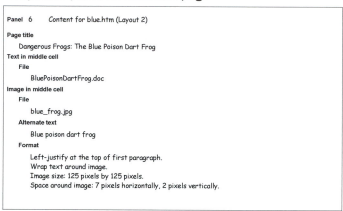

Panel 6   Content for blue.htm (Layout 2)

Page title
     Dangerous Frogs: The Blue Poison Dart Frog
Text in middle cell
     File
         BluePoisonDartFrog.doc
Image in middle cell
     File
         blue_frog.jpg
     Alternate text
         Blue poison dart frog
     Format
         Left-justify at the top of first paragraph.
         Wrap text around image.
         Image size: 125 pixels by 125 pixels.
         Space around image: 7 pixels horizontally, 2 pixels vertically.

3. Follow storyboard panel 7, shown in Figure 4, to build the content for the black.htm page, such as text descriptions, images, and links.

FIGURE 4
Storyboard panel for black.htm

Panel 7   Content for black.htm (Layout 2)

Page title
  Dangerous Frogs: The Dyeing Poison Dart Frog
Text in middle cell
  File
    DyeingPoisonDartFrog.doc
Image in middle cell
  File
    black_frog.jpg
  Alternate text
    Dyeing poison dart frog
  Format
    Left-justify at the top of first paragraph.
    Wrap text around image.
    Image size: 125 pixels by 125 pixels.
    Space around image: 7 pixels horizontally, 2 pixels vertically.

4. After completing the pages, save them and test all the links in the site to make sure all of the links work on all of the pages.

ACTIVITY 2: CREATE A CSS RULE

You learned how to create CSS styles for text and then export those styles into an external style sheet using Dreamweaver. Apply these same techniques to add a new style to the Dangerous Frogs style sheet.

You can review techniques for creating new CSS rules in Lesson 2.

The footer in the Dangerous Frogs Web site has text that is the same size as the body text. However, in most sites, the footer text is considered to be of lesser importance than the main content, so it is reduced in size. For this activity, create a footer style that you can apply to the footer text on each page.

1. In the Dangerous Frogs Web site, open the **index.htm** page.

2. Open the CSS panel and make sure the **All** button is selected. In the panel, make sure that **frogs.css** is selected.

3. At the bottom of the panel, click the **New CSS Rule** button.

4. In the New CSS Rule dialog box, make sure that **Class** is the Selector Type. For Name, key **footer**. Then click **OK**.

5. In the Type category, change the font to **Verdana, Arial, Helvetica, sans-serif**. Set the size to **70%**. The New CSS Rule dialog box should appear as in Figure 5. Click **OK**.

FIGURE 5
New CSS Rule dialog box

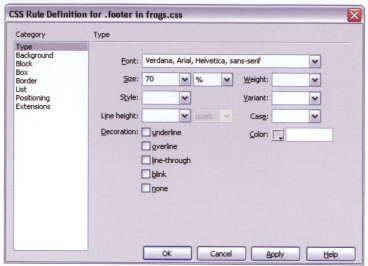

6. In each of the pages of the Dangerous Frogs Web site, select the footer text and and use the Property inspector to change the style of the text to the **footer** style.

7. Save the pages and view the pages to see the style changes.

BANKING SITE

GOALS

- Follow a design document to create pages in a large commercial Web site.
- Implement others' designs by assembling page elements in Dreamweaver.

TECHNICAL SKILLS

- Create a table.
- Modify table properties, including the properties of table rows and cells.
- Import data from a spreadsheet into a Web page.
- Attach and detach external style sheets.
- Use div tags to lay out a Web page.
- Create a Dreamweaver template.
- Create a new Web page from a Dreamweaver template.
- Update a Dreamweaver template.
- Update an image in Fireworks from within Dreamweaver.
- Insert a Flash movie on a Web page.
- Update a Flash movie from within Dreamweaver.
- Insert Flash Video on a Web page.

Estimated time to complete this project: 2 hours, 40 minutes

Summary

Working on a large corporate Web site presents a number of challenges that a small personal Web site does not. First, the larger a Web site is, the more difficult it becomes to manage. Updating one or two pages on a small Web site can take just a few minutes. But even a small change on a large site can result in an hours-long task. Say you decide to add or change a button on the main navigation bar—one that appears on each of a site's 200 pages. You not only have a lot of work to do, but you also have that many opportunities to make a mistake. In this situation, you not only have to make 200 changes, but you have to test 200 pages to make sure that the pages were updated correctly.

So it is important to use strategies that allow you to update many pages at once. In the following project, you experience two such strategies: Cascading Style Sheets and Dreamweaver templates.

The second challenge posed by a commercial site is that of sophistication. The nature of competition typically means that the site not only requires constant updates, but those updates must be more compelling than updates made by the competition. As the Web matures, different types of media, such as video and animation, are becoming more commonplace, so you need to know how to implement these.

Finally, you will find that the need to deal with large numbers of pages requires that a Web site be managed by a team and that the team coordinate its efforts. On such a team, you must incorporate sophisticated data and media elements created by others. You must be prepared to work from the team's design documents to make the project come to life. You may find that you lose control over certain aspects of the site, but the trade-off is that—as a team—you will be able to accomplish much, much more.

The Assignment

In this project, you use Dreamweaver to work on a Web site belonging to the fictitious financial institution, Experience Bank—a sample page from the site is shown in Figure 1. In this scenario, you are part of a team that is updating the site's look, and you will implement choices made by the team designers and content contributors. This project calls for you to:

- Work with tables to lay out data

- Implement consistency across the site using Cascading Style Sheets and Dreamweaver templates

- Use rich media to enhance pages

Along the way, you import data, switch out the CSS external style sheets to alter the site's design, implement a new navigation system, create page templates, and use those templates for new pages. You also add a bit of pizzazz to the pages, with Macromedia Flash animations and Flash Video.

> **Note**
>
> A Web site belonging to a real bank would consist of dozens, perhaps hundreds, of files. For this project, we have provided only those assets required to accomplish the activities in each lesson. Many files that you would expect to find in a site of this size have been omitted to make it easier to find the files you need to use.

FIGURE 1
Experience Bank Web site

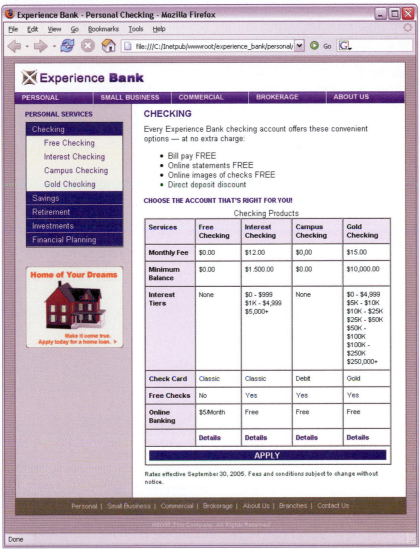

Web Site Design

The Experience Bank team uses a design document and storyboards that are a bit more sophisticated than the documents you used in the previous project. In some ways, they are more detailed, since more people have to be able to use them. In other ways, they are shorter, since the team uses documents that assume that a template is being used—which means that the story-board for a particular page does not have to describe every element on the page.

Instead, there is one storyboard panel for the standard page layout (the template), and this layout is referenced by the storyboard for each individual page. The template layout describes the standard elements that are consistent from one page to the next, as shown in Figure 2. The storyboards for the individual pages contain only the information required for that page—see the example in Figure 3.

FIGURE 2

Storyboard panel for a standard layout in the Experience Bank Web site

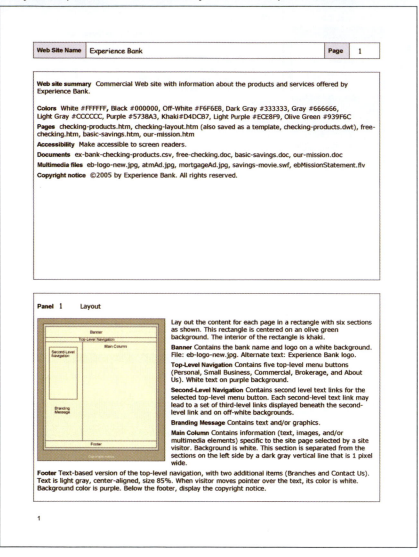

| Web Site Name | Experience Bank | | Page | 1 |

Web site summary Commercial Web site with information about the products and services offered by Experience Bank.

Colors White #FFFFFF, Black #000000, Off-White #F6F6E8, Dark Gray #333333, Gray #666666, Light Gray #CCCCCC, Purple #5738A3, Khaki#D4DCB7, Light Purple #ECE8F9, Olive Green #939F6C

Pages checking-products.htm, checking-layout.htm (also saved as a template, checking-products.dwt), free-checking.htm, basic-savings.htm, our-mission.htm

Accessibility Make accessible to screen readers.

Documents ex-bank-checking-products.csv, free-checking.doc, basic-savings.doc, our-mission.doc

Multimedia files eb-logo-new.jpg, atmAd.jpg, mortgageAd.jpg, savings-movie.swf, ebMissionStatement.flv

Copyright notice ©2005 by Experience Bank. All rights reserved.

Panel 1   Layout

Lay out the content for each page in a rectangle with six sections as shown. This rectangle is centered on an olive green background. The interior of the rectangle is khaki.

Banner Contains the bank name and logo on a white background. File: eb-logo-new.jpg. Alternate text: Experience Bank logo.

Top-Level Navigation Contains five top-level menu buttons (Personal, Small Business, Commercial, Brokerage, and About Us). White text on purple background.

Second-Level Navigation Contains second level text links for the selected top-level menu button. Each second-level text link may lead to a set of third-level links displayed beneath the second-level link and on off-white backgrounds.

Branding Message Contains text and/or graphics.

Main Column Contains information (text, images, and/or multimedia elements) specific to the site page selected by a site visitor. Background is white. This section is separated from the sections on the left side by a dark gray vertical line that is 1 pixel wide.

Footer Text-based version of the top-level navigation, with two additional items (Branches and Contact Us). Text is light gray, center-aligned, size 85%. When visitor moves pointer over the text, its color is white. Background color is purple. Below the footer, display the copyright notice.

1

FIGURE 3
Storyboard panel for an individual page in the Experience Bank Web site

Web Site Name	Experience Bank	Page	2

Panel 2   Content for checking-products.htm

Page title
Experience Bank – Personal Checking

Main Column heading
CHECKING

Main Column content
Every Experience Bank checking account offers these convenient options—at no extra charge.
- Bill pay FREE
- Online statements FREE
- Online images of check FREE
- Direct deposit discount

Choose the Account That's Right for You!

Checking Products

Services	Free Checking	Interest Checking	Campus Checking	Gold Checking
Monthly Fee	$0.00	$12.00	$0.00	$15.00
Minimum Balance	$0.00	$1.500.00	$0.00	$10,000.00
Interest Tiers	None	$0 - $999 $1K - $4,999 $5,000+	None	$0 - $4,999 $5K - $10K $10K - $25K $25K - $50K $50K - $100K $100K - $250K $250,000+
Check Card	Classic	Classic	Debit	Gold
Free Checks	No	Yes	Yes	Yes
Online Banking	$5/Month	Free	Free	Free
	Details	Details	Details	Details
APPLY				

Rates effective September 30, 2005. Fees and conditions subject to change without notice.

Notes for Checking Products table
The table should fill the width of the Main Column region. Border color is dark gray.

File for text in rows 2–7: Exp-bank-checking-products.csv

Text for the summary attribute of the table: This table of Experience Bank checking products lists the four different types of checking products (column headings) and the features of each one: monthly fee, minimum balance, interest tiers, check card, and free checks (row headings).

Column and row headers: Bold, center alignment, background color is light purple.

All cells: Add white space around the text in each cell. Display the text at 90%, vertically aligned at the top of the cell.

The instances of "Details" in the eighth row are links to the site pages free-checking.htm, interest-checking.htm, campus-checking.htm, and gold-checking.htm, respectively.

"APPLY" in the ninth row is white text on a purple background, a link to the site page application.htm.

The Experience Bank Web site is large enough that it would be impossible to build all of it—or even a main section—in the course of this project. When you complete the following lessons, you will have constructed only a representative sample of the site's pages. However, you will learn a number of techniques that professional development teams use to build pages on such sites. The flowchart in Figure 4 shows the sections of the site that you will work on.

FIGURE 4
Flowchart for the Experience Bank Web site

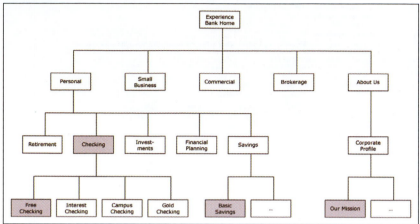

To print the design document and storyboards for the Experience Bank Web site, open the files named *DW_Project2_Design.pdf* and *DW_Project2_Storyboard.pdf*. These files are located in the Design folder for this project.

WORKING WITH TABLES

OBJECTIVES

Upon completion of this lesson, you will be able to:

- Create a table.
- Modify table properties, including the properties of table rows and cells.
- Import data from a spreadsheet into a Web page.

Estimated time to complete this lesson: 40 minutes

Introduction

Your first task for the Experience Bank Web site is to set up a table that displays information about products related to checking accounts. You set up the site and open the checking page, and then use this page to display the information. Although this table displays quite a bit of information, you will not enter all the data by hand. Instead, you import the data from a spreadsheet.

Before you begin, you need to set up a site definition for the Experience Bank Web site.

 ## Create a Site Definition for Experience Bank

1. Using the file management tools on your system, copy the entire **experience_bank** folder from the data files for this unit to the location where you will store your solution files (ask your instructor for specific directions).

2. Open Dreamweaver. Create a new site just as you did for the Dangerous Frogs Web site, with these differences:

   a. For the site name, use **Experience Bank** followed by your initials.

   b. For the local root folder, use the **experience_bank** folder that you copied in step 1.

Creating Tables

The Experience Bank Web site is divided into several main sections. Experience Bank wants to add more information to the page that describes its checking products. Similar information about each product needs to be displayed together so the site visitors can easily compare products. You can use tables in HTML either to present data in columns and rows or to lay out text and graphics on the page. If you have ever used a spreadsheet, then you are probably familiar with the concept of a data table as it appears on a Web page (for additional information, see the Learn More feature "HTML Tables").

You can use two methods to create a table for displaying data: you can create tables in Standard mode or Layout mode (for additional information, see the Learn More feature "Standard Mode and Layout Mode"), or you can import a spreadsheet. Creating your own tables provides you with the most flexibility for adjusting the table properties and contents. Importing a spreadsheet helps you quickly bring in content, but does not afford as much flexibility. To enter the product data into a table, you first create a table to hold some data, import a spreadsheet to quickly bring in additional data, and then use copy and paste to transfer the data from the spreadsheet table to the standard table to give yourself the most flexibility in setting table properties. To use Standard mode, make sure Standard Mode is selected in the Layout category of the Insert bar.

Learn More

HTML TABLES

If you were to look at the HTML tags that make up a table, you would see that these tables are defined not by rows and columns, but by rows (the <tr> tag) and cells (the <td> tag or the <th> tag). A table consists of one or more rows; each row consists of one or more cells. Fortunately, Dreamweaver enables you to manipulate columns as well as rows and cells.

When the table is selected or when the insertion point is in the table, Dreamweaver displays the table width and the column width for each table column at the top of the table. Next to the widths are arrows for the table header menu and the column header menu. Use the menus for quick access to some common table-related commands.

If you do not specify a width for a column or a height for a row, the browser uses the cell contents to determine the dimensions for each column or row. To control the dimensions, you can specify the width either in pixels or as a percentage.

When formatting tables in Design view, you can set properties for the entire table or for selected rows, columns, or cells in the table. When a property, such as background color or alignment, is set to one value for the whole table, a different value for rows, and yet another value for individual cells, cell formatting takes precedence over row formatting, which in turn takes precedence over table formatting.

The order of precedence for table formatting is:

1. Cells
2. Rows
3. Table

For example, if you set the background color for a single cell to blue and then set the background color of the entire table to yellow, the blue cell does not change to yellow, since cell formatting takes precedence over table formatting.

You can change the attributes, or characteristics, of a cell, row, or column by using options in the Property inspector. Following are definitions of the options in the cell, column, and row Property inspectors:

- **Horz:** Sets the horizontal alignment of the contents of selected cells to *Left*, *Right*, *Center*, or the browser's *Default* (usually Left for regular cells and Center for header cells).

(Continued . . .)

- **Vert:** Sets the vertical alignment of the contents of selected cells to *Top, Middle, Bottom, Baseline,* or the browser's *Default* (usually Middle).
- **W** and **H:** Sets the width and height of selected cells in pixels. To use a percentage, type a percent sign (%) after the value.
- **Bg (top):** Sets the background image for selected cells.
- **Bg (bottom):** Sets the background color for selected cells. Background color appears only inside the cells—that is, it does not flow over cell spacing or table borders. This means that if your cell spacing and cell padding are not set to zero, gaps will appear between the colored areas even if the border is set to zero.
- **Brdr:** Sets the border color for selected cells. Borders must be set for the entire table in order for this attribute to be recognized.
- **No Wrap:** Prevents word wrapping, so selected cells expand in width to accommodate all data. Normally, cells expand horizontally to accommodate the longest word and then expand vertically.
- **Header:** Formats the selected cells as table headers. The contents of table header cells are bold and centered by default.

Insert a Table

1. In the Files panel, open the **personal** folder. Then open the **checking** folder. Double-click the file **checking-products.htm** to open it.

   This is the Checking home page.

2. On the Insert bar, click the **Layout** category. Make sure the **Standard Mode** button is selected, as shown in Figure 1-1 (see the Learn More feature "Standard Mode and Layout mode" for more information about these options).

Note

Another way to refer to the Checking home page is by using the file path: /personal/checking/checking-products.htm. Throughout this unit, you may see a file path used to refer to a file. These file paths will help you find the location of the file.

FIGURE 1-1
Standard mode selected in the Layout category of the Insert bar

Table   Standard mode

3. Place the insertion point at the end of the line **Choose the Account That's Right for You!** Then press **Enter** (Windows) or **Return** (Macintosh) to create a new paragraph.

4. In the Layout category of the Insert bar, click **Table**, or click **Insert** on the menu bar and then click **Table**.

   The Table dialog box opens.

Inside the Design

The table is inside a div tag—a container that defines an area of the page. The designer wants the table to fill the width of the div tag. Setting the width as a percentage means that if the width of the div changes, the table will adjust accordingly.

5. Make the following changes in the Insert Table dialog box, as shown in Figure 1-2:

FIGURE 1-2
Table dialog box

a. Key **2** in the Rows box and **4** in the Columns box.

b. Change the Width to **100** and make sure the menu next to Table width is set to **Percent**.

c. Set the Border thickness to **1**.

This represents the width of the table border.

d. Set both the Cell padding and the Cell spacing to **0**.

e. For the Header, select the icon for **Top**.

The table will have labels for both rows and columns. However, because you will be importing data into the table, you will have to set the header attribute for the left column after the data has been imported into the table.

f. In the Caption box, key **Checking Products**.

g. In the Summary box, key **This table of Experience Bank checking products lists the four different types of checking products (column headings) and the features of each one: monthly fee, minimum balance, interest tiers, check card, and free checks (row headings).**

6. Click **OK** to close the dialog box.

The table appears in the page.

7. In the first cell of the first row, key **Services**. Then press **Tab** to move to the next cell. Key **Free Checking**. Press **Tab** again and key **Interest Checking**. Press **Tab** again and key **Gold Checking**.

Hot Tip

Tables specified in pixels are better for precise layout of text and images. Tables specified in percentages are a good choice when the proportions of the columns are more important than their actual widths.

Did You Know?

Cell padding refers to the amount of spacing between the cell content and the cell walls. Browsers use a default value of 0 pixels if you do not specify a value for the cell padding. *Cell spacing* refers to the amount of spacing between table cells, not including the border. Browsers use a default value of 0 pixels if you do not specify a value for the cell spacing (that is if you do not specify a border for the table—if a border is specified, the default value is 2).

8. You can change the number of columns or rows, even after you have created the table. With the insertion point in the **Gold Checking** cell, click **Insert** on the menu bar, point to **Table Objects**, and click **Insert Column to the Left**.

A new column appears.

9. In the cell at the top of the new column, key **Campus Checking**.

10. Click to the right of the table and then press **Enter** (Windows) or **Return** (Macintosh).

The insertion point is in a new paragraph below the table.

11. Save the file.

You could continue to enter the remaining text for the table. In the next Step-by-Step exercise, however, you use another method to fill the table.

Did You Know?

A table *header* is the cell used to hold the label for the column or row. Most browsers display a cell marked as a header slightly differently from other cells—boldface and centered by default. Setting the header property for a cell not only helps distinguish it from other cells, but some screen readers will recognize it and use it to read the table data in an intelligible manner.

Inside the Design

Captions and summary attributes help screen readers decipher content in a table and make it easier to understand that content. The Experience Bank design calls for both the caption and the summary attributes of a table to be implemented. The caption will be displayed at the top of the table, but the summary will not appear on the page—it is tucked away in the HTML, available to anyone who needs it.

Hot Tip

You can also use context menus to insert rows or columns before the cell you click. Right-click (Windows) or Control-click (Macintosh) a cell and then point to Tables. Then click *Insert Row* or *Insert Column*. If you choose the *Insert Columns or Rows* command instead, you can insert multiple rows or columns.

STANDARD MODE AND LAYOUT MODE

Dreamweaver provides two ways to view and manipulate tables: Standard mode, in which tables are presented as a grid of rows and columns (similar to a spreadsheet), and Layout mode, which allows you to draw, resize, and move boxes on the page while still using tables for the underlying structure.

Standard mode is better for tables that present data in columns. Layout mode is useful when you are using tables to lay out text and graphics on the page. (Recently, however, many designers have moved away from the use of tables for layout—they are relying on CSS positioning instead.)

Dreamweaver also offers an Expanded Tables mode, which temporarily adds cell padding and spacing to all tables in a document and increases the tables' borders to make editing easier. While in this mode, you won't necessarily see your tables the way they will appear in the browser, but you will be able to select items in tables or precisely place the insertion point. If you find yourself trying to select a cell but selecting its contents instead, try turning on Expanded Tables mode.

You can use the *Layout* category of the *Insert* bar to switch among these modes.

Importing Tabular Data

If you have information in a spreadsheet or even in a table in Microsoft Word, you can very easily insert it into Dreamweaver. Experience Bank has provided a spreadsheet containing information for its checking products.

Note

To make sure that the data comes in as expected, first save or export the text as a tab- or comma-delimited file.

Import Data as a Table

1. With the **checking-products.htm** page still open, make sure the insertion point is in the new paragraph after the table you created.

2. Click **Insert** on the menu bar, point to **Table Objects**, and then click **Import Tabular Data**, or click the **Tabular Data** button in the Layout category of the Insert bar.

   The Import Tabular Data dialog box opens, as shown in Figure 1-3.

FIGURE 1-3
Import Tabular Data dialog box

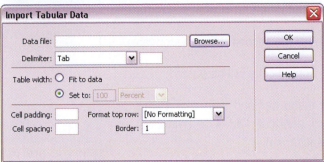

3. Click **Browse**; then navigate to the **exp-bank-checking-products.csv** file in the **_documents** folder and double-click it.

4. In the Import Tabular Data dialog box, do the following:
   a. Be sure Delimiter is set to **Comma.**
   b. For Table Width, click the **Set To** option and enter **100** in the text box and make sure that the menu next to it is set to **Percent**.
   c. Make sure that **[No Formatting]** is selected in the *Format top row* menu and that **1** appears in the Border box.

5. Click **OK**.

   The data is imported, and a table is built for you with the settings you chose.

6. Save the file.

You now have two tables: the first you created with the row headers and the second you imported with the data. But the design calls for only one table, so you must combine the two. You will copy the data from the imported spreadsheet into your existing table to provide the most flexibility with adjusting table properties.

Copying and Pasting Table Cells

You can copy and paste multiple table cells at once, preserving the cells' formatting, or you can copy and paste only the contents of the cells.

Cells can be pasted at an insertion point or in place of a selection in an existing table. To paste multiple table cells, the contents of the Clipboard must be compatible with the structure of the table or the selection in the table in which the cells will be pasted.

 Copy and Paste Cell Content

1. With the **checking-products.htm** page still open, select all the cells in the second table by dragging across the cells. Start in the upper-left cell and drag to the lower-right cell.

   The selected cells are displayed with a black border. To be cut or copied, the selected cells must form a rectangle.

2. Click **Edit** on the menu bar and then click **Copy**, or use the keyboard shortcut **Ctrl + C** (Windows) or **Command + C** (Macintosh).

3. Click in the first cell of the second row in the top table.

   This is where the copied cells will be pasted.

4. Click **Edit** in the menu bar and then click **Paste**, or use the keyboard shortcut **Ctrl + V** (Windows) or **Command + V** (Macintosh).

   All the cells from the second table should now be inserted in the first table.

5. Save the file.

Deleting Cells and Content

The first table on the Checking Products page is the one you will keep. You will remove the second table shortly. But before you remove it, use it to learn a few of the differences between working with cells and working with cell content.

Note

You may have to click away from the second table to deselect it before you can access the second row in the top table.

Note

If you are pasting entire rows or columns, the rows or columns are added to the table. If you are pasting an individual cell, the contents of the selected cell are replaced if the Clipboard contents are compatible with the selected cell. If you are pasting outside a table, the rows, columns, or cells are used to define a new table.

Delete Cell Content, Rows, Columns, and a Table

1. With the **checking-products.htm** page still open, select two or more cells in the second table, but not an entire row or column.

2. Click **Edit** on the menu bar and then click **Clear** or press **Delete**.

   This removes cell content but leaves the cells intact.

3. Drag across all the cells in a row of the second table to select the entire row.

4. Press **Delete**.

   The row and all its contents are deleted.

5. Practice selecting an entire table by doing the following:
   a. Position the pointer on the upper-left corner of the second table or anywhere on the bottom edge. The pointer turns to a white arrow with a small table icon when you are close to the edge. Click when you see the pointer. Click outside the table to deselect it.
   b. Click once in the second table. Click **Modify** on the menu bar, point to **Table**, and then click **Select Table**. Click outside the table to deselect it.

c. Position the insertion point anywhere inside the second table and select the **\<table\>** tag in the tag selector at the lower left of the Document window.

Selection handles appear around the table when it is selected. When the table is selected, you cannot see the black border around any of the cells.

6. With the second table selected, press **Delete** to remove the second table.

Your page should now look similar to the page shown in Figure 1-4.

FIGURE 1-4
Checking Products page

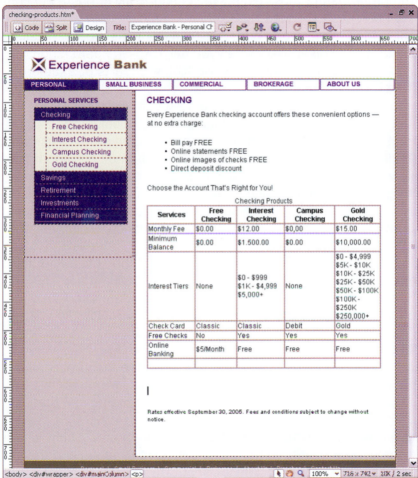

7. Save your file and preview it in the browser.

8. Close the browser.

For more about working with table cells, see the Learn More feature "Selecting Table Elements."

SELECTING TABLE ELEMENTS

To change or delete a table, you need to select the table. Dreamweaver provides several methods for selecting a table. You will find that some methods are easier than others, depending on the complexity of the table structure. You can easily select a row, a column, or all the cells in a table. You can also select noncontiguous cells in a table and modify the properties of those cells. (You cannot copy or paste noncontiguous cell selections.) You can use Expanded Tables mode to more easily select and edit cells. Expanded Tables mode temporarily adds space inside cells, between cells, and to the table border. That space disappears when you revert to Standard mode.

Following are options for selecting and working with parts of a table:

- **Selecting rows or columns:** Position the pointer at the left margin of a row or at the top of a column and click when the selection arrow appears. Or click in a cell and drag across or down to select multiple rows or columns.
- **Selecting one or more cells**: Click in a cell and drag down or across to another cell. Or click in one cell and then hold down Shift and click another cell to select all cells within the rectangular region defined by the two cells.
- **Selecting noncontiguous cells:** Press Ctrl (Windows) or Command (Macintosh) and click to add cells, rows, or columns to the selection. To deselect multiple cells in the table, press Ctrl (Windows) or Command (Macintosh) and click cells, rows, or columns.
- **Resizing a column:** Move the pointer over one of the column borders. When the pointer changes to a two-headed arrow, drag the column border.
- **Adding a new row**: Click in the last cell of a row and press Tab, or click Modify on the menu bar, point to Table, and then click Insert Row. You can also right-click (Windows) or Ctrl-click (Macintosh) in the table, select the Table menu, and then, in the submenu, click Insert Row.
- **Deleting a row:** Click in the row, click Modify on the menu bar, point to Table, and then click Delete Row. You can also use right-click (Windows) or Ctrl-click (Macintosh) while in the table row, click the Table menu, and then, in the submenu, click Delete Row.
- **Adding a row in the middle of the table:** Click in the row below where you want the new one, click Modify on the menu bar, point to Table, and then click Insert Row. You can also right-click (Windows) or Ctrl-click (Macintosh) in the row below, click the Table menu, and then, in the submenu, click Insert Row.
- **Inserting a row and controlling placement before or after the current row:** Click Modify on the menu bar, point to Table, and then click Insert Rows or Columns. A dialog box opens in which you can specify whether to insert before or after the current row.
- **Merging columns or rows:** Drag to select multiple cells and then, in the Property inspector, click Merge Cells. You can also click Modify on the menu bar, point to Table, and then click Merge Cells.
- **Splitting a cell**: Select the cell and then, in the Property inspector, click Split Cell, or click Modify on the menu bar, point to Table, and then click Split Cell to return the number of cells to the original setting (if you previously merged them) or to split a cell into any number of rows or columns.

Formatting Tables

The design for the table on the Checking Products page requires that information be formatted in line with design principles that enable better readability and accessibility. In the following steps, you format the table to add more white space around the text, which will improve readability. To increase accessibility, you designate header rows so that screen readers will be able to read the information in order.

 Format a Table

1. With the **checking-products.htm** page still open, select the **Checking Products** table.

   The Property inspector should look like that shown in Figure 1-5.

> **Inside the Design**
>
> Designers use different techniques to increase readability and accessibility of dense information. In the Experience Bank site, the designer calls for adding white space around the text in each cell to separate dense pieces of information, bold text to divert the eye first to heading information, and border and text color to set the table apart visually from the rest of the page. To improve accessibility, the designer specifies a heading row, which will show screen readers the order in which text in the table should be read.

FIGURE 1-5
Table Property inspector

Brdr color box

2. In the Property inspector, make these changes:

   a. In the CellPad box, key **6**. This will increase the space between the content of the cell and the cell border and make the text more readable.

   If you do not see the CellPad box in the Property inspector, make sure that you have selected the entire table, not just the cells in the table.

   b. In the box next to the *Brdr color* color picker, key **#333333**. This will darken the border color from its default gray and emphasize the table's presence on the page.

3. Select all of the cells in the table. The easiest way to do this is to drag from the upper-left corner cell to the lower-right corner cell.

Each cell should now be outlined with a selection border, as shown in Figure 1-6. (Make sure you do not select the table instead of the cells in the table. If you select the table as a whole, you will see a selection border around the table, [including the caption], instead of around each cell.)

FIGURE 1-6
Checking Products table with all cells selected

Services	Free Checking	Interest Checking	Campus Checking	Gold Checking
Monthly Fee	$0.00	$12.00	$0,00	$15.00
Minimum Balance	$0.00	$1.500.00	$0.00	$10,000.00
Interest Tiers	None	$0 - $999 $1K - $4,999 $5,000+	None	$0 - $4,999 $5K - $10K $10K - $25K $25K - $50K $50K - $100K $100K - $250K $250,000+
Check Card	Classic	Classic	Debit	Gold
Free Checks	No	Yes	Yes	Yes
Online Banking	$5/Month	Free	Free	Free

4. Make these changes in the Property inspector:

  a. In the Size box, key **90%**. This reduces the font size slightly to make the text fit more neatly into the cells.

  b. In the Vert menu, select **Top**.

5. Select all the cells in the left column.

When you created the table on the Checking Products page, you chose a setting to make the top row of cells header cells. You must also set the left column cells as header cells.

6. In the Property inspector, click the **Header** check box so that it is checked.

The text in the selected cells is now boldface and centered.

7. With the left column still selected, press **Ctrl** (Windows) or **Command** (Macintosh) and click each of the unselected cells in the top row.

Now all of the cells in the top row and all of the cells in the left column should be selected. You are going to set the colors for just these boxes, so that the headers stand out from the rest of the table. Changes that you make in the Property inspector, shown in Figure 1-7, will affect all of the selected cells.

FIGURE 1-7
Table cell Property inspector

Font color box

Bg color box

8. In the box next to the Bg color picker, key **#ECE8F9**. Then press **Tab**.

The background color of the selected cells is now light purple.

9. The bottom row of the table is empty. You can see in Figure 1-8 that the storyboard shows that each product should have a link to Details displayed in this row, so in the bottom cell of the Free Checking column, key the word **Details**.

FIGURE 1-8
Storyboard document for the Checking Products table

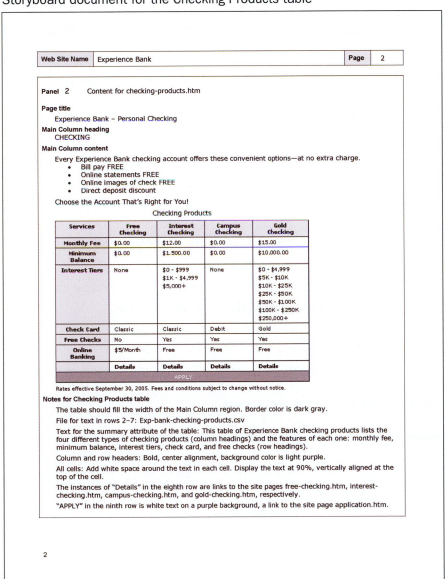

10. Select the word **Details**. In the Property inspector, key **free-checking.htm** in the Link box.

The free-checking.htm page has not been built yet, but the storyboard indicates this link will be required.

11. Repeat steps 9 and 10 for the other products in the table, keying the word **Details** in the bottom cell under each product and linking Details as follows:

a. For Interest Checking, key **interest-checking.htm**.

b. For Campus Checking, key **campus-checking.htm**.

c. For Gold Checking, key **gold-checking.htm**.

12. Select the four cells containing the word **Details**. In the Property inspector, use the **Style** menu to set the style of these cells to **DetailLink**.

13. You can add a row at the end of the table very easily. Click in the cell in the lower-right corner (the Details cell for Gold Checking). Press **Tab**.

A new empty row appears at the bottom of the table.

14. Select all of the cells in the new row. In the Property inspector, click the **Merge Cells** button, shown in Figure 1-9.

The row is now formed into a single cell. The Property inspector should now look like that in Figure 1-9.

FIGURE 1-9
Merge Cells button in the Property inspector

15. Make sure the merged cell is still selected. In the Property inspector, do the following:

a. Click the **Header** check box to uncheck the Header setting.

b. In the text box next to the Bg color picker, delete **#ECE8F9** to clear the background color setting.

c. Use the Style menu to apply the **ApplyLink** style for the cell.

16. Key the word **Apply** in the cell.

17. Select the word **Apply**. In the Property inspector, key **application.htm** in the **Link** text box.

18. Save your file and preview it in the browser.

19. Close the browser, close the document, and close Dreamweaver.

MAINTAINING CONSISTENCY WITH TEMPLATES AND CSS

OBJECTIVES

Upon completion of this lesson, you will be able to:

■ Attach and detach external style sheets.

■ Use div tags to lay out a Web page.

■ Create a Dreamweaver template.

■ Create a new Web page from a Dreamweaver template.

■ Update a Dreamweaver template.

Estimated time to complete this lesson: 1 hour, 30 minutes

Introduction

The Experience Bank Web site is too large for any one person to be responsible for. To reduce the number of tasks required to build or update a page, the team that works on the site uses both Cascading Style Sheets (CSS) and Dreamweaver templates. CSS enables you to quickly make design changes across the site. Dreamweaver templates enable you to make structural changes across the site. In addition, templates control which page elements other team members or contributors to the site—such as writers, graphic artists, or other Web developers—can edit.

As the number of pages in a Web site increases, consistency becomes a struggle. Good planning becomes a necessity. When there are only a handful of pages, correcting a navigation link is not difficult to do by hand. When there are 10 pages, you can use copy and paste. But when there are dozens of pages that need the same update, a good developer will take advantage of templates, CSS's, and reuseable content such as images and library objects.

As you proceed through this lesson, you will apply style sheets, create templates, and create pages from those templates, taking your cues from the design document and storyboards created by other members of the Experience Bank Web team.

Consistency in Design

Consistency is a simple concept that benefits both site developers and site visitors. It's the idea of sameness from one page to the next. While it's true that every page should hold different content from the others (or there'd be no reason for it to exist), it's also true that there are elements on every page that help to hold the distinct content (and, in fact, identify it as distinctive).

Confidence in your site will be conveyed in the consistent use of colors, placement of site navigation tools, text styles, layout, and menus (for additional information, see the Tips & Techniques feature "Trusting a Web Site").

Using Cascading Style Sheets

The Experience Bank Web site uses external style sheets to enforce a consistent look and feel across the site. CSS lets you control many properties that cannot be controlled using HTML alone (for additional information, see the Tips & Techniques feature "Understanding Cascading Style Sheets"). For example, you can specify different font sizes and units (pixels, points, and so on) for selected text. By using CSS to set font sizes in pixels, you can also ensure a more consistent treatment of your page layout and appearance in multiple browsers.

You can use CSS for design, and you can also use it for layout. In the Dangerous Frogs project, you saw how CSS can be used for design. Discussion of how CSS works to position elements on a page is beyond the scope of this book. However, in this lesson, you will build the layout for the checking products template and you will see how the CSS determines the size and position of the various sections of the page.

The best place to store a collection of styles is in an external style sheet. You could store your styles in the document that is using them, but then you would have to copy and paste the styles from one page to another. And if you ever wanted to change a style that is used in multiple pages, you would have to make the change on every page.

Instead, most developers store their styles in external style sheets. These style sheets can then be linked to a Web page with a single line of code. When the browser sees this line of code, it downloads the style sheet and displays the page using the rules specified in the style sheet. Not only does this allow a single group of rules to govern the look of all pages, but it also allows you to change the look of a page very quickly, simply by switching the page to a different style sheet.

Tips & Techniques

TRUSTING A WEB SITE

Think about your own behavior when you visit a new site. At first, you notice everything: the logo, the navigation bar, an image here, text there, and eventually your eye will settle on the "important" content on the page. As you move from one page to the next, there are certain elements you will begin to expect and thus ignore, so your focus will go more directly to the content that is unique to the page.

This happens because you develop a sort of "trust" of the items that are consistent from one page to the next. Having investigated them once, you come to assume that when you see them again, they will have the same properties on the new page that they had the first time you saw them. Any deviation from the standard look and feel will cause visitors to question whether they are still on the site and thus distract their attention from the important content. Imagine that you visit a site with a logo in the upper-right corner of each page, but on some pages, clicking this logo takes you to the home page, while on others it does nothing. Many visitors would be annoyed by such an inconsistency—and though you may assume that the inconsistency wasn't intentional, you may find your sense of confidence in the site as a whole undermined.

The ability to quickly switch style sheets will help you in your next assignment.

Experience Bank has asked your team to update the look of its site. The designers on the team have come up with three different proposals for the new look. They want you to prepare pages that show each of the new presentations (such pages are often referred to as *comps*, short for *comprehensive layout*). The comps will help the brand managers at Experience Bank determine which new look to use.

 ## Detach and Attach Style Sheets to a Web Page

1. Start Dreamweaver and make sure you have the Experience Bank site open. In the Files panel, click the site folder (the **Site - Experience Bank** folder at the top of the list of files in the Files panel).

   This folder represents the site root.

2. Create a new folder by clicking the Files panel **Options** menu, pointing to **File**, and clicking **New Folder**. Name the new folder **design-reviews**.

3. Open the file **personal/checking/index.htm**.

4. Click **File** on the menu bar and then click **Save As**. Name the file **exp-bank-design-a.htm** and save it in the **design-reviews** folder. If a message appears asking if you want to update links, click **Yes**.

5. Open the CSS Styles panel, shown in Figure 2-1. If you do not see the CSS Styles panel, click **Window** on the menu bar and then click **CSS Styles**.

> **Note**
>
> The file personal/checking/ index.htm should be identical to the final version of the personal/checking/checking-products.htm file you worked on in Lesson 1. If you feel confident in your completion of that file, you can continue this activity with your version of checking-products.htm instead of index.htm.

FIGURE 2-1
CSS Styles panel

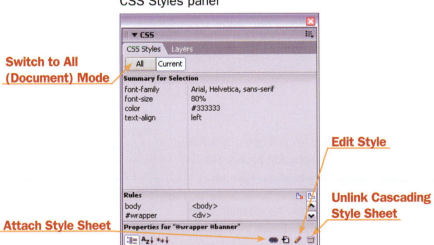

6. Click the **All** button.

   The name of the external style sheet attached to this page—experience-bank.css—is displayed at the top of the panel.

7. Click the name of the external style sheet—**experience-bank.css**—to select it.

8. Click the **Unlink CSS Stylesheet** button at the bottom of the CSS Styles panel (the trash can icon).

9. Click the **<style>** tag at the top of the CSS Styles panel. This is the collection of styles embedded in this page. Delete these styles from the page by clicking the **Delete Embedded Stylesheet** button at the bottom of the panel (the same trash can icon you clicked in the previous step).

   Note that the text on the page is now very plain and that the layout has disappeared.

10. At the bottom of the CSS styles panel, click the **Attach Style Sheet** button.

    The Attach Style Sheet dialog box appears, as shown in Figure 2-2.

FIGURE 2-2
Attach Style Sheet dialog box

11. Click the **Browse** button to open the Select Style Sheet File dialog box. Navigate to **/css/eb-main-a.css**, click the file, and click **OK** (Windows) or **Choose** (Macintosh).

12. Back in the Attach Style Sheet dialog box, make sure that **Add as Link** is selected. Then click **OK**.

    The page appears in a new layout.

13. Save the file.

14. With the **exp-bank-design-a.htm** file still open, click **File** on the menu bar and then click **Save As**. Save the file in the **design-reviews** folder as **exp-bank-design-b.htm**.

15. Use the CSS files panel to unlink the **eb-main-a.css** style sheet and attach the **eb-main-b.css** style sheet.

16. Save the file.

Inside the Design

Note the differences in the page. The designers want to show the clients something warmer, so this page has orange, tan, and gold colors whereas the old design used blues and grays. The caption has now been styled, the borders of the table are softer, and the pinstripe of the old design is gone, replaced by a darker color that brings the eye into the middle of the page, rather than drawing it out to the margins.

17. Repeat steps 14 through 16, unlinking **eb-main-b.css** from the page and attaching **eb-main-c.css**. Save the page in the **design-reviews** folder as **exp-bank-design-c.htm**.

You now have three sample pages ready to show to the Experience Bank brand managers.

18. Preview each page in the browser. Note the differences in the background colors of each section of the page and the color of text and headings.

19. Close the browser and close the design review pages in Dreamweaver.

Tips & Techniques

UNDERSTANDING CASCADING STYLE SHEETS

Cascading Style Sheets are a collection of formatting rules that control the appearance of content in a Web page. When you use CSS to format a page, you separate content from presentation. The content of your page—the HTML code—resides in the HTML file itself, while the CSS rules defining the presentation of the code reside in another file (an external style sheet) or in another part of the HTML document (usually the head section). With CSS, you have great flexibility and control over the exact appearance of your page, from precise positioning of layout to specific fonts and styles.

In addition to text formatting, you can use CSS to control the format and positioning of block-level elements in a Web page. For example, you can set margins and borders and float text around other text.

The term *cascading* refers to your ability to apply multiple styles to the same element. For example, you can create one CSS rule to apply color and another to apply margins, and apply them both to the same text on a page. The defined styles "cascade" down to the elements on your Web page, ultimately creating the design you want.

A major advantage of CSS is that it provides easy update capability; when you update a CSS rule in one place, the formatting of all the documents that use the defined style are automatically updated to the new style.

CSS rules can reside in the following locations:

- **External CSS style sheets** are collections of CSS rules stored in a separate, external CSS (.css) file (not an HTML file). This file is linked to one or more pages in a Web site using a link in the head section of a document.
- **Internal (or embedded) CSS style sheets** are collections of CSS rules included in a style tag in the head portion of an HTML document.
- **Inline styles** are defined with specific instances of tags throughout an HTML document.

Dreamweaver recognizes styles defined in existing documents as long as they conform to CSS style guidelines.

Using a Storyboard to Lay Out a Page

The Experience Bank Web team works together by using design documents such as storyboards, flowcharts, and user scenarios to make sure that everyone on the team knows what to do. Storyboards may differ in format from one design studio to another, but their purpose is the same: to make sure that as developers move from page to page, they know which parts of the page stay the same and which parts change. They also give developers confidence that their co-workers are building their pages according to the same plan.

Your next task for Experience Bank is to build a page layout according to the specifications of a storyboard, shown in Figure 2-3. This layout will eventually become a template for use across the site. Before you begin, look over the storyboard so that you have a sense of what the end product will be.

The page you build will be used to create a template from which other pages can be built, so the page will not have much in the way of content. Instead, you focus on creating the structure for the page and adding those elements that should be consistent from one page to the next.

To build this page, you start by creating a series of div tags. Each div tag acts as a container to hold a certain portion of the page—this is how you will block out the page layout. You will assign each div tag a style by giving it an ID. Just as you can assign a collection of CSS rules to text by applying a style to the text, you can assign a collection of CSS rules to a div tag by giving the div tag a particular ID.

After creating div tags, you will go back and populate each one with content appropriate to that section of the page.

Did You Know?

A div tag is used to identify a region of a Web page. The tag takes its name from the word *division*, and it is used to divide one portion of a page from the others. A div tag acts as a container of page elements. It can have width, height, border, background color, and a number of other properties. It can also be positioned on the page in many ways. A div tag is the main tool for implementing layout using CSS rules.

FIGURE 2-3

Storyboards for the Experience Bank checking template

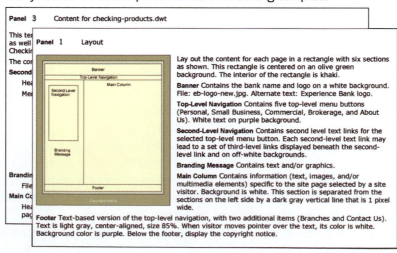

Create Basic Page Structure Using Div Tags

1. In the Files panel, create a new file in the root folder of the Experience Bank Web site and name it **checking-layout.htm**. Open the file.

2. Change the title of the page to **Experience Bank – Personal Services**.

3. Use the CSS panel to attach the external style sheet named **eb-main.css** to the page.

4. In the Layout category of the Insert bar, click the **Insert Div Tag** button, shown in Figure 2-4.

> **Important**
>
> The designers on your team have created a style sheet that will help you with the layout. As you assign each div tag a CSS style, you will find that many of the properties of the div tags have already been set, but you must review the properties to make sure that they conform to the storyboard.

FIGURE 2-4
Layout Category of the Insert bar

Insert Div Tag

The Insert Div Tag dialog box appears.

5. On the Insert menu, select **At Insertion Point**. On the ID menu, select **wrapper**. Then click **OK**.

A new div tag appears as a box in your document with placeholder text ("Content for id 'wrapper' Goes Here"). When you move the pointer over the edge of the box, Dreamweaver highlights it. This area will hold the div tags for the different content elements that will be placed on the page.

> **Note**
>
> Dreamweaver automatically inserts placeholder text whenever you insert a new div tag. Do not delete the placeholder text until you are ready to add real content in the div tag, or you may be forced to repeat the step.

In the next few steps, you will create six more div tags inside this one. Each of these will correspond to the sections blocked out on the storyboard: banner, navigation, subNavColumn (used to create a column on the left side of the page), vertnav (a div tag placed inside subNavColumn to hold the sub-section navigation), mainColumn (used to hold the main content of the page), and footer.

6. Place the insertion point at the end of the placeholder text. Click the **Insert Div Tag** button. In the Insert Div Tag dialog box, set the Insert menu to **At Insertion Point** and the ID menu to **banner**. Click **OK**.

The banner div tag appears inside the wrapper div tag. Your logo will be placed in this area.

7. Click the **Insert Div Tag** button. In the Insert Div Tag dialog box, set the Insert menu to **After Tag**. A second menu becomes active. On this menu, select **<div id = "banner">**. Then on the ID menu, click **navigation**. Click **OK**.

The navigation div tag appears under the banner div tag. Your button navigation will be placed in this area.

8. Click the **Insert Div Tag** button. In the Insert Div Tag dialog box, set the Insert menu to **After Tag**. On the menu to the right, click **<div id = "navigation">**. Then on the ID menu, click **subNavColumn**. Click **OK**.

Unlike the other div tags you have created thus far, the subNavColumn div tag does not stretch across the entire wrapper div tag. It appears on the left side of the wrapper. This restriction appears because of the CSS rules being applied from the style sheet.

9. Place the insertion point at the *beginning* of the placeholder text in the subNavColumn div tag. Key **Personal Services** at the top of the subNavColumn div tag and press **Enter** (Windows) or **Return** (Macintosh) to create a new paragraph.

10. In the Property inspector, set the format of the text **Personal Services** to **Heading 4**.

11. Again place the insertion point at the beginning of the placeholder text in the subNavColumn div tag. Click the **Insert Div Tag** button. In the Insert Div Tag dialog box, set the Insert menu to **At Insertion Point** and the ID menu to **vertnav**. Click **OK**.

The vertnav div tag appears inside the subNavColumn div tag. Your subsection navigation will be placed in this area.

12. Click the **Insert Div Tag** button. In the Insert Div Tag dialog box, set the Insert menu to **After Tag**. On the menu to the right, click **<div id = "subNavColumn">**. Then on the ID menu, click **mainColumn**. Click **OK**.

The mainColumn div tag appears. Your main content will be placed in this area.

13. Click the **Insert Div Tag** button. In the Insert Div Tag dialog box, set the Insert menu to **After Tag**. On the menu to the right, click **<div id = "mainColumn">**. Then on the ID menu, click **footer**. Click **OK**.

The footer div tag appears. The structure of the page is complete.

14. Save your work.

The page should look similar to Figure 2-5.

FIGURE 2-5
Experience Bank layout

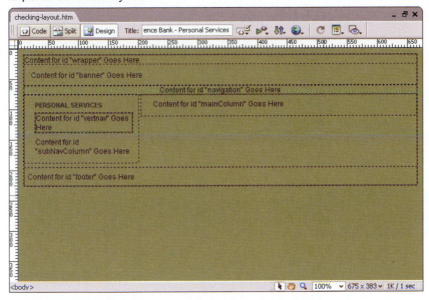

The page does not look like much yet. That is going to change as you add the content for each of the div tags in the following exercises. First you will add the Experience Bank logo to the page, then the navigation bar, then the subnavigation bar, and finally the footer material.

As you proceed, you will also have to make some corrections to the CSS rules that govern each div tag, so that the page will match the expected outcome in the storyboard.

Set the Properties for a Div Tag

1. With the **checking-layout.htm** file still open, open the CSS panel. Click the **All** button. If necessary, click the **+** button (Windows) or the **Right arrow** button (Macintosh) next to the name of the external style sheet so that you can see the list of rules in the sheet, as shown in Figure 2-6.

The list of CSS rules appears in the panel.

FIGURE 2-6
CSS panel showing eb-main.css

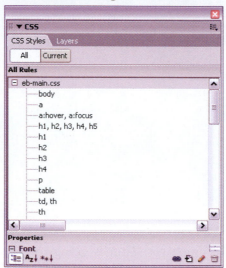

2. Scroll down the list of rules and click the rule named **#wrapper** to select it. Click the **Edit Style** button (the pencil icon at the bottom of the panel) to open the CSS Rule Definition dialog box, as shown in Figure 2-7.

 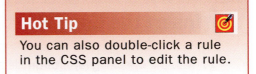
FIGURE 2-7
CSS Rule Definition dialog box for #wrapper in eb-main.css

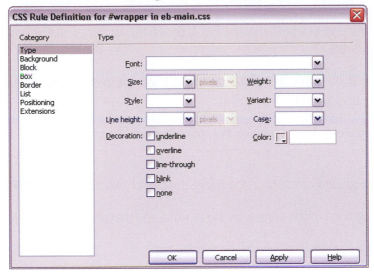

3. Click the **Background** category. In the Background color text box, key **#D4DCB7**. Then click **OK**.

When you use the CSS panel to edit a CSS rule in an external style sheet, Dreamweaver automatically opens the style sheet and makes the change. The document containing the style sheet (eb-main.css) should now be open in a new Document window behind checking-layout.htm.

4. In **checking-layout.htm**, select the placeholder text for the wrapper div tag and delete it.

5. Save your work.

6. Preview the page in the browser. If you see a message that says "Some files needed to accurately preview this page have been modified but not saved. Save them now?" click **Yes**.

This saves the CSS file that you edited when you changed the CSS rule definition for the wrapper div tag.

7. Close the browser.

Note

It may seem as if the wrapper div tag has disappeared, but it has not. You can tell because you can still see it listed in the tag selector at the bottom of the Document window. The other div tags serve as content for the wrapper div tag, even though the wrapper itself is not visible.

Now it's time to put content in each of the sections of the page.

Insert the Logo

1. With the **checking-layout.htm** file still open, place the insertion point at the beginning of the place-holder text for the **banner** div tag. Click **Insert** on the menu bar and then click **Image**. In the Select Image Source dialog box, navigate to the **images** folder. Insert the image **eb-logo-new.jpg**.

   The Image Tag Accessibility Attributes dialog box appears.

2. In the Alternate text box in the Image Tag Accessibility Attributes dialog box, key **Experience Bank logo**. Then click **OK**.

   An Experience Bank logo with a white background appears in the banner; it does not match the color of the banner background.

3. Use the CSS panel to select the rule **#wrapper #banner**. Open the CSS Rule Definition dialog box for this rule.

4. Click the **Background** category. In the Background color text box, key **#FFFFFF**. Then click **OK**.

   Now the background of the banner div tag is white and the logo looks more integrated.

5. Delete the placeholder text from the banner div tag.

6. Save your work. Preview the page in the browser. If asked whether to save the files needed to preview the page, click **Yes**.

7. Close the browser.

Insert the Navigation Bar Using Fireworks HTML

1. With the **checking-layout.htm** file still open, place the insertion point at the beginning of the place-holder text for the **navigation** div tag. Click **Insert** on the menu bar, point to **Image Objects**, and then click **Fireworks HTML**.

   The Insert Fireworks HTML dialog box opens, as shown in Figure 2-8.

   FIGURE 2-8
   Insert Fireworks HTML dialog box

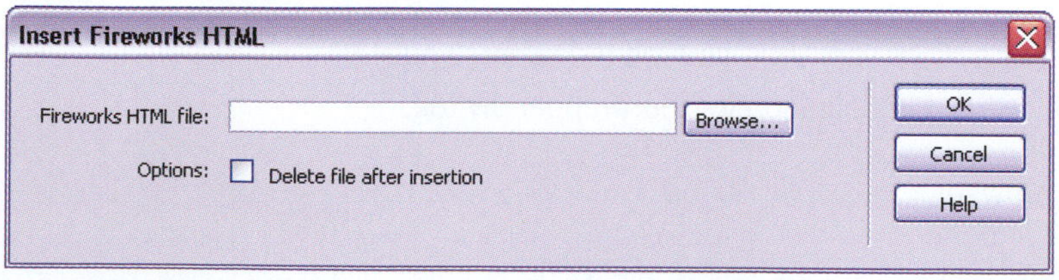

2. Click the **Browse** button and select the file **import-navigation.htm** in the site root. Click **Open** to return to the Insert Fireworks HTML dialog box and then click **OK**.

3. Delete the placeholder text from the navigation div tag.

4. Use the CSS panel to select the rule **#wrapper #navigation**. Open the CSS Rule Definition dialog box for this rule.

5. In the **Background** category, change the Background color to **#5738A3**. Then click **OK**.

6. Save your work. Preview the page in the browser. If asked whether to save the files needed to preview the page, click **Yes**.

7. Close the browser.

The design for the Experience Bank Web site calls for navigation on the left side of each page. This navigation is different from the main navigation bar across the top—it is reserved for links within a particular section of the site.

In the next exercise, you create the links for the Personal Services section of the site. The Personal Services section has several subsections, including Checking Products. The page you are building will be used for the Checking Products subsection, so you will also create links to each of the pages in that subsection.

 ## Create a Navigation Menu Using List Items

1. With the **checking-layout.htm** file still open, place the insertion point at the beginning of the placeholder text for the **vertnav** div tag. Press **Enter** (Windows) or **Return** (Macintosh) to create a new paragraph.

2. Place the insertion point in the first line of the **vertnav** div tag. In the Property inspector, click the **Unordered List** button. Then key the following list into the vertnav div tag:

Checking

Free Checking

Interest Checking

Campus Checking

Gold Checking

Savings

Retirement

Investments

Financial Planning

Inside the Design

Designers will use CSS rules to change the appearance of commonly used HTML items. In the Experience Bank template you are creating, even though there are list items used in the navigation, you won't see bullets in front of them because the designer has used a CSS rule in eb-main.css to change the appearance of list items in the vertnav div. The structure of the list is useful in this situation, but the decorative element of the bullet would be distracting.

3. Select the text of each of the items in the list in turn, and use the Property inspector to key **#** (a pound sign or number sign) in the Link field.

Here's an easy way to select this text: click in the line containing the text, and use the tag selector at the bottom of the Document window to click on the <li> tag.

4. Select the four lines containing the text **Free Checking**, **Interest Checking**, **Campus Checking**, and **Gold Checking**. In the Property inspector, use the **Style** menu to set the style of these four lines to **subnav**.

The page should look like that shown in Figure 2-9.

Did You Know?

You learned in the previous project that the # (also known as the octothorpe, pound sign, or number sign) can be used in a URL to link to a specific part of a page, if the page contains an anchor tag. If you use the # character to link to an anchor tag that does not exist on the page, the browser will simply jump to the top of the page. So if you use just # for a URL, clicking the link will take you to the top of the same page that the link is on.

Web developers often use this technique to create dummy links, so that they can show clients how the links will appear even if they do not yet know what pages should be linked to. If clients test the page, they will simply stay on the page, instead of getting a "File Not Found" error message, which may make the site look broken.

FIGURE 2-9
Checking submenu items in the Checking Products layout

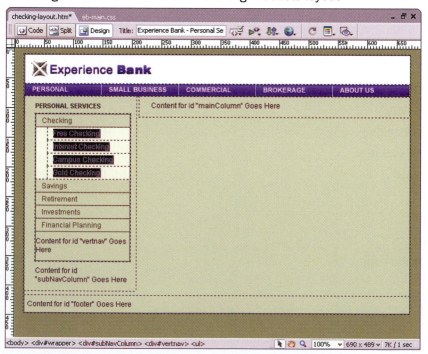

5. Delete the placeholder text from the vertnav div tag. Make sure to backspace if necessary to delete the line that the placeholder text was on.

6. Place the insertion point at the beginning of the placeholder text for the **subNavColumn** div tag. Click **Insert** on the menu bar and then click **Image**. In the Select Image Source dialog box, navigate to the **images** folder. Insert the graphic **images/checking/atmAd.jpg**. For the Alt text, key **Find an ATM near you.** Then click **OK**.

7. Select the image. In the Property inspector, key **#** in the Link field.

8. Delete the placeholder text from the subNavColumn div tag.

9. Save your work. Preview the page in the browser. If asked whether to save the files needed to preview the page, click **Yes**.

10. Close the browser.

To create a more defined division between the main column and the navigation elements on the left, the page design calls for a vertical line to separate them. To create the line, you will set attributes for the left border of the mainColumn div tag.

Inside the Design

If you work on a commercial Web site, you will often experience a tension between showing the site visitors what they want to see and showing them what the client wants them to see. Often clients will want to advertise their products, and you will have to discover creative ways of letting them do that while still keeping the page focused on its purpose—if you do not keep the page focused, visitors will get distracted or even determine that the site as a whole is not useful.

The designers of the Experience Bank Web site have chosen to place an advertising badge (such as the "Locate an ATM near you" graphic) at the bottom of the subNavColumn div tag on each page. This placement takes advantage of space that would otherwise go to waste and allows Experience Bank to advertise other products to existing customers without interrupting the main content on the page.

Set the Border Property for a Div Tag

1. With the **checking-layout.htm** file still open, place the insertion point at the beginning of the placeholder text for the **mainColumn** div tag. Key the word **Checking** and press **Enter** (Windows) or **Return** (Macintosh) to put the new word on its own line.

2. Click anywhere in the new line that contains the word *Checking* and use the Property inspector to change the format to **Heading 2**.

3. Use the CSS panel to select the rule **#wrapper #mainColumn**. Open the CSS Rule Definition dialog box for this rule.

4. Click the **Background** category. In the Background color text box, key **#FFFFFF**.

Inside the Design

Designers use colors to contrast information sections on a page so that areas that contain important information will be the most prominent. Setting the background color to white creates the highest degree of contrast on the page. As a result, the main column content will be the most prominent on the page.

5. Click the **Border** category. This category lets you set three attributes for a border: **Style**, **Width**, and **Color**. Click the **Same for all** check box under each of these three attributes so that it is unchecked.

Now you can set the properties for just the left border, instead of for all of the borders at once.

6. Make these changes in the **Left** row of controls:
   a. For Style, use the menu to select **Solid**.
   b. For Width, key **1** in text box.
   c. For Color, key **#666666**.

The CSS Rule Definition dialog box should now look like Figure 2-10.

FIGURE 2-10
CSS Rule Definition dialog box with left border attributes set for the mainColumn div tag

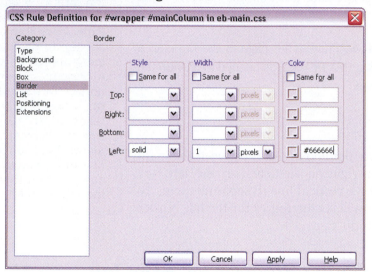

7. In the CSS Rule Definition dialog box, click **OK**.

8. Leave the placeholder text in the mainColumn div tag. When other developers use this page as a template, this will show them where to place new content.

9. Save your work. Preview the page in the browser. If asked whether to save the files needed to preview the page, click **Yes**.

10. Close the browser.

The footer of the page contains a series of text links that are similar to those in the main navigation bar. The repetition of these links makes the page more accessible to visitors with disabilities. Most of the technologies used to create sophisticated navigation using image rollovers or pop-up menus are complex and difficult for screen readers to navigate. Text links are the best way to enable people who rely on screen readers and other assistive technologies to navigate your site.

At the same time, placement of these links at the bottom of the page is convenient for all of your visitors. The links are useful for anyone who has scrolled down through the page where the main navigation bar is no longer visible.

Create Redundant Navigation Links

1. With the **checking-layout.htm** file still open, place the insertion point at the beginning of the place-holder text for the **footer** div tag. Key the following text:

   Personal | Small Business | Commercial | Brokerage | About Us | Branches | Contact Us

2. Remove the placeholder text for the footer div tag.

   The footer should now look like that shown in Figure 2-11.

   FIGURE 2-11
   Footer for the Checking Products layout

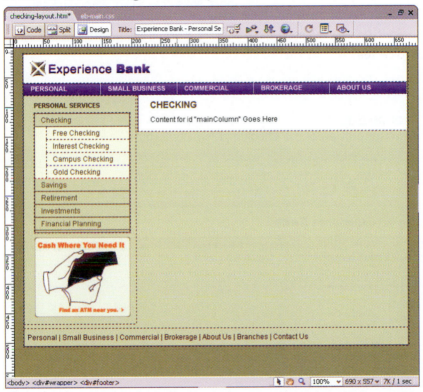

3. Select each word or phrase between the text lines and use the Property inspector to link it to **#**, as you did previously for the Personal Services navigation elements.

4. Use the CSS panel to select the rule **#wrapper # footer**. Open the CSS Rule Definition dialog box for this rule. Make these changes:

   a. In the **Type** category, key **85%** in the Size box. In the Color box, key **#CCCCCC**.

   b. Switch to the **Background** category. In the Background color box, key **#5738A3**.

   c. Switch to the **Block** category. On the Text align menu, click **Center**. Then click **OK**.

5. In the CSS panel, open the CSS Rule Definition dialog box for **#wrapper #footer a, #wrapper #footer a:visited**. Make these changes in the **Type** category:

   a. In the Color box, key **#CCCCCC**.

   b. For Decoration, click the **None** check box to check it. Then click **OK**.

   This will set the style of links in the footer to light gray, with no underline.

6. In the CSS panel, open the CSS Rule Definition dialog box for **#wrapper #footer a:hover, #wrapper #footer a:focus**. Make these changes in the **Type** category:

   a. In the Color box, key **#FFFFFF**.

   b. For Decoration, click the **underline** check box to check it. Then click **OK**.

   This will set the rollover state of the links in the footer to white with an underline. The next effect is that when a visitor rolls the mouse over these links, they will brighten and gain an underscore.

7. Save your work. Preview the page in the browser. If asked whether to save the files needed to preview the page, click **Yes**.

   The footer should now look like that shown in Figure 2-12.

FIGURE 2-12
Browser preview of the Checking Products layout

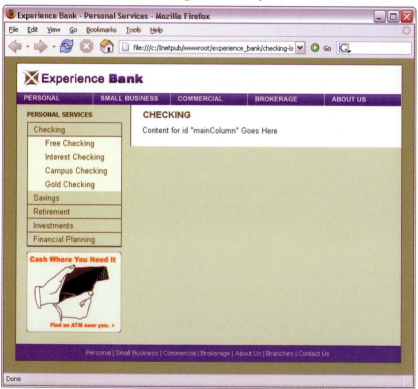

8. Close the browser.

The last thing that the page needs is a copyright notice.

Create a Copyright Notice

1. With the **checking-layout.htm** file still open, click in the Document window underneath the wrapper div tag (that is, under the footer). This should place the insertion point below and outside of the div tag. Press **Enter** (Windows) or **Return** (Macintosh).

2. On the new line, key **©2005 by Experience Bank. All rights reserved.**

   You can use the Text category on the Insert bar to insert the copyright symbol. Click the Characters menu on the right end of the Insert bar, and click the copyright symbol.

3. Select the text. In the Property inspector, use the Format menu to set the format of the text to **None**. Use the Style menu to set the style of the text to **copyright**.

4. Save your work. Preview the page in the browser. The page should look like that in Figure 2-13.

FIGURE 2-13
Completed Checking Products layout

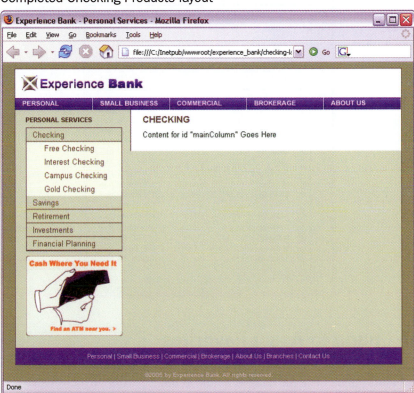

5. Close the browser. Close **checking-layout.htm** and **eb-main.css**.

Reusing Page Elements by Adding Images to Asset Favorites

As you worked on the Checking Products layout, you used images that will likely be used throughout the site. One was the logo (which probably appears on every page in the site). The other was the advertising badge for ATMs. Since these images will likely be used elsewhere, it may be helpful to bookmark them so that they are easy to find again.

All images used within a site are listed as site assets on the Assets panel, as shown in Figure 2-14. As the site grows, the number of images listed in this panel can become quite large. For images that are used repeatedly, placing them in the Favorites list can be a time-saver. You can organize your images into folders to make them easy to locate.

Note

When you add a new asset to your site, it may not immediately appear on the Assets panel. To update the Assets panel to include all the images in your site, you need to refresh the site catalog. Click the *Refresh Site List* button at the bottom right of the Assets panel (this button is available only when Site is selected in the Assets panel).

FIGURE 2-14
Image category of the Assets panel

Image category

Refresh Site List

Add to Favorites

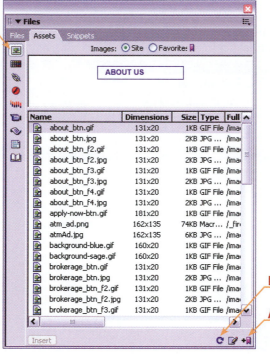

 Add an Image to Asset Favorites

1. Open the Assets panel. Click the **Images** button at the upper left of the panel and then click **Site** at the top of the Assets panel.

2. From the list of images, select the **eb-logo-new.jpg** graphic.

3. Click **Add to Favorites** at the lower right of the panel. If a message box appears, click **OK**.

Note

The first time you try to access the Assets panel, it may take a few seconds for the panel to create a listing of all the assets used by files in your site. If you have not created a site cache for this site, the Assets panel prompts you to do so—the asset catalog can not be created without a site cache.

4. Repeat steps 2 and 3 for the images **atmAd.jpg** and **mortgageAd.jpg**.

5. Click **Favorites** at the top of the Assets panel.

The images appear in the Favorites list.

6. Click **New Favorites Folder** at the bottom of the panel. Name the new folder **Advertising Badges**.

7. Drag **atmAd** and **mortgageAd** to the new folder.

Once you have created a folder, you can collapse it or expand it by clicking the **+** button (Windows) or the **Right arrow** button (Macintosh) next to the folder. The Assets panel should now look like that in Figure 2-15.

FIGURE 2-15
Assets panel showing Image Favorites

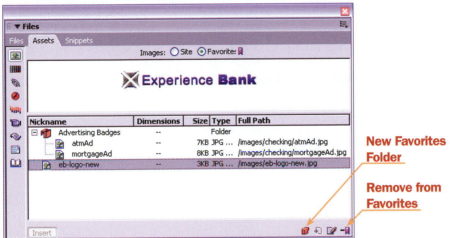

New Favorites
Folder

Remove from
Favorites

Using Templates

Previously, you created a standard layout for the Experience Bank Web site. Anyone on your team can copy this page and create a new page with the same elements on it. However, if your layout ever needs to be updated, all the pages that are copied from it will have to be updated individually. In addition, there's always the chance that someone working on a copy of the page may accidentally alter some portion of the page that shouldn't be altered.

Dreamweaver provides a mechanism to help you avoid these problems: the template.

A template author designs a fixed page layout, just as you did for the Checking Products layout. The author then saves the page as a template and creates regions in the template that are editable in documents based on that template; if the author does not define a region as editable, then template users cannot edit content in that area. Templates enable the template author

Hot Tip

To remove an image from the Favorites list, select the image from the list of images and then click *Remove from Favorites*. The image is no longer listed as a Favorite. You have not deleted the image—it is still in its original location. You have simply removed the image from the list of Favorites. To remove a folder from the Favorites list, select the folder you want to delete and then click *Remove from Favorites* at the bottom of the panel. But if a Favorites folder you want to remove contains any images you want to keep as Favorites, first move the images to another folder.

to control which page elements template users can edit, so the author can protect elements like navigation and copyright notices from unintentional changes.

One of the most powerful benefits of templates is the ability to update multiple pages at once. A document that is created from a template remains connected to that template (unless you detach the document later). If you modify a template created from the Checking Products layout, any change to the template can prompt a change in all of the pages that have been created from it.

Did You Know?

You can create a template from an existing Web page, or you can create a template from a new, blank document.

Creating a Template

You will create a template that you and your team can use to build other pages for the Checking Products section of the Experience Bank Web site.

Create a Template

1. Open the **checking-layout.htm** file. Click **File** on the menu bar and click **Save as Template**.

   The Save As Template dialog box appears, as shown in Figure 2-16.

FIGURE 2-16
Save As Template dialog box

2. On the Site menu, make sure that **Experience Bank** is selected.

3. In the Description text box, key **Use for Checking Products in Personal Services pages.**

4. In the Save As text box, key **checking-products**. Then click **Save**.

5. A message appears asking if you want to update links. Click **Yes**.

6. Select the text **Checking** at the top of the mainColumn div tag. Click **Insert** on the menu bar, point to **Template Objects**, and click **Editable Region**.

The New Editable Region dialog box appears, shown in Figure 2-17.

FIGURE 2-17
New Editable Region dialog box

7. In the Name text box, key **Main Heading**. Then click **OK**.

8. Select the text **Content for id "mainColumn" Goes Here**. Click **Insert** on the menu bar, point to **Template Objects**, and click **Editable Region**. Name the region **Main Content** and click **OK**.

Your template now has two editable regions and should look like Figure 2-18.

FIGURE 2-18
Checking Products template

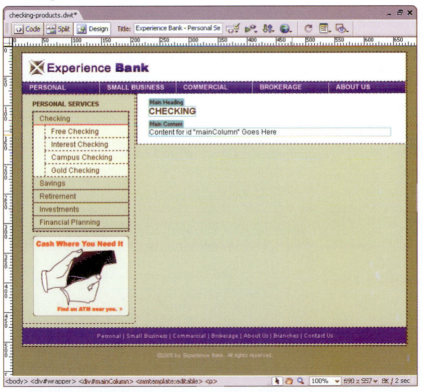

9. Save the template. You may see a message warning you that you placed the Main Heading editable region inside a block tag. Click **OK** and close all files open in Dreamweaver.

Dreamweaver saves the template file in the site's Templates folder in the local root folder of the site, with a .dwt filename extension. If the Templates folder does not already exist in the site, Dreamweaver automatically creates it when you save a new template.

Creating New Pages from Templates

Now that you have a template to work with, you can create any number of pages for the Checking Products section of the Experience Bank Web site. You can even copy the template and modify it for use in other sections of the site.

> **Important**
>
> Do not move your templates out of the Templates folder or put any non-template files in the Templates folder. Also, do not move the Templates folder out of your local root folder. Doing so causes errors in paths in the templates.

You can select, preview, and create a new document from an existing template. You can use the New Document dialog box to select a template from any of your Dreamweaver-defined sites. You can also use the Assets panel to create a new document from an existing template. The Experience Bank Web site requires you to use your new Checking Products template to create a new Free Checking page.

Create a New Page From a Template

1. Open the **Assets** panel.

2. In the Assets panel, click the **Templates** icon on the left to view the list of templates in your current site, as shown in Figure 2-19.

   Your checking-products template is listed here.

> **Note**
>
> If you just created the template you want to apply, you may need to click the *Refresh Site List* button to see it.

FIGURE 2-19
Templates category of the Assets panel

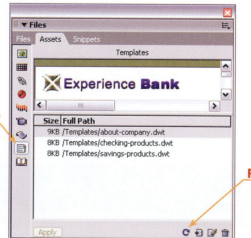

Templates category

Refresh Site List

3. Click the template **checking-products** in the list. Click the **Options** menu and click **New from Template**.

A new document opens in the Document window. Note the two editable regions: Main Heading and Main Content. If you try to select or change anything on the page that is outside of these two areas, the cursor becomes a circle with a slash through it. You cannot select anything on the page that isn't inside an editable region.

4. In the Document bar, change the title of the page to **Experience Bank – Personal Services – Free Checking**.

5. In the Main Heading editable region, replace the existing text with **Free Checking**.

6. Open the **_documents** folder and find the document **free-checking.doc**. Insert the contents from **free-checking.doc** into the Main Content editable region. Delete the placeholder text.

7. Select the last paragraph of the new text in the Main Content region. In the Property inspector, set the style of this paragraph to **Small**.

8. Save the document in **/personal/checking** and name it **free-checking.htm**.

9. Preview **free-checking.htm** in a browser.

10. Close the browser. Then close the document in Dreamweaver.

Updating a Template

When you created the Checking Products layout, you used a series of dummy links in the Personal Services navigation. Now that you have a page for the Free Checking product, you can update the template with a link to that page.

 ## Update a Template

1. In the Files panel, open the **Templates** folder. Then open **checking-products.dwt**.

2. In the **vertnav** div tag on the left side of the page, select the text **Checking**.

3. In the Property inspector, delete the **#** sign from the Link field.

4. Click the folder icon next to the Link field. Navigate to **/personal/checking** and select the file **index.htm** as the page to link to.

5. Repeat steps 2 through 4, selecting the text **Free Checking** and linking it to **free-checking.htm**.

> ### Hot Tip
>
> To create a link in a template file, use the folder icon or the *Point to File* icon in the Property inspector—don't type the name of the file to link to. If you type the name, the link may not work correctly in pages created from this template.

6. Save the template. If you see a message about placing an editable region inside a block tag, click **OK**.

The Update Template Files dialog box appears, as shown in Figure 2-20, with a list of the files that are based on this template.

7. Click **Update**.

FIGURE 2-20
Update Template Files dialog box

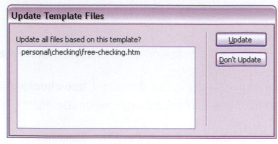

8. The Update Files dialog box appears, showing the progress of the updates. Since you only have one page to update, this process should happen quickly. Click the **Close** button when it appears.

9. Close the checking-products template.

10. Open **/personal/checking/free-checking.htm**. Preview the page in the browser.

Note that clicking the Checking link takes you to /personal/checking/index.htm.

11. Close the browser. Close **free-checking.htm**.

ENHANCING A WEB PAGE WITH RICH MEDIA

OBJECTIVES

Upon completion of this lesson, you will be able to:

- Update an image in Fireworks from within Dreamweaver.

- Insert a Flash movie on a Web page.

- Update a Flash movie from within Dreamweaver.

- Insert Flash Video on a Web page.

Estimated time to complete this lesson: 30 minutes

Introduction

Experience Bank not only wants to update the look of its site; it also wants to enhance the site with more than just text and graphics.

Dreamweaver lets you add sound and movies to your Web site quickly and easily. You can incorporate the following media files into your Dreamweaver pages: Flash and Shockwave movies, QuickTime movies, AVI movies, Java applets, Active X controls, and audio files of various formats.

Roundtrip editing and Design Notes enable Dreamweaver to integrate operations with Fireworks and Flash. Roundtrip editing ensures that code, image, and animation updates transfer correctly between Dreamweaver and these other applications (for example, to preserve rollover behaviors or links to other files). When you select an image or a movie in the Document window, note that there is an Edit button in the Property inspector. This button launches the appropriate application to edit the object and minimizes the number of steps required to implement the edit.

Design Notes are small files that allow Dreamweaver to locate the appropriate source document for an exported image or movie file. When you export files from Fireworks or Flash directly to a Dreamweaver-defined site, Design Notes, which contain references to the PNG or Flash authoring file (FLA), are automatically exported to the site along with the Web-ready (GIF, JPEG, or SWF format) file.

In this lesson, you use roundtrip editing to update an image in Fireworks, add a Flash animation to a page and edit that animation, and add Flash Video to a page.

> **Important**
>
> Dreamweaver collects the Design Notes for a site in folders called _notes. Do not remove these folders; if you do, Dreamweaver won't know which images or movies belong to a particular Fireworks or Flash source file.

Editing Fireworks Images

The new look for the Experience Bank Web site incorporates advertising badges in the lower-left portion of the layout. You can start Fireworks from Dreamweaver to update these badges. When you open and edit an image, Dreamweaver starts Fireworks, which opens the PNG file from which the image or table was exported.

You use this feature of Dreamweaver to update the advertising badge being used in the Savings Products template.

 Update an Image in Fireworks

1. Use the Assets panel to open the Savings Products template (/**Templates/savings-products.dwt**).

2. On the left side of the page, click the advertising badge that says "Dream Home."

3. In the Property inspector, click the **Edit** button, shown in Figure 3-1.

   Fireworks launches.

> **Note** ✓
>
> If the Find Source dialog box appears, click the Use PNG button. In the Select Image Source dialog box, open the _fireworks folder and select the mortgage_ad.png file.

FIGURE 3-1
Image Property inspector

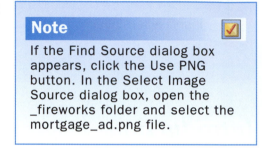

Edit in Fireworks

4. In Fireworks, double-click the text **Dream Home** so that you can edit the text block. Edit the text so that it now says **Home of Your Dreams**.

5. Click the **Done** button, shown in Figure 3-2.

FIGURE 3-2
Fireworks Document window

Done

6. In the Dreamweaver Document window, verify that the ATM advertising badge has been updated.

7. Close the template file. If Fireworks is still open, close Fireworks.

Inserting Flash Movies

An animator on the Experience Bank Web team has created an animation promoting the company's mortgage services. Your task is to create a new page and load the animation.

You can use Dreamweaver to set playback and display options for a Flash file in a Web page or to update the links in the movie. If Macromedia Flash 8 is installed, you can also select a SWF file in a Dreamweaver document and start Flash to edit it. Flash does not directly edit the SWF file; it edits the source document (FLA file) and re-exports the SWF file.

To find out about the types of Flash files you will be working with, see the Tips & Techniques feature "Flash File Formats."

Did You Know?

When you closed the template file, you may have expected Dreamweaver to ask if you want to update the pages created with the template. However, you didn't make any updates to the template file—just to the image file. Because the image file was altered, each of the pages using this image will automatically be updated with the new version, whether those pages belong to a template or not.

Insert a Flash Movie on a Web Page

1. In the Assets panel, use **savings-products.dwt** to create a new page. Save the page in /personal/savings as **basic-savings.htm**.

2. Make these changes to the new page:
   a. Change the page title to **Experience Bank – Personal Services – Basic Savings**.
   b. Change the contents of the Main Heading region to **Basic Savings**.
   c. In the **_documents** folder, find the document **basic-savings.doc**. Insert the contents of basic-savings.doc into the Main Content region of the page.
   d. Remove the placeholder text.
   e. Set the style of the text in the final paragraph to **Small**.

The page should now look similar to that shown in Figure 3-3.

FIGURE 3-3
Basic Savings page

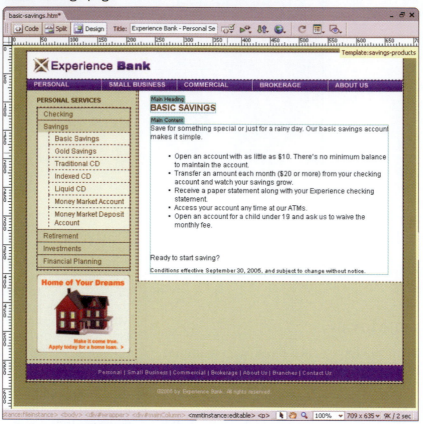

Tips & Techniques

FLASH FILE FORMATS

Dreamweaver comes with Flash objects you can use whether you have Flash installed on your computer or not. Before you use the Flash commands available in Dreamweaver, here are some of the Flash file types you should know about:

■ **The Flash document (.fla)** is the source file for any Flash project and is created in the Flash program. This type of document can be opened only in Flash (not in Dreamweaver or in browsers). You can open the Flash document in Flash and then export it as a SWF or SWT file to use in browsers.

■ **The Flash SWF file (.swf)** is a compressed version of the Flash document (.fla), optimized for viewing on the Web. This file can be played back in browsers and previewed in Dreamweaver, but it cannot be edited in Flash. This is the type of file you create when you use the Flash button and Flash text features in Dreamweaver.

■ **The Flash Video file format (.flv)** is a video file that contains encoded audio and video data for delivery through the Macromedia Flash Player. For example, if you had a QuickTime or Windows Media video file, you would use an encoder (such as Flash 8 Video Encoder or Sorensen Squeeze) to convert the video file to an FLV file.

3. Add a new line before the first paragraph in the Main Content region. With the insertion point in the new line, click **Insert** on the menu bar, point to **Media**, and click **Flash**.

The Select File dialog box appears, as shown in Figure 3-4.

FIGURE 3-4
Select File dialog box for inserting a Flash movie

4. Navigate to the **movies** folder and select the movie **savings-movie.swf**. Then click **OK** (Windows) or **Choose** (Macintosh).

The Object Tag Accessibility Attributes dialog box appears, as shown in Figure 3-5.

FIGURE 3-5
Object Tag Accessibility dialog box for Flash movies

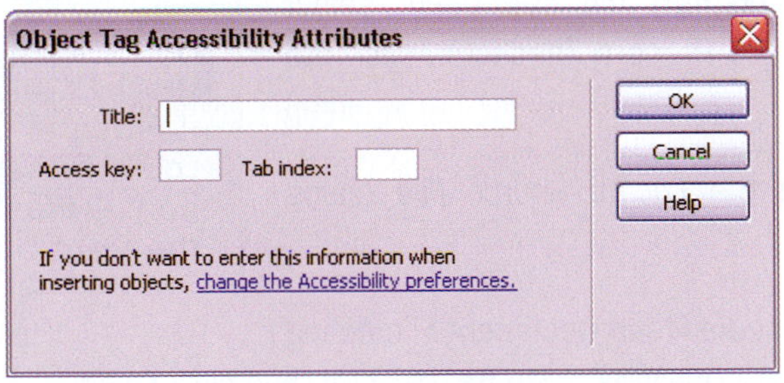

5. In the Title text box of the Object Tag Accessibility Attributes dialog box, key **Savings movie**. Then click **OK**.

   A placeholder for the Flash movie appears on the page.

6. Select the movie. Uncheck the **Loop** check box in the Property inspector.

   Note that the movie's size does not correspond with the specifications in the storyboard. The movie has a width of 350 pixels and a height of 200 pixels, but the storyboard indicates that the movie should be 410 pixels wide and 233 pixels high.

7. In the Property inspector, key **410** in the W text box and key **233** in the H text box to resize the movie.

8. Click the **Play** button in the Property inspector to see the movie play.

   Notice that the movie contains a misspelling of the word *for*. You will correct this in the next Step-by-Step.

9. Click the **Stop** button in the Property inspector.

10. Save the file. Preview the page in the browser.

11. Close the browser.

Editing Flash Movies from Dreamweaver

You may find that you need to make quick edits to a Flash movie. If you have Macromedia Flash 8 installed, you can do this easily directly from Dreamweaver. The Savings movie you worked with in the previous Step-by-Step had a typographical error that needs to be corrected.

 Edit a Flash Movie

1. With the **basic-savings.htm** file still open, select the Flash movie. In the Property inspector, click the **Edit** button.

   Flash launches and the *Locate Source File* dialog box appears.

   > **Note**
   >
   > If Flash is already open, then you may have to switch applications—Flash may not come to the front automatically.

2. In the Locate Macromedia Flash Document File dialog box, navigate to **/_flash/savingsmovie.fla**, select it, and click **Open**.

3. In the Flash Document window, double-click the text **Saving ofr a Home?** to edit it. Change **ofr** to **for**.

4. Click the **Done** button at the upper left of the Flash Document window.

   Flash automatically publishes an update to the SWF file and saves and closes the source file. The Dreamweaver Document window appears.

5. Save your work and preview the page in the browser.

6. Close your browser. In Dreamweaver, close **basic-savings.htm**.

Inserting Flash Video

Experience Bank has requested a page that explains the company mission. The president of the bank has recorded a short video clip to accompany the page. Your job is to implement it.

 Insert Flash Video

1. In the Assets panel, use **about-company.dwt** to create a new page. Save the page in the **about** folder as **our-mission.htm**. Change the title of the new page to **Experience Bank – About Us – Our Mission**.

2. Change the contents of the Main Heading region to **Our Mission**.

3. Open the **_documents** folder and find the document **mission-statement.doc.** Insert the contents of the document into the Main Content editable region. Make sure the new text is set to **Paragraph** format. Delete the placeholder text.

4. Place the insertion point at the beginning of the first paragraph in the Main Content region. Press **Enter** (Windows) or **Return** (Macintosh) to start a new line.

5. With the insertion point at the beginning of the new line, click **Insert** on the menu bar, point to **Media**, and click **Flash Video**.

   The Insert Flash Video dialog box appears, as shown in Figure 3-6.

FIGURE 3-6
Insert Flash Video dialog box

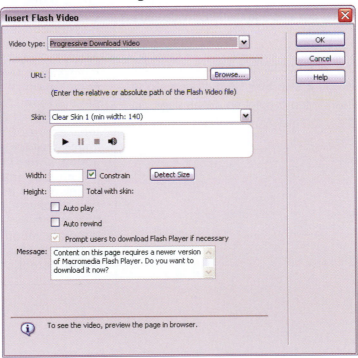

6. For Video type, make sure **Progressive Download Video** is selected.

7. Click the **Browse** button next to the URL text box. In the Select File dialog box, navigate to the movies folder and select **ebMissionStatement.flv**. Click **OK** (Windows) or **Choose** (Macintosh).

8. Click the **Skin** menu and then click **Halo Skin 2**.

When you insert a Flash Video file, Dreamweaver will add playback controls to the movie. The skin you choose determines which controls are included and how they appear. A preview of the selected skin appears beneath the Skin menu.

9. Click the **Detect Size** button.

Dreamweaver automatically determines the exact height and width for the Flash Video movie, based on information it gathers from the FLV file.

10. Check **Auto Play**.

This will cause the movie to start playing as soon as the page is loaded in the browser.

11. Check **Auto Rewind**.

This will cause the playback control to return to its starting position after the video finishes playing.

12. Make sure the **Prompt users to download Flash Player if necessary** box is unchecked. Then click **OK** to close the dialog box and add the Flash Video content to your Web page.

The *Insert Flash Video* command generates a video player SWF file and a skin SWF file that are used to display your Flash Video content on a Web page. (To see the new files, you may need to click the Refresh button in the Files panel.)

> **Note**
>
> On the Macintosh, you must use an absolute path if you are pointing to FLV files in directories that are two or more levels up from the HTML file.

> **Important**
>
> Typically, you should prompt users to download the Macromedia Flash Player if they do not already have it (or have an outdated version). Otherwise, they will not be able to view the Flash Video movie. So usually you would check the *Prompt users to download Flash Player if necessary* check box. In this case, however, you are using a page created from a template, and it will not allow you to use this feature. Checking this check box causes code to be added to the <head> tag, but the <head> tag is not included in any of the editable regions of this template. In anticipation of this event, the developer of this template modified the template to include Macromedia Flash Player detection code.

13. Save the file and preview the page in a browser.

You should see the video of the bank president explaining the company's mission. It should look similar to Figure 3-7.

FIGURE 3-7
Mission statement page for Experience Bank

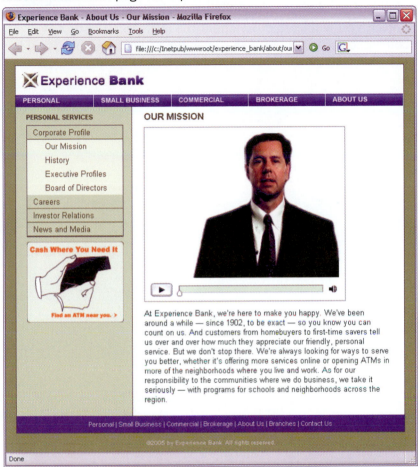

14. Close your browser. Close the document and close Dreamweaver.

Note ☑

The FLV movie needs to be hosted on a Web server. The Web server can be local, such as IIS (localhost) in Windows or Apache on a Macintosh. If your instructor had you place the asset files for this site in a local Web server, then you should be able to see the video. Otherwise, the video will not play successfully when you preview it.

SUMMARY

You have successfully updated the Experience Bank Web site.

In this project, you worked with tables to present information, you implemented a new layout using CSS and Dreamweaver templates, and you enhanced the site with rich media. The collaboration skills you learned will be formational in your success on a Web development team.

In the next project, you will learn more about the infrastructure of a Web site. You will learn how to create a connection to a remote Web server, how to manage files, and how to run reports on your site.

ON YOUR OWN – TEMPLATES AND CSS

ACTIVITY 1: BUILD A TEMPLATE FOR THE DANGEROUS FROGS 2 WEB SITE

You have learned how to use templates in Dreamweaver. Apply these same techniques to build a template for the Dangerous Frogs 2 personal Web site. The Dangerous Frogs 2 site is similar to the site you completed in Project 1. Four of the five pages in that site used the same basic layout, and all of the pages used the same basic three-cell table structure. Build a template for that structure so you can complete the remaining pages in the Dangerous Frogs 2 site.

You can review the techniques for saving a file as a template and inserting editable regions in a template in Lesson 2.

1. Create a site definition in Dreamweaver for the Dangerous Frogs 2 Web site. This site is provided in the data files for On Your Own Project 2 Activity 1.

2. Open the **green.htm** page. Save the file as a template and name the template **frog-species**.

3. In the new **frog-species.dwt** template, select the page heading **Dangerous Frogs: The Monkey Frog**. Insert an editable region and name the region **Page Heading**.

4. Select the text **Phyllomedusa bicolor** and insert a new editable region called **Scientific Name**.

5. Select all of the text starting with the heading **Habitat** and including the paragraph that follows it, the heading **Description**, and the final two paragraphs. Insert a new editable region called **Frog Data.**

6. Save the template.

7. Use the new template to create **gold.htm**, **black.htm**, and **blue.htm**.

8. Use the storyboard for Project 1 to determine the content for each new page. Open the storyboard, DW-Project1_Storyboard.pdf, from the data files for Project 1 of this unit. Follow storyboard panel 5 to insert the content for **gold.htm**. Follow storyboard panel 6 to insert the content for **blue.htm**. Follow storyboard panel 7 to insert the content for **black.htm**.

9. After completing the pages, save them and make sure all of the links work on all of the pages.

ACTIVITY 2: CREATE A CSS STYLE SHEET

In both Project 1 and Project 2, you learned about Cascading Style Sheets and how you can use them to control the appearance of different kinds of text. You learned how to create styles and how to export them to an external style sheet. You learned how an external style sheet can improve the consistency of your site design and how it can save you time and effort.

A good style sheet requires good planning. In this activity, you use text-styles.htm, a page that contains sample text formatted according to basic HTML formats. You use this page to create CSS rules for several HTML tags, such as the top five header styles, paragraphs, links, and lists. You also create a rule for a *footer* class, which you can use on certain paragraphs. Once you have defined the rules, you export the style sheet so that it can be used on a site.

You can review the techniques for creating a new CSS rule and for exporting an external style sheet in Project 1, Lesson 2. If you want to use the style sheet you create in this activity for your own Web pages, review the techniques for attaching external style sheets in Project 2, Lesson 2.

Did You Know?

The text-styles.htm page includes what is known as *lorem ipsum* text. This text looks a bit like Latin. It starts "Lorem ipsum dolor sit amet, consectetuer adipiscing elit. Cras malesuada sagittis neque." While the text looks like Latin, it doesn't actually mean anything—it's a scrambled version of an ancient text by Cicero. A longer version of this text is commonly used by printers and other designers as a placeholder to get an idea of what a design will look like.

1. In Dreamweaver, open the **text-styles.htm** page from the data files for On Your Own Project 2 Activity 2.

2. Create a new CSS rule for the body tag. In the New CSS Rule dialog box, set Selector Type to **Tag**. Use the Tag menu to select **body**. For Define in, choose **This document only**. Then click **OK**.

3. In the *CSS Rule Definition for body* dialog box, make these changes:
   A. In the Type category, set Font Family to **Verdana, Arial, Helvetica, sans-serif**.
   B. In the Type category, set Color to **#444444**.
   C. In the Background category, set Background color to **#D4DCB7**.

All of the changes in the Type category, shown in Figure 1, will apply to all of the text, unless a specific rule for a particular text format overwrites the setting.

FIGURE 1
CSS Rule Definition dialog box

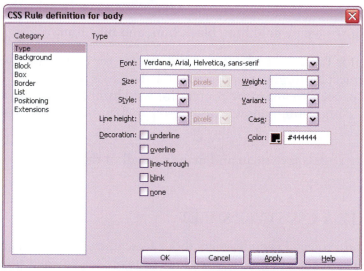

4. Set the style for Heading 1 by creating a new CSS rule for the **h1** tag. Make these changes to the CSS rule definition for the tag:
   A. In the Type category, set Size to **180%**.
   B. In the Type category, set Color to **#616945**.
   C. In the Type category, set Weight to **bold**.
   D. In the Block category, set Text align to **center**.

5. Set the style for Heading 2 by creating a new CSS rule for the **h2** tag. Make these changes to the CSS rule definition for the tag:
   A. In the Type category, set Size to **140%**.
   B. In the Type category, set Color to **#616945**.
   C. In the Type category, set Weight to **Bold**.
   D. In the Type category, set Case to **Uppercase**.
   E. In the Border category, under Style, uncheck the **Same for all** check box and set Bottom to **solid**.

6. Set the style for Heading 3 by creating a new CSS rule for the **h3** tag. Make these changes to the CSS rule definition for the tag:
   A. In the Type category, set Size to **110%**.
   B. In the Type category, set Color to **#616945**.
   C. In the Type category, set Weight to **bold**.
   D. In the Type category, set Case to **uppercase**.

7. Set the style for Heading 4 by creating a new CSS rule for the **h4** tag. Make these changes to the CSS rule definition for the tag:
   A. In the Type category, set Size to **90%**.
   B. In the Type category, set Color to **#616945**.
   C. In the Type category, set Weight to **bold**.

8. Set the style for Heading 5 by creating a new CSS rule for the **h5** tag. Make these changes to the CSS rule definition for the tag:
   A. In the Type category, set Size to **60%**.
   B. In the Type category, set Weight to **bold**.

9. Set the style for paragraph text by creating a new CSS rule for the **p** tag. For this tag, make a single change to the Type category: set Size to **80%**.

10. Set the style for text used in lists by creating a new CSS rule for the **li** tag. For this tag, in the Type category, set Size to **80%**. This setting ensures that list text is the same size as paragraph text.

11. Specify the style of bullet used for unordered lists by creating a new CSS rule for the **ul** tag. For this tag, in the List category, set Type to **square**.

12. The copyright text at the bottom uses the *footer* style. To define this style, in the New CSS Rule dialog box, set Selector Type to **Class**. In the Name text box, key **footer**. Make sure the rule will be defined using the **This document only** setting. Then click **OK**. Make these changes to the footer rule definition:
    A. In the Type category, set Size to **60%**.
    B. In the Type category, set Color to **#616945**.
    C. In the Block category, set Text align to **center**.

13. To set the style for links, click **Modify** on the menu bar, and then click **Page Properties**. In the Page Properties dialog box, click the **Links** category and make these changes, shown in Figure 2, before clicking **OK**:

A. Set Link color to **#993300**.

B. Set Underline style to **Show underline only on rollover**.

FIGURE 2
Page Properties dialog box

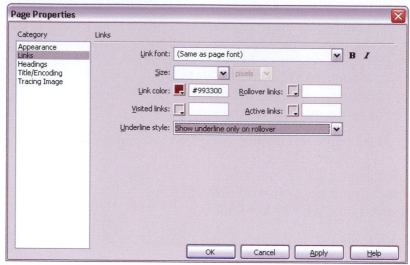

14. Export the style sheet as **mystyles.css**.

15. In the CSS panel, delete the **<style>** rule collection and attach **mystyles.css** to the **text-styles.htm** page.

As you plan a site, collect all of the different kinds of text you intend to use throughout the site on a single HTML page such as text-styles.htm. You can use this page as a starting point whenever you prepare styles for a site. This page will allow you to easily compare the styles to each other. It will serve as an easy reference, help you create all the styles you need, and help you eliminate redundant styles.

LOCAL CATERER WEB SITE

GOALS

- Learn collaboration techniques for working with others on a Web site.
- Verify that a Web site meets guidelines for best practices.

TECHNICAL SKILLS

- Publish to a remote server.
- Download and upload files to and from a remote Web site.
- Use the Dreamweaver Check In/Check Out system.
- Run site reports in Dreamweaver.
- Check spelling on a Web page.
- Add keywords to a page.
- Check a site for broken links and orphaned files.
- Move or rename a Web file.

Estimated time to complete this project: 1 hour, 40 minutes

Summary

If you work professionally as a Web developer, you won't always have the luxury of creating the sites you work on. Sometimes you will inherit a site along with a mandate to add new features, improve the design, or simply maintain it.

In previous projects, much of the focus was on page design and structure. In this project, you look at the site as a whole as you run through a test plan, running site reports and thinking about site structure.

You also get experience with the Check In/Check Out features of Dreamweaver and the features that Dreamweaver provides for managing a remote site.

The Assignment

Café Townsend is a local catering business that has an established Web site. Your team has been asked to take over the maintenance of the site. The site seems to be working well, but to make sure that it is in good shape and that it accommodates current best practices, you have been asked to run a simplified test plan in which you run some reports on the site and make updates as necessary.

As you work on the project, you will:

- Create a site definition to connect to a remote site
- Check files into and out of a site
- Run reports on a site
- Organize files on a site

Figure 1 shows the home page of the Café Townsend Web site.

FIGURE 1
Café Townsend Web site

Web Site Review and Testing

In the Dangerous Frogs and Experience Bank projects, you used storyboards to determine the design of the pages. But there may be times you have to work on a site that you did not build. In such a case, it is a good practice to have a test plan that you can run on the files that you inherit.

A test plan is a checklist of those aspects of a page or site that you need to review to ensure that the site accommodates current best practices, that the site technically works, and that the site is organized well.

Dreamweaver can greatly simplify the testing process, but a thorough test plan includes a number of checkpoints that only a human can verify. For instance, Dreamweaver can tell you if a link is broken (a link to a page that does not exist), but it cannot tell if a link is wrong (a link to the menu.html page instead of the location.html page, for instance). The following lessons cover only some aspects of a full test plan for a Web site such as Café Townsend, primarily those that Dreamweaver can assist with. The test plan for the Web site is shown in Figure 2.

FIGURE 2
Test plan for the Café Townsend Web site

Test Plan – Café Townsend Web Site

Technical Testing

Links
On each page of the site, test all links to pages of the site, links to external sites, and e-mail links. Note links that have incorrect destinations, links that are broken, and orphaned files (files that are not linked from any page).

Layout Structures
Are standard layout structures consistently implemented on each page of the site? (banners; navigation schemes; color schemes; fonts; blocked regions for text, graphics, or multimedia elements)

Browsers
Test each page of the site in targeted browsers.
Is the contrast between the colors of text and its background sufficient to make the text readable?
Are images clear?
Are videos playable? Do all video controls function properly?
Are sound elements clear?
Are Flash movies playable? Do all movie controls function properly?

Computer Platforms
Does the site function properly in major operating systems, such as Windows and Macintosh?
Test in targeted browsers on each platform.

Spelling
Check the spelling of all text content on the site.

Usability Testing

General
Do pages appear in reasonable amounts of time? If a page is slow to appear, is there some provision for informing a site visitor of progress in providing the page?
How well are elements of the page organized? Are the most important elements emphasized?
Is the text readable? (font, text size, color contrast with background)

Accessibility
Does the site meet the Priority 1 checkpoints for the W3C Web Content Accessibility Guidelines?
Does every image have alternate text?
Is the language on every page as clear and simple as possible?
In data tables, are there appropriate row or column headers?

Navigation
Are links labeled clearly? Is the link destination predictable?
How easy is it for site visitors to find specific information?
How long does it take (number of clicks) to reach a typical destination?
How easily can visitors return to essential sections of the site?
Is the site structure apparent?

Café Townsend Web Site – Test Plan   1

To print the test plan for the Café Townsend Web site, open the file named *DW_Project3_Testplan.pdf*. This file is located in the Design folder for this project.

REVIEWING, TESTING, AND PUBLISHING A WEB SITE

OBJECTIVES

Upon completion of this lesson, you will be able to:

- Publish to a remote server.
- Download and upload files to and from a remote Web site.
- Use the Dreamweaver Check In/Check Out system.
- Run site reports in Dreamweaver.
- Check spelling on a Web page.

Estimated time to complete this lesson: 55 minutes

Introduction

Before you can work on the Café Townsend Web site, you have to download the files from the site. First you set up a site definition that simulates a remote site, and you enable the Check In/Check Out system. Once that is done, you run several reports.

In the course of this lesson, you will not run all of the reports that Dreamweaver provides. But you will see that implementing best practices is much easier when you have the right tools for the job.

The Café Townsend Web site test plan calls for a number of assessments. In this lesson, you verify that the site is compliant with the Web Content Accessibility Guidelines Priority 1 checkpoints. You also meet the test plan's requirement to check for broken links and orphaned files. Finally, you run a spelling check on a Web page.

Publishing to a Remote Server

In previous projects, you created a local site—that is, a folder on your hard drive to store all the folders and files needed for your site. For visitors to see your Web pages, however, you need to copy your files to a remote Web server. Typically, the remote site is on a server specified by your Web administrator or client, but it could also be on a local network.

After you create your local site, you choose the remote site to connect to and the attributes of that remote site. For this project, you will simulate a remote site by using a folder on your desktop (or wherever your instructor indicates). This will enable you to experiment with the Get and Put functions without the possibility of corrupting an actual remote site.

Set Up a Connection to a Remote Site

1. Using the file management tools on your system, copy the **cafe_townsend_remote** folder from the data files for this unit to the location where you will store your solution files. Also create a new, empty folder named **cafe_townsend_local**. Ask your instructor for specific directions about where these folders should go.

   Whenever you work on a site that someone else built, you first connect to the remote site and download the files to your local site. That's why you are creating an empty folder for the local site. In the next activity, you download the Web site files from the remote folder into the empty local folder.

2. Open Dreamweaver. Click **Site** on the menu bar and then click **New Site** to open the Site Definition dialog box. If the dialog box opens in Advanced mode, click the **Basic** tab to start the Site Definition Wizard.

3. The wizard starts with *What would you like to name your site?* Key **Cafe Townsend**, followed by your initials, as the site name. Then click **Next**.

4. Under *Do you want to work with a server technology such as ColdFusion, ASP.NET, ASP, JSP, or PHP?* click **No, I do not want to use a server technology**. Then click **Next**.

5. Under *How do you want to work with your files during development?* click **Edit local copies on my machine, then upload to server when ready (recommended)**.

6. Under *Where on your computer do you want to store your files?* click the folder icon next to the text box, locate the **cafe_townsend_local** folder that you created in step 1, and click **Select** (Windows) or **Choose** (Macintosh). Then click **Next**.

7. Under *How do you connect to your remote server?* click the arrow to see the list of options and then select **Local/Network**.

8. Under *What folder on your server do you want to store your files in?* click the folder icon next to the text box and select the **cafe_townsend_remote** folder. Make sure the **Refresh Remote File List Automatically** check box is checked. Then click **Next**.

9. Under *Do you want to enable checking in and checking out files, to ensure that you and your co-workers cannot edit the same file at the same time?* click **Yes, enable check in and check out**.

   New questions appear regarding how Dreamweaver should check out files for you.

10. Under *When you open a file that isn't checked out, should Dreamweaver check it out, or do you want to view a read-only copy?* choose **Dreamweaver should check it out**.

11. Under *What is your name?* key your name. Under *What is your email address?* key your e-mail address.

12. Click **Next** to move to a summary of your site definition settings. Review your settings.

13. Click **Done** to finish defining your site. A message box may appear to notify you that the initial site cache will be created. Click **OK**.

Since you created an empty folder as your local folder, you will notice that the Files panel remains empty. In the next activity, you will get the files from the simulated remote server where you copied the data files.

Getting and Putting Files

Dreamweaver includes a number of features for managing files and transferring files to and from a remote server. Moving a file from your computer to the Web server is called *uploading* or *putting* a file. Moving a file from a Web server to your computer is called *downloading* or *getting* a file. There are a number of different means by which files can be transferred between servers. The most popular is probably FTP (see the Learn More feature "File Transfer Protocol" to find out what information you need to set up a site definition to use FTP).

When you transfer files between local and remote sites, Dreamweaver maintains parallel file and folder structures on the sites. When transferring files between sites, Dreamweaver automatically creates necessary folders if they do not yet exist on a site.

When you transfer a document between local and remote folders using the Files panel, Dreamweaver gives you the option of transferring the document's dependent files. Dependent files are images, external style sheets, and other files referenced in your document that a browser loads when it loads the document.

Dreamweaver provides two methods for transferring files: you can use either the Get and Put commands or the Check In and Check Out commands. You explore the Check In and Check Out system later in this lesson.

Now that you have created a site definition for the Café Townsend Web site, you need to download the files for the site so that they will be available for you to work on. Since you do not want to change the checked-out status of any of the files, you use the Get command.

Learn More

FILE TRANSFER PROTOCOL

File Transfer Protocol (FTP) access is commonly used to get files from or put files on a remote site. If you want to create a site definition that uses FTP to connect to your remote site, consult your network administrator to correctly set the options explained here.

- **FTP hostname:** The host name of your Web server: for example, ftp.everyone.com or www.mysite.com.
- **Host folder:** The directory on the remote site where documents visible to the public are stored. Ask your FTP service provider what directory, if any, you should use.
- **Login and password:** Your login name and password for the server. If you deselect the Save option, you will be prompted for a password when you connect to the remote site.

Step by Step

Get Files from a Remote Site

1. In the Files panel, make sure your new **Cafe Townsend** site is selected. Then click the **Expand/Collapse** button, shown in Figure 1-1.

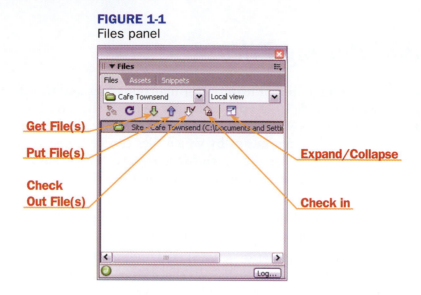

FIGURE 1-1
Files panel

The Files panel expands to show two panes instead of one, as shown in Figure 1-2. On the left are the files in the remote site, and on the right are the files in the local site.

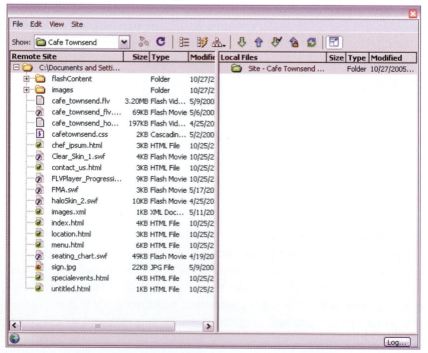

FIGURE 1-2
Expanded Files panel showing the Café Townsend Web site

2. Click the site folder at the top of either pane. Then click the **Get File(s)** button. A message appears, asking if you are sure you want to get the entire site. Click **OK**.

The files download to the local version of the site, and a list of the files appears in the local pane.

3. Click the **Expand/Collapse** button to reduce the Files panel to a single pane.

Hot Tip

You do not have to expand the Files panel to get files from the remote site, but having two panes open is helpful for quickly comparing the local and remote sites.

Checking Files In and Out

If you were the only person working on the Café Townsend Web site, then you could simply use the Get and Put commands. But you are part of the Café Townsend Web team, and team members must avoid overwriting each other's files or undoing each other's work. To keep track of who is working on what file, the team uses Dreamweaver to check files in and out from the Web server.

Checking out a file is the equivalent of declaring "I'm working on this file now—don't touch it!" When a file is checked out, Dreamweaver displays the name of the person who checked out the file in the Files panel, along with a red check mark (if a team member checked out the file) or a green check mark (if you checked out the file) next to the file's icon.

Checking in a file makes the file available for other team members to check out and edit. When you check in a file after editing it, your local version becomes read-only and a lock symbol appears beside the file in the Files panel to prevent you from making changes to the file.

Dreamweaver does not make checked-out files read-only on the remote server. If you transfer files with an application other than Dreamweaver, you can overwrite checked-out files. However, in file transfer applications other than Dreamweaver, a file with an LCK extension is visible next to the checked-out file in the file hierarchy to help prevent such accidents. The LCK file is created on the remote server by Dreamweaver and contains information about who has checked out the file. When the file is checked in, Dreamweaver deletes the LCK file.

Note

There are two common situations in which you might use the Put command instead of Check In:
- You're not in a collaborative environment, and you aren't using the Check In/Check Out system.
- You want to put the current version of the file on the server, but you are also going to continue editing it.

Check a File Out and Check It Back In

1. In the Files panel, notice that the files all have lock icons next to them. This icon shows that the file is checked in. Double-click the **chef_ipsum.html** file to open it.

   Because of the way you defined this site, when you open this file, you will also be checking it out.

2. A message appears asking if you want to get dependent files. Check the **Don't Show Me This Message Again** check box and click **No**.

   When the file opens, notice that the **chef_ipsum.html** file now has a green check next to it, indicating that the file is checked out to you.

3. In the Files panel, click the **Expand/Collapse** button.

   Notice that the green check next to **chef_ipsum.html** is also present in the remote pane. Other collaborators who have connections to this site will also be able to see that you have the file checked out.

4. Collapse the Files panel back to a single pane.

5. On the **chef_ipsum.html** page, find the sentence that says "In his fourth DVD, the cooking legend Chef Ipsum shows you how to be a world-class chef!" Insert the word **Lorem** between **Chef** and **Ipsum**.

6. Save your work and preview it in a browser. Then close the browser.

7. In Dreamweaver, close the **chef_ipsum.html** page. Select the **chef_ipsum.html** file in the Files panel and click the **Check In** button. When asked if you want to check in dependent files, check the **Don't Show Me This Message Again** check box and click **No**.

   Note that the icon next to the file is now a lock again, indicating that the file is locked in the local site and checked in with regard to both the local and remote sites.

Conducting Site Reviews

Before uploading your site to a server and declaring it ready for viewing, it's a good idea to test it locally. Throughout the site's construction, you should test and troubleshoot your site so that you can catch problems early and avoid repeating them.

You should make sure that your pages look and work as expected in the browsers you are targeting, that there are no broken links, and that the pages do not take too long to download. You can also test and troubleshoot your entire site by running a site report.

The following guidelines will help you create a good experience for visitors to your site:

■ Make sure your pages function as expected in the browsers you are targeting and that they either work or "fail gracefully" in other browsers. Pages that fail gracefully should remain legible and functional in browsers that do not support styles, layers, plug-ins, or JavaScript.

■ Preview your pages in as many different browsers and on as many different platforms as possible. This gives you an opportunity to see differences in layout, color, font sizes, and default browser window size that cannot be predicted in a target browser check.

■ Check your site for broken links. Then fix them. Other sites undergo redesign and reorganization, too, and a page you are linking to may have been moved or deleted. You can run a link check report to test your links.

■ Monitor the file size of your pages and the time the pages take to download. Keep in mind that if a page consists of one large table, in some browsers visitors will see nothing until the entire table finishes loading. Consider breaking up large tables; if this is not possible, consider putting a small amount of content—such as a welcome message or an advertising banner—outside the table at the top of the page so users can view this material while the table downloads.

■ Run a few site reports to test and troubleshoot the entire site. These reports allow you to check your entire site for problems, such as untitled documents, empty tags, and redundant nested tags.

■ Validate your code to locate tag or syntax errors.

■ Once the bulk of the site has been published, continue to update and maintain it. Publishing your site—that is, making it live—can be accomplished in several ways and is an ongoing process. An important part of the process is defining and implementing a version-control system, either with the tools Dreamweaver includes or with an external version-control application.

Conducting Usability Tests

When evaluating a site for usability, consider these questions:

■ How clearly are links labeled? When you click a link, do you find the information you are expecting?

■ Is the time a page takes to load worth the wait? (Typical users will wait seven seconds for a page to load before moving on.)

■ How easily can users find information?

■ How easily can users return to essential sections of the site (if at all)?

■ What types of navigation elements are used: buttons, hyperlinks, images, something else? One type or many? Provide a description of the types of navigation elements.

■ Is the site structure apparent?

■ What are the elements of the visual layout?

■ How do the visual elements help or hinder the message or make the message easier or more difficult for users to understand?

■ Can you tell when the page was last updated or whether any of the information is new?

■ As you navigate, how many clicks does it generally take to get to the information you are seeking?

■ How does the use of text, navigation, and site structure make the site easier or more difficult for users?

■ Do pages contain clear titles, headings, or other visual elements that specifically help organize the information?

■ Do the images have alternative text (Alt tags), so descriptive text appears when you roll the pointer over the image?

■ Is the text readable? Is the text uniquely styled? If so, does the styling add value to the message?

■ Is color the only element used to convey emphasis?

Using Validation Reports

Dreamweaver provides several features to help you test your site, including features to help you preview pages and check for browser compatibility. You can also run various reports, such as a broken links report.

You can run site reports on workflow or HTML attributes, including accessibility for the current document, selected files, or the entire site. You can also run workflow reports that indicate who has checked out a file.

HTML reports enable you to compile and generate reports on several HTML attributes. You can check for accessibility, missing Alt text, redundant nested tags, removable empty tags, and untitled documents.

Your task is to run an accessibility report to find out if the Café Townsend Web site meets WCAG Priority 1 checkpoints for Web accessibility (for additional information, see the Tips & Techniques feature "Web Content Accessibility Guidelines").

 ## Run a Report to Test a Site

1. In the Café Townsend site, make sure all Document windows are closed. Click **Site** on the menu bar and click **Reports**. The Reports dialog box appears, as shown in Figure 1-3.

FIGURE 1-3
Reports dialog box

2. In the Reports dialog box, click the **Report On** menu and then click **Entire Current Local Site**.

3. Under **Select Reports**, check the **Accessibility** check box.

The Report Settings button is now active.

4. Click the **Report Settings** button to open the Accessibility dialog box.

A full report of all of the available accessibility options would be far too long for this lesson and would list many items that require more training in accessibility issues than this lesson provides. In the next few steps, you will limit the scope of the report to address only the most critical issues.

5. In the Category – Rule list, make sure that **ALL** (the first item in the list) is selected. Then click the **Disable** button.

This button turns off the selected settings so that in the next few steps you can turn on only the settings that you want in the report.

6. Select the **W3C/WCAG P.1 accessibility** category. Click the **Enable** button.

This turns on the Priority 1 checkpoints, which the site test plan calls for you to test. That plan also indicates that the report should review only non-manual checks.

7. In the Category – Rule list, select the **manual** category. Click the **Disable** button.

This turns off any Priority 1 checkpoints that are manual checks. Manual checks are those that require you to review the indicated content and consider whether the content meets accessibility standards. For instance, you would need to check manually to decide whether a color provides enough contrast with its background to serve as text color, or whether an image needs a long description instead of just alternative text. If you left the manual checks on, you would get dozens of items in the report, all of which you would have to check manually.

The Accessibility dialog box should now look that in Figure 1-4.

FIGURE 1-4
Accessibility dialog box with manual reports disabled

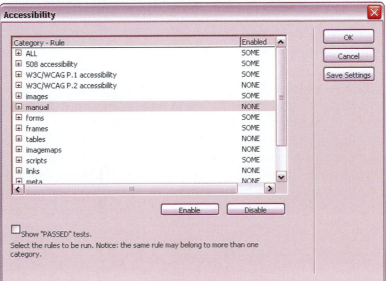

8. Click **OK** to close the Accessibility dialog box. In the Reports dialog box, click the **Run** button.

The Accessibility dialog box closes, and the Site Reports panel opens in the Results panel group, showing the results of the report. Your report should look similar to that in Figure 1-5.

FIGURE 1-5
Site Reports panel

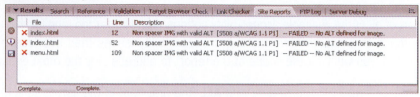

The Site Report panel displays a list of accessibility errors, each marked by a red X. For each error, the report lists the name of the file in which the error occurs, the line number on which the error can be found, and a description of the problem. In each case, the problem is that no alternative text has been supplied for an image.

You can use the report to go quickly to the source of the problem and correct it.

Tips & Techniques

WEB CONTENT ACCESSIBILITY GUIDELINES

Accessibility standards help designers and developers of Web content identify and address accessibility issues.

The Web Content Accessibility Guidelines (WCAG) from the World Wide Web Consortium (W3C) represented the first major effort to establish guidelines for accessible design. This standard consists of 14 guidelines, each with three checkpoint levels for Web developers to meet: Priority 1, Priority 2, and Priority 3.

Priority 1 checkpoints identify issues that, if not addressed, will make it impossible for one or more groups of people to access information in the site.

Priority 2 checkpoints identify issues that will make it difficult for one or more groups to access information.

Priority 3 checkpoints identify ways in which Web developers can improve access to Web-based information.

Use a Report to Update a Page

1. In the Site Reports panel, double-click the first item on the list, **index.html**.

The file was checked in, so Dreamweaver automatically checks it out for you to work on. It opens in split view—both Code view and Design view are visible, as shown in Figure 1-6. When the file opens, the focus is on the code that causes the error in line 12. The problem turns out to be that a photo image does not have alternative text.

FIGURE 1-6
Index.html open in split view

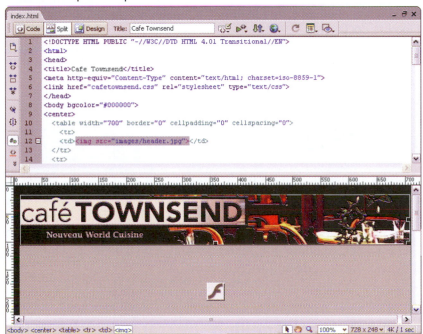

2. With the banner image selected, in the Property inspector, key **Cafe Townsend - Nouveau World Cuisine** in the **Alt** text field. Then press **Tab**.

The alternative text should be the same as the words in the graphic.

3. Save the page. Preview it in a browser. Then close both the browser and the **index.html** Document window.

You should not see a visible change in the page (since all you did was change the alternative text), but it is always a good idea to preview any page you edit to make sure you haven't made any unintentional changes to the page.

4. In the Site Reports panel, find the next result in the list. This problem is also on the **index.html** page. Double-click the result to open the page at line 52, the line that contains the error.

This time the page opens to show an image of a street corner and its corresponding HTML code. You may need to click the image in Design view in order to use the Alt field in the Property inspector.

5. In the Property inspector, key the Alt text **Building on Townsend Street** and press **Tab**. Save and preview the page to check the change. Then close both the browser and the index.html Document window.

6. In the Site Reports panel, find the third item in the list. This time the problem is on the **menu.html** page. Double-click the result to view the corresponding code in line 109 on the menu.html page.

   The page opens to show the footer image and its corresponding HTML code.

7. Set the Alt text for this image to **Cafe Townsend, a fictional company** so that it matches the text in the image.

8. Save the page. Preview it in a browser. Then close both the browser and the **menu.html** Document window.

9. Check in the two documents that you edited.

10. To verify that all of the issues have been resolved, rerun the accessibility report that you ran in the previous activity.

Checking Spelling

Checking spelling is just as important as making sure your code and accessibility features are correct. You can use the *Check Spelling* command on the *Text* menu to check the spelling in any current document you have open. The Check Spelling command ignores HTML tags and other source code and focuses only on the text.

Check and Correct Spelling

1. Open the **location.html** page.

2. Click **Text** on the menu bar and then click **Check Spelling**.

> **Note**
>
> By default, the spelling checker uses the U.S. English spelling dictionary. To change the dictionary, click Edit on the menu bar, click Preferences, and then click the General category (Windows), or click Dreamweaver in the menu bar, click Preferences, and then click the General category (Macintosh). In the Spelling Dictionary menu, select the dictionary you want to use. Dictionaries for additional languages can be downloaded from the Dreamweaver Support Center at www.macromedia.com/ support/dreamweaver.

When Dreamweaver encounters an unrecognized word—in this case, the word *Ipsum*—the Check Spelling dialog box opens with a list of suggested corrections. However, this word is someone's name and does not need to be corrected.

3. Click the **Ignore All** button.

   Dreamweaver immediately continues the check and flags the word *gigiantic*.

4. In the Check Spelling dialog box, make sure that the suggestion **gigantic** is selected. Then click the **Change** button.

   The word on the page changes to *gigantic*.

5. When a message appears indicating that the spelling check is complete, click **OK**.

6. Save the page and preview it in a browser. Then close both the browser and the **location.html** page in the Document window.

7. Check the page in. Then close Dreamweaver.

MANAGING A SITE

OBJECTIVES

Upon completion of this lesson, you will be able to:

- Add keywords to a page.
- Check a site for broken links and orphaned files.
- Move or rename a Web file.

Estimated time to complete this lesson: 45 minutes

Introduction

When you manage a Web site, whether one you created yourself or one you inherited, you must take pains to pay attention to little details: Do all of the links work? Are all of the files in the right places? Good organization helps you return to a site later and find everything easily.

In this lesson, you address two of the items on the site test plan related to broken links and site organization. You will review the Café Townsend Web site to make sure that the pages use well-chosen keywords so that search engines can easily find the site, and you will review the links used in the site to make sure that none of them are broken and that the site files are well organized.

Adding Meta Tags

One of your tasks for the Café Townsend Web site is to add keywords to the pages so that search engines can more easily find the site.

Keywords were originally intended to help Web developers ensure that search engines properly indexed their sites. This, in turn, should have helped Web users find the information they were looking for. Unfortunately, keywords were abused so much in the early history of the Web that some search engines now downplay their significance.

However, keywords can still have some influence on how a page is indexed in a Web search engine, so it is always a good idea to implement them. Many search engine robots (programs that automatically browse the Web gathering information for search engines to index) read the keywords in the *meta* tag, an HTML element that provides information about the site to servers, and use the information to index your pages in their databases. Because some search engines limit the number of keywords or characters they index, or ignore all keywords if you go beyond the limit, it is a good idea to use just a few well-chosen keywords.

⬤ Add Keywords to a Web Page

1. Open the **index.html** page. Make sure the page is shown in Design view. On the **Insert** bar, select the **HTML** category, shown in Figure 2-1.

FIGURE 2-1
HTML category on the Insert bar

2. Click the down arrow next to the **Head** button. On the menu, click **Keywords**.

   The Keywords dialog box appears.

3. In the Keywords dialog box, key **Cafe Townsend, gourmet, cuisine, restaurant, San Francisco** (including the commas). Then click the **OK** button.

4. Repeat steps 1 through 3 for each of the other pages in the site using the keywords listed here:
   a. chef_ipsum.html: **Cafe Townsend, gourmet, cuisine, restaurant, San Francisco, chef, Lorem Ipsum**
   b. location.html: **Cafe Townsend, gourmet, cuisine, restaurant, San Francisco, historic, 601 Townsend Street, Spectacular Drive**
   c. menu.html: **Cafe Townsend, gourmet, cuisine, restaurant, San Francisco, menu, appetizer, entrée, dessert**
   d. specialevents.html: **Cafe Townsend, gourmet, cuisine, restaurant, San Francisco, catering, parties, seating, floor plan**
   e. contact_us.html: **Cafe Townsend, gourmet, cuisine, restaurant, San Francisco**

5. Save all of the pages and close all of the Document windows. Check in all of the files.

Managing Broken Links

Use the Check Links feature to search for broken links and orphaned files (files that still exist in the site but are not linked to by any other file in the site) in an open file, a portion of a local site, or an entire local site.

The only links that Dreamweaver verifies are links to documents within the site; Dreamweaver compiles a list of external links that appear in the selected document or documents, but does not verify them.

Check a Site for Broken Links

1. Click **Site** on the menu bar and then click **Check Links Sitewide**.

   The Link Checker panel opens in the Results panel group, showing broken links. The Café Townsend Web site has a single broken link in the **chef_ipsum.html** page, as shown in Figure 2-2.

   FIGURE 2-2
   Link Checker panel showing broken links

2. In the Link Checker panel, in the Broken Links column, click the text **contract_us.html**.

   The text becomes a text field, and you can now edit it.

3. Change **contract_us.html** to **contact_us.html** (remove the *r* from *contract*). Then press **Enter** (Windows) or **Return** (Macintosh).

4. A message appears, indicating that you cannot update this file unless you check it out. Click **Yes** to check out the file.

   Once the file is checked out, Dreamweaver updates the file and clears the broken link from the list in the Link Checker panel. Note that **chef_ipsum.html** is now checked out in the Files panel.

5. Open the **chef_ipsum.html** page and preview it in a browser. On the left side of the page, click the link **Contact Us** and verify that it opens to the **contact_us.html** page.

6. Close the browser. Close the **chef_ipsum.html** page and check the file in.

Managing Orphaned Links

Y ou can also use the Link Checker panel to find orphaned files. An orphaned file is one that is not referred to by any link in the site. Looking for orphaned files is a good way to discover, for instance, images that are no longer being used. You would know that you could delete those images without harming a Web page.

Be careful, though. Many developers keep their source files in the local site, and these would show up on the Orphaned Files list. And in the Café Townsend site, several files used by a Flash movie will appear on the list, because Dreamweaver does not check links embedded in Flash movies. You can delete a file from the Orphaned Files list, but keep in mind that this deletes the file from the site as well.

Review the List of Orphaned Files

1. If you are continuing from the previous activity, the Link Checker panel should still be open. If not, use the same Check Links Sitewide command you used in the previous activity to get an updated list of links in the Link Checker panel. Then click the **Show** menu in the Link Checker panel and click **Orphaned Files**.

   The Link Checker panel now displays a list of files that are not referred to by any link in the site, as shown in Figure 2-3.

   FIGURE 2-3
   Link Checker panel showing orphaned files

   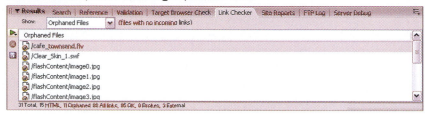

2. In the list of orphaned files, scroll down if necessary and double-click the file **untitled.html**.

   Double-clicking a filename in the Link Checker panel opens the file. The **untitled.html** page opens to show an empty page. This page seems to be unused. It was not checked out by anyone. Someone must have created this file and then decided not to use it.

3. Close the **untitled.html** page. In the Files panel, check in the **untitled.html** page.

4. In the Files panel, click **untitled.html** and then press the **Delete** key. A confirmation message appears, asking if you really want to delete the file. Click **Yes**. Click **Yes** again when asked if you want to delete the read-only file untitled.html.

   You downloaded this file from the remote site. You should delete it from the remote site as well so that the local and remote versions of the site correspond as closely as possible.

5. In the Files panel, click the **Expand/Collapse** button to display the remote site.

6. In the remote pane of the Files panel, select the **untitled.html** page, shown in Figure 2-4. Press the **Delete** key. When asked if you really want to delete the file, click **Yes**.

FIGURE 2-4
Untitled.html in the remote pane of the Files panel

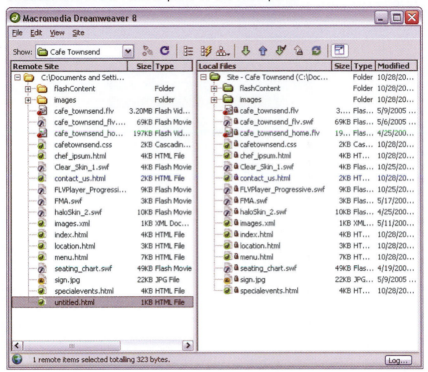

7. Click the **Expand/Collapse** button to return the Files panel to single-pane view. Collapse the Results panel group.

Hot Tip

You can also use the Link Checker panel to see a list of all of the URLs in your site that link to other Web sites. In the Link Checker, use the Show menu to view the External Links. Pages on the Web may change or disappear over time. If you typically link to external Web sites in your pages, you can periodically review this list to test those links and make sure that they still work.

Renaming and Moving Files

The Café Townsend Web site includes a JPG file that is not inside the images folder, as shown in Figure 2-5. In addition, the file's name—sign.jpg—is not very descriptive. Investigate and then rename the file so that in the future you will not have to guess what the image shows.

FIGURE 2-5
Files panel showing sign.jpg

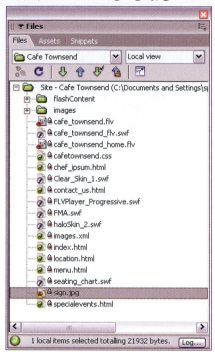

If you need to change the name of one of your files, change the name on the Files panel. This preserves the link information maintained by Dreamweaver. If you change the filename outside of Dreamweaver for either an HTML file or a graphics file that is linked, Dreamweaver has no way to track your changes. If you make the change on the Files panel, Dreamweaver updates all pages that link to the file or contain the graphic.

 **Rename a File**

1. Double-click the **sign.jpg** image to open it in Fireworks.

   Fireworks opens, and you see that the image shows part of a building and a street sign that says "Townsend," as shown in Figure 2-6.

   FIGURE 2-6
   Sign.jpg

2. Close Fireworks.

3. In Dreamweaver, in the Files panel, click the name of the **sign.jpg** file once so that the text is editable. Key **townsend_street_sign.jpg** to change the name of the file. Then press **Enter** (Windows) or **Return** (Macintosh).

4. A message appears asking you to confirm that you want to rename the checked-out file. Click **OK**.

   The Update Files dialog box appears, as shown in Figure 2-7.

   FIGURE 2-7
   Update Files dialog box

   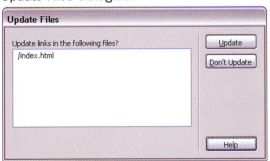

5. In the Update Files dialog box, click **Update**.

6. A message appears, telling you that index.html cannot be updated unless it is checked out, as shown in Figure 2-8. Click **Yes** to check out the **index.html** page.

FIGURE 2-8
Confirmation message for checking out index.html

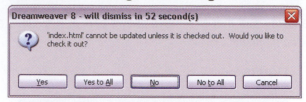

7. Open the **index.html** page and preview it in a browser. Close the browser.

The image file you have been working with is also in an odd location. All of the other image files are in either the images folder or the flashContent folder, while the townsend_street_sign.jpg file is in the site root.

If a file or folder is not in its proper place, you can easily move the file or folder to its correct location. Doing this on the Files panel in Dreamweaver ensures that all the link information remains correct and intact.

When you drag a file from one Dreamweaver site to another, or to a folder that is not part of a Dreamweaver site, Dreamweaver copies the file to the location where you drop it. If you drag a file within the same Dreamweaver site, Dreamweaver moves the file to the location where you drop it. If you drag a file that is not part of a Dreamweaver site to a folder that is not part of a Dreamweaver site, Dreamweaver moves the file to the location where you drop it.

 Move a File to a Different Directory

1. In the Files panel, drag the **townsend_street_sign.jpg** file to the **images** folder.

   The Update Files dialog box appears.

2. In the Update Files dialog box, click **Update**.

3. Save the **index.html** page and preview it in a browser. Close the browser and close the **index.html** Document window.

4. In the Files panel, click the **+** button (Windows) or the **Right Arrow** button (Macintosh) next to the **images** folder.

The folder opens to display all of the images inside, as shown in Figure 2-9.

FIGURE 2-9
Files in the images folder

5. Select the **townsend_street_sign.jpg** file and check it in. Check in the **index.html** file.

6. In the Files panel, click the **Expand/Collapse** button to display the remote site.

Notice that the sign.jpg file is still in the site root of the remote site.

7. In the remote pane of the Files panel, click the **+** button (Windows) or the **Right Arrow** button (Macintosh) next to the **images** folder to open it. Verify that the **townsend_street_sign.jpg** file is in the folder.

8. In the remote pane, in the site root, select the **sign.jpg** file, shown in Figure 2-10. Press the **Delete** key. When asked if you really want to delete the file, click **Yes.**

FIGURE 2-10
Files in the images folder

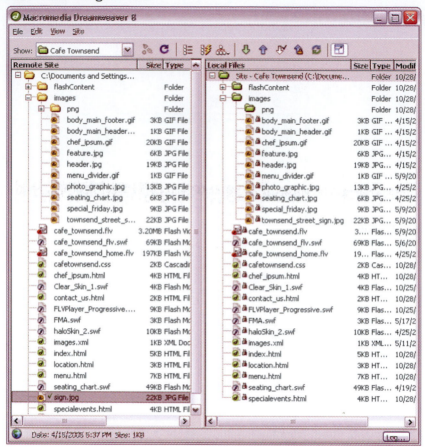

9. Make sure that all files are checked in. Then collapse the Files panel and close Dreamweaver.

SUMMARY

You have successfully reviewed and cleaned up the Café Townsend Web site.

In this project, you learned to create a site definition to connect to a remote site, check files into and out of a site, run reports on a site, and organize files on a site.

This project concludes the Macromedia Dreamweaver Unit of this program.

ON YOUR OWN – SITE REPORTS

ACTIVITY 1: RUN ACCESSIBILITY REPORTS ON THE DANGEROUS FROGS 3 WEB SITE

You learned how to use reports in Dreamweaver to improve the quality of your site. Apply these same techniques to run accessibility reports on the Dangerous Frogs 3 personal Web site. The Dangerous Frogs 3 site is very similar to the site you completed in Project 1.

You can review the techniques for running accessibility reports with Priority 1 checkpoints in Lesson 1.

1. Create a site definition in Dreamweaver for the Dangerous Frogs 3 Web site. This site is provided in the data files for On Your Own Project 3 Activity 1.

2. Run an accessibility report on the site, enabling only the Priority 1 checks and disabling the manual checks.

3. Fix any items that the report turns up. Run the report again and make sure that no items remain unresolved.

ACTIVITY 2: CHECK LINKS ON THE DANGEROUS FROGS 4 WEB SITE

You learned how to check links in Dreamweaver to improve the quality of your site. Apply these same techniques to check links on the Dangerous Frogs 4 personal Web site. The Dangerous Frogs 4 site is very similar to the site you completed in Project 1.

You can review techniques for checking site links in Lesson 2.

1. Create a site definition in Dreamweaver for the Dangerous Frogs 4 Web site. This site is provided in the data files for On Your Own Project 3 Activity 2.

2. Use the Check Links feature in Dreamweaver to check the links in the site.

3. Use the results in the Link Checker panel to make sure there are no broken links in the site. In the Orphaned Files list, keep any files that are in the _documents folder or in the _fireworks folder. If the list contains other files, remove them from the site.

4. After fixing the broken links, manually test all the links in the site to make sure the links send the site visitor to the expected pages.

Macromedia Fireworks 8

MACROMEDIA FIREWORKS 8

IN THIS UNIT YOU WILL LEARN TO:

- Follow a design document to prepare images for inclusion in a Web page.
- Run a batch process to prepare multiple images in one step.
- Use Web site specifications to draw logo images.
- Use Web site design criteria to define effects and blends.
- Integrate text and drawn images to generate a design described in Web site specifications.
- Use the Web site design document to generate a page comp and define elements of a navigation bar.
- Use the Web site design document to define colors and fonts of a page and a navigation bar.
- Generate and save a page comp.
- Build, optimize, and export a navigation bar for use in a Web site.

Summary

Macromedia Fireworks 8 is a graphics program used to create and edit sophisticated images for the Web. With Fireworks, you can quickly manipulate and create images, rollover buttons, and navigation bars. You can then use the optimization features to shrink the file size of your graphics without sacrificing quality. When you are ready, simply export the HTML code to your favorite editor, such as Macromedia Dreamweaver 8. The professional design tools in Fireworks even let you import digital camera files and scanned images, as well as files from popular image-editing programs and other graphics applications.

In this unit you build three projects that will help you develop the skills needed to understand graphic design as well as the technical skills needed to implement the designs. To begin engaging in these projects, you first need to become familiar with Fireworks and basic graphic design.

Getting to Know Macromedia Fireworks 8

Understanding Macromedia Fireworks

In Macromedia Fireworks, you can create and manipulate images for print or the Web. Fireworks allows you to balance the quality of the design with the file size of the image when creating graphics for use in different contexts. You can create many types of graphics, which fall into two main categories: bitmap and vector.

Bitmap versus Vector Graphics

Macromedia Fireworks functions as both a bitmap editor and a vector drawing program. Most images on the Web are bitmap graphics, such as GIF and JPEG files. Bitmaps record information pixel by pixel and color by color. The file size of a bitmap is determined by the number of pixels and colors used to define the image. Creating and editing bitmaps has its limitations. As with paint on a canvas, you need to completely remove a mistake. When editing bitmaps, you need to completely erase or "paint" over the mistake.

Vector graphics, on the other hand, store mathematical formulas they use as recipes to construct an image at the time it is presented. Vector graphics give you more precise control in creating an image and allow for more advanced editing and modification. Figure 1 illustrates the difference between bitmap and vector graphics.

By combining bitmap and vector drawing methods in the same application, Fireworks gives you a powerful and versatile set of tools. You get the features of photo editing and paint programs along with the precision of a vector drawing program, and your finished graphics are optimized for use in Web pages.

FIGURE 1
Bitmap and vector images

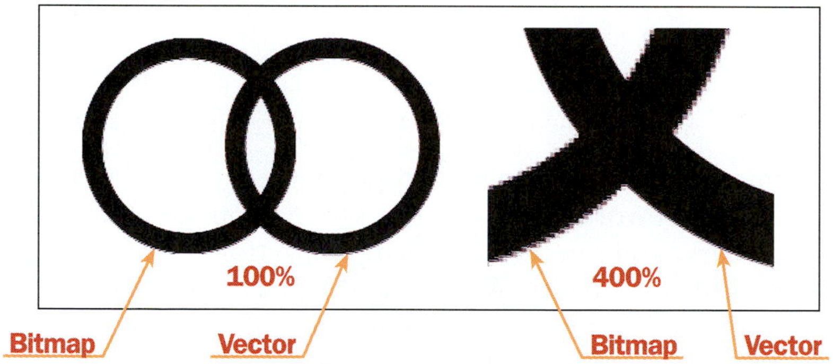

100%   400%

Bitmap   Vector   Bitmap   Vector

Finding Your Way Around the Fireworks Interface

Fireworks helps you create and manipulate images. When you are creating a new document, the area that opens is called the canvas. When you open a document in Fireworks for the first time, Fireworks activates the work environment, including the Tools panel, Property inspector, menus, and other panels, as shown in Figure 2 and described in Table 1. The Tools panel, on the left of the screen, contains labeled categories, including bitmap, vector, and Web tool groups. The Property inspector appears along the bottom of the document by default and initially displays document properties. It then changes to display properties for a newly selected tool or currently selected object as you work in the document. The panels are initially docked in groups along the right side of the screen. The document window appears in the center of the application.

FIGURE 2
Fireworks Canvas and Panels

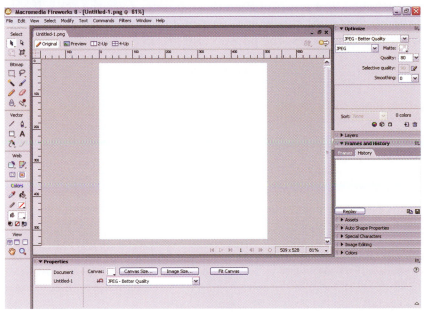

TABLE 1

Document window	The document contains the characteristics for the content, such as size and color of the canvas and resolution of the image.
Panels	Panels help you view, organize, and modify the elements in the document.
Tools panel	The Tools panel contains the tools for creating, placing, and modifying text and graphics.
Property inspector	You use the Property inspector (titled "Properties") to specify the properties of a selected object, such as text and graphics.

Fireworks Editing Modes

Fireworks knows whether you want to create and edit vector objects, bitmap objects, or text, based on the current tool or selection. The Tools panel is divided into clearly labeled sections for easy tool selection.

Floating and Docked Panels

Panels provide easy access to controls that help you edit selected objects or elements of the document. You can use panels to work on frames, layers, symbols, color swatches, and more. Each panel can be dragged so you can group panels together in custom arrangements. By default, the panels are docked to the right side of the workspace. You can undock panel groups, add panels to a group, undock individual panels, rearrange the order of docked panel groups, and collapse and close panel groups. To undock a panel, drag the panel gripper in the upper-left corner of the panel's title bar. Many of the panels are tabbed, with two or more panels combined.

Tools Panel

The Fireworks Tools panel, shown below in Figure 3, is divided into clearly labeled sections for easy tool selection. If the Tools panel is not visible, you can display it by selecting Window from the menu bar, and then clicking Tools. To select a tool, just click it or use the shortcut key shown in parentheses when you position the mouse pointer over the tool. If a tool has a small black triangle in the bottom-right corner, it is part of a group of tools; click and hold down the mouse pointer over the tool to access the pop-up tool group.

FIGURE 3
Tools panel

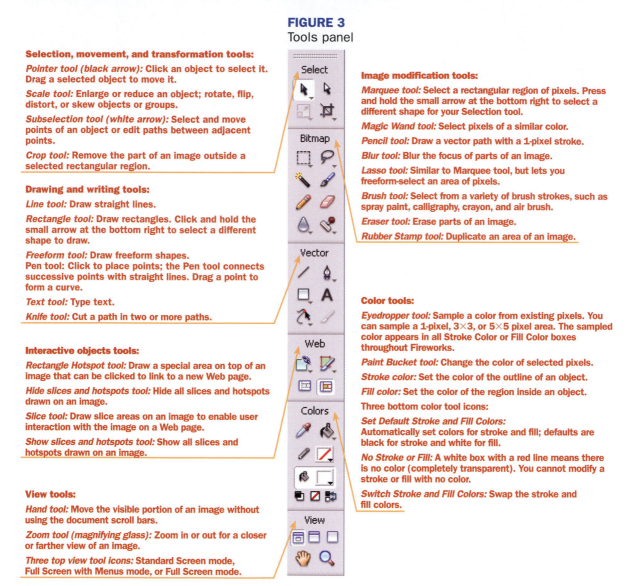

Selection, movement, and transformation tools:

Pointer tool (black arrow): Click an object to select it. Drag a selected object to move it.

Scale tool: Enlarge or reduce an object; rotate, flip, distort, or skew objects or groups.

Subselection tool (white arrow): Select and move points of an object or edit paths between adjacent points.

Crop tool: Remove the part of an image outside a selected rectangular region.

Drawing and writing tools:

Line tool: Draw straight lines.

Rectangle tool: Draw rectangles. Click and hold the small arrow at the bottom right to select a different shape to draw.

Freeform tool: Draw freeform shapes.
Pen tool: Click to place points; the Pen tool connects successive points with straight lines. Drag a point to form a curve.

Text tool: Type text.

Knife tool: Cut a path in two or more paths.

Interactive objects tools:

Rectangle Hotspot tool: Draw a special area on top of an image that can be clicked to link to a new Web page.

Hide slices and hotspots tool: Hide all slices and hotspots drawn on an image.

Slice tool: Draw slice areas on an image to enable user interaction with the image on a Web page.

Show slices and hotspots tool: Show all slices and hotspots drawn on an image.

View tools:

Hand tool: Move the visible portion of an image without using the document scroll bars.

Zoom tool (magnifying glass): Zoom in or out for a closer or farther view of an image.

Three top view tool icons: Standard Screen mode, Full Screen with Menus mode, or Full Screen mode.

Image modification tools:

Marquee tool: Select a rectangular region of pixels. Press and hold the small arrow at the bottom right to select a different shape for your Selection tool.

Magic Wand tool: Select pixels of a similar color.

Pencil tool: Draw a vector path with a 1-pixel stroke.

Blur tool: Blur the focus of parts of an image.

Lasso tool: Similar to Marquee tool, but lets you freeform-select an area of pixels.

Brush tool: Select from a variety of brush strokes, such as spray paint, calligraphy, crayon, and air brush.

Eraser tool: Erase parts of an image.

Rubber Stamp tool: Duplicate an area of an image.

Color tools:

Eyedropper tool: Sample a color from existing pixels. You can sample a 1-pixel, 3×3, or 5×5 pixel area. The sampled color appears in all Stroke Color or Fill Color boxes throughout Fireworks.

Paint Bucket tool: Change the color of selected pixels.

Stroke color: Set the color of the outline of an object.

Fill color: Set the color of the region inside an object.

Three bottom color tool icons:

Set Default Stroke and Fill Colors: Automatically set colors for stroke and fill; defaults are black for stroke and white for fill.

No Stroke or Fill: A white box with a red line means there is no color (completely transparent). You cannot modify a stroke or fill with no color.

Switch Stroke and Fill Colors: Swap the stroke and fill colors.

Property Inspector

The Property inspector displays options that change according to the current object or tool selection. Open a document, and the Property inspector displays document properties. Select a tool, and it displays tool options. Select a vector object, and it displays options such as stroke and fill. You can change these and other options right from the Property inspector. By default, the Property inspector is visible, but you can hide or show it by selecting Window from the menu bar, then clicking Properties. The following examples show the properties for a text object, shown in Figure 4, and a rectangle shape, shown in Figure 5. The options vary depending on the type of object or tool you have selected.

FIGURE 4
Text Property inspector

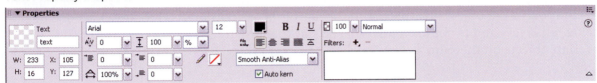

FIGURE 5
Rectangle Shape Property inspector

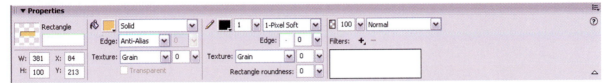

The left side of the Property inspector provides information about the selected object. You can also use this area to size or position the object on the canvas. Additional options available on the Property inspector are described in Table 2.

TABLE 2

Fill	Change the Fill color by clicking the color box. For example, you can select the fill type for a shape, such as solid, patterned, or dithered, from the menu beside the color box. This menu also provides various gradient effects. Other options include changing the type and amount of texture.
Stroke	Change the Stroke category or color. Change the tip size (thickness of the stroke) by typing a number in the text box beside the color box or by clicking the down arrow and then setting the slider. Select the Stroke category, such as pencil, felt tip, or crayon, from the menu on the upper right. Other options include changing the edge softness, the type and amount of texture, and the degree of corner roundness.
Filters	Add effects by clicking the Add Live Filters (+) button. You can add filters to either the inside or the border of objects. Filters include glows, shadows, bevels, and color adjustments. Delete existing filters by selecting the filter and clicking the Delete Current Selected Live Filter (-) button. After you select a filter from the menu, you can vary the opacity and blend mode.

Fireworks Layers Panel

Layers divide a Fireworks document into discrete planes, as though the components of the illustration were drawn on separate tracing paper overlays. A document can be made up of many layers, and each layer can contain many objects. In Fireworks, the Layers panel lists layers and the objects contained on each layer, as shown in Figure 6. If you draw or place each object on a separate layer, it is easier for you to control or change each object. Layers enable you to divide your artwork when building complex vector objects or composite images.

You can rearrange the order of layers and of objects within layers. Different portions of an image can be stored on different layers and selectively turned off or on so you can isolate just the portion you are working with. Layers can contain either vector or bitmap objects, or a combination of both. On each layer, you can place one object or multiple objects. If you place multiple objects on the same layer, each object appears in a stack of objects contained within the layer and can be selected and manipulated separate from other objects on the same layer. A thumbnail representation of the object is displayed to the left of the object name. The canvas, or document, is below all layers and is not itself a layer. The stacking order determines how objects on one layer overlap objects on the same layer as well as on other layers.

FIGURE 6
Layers panel

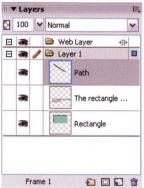

Fireworks History Panel

The History panel, shown below in Figure 7, lists commands you have recently used so you can quickly undo and redo them. In addition, you can select multiple actions and then save and reuse them as commands.

FIGURE 7
History panel

Fireworks Optimize Panel

You can use the Optimize panel to select your optimization settings. The first step is to determine which type of file you plan to export, such as GIF or JPEG. You can then select the detailed settings. GIF images are generally used for line art and images with solid colors. GIF images can contain transparent areas and can be used for animation files. The disadvantage of GIF images is they are restricted to 256 colors. JPEG is generally used for photographic images or images with gradients and more colors. JPEG files cannot be transparent or animated.

Options for GIF Optimization

The options for optimization of GIF images are shown in Figure 8 and described in Table 3.

FIGURE 8
Optimize panel with options for GIF images

TABLE 3

Settings	Use Settings to select a preset image-quality setting for export. For GIF, these include GIFs Web 216, GIF WebSnap 256, GIF WebSnap 128, GIF Adaptive 256, and Animated GIF WebSnap 128.
Matte	If you want to anti-alias an image, or smooth jagged edges, for multiple exports with different-colored backgrounds, click the Matte color box and select a color for the background of the image. This is useful if the image will appear on Web pages with different-colored backgrounds.
Colors	Control the number of colors in the image. This number is automatically configured from the Settings selection. Decreasing the number of colors decreases the file size and can lower image quality.
Dither	The Dither option is useful for images with many color gradations. Dithering approximates colors not in the current color palette by alternating two similar colors. Increasing the Dither setting can greatly increase file size.
Loss	Lower the image quality on export. Higher loss settings can yield smaller files but lower image quality. A loss setting between 5 and 15 typically yields the best results.
Transparency	Remove the background color or halos around an image so that in a Web browser the background of the Web page is visible through those areas. (This capability is a key advantage of exporting images as GIFs.) Index Transparency removes the background color. Alpha Transparency removes the background of an image if its canvas color is transparent. Use the Add to Transparency button to remove specific colors from the image.

Options for JPEG optimization

The options for optimization of JPEG images are shown in Figure 9 and described in Table 4.

TABLE 4

Settings	Select from preset image-quality settings for export. For JPEG, these include JPEG Better Quality and JPEG Smaller File.
Matte	If you want to anti-alias an image, or smooth jagged edges, for multiple exports with different-colored backgrounds, click the Matte color box and select a color for the background of the image. This is useful if the image will appear on Web pages with different-colored backgrounds.
Quality	Adjust the quality of the image. Lower quality decreases file size; higher quality increases file size.
Selective Quality	Adjust the quality of only the selected part of the image while leaving the rest of the image intact. Used with a JPEG mask.
Smoothing	Blurs hard edges in the image and reduces file size.

Fireworks File Types

You can create a variety of file types with Fireworks for the Web or print and you can also use the Fireworks tools to edit imported graphics. You can import and edit files in JPEG, GIF, PNG, PSD, and many other file formats. You can save to the following file formats directly: Fireworks PNG, GIF, animated GIF, JPEG, BMP, WBMP, TIF, SWF, AI, PSD, and PICT (Macintosh only).

Files of other types, such as PSD and HTML, open as PNG files so you can use the Fireworks PNG document as your source file. Any edits you perform are applied to the PNG file and not the original.

Use Table 5 to become familiar with the file types you can save or export with Macromedia Fireworks.

TABLE 5

Fireworks PNG	PNG, or Portable Network Graphic, is a versatile Web graphic format. Fireworks PNG files contain additional application-specific information that is not stored in an exported PNG file or in files created in other applications.
GIF	GIF, or Graphics Interchange Format, is a popular Web graphic format. A GIF is usually ideal for cartoons, logos, graphics with transparent areas, and animations.
Animated GIF	An animated GIF is made up of a series of GIF images that change over time.
JPEG	JPEG is used for high-color images. The JPEG format is best for scanned photographs, images using textures, images with gradient color transitions, and any images that require more than 256 colors.
BMP	BMP, the Microsoft Windows graphic file format, is a common file format used to display bitmap images. BMPs are used primarily on the Windows operating system. Many applications can import BMP images.
WBMP	WBMP, or Wireless Bitmap, is a graphic format created for mobile computing devices such as cell phones and PDAs. This format is used on Wireless Application Protocol (WAP) pages. WBMP can be only black and white.
TIF	TIFF, or Tagged Image File Format, is a graphic format used for storing bitmap images. TIFFs are most commonly used in print publishing. Fireworks saves 16-bit TIF images at 24-bit color depth.
SWF	A SWF, or Small Web Format, is a file that is normally exported from Macromedia Flash. You can use this file for animations or rich objects you will import to Flash.
PSD	A PSD is a native file format for documents used in Adobe Photoshop.
PICT (Macintosh only)	PICT, developed by Apple Computer, is a graphic file format commonly used on Macintosh operating systems. Most Macintosh applications are capable of importing PICT images.

Arranging the Fireworks Window

You can open and close panels to see more or less of the document. You can also collapse a panel, leaving only the title bar visible, or hide a panel to remove it completely.

To view items close up or to see the entire object on the canvas at once, use the Zoom tool on the Tools panel, or select a new magnification from the Set Magnification pop-up menu.

 Expand and collapse panels

1. Start Fireworks 8.

2. To expand or collapse the Frames and History panel, click the panel's title, as shown in Figure 10.

FIGURE 10
History panel title

Click the title of a panel to collapse or restore the panel

When you collapse a panel, only its title bar remains visible.

 Show and hide panel groups

1. To hide a group of panels that are docked (attached to the side or bottom of the window), click the **Show/Hide** button, as shown in Figure 11.

FIGURE 11
Show/Hide button

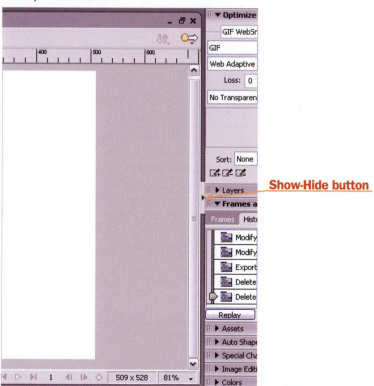

Show-Hide button

The group of panels is hidden.

2. Click the **Show/Hide** button again to restore the group of hidden panels.

The group of panels is again visible.

Open new panels by using the Window menu

1. Click **Window** on the menu bar, and then click **History** to open the History panel.

Panels are often grouped together. To switch between panels, select the tab for the panel you want to view.

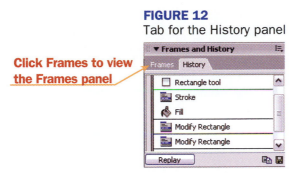

FIGURE 12
Tab for the History panel

Click Frames to view the Frames panel

2. To close the History panel, click the **Options** menu on the panel, as shown in Figure 13, and then click **Close Panel Group**.

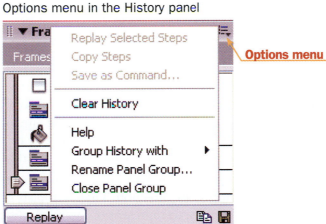

FIGURE 13
Options menu in the History panel

Options menu

As you add objects to the canvas, you will find yourself zooming in to see detail and out to see the bigger picture. One way to quickly adjust the magnification of the window is to use the Set Magnification menu.

 ## Change the window magnification and adjust the size of the Timeline

1. Select the **Set Magnification** menu, as shown in Figure 14.

2. Select **100%**.

FIGURE 14
Set Magnification menu

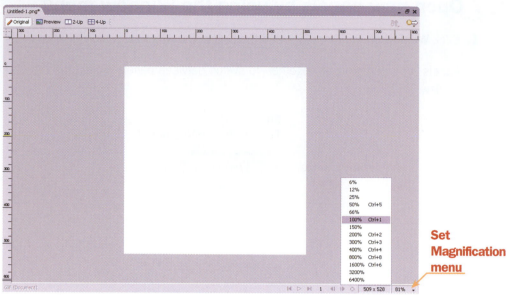

Set
**Magnification
menu**

The size of the object adjusts automatically to be viewed at its full size.

2. To see a greater level of detail, select a larger percentage, such as **200%**.

Understanding Basic Graphic Design

When building graphics for use on the Web, it is important to keep in mind the goals of the site where they will be used. Applying graphic design principles can help you build graphics that meet the goals of the Web site while drawing in and keeping site visitors. Two main components to apply are *graphic design elements*, which are the building blocks of graphics, and *graphic design principles*, which are the ways in which elements are used together.

Graphic design elements include the use of lines, colors, shapes, and textures. Lines can be straight or curved to indicate motion or direction. Lines can also be used to form shapes. Colors can be used to label or show hierarchy, to represent or imitate reality, to unify, separate, or emphasize, or to decorate. Textures are created by varying light and dark areas on the composition. These separate elements together can evoke different characteristics.

The way lines, colors, shapes, and textures are used can produce movement in an image, balance the composition, emphasize an element of the composition, or unify the composition with its surrounding site. For example, you can use lines, color, and repetition to create the illusion of motion, such as curved lines or repetitive geometric shapes. You can create balance by comparing or estimating two things, one against the other, or by contrasting empty space (white space) and filled space or textures against flat colors.

The basis of good graphic design is the use of design elements and their thoughtful application in the form of design principles. You can accomplish good design by clearly identifying the message you are trying to convey.

Macromedia Fireworks 8 Projects

This unit contains three projects that will help you build your skills in recognizing graphic design decisions and the building and manipulating of images.

Project 1: Pictures for a Web Site

You follow the specification for images on a Web site to process multiple photographs quickly and easily for use on that Web site. Each of the steps used to process the images can be saved and run as an automatic command, providing you with reusable tools for other images of the same type.

Project 2: Experience Bank Logo

You build the logo for the Experience Bank Web site. You use the drawing and manipulation tools to draw part of the logo. You then use effects to finalize the look of the logo. You incorporate the use of text, imagery, and effects to produce a logo that evokes the professionalism and integrity of the bank.

Project 3: Page Layout and Navigation Bar for a Web Site

You build the page comp that will guide the developer of the Experience Bank Web site. You lay out the elements of the page to help determine relative sizing and build the navigation bar that will be used on the page. You use a variety of image manipulation and creation tools to generate the guiding design and navigation for the Web site.

PICTURES FOR A WEB SITE

GOALS

- Follow a design document to prepare images for inclusion in a Web page.

- Run a batch process to prepare multiple images in one step.

TECHNICAL SKILLS

- Open an image.

- Save an image.

- Resize an image.

- Add a border to an image.

- Add a drop shadow to an image.

- Create white space by using an object behind an image.

- Trim the canvas around an image.

- Optimize an image.

- Store a set of actions on an image as a reusable command.

- Apply batch processing to images by using stored commands.

Estimated time to complete this project: 2 hours

Summary

Before you add images to a Web site, you need to prepare them to integrate with the Web site's design. You may need to resize, crop, or rotate images. Other embellishments can enhance the impact of images and contribute to overall page design. When images serve as links to other pages, you can add borders and shadows to make the images appear more clickable. It is important to optimize images, because they contribute to the file size of a Web page. *Optimization* is a process of decreasing the file size of an image as much as possible while maintaining a sufficient level of image quality. You can store commands that apply one or more actions you have performed on an image to reuse for other images. You can then use these commands to apply the saved actions to many images at once by running a *batch process*.

The Assignment

In this project, you use Macromedia Fireworks to prepare six different images for inclusion on a personal Web page. The images are photographs taken by the site owner during visits to various locations. You prepare these images according to the site's *design criteria*, a set of specifications that describe how the Web page will look. You use the design document for this project to:

- Import, resize, and save an image.

- Add effects to images.

- Add white space around an image.

- Optimize and export images.

Site Design Criteria and Technical Requirements

When you prepare images for a Web page, you first need general information about the page's design criteria. A design document gives you background about the goals, purpose, and audience for the page. It describes design requirements such as image dimensions and border colors. The design document also provides key content elements and technical requirements. The site's technical requirements dictate file sizes and types of files used, among other characteristics. Image file size can be addressed through image optimization. You use the information contained in the design document throughout the project.

The design criteria for a Web page define the size of the page, which can be used to interpret and the size and appearance of images on that page. As a designer, you will often have to process images according to such a specification. Processing includes the use of such features as resizing, cropping, adding a border, and adding a drop shadow. The design document for the Likeable Places Web site is shown in Figure 1.

FIGURE 1
Design document for Likeable Places Web site

Design Document – Pictures for a Web Site

Goals and Purpose

A page on the client's Web site will present information and photographs about vacation sites visited by the client.

Audience

The target audience is primarily the family and friends of the client. Their age range is 6 and older. Some, but not all, are frequent web users. Some adjectives to describe the audience are: curious, ready for a challenge, friendly.

Design Requirements

Photographs provided by the client should be prepared so as to present a relatively uniform appearance on the page, even through the original photographs are not all the same size or orientation. The photographs should be the main focus of the page.

The photographs should be prepared at a size that allows three images to be presented side by side on a Web page that is 700 pixels wide.

Each photograph should be presented within a border and should appear to "float" slightly above the page.

Delivery Requirements

The Web site should display as required on the following browsers.

- Internet Explorer, v6
- Safari 1.0 or later
- AOL 8 or later
- Mozilla Firefox 1.04 or later

The Web site should display on the following operating systems.

- Macintosh OS X 10.3 or later
- Windows XP Home or Professional

The file sizes of the prepared photographs should be as small as possible, so the Web page will load quickly in site visitors' browsers. However, the quality of the prepared photographs should not be noticeably different from the quality of the originals.

Content

Six photographs are provided for the Web page. These photographs were taken at the following locations:

- Colorado River
- Grand Canyon
- Hawaii
- Lake Powell
- Forest in Northwestern US
- San Francisco

Pictures for a Web Site – Design Document   1

To print the design document for this page, open the file named *FW_Project1_Design.pdf*. This file is located in the Design folder of the data files for this project.

IMPORTING, RESIZING, AND SAVING IMAGES

OBJECTIVES:

Upon completion of this lesson, you will be able to:

- Open an image.

- Save an image.

- Adjust the size of an image.

- Save an action as a command.

Estimated time to complete this lesson: 15 minutes

Introduction

The photographs the site designer wants to include are all taken larger than are necessary to post on his site. Designers often resize images so they can include multiple images on a site and so they can reduce some of the overall file size. Because the same action needs to be taken with all the photographs, you can save much time by doing the step once and reapplying it in an automated way to other photographs. This is called a batch process.

Preparing a batch of images is repetitive work, so many developers save series of commonly used steps as *commands*. Selecting a single previously saved command from a menu executes all the steps contained in the command.

In this lesson you begin by opening one of the images, resizing it, and saving the resizing action as a command to use later when you apply a batch process to the other images.

Take a moment to review the design document shown in Figure 1-1 before completing this lesson.

FIGURE 1-1
Design document for Likeable Places Web site

Design Document – Pictures for a Web Site

Goals and Purpose

A page on the client's Web site will present information and photographs about vacation sites visited by the client.

Audience

The target audience is primarily the family and friends of the client. Their age range is 6 and older. Some, but not all, are frequent web users. Some adjectives to describe the audience are: curious, ready for a challenge, friendly.

Design Requirements

Photographs provided by the client should be prepared so as to present a relatively uniform appearance on the page, even through the original photographs are not all the same size or orientation. The photographs should be the main focus of the page.

The photographs should be prepared at a size that allows three images to be presented side by side on a Web page that is 700 pixels wide.

Each photograph should be presented within a border and should appear to "float" slightly above the page.

Delivery Requirements

The Web site should display as required on the following browsers.

- Internet Explorer, v6
- Safari 1.0 or later
- AOL 8 or later
- Mozilla Firefox 1.04 or later

The Web site should display on the following operating systems.

- Macintosh OS X 10.3 or later
- Windows XP Home or Professional

The file sizes of the prepared photographs should be as small as possible, so the Web page will load quickly in site visitors' browsers. However, the quality of the prepared photographs should not be noticeably different from the quality of the originals.

Content

Six photographs are provided for the Web page. These photographs were taken at the following locations:

- Colorado River
- Grand Canyon
- Hawaii
- Lake Powell
- Forest in Northwestern US
- San Francisco

Pictures for a Web Site – Design Document   1

Opening an Image

The design document requires you to process a set of photographs. So you will not have to repeat your steps manually, you first open one of the images to start the process and later save the resizing steps to use again. First, open one of the image files in Fireworks.

 Open an Image

1. Start Macromedia Fireworks 8.

2. Click **File** on the menu bar and click **Open**.

The Open dialog box opens (Windows), as shown in Figure 1-2, or the Open File dialog box opens (Macintosh).

FIGURE 1-2
Open dialog box

3. Navigate to the **likeable_places** folder and select **colorado_river.jpg**.

4. Click **Open**.

The image opens in Fireworks. The blue outline around the image, as shown in Figure 1-3, indicates that it is selected.

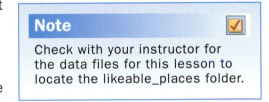

Note ☑

Check with your instructor for the data files for this lesson to locate the likeable_places folder.

FIGURE 1-3
Image in Fireworks canvas

Saving an Image as a Fireworks PNG

It is good practice to save an image as a Fireworks PNG. When you save an image as a PNG, all the changes you make to the image remain editable in Fireworks so you can reverse or modify such changes at any time.

Save an image as a Fireworks PNG

1. Click **File** on the menu bar and click **Save As**.

2. Create a new folder on your desktop called **formatted_images**.

3. Click the **Save as Type** (Windows) or **Save as** (Macintosh) menu and select **Fireworks PNG**.

4. Make sure **colorado_river.png** appears in the File name box and click **Save**.

Hot Tip

Give images and folders meaningful names. This will make it easier for you and your teammates to find the right image later.

Resizing an Image

The site's design criteria designate the page dimensions for the site and how many images will appear on the site. To put multiple images across the page, the images will need to be reduced in size. To allow multiple images to fit next to each other, you reduce the first image to 45 percent of its original size.

Inside the Design

Designers use Web page design criteria to make decisions about the size of the images used on a page. In the Likeable Places Web site, the width of the Web page is assumed to be 700 pixels. With original images around 300 pixels, the designer chooses to reduce the images to 45 percent so that three thumbnail images can be placed side by side on a page.

Adjust the Size of an Image

1. With the **colorado_river.png** file still open, make sure the image is selected. If it is not selected, click the image to select it.

2. Click **Modify** on the menu bar, point to **Transform**, and then click **Numeric Transform**.

   The Numeric Transform dialog box opens, as shown in Figure 1-4.

Note

When an image is selected, it has a blue border around it.

FIGURE 1-4
Numeric Transform dialog box

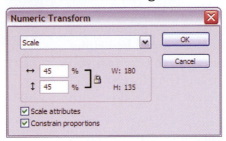

3. Make sure **Scale** is selected on the Numeric Transform Type menu, and make sure the **Scale Attributes** and **Constrain Proportions** options are both selected.

4. In the Width percentage box, key **45**. Notice that the Height percentage changes to 45 automatically.

5. Click **OK** to close the Numeric Transform dialog box.

The image is resized. It should appear similar to the image in Figure 1-5.

> **Note**
>
> When you constrain the proportions, you prevent the image from being distorted, such as being stretched more in one direction than the other. This is especially important for photographs.

FIGURE 1-5
Resized image

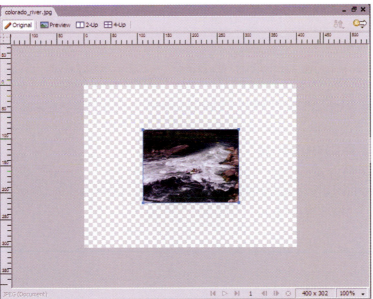

6. Save the file.

Creating a Command

Because the site designer has many photographs for you to process in a similar manner, it will be helpful for you to save a step or action you have taken so you can reapply it to other photographs. The History panel lists every step or action you take in a session with Fireworks.

For example, the History panel in Figure 1-6 shows the steps taken to draw a rectangle, add an effect, add a text label, and align the text to the center of the rectangle.

FIGURE 1-6
History panel

You can save one or more such steps or actions as a *command* that appears in the Commands menu. In this Step-by-Step you capture your work on the first image to create a command that transforms an image to 45 percent of its original size.

 Create a Command

1. With the **colorado_river.png** file still open, open the History panel by clicking **Window** on the menu bar and then clicking **History**.

Your History panel should include the steps shown in Figure 1-7.

FIGURE 1-7
History panel

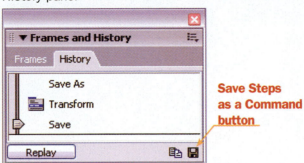

Save Steps
as a Command
button

2. Select the **Transform** step.

3. Click the **Save Steps as a Command** button as in Figure 1-7.

The Save Command dialog box opens, as shown in Figure 1-8.

4. Key **scale45** as the name for the command.

FIGURE 1-8
Save Command dialog box

5. Click **OK**.

6. Click **Commands** on the Menu bar. Observe that "scale45" has been added to the bottom of the menu. You can use this command to apply 45 percent scaling to other images.

7. Save the file.

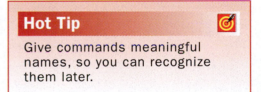

Hot Tip

Give commands meaningful names, so you can recognize them later.

ADDING EFFECTS TO IMAGES

OBJECTIVES:

Upon completion of this lesson, you will be able to:

- Add a bevel effect to an image.

- Add a drop shadow effect to an image.

The estimated time to complete this lesson is: 25 to 30 minutes

Introduction

The photographs will be the main focus of the personal Web site and therefore should draw the attention of site visitors. Designers often add effects such as borders and drop shadows to images. Borders make images look clickable and add interest. Shadows give images a slight lift from the page, adding depth and interest to the page.

In this lesson, you add a beveled border and a drop shadow to the image you opened and saved in the previous lesson. You then save the steps for adding the bevel and shadow as a command to reuse later in the project.

Take a moment to review the design document shown in Figure 2-1 before completing this lesson.

FIGURE 2-1
Design document

Design Document – Pictures for a Web Site

Goals and Purpose

A page on the client's Web site will present information and photographs about vacation sites visited by the client.

Audience

The target audience is primarily the family and friends of the client. Their age range is 6 and older. Some, but not all, are frequent web users. Some adjectives to describe the audience are: curious, ready for a challenge, friendly.

Design Requirements

Photographs provided by the client should be prepared so as to present a relatively uniform appearance on the page, even through the original photographs are not all the same size or orientation. The photographs should be the main focus of the page.

The photographs should be presented at 45% of their original size, so that several images may be presented side by side on the Web page.

Each photograph should be presented within a border and should appear to "float" slightly above the page.

Each photograph should be framed in a 220-pixel square of white space.

Delivery Requirements

The Web site should display as required on the following browsers.
- Internet Explorer, v6
- Safari 2.0
- AOL 8 or later
- Mozilla Firefox 1.04 or later

The Web site should display on the following operating systems.
- Macintosh OS X 10.3 or later
- Windows XP Home or Professional

The file sizes of the prepared photographs should be as small as possible, so the Web page will load quickly in site visitors' browsers. However, the quality of the prepared photographs should not be noticeably different from the quality of the originals.

Content

Six photographs are provided for the Web page. These photographs were taken at the following locations:
- Colorado River
- Grand Canyon
- Hawaii
- Lake Powell
- Forest in Northwestern US
- San Francisco

Pictures for a Web Site – Design Document   1

Effects

Fireworks has built-in enhancements, called Live Filters, that you can apply to images, drawn objects, or text. Live Filters include bevels, embossing, shadows, glows, color correction, blurring, and sharpening. You apply Live Filters to a selected object directly from the Property inspector. As soon as you add a filter, you see its effects on-screen. This lets you make changes to the filter and view the effect of these changes immediately. You can also apply multiple filters in combinations to a single object.

The text in Figure 2-2 illustrates a blur effect.

FIGURE 2-2
Text with blur effect

The text in Figure 2-3 illustrates a drop shadow effect.

FIGURE 2-3
Text with drop shadow effect

Used carefully, effects can brighten washed out colors, add the impression of motion or depth, or simply add an interesting look to a page. As with all design features, though, be careful not to overuse effects—they can distract from the composition and they will also increase the file size of the image.

Adding a Border

To create a border for the image you imported in the previous lesson, select the image and apply a bevel effect. Although bevel effects often add depth to the object itself, the type of bevel you use here adds a raised border around the image.

> **Note**
>
> Filters are stackable and are applied in the order you use them. For example, a bevel effect added after a drop shadow will make the shadow appear slightly beveled, whereas a shadow effect added after a bevel will give a shadow to the image and the bevel.

> **Inside the Design**
>
> Designers use bevel effects to add dimensionality to an image. The site designer for this Web site wants to have some dimension added to the images so they appear clickable to site visitors.

 Add a Border to an Image

1. With the **colorado_river.png** file still open, select the **Pointer** tool on the Tools panel, and click the image to select it.

2. Click the **Add Live Filters** button (+ icon) on the Property inspector, point to **Bevel and Emboss**, and then click **Outer Bevel**, as shown in Figure 2-4.

FIGURE 2-4
Add Live Filters menu

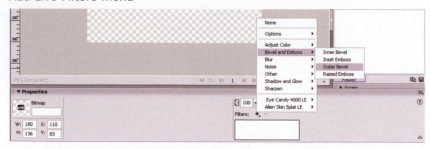

The Outer Bevel window opens, as shown in Figure 2-5.

FIGURE 2-5
Outer Bevel window

Bevel Edge Shape · Width · Color · Contrast · Softness · Angle

3. Select **Ring** on the Bevel Edge Shape menu and key **6** for width.

4. Click the bevel **Color** box and select **gray (#999999)**. Leave the default vales for the other settings.

5. The bevel is applied to the image. Press **Enter** (Windows) or **Return** (Macintosh) or click anywhere in the workspace to close the Outer Bevel window.

The filter is added to the Filters list.

> **Note**
>
> The Contrast percentage controls the difference between the look of the base and the look of the top of the bevel. The Softness setting controls the blurring of the edge of the bevel, and the Angle setting controls the angle at which light appears to fall on the bevel.

Adding a Drop Shadow

The design also calls for a drop shadow to be added to each image, to give the image a slight lift from the page. Drop shadows are not usually drawn with a strong black. A gradation lower—50 percent black—gives the impression of depth but avoids overpowering the image.

A drop shadow's *distance* refers to how far from the background the image will appear. A shadow set to a distance of 10, for example, will appear to be 10 pixels away from the background. Because the current image

> **Hot Tip**
>
> You can change these settings at any time by clicking the info button next to Outer Bevel in the Filters list in the Property inspector.

already has a border, the shadow here doesn't need to be a distinctive piece on its own, so the distance is kept short.

Add a Drop Shadow

1. With the **colorado_river.png** file still open, click the image to select it.

2. Click the **Add Live Filters** button on the Property inspector, point to **Shadow and Glow**, then click **Drop Shadow**.

   The Drop Shadow window opens, as shown in Figure 2-6.

FIGURE 2-6
Drop Shadow window

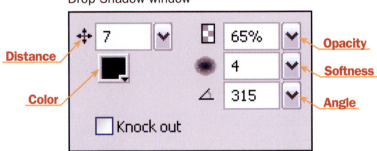

3. Key **6** for distance and **50%** for opacity. Make sure the color is set to **black (#000000)**. Leave the default vales for the other settings.

   The drop shadow is applied to the image.

4. Press **Enter** (Windows) or **Return** (Macintosh) or click anywhere in the workspace to close the Drop Shadow window.

   The filter is added to the Filters list.

5. Save the file.

   The image should now appear as in Figure 2-7.

Note

The Softness setting controls the sharpness of the end of the shadow. The Angle setting controls the angle from which the light appears to fall in forming the shadow. The Knock Out option removes the image color to leave just the shadow.

Hot Tip

You can change these settings at any time by clicking the info button next to Drop Shadow in the Filters list in the Property inspector.

FIGURE 2-7
Image with outer bevel and drop shadow

Creating a Command

As in the previous lesson, you can create a command to capture the application of these filters for later use.

 Create a Command

1. With the **colorado_river.png** file still open, make sure the **History** panel is open. If it is not open, click **Window** on the menu bar and click **History**.

2. Select the two **Set Live Filter** steps.

3. Click the **Save Steps as a Command** button. The **Save Command** dialog box opens.

4. Key **add_border_shadow** as the name for the command, and click **OK** to close the dialog box.

> **Note**
>
> To select multiple steps at once, hold down Shift and click the steps.

ADDING WHITE SPACE AROUND AN IMAGE

OBJECTIVES:

Upon completion of this lesson, you will be able to:

- Draw and resize a rectangle.

- Arrange one object behind another object.

- Align objects.

- Trim the canvas to the size of an object.

Estimated time to complete this lesson: 15 to 20 minutes

Introduction

Designers can choose specific sizes for images to help Web developers lay out their Web pages. When images are different shapes, designers often add white space or "air" around images so the different shapes are each displayed within a common frame.

The design criteria for the personal Web page specify that each image should be framed in a square of white space that is 220 pixels × 220 pixels.

In this lesson, you add a white square to the image you have been editing. After you align the image within this square, you trim the excess canvas. Then you capture this process as a command to use later in the project.

Adding a Square White Space

In addition to modifying images, designers often use drawing tools to add visual elements directly to an image, which will help with its eventual function on the Web site. The photographs to be processed for the personal Web site have different orientations. To give these images uniformity on the site, the site designer has recommended adding a white space to the background of the image to frame all the images within equal-sized spaces.

 Step by Step **Add a White Square**

1. With the **colorado_river.png** file still open, click the **Rectangle** tool in the Vector section of the Tools panel as shown in Figure 3-1. If the Rectangle tool is not visible, click the small triangle next to the current shape icon and then click the Rectangle tool.

FIGURE 3-1
Rectangle tool selected in Tools panel

Rectangle tool

2. Drag across the canvas to draw a rectangle. The size does not matter because you will set the size precisely in the Property inspector.

   After you release the mouse, the rectangle remains selected. Selection is indicated by blue dots at the corners of the rectangle.

3. Click the **Fill Color** box in the Property inspector, shown in Figure 3-2, and select **White (#FFFFFF)**. Click the **Stroke Color** box and select **White (#FFFFFF)**.

FIGURE 3-2
Fill and stroke color boxes in the Property inspector

Fill   Stroke

4. In the Property inspector, key **220** in both the Width (**W**) and Height (**H**) boxes.

5. Press **Enter** (Windows) or **Return** (Macintosh). The rectangle is now a white square, 220 pixels wide by 220 pixels high.

Note

Do not worry if all or part of the image is temporarily hidden by the white square at this point.

Aligning the Square and Trimming the Canvas

Your next step is to change the stacking order of the white square and the river image so the image is on top. Then you trim the canvas around the white square. The design criteria call for images that are 220 by 220 (including the white space around them). Trimming the canvas eliminates unused space, cropping the document to the size of the white square you created.

 ### Align the White Square with the Image and Trim the Canvas

1. With the **colorado_river.png** file still open, click the **Pointer** tool to select it.

2. Leaving the white square selected, click **Modify** on the menu bar, point to **Arrange**, and click **Send to Back**.

   The square moves behind the river image.

3. Leaving the square selected, hold down **Shift** and click on the river image. Both the square and the image are now selected, as shown in Figure 3-3.

Hot Tip

You can also change the stacking order of objects by dragging their positions up or down on the Layers panel.

FIGURE 3-3
Both square and image selected

4. Click **Window** on the menu bar and click **Align**. The Align panel opens, as shown in Figure 3-4.

FIGURE 3-4
Align panel

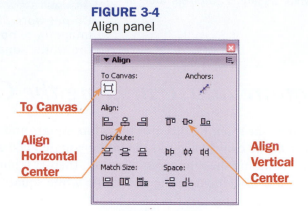

5. On the Align panel, make sure the **To Canvas** button is selected, click **Align Horizontal Center**, and click **Align Vertical Center**. This centers the square behind the image.

Look at the To Canvas button carefully. Click it several times to see the difference between having the button selected and having it not selected, as shown in Figure 3-5.

FIGURE 3-5
To Canvas button

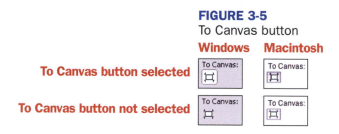

6. Close the Align panel.

The canvas should now look like Figure 3-6.

FIGURE 3-6
Square centered behind image

7. Click **Modify** on the menu bar, point to **Canvas**, and click **Fit Canvas**. The canvas is cropped to fit around the square.

8. Save the file.

How Fireworks Aligns and Distributes Objects

Aligning or distributing objects is different from centering them. Fireworks aligns objects on the left based on the leftmost object in the selected group and aligns objects on the right based on the rightmost object in the selected group. The topmost object controls Align Top, and the bottommost object controls Align Bottom. For Distribute Widths, Fireworks creates an equal amount of space between the objects, divided between the right edge of the leftmost objects and the left edge of the rightmost objects. For Distribute Heights, Fireworks creates an equal amount of space between the objects, divided between the bottom edge of the highest and the top edge of the lowest objects.

Creating Commands

Create a command for the process of adding the white square and resizing it. Create another command to center the image on the white square and trim the canvas. Notice in the History panel that a *separator* line appears between the Move to Back step and the Command Script step, indicating that a different object has become selected. A saved command should not include steps from both sides of this separator. That is the reason you must save your steps in this lesson as two separate commands.

 ## Create Commands

1. With the **colorado_river.png** file still open, in the **History** panel, select the steps from **Rectangle Tool** to **Move to Back**, and click the **Save Steps as a Command** button.

The two instances of Transform in the list are changing the width of the rectangle to 220 pixels and changing the height to 220 pixels.

2. Key **draw_white-square** as the name for the command.

3. Click **OK**.

4. In the **History** panel, select the steps from **Command Script** to **Crop Document**, and click the **Save Steps as a Command** button.

The two instances of Command Script in the list are centering the square and the image horizontally and centering them vertically. Be sure to select both of these steps.

5. Key **center-image_fit-canvas** as the name for the command.

6. Click **OK**.

7. Save the file.

OPTIMIZING AND EXPORTING AN IMAGE AND RUNNING A BATCH PROCESS

OBJECTIVES:

Upon completion of this lesson, you will be able to:

- Optimize an image for the Web.

- Export an image for the Web.

- Run a batch process on multiple images.

Estimated time to complete this lesson: 15 to 20 minutes

Introduction

A good practice is to make optimizing any image the last step in preparing it for the Web. Optimization reduces the file size of an image. You must optimize JPEG images thoughtfully, however, because smaller file size is achieved by loss of some image quality.

In this lesson you optimize and export the image you have been preparing in the previous lessons. Because the settings you will choose for optimization are part of a standard export setting in Fireworks, you will not need to save either your optimization or export steps as separate commands. Finally, you set up a batch process to prepare and export the remaining images for the site.

Optimizing an Image

Because the image you have prepared for use on this site is a photograph, you should optimize and export it in the JPEG format. With optimization, you can make the file somewhat smaller without notable loss of quality. For example, the image on the right in Figure 4-1 has been compressed to a quality of 80 percent. Note that the file size is much smaller and the quality is basically the same.

Did You Know?

JPEG stands for Joint Photographic Expert Group, the original name of the committee that wrote the standard.

Hot Tip

The 2-Up and 4-Up features in Fireworks let you preview different optimization settings before exporting images. The windows show the projected file size and download time.

FIGURE 4-1
2-Up feature in Fireworks

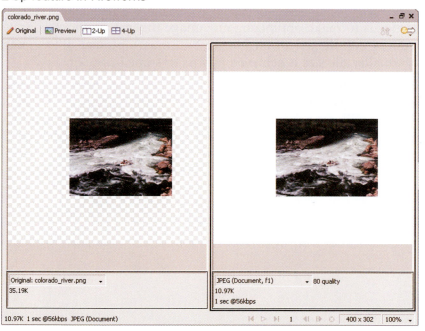

The image on the right has been reduced from 35K to 11K without losing quality. This reduction is substantial, especially when you put multiple images on one page.

Optimize and Export an Image

1. With the **colorado_river.png** file still open, make sure the Optimize panel is open, as shown in Figure 4-2. If it is not open, click **Windows** on the menu bar and click **Optimize**.

FIGURE 4-2
Optimize panel

2. In the **Optimize** panel, click the **Saved settings** menu at the top of the panel and click **JPEG— Better Quality**. Observe that Quality changes to 80. The settings in the Optimize panel determine how the file exports.

3. Save the file.

For information about types of image files, see the Tips & Techniques feature "Bitmap Image File Types for the Web."

Note

The Optimize panel, like other Fireworks features, can also be accessed through a shortcut key—the F6 button.

Note

You can set Quality to any number from 1 to 100, but 80 offers very little loss of quality while still reducing file size.

Exporting an Image File

Once you have specified the optimization setting for an image, it is a simple matter to apply those settings by exporting the image file. The image is then ready to place on a Web page.

Export an Image File

1. With the **colorado_river.png** file still open, click **File** from the menu bar and click **Export**. The Export dialog box opens, as shown in Figure 4-3.

FIGURE 4-3
Export dialog box

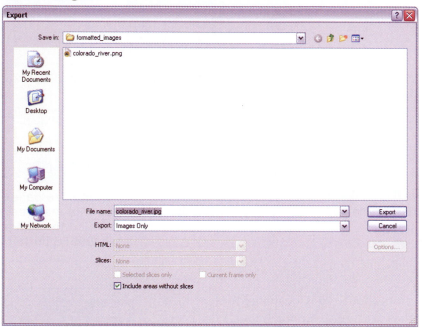

2. Make sure **colorado_river.jpg** is entered as the File name and that the Save in box (Windows) or the Where box (Macintosh) is pointing to your formatted_images folder. Leave the default values for the other settings.

3. Click **Export** to close the dialog box.

4. Open **colorado_river.jpg** from your formatted_images folder to confirm that it has been formatted correctly. It should have the same appearance as colorado_river.png, with a border and drop shadow on the river image and the image centered in a white square.

5. Close the **colorado_river.jpg** file. Save and close the **colorado_river.png** file.

> **Note** ☑
>
> You can also use Save As to export an image. Click File on the menu bar, and click Save As to open the Save As dialog box. Select the file type you want to export. When you click Save, the image will be converted to the file type you selected and saved.

Tips & Techniques

BITMAP IMAGE FILE TYPES FOR THE WEB

The two most common bitmap file types used on the Web are GIF and JPEG.

GIFs are generally used for line art and images with solid colors; these might include logos, page banners, page headers, navigation bars, and clickable buttons. Such images are generally drawn images rather than photographs. GIF images can contain transparent areas and can be used for animation files. If you choose GIF as your export file format, you need to pick the color palette for the export. GIFs offer the advantage of smaller file sizes. The disadvantage of GIF images is that they are restricted to 256 colors.

JPEGs are generally used to export photographs or any artwork with gradations or millions of colors in the image. JPEG files cannot be transparent or animated. Unlike GIF images, JPEG images don't need a color palette. JPEG uses a *lossy* compression scheme, meaning it looks at your image and removes information as part of its compression algorithm. This causes a loss in quality. You set the level of quality for the compression on the Optimize panel.

Running a Batch Process

Now that you have created commands for each of the steps you took for processing the initial image in the site, you can collect these commands into a batch process to run on all the images you need to prepare for the personal Web site. Batch processes save time by eliminating the need for you to carry out repetitive commands on each image in a set. They also help you make all the images on your site look consistent. In this Step-by-Step, you incorporate the commands you created earlier to create a batch process that prepares all the images just as you prepared the Colorado River image.

Run a Batch Process

1. Click **File** from the menu bar and click **Batch Process**. The Batch dialog box opens, as shown in Figure 4-4. (Note that you do not need to have an image file open when you execute a batch process.)

FIGURE 4-4
Batch dialog box

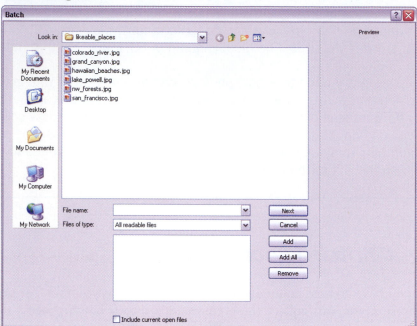

2. Browse to the **likeable_places** folder.

3. Click **Add All**.

All the images (colorado_river.jpg, grand_canyon.jpg, hawaiian_beaches.jpg, lake_powell.jpg, nw_forests.jpg, and san_francisco.jpg) from the data files are put into the list of images to be batch processed.

4. Click **Next**.

The Batch Process dialog box opens, as shown in Figure 4-5.

5. In the Batch Options pane, common actions are listed at the top. Click the plus (**+**) button (Windows) or the **Right arrow** button (Macintosh) next to **Commands** to expand the list of specific commands.

FIGURE 4-5
Batch Options pane of the Batch Process dialog box

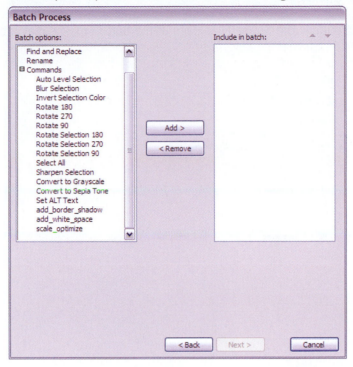

6. Click **scale45**, then click the **Add** button. Repeat this step for **add_border_shadow**, **draw_white-square**, and **center-image_fit-canvas**.

7. Click **Export** on the list of common actions at the top of the Batch options pane, then click the **Add** button.

8. Make sure the commands in the Include in Batch pane are in the order shown in Figure 4-6. Select any commands that are not in the proper order and click the **Remove** button; then you can add them back in the proper order.

FIGURE 4-6
Include in Batch pane of the Batch Process dialog box

9. Make sure Export is selected in the *Include in batch* pane. In the Export Settings menu, click **JPEG – Better Quality**.

10. Click the **Next** button. The Saving Files page of the Batch Process dialog box opens, as shown in Figure 4-7.

FIGURE 4-7

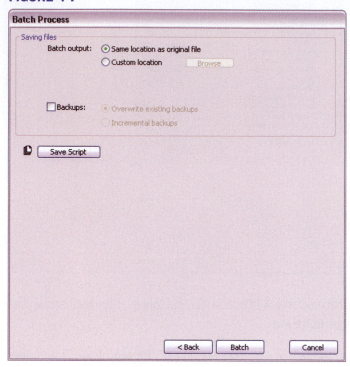

11. In the Batch output section, click **Custom Location**. If the Select Images Folder dialog box does not open, click the **Browse** button beside "Custom location" to open the Select Images Folder dialog box.

12. Browse to the **formatted_images** folder you created in Lesson 1, and open it (Windows) or select it (Macintosh).

13. Click **Select "formatted_images"** (Windows) or **Choose** (Macintosh).

14. Click **Batch**. A message appears, confirming that the batch has run, as shown in Figure 4-8.

FIGURE 4-8
Batch Progress message

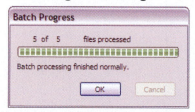

15. Click **OK**.

16. Open one or more of the images from your formatted_images folder to confirm that they have been formatted correctly. They should appear like the images in Figure 4-9. Note that although the photos are different shapes, the white space around them gives the images the same size.

FIGURE 4-9
Successfully formatted images

17. Close all the files and close Fireworks.

SUMMARY

You have successfully formatted a batch of images for a Web page.

In this project, you learned to follow a design document to prepare one image for a Web page and then saved the steps you used so you could use a batch process to prepare multiple images at the same time.

These basic skills provide the necessary foundation for preparing images for Web pages, whether for yourself or as part of a design team.

The next project in this unit builds on what you have already learned, reinforcing these skills and introducing several new ones, including drawing and manipulating images for use in a logo.

ON YOUR OWN – PICTURES FOR A WEB SITE

ACTIVITY 1: IMPORTING AND RESIZING IMAGES

You learned how to use the transformation tools in Fireworks to adjust the size of an image. Apply these same techniques to adjust the size of the images in the landscapes folder. (The landscapes folder is in the data files for this project.)

You can review the resizing techniques in Lesson 1.

There are five pictures in the landscapes folder and they must all be set to half their original height and width so they can be included on a Web site. (The landscapes folder is in the data files for this project.)

1. Resize one of the images from the landscapes folder to half its original height and width. Save it in a new folder as a JPEG image.

2. Create and run the new resize command on all the images so that all the images in the new folder are half the height and width of the images in the landscapes folder.

ACTIVITY 2: ADDING EFFECTS TO IMAGES

You learned how to apply different types of effects to images such as beveling and drop shadows. You also learned to adjust the elements of these effects to customize a particular look for your images.

Apply these same techniques to change the landscapes images from color to black and white. You can review adding effects techniques in Lesson 2.

There are five pictures in the landscapes folder and they must all be changed to black and white images before you put them on a Web site. (The landscapes folder is in the data files for this project.)

1. Add a Hue/Saturation effect to one of the images in the landscapes folder that turns the image to a black-and-white image. Save the image in a new folder as a JPEG image.

    Hint: The shade of a color is known as its hue; the intensity of a color is known as its saturation. Removing all the hue and saturation from an image will change it to black and white.

2. Create a command that adjusts the Hue/Saturation of an image so the image appears black and white.

3. Run the command on the images in the landscapes folder and save them in a new folder.

ACTIVITY 3: OPTIMIZING AND EXPORTING IMAGES

You learned how to optimize and export images for use on a Web site by changing the type of image and adjusting its properties in the Optimize panel.

Apply these same techniques to optimize and export an image from the landscapes folder. (The landscapes folder is in the data files for this project.) You can review these techniques in Lesson 4.

1. Optimize an image from the landscapes data folder as a JPEG image. Experiment with the optimization settings to keep as much quality as possible while reducing the file size to be between 30K and 50K.

2. Export the image to a new folder as a JPEG image.

EXPERIENCE BANK LOGO

GOALS

- Use Web site specifications to draw logo images.
- Use Web site design criteria to define effects and blends.
- Integrate text and drawn images to generate a design described in Web site specifications.

TECHNICAL SKILLS

- Set up a new document.
- Use grids to align image elements.
- Draw and edit images by using a Pen tool.
- Select and modify images by using selection tools.
- Apply gradient and drop shadow effects.
- Copy and paste objects.
- Use transformation tools to rotate objects.
- Use alignment tools to position objects.
- Adjust a drop shadow effect.
- Group objects to create a single image.
- Create text and modify its properties.
- Position text.
- Apply and modify gradients on text.
- Apply drop shadow effects to text.
- Group and resize an image.
- Optimize and export an image.

Estimated time to complete this project: 2 hours

Summary

A logo is a graphical element that represents an organization. The logo helps people identify the organization with certain traits that represent the organization's business. Logos are used in many media, such as print materials, products, advertisements, and Web sites. On Web sites, logos unify the look and feel of a site and help site visitors orient themselves to the site they are on, especially as they navigate through pages of the site.

The Assignment

In this project, you use Macromedia Fireworks to produce a Web-based logo for Experience Bank, redesigned from the print-based logo presently used by the bank. The logo has been redesigned to use colors that evoke the professionalism and integrity of Experience Bank. The design specifications for this logo have been determined by the needs of the company and the design features of their Web site. The designer of the Experience Bank Web site has provided a design document shown in Figure 1. You use the specifications in the design document as you:

■ Draw and modify objects.

■ Generate and position objects.

■ Add and adjust text.

Experience Bank Logo Design Document

The design document for the Experience Bank logo requires final dimensions that are 209 pixels wide and 30 pixels high so the logo can be integrated appropriately into the bank's Web site pages. The gradient and drop shadow effects required for this logo are based on the goals and needs of Experience Bank.

Take a moment to review the project design document before you start the project.

FIGURE 1
The design document for the Experience Bank logo

Design Document – Experience Bank Logo

Client: Experience Bank

Goals and Purpose

The client wants to redesign their logo that appears on printed materials to create a more dynamic look for the pages on their Web site. The Web-based logo should be serious but vibrant. It should reflect the spirit of Experience Bank—confident but friendly, modern but rock-solid, and community oriented.

Audience

The target audience is looking for an established, proven financial institution that still cares about the individual. They want to be assured that their bank is always working for them, that their money is safe, and that they can get personal service. Their age range is 18 and older. They can be visually astute, but don't need to be. Some adjectives to describe the audience are: busy, intelligent, focused.

Design Requirements

The print-based logo for the bank is pictured below for reference. This section describes the redesigned features of the Web-based logo.

The rectangular space reserved for the logo on the Web site is 209 pixels wide and 30 pixels high.

Each of the four triangles on the left should be filled with a green khaki (hexadecimal color code #8A995A) that gradually fades to a lighter color (#DFE5D0) toward both ends of the curved side.

The triangles should have no borders.

Each triangle should have a small drop shadow.

The text in the logo should use two different fonts, just as in the print version: "Experience" is Arial and "Bank" is Arial Black. The height of the text should be slightly less than the curved side of one of the triangles.

The text should be filled with a blue gradient that gradually changes from lighter at the top (#330066) to darker at the bottom (#6666FF).

The text should have a drop shadow, as subtle as the drop shadow on the triangles.

Delivery Requirements

The Web site should display as required on the following browsers.

- Internet Explorer, v6
- Safari 2.0
- AOL 8 or later
- Mozilla Firefox 1.04 or later

The Web site should display on the following operating systems.

- Macintosh OS X 10.3 or later
- Windows XP Home or Professional

The file size of the logo should be as small as possible, so the Web pages will load quickly in site visitors' browsers. However, the image should be crisp.

Print-Based Logo

Experience Bank Logo – Design Document   1

To view the design document, open the file named *FW_Project2_Design.pdf*. This file is located in the Design folder for this project.

DRAWING AND MODIFYING OBJECTS

OBJECTIVES

Upon completion of this lesson, you will be able to:

- Set up a new document.

- Use grids to align image elements.

- Draw and edit images by using a Pen tool.

- Select and modify images by using selection tools.

- Apply gradient and drop shadow effects.

Estimated time to complete this lesson: 50 to 60 minutes

Introduction

The object, or mark, on the left side of the Experience Bank logo is a grouping of four instances of a single drawn object that has been positioned and rotated in different ways. It will be easier to make the logo if you first build the basic element of the mark and then replicate that element in the next lesson. Together, the basic element and the variation compose the complete mark.

Most drawn objects are made from a variety of basic lines and shapes. Fireworks provides basic tools to create vector shapes, such as the Rectangle, Ellipse, and Polygon tools, as well as tools to create free-form drawings, such as the Pen tool.

In this lesson, you set up a document and use the Pen tool to draw an element of the mark for the Experience Bank logo. You add a gradient fill and drop shadow to this element so that you can create the complete mark in the next lesson.

Setting Up a New Document

To fit properly on the Experience Bank Web site, the logo must be fairly small. However, you can more easily draw the parts of the logo if you work with a larger image and then reduce its size after the logo is completed. You use an initial size of 1045 pixels wide and 160 pixels high.

To better blend into the bank's Web site, the logo will sit on a white background. The canvas color is the background color of your document.

 Set Up a New Document

1. Start Fireworks. Click **File** on the menu bar, and then click **New** to create a new empty document. The New Document dialog box opens.

2. Set the Canvas size to **1045** pixels wide by **180** pixels high, as shown in Figure 1-1. Set the resolution to **72** pixels per inch, which is the resolution at which most Web graphics are saved.

FIGURE 1-1
New document dialog box

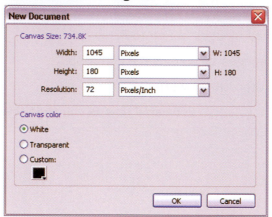

3. Click **OK** to close the dialog box.

4. Make sure the **Pointer** tool on the Tools panel is selected.

5. Click the **Canvas Color** box on the Property inspector, as shown in Figure 1-2. The pointer becomes an eye-dropper you can use to select colors from anywhere on the screen, including the color window. In the color window, select the color white (**#FFFFFF**).

Hot Tip

You can set the Canvas size in the New Document dialog box using pixels, inches, or centimeters. Other ways you can change the canvas size are by selecting **Canvas Size** on the Property inspector or by clicking **Modify** on the menu bar, pointing to **Canvas**, and then clicking **Canvas Size**.

FIGURE 1-2
Property inspector

Canvas
Color box

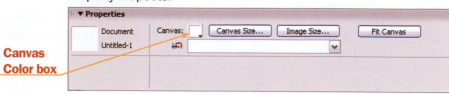

Using the Grid, Guides, and Rulers

You can use rulers and guides to lay out objects precisely and to help you draw. You can place guides in the document and snap objects to those guides.

To make it easier to draw an element of the Experience Bank mark precisely, you will use gridlines and guides. The gridlines make it easier to size objects, and the guides help you align objects as you draw them.

Set Up a Grid

1. Click **View** on the menu bar, point to **Grid**, and then click **Edit Grid**. The Edit Grid dialog box opens, as shown in Figure 1-3. On a Macintosh, the dialog box is named Grids and Guides.

FIGURE 1-3
Edit Grid dialog box

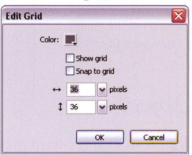

2. Set the grid size to **30 × 30** pixels. Make sure the **Show Grid** and **Snap to Grid** options are checked.

3. Click the **Color** box and choose a pale blue color such as **#99CCFF** for the grid. Make sure you select a color you can easily see.

4. Click **OK**. Pale blue gridlines appear on the canvas.

5. Make sure rulers are visible along the left and top edges of the canvas. If they are not, click **View** on the menu bar, and then click **Rulers**.

6. Position the pointer over the vertical ruler (at the left). Drag from the ruler a distance of three grid spaces right onto the canvas, and then release to add a vertical guide to the document, as shown in Figure 1-4.

Inside the Design

Designers adjust the grid size to be the number of pixels necessary to help them draw an object. When objects have fine features, designers use smaller grids. In the Experience Bank mark, the designer chose a grid size of 30 × 30 pixels because only a few vertices on the mark need to be drawn and aligned.

Hot Tip

To turn the grid on or off, click **View** on the menu bar, point to **Grid**, and then uncheck **Show Grid**.

7. Position the pointer over the horizontal ruler (at the top). Drag from the ruler a distance of three grid spaces down onto the canvas, and then release to add a horizontal guide to the document.

You are going to use the intersection of the guides as the center of the mark in the Experience Bank logo.

Did You Know?

Because Fireworks images are intended for the Web, where graphics are measured in pixels, the rulers in Fireworks always measure in pixels as well, regardless of the unit of measurement you specify when you create a document.

Drawing a Basic Object

The Experience Bank mark is made of slightly curved triangles. You can use the Pen tool to draw points, straight lines, and curved lines. Drawing straight line segments with the Pen tool is a simple matter of clicking to place the points. Each click with the Pen tool plots a corner point. Clicking and then dragging while holding generates curves.

Step by Step Draw a Triangle with a Curved Side

1. Select the **Pen** tool on the Tools panel, as shown in Figure 1-5.

FIGURE 1-5
Tools panel

2. Click the **Stroke color** box on the Tools panel, as shown in Figure 1-5, and select the color black.

   You will not see the effect of this color selection until you complete this Step-by-Step.

3. With the Pen tool selected, click once at the intersection of the guides to place the first corner point.

4. Move the pointer diagonally down two grid spaces and left two grid spaces, and then double-click to place the endpoint. A line segment joins the two points.

   Double-clicking creates an open path. This means the Pen tool "closes off" the path where you double-clicked, leaving you with a line segment.

5. Start a new line segment by clicking the starting point (the intersection of the guides). Move the pointer diagonally down two grid spaces and right two grid spaces, and then double-click to place the endpoint. A line segment joins the two points.

There are now two line segments that meet at the intersection of the guides, as shown in Figure 1-6.

FIGURE 1-6
Open paths create the sides of the triangle

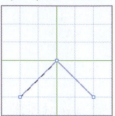

Now you will join the two endpoints with a curve. Drawing a curve is tricky until you learn how. If you make mistakes, remember that you can click Edit on the menu bar and then click Undo to reverse your most recent action. If you want to start over, you can delete any part or all of your drawing by selecting it and pressing Backspace (Windows) or Delete (Macintosh).

6. Click the endpoint on the left (the first line segment) and move the pointer to the endpoint of the second line segment. Click once on the second endpoint and hold the mouse button down as you drag the pointer down and to the right. Continue to drag until the point handle is about halfway between the curved base of the triangle and the tip, as shown in Figure 1-7. Release the mouse button.

FIGURE 1-7
Curved line drawn with the Pen tool

Point handle

Notice that as you drag the mouse pointer, the line segment curves in the opposite direction. This is one way to create curves.

7. Select the **Pointer** tool on the Tools panel to stop drawing.

If you use the Pointer tool to click away from the drawing, you can see that the stroke color of the drawing is black, reflecting your choice in step 2. Selected objects are blue. Otherwise, objects are displayed in the stroke and fill colors of your choice.

8. Click **File** on the menu bar, and then click **Save**.

9. Key a name for your logo file, such as **Exp_Bank_logo_[YourName]**.

10. Navigate to the folder where you want to save the new file, and click **Save**.

The document is saved as a Fireworks PNG. Note that within Fireworks you can also save a document as other types of image files.

Creating and Applying a Gradient Fill

The Experience Bank mark is made of two colors that seem to blend from one to the next. The pattern makes the elements in the mark appear to be curved up from the page. You can create these types of effects by using simple colors and gradients. You can change fills to display a variety of solid, dithered, pattern, or gradient characteristics. When you apply these characteristics to an object, the characteristics conform to the object's contours and resemble satin, ripples, folds, or gradients. Additionally, you can change various attributes of a fill, such as color, edge, texture, and transparency.

For further information on using colors on the Web, see the Tips & Techniques feature "Web-Safe Colors."

Now that you have drawn one element in the mark of the logo, you can apply a gradient fill to the element so it appears to have lighter edges and a darker center.

> ### Inside the Design
>
> Designers use colors and combinations of colors to add depth and dimensionality to objects. In the Experience Bank logo, the designer uses a gradient fill to add depth and create a layered effect.

 ## Create and Apply a Gradient Fill

1. Make sure the **Pointer** tool is selected, and select the curved triangle.

2. Click the **Fill category** menu on the Property inspector, as shown in Figure 1-8. Point to **Gradient**, and then click **Linear**.

FIGURE 1-8
Fill category menu

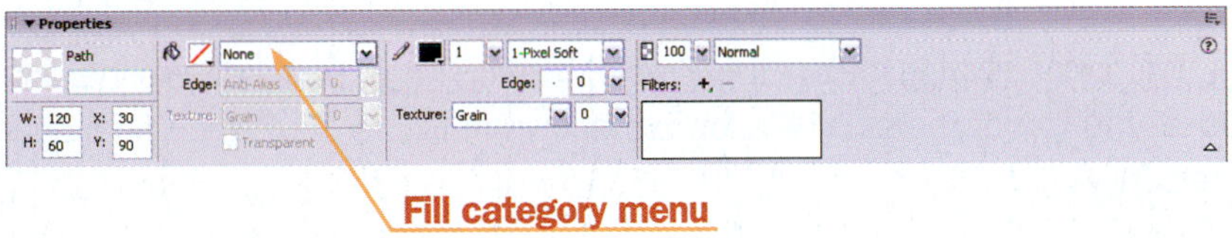

Fill category menu

The fill pattern changes from None to a black-and-white gradient. The black line that appears across the middle of the object has a round handle on the left end and a square handle on the right end. You will use these handles later to adjust the gradient. The handles do not appear in your final image. You will now change the colors of this gradient to match the Experience Bank's company colors.

Set the Colors of a Gradient Fill

1. Click the **Fill Color** box to the left of the Fill Category menu to open the Edit Gradient window, as shown in Figure 1-9.

FIGURE 1-9
Edit Gradient window

Although a number of preset colors are available, you will use the Experience Bank colors.

2. Click below the center of the gradient color ramp to add a new color swatch halfway between the outer swatches, as shown in Figure 1-10.

Note

If the new color swatch is not centered well enough, you can reposition it by dragging it along the gradient color ramp.

FIGURE 1-10
Color swatches

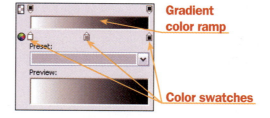

Gradient color ramp

Color swatches

3. Click the left color swatch below the gradient color ramp and key the hexadecimal color code **#DFE5D0** at the top of the color window, as shown in Figure 1-11. (The final character in the color code is zero.)

FIGURE 1-11
Hexadecimal color code at the top of the color window

4. Press **Enter** (Windows) or **Return** (Macintosh) to return to the Edit Gradient window.

5. Click the center color swatch below the gradient color ramp and key the hexadecimal color code **#8A995A** at the top of the color window. Press **Enter** (Windows) or **Return** (Macintosh).

6. Click the right color swatch and key the hexadecimal color code **#DFE5D0** at the top of the color window. (The final character in the color code is zero.) Press **Enter** (Windows) or **Return** (Macintosh).

7. Click outside the Edit Gradient window to close it and update the object.

Your gradient fill should look similar to the one in Figure 1-12.

FIGURE 1-12
Triangle with gradient

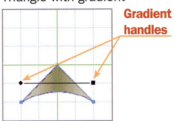

Gradient handles

8. Save the file.

Now that you have added the gradient fill to the triangle shape, you can manipulate the gradient's width and angle to get just the right sense of depth and texture for your object by using the gradient handles.

 Use Gradient Handles to Adjust a Gradient

1. Drag the round (left) handle inward so it is only half a grid space beyond the side of the triangle.

Dragging the round handle moves the fill within an object.

2. Drag the square handle (right endpoint) inward so it is only half a grid beyond the side of the triangle.

Dragging the square handle changes the fill width and skew. Your object should now look similar to the one in Figure 1-13.

> **Note**
>
> To rotate a gradient fill, drag the line connecting the handles.

FIGURE 1-13
Triangle with adjusted gradient

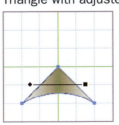

3. Save the file.

Removing the Stroke

The Experience Bank mark appears as if each element floats. To create this appearance, each element of the mark should have no border around the gradient fill. You will now remove the border (stroke) of the curved triangle.

Remove the Stroke of an Object

1. Make sure the **Pointer** tool on the Tools panel is selected. Click the triangle to select it.

   The triangle shape has a black outline that becomes blue when the shape is selected.

2. With the triangle selected, click the **Stroke Color** box on the Tools panel to open the color window.

3. At the top of the color window, click the **Transparent** button (red diagonal icon), as shown in Figure 1-14.

Hot Tip

You can select objects by dragging a marquee around them. It is easy to select multiple objects at once with this technique.

Hot Tip

The red diagonal is a Fireworks convention to represent no color or transparency. It appears in all color menus.

FIGURE 1-14
Transparent button in the color window

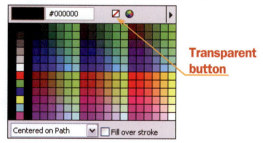

Transparent button

The 1-pixel stroke path has been removed (made transparent). When you select the triangle, the blue selection outline still appears, but the black border is no longer visible when you click away from the triangle to deselect it.

4. Save the file.

Tips & Techniques

WEB-SAFE COLORS

If you have worked with Web tools such as Fireworks, you have probably heard the term *Web-safe colors*. You might have also heard these colors referred to as *browser-safe*, *the 216 palette*, *the Netscape cube*, or *Explorer colors*. These all refer to a set of 216 colors that can be viewed with computer systems set to display 8-bit colors. Now, however, most computers can display 64,000 colors or more. Many Web designers now use a WebSnap Adaptive palette or an Exact palette instead. A WebSnap Adaptive palette creates a bridge between Web-safe colors and a custom palette containing the majority of the colors in an image by snapping colors within a tolerance of seven color steps to the closest Web-safe color. An Exact palette contains the exact colors in an image when the image contains 256 or fewer colors.

You might choose not to work at 16-bit color depth, because Web-safe colors might dither (making the image look grainy), and the Eyedropper tool in Fireworks may sample colors incorrectly at that depth.

When you select fill and stroke colors in Fireworks, you are presented with a palette of Web-safe colors, but you can also sample colors from any image by using the Eyedropper tool. Keep in mind that to get accurate color sampling, your monitor needs to be set to 24-bit or greater color depth.

GENERATING AND POSITIONING OBJECTS

Introduction

The Experience Bank mark is composed of four objects positioned in a rectangular formation that resembles a shield. To create this mark without having to redraw and adjust each element individually, you replicate the element you created in the previous lesson, and position the elements in the final formation. This technique allows you to reuse previous work and ensure all the elements in the mark are identical.

In this lesson you replicate the basic object, position the objects into a rectangular shape, adjust the drop shadow on each object, and then group the objects together to create the mark.

Replicating Objects

Replicating the object you have drawn is an easy way to build the logo without repeating tasks you have already completed. In the following exercises, you copy the triangle object and paste multiple copies of it onto the canvas. Then you move the objects to make the final mark.

 Replicate an Object

1. Make sure the file you created in the previous lesson is open, or open the file named **Exp_Bank_logo_Lesson2.png**. This file is located in the data files for this project. If you use the data file, save it as **Exp_Bank_logo_[YourName].png**.

2. Make sure the **Pointer** tool on the Tools panel is selected, and click the triangle object to select it.

3. Click **Edit** on the menu bar, and then click **Copy** to save a copy of the triangle object to the Clipboard.

4. Click **Edit** on the menu bar, and then click **Paste** to paste a copy of the triangle object.

   Fireworks pastes the copy directly on top of the original image. You will not see two objects until you move the copy.

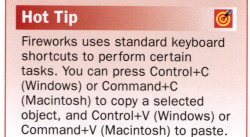

Hot Tip

Fireworks uses standard keyboard shortcuts to perform certain tasks. You can press Control+C (Windows) or Command+C (Macintosh) to copy a selected object, and Control+V (Windows) or Command+V (Macintosh) to paste.

5. Twice more, click **Edit** on the menu bar, and then click **Paste** to create a total of four objects.

   You will notice four Path objects in the Layers panel, as shown in Figure 2-1. If the Layers panel is not open, click **Window** on the menu bar, and then click **Layers**.

FIGURE 2-1
Four objects in the Layers panel

6. Save the file.

Positioning Objects

Now that you have created all the elements of the mark, you will rotate and position each element to match the sketch drawn by the designer. Because the objects are small, you will draw four additional guides to help you precisely position each object.

 ## Position Objects

1. Position the pointer over the horizontal ruler (at the top of the canvas). Drag from the ruler a distance of two and a half grid spaces onto the canvas, and then release to add a horizontal guide to the document.

2. Drag another horizontal guide a distance of two grid spaces down from the ruler.

3. Position the pointer over the vertical ruler (at the left). Drag from the ruler a distance of two and a half grid spaces onto the canvas, and then release to add a vertical guide to the document.

4. Drag another vertical guide a distance of three and a half grid spaces from the ruler.

   You now have a set of guides that form four small grids squares above the original triangle, as shown in Figure 2-2.

FIGURE 2-2
New set of guides

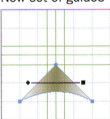

Now you are ready to rotate and position the objects you have pasted.

Arrange Objects to Match a Design

1. Use the **Pointer** tool to select the visible curved triangle.

   Only the top triangle is selected because the images are stacked.

2. Click **Modify** on the menu bar, point to **Transform**, and click **Rotate 90° CW**.

   The shape rotates 90 degrees clockwise, as shown in Figure 2-3.

FIGURE 2-3
Rotated triangle

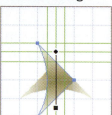

3. Drag the rotated triangle until the tip is on the intersection of the guides to the left and above the tip of the original triangle (half a grid space up and to the left), as shown in Figure 2-4. The rotated triangle forms the left side of the mark in the Experience Bank logo.

> **Note**
>
> Before you drag an object that contains a gradient fill, move the pointer over the object until the pointer does not have a curved arrow beside it. (If you drag while the curved arrow is visible, you will adjust the gradient fill instead of moving the object.) If you have difficulty dragging the triangle by using the mouse, you can use the arrow keys instead.

FIGURE 2-4
Rotated and moved triangle

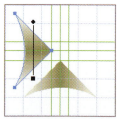

4. Select the visible triangle on the remaining stack of replicated triangles.

5. Click **Modify** on the menu bar, point to **Transform**, and click **Rotate 180°**.

6. Drag the rotated triangle until the tip is one full grid space directly above the tip of the original triangle, as shown in Figure 2-5.

Hot Tip

You can use the arrow keys to move selected shapes one pixel at a time. You can also drag an object close to where you want it, and then use the arrow keys to move it pixel by pixel to locate it more precisely.

FIGURE 2-5
Second rotated and moved triangle

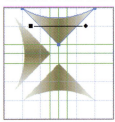

7. Select the visible triangle on the remaining stack of replicated triangles.

8. Click **Modify** on the menu bar, point to **Transform**, and click **Rotate 90° CCW**.

9. Drag the rotated triangle until the tip is on the intersection of the guides to the right and above the tip of the original triangle (half a grid space up and to the right), completing the mark as shown in Figure 2-6.

FIGURE 2-6
Completed mark

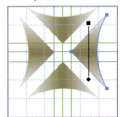

10. Save the file.

Adding a Drop Shadow

The Experience Bank mark appears to have dimensionality and float above the page with the use of the gradient fill and the loss of the stroke. A final aspect you can apply to the elements to reinforce its dimensionality is to add drop shadows to each object. The shadows serve to lift the objects from the background and thereby add depth to the overall composition.

Fireworks makes it easy to apply solid shadows, drop shadows, inner shadows, and glows to images. You can also specify the angle of the shadow to simulate the angle from which the light is shining. Because each object sits in a different position, a single light source would impact each object differently. Although you drew only one object, added its gradient fill, and then replicated it, you need to set a unique drop shadow for each object now that you have formed and positioned the elements of the mark correctly.

 ### Add a Drop Shadow

1. Select the **Pointer** tool and select the triangle on the left side of the mark.

2. Click the **Add live filters** button (**+** icon) on the Property inspector, as shown in Figure 2-7, point to **Shadow and Glow**, and then click **Drop Shadow**.

FIGURE 2-7
Add live filters button

Add live filters button

The Drop Shadow window opens, as shown in Figure 2-8.

FIGURE 2-8
Drop Shadow window

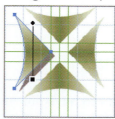

3. Key **9** for distance, **45%** for opacity, **0** for softness, and **315** for the angle of the shadow. Set the color to **black**.

4. Click outside the window or press **Enter** (Windows) or **Return** (Macintosh) to close the window.

The triangle on the left now has a drop shadow, as shown in Figure 2-9.

FIGURE 2-9
Triangle with drop shadow

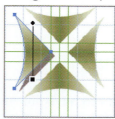

5. In turn, select each of the other triangles and repeat steps 2–4.

The mark is now complete, as shown in Figure 2-10.

FIGURE 2-10
FIGURE 2-10
Completed mark with drop shadows

6. Save the file.

Grouping Objects

Now that you have completed the mark, it is good practice to group the elements into a single object so you cannot mistakenly alter one part of it. Having the mark grouped as a single object is also helpful for scaling or fine-tuning the placement of the objects for the final logo.

 ## Group Objects

1. With the **Pointer** tool selected, click the top triangle.

2. Hold down **Shift**, and click the remaining triangles.

3. With all four objects selected, click **Modify** on the menu bar, and then click **Group**.

   Instead of selection points (handles) on each of the shapes, the group now has only four selection points—one at each corner—as shown in Figure 2-11. Fireworks has grouped these objects and it will now treat these objects as a single object. Any actions, filters, or other effects you apply will be applied to the whole group.

FIGURE 2-11
Grouped mark

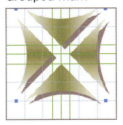

> **Note**
>
> To ungroup a grouped object into its original elements, select the group, click **Modify** on the menu bar, and then click **Ungroup**.

4. Select the group and use the arrow keys to move it to the left edge of the canvas, as shown in Figure 2-12.

FIGURE 2-12
Mark aligned with left edge of canvas

5. Save the file.

ADDING AND ADJUSTING TEXT

OBJECTIVES

Upon completion of this lesson, you will be able to:

- Create text and modify its properties.
- Position text.
- Apply and modify gradients on text.
- Apply drop shadow effects to text.
- Group and resize an image.
- Optimize and export an image.

Estimated time to complete this lesson: 20 to 30 minutes

Introduction

The text on a logo generally names the organization and, together with the mark, creates an identity for the organization.

In this lesson, you finalize the logo. You add and format text. You apply text effects to evoke the qualities of integrity and professionalism. You position and group the elements of the completed logo. You optimize it for use on a Web site, and then resize and export it for use on the Experience Bank Web site.

Adding Text to the Canvas

The Experience Bank logo contains two major elements: the mark and the text. You create this text as shown in the drawn logo and use the design guidelines set by the company for formatting the text.

 ## Add Text and Modify Its Properties

1. Make sure the file you created in the previous lesson is open, or open the file named **Exp_Bank_logo_Lesson3.png**. This file is located in the data files for this project. If you use the data file, be sure to save it as **Exp_Bank_logo_[YourName].png**.

2. Select the **Text** tool on the Tools panel, as shown in Figure 3-1.

FIGURE 3-1
Tools panel

Text tool

3. Click on the canvas to the right of the mark and key **Experience Bank**, as shown in Figure 3-2. If you have difficulty seeing the text as you key it, click **Text** on the menu bar, point to **Align**, and click **Left** to left-align the text.

FIGURE 3-2
Mark and text

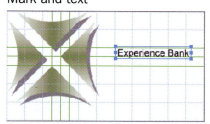

4. Use the **Pointer** tool to select the text **Experience Bank**.

5. On the Property inspector, click the **Font** menu, and click **Arial**.

6. Set font Size to **117**.

7. Set Kerning or Range Kerning to **2**.

Hot Tip

To format only a portion of text, use the Text tool to highlight the portion you want to format. To format an entire text object, select it by using the Pointer tool (or use the Text tool to highlight the entire text).

8. Set Horizontal Scale to **91%**, as shown in Figure 3-3.

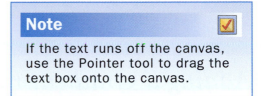

Horizontal Scale   Kerning or Range Kerning

9. Use the **Text** tool to drag over the word **Bank** to select that text.

10. On the Property inspector, click the **Font** menu, and click **Arial Black**. The two words have a different appearance, as shown in Figure 3-4.

> **Note** ☑️
>
> If the text runs off the canvas, use the Pointer tool to drag the text box onto the canvas.

FIGURE 3-4
Logo text with two different fonts

11. Save the file.

Adjusting Text on the Canvas

The text may run off the canvas, and may not be in line with the mark you created earlier. You need to move the text, using the grids on the canvas to help you better align the text with the mark.

Position Text

1. Select the **Pointer** tool from the Tools panel.

2. Select the text box. A blue outline defines a border around the text.

3. Drag the text until the left border is five grid spaces in from the left edge of the canvas and the top border is one grid space from the top of the canvas, as shown in Figure 3-5.

FIGURE 3-5
Text aligned on grid

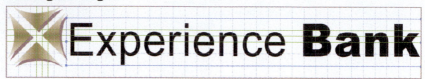

4. Save the file.

Adding a Gradient Fill and Drop Shadow to Text

At this point, the mark has dimensionality and color, but the text is plain. The complete logo for Experience Bank needs to be unified. You will apply a gradient fill, as well as a drop shadow to the text, to match the gradient and drop shadow on the mark.

Add a Gradient Fill to Text

1. Use the **Pointer** tool to select the text.

2. Click the **Fill color** box on the Property inspector to open the color window.

3. In the color window, click **Fill Options**. At the top of the second color window, select **Gradient** for the **Fill category**. In the second menu that appears, select **Linear**, as shown in Figure 3-6.

FIGURE 3-6
Color windows

 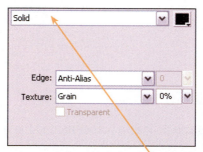 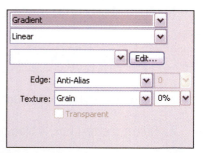

Fill category menu

4. In the color window, click the **Edit** button.

5. Click the left color swatch under the gradient color ramp and key hexadecimal color code **#6666FF** at the top of the color window.

6. Click the right color swatch under the gradient color ramp and key hexadecimal color code **#330066**.

7. Click out of each of the two windows to close them. The text now has a gradient fill, as shown in Figure 3-7.

FIGURE 3-7
Logo text with gradient applied

The gradient runs the length of the text, with the lightest text on the left and the darkest on the right. However, you need to adjust the gradient handles to rotate the gradient so the darkest color in the gradient is at the bottom of the text and the lightest is at the top.

 ## Adjust a Gradient Fill

1. Drag the round handle to the top left corner of the text box.

2. Drag the square handle to the bottom left corner of the text box, as shown in Figure 3-8.

Now the gradient shades vertically, from lighter blue at the top of the text to darker blue at the bottom, as shown in Figure 3-8.

FIGURE 3-8
Logo text with vertical gradient applied

Square handle   **Round handle**

3. Save the file.

 ## Apply a Drop Shadow to Text

1. Use the **Pointer** tool to select the text.

2. Click the **Add Live Filters** button (**+** icon) on the Property inspector, point to **Shadow and Glow**, and then click **Drop Shadow**.

3. In the Drop Shadow window, key **6** for distance, **65%** for opacity, **6** for softness, and **315** for the angle of the shadow. Set the color to **black**.

4. Click outside the window or press **Enter** (Windows) or **Return** (Macintosh) to close the window.

The text should appear as in Figure 3-9.

FIGURE 3-9
Text with drop shadow applied

5. Save the file.

Optimizing, Resizing, and Exporting an Image

Now that the logo is complete, you group the mark and text together. Because the logo is to be incorporated into a Web site, you optimize it to the smallest file size possible without losing the design integrity of the image. Finally, you resize the logo to fit into the space reserved for it on the Web pages.

 ## Group Objects

1. Click the mark, hold down **Shift**, and click the Experience Bank text to select them both.

2. With both objects selected, click **Modify** on the menu bar, and then click **Group**.

 ## Optimize Objects

1. Make sure the Optimize panel is open. If it is not open, click **Window** on the menu bar, and click **Optimize**.

2. In the Optimize panel, click the **Export file format** menu, and click **JPEG**.

3. Change the Quality setting to **75%**, as shown in Figure 3-10, and press **Enter** (Windows) or **Return** (Macintosh).

> **Note**
>
> The Optimize panel, like other Fireworks features, can also be opened by using a shortcut key, F6.

FIGURE 3-10
Optimize panel

Export
file format

Quality

4. Save the file.

You need to resize the logo to fit into the Experience Bank Web site.

Inside the Design

Designers use the 2-Up view or 4-Up view in Fireworks to test different optimization settings such as GIF image type or JPEG image type, as well as to adjust the qualities of these image types. For the Experience Bank logo, the designer tested these different options and found that using a JPEG file format best retained the smoothness of the gradient fill and shadow. Because the image is displayed in a very small size on the site, lowering the quality to 75 percent still yields a good-quality image.

Resize an Object

1. With the logo still selected, click **Window** on the menu bar, and click **Image Editing** to open the Image Editing panel, as shown in Figure 3-11.

FIGURE 3-11
Image Editing panel

2. Click **Transform Commands** on the Image Editing panel, and then click **Numeric Transform** on the Transform Commands menu, as shown in Figure 3-12.

FIGURE 3-12
Transform Commands menu

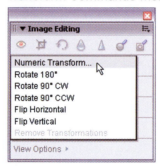

3. Select **Resize** from the menu at the top of the Numeric Transform dialog box, as shown in Figure 3-13.

FIGURE 3-13
Numeric Transform dialog box

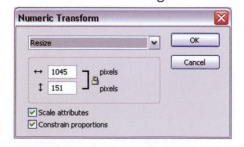

4. Make sure **Constrain proportions** is checked, key **209** pixels as the width, and click **OK**.

5. Click **Modify** on the menu bar, point to **Canvas**, and click **Fit Canvas**.

The excess canvas area is removed, leaving only what is necessary for the logo image, as shown in Figure 3-14.

FIGURE 3-14
Canvas fit around final logo

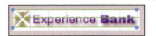

6. Save the file (as a PNG).

 Export an Object

1. Click **File** on the menu bar, and click **Save As**.

2. Navigate to the same folder in which you saved the PNG, and select **JPEG** as the type of file to save.

3. Click **Save**.

4. Close the file.

When you see a message asking whether you want to save this file as a Fireworks PNG, you can safely click No if you saved the file as a PNG in step 6 in the previous exercise. (Fireworks displays this message because it interprets saving the file as a JPEG as a change to the original image.)

Note

Using Save As and specifying to save as a JPEG is equivalent to exporting the file as a JPEG (by using Export in the File menu). Either way, the file is saved as a Web-ready JPEG.

Did You Know?

The settings you specify in the Optimize panel are applied when you save or export an image using the same file type you selected in the Optimize panel.

SUMMARY

You have successfully created the Experience Bank logo for the Experience Bank Web site.

In this project, you learned to use Fireworks tools to draw an image, to apply and adjust gradient fills, to apply and adjust effects, and to reduce file size.

These basic skills provide the necessary foundation for creating more complex logos or other types of drawings.

The last project in this unit builds on what you have learned, reinforcing these skills and introducing several new ones, including generating page layout and creating an interactive navigation button.

ON YOUR OWN — LOGOS

ACTIVITY 1: DRAWING LINES AND CURVES

You have learned how to use the Pen tool to draw simple lines and curves in Fireworks. Apply these same techniques to build the outline for the Mountain Arts logo.

You can review the Pen tool techniques in Lesson 1.

1. Open a new document in Fireworks and set the size larger than you will need, such as 500 × 500 pixels.

2. Use the **Pen** tool to draw the mountain image. Use three anchor points for the left base, the tip, and the right base. Close the shape.

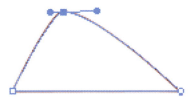

3. Use the **Pointer** tool to select the mountain outline. Change the stroke color to dark brown

4. Save the file as **mountain_outline_[YourName].png**.

Hint

Start by building the base of the mountain: Click to create the left base point and click to create the right base point. To generate the curved top, move to where you want the peak, then click, hold, and drag to draw the curve at the peak. After you release, move to the first point (the left base), and click once. Be sure to select the Pointer tool after the mountain outline is complete. If you continue to use the Pen tool, you will draw additional lines. If you wish to adjust the curve after it is completed, use the Subselection tool (white pointer icon) to select the anchor point at the peak, and then drag either of the handles at the point.

ACTIVITY 2: USING GRADIENTS AND ADDING EFFECTS

You have learned how to apply gradients and manipulate their properties in Fireworks. You also learned to apply effects to add dimensionality. Apply these same techniques to build the mountain for the Mountain Arts logo.

You can review using gradients in Lesson 1.

1. Open the mountain outline you drew in activity1 or **open mountain_outline.png** from the data files.

2. Select linear gradient as the fill category.

3. Adjust the gradient so that there are four gradient swatches, with white swatches on either end of the gradient color ramp and dark brown in the center and also closest to the left-most white swatch.

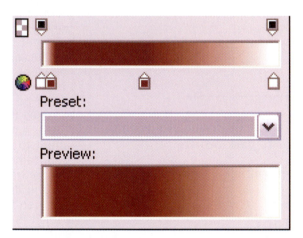

4. Adjust the gradient handles so that the round handle is below the base of the mountain and the square handle is just below the vertex inside the mountain.

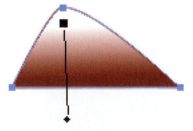

5. Use the **Pointer** tool to select the mountain and add an inner bevel to give the object smooth dimensionality.

6. Save the file as **mountain_[YourName].png**.

ACTIVITY 3: ADDING TEXT

You have learned how to create text and apply gradients and other effects to text in Fireworks. Apply these same techniques to complete the Mountain Arts logo.

You can review using gradients in Lesson 3.

1. Open the mountain file you completed in activity 2 or open **mountain.png** from the data files.

2. Key **Mountain Arts**, using the font Bradley Hand ITC or a similar script type font. Apply a gradient to the text. The gradient should have four swatches, with white swatches at either end and dark brown swatches as the next swatches in on the gradient ramp.

3. Add a drop shadow to the text.

4. Adjust the gradient handles so that the round handle extends to the right of the word "Arts" and the square handle is directly to the left of the word "Arts."

5. Position the text so that the word "Mountain" is on the brown background of the mountain image.

6. Fit the canvas and save the image as **mountain_logo_[YourName].png**.

PAGE LAYOUT AND NAVIGATION BAR FOR A WEB SITE

GOALS

- Use the Web site design document to generate a page comp and define elements of a navigation bar.
- Use the Web site design document to define colors and fonts of a page and a navigation bar.
- Generate and save a page comp.
- Build, optimize, and export a navigation bar for use in a Web site.

TECHNICAL SKILLS

- Lay out Web pages.
- Create layers.
- Group and ungroup objects.
- Create and edit buttons for navigation.
- Apply effects to buttons.
- Copy and paste a navigation bar into a new document.
- Optimize a navigation bar.
- Export a navigation bar.

Estimated time to complete this project: 2 – 3 hours

Summary

A clean, simple page layout and neat navigation enhances the look of your Web site. This also helps visitors find what they need and makes your site design a success. Where elements are laid on the page dictates how a site visitor will digest the information. Not only should the page design be clean, but you also should use your navigation space efficiently. Short, clear, specific words in links provide visitors to your site with information about what the corresponding page will contain and how to easily find the information they seek.

Assignment

In this project, you use Macromedia Fireworks to produce a page composition (known as a *page comp*) for the design of the Experience Bank Web site and a navigation bar for this site. Page comps are used to help clients visualize what a page in the site will look like to make sure it meets their expectations. Once a page comp is approved, the rest of the pages on the site are designed, using the approved design elements of the comp. The clients have provided information in the design document that will help you to:

- Lay out the elements of a checking account page for the Experience Bank Web site and create a page comp.

- Build a navigation bar for the Experience Bank Web site.

- Optimize and export the navigation bar so it is ready to use in the Web site.

Web Site Design Document

The Experience Bank Web site project includes a design document that contains the flow-chart for the site and the goals of the client. The pages linked directly from the home page form the main navigation. A designer will translate the goals into a general look and feel by making color and layout design choices—see the example in Figure 1.

Experience Bank design document

Design Document – Banking Site

Client: Experience Bank

Goals and Purpose

A team will update the Experience Bank Web site. The goals of the update are to improve:

- The look of the site
- The usability of the site
- The readability and accessibility of the site
- The competitive stance of the site

The bank's Web site should reflect the spirit of Experience Bank—confident but friendly, modern but rock-solid, and community oriented.

Audience

The target audience is looking for an established, proven financial institution that still cares about the individual. They want to be assured that their bank is always working for them, that their money is safe, and that they can get personal service. Their age range is 18 and older. They may have visual or other impairments. They can be frequent web users, but don't need to be. On a Web site they expect to be able to find answers to their questions easily and quickly. Some adjectives to describe the audience are: busy, intelligent, focused.

Design Requirements

There should be a consistent page design to improve the look and usability of the site. Include a streamlined, easy-to-use navigation scheme in the page design to enhance the usability of the site.

In order to improve readability, use white space to break up dense blocks of information, text emphasis to draw the eye initially to heading information, and color to group related pieces of information and separate them from other information.

The site should provide a graphic navigation scheme, as well as a text-based navigation alternative that will be accessible to screen readers. Navigation presents a significant challenge because of the large number of pages in this site, reflecting the range and complexity of the products offered by Experience Bank.

Provide captions, headings, and summaries for data tables to make the data more accessible to visitors who use screen readers.

Delivery Requirements

The Web site should display as required on the following browsers.

- Internet Explorer, v6
- Safari 2.0
- AOL 8 or later
- Mozilla Firefox 1.04 or later

The Web site should display on the following operating systems.

- Macintosh OS X 10.3 or later
- Windows XP Home or Professional

Content

In the current phase of implementation, the revised design should be applied to the following pages as representative samples:

- Checking home page in the Personal Services section of the site. This page provides information about the various checking account products available from Experience Bank. It includes links to pages that provide additional information about each of these checking products.

Banking Site – Design Document   1

To view the design document for the Experience Bank Web site, open the file named *FW_Project3_Design.pdf*. This file is located in the Design folder for this project.

CREATING PAGE LAYOUTS

OBJECTIVES:

Upon completion of this lesson, you will be able to:

- Lay out Web pages.
- Create layers.
- Group and ungroup objects.

Estimated time to complete this lesson: 50 – 60 minutes

Introduction

In this project you create a look and feel for Experience Bank, a fictional bank. During the early planning stages of a project like this, members of the design team meet with the client to gather ideas for the site. The team incorporates this information in a design document to guide color and layout choices.

In this lesson, you build a page design comp for a checking account Web page. The page mock-up should look like a Web page, but it will not function like one.

Setting Up the Document

The Web pages for the Experience Bank Web site should have final dimensions of 700 pixels wide and 800 pixels high. Because these dimensions include some image padding around the main content, it ensures that the main content will fit horizontally at screen resolutions of 1024×768 and at 800×600.

To begin laying out the regions of the page, you first create a document that will simulate a full open page.

 Set Up the Document

1. Start Fireworks. Click **File** on the menu bar, and then click **New** to create a new empty document. The New Document dialog box opens.

2. Set the canvas size to **700** pixels wide by **800** pixels high, as shown in Figure 1-1. Set the resolution to **72** pixels per inch.

FIGURE 1-1
New Document dialog box

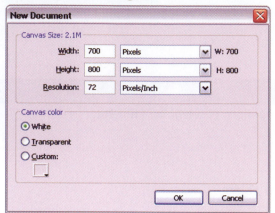

3. Set canvas color to olive green (**#939F6C**).

4. Click **OK** to close the dialog box.

5. Save your comp file, giving it a name such as **Exp_Bank_comp_[YourName].**

Using Layers

A Fireworks document can consist of many lay-ers, and each layer can contain many objects. The Layers panel lists the layers in a document as well as each of the objects the layers contain. Layers help organize a document that contains multiple elements.

When you create a page comp, all the text, graphical, and animation elements are represented by objects. With a large number of objects, you should use layers to help organize these objects.

The objects and layers in the Layers panel show the order in which elements are stacked. Layers or objects high in the panel list cover layers and objects that are below them in the list. By rearranging the stacking order of layers or of objects within a layer, you can make higher objects mask or block out certain other objects.

Fireworks starts with two default layers: Web Layer and Layer 1. The Web Layer is a special layer that appears as the top layer in every Fireworks document. The Web layer contains any interactions you create, such as rollovers or buttons. You work with this layer when you create buttons in the next lesson. Layer 1 is the name of the active layer.

> **Inside the Design**
>
> The Experience Bank Web site requires colors that evoke the spirit of the bank. For this rea-son, the designer has chosen colors such as khakis and greens to suggest that the bank is confident but friendly, modern but rock-solid, and community oriented.

You will designate a few layers in your document as design areas or content areas on the checking page so you can organize the content of the comp. According to the design document, as shown in Figure 1-2, you need to set off parts of the page with colors to designate different areas of content. To accomplish this, you will create four layers, one to hold the background colors, one to hold the main navigation, one for the left sub-navigation, and one for page-specific content.

FIGURE 1-2
Experience Bank design document

Design Document – Banking Site

Client: Experience Bank

Goals and Purpose

A team will update the Experience Bank Web site. The goals of the update are to improve:
- The look of the site
- The usability of the site
- The readability and accessibility of the site
- The competitive stance of the site

The bank's Web site should reflect the spirit of Experience Bank—confident but friendly, modern but rock-solid, and community oriented.

Audience

The target audience is looking for an established, proven financial institution that still cares about the individual. They want to be assured that their bank is always working for them, that their money is safe, and that they can get personal service. Their age range is 18 and older. They may have visual or other impairments. They can be frequent web users, but don't need to be. On a Web site they expect to be able to find answers to their questions easily and quickly. Some adjectives to describe the audience are: busy, intelligent, focused.

Design Requirements

There should be a consistent page design to improve the look and usability of the site. Include a streamlined, easy-to-use navigation scheme in the page design to enhance the usability of the site.

In order to improve readability, use white space to break up dense blocks of information, text emphasis to draw the eye initially to heading information, and color to group related pieces of information and separate them from other information.

The site should provide a graphic navigation scheme, as well as a text-based navigation alternative that will be accessible to screen readers. Navigation presents a significant challenge because of the large number of pages in this site, reflecting the range and complexity of the products offered by Experience Bank.

Provide captions, headings, and summaries for data tables to make the data more accessible to visitors who use screen readers.

Delivery Requirements

The Web site should display as required on the following browsers.
- Internet Explorer, v6
- Safari 2.0
- AOL 8 or later
- Mozilla Firefox 1.04 or later

The Web site should display on the following operating systems.
- Macintosh OS X 10.3 or later
- Windows XP Home or Professional

Content

In the current phase of implementation, the revised design should be applied to the following pages as representative samples:
- Checking home page in the Personal Services section of the site. This page provides information about the various checking account products available from Experience Bank. It includes links to pages that provide additional information about each of these checking products.

Banking Site – Design Document   1

Create Comp Layers

1. Open the **Layers panel**, if it is not already open, by clicking **Window** on the menu bar and selecting **Layers**.

Inside the Design

Designers research existing sites to gather ideas on how to use colors and layouts for sites of a particular genre. In the Experience Bank example, the designer has researched how other banks tend to organize and block content and has applied similar principles to the current site.

2. Double-click the words **Layer 1** in the Layers Panel, as shown in Figure 1-3, to rename the layer.

FIGURE 1-3
Renaming in the Layers panel

3. Key **Background** as the new name and press **Enter** (Windows) or **Return** (Macintosh).

4. Click the **New/Duplicate Layer** icon, as shown in Figure 1-4, to add a new layer.

FIGURE 1-4
Add new layer

New/Duplicate
Layer icon

A new layer, named Layer 1, appears in the Layers pane.

5. Double-click the new layer name and key **Left Navigation** in the Layer name text box.

6. Add two more layers named **Main Navigation** and **Content**, as shown in Figure 1-5.

FIGURE 1-5
Layers named

Setting Up the Background

Now that the document is organized into layers, you are ready to work on the individual elements of the page. Maintaining consistency in your page layout and design helps ensure a good site visitor experience. Visitors should be able to scan a page and click through the different pages in your site without becoming confused. Visitors may be frustrated if all the pages have a different look or if the navigation is in a different place on each page. For this reason, the design document calls for a set of background elements in the comp to provide the basis for all the pages. The elements on the other layers may change slightly, but the stable background elements unify the design of the site.

In the next set of steps you implement the ideas from the design document requiring "color to group related pieces of information and separate them from other information" and "white space to break up dense blocks of information." You generate different regions, using color blocks to designate the content areas. First you create the following regions on the background: a white region for most of the content, a khaki region for the left navigation content, and blue regions for the main navigation and footer navigation. Then you will draw lines to separate these color areas.

Create the Background

1. Make sure the **Background** layer is selected. If a grid is displayed on the canvas, click **View** on the menu bar, point to **Grid**, and click **Show Grid** to hide the grid.

2. In the Tools panel, select the **Rectangle** tool, as shown in Figure 1-6.

3. Draw a rectangle in the Document window by positioning the cross-hair pointer over the canvas and dragging downward and to the right. Don't worry about the size and position of the rectangle. You will address these issues later in this exercise.

4. Use the **Pointer** tool to select the rectangle. Select white (**#FFFFFF**) for the fill color and dark gray (**#666666**) for the stroke color.

5. In the Property inspector, set the width of the rectangle to **657** and the height to **760**.

Inside the Design

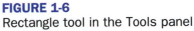

Designers tend to place objects high on a page and leave a greater margin at the bottom to increase the balance of content-heavy pages. With lots of text on a page, centering content somewhat higher than the center of the page creates the illusion of page balance. On the Experience Bank site, the white wrapper rectangle will "wrap" or hold the majority of the content, so it is centered slightly above the center of the canvas.

6. Set the position of the rectangle in the Property inspector by setting X to **22** and Y to **10**. Press **Enter** (Windows) or **Return** (Macintosh) to accept the changes. See Figure 1-7.

7. Double-click the object **Rectangle** in the Layers panel and rename it **wrapper**. Press **Enter** (Windows) or **Return** (Macintosh).

FIGURE 1-7
Background page layout

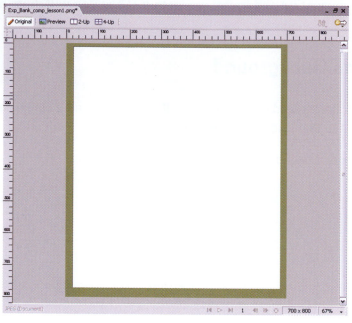

8. Save the file.

   Now that the region for the main content is set, you create the regions for the main navigation and the footer navigation.

9. Make sure you are still on the **Background** layer. Select the **Rectangle** tool and draw a new rectangle to represent the footer navigation region.

10. Set the rectangle properties as shown in Figure 1-8.

    • Width: **655**
    • Height: **20**
    • Fill Color: Dark Blue (**#000099**)
    • Stroke Color: **None**
    • X position: **23**
    • Y position: **749**

FIGURE 1-8
Rectangle for footer navigation

11. Select the **Line** tool and draw a straight line across the page. Set the stroke properties of the line as follows:
- Width: **655**
- Height: **1**
- Fill Color: **None**
- Stroke Color: Darker Blue (**#330099**)
- Stroke Tip size: **2**
- Stroke category: **Pencil, 1-Pixel Hard**
- X position: **23**
- Y position: **749**

FIGURE 1-9
Outline for footer navigation

The dark blue rectangle and darker blue line create the region for the footer. You use the darker blue line to outline the shape on only one side instead of using a stroke for the full rectangle. This outline creates a sharp visual distinction between the main content region and the footer region. You use this same technique to create the region for the main navigation. Because these regions consist of two objects, you group them together in the next section.

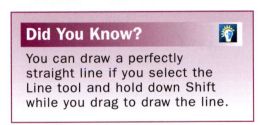

Did You Know?

You can draw a perfectly straight line if you select the Line tool and hold down Shift while you drag to draw the line.

12. Save the file.

13. Make sure you are still on the **Background** layer. Use the **Rectangle** tool and draw a new rectangle to represent the main navigation region.

14. Set the rectangle properties to be as shown in Figure 1-10.
- Width: **655**
- Height: **21**
- Fill Color: Dark Blue (**#000099**)
- Stroke Color: **None**
- X position: **23**
- Y position: **61**

FIGURE 1-10
Rectangle for main navigation

15. Use the **Line** tool to draw a straight line across the page. Set the stroke properties of the line as follows:
- Width: **655**
- Height: **1**
- Fill Color: **None**
- Stroke Color: Dark Blue (**#330099**)
- Stroke Tip size: **1**
- Stroke category: **Pencil, 1-Pixel Hard**
- X position: **23**
- Y position: **81**

16. Save the file.

The last region to create is the area for the left navigation.

17. Draw a rectangle to represent the left navigation and set its properties as follows:
- Width: **200**
- Height: **666**
- Fill Color: Khaki (**#D4DCB7**)
- Stroke Color: **None**
- X position: **23**
- Y position: **82**

18. Use the **Line** tool to draw a straight line down the page. Set the stroke properties of the line as follows:
- Width: **1**
- Height: **665**
- Fill Color: **None**
- Stroke Color: Pale Khaki (**#C9CFB6**)
- Stroke Tip size: **2**
- Stroke category: **Basic, Soft Line**
- X position: **224**
- Y position: **83**

19. Save the file.

Grouping and Naming Objects in Layers

To block out the page, you created regions corresponding to the main content areas on the Experience Bank checking page. The regions for the main navigation, the footer navigation, and the left navigation are made up of multiple objects. To better organize these areas, you will group these objects together and rename the resulting object.

Group and Name Objects in Layers

1. Open the **Layers** panel and make sure the **Background** layer is expanded. If it isn't, click the **Plus (+)** icon (Windows), as shown in Figure 1-11, or the arrow (Macintosh) to the left of the layer name.

   You can see all the objects you've drawn, such as rectangles and lines (paths). You can select the objects either on the canvas or on the Layers panel. Selecting objects on the Layers panel makes it easier to select objects that sit on top of each other.

> ### Inside the Design
>
> Designers create regions on a page by using multiple colors and textures. They group related regions so team members can easily understand and update the design based on client feedback.

FIGURE 1-11
Layers panel

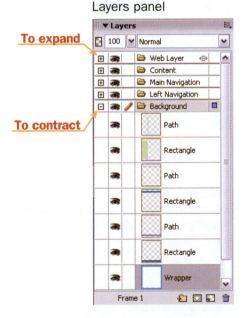

2. Click in the Layers panel to select the dark blue rectangle you drew for the footer navigation.

3. Hold down **Shift** and click to select the line (path) you drew as an outline near the footer in the Layers panel.

The two elements that make up the footer are now selected, as shown in Figure 1-12.

FIGURE 1-12
Footer elements selected

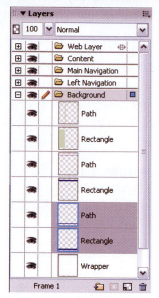

4. Select **Modify** on the menu bar and then select **Group**. The objects are now grouped, as shown in Figure 1-13.

FIGURE 1-13
Grouped objects in the Layers panel

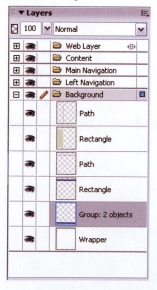

5. Double-click the new grouped object name, and rename it **Footer Nav**.

6. Click in the **Layers** panel to select the dark blue rectangle you drew for the main navigation.

7. Hold down **Shift** and click to select the line (path) you drew as an outline near the main navigation in the Layers panel.

8. Select **Modify** on the menu bar and then select **Group**. The objects are now grouped.

9. Double-click the new grouped object name, and rename it **Main Nav**.

10. Repeat the same steps to group the color block and path you drew for the left navigation, and rename the new object **Left Nav**.

   You now have four objects that make up the background as shown in Figure 1-14.

FIGURE 1-14
Color blocks for the background

11. Save the file.

Creating the Left Navigation

Now that the document is blocked into content areas, you add specific details to create the page comp. According to the design document, the size of the site is large enough to warrant multiple types of navigation. When blocking the document, you created a color block for the left navigation. This will serve as a sub-navigation for each section of the site a visitor selects on the main navigation. In the next set of steps, you build a sample sub-navigation to illustrate how button areas might appear and the type of text the sub-navigation can contain.

   The sample sub-navigation will have five button areas that are not expanded and one area that is

Inside the Design

Designers create page comps that vary in specificity. Usually they create a comp that shows examples of different page configurations. In the Experience Bank comp, the sub-navigation is created to show how information is to be organized in the site and the types of button effects that can be used.

expanded to illustrate how a multi-tiered navigation can appear. The sample will show the sub-sections of the Personal Services section of the site—specifically, the Checking pages to which a site visitor can navigate.

 ## Create the Left Navigation

1. Make sure the **Left Navigation** layer is selected in the Layers panel.

2. Use the **Rectangle** tool to draw a small rectangle, and set its properties as follows:
   - Width: **160**
   - Height: **21**
   - Fill Color: Olive green (**#C0CC95**) (The second character is zero.)
   - Stroke Color: Dark olive green (**#616945**)
   - X position: **43**
   - Y position: **109**

3. Make sure the **Left Navigation** layer is selected in the Layers panel. Using the **Text** tool, key **Checking** on the rectangle you just drew. Select the text with the **Pointer** tool. Set the font properties to **Arial**, **12 pt**, **bold**, dark olive green (**#616945**), Horizontal Scale **80%**, and anti-aliasing level to **Strong Anti-Alias**, as shown in Figure 1-15.

FIGURE 1-15
Properties for Checking text

4. To be sure the text is aligned near the left side of the rectangle, set its coordinates in the Property inspector to X: **46** and Y: **111**.

The button area in the Left Nav area for Checking should appear as in Figure 1-16.

FIGURE 1-16
Checking button area

Next you create button areas for Savings, Retirement, Investments, and Financial Planning that are similar to the button area for Checking. As you place these areas, you will leave space for an expanded button area between Checking and Savings that you will create later in the lesson.

5. Make sure the **Left Navigation** layer is selected in the Layers panel. Use the **Rectangle** tool to draw four rectangles with the following properties, and use the **Text** tool to create the specified text and align it according to the specified coordinates.

Savings button area
- Width: **160**
- Height: **21**
- Fill Color: Olive green (**#C0CC95**)
- Stroke Color: Dark olive green (**#616945**)
- X position: **43**
- Y position: **209**
- Text: **Savings**
- Text font, size, color, and style: **Arial**, **12 pt**, dark olive green (**#616945**), **bold**
- Text horizontal scale: **80%**
- Text anti-aliasing level: **Strong Anti-Alias**
- Text X position: **46**
- Text Y position: **211**

Retirement button area
- Width: **160**
- Height: **21**
- Fill Color: Olive green (**#C0CC95**)
- Stroke Color: Dark olive green (**#616945**)
- X position: **43**
- Y position: **229**
- Text: **Retirement**
- Text font, size, color, and style: **Arial**, **12 pt**, dark olive green (**#616945**), **bold**
- Text horizontal scale: **80%**
- Text anti-aliasing level: **Strong Anti-Alias**
- Text X position: **46**
- Text Y position: **231**

Investments button area
- Width: **160**
- Height: **21**
- Fill Color: Olive green (**#C0CC95**)
- Stroke Color: Dark olive green (**#616945**)
- X position: **43**
- Y position: **248**
- Text: **Investments**
- Text font, size, color, and style: **Arial**, **12 pt**, dark olive green (**#616945**), **bold**
- Text horizontal scale: **80%**
- Text anti-aliasing level: **Strong Anti-Alias**
- Text X position: **46**
- Text Y position: **250**

Financial Planning button area
- Width: **160**
- Height: **21**
- Fill Color: Olive green (**#C0CC95**)
- Stroke Color: Dark olive green (**#616945**)
- X position: **43**
- Y position: **268**
- Text: **Financial Planning**
- Text font, size, color, and style: **Arial**, **12 pt**, dark olive green (**#616945**), **bold**
- Text horizontal scale: **80%**
- Text anti-aliasing level: **Strong Anti-Alias**
- Text X position: **46**
- Text Y position: **270**

The sub-navigation now includes five button areas to navigate within the Personal Services section of the site, as shown in Figure 1-17, with an open space for the expanded button area you build in the next set of steps.

FIGURE 1-17
Sub-navigation with five button areas

6. Save the file.

Next, you complete the sub-navigation by creating an illustration of an expanded button area.

7. Make sure the **Left Navigation** layer is selected in the Layers panel. Create a rectangle with the following properties:
- Width: **160**
- Height: **80**
- Fill Color: Cream (**#EFF2E6**)
- Stroke Color: Dark olive green (**#616945**)
- X position: **43**
- Y position: **130**

8. Make sure the **Left Navigation** layer is selected in the Layers panel. Create a text block with the following terms, as shown in Figure 1-18. Press **Enter** (Windows) or **Return** (Macintosh) between terms. Set the font properties to **Arial 10 pt**, dark olive green (**#616945**), Horizontal Scale **80%**, Leading **180%**, anti-aliasing level **Strong Anti-Alias**, X position **49**, Y position **135**, and **Left** alignment.

Free Checking

Interest Checking

Copper Checking

Titanium Checking

FIGURE 1-18
Completed sub-navigation

9. Group each object that holds a button area rectangle with its respective text block and rename it with the name of the text block as shown in Figure 1-19. For the last text block you created, you can group it with its expanded rectangle area and rename it Free Checking. You should now have the following objects on the Left Navigation layer: Free Checking, Financial Planning, Investments, Retirement, Savings, and Checking.

FIGURE 1-19
Grouped and renamed objects on Left Navigation layer

10. Save the file.

Adding Content

A final step in creating the Experience Bank comp is to add some mock content to the page so the client can visualize how the design will come together with their content. In the next set of exercises, you add mock content to illustrate a page from the Checking section of the site.

Inside the Design

Designers research what type of content is on other sites of the same genre so they can mock up a realistic page for the client. In the Experience Bank comp, some realistic content and some gibberish is used to show how different blocks of text and data might appear on the page.

Add Content

1. Make sure the **Content** layer is selected in the Layers panel.

2. Use the **Text** tool to key **PERSONAL SERVICES** and set the properties in the Property inspector to be as shown in Figure 1-20.

   - Font: **Arial 11 pt**, **bold**
   - Color: Dark olive green (**#616945**)
   - Kerning: **2**
   - Horizontal scale: **100%**
   - Anti-aliasing level: **No Anti-Alias**
   - Leading: **100%**
   - X position: **44**
   - Y position: **92**

FIGURE 1-20
Personal Services text properties

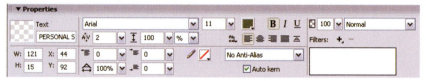

3. Use the **Text** tool to key **CHECKING** and set the properties in the Property inspector to be as shown in Figure 1-21.

- Font: **Arial 15 pt**, **bold**
- Color: Dark olive green (**#616945**)
- Kerning: **2**
- Horizontal scale: **100%**
- Anti-aliasing level: **No Anti-Alias**
- Leading: **100%**
- X position: **247**
- Y position: **92**

FIGURE 1-21
Checking text properties

4. Use the **Text** tool to key **Personal | Small Business | Commercial | Brokerage | About Us | Branches | Contact Us | Help | Careers** and set the properties in the Property inspector to be as shown in Figure 1-22.

- Font: **Arial 10 pt**
- Color: White (**#FFFFFF**)
- Kerning: **0**
- Horizontal scale: **100%**
- Anti-aliasing level: **Strong Anti-Alias**
- Leading: **130%**
- X position: **123**
- Y position: **753**
- Alignment: **Center**

FIGURE 1-22
Footer text properties

5. Use the **Text** tool to click in the footer text you just created and place the cursor after the word "Careers." Press **Enter** (Windows) or **Return** (Macintosh) and key **A Fictitious Company**. Select that text and set the properties in the Property inspector to be as shown in Figure 1-23.

- Font: **Arial 8 pt**
- Color: White (**#FFFFFF**)
- Kerning: **0**
- Horizontal scale: **100%**
- Anti-aliasing level: **Strong Anti-Alias**
- Leading: **130%**
- Space preceding paragraph: **5**

FIGURE 1-23
Second part of footer text properties

The footer now appears on two lines, as shown in Figure 1-24, centered in the footer color block you created earlier.

FIGURE 1-24
Footer

6. Double-click the name of this footer object in the Layers panel and rename it **Footer**.

Next you import two text blocks to serve as placeholder text, demonstrating how the design accommodates large blocks of text.

7. Make sure the **Content** layer is selected. Click **File** in the menu bar, and then click **Import**.

8. Navigate to and select **gibberish_text_1.jpg**, in the data files for this project. Click **Open**.

The image does not immediately appear on the canvas, but notice the bracket shape of the import pointer, as shown in Figure 1-25.

FIGURE 1-25
Import pointer

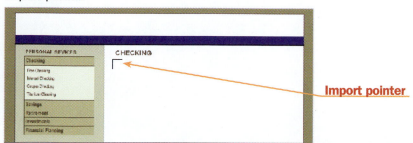

Import pointer

9. Position the import pointer where you want to place the upper-left corner of the image. Click to place the image under "Checking." You will fine-tune the placement in the next step, so don't worry about being precise.

10. Be sure the text block is selected and set X to **253** and Y to **122**. Rename the object in the Layers panel to **Textblock 1**.

11. Import the second text block, **gibberish_text_2.jpg**, to the Content layer under Textblock 1 and set X to **250** and Y to **650**. Rename this new object **Textblock 2**.

Your comp now has two text blocks—one at the top of the comp and one near the bottom, as shown in Figure 1-26.

FIGURE 1-26
Text blocks on comp

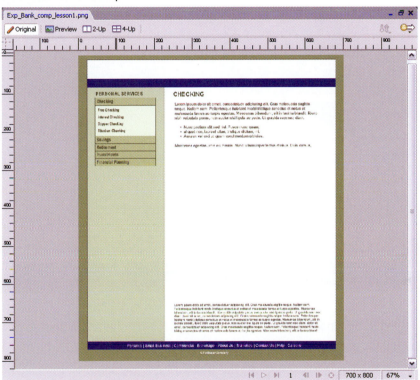

Bank Web pages also tend to have advertisements for other services offered by the bank. Next you add some sample ads to the comp, illustrating how these would work in the design.

12. Make sure the **Content** layer is selected.

13. Import the first advertisement, **atm_ad.gif,** in the data files for this project.

14. Click anywhere on the canvas to place the imported image.

15. Be sure the new image is selected and set X to **43** and Y to **455**. Rename this new object **ATM ad**.

16. Import the second ad, **mortgage_ad.gif**, to the Content layer and set X to **43** and Y to **302**. Rename this new object **Mortgage ad**.

Your comp now has two ads on the page, as shown in Figure 1-27.

FIGURE 1-27
Ads on comp

Next you bring in the final content aspects: the logo for the site and a sample data table that might appear on a page in the Checking section of the site.

17. Make sure the **Content** layer is selected.

18. Import **Exp_Bank_logo.jpg**, in the data files for this project.

19. Click anywhere on the canvas to place the imported image.

20. Be sure the new image is selected and set X to **32** and Y to **25**. Rename this new object **Logo**.

21. Import the data table image, **checking_table.jpg**, to the Content layer and set X to **251** and Y to **252**. Rename this new object **Checking table** and save the file.

Your comp now has sufficient sample content and placeholder content to illustrate the design of the site and how it might apply to a page in the site, as shown in Figure 1-28. In the next lesson, you complete this comp by adding the main navigation bar.

FIGURE 1-28
Checking page comp

CREATING NAVIGATION BARS

OBJECTIVES:

Upon completion of this lesson, you will be able to:

- Create and edit buttons for navigation.
- Apply effects to buttons.

Estimated time to complete this lesson: 30 – 45 minutes

Introduction

Creating a comp for the Experience Bank site involves laying out the regions for content, inserting sample and placeholder content, and creating a main navigation bar. Because the navigation bar will complete the comp, you build it in on the comp page to best match any rollover effects you create. A rollover is an image that changes appearance when you move the mouse pointer over it or click it.

In this lesson, you learn how to create a button symbol and how to use that button symbol to build the other buttons in the navigation bar.

Creating Buttons

A *navigation bar*, or *nav bar*, is a group of buttons that provide links to different areas of a Web site. The nav bar generally remains consistent throughout the site, providing a constant method of navigation, no matter where the visitor is within the site. The nav bar looks the same from Web page to Web page, but in some cases, the links may be specific to the function of each page.

A navigation bar is made up of *buttons*, which are simply objects that perform some action when you click them. Most Web pages contain buttons that direct you to other information on the Web. Buttons are made up of different states to give site visitors feedback on their actions, such as changing appearance when visitors move the mouse pointer over the button or when they click the button. There are four common button states, and each state reflects a particular type of visitor interaction with the button:

- Up   The visitor is not interacting with the button.
- Over   The visitor moves the pointer over the button.
- Down   The visitor clicks the button.
- Over While Down   The visitor holds the pointer over the button on a page where that button is already depressed.

A button will always have the Up and Over states; the Down and Over While Down states are optional. For additional information on buttons, see the Learn More feature, "Button States."

The Experience Bank Web site flowchart shows five main areas of the site that site visitors should be able to reach from any page. These areas will make up the buttons in the main navigation. You will create the first button for the navigation by using the Button Editor and then reuse this button to help create similar buttons for the rest of the navigation.

 ## Create a Button

1. Make sure the file you created in the previous lesson is open, or open the file named **Exp_Bank_comp_Lesson2.png**. This file is located in the data files for this project. If you use the data file, save it as **Exp_Bank_comp_[YourName].png**.

2. Make sure the **Main Navigation** layer is selected. Click **Edit** in the menu bar, click **Insert**, and then click **New Button**.

   The Button Editor opens on the Up state by default, and the color of the background in the editor is the same as the canvas color, as shown in Figure 2-1.

FIGURE 2-1
Button Editor

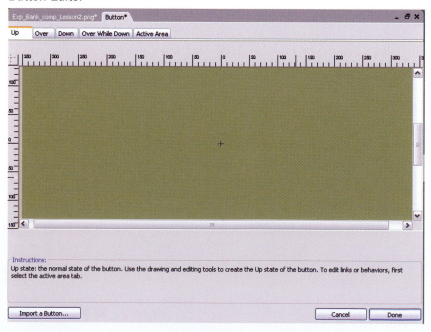

3. Create a rectangle shape with a width of **131** and height of **20**.

4. Set the stroke color to black (**#000000**). Create a gradient fill for the rectangle and choose the **Bars** gradient as the type.

5. Set three gradient swatches: a blue (**#625EF3**) swatch to the far left, a darker blue (**#513CC0**—the final character is zero) swatch a fifth of the way along the gradient color ramp, and a midnight blue (**#3E1586**) swatch a sixth of the way back from the right edge of the color ramp as shown in Figure 2-2.

Inside the Design

Designers experiment with different sizes and shapes for buttons before settling on a size that is best for a site. The button needs to be large enough to draw attention while not distracting from the overall design of the page. For the Experience Bank navigation bar, you implement the final decision made by the designer.

FIGURE 2-2
Gradient swatches for button

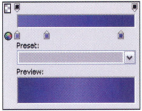

6. Set the gradient handles so the round handle is near the top of the button and the square handle is near the base of the button, as shown in Figure 2-3.

FIGURE 2-3
Gradient handles for button

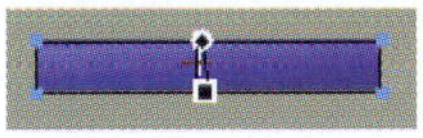

Next add placeholder text for the button; you will reuse this button to create the other buttons in the navigation bar.

7. While still in the Button Editor, use the **Text** tool to key **Label** in the rectangle you just created.

8. Use the **Pointer** tool to drag the middle anchor point on each side of the text, which expands the edges of the text box. Expand them to match the edges of the rectangle, as shown in Figure 2-4. (You set the text size in the next step.) Note that only the width needs to be expanded, not the height.

Note

The name Label is temporary. You rename the buttons later in this exercise.

FIGURE 2-4
Text box expanded

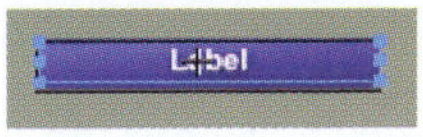

9. Set the properties for the text in the Property inspector as follows:
- Font: **Arial 11 pt**, **bold**
- Color: White (**#FFFFFF**)
- Kerning: **1**
- Horizontal scale: **100%**
- Leading: **100%**
- Live Effects: **Drop Shadow** with a distance of **2** (leave all other properties as default)

The Up state for the button is now complete, as shown in Figure 2-5. Next you build the other states of the button.

FIGURE 2-5
Up state of the button

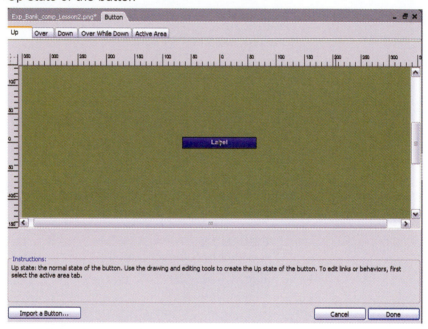

10. Select the **Over** tab in the Button Editor to create the Over state of the button.

11. Click the **Copy Up Graphic** button. The Up state graphic displays in the editor.

12. Using the **Pointer** tool, select the rectangle and change its opacity in the Property inspector to **70%**, as shown in Figure 2-6.

FIGURE 2-6
Opacity setting in Property inspector

13. Select the **Down** tab in the Button Editor to create the Down state of the button.

14. Click **Copy Over Graphic**. The Over state graphic displays in the editor. Be sure **Include nav bar Down state** is checked, as shown in Figure 2-7.

FIGURE 2-7
Check box to include the Down state

15. Using the **Pointer** tool, select the rectangle and change its opacity in the Property inspector to **100%**.

16. Make sure the rectangle is selected and add an **Inner Glow** Live Effect for which the width is **10**, the opacity is **30%**, and the color is black, as shown in Figure 2-8. (Accept the default values for the other two settings.)

FIGURE 2-8
Inner glow for Down state

17. Click **Done** to exit the Button Editor. Your new button appears on the center of the canvas.

18. Use the **Pointer** tool to select this button and set X to **23** and Y to **61**.

19. With the button still selected, change the text in the Property inspector from Label to **PERSONAL**, as shown in Figure 2-9.

FIGURE 2-9
Change text to PERSONAL in Property inspector

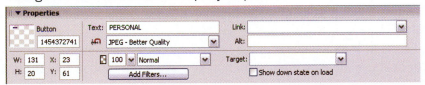

20. Double-click the name of the object in the Main Navigation layer and rename it **personal_button**. Save the file.

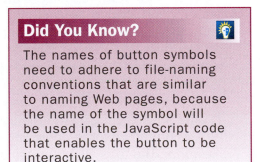

Did You Know?

The names of button symbols need to adhere to file-naming conventions that are similar to naming Web pages, because the name of the symbol will be used in the JavaScript code that enables the button to be interactive.

Using the Library to Create the Navigation Bar

When you created the button, Fireworks stored it in the library as a symbol. Symbols are useful whenever you want to reuse a graphic element, such as when you need similar buttons for a navigation bar. After you create a button symbol, you can use the button over and over by placing instances throughout your document. An instance is a representation of a Fireworks symbol. When you edit the symbol object (the original), the instances (copies) automatically change to reflect the modifications to the symbol. Buttons are a special kind of symbol because you can edit the text on an instance without changing the original symbol. For additional information on the types of symbols that can be stored in the library, see the Tips & Techniques feature "Symbols and the Library."

You continue to build the navigation bar by adding instances of the reusable button symbol you created in the previous exercise. The button symbol is stored in the Library panel.

Learn More

BUTTON STATES

A button can have up to four different states. Each state represents the button's appearance in response to a mouse event:

The Up state is the default or at-rest appearance of the button.

The Over state is the way the button appears when the mouse pointer is moved over it. This state alerts the visitor that clicking the mouse is likely to result in an action.

The Down state represents the button after it is clicked. Often a concave image of the button is used to signify that it has been pressed. This button state typically represents the current Web page on multi-button navigation bars.

The Over While Down state is the appearance when the visitor moves the pointer over a button that is in the Down state. This button state typically shows that the pointer is over the button for the current Web page on multi-button navigation bars.

With the Button Editor, you can create all these different button states, as well as an area for triggering the button action.

The Button Editor is where you create and edit a JavaScript button symbol in Fireworks. The tabs along the top of the Button Editor correspond to the four button states and the active area. The tips on each option in the Button Editor help you make design decisions for all four button states.

Create Additional Buttons

1. Open the **Library** panel by clicking **Window** on the menu bar and selecting **Library**.

   The Library panel opens and displays the button you just created, as shown in Figure 2-10.

   FIGURE 2-10
   Library with button symbol

2. Make sure the **Main Navigation** layer is selected and drag the button from the library onto the canvas to create an instance of the button, as shown in Figure 2-11.

   FIGURE 2-11
   New button instance on the canvas

3. With the new button instance selected, set X to **154** and Y to **61**.

   These settings place the new button directly beside the Personal button, as shown in Figure 2-12.

   FIGURE 2-12
   Button placement

4. Make sure the new button instance is selected, and change its text in the Property inspector to **SMALL BUSINESS**.

5. Double-click the object in the Main Navigation layer and rename it **sm_business_button**.

6. Drag a new instance of the button symbol to the canvas on the Main Navigation layer and set its properties in the Property inspector as follows:
   • Text: **COMMERCIAL**
   • X value: **285**
   • Y value: **61**

7. Rename the object **commercial_button**.

8. Drag a new instance of the button symbol to the Canvas on the Main Navigation layer and set its properties in the Property inspector as follows:
- Text: **BROKERAGE**
- X value: **416**
- Y value: **61**

9. Rename the object in the Main Navigation layer to **brokerage_button**.

10. Drag a new instance of the button symbol to the Canvas on the Main Navigation layer and set its Properties in the Property inspector as follows:
- Text: **ABOUT US**
- X value: **547**
- Y value: **61**

11. Rename the object in the Main Navigation layer to **about_us_button**.

You now have a complete navigation bar, as shown in Figure 2-13.

FIGURE 2-13
Button navigation bar completed

12. Click **Image Preview** view, as shown in Figure 2-14, and move the pointer over each button in turn to test the rollovers of the buttons and how they appear on the comp.

FIGURE 2-14
Preview view

Now that the comp is complete, you will save the comp as an image file that can be shared with the client.

Note to Macintosh users: If you can not complete step 12 and you see a message that Fireworks could not render the data base because the file is open in another application, close the PNG file. In the Finder, locate and select the file. Click **File** in the menu bar, and click **Get Info**. If the file **Kind** is not **Fireworks document**, select **Fireworks 8** on the **Open with** menu. Open the PNG file in Fireworks, and repeat step 12.

13. Save the file.

14. Click **File** in the menu bar, and click **Save as**.

15. Navigate to the folder where you will save your work. Leave the filename as it is and select **JPEG** in the **Save as type** menu (Windows), as shown in Figure 2-15, or in the **Save as** menu (Macintosh). Click **Save**.

FIGURE 2-15
Save as JPEG

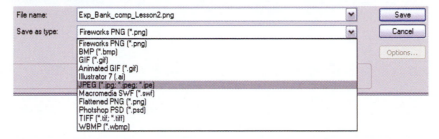

16. Close the file. If you followed step 13 and saved the PNG file before you saved the file as a JPEG in step 15, you can click **No** if Fireworks asks whether you want to save a Fireworks PNG before closing the file.

Your comp is now saved to show the design and sample content with that design. The buttons you created are not active in the comp because this is an image file for the client to review. In the next lesson, you save a working navigation bar separate from the comp to provide to the Web site developer to use in the site.

Tips & Techniques

SYMBOLS AND THE LIBRARY

Fireworks has three types of symbols: graphic, animation, and button. Each has unique characteristics for its specific use. Instances are representations of Fireworks symbols. When the symbol object (the original) is edited, the instances (copies) automatically change to reflect the modifications to the symbol.

Symbols are useful whenever you want to reuse a graphic element. You can place instances in multiple Fireworks documents and retain the association with the symbol. Symbols are helpful for creating buttons and animating objects across multiple frames.

When you double-click an instance to edit it, you're actually editing the symbol itself in the Symbol Editor or Button Editor. To edit only the current instance, you need to break the link between the instance and the symbol. This permanently breaks the relationship between the two, however, and any future edits you make to the symbol won't be reflected in the former instance.

Button symbols have several convenient features that allow you to retain the symbol-instance relationship for a group of buttons while assigning unique button text and URLs to each instance.

The Library panel stores animation, graphic, and button symbols you create in the current document. It also stores symbols you import into the current document. The Library panel is specific to the current document, but you can use the symbols from one library in more than one Fireworks document by importing and exporting, cutting and pasting, or dragging and dropping.

OPTIMIZING AND EXPORTING FOR THE WEB

OBJECTIVES:

Upon completion of this lesson, you will be able to:

- Copy and paste a navigation bar into a new document.
- Optimize a navigation bar.
- Export a navigation bar.

Estimated time to complete this lesson: 15 – 20 minutes

Introduction

The navigation bar was created on the comp to best gauge the colors that are used for the different states of the button and to build a complete comp to share with the client. Now that you have saved the comp, the last step is to save the navigation bar in a format that a developer can put into a Web page.

In this lesson, you will take the navigation bar from the comp and place it in a new document. You will make sure the different states of the button are seen in the new document and then optimize and export the navigation bar.

Copying the Navigation Bar

The navigation bar is currently in the comp. It also needs to be in a separate document so you can save it for use in a Web site. Fireworks opens a new document with the dimensions of whatever is saved in the Clipboard. To be sure the dimensions are correct, you copy the current navigation bar and then paste it into a new document.

 Copy the Navigation Bar

1. Open the PNG file you created in the previous lesson, or open the file named **Exp_Bank_comp_Lesson3.png**. This file is located in the data files for this project. If you use the data file, save it as **Exp_Bank_comp_[YourName].png**.

2. Hold down **Shift** and click each of the buttons in the Main Navigation layer to select them all at once, as shown in Figure 3-1.

FIGURE 3-1
Select all buttons

3. Click **Edit** on the menu bar, and then click **Copy** to copy the navigation bar. The full navigation bar is now copied to the Clipboard.

4. Click **File** on the menu bar, and then click **New** to create a new document. The New Document dialog box opens, with the dimensions of the Clipboard set as its width and height, as shown in Figure 3-2.

Note ✅

When a button is selected, note the small arrow. If you were to double-click the object, you would enter its editing mode. If your view is set to see slices, which indicate the interactive regions, you will also see a small pinwheel object in the center of the object. You can use this shortcut tool in Fireworks to create simple rollovers and pop-up menus.

FIGURE 3-2
New Document dialog box with Clipboard dimensions

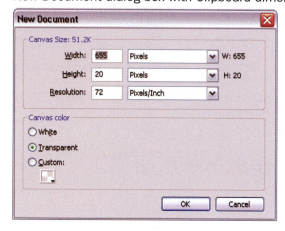

5. Click **OK**. A new canvas opens with the dimensions as set in the dialog box.

6. Click **Edit** on the menu bar, and then click **Paste**. The navigation bar is pasted on the new canvas.

7. Save this new file and name it **Exp_Bank_nav_[YourName].png**.

Optimizing Navigation Bars

A good practice is to optimize any image as the last step in preparing it for the Web. Optimization reduces the file size of an image. Because this navigation bar has a gradient in the buttons, the best way to preserve it is to use JPEG compression.

 ## Optimize the Navigation Bar

1. Make sure the navigation bar file is open and expand the Optimize panel. If the Optimize panel is not open, open it by clicking **Window** on the menu bar, and then clicking **Optimize**.

2. Select **JPEG - Better Quality** from the Saved settings menu, as shown in Figure 3-3.

FIGURE 3-3
Optimize panel saved settings

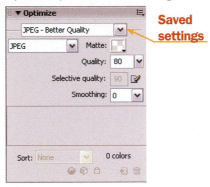

3. Save the file.

Exporting the Navigation Bar

The navigation bar is made up of images and interactivity in the Web layer of the document. The file needs to be exported to include both the JavaScript interactivity and the images. For this reason, you will export an HTML file with the JavaScript and a folder of images.

 Export the Navigation Bar

1. Make sure the navigation bar file is open. Click **File** on the menu bar, and then click **Export**. The Export dialog box opens, as shown in Figure 3-4.

FIGURE 3-4
Export dialog box

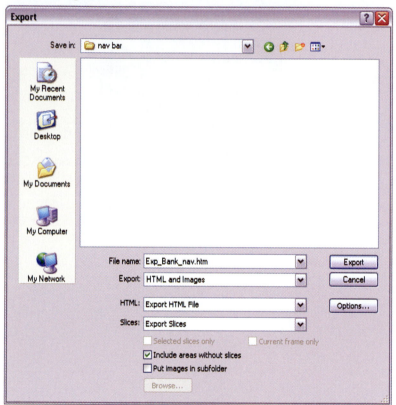

2. Navigate to the location where you will save the HTML file and select the option **Put Images in subfolder**, as shown in Figure 3-5.

FIGURE 3-5
Options for export

3. To create a subfolder for the images, click the **Browse** button in the dialog box and navigate to the same location where you will save the HTML file.

4. Create a new folder and name it **images**. In Windows, select that new folder and click **Open**; then click **Select "images"** as shown in Figure 3-6. On a Macintosh, select that new folder and click **Choose**.

FIGURE 3-6
Create and select subfolder

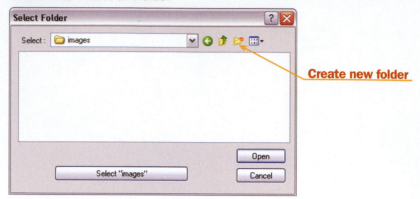

Create new folder

5. In the Export dialog box, click **Export**.

   The HTML file is saved in the folder and the images are saved in the images subfolder you created. You can open your HTML file in a browser window to see button rollovers on a page; however, the Web site developer will need to assign a link to each button when adding the nav bar to a Web page.

SUMMARY

You have successfully created a page composition and navigation bar for use on the Experience Bank Web site.

In this project, you learned to implement the goals of the design document to produce a page design and comp with sample content. You also learned to create an interactive button navigation bar to use on a Web site.

This project concludes the Macromedia Fireworks unit of this program.

ON YOUR OWN – NAVIGATION BARS

ACTIVITY 1: CREATING BUTTON NAVIGATION BARS

You have learned how to build the different states of a button navigation bar and then export this navigation bar for use on a Web site. Apply these same techniques to build the navigation bar for the Poisonous Frogs Web site, which requires buttons for the following pages: Home, Green Frog, Gold Frog, Blue Frog, and Black Frog. The navigation bar itself should measure 600 × 40 pixels.

You can review techniques on how to create buttons in Lessons 2 and 3.

1. Open a new document in Fireworks and set the size larger than you will need, such as 700 × 700 pixels.

   Since the width of the navigation bar should be 600 pixels and the height should be 40 pixels, each of the five buttons should be 120 pixels wide and 40 pixels tall.

2. Draw a rectangle that measures 120 × 40 pixels, set the stroke and fill colors to dark green, and add a smooth inner bevel.

3. Use the **Pointer** tool to select the rectangle image. Click **Modify** on the menu bar, click **Symbol**, and then click **Convert to Symbol**. Select **Button** as the type, to convert the rectangle image to a button symbol.

4. Click **Modify** on the menu bar, click **Symbol**, and then click **Edit Symbol** to open the Button Editor.

5. On the Up state in the Button Editor, use the **Text** tool to key **Home** on the button in the Up state. Adjust the font and size to **Arial, 20-point**. Set the text color to yellow. Extend the ends of the text box to the ends of the button and center the text so that future instances of your button can hold longer text that will fit correctly.

6. Click the **Over** tab and click **Copy Up Graphic**. Make the following changes to the rectangle:
   - Change the stroke color to yellow, with a tip size of **2** pixels.
   - Adjust the inner bevel to be **Highlighted** rather than **Raised**.

7. Click the **Down** tab and click **Copy Over Graphic**. Make the following change to the rectangle:
   - Adjust the inner bevel to be **Inset** rather than **Highlighted**.

8. Click **Done** in the Button Editor to see your new button on the canvas.

9. In the Property inspector, select **JPEG Better Quality** in the **Button export options** menu.

10. Open the **Library** panel and drag four more instances of the button onto the canvas. Align the tops of these instances, and arrange them side-by-side.

11. Select the second button and use the Property inspector to change the text to **Green Frog**. Repeat this process with the remaining buttons:
    - Text for the third button: **Gold Frog**
    - Text for the fourth button: **Blue Frog**
    - Text for the fifth button: **Black Frog**

12. Fit the canvas and save the file as **button_nav.png**.

13. Export the navigation bar for use on a Web site. Be sure to save the slice images in a subfolder.

MACROMEDIA FLASH 8

MACROMEDIA FLASH 8

IN THIS UNIT YOU WILL LEARN TO:

- Follow a design document and storyboard to define the properties of an animated billboard.

- Draw and animate simple shapes and text to create an animated billboard for a Web site.

- Follow a design document and storyboard to produce an online documentary.

- Use Flash to simulate film-style techniques and effects to tell a story.

- Create user-friendly navigation and features that provide ongoing feedback and put the audience in control of their online experience.

- Follow a design document and storyboard to produce an online gallery of video clips.

- Create Flash Video (FLV) files and prepare video for display on the Web.

- Learn methods for improving Flash performance by storing and accessing content outside the main FLA document.

- Ensure that your Flash documents are readable, usable, and accessible for the entire target audience.

Summary

Although best known for its animated text and graphics, Macromedia Flash 8 is an excellent tool for producing advanced interactivity, rich content for mobile devices, and high-quality video for Web sites.

In this unit you build three projects that will help you understand rich media design as well as develop the technical skills needed to implement the designs. To begin engaging in these projects, you first need to become familiar with Flash 8 and rich media design on the Web.

Getting To Know Macromedia Flash 8

Understanding Macromedia Flash

Animation, synchronized sound, engaging interactivity, film-style transitions, and high-quality Web video are all signs that you are viewing content created with Macromedia Flash.

You might think a Web experience this compelling would take an unbearably long time to download. But fast downloads is one of the reasons Flash has become so popular with Web developers and site visitors alike.

Flash content is smaller than HTML content because it uses its own compression scheme that optimizes vector and bitmap content differently than images typically added to HTML pages.

What are Vectors and Bitmaps?

Most graphics on the Web are *bitmap* images (JPEG or GIF). Bitmap files (also called raster images) are made up of a fixed number of individual picture elements called pixels. There are several disadvantages to using bitmap images:

- If a bitmap is stretched beyond its intended size, it appears distorted (pixilated), as shown in Figure 1.

- As the image size gets bigger, so does the file size, meaning it takes longer to download from the Internet to your computer.

- When you view a bitmap image on the Web, it is reproduced on your computer pixel-by-pixel and color-by-color.

Graphics created with Flash are *vectors*. Vector images are created by using mathematical lines and curves as well as descriptions of their properties. Commands within the vector tell your computer how to display the lines and shapes, what colors to use, how wide to make the lines, and so on. Such vector commands typically require much less computer memory than the corresponding collection of pixels that would produce the same image as seen in Figure 1. This means smaller file sizes and faster download times when you create content with Flash.

Vector graphics have important benefits as well as some limitations. They are small in file size and they scale wonderfully; however, vectors are not the best choice for images with gradations of color, such as photographs. For images such as photographs, the better choice is to import the bitmaps into Flash and optimize them for use in your finished document.

FIGURE 1
Bitmap and vector images

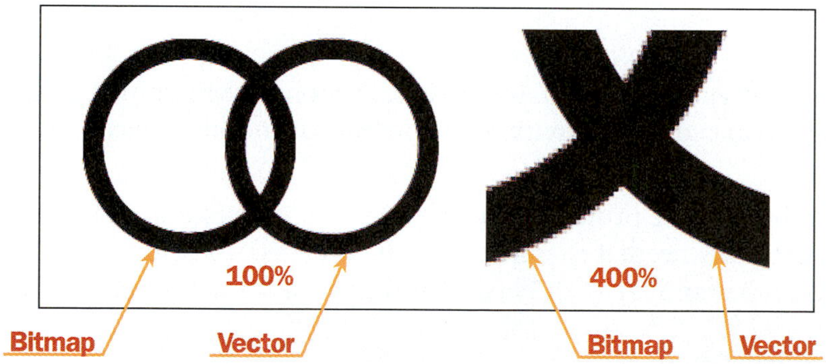

Streaming Content

Flash improves site usability by *streaming* content to the viewer's computer. This means the animation can begin before it has completely downloaded. When you make your Flash movies correctly, visitors can start viewing your site within seconds without waiting for the whole movie to download. They have something to look at right away, keeping them from losing interest and missing important information.

Macromedia Flash Player

A requirement for viewing Flash content on the Web is having Macromedia Flash Player installed. Macromedia Flash Player is the most widely distributed software in the history of the Internet and is bundled with most current Web browsers.

In some cases, you may need to deliver Flash content to people without an Internet connection, a Web browser, or Flash Player. You can do this by turning the Flash document into a *projector*, which is a stand alone executable version of the movie. Anyone with access to the projector file can view the movie. However, these files are considerably larger and require people to download the file to their desktop to view, which could pose problems for those with slower connections.

Macromedia Flash also includes a stand alone version of Flash Player (not a plug-in to a Web browser) so you can view and test projects without using a Web browser or creating projector movies.

Flash File Types

The name Flash can sometimes be a source of confusion for developers. The term "Flash" is used to describe both the authoring environment and the rich media files you produce from a Flash authoring document. The two main file types associated with Flash are FLA (pronounced "flaw") and SWF (pronounced "swif").

The FLA file is the source document used to create and edit your content. This file is used strictly for development. When you finish authoring content in the FLA document, you publish the SWF file, which can be viewed on the Web. The SWF file cannot be edited. You must return to the source FLA document to make changes and publish a new SWF file.

Figure 2 illustrates the icons used for each of the Flash file types. Use the list in Table 1 to become familiar with the file types associated with Macromedia Flash.

FIGURE 2
Flash file types

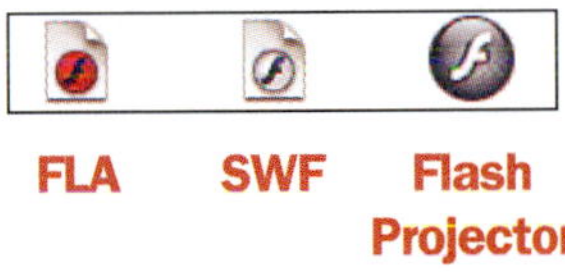

FLA   SWF   Flash
                  Projector

TABLE 1
Flash File Types

FLA	The FLA is the master project document, which stores the settings and resources for a Flash project. The FLA contains the Timeline and Stage for producing new content. FLA files have the .fla filename extension.
SWF	The SWF (Small Web File) is a file that can be added to an HTML Web page or another FLA document. SWF files are produced when you test, preview, or publish your FLA document.
HTML	When you publish a FLA document, you can choose to produce a new HTML file that can be used to display the SWF on the Web.
EXE-Projector (Windows) HQX-Projector (Mac)	EXE (Windows) and HQX (Mac) files are produced when you publish a Flash document as a projector file. A projector is a stand alone file that can play on any computer, even without a Web browser or Flash Player.

Finding Your Way Around the Flash Interface

The development environment in Flash is based on a movie metaphor. In fact, the terms Flash document and Flash "movie" are often used interchangeably. You create scenes on a Stage and these scenes play out frame-by-frame along a Timeline.

Figure 3 shows the default user interface for Flash. The key elements of this interface are shown below.

FIGURE 3
Flash 8 interface

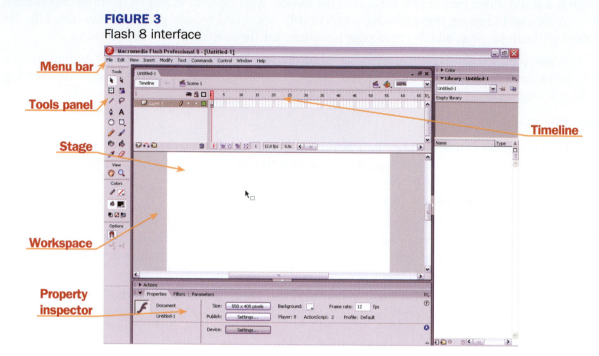

The main components of the Flash interface are the Stage, workspace, Timeline, panels, Tools panel, and Property inspector. These are detailed in Table 2.

TABLE 2
Flash 8 interface

Stage	The Stage is where your text, images, and animations appear. Objects on the Stage are visible to viewers.
Workspace	The workspace is the gray space surrounding the Stage. This is much like backstage at a theater or the area beyond the view of a camera lens. Objects can begin in the workspace and then be animated into view as if entering from offstage or out of frame.
Timeline	You use the Timeline to control the elements of your movie over time. The Timeline indicates when objects (such as text, images, or sounds) arrive onstage, how long they remain, and when changes occur.
Panels	Panels help you view, organize, and modify the elements in the document.
Tools panel	The Tools panel contains the tools for creating, placing, and modifying text and graphics.
Property inspector	You use the Property inspector to specify the properties of a selected object, such as text and graphics.

The Timeline

Use the Timeline to organize and control the movie's contents by specifying when each object appears on the Stage. By stacking objects on separate layers, you create the illusion of depth and gain more control over each object on the Stage. The Timeline can contain frames, keyframes (indicating a change), and blank (empty) keyframes, as illustrated in Figure 4. When the Flash movie is played, a playhead moves from frame to frame on the Timeline, causing each frame to appear on the Stage in a linear sequence. Each of the elements of the Timeline are described in Table 3.

FIGURE 4
Flash timeline

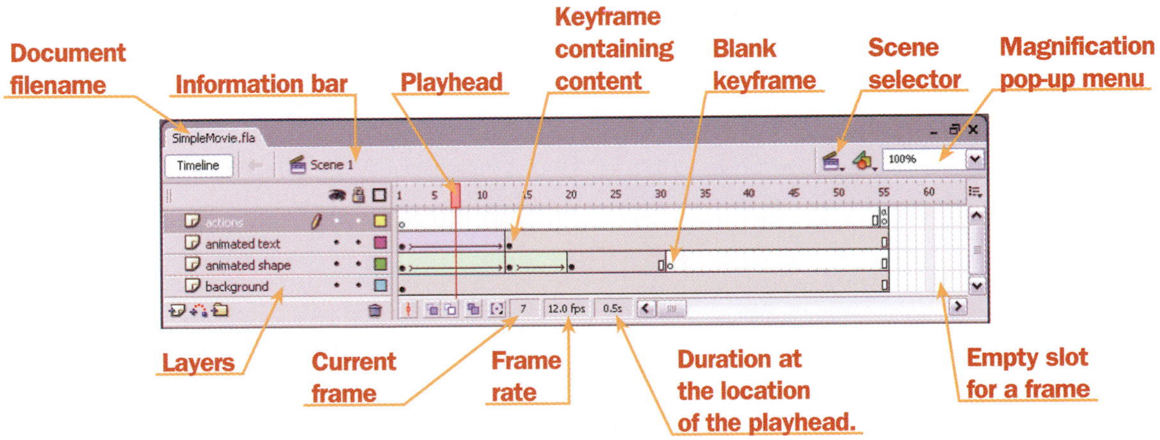

TABLE 3
Flash timeline

Layers	Layers are a way of organizing objects on the Stage. Use separate layers to draw overlapping shapes. Or use a layer for each object on the Stage so you can control the objects independently. Each layer has controls that enable you to hide or show the layer and lock it (so you can not move its contents accidentally). A new Flash project starts with one empty layer. Use the buttons below the layers to add and delete layers.
Frames	Frames are like the individual frames of a movie. The Timeline in a new Flash project appears to have many frames, but these are actually empty slots that you can define as frames or keyframes.
Keyframe	A keyframe containing content is indicated by a solid circle in the frame. A keyframe usually indicates a change is going to occur on the Stage.
Blank keyframe	A blank keyframe has no visual content on the Stage. The Timeline opens with one blank keyframe when you start a new project.
Playhead	The playhead indicates which frame of the Timeline is currently being shown on the Stage. You can drag the playhead to a specific frame to view it, or scan through the Timeline by dragging the playhead. This is called "scrubbing."
Current frame	The current frame is the frame on which the playhead is positioned.
Frame rate	Frame rate is the number of frames that will play each second when the movie is viewed. Increasing frame rate creates smoother animation but requires a faster computer processor for playback.
Elapsed time	Elapsed time is the amount of time it will take for the movie to play from the first frame to the currently selected frame. You select a frame by clicking it.

The Tools Panel

The Tools panel, shown in Figure 5, contains tools for drawing shapes, adding text, modifying objects, and controlling color. The Options section at the bottom of the Tools panel displays options for modifying the selected tool. When selecting a tool, it's always a good idea to see which options are selected. These options can significantly change the function of the tool.

FIGURE 5
Tools panel

In this introduction, you create a new document and take a moment to get familiar with the basic layout of the window by organizing panels. You then open and view an example of a completed Flash project. Viewing a completed project is a good way to see how Flash elements such as layers, frames, keyframes, and the Timeline all work together to produce a finished movie.

Opening a New Document and Selecting a Layout

The first step to creating new Flash content is to open a new document (FLA file). You can arrange the document window for easy access to the tools and features you rely on most. For example, as a designer you may prefer to open panels for working with color and manipulating images. On the other hand, an application developer might prefer easy access to features such as Flash Components and Classes. You can change the arrangement of panels at any time by selecting and deselecting panels on the Windows menu.

Each new Flash document opens with one empty layer on the Timeline and one blank keyframe for adding content to the Stage. You can modify the document according to your design specifications by adding additional layers and setting document properties, such as changing the size and color of the Stage and selecting a frame rate for the movie.

 ## Open a Document and Select a Layout

1. Start Macromedia Flash 8.

2. Click **Flash Document** in the Create New column.

   A new untitled Flash (FLA) document opens. The window displays whichever panels were open the last time Flash was used.

3. Click **Window** on the menu bar, point to **Workspace Layout**, and then click **Default.**

The default layout shows the Library panel and the Color Mixer docked along the right side of the window. The Tools panel is on the left side of the Window. On Windows computers, the Property inspector and Actions panel are docked at the bottom of the window. The Actions panel is collapsed, but its title bar is visible. On Macintosh computers, the Actions panel may not be open.

Arranging the Flash Window

You can open and close panels or resize the Timeline to see more or less of the Stage and workspace. You can also collapse a panel, leaving only the title bar visible, or hide a panel to remove it completely.

To view items close up or to see the entire Stage and workspace at once, use the Zoom tool on the Tools panel, or select a new magnification from the Magnification pop-up menu.

Expand and Collapse Panels

1. To collapse the Library panel, click the panel's title.

FIGURE 6
Library panel

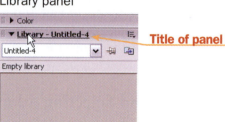

Title of panel

When you collapse a panel, only its title bar remains visible.

2. To restore the panel, click the panel's title again.

The entire panel is visible.

Show and Hide Panel Groups

1. To hide a group of panels that are docked (attached to the side or bottom of the window), click the **Show/Hide** button. (Note: This button is not available on Macintosh computers. To show or hide a panel group on the Macintosh, open the Options menu for the panel and select a command.)

FIGURE 7
Show/Hide button

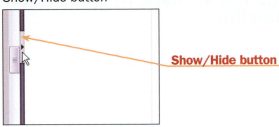

Show/Hide button

The group of panels is hidden.

2. Click the **Show/Hide** button again to restore the group of hidden panels.

The group of panels is again visible.

 ## Open New Panels by Using the Window Menu

1. Click **Window** on the menu bar, and then click **Info** to open the Info panel.

The Align, Info, and Transform panels are grouped together. To switch between panels, select the tab for the panel you want to view.

FIGURE 8
Align, Info, and Transform panels

Options menu

3. To close the Info panel, click the **Options** menu in the panel's title bar, and select **Close panel group** from the pop-up menu.

FIGURE 9
Options pop-up menu

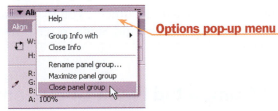

Options pop-up menu

As you add objects to the Stage and workspace, you will find yourself zooming in and out to see both detail and the bigger picture. One way to quickly adjust the magnification of the window is to use the Magnification pop-up menu.

Change the Window Magnification and Adjust the Size of the Timeline

1. Click the down arrow to open the Magnification pop-up menu, and then select **Fit in Window**.

FIGURE 10
Magnification pop-up menu

The size of the Stage adjusts automatically to fit in the available space. With this selection, the Stage adjusts automatically as you resize, collapse, expand, or hide panels.

2. To size the Timeline, position the mouse pointer along the bottom edge of the Timeline. When it changes to a two-headed arrow, click and drag to make the Timeline taller or shorter.

FIGURE 11
Resize Timeline

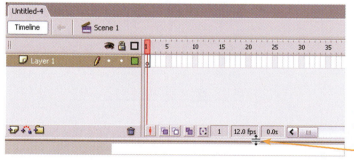

Drag the bottom edge of the Timeline to make it taller or shorter

Viewing a Completed Flash Document

Before creating your first Flash document, you may find it helpful to open a completed document and view the Timeline, Layers, and Stage to see how these features work together to produce a finished movie.

View a Completed Flash Document

1. Click **File** on the menu bar and then click **Open**.

2. Navigate to the location of the data files for this unit and double-click the file named **Animated_Billboard.fla**.

3. Click **Control** on the menu bar and then click **Play**. The playhead advances in the Timeline and the document plays on the Stage.

You can also press **Enter** (Windows) or **Return** (Mac) to play and stop the playhead on the Timeline.

Explore the Timeline.

4. Move the playhead – by dragging or by simply clicking on the frame location – to frame 30 (the beginning of an animation) and then, using the Control menu, click **Step Forward One Frame** and **Step Backward One Frame** to advance and back up one frame at a time.

> **Did You Know?**
>
> You can also use the period and comma keys on the keyboard to advance or back up one frame at a time.

5. Click **File** on the menu bar, and then click **Close** to close document. Do not save changes.

Identifying Rich Media Content On The Web

With nearly every desktop computer capable of displaying Macromedia Flash content, you might be tempted to include animation, sound, and video on *every* Web site you build. But, just because you can, doesn't mean you should.

As a Flash developer, it's often your responsibility to determine when to use Flash and when it's best to restrict a site to simple text and static images.

For the purpose of this training, *rich media content* refers to the use of animation, sound, or video on a Web page, or Web content that dynamically changes based on a visitor's unique interaction.

Deciding When to Use Rich Media Content

Long before the Internet, people embraced the realism of film and video as a means to communicate more effectively. Whether to inform, educate, train, sell, inspire, raise awareness, or simply to entertain, a message artfully packaged with sound and motion has tremendous potential for affecting the behavior of your target audience.

But, just as newspapers and books have not been replaced by radio, television, and cinema, static HTML text and images are sometimes *preferred* and can be more effective than a Web page filled with sound and motion.

Sound, motion, and video provide the *most* benefit when they serve a specific purpose, clearly improve communication, and help achieve the stated goals of a Web site.

Ask yourself the following questions when deciding if content should be implemented by using rich media:

- Does the content require illustration of change over time?
- Does the message *depend* on motion, sound, or video?
- Is synchronized audio necessary?
- Is the purpose of the content to attract attention?
- Is the content intended to entertain?

- Will the content present cross-platform browser issues?

- Does the content require unique fonts that visitors might not have installed?

If you answered yes to one or more of the questions listed, you should consider using Macromedia Flash to produce your Web content.

Table 4 lists a few things to consider when using Macromedia Flash to produce rich Web content.

TABLE 4

BEST PRACTICES	THINGS TO AVOID
Keep animated intros short. Long introductions may look nice but can take a long time to load and could turn away visitors.	Avoid bells & whistles-adding features, graphics, motion, sound, or music just for the sake of having them.
Follow established user interface, graphic design, and usability principles.	Avoid sound effects or animations that loop repeatedly.
Clearly identify areas of the screen that are "clickable."	Avoid navigation bars or buttons that require effort to locate or identify.
Provide a simple method for turning off or reducing the volume of sounds.	Avoid labels or buttons that automatically disappear or change.
Take advantage of the Flash Accessibility features to ensure content is accessible to people with disabilities.	Avoid nonstandard user controls. Most Web users are accustomed to Web links, scrollbars, and other conventions.
Add carefully selected rich media elements to sites built by using primarily HTML pages.	Avoid sites built entirely in Flash with no alternative for visitors who may not have Flash Player installed.

Examples of Rich Media Content on the Web

With every new project comes experience and inspiration for future development. In addition to experience, a common source for learning and innovation is the work of others. By analyzing and evaluating Web sites, you can build and maintain good development practices, prevent common mistakes, and get inspiration for future designs.

There are different types of examples that illustrate effective uses of rich media content on a Web page. Following are some ways to use rich media on the Web.

Virtual Tours

Virtual tours use Flash to create a virtual experience of a particular location or destination. Visitors to virtual tours get an audio and visual glimpse of a location, its people, and history. The use of Flash allows for a richer experience and faster downloads.

Interactive Personalized Shopping Experiences

Some Web sites transform the search for products into an interactive shopping experience with Macromedia Flash. Visitors can choose from a variety of colors and patterns to build, personalize, and buy products.

Hybrid HTML Sites Enriched with Flash Elements

Some sites use Macromedia Flash to add just the right amount of rich media, including Flash animation and video, to an e-commerce site built by primarily using HTML pages. Visitors can be immersed into the content of the site with video and animation and at the same time engage in other tasks such as purchasing or browsing products.

Macromedia Flash 8 Projects

This unit contains three projects that will help you develop your skills in making rich media design decisions and building rich media elements.

Project 1: Animated Billboard

In this project, you follow a design document and storyboard to produce an animated billboard for a client's Web site. The animated billboard promotes an upcoming film festival, and includes rich graphic elements, text, and simple animation.

Project 2: Digital Documentary

In this project, you incorporate rich graphics, photographs, text, and sound to tell a brief history of the Paradise Beach Boardwalk amusement park. Combining rich graphics, film-style techniques, narration, sound effects, and simple navigation, your story will guide viewers through a brief history of the park.

Project 3: Video Gallery

In this project, you produce a video gallery featuring short video clips from recent surfing events held at the world-famous surfing location knows as Mavericks. The video clips are samples taken from a video that can be purchased on the client's Web site. The client, Blue Mountain Riders, will host the video gallery on their Web site designed for big wave surfers and other surfing enthusiasts.

ANIMATED BILLBOARD

GOALS

- Follow a design document and storyboard to define the properties of an animated billboard.

- Draw and animate simple shapes and text to create an animated billboard for a Web site.

TECHNICAL SKILLS

- Create a new Flash document.
- Use the Flash drawing tools.
- Create text and basic shapes.
- Work with symbol instances and the library.
- Animate shapes, symbols, and text.
- Make a Flash document accessible.
- Publish Flash content for the Web.

Estimated time to complete this project: 2.5 hours

Summary

Animated billboards combine images and text that incorporate motion to achieve a particular goal of the Web site. You can use animated billboards effectively to explain a concept, define a process or flow, attract attention, introduce new or updated information, cause an emotional response, or simply to entertain viewers, depending on the goals of your Web site.

The Assignment

In this project, you use Macromedia Flash to produce a brief animated billboard to promote an upcoming film festival in Detroit. The billboard is designed to add a focal point on the left side of the home page of an HTML Web site for the film festival sponsor, SMV. They have provided you with a design document, illustrated in Figure 1, and storyboards to help you produce the billboard. You will use the design document and storyboards to:

■ Set the properties for your billboard

■ Create the necessary graphics and text

■ Create and generate graphical objects to reuse

■ Animate graphics and text

FIGURE 1
SMV Web site example showing placement of the animated billboard

Billboard Design

When you start a new Flash document, you first need general information about the structure and content. A design document gives you background about the goals, purpose, and audience. It describes design requirements such as dimensions, colors, fonts, and logos. It details delivery requirements for the Flash Player and browsers. The design document also provides key content elements. You will use this information throughout the project.

FIGURE 2
Design document

> **Design Document – Animated Billboard**
>
> **Client: SMV Digital Impact Film Festival**
>
> **Goals and Purpose**
>
> The billboard will display on the Digital Impact Film Festival website home page. Its goals are to:
> - Publicize that the film festival will occur in Detroit in April 2007.
> - Make people want to purchase tickets for the film festival.
> - Provide information about the films.
> - Inform people of the film festival location and where to purchase tickets.
>
> Key information on the billboard should be general information about the film festival in Detroit:
>
> **Audience**
>
> Our target audience is interested in digital video, movies, short films, and activities in Detroit. Their age range is 18 and older. They can be frequent web users, but don't need to be. Some adjectives to describe the audience are: forward-thinking, media-savvy, colorful.
>
> **Design Requirements**
>
> The Digital Impact website is gray with white text. The billboard should keep that color scheme. The site uses bright shades of red, blue, green, and orange as accents with the following hexadecimal values: Green: #009900, Red: #FF0000, Blue: #0000FF and Orange: #FF9900
>
> The Digital Impact Film Festival logo, including the DVD symbol, should appear prominently at the top of the billboard.
>
> The client would prefer some type of animation that calls attention to the festival details and uses movie themes.
>
> Billboard duration: 5 seconds maximum
>
> Frame rate (FPS): 12
>
> Dimensions: 360 px x 360 px
>
> **Delivery Requirements**
>
> The billboard will be built with Macromedia Flash and run with Macromedia Flash Player 8.
> - Internet Explorer, v6
> - Safari 2.0
> - AOL 8 or later
> - Mozilla Firefox 1.04 or later
>
> The billboard should run on
> - Macintosh OS10.3 or later
> - Windows XP Home or Professional
>
> **Content**
>
> The following content should be displayed in the billboard.
> - *Title*: Digital Impact Film Festival
> - *Information*: 10 Short Films, Special Guest Santosh Chopra
> - *Location*: Lakeview Theater, Detroit
> - *Dates*: April 12-14, 2007
> - *Purchase tickets*: 313-123-4567
> - *Logo*: Digital Impact Film Festival (words plus DVD image)
>
> Special Instructions: The title should appear first, and all text should continue to display on the billboard when the animation completes.
>
> Digital Impact Billboard – Design Document   1

To view the design document for the animated billboard, open the file named **FL_Project1_Design.pdf**. This file is located in the Design folder for this project.

Project Storyboards

A storyboard is a series of panels with pictures and words. Each panel describes images and actions over time. Designers create storyboards for Flash documents that describe what happens on the Stage as the document plays. Designers use storyboards to share their design with team members and clients without having to build anything in Flash.

A storyboard starts with general information, followed by drawings and descriptions of what appears or changes on the Stage. A Flash producer follows the storyboard to produce the document to the specifications of the designer and the client. You can also use a storyboard to test a Flash document. Testers compare what happens on the screen to what is described on the storyboard. The storyboard for the animated billboard project includes a series of images and descriptions of how each section of the finished movie should look. In this case, the designer created the images by using Macromedia Fireworks.

FIGURE 3
Storyboard

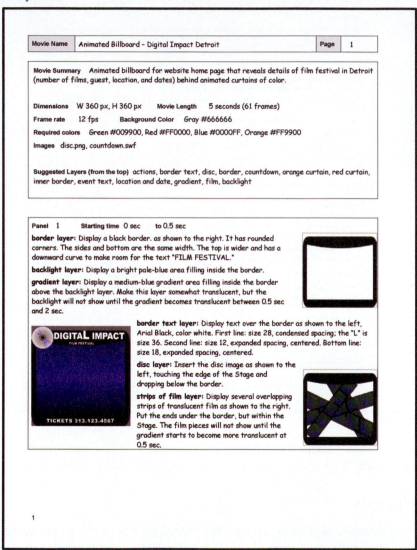

To view the storyboard for this project, open the file named **FL_Project1_Storyboard.pdf**. This file is located in the Design folder for this project.

CREATING A NEW FLASH DOCUMENT

OBJECTIVES:

Upon completion of this lesson, you will be able to:

- Set document properties.

- Set the duration of a document by extending the Timeline.

- Add and name layers on the Timeline.

- Save and name a document.

Estimated time to complete this lesson: 15 minutes

Introduction

The requirements defined on the storyboard will help the animated billboard easily integrate with the Web site. The best way to begin a Flash project is to identify requirements from the design document that you can implement as properties of the Flash document, such as size, background color, frame rate, and duration. If the design document suggests layers for the project, you can easily create and name those layers after you have set document properties. Finally, you should save and name your Flash document.

Take a moment to review the design document and the first page of the storyboard, shown in Figure 1-1, before completing this lesson.

FIGURE 1-1
Storyboard summary information

Movie Summary   Animated billboard for website home page that reveals details of film festival in Detroit (number of films, guest, location, and dates) behind animated curtains of color.

Dimensions W 360 px, H 360 px	**Movie Length** 5 seconds (61 frames)	
Frame rate 12 fps	**Background Color** Gray #666666	

Required colors   Green #009900, Red #FF0000, Blue #0000FF, Orange #FF9900

Images   disc.png, countdown.swf

Suggested Layers (from the top)   actions, border text, disc, border, countdown, orange curtain, red curtain, inner border, event text, location and date, gradient, film, backlight

Setting Document Properties

The design specification for the animated billboard requires it to fit into an area of the Web page that is 360 pixels wide and 360 pixels high. The background of the graphic needs to match the color of the Web page so it blends in, and the frame rate should be 12 frames per second. For additional information, see the Tips & Techniques feature "Guidelines for Selecting Frame Rate."

You set these values in the Document Properties dialog box. Setting document properties is the first step to creating any new Flash document.

Did You Know?

A frame rate of 12 is recommended for very simple animations. This is the rate chosen for the countdown and moving text in the animated billboard.

Inside the Design

The dimensions of a Web page impact the size and position of the elements on that page. In the animated billboard, the designer based the size of the billboard on the width and height of the Web page, which needs to accommodate text next to the billboard. Keeping the width and height at 360 pixels allows viewers to see the full billboard without scrolling when they open the Web page and to view the text next to the billboard.

Tips & Techniques

GUIDELINES FOR SELECTING FRAME RATE

Frame rate is the number of frames or images that are projected or displayed per second. For example, motion pictures play back 24 individual pictures every second. Television and professional video play back 30 frames per second (in the United States).

In computer animation and video, the frame rate directly relates to the perceived smoothness of its playback. The higher the number of frames playing per second, the smoother the video or animation appears to the user. Lower rates can result in choppy-looking playback. Several factors affect the actual frame rate you get on your computer. For example, your computer's processor or graphics hardware may be only capable of playing 10–15 frames per second.

A frame rate of 12 frames per second is recommended for simple computer animation. This setting allows for reasonably smooth animation and is more likely to play back at the intended frame rate on most computers.

Sometimes the complexity of animation requires you to increase the intended frame rate. For example, an animation might include a long slow fade between two or more images. Or the movie may include video, which appears more life-like at a higher frame rate.

Some important points to remember when selecting a frame rate:
- Most computers are capable of playing simple animation with a frame rate of 12 fps.

(Continued . . .)

- Animation with a frame rate lower than 12 fps can appear choppy (less smooth).
- The human eye perceives frame rates above 20 fps as smooth.
- Animations with frame rates higher than 30 fps do not look noticeably superior when compared with animations set at between 24 and 30 fps.
- The higher the frame rate, the more difficult it is for a computer to display an animation at the specified frame rate.
- Slower computers are especially prone to animation slowdowns. Always take into consideration the speed of the typical computer you expect will be used by the target audience.

A good rule is to select the lowest frame rate possible to achieve what you consider to be an acceptable quality of playback. You will probably find this to be somewhere between 12 and 24 frames per second.

Set Document Properties for the Animated Billboard Graphic

1. Open a new blank Flash document.

2. Open the **Modify** menu, and then click **Document**.

The Document Properties dialog box shown in Figure 1-2 opens with the width dimension selected.

FIGURE 1-2
Document Properties dialog box

3. Make sure the Ruler units is set to Pixels, and then enter a new width of **360 px**.

4. Double-click in the height box and enter a new height of **360 px**.

5. Click the Background color box to open the color palette shown in Figure 1-3.

FIGURE 1-3
Color palette

6. As you position the eyedropper over each color swatch, the hexadecimal color value displays at the top of the color palette. Using the eyedropper, select the gray color swatch (**#666666**).

7. Make sure the *Frame rate* is set to **12**.

8. Click in the Title box and key **SMV Digital Impact Trailer**.

9. Click in the Description box and key **Detroit Film Festival**. (The film festival takes place in Detroit.)

10. Click **OK** to confirm the changes and close the dialog box.

The size and color of the Stage are adjusted and a frame rate of 12.0 fps is shown at the bottom of the Timeline.

FIGURE 1-4
Frame rate set to 12 frames per second

Frame rate

1   12.0 fps   0.0s

Setting Duration by Extending the Timeline

If you know how long the movie is supposed to be (by referencing the storyboard), you can save development time by adding the correct number of frames to the Timeline. This eliminates the need to repeatedly extend individual layers.

As the storyboard indicates, the animated billboard is intended to run for 5 seconds. At 12 frames per second, the Timeline will play for 60 frames (5 seconds × 12 frames = 60).

The playhead starts at frame 1, which is at zero seconds, so to make the movie 5 seconds long, extend the Timeline to frame 61.

Set the Movie Duration by Extending the Timeline

1. Click the empty slot for frame **61** as shown in Figure 1-5.

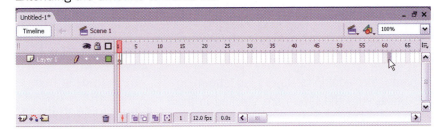

2. Open the **Insert** menu, point to **Timeline**, and then click **Frame**.

As Figure 1-6 reflects, the Timeline extends to frame 61 and the duration of the movie is 5 seconds. When you add new layers, they will automatically include 61 frames.

FIGURE 1-6
The duration of the movie is five seconds

Adding and Naming Layers on the Timeline

The animated billboard contains multiple objects, including graphics and text. If you draw or place each object on a separate layer, it is easier for you to control or change each object and to coordinate interactions between objects.

Layers are arranged vertically and represent the stacking order of objects as they appear on the Stage. In other words, layers at the top of the list appear in front of or on top of other objects on the Stage. As a result, you can arrange layers to cause objects to appear in the background or foreground; or cause an object to pass in front of or behind another object when animated, adding dimension and realism to the movie.

The animated billboard includes a border, a background effect, a disc, text, and an animated film reel countdown. Each of these elements will appear on a separate layer of the Timeline.

Add and Name Layers

1. Look at the Layers area of the Timeline.

By default, each new movie includes one layer, named *Layer 1*.

Hot Tip

If you double-click the icon to the left of a layer name, the Layer Properties dialog box opens in which you can edit several layer properties, including the layer name.

2. Double-click the name **Layer 1**, key **backlight**, and press **Enter** (Windows) or **Return** (Macintosh).

Layer 1 is renamed.

3. Open the **Insert** menu, point to **Timeline**, and then click **Layer**.

A new layer is added above the current layer.

4. Rename the new layer **film**.

5. Add and name the additional layers as shown in Figure 1-7. Make sure the layers are stacked in the following order from top to bottom: border text, disc, border, countdown, event text, location and date, gradient, film, backlight.

Hot Tip

You can also insert a new layer by clicking the Insert Layer button located below the list of layers. To delete a layer, click the layer name and click the Delete Layer button (trash can).

Note

You can drag layers to move them after they are created. If you accidentally add an extra layer, delete it by selecting it and then clicking the Delete Layer button (trash can).

Note

There should be nine layers in the document.

FIGURE 1-7
Named layers

Insert Layer   Delete Layer

Saving and Naming a Document

As you continue your work on the animated billboard, it is a good idea to save your work before getting too far. The first time you save a new Flash document, you need to give the file a name and indicate where on your computer to save the file. Flash documents are saved with the .fla filename extension.

After saving and naming a document, you can save additional changes by using the Save command on the File menu. Save your file often to avoid losing valuable work.

Save and Name the Document

1. Open the **File** menu, and then click **Save**.

Because this is a new document, the Save As dialog box opens.

2. Key a name for the file, such as **FL_Project1_YourName**.

3. Click the arrow beside the Save in box and navigate to the folder where you want to save the new file. You may want to create a new folder, such as MyFiles, for storing your project documents.

Notice the *Save as type* box is set to save the document as a Flash 8 document. You can also save the document as a Flash MX 2004 file.

FIGURE 1-8
Save As dialog box

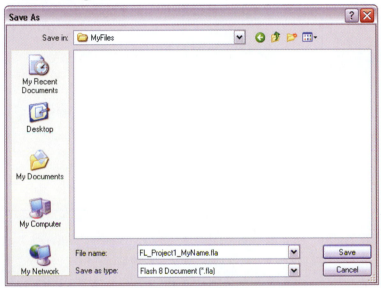

4. Click **Save** (Windows) or **Save As** (Macintosh) to confirm the changes and close the dialog box.

5. If you are continuing with the next lesson, keep the Flash document open. If you are not continuing at this time, close the document and close Flash.

ADDING SHAPES AND TEXT TO THE TIMELINE

Introduction

The animated billboard contains specific drawn elements such as a border and background, typed elements such as title and information text, and imported elements such as the disc logo. In this lesson, you use simple shapes and lines to draw the border and background for the animated billboard. You also add descriptive text that provides information about the Digital Impact Film Festival and import the logo to create the title outlined on the storyboard. The design document will help you create the appropriate look and feel for the background.

Take a moment to review the next page of the storyboard, shown in Figure 2-1, before creating the border and adding text.

FIGURE 2-1
Storyboard

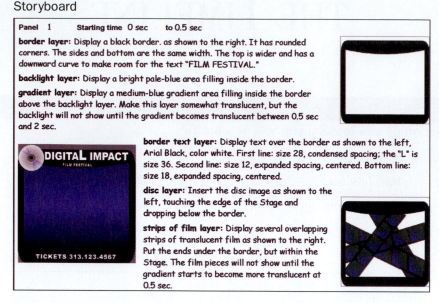

Drawing Shapes

The border and background images are objects you produce by using the drawing tools in Flash and they are called *shapes*.

When using the drawing tools to paint new shapes on top of existing shapes, the portion underneath is replaced by whatever is on top. Paint of the same color merges together to create a single object. Paint of different colors remains distinct. You can use these features to create masks, cutouts, and other negative images.

For example, the cutout in Figure 2-2 was made by moving the red circle shape onto the green rectangle shape and then moving the filled portions of the circle away from the green shape.

FIGURE 2-2
Drawing with ungrouped shapes

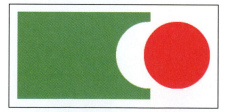

To avoid inadvertently altering shapes by overlapping them, you can group the shapes or draw them on separate layers. You can also use the Object Drawing option at the bottom of the Tools panel to draw shapes that are grouped together automatically as you make them.

FIGURE 2-3
Drawing with the Object Drawing option selected on the Tools panel

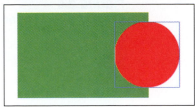

This option lets you overlap shapes without altering their appearance if you choose to move them apart. When using this option Flash creates each shape as a separate object you can individually manipulate.

Once you have added shapes to the Stage, you can use the options on the Property inspector to apply formatting, such as size and color.

Drawing the Border

To create the border for the animated billboard, you will draw a black rectangle about the same size as the Stage. Then you will draw a smaller rectangle (any color) and use it to cut a hole in the first rectangle, resulting in a rectangular border with an empty center.

 ### Create the Border for the Animated Billboard

1. If necessary, open the file you created in the previous lesson, or open the practice file named **FL_Project1_Lesson2.fla**. This file is located in the Practice folder for this project. If you use the practice file, be sure to save it as **FL_Project1_YourName.fla**.

2. Click frame **1** on the *border* layer of the Timeline.

Inside the Design

In the billboard, the designer uses the border to frame content and reinforce the film motif by shaping the border similar to a stage. Elements will be inside and along this border to add interest and attract the eye.

Hot Tip

You may have to expand the Timeline in order to see all the layers.

FIGURE 2-4
Click to select a frame

Click to select frame 1

3. Select the **Rectangle Tool** on the Tools panel.

4. Make sure the Object Drawing option in the Options section of the Tools panel is not selected.

FIGURE 2-5
Rectangle Tool options on the Tools panel

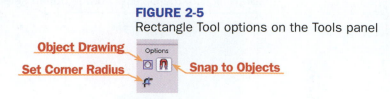

The rectangle you draw will be an ungrouped shape, and you can use a smaller rectangle to cut a hole in the center.

5. Click the **Set Corner Radius** button in the Options section of the Tools panel.

The Rectangle Settings dialog box opens as shown in Figure 2-6.

FIGURE 2-6
Rectangle Settings dialog box

6. Key **20** for the corner radius and click **OK**. The higher the radius setting, the larger the curve of the rounded corner.

7. Click the **Stroke color** box in the Colors section of the Tools panel and click the **No Stroke** button shown in Figure 2-7.

FIGURE 2-7
Stroke color palette

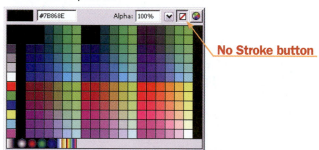

No Stroke button

8. Click the **Fill color** box on the Tools panel and select black (**#000000**).

9. Click and drag to draw a rectangle on the Stage. (The exact size and shape do not matter. It will be adjusted later.)

10. Click the **Selection Tool** on the Tools panel, and then click the rectangle to select it.

Did You Know?

When you click a shape with a fill and stroke, you select the fill but not the stroke. When you double-click the fill, you select both the stroke and fill. If you select the stroke of a multi-sided shape, only one side of the stroke is selected. If you double-click the stroke, you select the stroke on all sides of the shape.

11. Make sure the Constrain Dimensions padlock is unlocked on the Property inspector. You can click the padlock to lock or unlock it.

FIGURE 2-8
Constrain Dimensions padlock on the Property inspector

Constrain Dimensions padlock (shown unlocked)

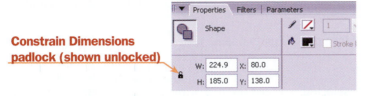

When the dimensions are constrained, or locked, changing the width automatically changes the height and width together to maintain the height-to-width ratio of the shape. To change the height and/or width individually, unlock the dimensions.

12. Double-click in the width box (W:) on the Property inspector and key **360**. Double-click in the height (H:) box, key **344**, and press **Enter** (Windows) or **Return** (Macintosh).

FIGURE 2-9
Width and Height boxes on the Property inspector

Width

Height

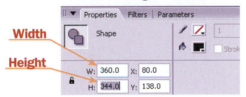

The rectangle is now the correct size for the outside portion of the border, as described on the storyboard.

The next step is to cut out the center of the rectangle to create the border. You do this by creating another rectangle of a different color, placing it directly on top of the black rectangle, and then deleting the interior to cut a hole. The size and position of the interior rectangle determines the width of the border.

Because overlapping shapes blend together, you will temporarily draw the top rectangle on a different layer.

13. Click frame **1** on the *disc* layer.

14. Select the **Rectangle Tool** and set the Corner Radius option to **0**.

15. Leave the Stroke color set to **No Stroke** and change the Fill color to red (**#FF0000**).

16. Draw a rectangle on the Stage.

> **Note**
>
> This rectangle is only being used to cut a hole in the first rectangle, so it can be any color other than black.

17. Use the Selection Tool to select the red rectangle and use the Property inspector to make the width **322** and the height **268.**

The next step is to center the top rectangle over the black rectangle.

18. Open the **Window** menu, and then click **Align** to open the Align panel.

19. The red rectangle is already selected, so hold down the Shift key and select the black rectangle.

Both rectangles are selected.

> **Note**
>
> The dimensions of the inside rectangle were selected to cut a hole and create a border with thinner sides and a thicker top and bottom. The storyboard does not provide the dimensions of the inner rectangle but does provide border thickness information. You could do the calculation yourself, or experiment with the size of the shape until you get it the size needed to create the cutout for the border.

20. In the Align panel, click the **Align horizontal center** and **Align vertical center** buttons, as shown in Figure 2-10.

FIGURE 2-10
Align panel

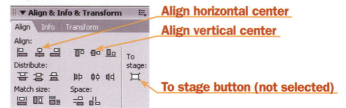

21. Click away from the rectangles to deselect the shapes.

The red rectangle is centered over the black rectangle, but the two shapes are still on separate layers.

22. Select the red rectangle, click **Edit** on the Menu bar, and then click **Cut.**

The red rectangle is temporarily placed on the computer's Clipboard.

23. Click frame **1** on the *border* layer.

24. Open the **Edit** menu, and then click **Paste in Place.**

25. Click away from the shape to deselect it.

The Paste in Place command places the contents of the Clipboard in the exact position from where the last object was cut. Now both shapes are on the same layer and combine to form one shape.

FIGURE 2-11
The red and black shapes blend together to form a single object

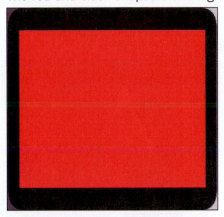

26. Click to select the red interior rectangle and press **Delete**.

The red portion of the combined shape is removed, cutting a hole and turning the black rectangle into a border. Objects placed on layers below the border will now show through the hole.

FIGURE 2-12
Deleting the red interior cuts a hole and creates the outer border

The next step is to position the border on the Stage.

Position the Border on the Stage

1. Click the black border shape to select it, and then enter **0** for the horizontal (X:) position and **16** for the vertical (Y:) position on the Property inspector as shown in Figure 2-13. Press **Enter** (Windows) or **Return** (Macintosh).

FIGURE 2-13
The border positioned on the Stage

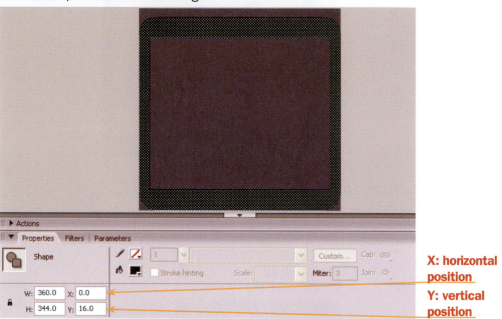

X: horizontal position

Y: vertical position

As shown on the storyboard, this position centers the border horizontally and places it against the bottom edge of the Stage, allowing enough room for the disc logo to extend above the border.

2. Click away from the shape to deselect it.

Did You Know?

In Flash, X represents the horizontal position and Y represents the vertical position of objects on the Stage. Zero (0) is the upper-left corner of the Stage. Increasing the X value moves objects to the right, and increasing the Y value moves objects down.

Modify the Border Shape to Make Additional Room for the Title Text

1. Position the pointer along the top inside edge of the border, as shown in Figure 2-14.

   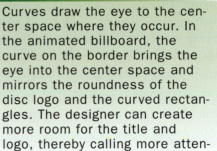
   FIGURE 2-14
   Use the Selection Tool to modify a shape

   The pointer changes to indicate you can curve the edge of the shape by dragging.

2. Drag the edge of the border down slightly to change its shape, as shown in Figure 2-15. You can drag the edge back up if you go too far. This gap is to create a space for the text "FILM FESTIVAL," as shown on the storyboard.

   FIGURE 2-15
   Drag the inside edge of the border to create a curved shape

3. Lock the *border* layer by clicking in the column below the padlock icon, as shown in Figure 2-16.

   As shown in Figure 2-16, a padlock appears on the border layer. A pencil with a slash also appears to indicate you cannot draw on that layer as long as it is locked.

   FIGURE 2-16
   Click below the padlock icon to lock or unlock a layer

Creating a Backlight for Background Effect

The background of the animated billboard changes from a dark background to illuminating strips of film. This design was chosen to add depth and style to the overall billboard. You will create the effect by using three layers: a dark semitransparent gradient background over a light background, with an image in between. In the animated billboard, a light blue layer, or backlight, is placed in back, and a darker blue semi-transparent gradient is in front.

Using the storyboard as a guide, you will create the backlight first, and then create the darker blue gradient. You will change the transparency of the gradient and draw the strips of film later in this project.

Inside the Design

Designers consider the entire composition of the piece when making design decisions about look and feel. Using lighter colors encased in and behind darker images can make objects appear illuminated. In the animated billboard, you use a light blue block of color to compose the backlight and reinforce the concept of cinema — that the illuminant center of the theater is the screen.

Draw the Background Layers for the Animated Billboard Graphic

1. Click frame **1** on the *backlight* layer.

2. Using the Rectangle Tool, draw a rectangle with no stroke, a light blue fill color (#00CCCC), and square corners that fills the interior of the border, as shown in Figure 2-17.

FIGURE 2-17
Draw a light blue rectangle that fills the interior of the border

3. Select the light blue rectangle, open the **Edit** menu, and then click **Copy**.

4. Click frame **1** on the *gradient* layer, open the **Edit** menu, and then click **Paste in Place**.

5. Lock the *backlight* layer.

The next step is to fill the top rectangle with a gradient blue fill. You do this by using the Color Mixer.

Creating Custom Fills by Using the Color Mixer

The colors you see on the Flash color palette are designed to display properly when viewed in a Web browser. These colors are referred to as the *Netscape* or *Web-safe* palette.

Most computer monitors are now capable of displaying millions of colors, so it has become less important to use only Web-safe colors in your design. To access colors that are not found on the Web-safe palette, use the Color Mixer. You can also use the Color Mixer to add gradient fills that fade from one color to another.

The background effect is made up of three layers. You have just created the backlight for the background effect. Next, you will create the darker blue gradient that will sit above the backlight.

 Create a Blue Gradient Fill for the Background

1. Click frame **1** on the *gradient* layer to select the rectangle if necessary.

2. Expand the Color Mixer panel and select **Linear** from the Type pop-up menu.

FIGURE 2-18
Select a Linear gradient

The fill is replaced by a linear gradient. Flash applies the last gradient used during the current session, or the default black-and-white gradient.

Did You Know?

By default, a feature called snapping is turned on when you start Flash. Snapping automatically snaps objects to the document grid, the nearest guide, or nearby objects. To adjust snapping settings, open the View menu, point to Snapping, and then select or deselect snapping options on the menu.

Inside the Design

Gradients of color can add shading and depth to an image. In the animated billboard, you overlay a gradient color to give further depth to the background.

You can modify the gradient by adding, removing, or modifying the color markers along the gradient definition bar, as shown in Figure 2-19.

FIGURE 2-19
Gradient definition bar on the Color Mixer panel

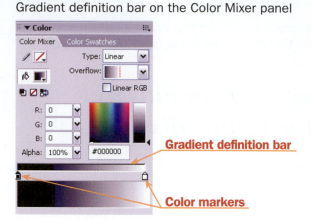

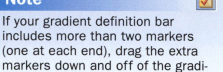

Gradient definition bar

Color markers

3. Click and hold the color marker at the far left end of the gradient definition bar. Release the mouse button to open the color palette.

4. Select black (**#000000**) on the palette.

5. Change the marker at the far right-end of the gradient definition bar to dark blue (**#000066**).

> **Note** ☑
>
> If your gradient definition bar includes more than two markers (one at each end), drag the extra markers down and off of the gradient definition bar to remove them.

6. Click below the center of the gradient definition bar to add an additional marker, as shown in Figure 2-20.

FIGURE 2-20
Click below the gradient definition bar to add a new marker

Using the Color Mixer, you can custom mix colors to create a new palette. If you know the hexadecimal value of a color, you can enter it in the Hex box. For additional information, see the Learn More feature "Understanding Hexadecimal Color Values."

7. On the Color Mixer, drag within the color spectrum to locate a color.

You can pick slight variations of the color by dragging in the box to the right of the Color Mixer.

FIGURE 2-21
Use the Color mixer or Hex box to specify a new color

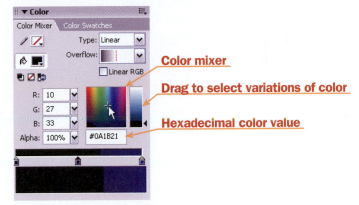

8. Double-click in the *Hex* box, key **3838AA**, and press **Enter** (Windows) or **Return** (Macintosh).

The Color Mixer locates the exact color you request, based on the hexadecimal value you enter. The color #3838AA is a medium shade of blue. The gradient now fades from black to medium blue and then to dark blue.

FIGURE 2-22
A sample of the gradient is shown at the bottom of the Color Mixer panel

9. Click the **Gradient Transform Tool** on the Tools panel.

10. Drag the rotation handle in the upper-right corner of the rectangle to the left. Rotate the rectangle 90 degrees.

The gradient is darker at the bottom, fades up to a medium shade of blue, and then fades to dark blue at the top.

FIGURE 2-23
Use the Gradient Transform Tool to rotate the gradient

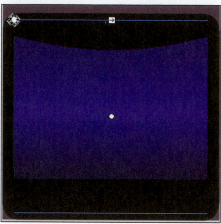

11. Lock the *gradient* layer.

In the next Step-by-Step exercise, you will finish creating the border by importing the disc logo and adding text.

> **Note**
>
> So far, you have created the backlight and the gradient for the background effect. You will complete the background effect by adding strips of film when you learn about creating symbols in Lesson 3.

Learn More

UNDERSTANDING HEXADECIMAL COLOR VALUES

The colors you see on your computer monitor are produced using various combinations of red, green, and blue (RGB). The levels of red, green, and blue are measured by using a numbering system that runs from 0 to 255. For example, the color black is created by mixing 0 red, 0 green, and 0 blue. White is represented by 255 red, 255 green, and 255 blue. Yellow is 255 each of red and green and 0 blue.

When specifying colors on a Web page, you must use hexadecimal values instead of RGB values. Flash does this for you automatically.

While RGB color values are based on the decimal system (base 10), hexadecimal color values are represented by a hexadecimal (base 16) numbering system. Do not worry if you do not fully understand the difference between decimal and hexadecimal values.   *(Continued . . .)*

Learn More

Simply remember the following when specifying hexadecimal colors for the Web:
- Hexadecimal color codes always consist of a number sign (#) followed by a combination of six characters.
- The first two digits determine how much red is in the color.
- The middle two digits determine how much green is in the color.
- The last two digits determine how much blue is in the color.
- You can manipulate and change the color by increasing or decreasing the amount of red, green, or blue in the color code.
- The hexadecimal code for white is #FFFFFF. The code for black is #000000.

Web-safe colors always consist of any three of the pairs 00, 33, 66, 99, CC, or FF in the hexadecimal value range. For example, #FF9900 would be a Web-safe color, whereas #39C6C5 does not appear on the Web-safe color palette.

Flash lets you create colors with RGB and hexadecimal values by using the Color Mixer.

Importing Vector Graphics

The animated billboard storyboard calls for a disc logo to be placed alongside the title. Although Flash has an extensive set of tools for producing graphics, you may want to include preexisting images created by a graphic artist. To add the disc logo to your Flash document you will import the graphic to the Stage.

Inside the Design

Design focuses on moving the eye where you want it and making it rest there or pushing it on. In the animated billboard, the disc logo creates a break in the top margin; this causes asymmetry in the design, and the eye is drawn to asymmetry. The disc logo ties the billboard to the rest of the site and draws attention to the title of the billboard.

Import and Position the Disc Graphic

1. Click frame **1** on the *disc* layer.

2. Open the **File** menu, point to **Import**, and then click **Import to Stage**.

   The Import dialog box appears.

3. Navigate to the data files for this project. Open the Graphics folder and double-click the file named disc.png. One advantage of using PNG files in Flash is that they can have transparent backgrounds. For additional information, see the Learn More feature "Importing Vector & Bitmap Images."

   The file is added to the Stage and a master copy is placed in the document library. You can reuse this graphic by dragging copies from the Library panel to the Stage.

4. Use the Selection Tool to select the disc. Use the Property inspector to position the disc at X:**1** and Y:**1**.

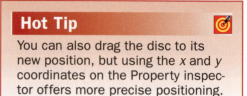

Hot Tip

You can also drag the disc to its new position, but using the *x* and *y* coordinates on the Property inspector offers more precise positioning.

FIGURE 2-24
The disc graphic positioned over the border

5. Lock the *disc* layer.

Learn More

IMPORTING VECTOR AND BITMAP IMAGES

The following vector or bitmap file formats can be imported into Macromedia Flash:

FILE TYPE	EXTENSION
Adobe Illustrator	.eps, .ai, .pdf
AutoCAD DXF	.dxf
Bitmap	.bmp
Enhanced Windows Metafile (Windows only)	.emf
Macromedia FreeHand 7, 8, 9, 10, or 11	.fh7, .fh8, .fh9, .fh10, .fh11
FutureSplash Player	.spl
GIF and animated GIF	.gif
JPEG	.jpg
PNG	.png
Flash	.swf
Windows Metafile	.wmf

If you have QuickTime 4 or later installed, you can also import the following file types:

FILE TYPE	EXTENSION
MacPaint	.pntg
Photoshop	.psd
PICT	.pct, .pic
Quick Time Image	.qtif
Silicon Graphics Image	.sgi
TGA	.tga
TIFF	.tif

Entering and Formatting Text for the Border

The animated billboard contains multiple blocks of text that are different sizes and in different positions on the billboard. For example, the top and bottom of the border display the name of the film festival and a phone number for purchasing tickets.

FIGURE 2-25
Storyboard

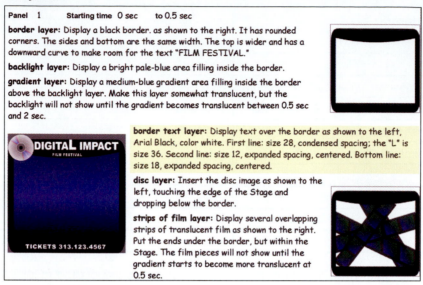

Entering, modifying, and positioning text in Flash is easy. Select the Text Tool on the Tools panel, click to begin a new text block, set properties on the Property inspector, and key the new text. After entering text, you can double-click a text block to activate it and then highlight some or all of the text and use the Property inspector to apply new formatting.

In the next Step-by-Step exercise you will follow the storyboard and use the Text Tool and the Property inspector to add the text for the top and bottom border of the animated billboard.

Inside the Design

Size and color of elements determines their ranking (importance). In the animated billboard, the word Impact is the most powerful; therefore, the large L placed prior to that word draws attention to the word Impact and adds interest to the "brand" of the film festival. It will also help viewers remember the name of the festival.

 Step by Step

Enter and Format Text for the Border of the Graphic

1. Click frame **1** on the *border text* layer (not the border layer).

2. Select the **Text Tool** on the Tools panel.

3. Click on the Stage to start a new text block.

   The Property inspector shows text formatting options.

4. Use the Property inspector to set the following properties:

Type: **Static Text**

Color: white (**#FFFFFF**)

Font: **Arial Black**

Size: **28**

Alignment: **Left**

Letter spacing: **– 1** (negative one)

Font rendering method: **Anti-alias for readability**

Auto kern: **Selected**

FIGURE 2-26
Text properties

Anti-alias for readability smoothes text so the edges of characters displayed on-screen look less jagged. For additional information, see the Tips & Techniques feature "Improving Text Readability."

5. Key **DIGITAL IMPACT** in uppercase letters.

6. Using the Text Tool, drag to highlight the letter **L** in the word DIGITAL. Use the Property inspector to change the size to **36**.

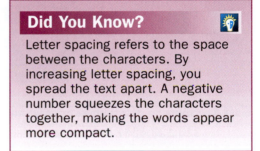

Did You Know?

Letter spacing refers to the space between the characters. By increasing letter spacing, you spread the text apart. A negative number squeezes the characters together, making the words appear more compact.

7. Click the Selection Tool. The text is surrounded by a blue outline, indicating it is selected.

8. Open the **Window** menu, and then click **Transform** to open the Transform panel.

9. Double-click the **Width** box in the Transform panel, key **105**. Double-click the Height box, key **120**, and press **Enter** (Windows) or **Return** (Macintosh).

FIGURE 2-27
Transform panel

By transforming the height and width of the text, you can change the appearance of text without adding additional fonts to the document. These settings make the text appear a little taller and wider than the standard Arial Black font.

10. Drag the text to position it to the right of the disc, as shown in Figure 2-28. Use the arrow keys to fine-tune the position of the text.

FIGURE 2-28
Text positioned over the border

11. Create a second text block that reads **FILM FESTIVAL** in all capital letters.

12. Use the Property inspector to change the size to **12** and the letter spacing to **1**. Use the Transform panel to change the width to **80%**.

13. Position the text in the curve of the top border, as shown in Figure 2-29.

FIGURE 2-29
Text positioned in the curve of the border

14. Create a third block of text that reads **TICKETS 313.123.4567** in all capital letters.

15. Change the size to **18** and the alignment to **Center.**

16. Position the text over the bottom border, as shown in Figure 2-30.

> **Note**
>
> If the curved area of the border is not deep enough to fit the text, unlock the border layer and adjust the shape to make more room. You can also reduce the curve.

FIGURE 2-30
Text positioned over the bottom border

17. Lock the *border text* layer.

18. Save your work. If you are continuing with the next lesson, leave the project open. If you are not continuing at this time, close the file and close Flash.

Tips & Techniques

IMPROVING TEXT READABILITY

The Anti-Alias option makes text more readable by aligning text outlines along pixel boundaries, and is particularly effective for more clearly rendering small font sizes. When anti-aliasing is enabled, all text in the current selection is affected. Anti-aliasing operates with text of all point sizes in the same way.

When using small text in a Flash document, keep in mind the following guidelines:

- Very small text (below 8 points) may not be displayed clearly even if you have selected anti-alias for readability.
- Sans serif text, such as Helvetica or Arial, appears clearer at small sizes than serif text.
- Some fonts or type styles, such as bold and italics, can reduce text readability at small sizes.

Working with Symbols, Instances, and the Library

OBJECTIVES:

Upon completion of this lesson, you will be able to:

- Define symbol, instance, and library.
- Create graphic symbols.
- Add instances of symbols to the Stage.
- Edit symbols.
- Change the properties of a symbol instance.

Estimated time to complete this lesson: 30 minutes

Introduction

The animated billboard background contains an effect that illuminates several strips of film. The strips of film are similar in composition, but they vary in size, position, angle, and transparency. To keep from drawing multiple graphics, you can create one strip of film and convert it to a reusable object called a symbol.

A *symbol* is a graphic, button, or movie clip you create once in Macromedia Flash and can use any number of times throughout your movie. Any symbol you create is automatically placed in a storage area called the *library* for the current document.

There are advantages to working with symbols. After adding a symbol to the library, you can drag any number of instances to the Stage without increasing the size of your published document. Adding and modifying instances also saves you the trouble of creating every individual object from scratch.

An *instance* is a copy of a symbol located on the Stage. An instance can be different from its symbol in color, size, and function. To create an instance of a symbol, drag the symbol from the Library panel to the Stage. Once you have created an instance, you can use the Color options on the Property inspector to change its brightness, tint, transparency, or color settings.

You can make changes to any instance of a symbol (on the Stage) without affecting the original symbol (in the library). On the other hand, if you edit the original symbol, every instance is updated to reflect your changes, which can save time and maintain consistency in design.

There are three types of symbols (called behaviors): *graphic*, *button*, and *movie clip*.

A concise definition of *instance*, *library*, and each of the types of *symbols* can be found in Table 2-1 for easy reference.

TABLE 2-1

TERM	DEFINITION
Symbol	A reusable object stored in the document library.
Instance	A copy of the original symbol. Color, size, shape, and position of an instance can be changed without affecting the original symbol.
Graphic Symbol	A graphic symbol includes artwork that can be either static or animated. A graphic symbol has its own timeline that is dependent on the main Timeline. The symbol timeline plays only if the main Timeline is playing.
Movie Clip Symbol	A movie clip includes a unique timeline that can play independent of the main Timeline. This allows you to create a movie within a movie. You will learn more about movie clip symbols later in this unit.
Button Symbol	A button includes four states that change appearance as a viewer interacts with the button. You can use button symbols to control interactivity, such as starting or stopping a movie, or for navigation within an application. You will learn more about button symbols later in this unit.
Library	Each document includes a storage area called the library. The library is used to store and manage symbols, as well as imported files such as bitmap images, vector drawings, and sounds. Open the Library panel to view, access, or manage objects in the library.

In Lesson 2, you created the first two layers for the background effect. The backlight layer is on the bottom, and the darker blue gradient layer is above it. In this lesson, you finish the background effect by creating the strips of film that go in the middle. Take a moment to review the storyboard, shown in Figure 3-1, before creating the symbols for the animated billboard graphic.

FIGURE 3-1
Storyboard

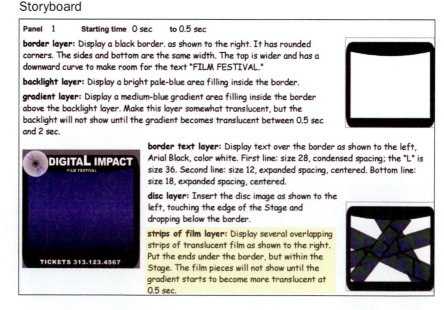

Creating Graphic Symbols

To complete the background effect, you will create a new graphic symbol that resembles a strip of film. You can then place instances (copies) on the Stage and modify each instance without affecting the integrity of the original symbol stored in the library.

There are two ways to create graphic symbols in Flash: open a new blank symbol and create the image from scratch, or convert existing objects, such as text, shapes, and imported graphics.

Create a New Symbol for the Filmstrip Graphic Used in the Background

1. If necessary, open the document you created in the previous lesson, or open the practice file named **FL_Project1_Lesson3.fla**. If you use the practice file, be sure to save it as **FL_Project1_YourName.fla**.

2. Open the **Insert** menu and then click **New Symbol**.

   The Create New Symbol dialog box opens. You can select the movie clip, button, or graphic symbol behaviors. You can also give the symbol a unique name.

   FIGURE 3-2
   Create New Symbol dialog box

   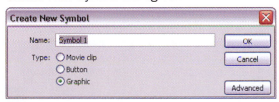

3. Key the symbol name **filmstrip**, select the **Graphic** type, and then click **OK**.

   A blank timeline and Stage open for the symbol. The name of the symbol is added to the library automatically. The icon beside the symbol in the library indicates this is a graphic symbol.

   FIGURE 3-3
   Timeline for the filmstrip symbol

   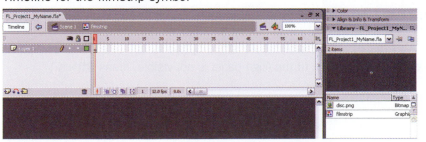

To create the interior cells of the filmstrip, you will draw a rectangle and convert the shape into another graphic symbol called film_cell. The film_cell symbol will be inside the filmstrip symbol.

Convert Objects to Symbols

1. Draw a small rectangle with no stroke and a white fill (**#FFFFFF**). Use the Property inspector to make the size of the rectangle approximately **50** pixels wide and **54** pixels high.

   Instead of creating more than one film cell, convert the shape into a symbol and reuse it.

2. With the white rectangle still selected, click the **Modify** menu, and then click **Convert to Symbol.**

3. Name the symbol **film_cell,** select the **Graphic** type, and then click **OK.**

   The symbol is added to the library.

> **Note**
>
> Generating symbols and reusing the symbols rather than re-drawing them helps you retain the shape, size, and color of objects. This technique also reduces file size because Flash only needs to generate the symbol once and then reuse it.

Add and Position Instances of the film_cell Symbol Inside the Filmstrip Symbol

1. Drag four additional instances of the film_cell symbol from the Library panel to the Stage, as shown in Figure 3-4.

FIGURE 3-4
Adding instances of the film_cell symbol to the Stage

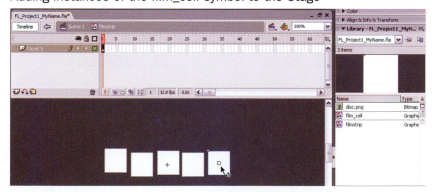

2. Open the **Edit** menu and then click **Select All** to select all five instances of the film_cell symbol.

3. On the Align panel, make sure the To stage button is not selected and click **Align top edge** and **Space evenly horizontally.** (If the Align panel is not visible, press **Ctrl+K**.)

FIGURE 3-5
Align panel

Align top edge

To stage button not selected

Space evenly horizontally

4. Select the Rectangle Tool, make sure the Object Drawing option is not selected, and then set the stroke color to **No Stroke** and the fill color to black (**#000000**).

5. Draw a rectangle that covers the cells, as shown in Figure 3-6.

>
> **Important**
>
> Flash automatically places the shapes you draw behind the symbols. If your rectangle appears on top of the film cells (hiding them), then you have the Object Drawing option turned on by mistake.

FIGURE 3-6
Draw a rectangle behind the film cells to create the strip of film

6. Click **Scene 1** on the Information bar (at the top of the Timeline) to close the symbol and return to the main Timeline.

Adding Symbol Instances to the Main Timeline

To continue creating the background effect, which has multiple strips of film, you will use instances of the symbol and then modify each instance to generate the look outlined on the storyboard.

> **Inside the Design**
>
> The designer chose to include objects that reinforce a theme and add interest to the composition. In the animated billboard, the designer creates interest through the use of multiple strips of film that appear in different orientations and opacities. This effect creates a subtle idea of dimensionality and is a metaphor for film without being busy or distracting.

 ## Add Instances of the Completed Filmstrip Symbol to the Stage

1. Temporarily hide the *gradient* layer by clicking in the show/hide column (below the eye) beside the layer name. This allows you to work on the film layer. Later, you will make the gradient layer semi-transparent so the strips of film show through.

FIGURE 3-7
Click below the eye icon to hide or show a layer

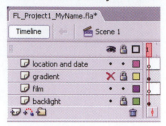

2. Click frame **1** on the *film* layer.

3. Drag four instances of the **filmstrip** symbol from the Library panel to the Stage.

4. Using the Free Transform Tool, size, rotate, and position the strips of film so they look similar to those shown in Figure 3-8. Make sure the ends of the filmstrips do not extend beyond the outside border of the animated graphic.

> **Hot Tip**
>
> Turn off the Snapping options on the View menu when sizing the strips of film. You can also skew the objects by positioning the mouse pointer along the edge of the selected symbol and dragging.

FIGURE 3-8
Four instances of the filmstrip symbol transformed and arranged on the Stage

5. Click to select any one of the filmstrip instances on the Stage.

The Property inspector changes to display symbol properties.

6. Select **Alpha** from the Color pop-up menu and then click and drag the slider to **80%**, as shown in Figure 3-9.

> **Hot Tip**
>
> When arranging more than one symbol or object on the same layer, you can use the Arrange commands to control their stacking order. For example, you can move one filmstrip to the top of the stack by opening the Modify menu, pointing to Arrange, and then clicking Bring to Front.

FIGURE 3-9
Changing the Alpha transparency to 80 percent

At 80 percent, the symbol is partially transparent. A setting of 100 percent makes the symbol opaque, and a setting of 0 percent makes the symbol completely transparent.

7. Change the transparency of the remaining symbol instances to **80%**. Notice that once you have set the transparency value for Alpha, each time you select it after that it defaults to that same value.

> **Hot Tip**
>
> You can apply properties to more than one symbol instance at the same time. Select the group of instances by holding down the Ctrl key while clicking on each instance; then click on any of the instances and make your selections on the Property inspector.

Editing Symbols

When you edit a symbol, Flash updates all instances of that symbol in your document. For example, you can change the fill of the film_cell symbol and update all instances that appear on the Stage.

 Add Gradient Fills to the Cells on the Filmstrip Symbol

1. Double-click the icon beside the *film_cell* symbol on the Library panel.

   The film_cell symbol opens in Symbol Editing mode. The name of the symbol appears on the Information bar.

FIGURE 3-10
Timeline for the film_cell symbol

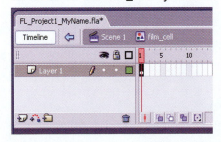

2. Select the white rectangle that represents the film cell if necessary.

3. Use the Color Mixer to add a linear gradient fill that fades from **violet** (#333399) to **green** #006600.

FIGURE 3-11
Linear gradient for the film_cell symbol

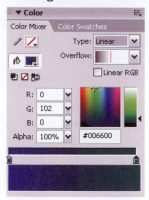

4. Use the Gradient Transform Tool to rotate the fill diagonally.

FIGURE 3-12
Rotating the gradient fill by using the Gradient Transform Tool

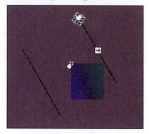

5. Click **Scene 1** on the Information bar to close the symbol and return to the main Timeline.

Every instance of the symbol is updated automatically.

FIGURE 3-13
All symbol instances change automatically

6. Show the *gradient* layer by clicking the red X beside the layer name. This hides the film layer. You will change the transparency of the gradient in the next lesson. This will make the strips of film visible in the background.

7. Lock the *film* layer and save your document. If you are continuing with the next lesson, leave the project open. If you are not continuing at this time, close the file and close Flash.

Hot Tip

You can edit a symbol by double-clicking a symbol instance on the Stage. The symbol opens on the Stage for easy editing, and all other objects on the Stage are dimmed. This is called *Edit in Place*. By using Edit in Place, you can see your changes as they will appear on the Stage.

ANIMATING SHAPES, SYMBOLS, AND TEXT

OBJECTIVES:

Upon completion of this lesson, you will be able to:

- Explain keyframe animation and tweening.
- Animate shapes by using shape tweens.
- Animate symbols and text by using motion tweens.
- Prevent the Timeline from looping by using ActionScript.

Estimated time to complete this lesson: 45 minutes

Introduction

The animated billboard uses motion to draw attention to the event it promotes. The motion occurs in the countdown graphic, the strips of film showing and illuminating, and the theater location text entering. In Flash, movement is created by changing the content of successive frames along the Timeline. These animations are outlined in the storyboard (see Figure 4-1).

There are two ways to produce animation in Flash: *frame-by-frame animation* and tweened animation or *tweening*. Flash includes two types of tweening: *shape tweening* and *motion tweening*. These will be explained in greater detail later in this lesson.

In this lesson, you will animate shapes, text, and symbols by using both frame-by-frame animation and tweening.

Creating Frame-by-Frame Animation

The countdown is an example of a frame-by-frame animation. To create frame-by-frame animation, insert or draw an image in the first frame on the layer where you want the animation to begin. Then, select the frame where you want a change to occur, insert a new keyframe (indicating a change), and modify (or replace) the image to create the change. Continue this process to create gradual changes over time, bringing images to life.

> **Note**
>
> The designer of the animated billboard chose to provide the graphic elements for the animated countdown. The graphic was created in Fireworks and exported as a single SWF image. By importing this image, you save the time of drawing the countdown graphic, but you can easily modify the image in Flash to create the four frames of the animation. Also, when you import the graphic to the library as a SWF file, it is automatically converted to a graphic symbol and can be reused and modified just like any other symbol in the document.

To create the animation of a film reel countdown, import the **countdown.swf** graphic, place a copy of the graphic in a series of consecutive frames, and then modify each frame of the countdown.

FIGURE 4-1
Storyboard

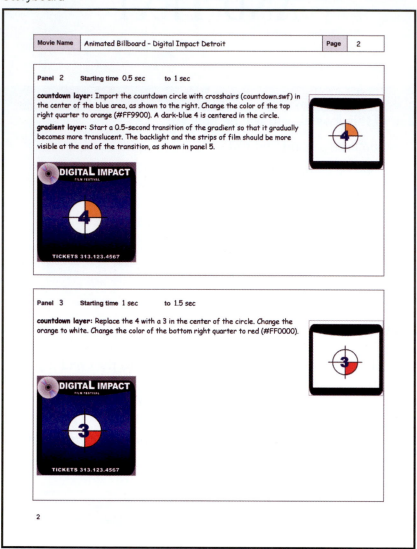

 ## Animate the Countdown Graphic by Using Frame-by-Frame Animation

1. Open the document you created in the previous lesson, or open the practice file named **FL_Project1_Lesson4.fla**. If you use the practice file, be sure to save it as **FL_Project1_YourName.fla**.

2. Click frame **7** on the *countdown* layer. At 12 frames per second, this is exactly one-half of a second into the movie.

Inside the Design

Adding elements that emphasize the overall theme draws viewer attention while keeping with the consistency of the design. In the animated billboard, a countdown reel creates an anticipatory effect by evoking the image of old-time film leaders that signaled the beginning of a film.

3. Open the **Insert** menu, point to **Timeline**, and then click **Keyframe**.

A keyframe indicates a change on the Timeline. When the Timeline reaches frame 7, or one-half of a second, the first graphic of the countdown will appear.

4. Open the **File** menu, point to **Import**, and then click **Import to Library**.

Hot Tip

By using the duration indicator on the Timeline, you can identify where along the Timeline to add objects, create animation, and identify changes by using keyframes.

5. Navigate to the data files for this project. Open the Graphics folder and double-click the file named **countdown.swf**.

The countdown.swf file is added as a graphic symbol on the Library panel.

6. Drag an instance of the countdown.swf symbol from the Library panel to the center of the Stage.

FIGURE 4-2
Instance of the countdown.swf graphic

The imported graphic is a grouped object. To edit each section of the graphic separately, you need to break the group apart.

7. With the countdown graphic still selected, click **Modify** on the Menu bar, and then click **Break Apart**. This separates the text from the shapes.

8. Open the **Modify** menu, and then click **Break Apart** a second time to break apart the shape elements.

9. Click frame **13** (at 1 second) on the *countdown* layer. Click the **Insert** menu, point to **Timeline**, and then click **Keyframe**.

Important

If you accidentally add a keyframe or blank keyframe, you can remove it. Select the keyframe, open the **Modify** menu, point to **Timeline**, and then click **Clear Keyframe**. You can also drag a keyframe to a new position on the Timeline.

10. Add additional keyframes at frames **19** (1.5 seconds) and **25** (2 seconds) on the *countdown* layer. When you are done, your Timeline should look like that shown in Figure 4-3.

FIGURE 4-3
Four instances of the countdown graphic appear at one-half second intervals along the Timeline

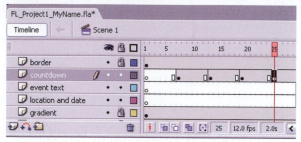

11. Click frame **7** on the *countdown* layer and click away from the Stage to deselect the objects. Using the Selection Tool, click the upper-right quadrant of the circle to select its fill. On the Property inspector, change the Fill color from white to orange (**#FF9900**).

FIGURE 4-4
Each instance of the countdown displays a different color and number

12. Click frame **13** on the *countdown* layer. Use the Selection Tool to select the lower-right quadrant and change the color to red (**#FF0000**). Double-click the number 4 and change it to **3**.

13. Click frame **19** on the *countdown* layer. Use the Selection Tool to select the lower-left quadrant and change the color to green (**#009900**). Change the number 4 to **2**.

14. Click frame **25** on the *countdown* layer. Use the Selection Tool to select the upper-left quadrant and change the color to blue (**#0000FF**). Change the number 4 to **1**.

15. Click frame **31** on the *countdown* layer. Open the **Insert** menu, point to **Timeline**, and then click **Blank Keyframe**.

The countdown image will disappear when the playhead reaches frame 31.

FIGURE 4-5
A blank keyframe clears the countdown graphic from the Stage

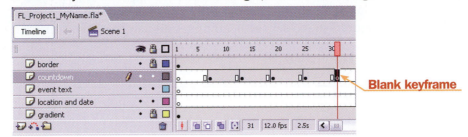

16. Position the playhead on frame **1** and press **Enter** (Windows) or **Return** (Macintosh) to play the movie on the Timeline.

17. Lock the *countdown* layer.

Animating Symbols with Motion Tweens

The background effect of the animated billboard has a gradient look that gradually shows and illuminates filmstrips as the movie plays. The effect of slowly showing these filmstrips can be created by "tweening" the gradient part of the background from opaque to semitransparent.

The term *tweening* is borrowed from traditional animators and is an abbreviation for the word *inbetweening*. In traditional cell animation, an artist known as the *inbetweener* would take the beginning and ending keyframes provided by the main artist and draw all the frames between them to create the illusion of motion. Fortunately, Flash does the work of the inbetweener, leaving you with the simple task of drawing only the beginning and ending keyframes for the animation.

Motion tweens are used to move text across the screen, animate grouped objects, or animate between two instances of a symbol that have different properties.

Hot Tip

You can right-click (Windows) or Control-click (Macintosh) frames on the Timeline to access a shortcut menu for inserting and removing frames, keyframe, blank keyframes, and motion tweens.

Inside the Design

Designers use different methods to reinforce a theme while drawing attention to information. In the animated billboard, the designer chose to have the countdown occur on a solid background and then create an effect that mimics lights coming up in a theatrical way. This is accomplished by having the background gradient fade out and reveal the strips of film, much like lights coming up on a stage or the screen getting brighter at the start of a movie. This effect draws the viewer into the main focus area and creates some anticipation.

For example, if you convert the dark blue gradient to a graphic symbol, you can use a motion tween to animate between two instances of the symbol, gradually making the gradient transparent and revealing the background and film layers below it. Use the specifications on the storyboard (shown in Figure 4-6) to set the beginning and length of the transparency.

FIGURE 4-6
Storyboard

> **gradient layer:** Display a medium-blue gradient area filling inside the border above the backlight layer. Make this layer somewhat translucent, but the backlight will not show until the gradient becomes translucent between 0.5 sec and 2 sec.

Fade the Gradient Blue Background Over Time by Using a Motion Tween

1. Unlock the *gradient* layer.

2. Click frame **1** on the *gradient* layer to select the rectangle shape with the gradient fill (on the Stage).

3. Convert the gradient to a graphic symbol named **gradient**. (*Hint*: Open the **Modify** menu and click **Convert to Symbol**.)

   The gradient will change transparency between one-half of a second and 2 seconds on the Timeline and slowly reveal the strips of film and backlight below it.

4. Insert keyframes at frames **7** and **25** on the *gradient* layer.

5. Using the Selection Tool, click the instance of the gradient symbol in frame 25. On the Property inspector, select **Alpha** from the Color pop-up menu, and change the transparency to **85%.**

FIGURE 4-7
Changing the Alpha transparency to 85%

6. Click anywhere between frames 7 and 25 on the *gradient* layer. On the Property inspector, select **Motion** from the **Tween** pop-up menu.

FIGURE 4-8
Applying a motion tween from the Property inspector

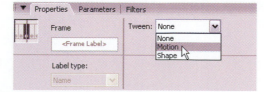

The motion tween is represented by light blue shading and an arrow running between the start and end frames on the Timeline.

FIGURE 4-9
Motion tweens are represented by light blue shading

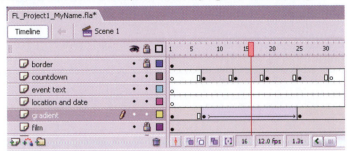

7. Position the playhead at frame **1** and press **Enter** (Windows) or **Return** (Macintosh) to play the movie on the Timeline.

   As the countdown animates, the gradient slowly becomes transparent, revealing the backlight and film layers.

8. Lock the *gradient* layer.

Hot Tip

You can also apply a motion tween by opening the **Insert** menu, pointing to **Timeline**, and then clicking **Create Motion Tween**; or by right-clicking where you want the tween to occur and clicking **Create Motion Tween**.

Animating Text with Motion Tweens

As the storyboard shows, the animated billboard displays information about the event after the countdown occurs. The location of the festival animates into view, drawing attention to the information. You can animate this text by using motion tweens.

FIGURE 4-10
Storyboard

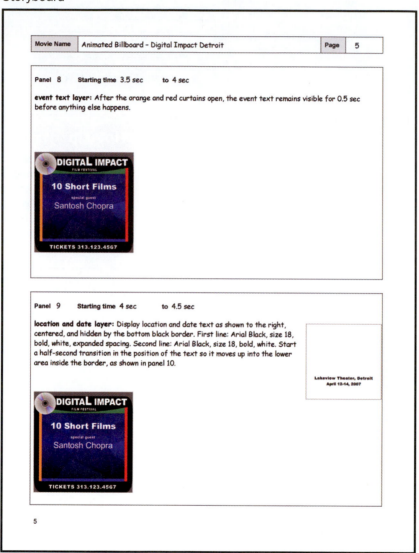

 Enter and Format the Interior Text Message

1. Insert a keyframe at frame **37** (at 3 seconds) on the *event text* layer.

   The *event text* layer will contain a description of the festival.

Inside the Design

Using minimal fonts enhances the consistency of the design. The designer chose to use Arial and Arial Black consistently throughout the billboard, providing a consistent look.

2. Create, format, and position the text, as shown in Figure 4-11.

FIGURE 4-11
Event text

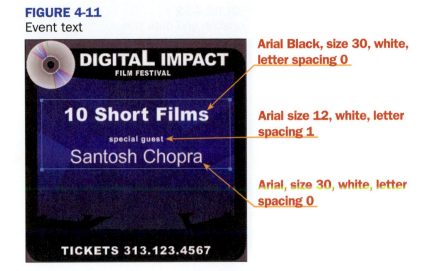

Arial Black, size 30, white, letter spacing 0

Arial size 12, white, letter spacing 1

Arial, size 30, white, letter spacing 0

3. Lock the *event text* layer.

Hot Tip

When positioning text or other objects on the Stage, you can use the up, down, right, or left arrow keys to move the object one pixel at a time.

Animate the Theater Location and Date Text by Using a Motion Tween

1. Insert a keyframe at frame **49** (at 4 seconds) on the *location and date* layer.

The *location and date* layer will show the location and date of the film festival.

Inside the Design

Motion on the screen attracts the eye. In the animated billboard, the designer chose to use motion to bring important pieces of text into focus.

2. Create, format, and position the text, as shown in Figure 4-12.

FIGURE 4-12
Location and date text

Arial Black, size 18, white, bold, letter spacing 1

Arial Black, size 18, white, bold, letter spacing 0

3. Insert a keyframe at frame **55** (at 4.5 seconds) on the *location and date* layer. This is the end frame for the animation.

4. Click frame **49** on the *location and date* layer. This is the start frame for the animation.

5. Press the down arrow key several times to slide the text down until it is hidden behind the border, as shown in Figure 4-13.

FIGURE 4-13
Starting position for the moving text

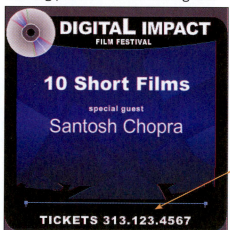

Use the down arrow key to position the location and date down behind the border

6. Click anywhere between frames 49 and 55 on the *location and date* layer. Open the **Insert** menu, point to **Timeline**, and then click **Create Motion Tween**.

FIGURE 4-14
The text will movie into position between frames 49 and 55

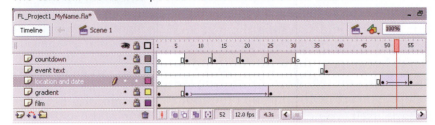

7. Position the playhead on frame **1** and press **Enter** (Windows) or **Return** (Macintosh) to play the movie on the Timeline.

8. Lock the *location and date* layer and save your document.

Did You Know?

The terms Easing In and Easing Out have to do with the speed of animation. Easing Out means the animation will gradually slow to the last frame. Easing In means the animation will gradually speed up to the last frame. You can apply easing by clicking anywhere in the shape or motion tween on the Timeline and then adjusting the Ease setting on the Property inspector.

Creating Shape Tweens

The storyboard describes orange and red curtains in the animated billboard that use the animation of shapes to draw attention to the billboard and create the effect of a curtain opening and revealing the text you just created. These shapes change size and shape during the animation. Flash lets you use shape tweening to animate between two shapes on the Stage. By moving the position of the shape, you create the illusion of motion. By altering the shape itself, you can create the illusion of one shape morphing into another shape.

FIGURE 4-15
Storyboard

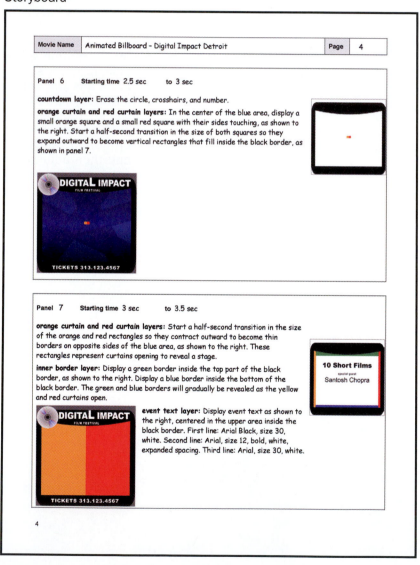

4

Create the Shape Tweens that Reveal the Message and Morph into Colored Borders

1. Insert two new layers above the *event text* layer. Name them **red curtain** and **orange curtain.**

FIGURE 4-16
Orange curtain and red curtain layers

2. Insert a keyframe at frame **31** (at 2.5 seconds) on the *red curtain* layer.

3. Select the Rectangle Tool and change the Stroke color to **No Stroke** and the Fill color to red (**#FF0000**). Make sure the Object Drawing option is not selected, because you cannot apply shape tweens to grouped objects.

4. Draw a rectangle that fills the right half of the border's interior, as shown in Figure 4-17. Use the Selection Tool to select the shape you have drawn and then make the shape W:**170** H:**286** and position it at X:**181** Y:**35**.

FIGURE 4-17
Red curtain shape

5. Insert keyframes at frames **37** (at 3 seconds) and **43** (at 3.5 seconds) on the *red curtain* layer.

The shape will begin small in frame 31, zoom out to fill half the screen in frame 37, and then morph to form the right inside border in frame 43.

6. Click frame **31** on the *red curtain* layer. Select the shape and use the Property inspector to change the width and height of the red shape to **10** pixels (W:**10** and H:**10**). When you do, the red shape seems to disappear, but it has just been moved out of position.

7. On the Align panel, make sure the **To stage** button is selected, and then click **Align vertical center**. The small red rectangle moves to X:**181** and Y:**175**.

FIGURE 4-18
Start position of the red curtain animation

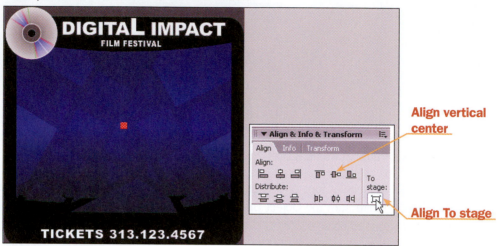

Align vertical
center

Align To stage

8. Click frame **43** on the *red curtain* layer. Select the shape and then change the width of the shape to **10** pixels and position it along the inside border, as shown in Figure 4-19. (The position is X:**331** and Y:**35**.)

FIGURE 4-19
End position of the red curtain animation

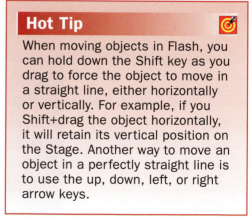

Hot Tip

When moving objects in Flash, you can hold down the Shift key as you drag to force the object to move in a straight line, either horizontally or vertically. For example, if you Shift+drag the object horizontally, it will retain its vertical position on the Stage. Another way to move an object in a perfectly straight line is to use the up, down, left, or right arrow keys.

9. Click between frames 31 and 37 on the *red curtain* layer. Select **Shape** from the **Tween** pop-up menu on the Property inspector.

FIGURE 4-20
Applying a shape tween from the Property inspector

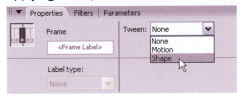

Shape tweens are represented on the Timeline by an arrow and light green shading.

FIGURE 4-21
Shape tweens are represented by light green shading

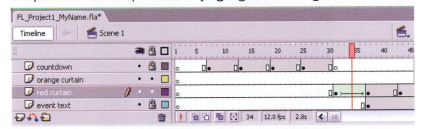

10. Apply another shape tween between frames 37 and 43 on the *red curtain* layer.

11. Drag the playhead back and forth between frames 31 and 43 to preview the animation.

This is called **scrubbing**.

The red shape opens horizontally, similar to a curtain, revealing the text behind it. For additional information, see the Tips & Techniques feature "Resolving Tween Errors."

12. Lock the *red curtain* layer.

Next, you will create the left half of the curtain by duplicating and modifying the shapes you just created.

13. Click frame **31** on the *red curtain* layer, hold down the **Shift** key, and then click frame **43** on the *red curtain* layer.

14. Hold down **Alt** (Windows) or **Option** (Macintosh) and click and drag the frames up to the *orange curtain* layer, as shown in Figure 4-22.

> **Important**
>
> Be sure to apply a shape tween, not a motion tween. Shape tweens are used for animating shapes, whereas motion tweens are used for animating text and symbols.

FIGURE 4-22
Copying layers from the red curtain layer to the orange curtain layer

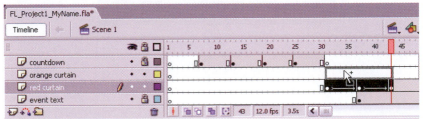

Copies of the frames and shape tweens are copied to the orange curtain layer.

15. Click frame **31** on the *orange curtain* layer and change the fill color of the small rectangle to orange (**#FF9900**)

16. With the small orange rectangle still selected, use the left arrow key to nudge it to the left, as shown in Figure 4-23. (The position is X:**171** and Y:**175**.)

FIGURE 4-23
Start position of the orange curtain animation

17. Click frame **37** on the *orange curtain* layer. Change the fill color of the rectangle to orange (**#FF9900**), and position the shape as shown in Figure 4-24. (The position is X:**11** and Y:**35**.)

FIGURE 4-24
Mid position of the orange curtain animation

18. Click frame **43** on the *orange curtain* layer. Change the color of the shape to orange (**#FF9900**), and position the shape as shown in Figure 4-25 (X:**19** Y:**35**).

FIGURE 4-25
End position of the orange curtain animation

The finished graphic also includes an inner green and blue border along the top and bottom inside edges of the outer border.

19. Insert a new layer above the *event text* layer and name it **inner border**.

FIGURE 4-26
Inner border layer

20. Insert a keyframe at frame **43** on the *inner border* layer.

21. Use the Rectangle Tool to draw and position blue (**#0000FF**) and green (**#009900**) shapes, as shown in Figure 4-27.

FIGURE 4-27
Green and blue inner border

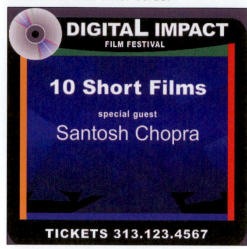

22. Click frame **43** on the *inner border* layer. Drag the keyframe back to frame **37** on the same layer.

FIGURE 4-28
The blue and green borders appear at frame 37

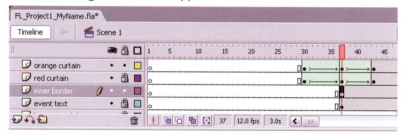

The blue and green borders will be revealed as the red and orange shapes animate into place.

23. Position the playhead on frame **1** and press **Enter** (Windows) or **Return** (Macintosh) to play the movie on the Timeline.

24. Lock the *orange curtain* and *inner border* layers and save your document.

Testing a Flash Document

As you create the animated billboard, it is helpful to see and test your progress. You can view the images and animation as they will appear when you publish the document as a movie. Testing allows you to see potential errors with positioning and timing of objects.

You can test your SWF file by viewing it in Flash Player, which provides a more realistic view of the finished movie than simply playing the movie on the Timeline.

Test the Animated Billboard in Flash Player

1. Open the **Control** menu, and then click **Test Movie**.

   When you test a movie, Flash generates a SWF file in the same directory as the FLA file (using the same file name as the FLA file) and opens the SWF file in a Flash Player window.

   You may have noticed that the movie plays to the end of the Timeline and then repeats. This is called **looping**. To prevent a movie from looping, you can add simple controls to the Timeline by using ActionScript.

2. Close the Flash Player window and return to the document.

> **Hot Tip**
>
> You can also press **Ctrl+Enter** (Windows) or **Command+Return** (Macintosh) to test the movie.

Controlling the Timeline with ActionScript

When the animated billboard plays, it is supposed to complete the animation and then stop. This allows viewers to read the rest of the Web site without distraction. You can control the looping of your billboard by adding ActionScript.

ActionScript is a sophisticated scripting language that allows people with programming expertise to develop powerful Web applications by using Macromedia Flash.

By using the Flash Actions panel, however, you can add basic controls to your movies without knowing a single line of code. For example, you can add simple actions that control the playback of the Timeline. Or, you can add buttons that pause, play, or jump to various parts of the Timeline when a site visitor clicks a button. You can build simple pre-loaders and navigation menus, or link objects to other pages on the Internet.

The most basic action in Flash is the *stop* action, used to prevent a movie from advancing to the next frame. You can apply the *stop* action to any frame, but when you apply it to the last frame of the Timeline, the *stop* action prevents the movie from looping back to the beginning and repeating.

It is a good idea to create a separate layer for actions that control your movie.

> **Inside the Design**
>
> Looping animation can be distracting on the Web. The animated billboard grabs attention and then stops on the most important information to allow viewers to see the content on the Web site.

Tips & Techniques

RESOLVING TWEEN ERRORS

A common mistake when creating tween animation in Flash is to apply a shape or motion tween to the wrong type of object. When you make a mistake creating shape or motion tweens, Flash identifies the mistake on the Timeline and in the Property inspector. On the Timeline, a good tween is shown by a solid line with an arrow. A broken tween displays a dashed line.

For help on repairing a broken tween, click the Tween error button on the Property inspector.

Most animation errors are caused by using the wrong type of tween. The basic distinction between the two types of tween animation is that with shape tweening, you use shapes to create the animation, whereas with motion tweening, you animate grouped objects, text, or symbols. Use the following rules to help determine when to use shape and motion tweens.

SHAPE TWEENING CAN	SHAPE TWEENING CANNOT
Animate between two shapes	Animate grouped objects
Animate between two colors of a shape (including color with transparency)	Animate between two symbols
Animate between two positions of a shape on the Stage	Animate text that has not been broken apart
Animate text that has been broken apart	
Animate between two gradient fills	

MOTION TWEENING CAN	MOTION TWEENING CANNOT
Animate between grouped objects	Animate ungrouped shapes
Animate between instances of symbols	Animate text that has been broken apart
Animate text blocks	

Add a Stop Action to the Timeline to Prevent the Movie from Looping

1. Insert a new layer above the *border text* layer (or whichever layer is at the top) and name it **actions**.

FIGURE 4-29
Actions layer

2. Insert a keyframe in frame **61** on the *actions* layer (the last frame in the movie).

3. Expand the Actions panel.

It appears above the Property inspector.

4. In the Actions toolbox (the pane on the left), click the **Global Functions** category to expand it.

5. Expand the **Timeline Control** category.

> **Note**
>
> You may need to drag to split the Actions panel to see both the Actions toolbox and the Script pane, as shown in Figure 4-30.

FIGURE 4-30
Actions panel

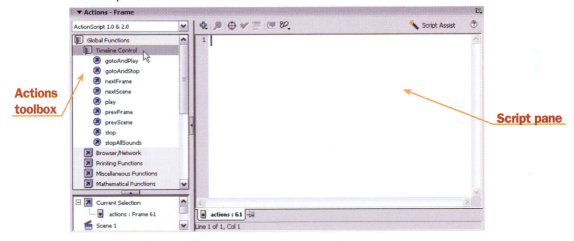

Actions toolbox

Script pane

6. Double-click the **stop** action.

A stop action is added to the Script pane and to frame 61 of the actions layer. The playhead will now stop when it reaches the end of the Timeline, preventing the movie from looping.

7. Collapse the Actions panel (to hide it).

8. Open the **Control** menu, and then click **Test Movie**.

The movie plays to the end of the Timeline and stops without looping.

9. Close the Flash Player window.

10. Lock the *actions* layer and save the document. If you are continuing with the next lesson, leave the project open. If you are not continuing at this time, close the file and close Flash.

Learn More

ANIMATING LETTERS BY USING BREAK APART

You can use the Break Apart command on the Modify menu to animate each letter of a text block independently. When you break apart a block of text, each letter becomes a separate object.

To apply separate animation to each letter, select the letters, click the Modify menu, point to Timeline, and then click Distribute to Layers. Flash places each letter on a separate layer automatically, making it possible for you to apply a unique animation to each letter.

This technique is often used to create the effect of letters animating separately into view to form a word or phrase.

Once a text block is broken apart, applying the Break Apart command to the individual letters converts them into shapes. By breaking apart text, you can apply shape tweens to the text, causing letters to morph into shapes or other objects. For example, you can morph one word or letter into another, or change a word into a related shape. To see an example of this, navigate to the data files for this project, open the Sample_Movies folder, and then view the file named **apple.swf**.

MAKING THE ANIMATED BILLBOARD ACCESSIBLE

OBJECTIVES

Upon completion of this lesson, you will be able to:

■ Define Accessibility.

■ Make a Flash document accessible.

Estimated time to complete this lesson: 10 minutes

Introduction

The animated billboard is intended to reach a wide audience, including people with visual or hearing impairment. The animated billboard was designed as a visual presentation with descriptive text and no audio. To make this information available to people with limited vision, you need to expose the movie to a special type of computer program called a screen reader. Visitors with screen-reader software hear a spoken description of what appears on the screen.

In this lesson, you use the Flash Accessibility panel to make the animated billboard accessible to screen readers.

Understanding Accessibility

"Accessibility" is broadly used to refer to efforts to make the Web usable for people with visual, auditory, and other disabilities.

A Flash document is considered *accessible* when it can be used by someone with a disability. Disabilities are broad and difficult to categorize, but according to the U.S. Census Bureau, one out of every five people in the United States has some sort of disability. One out of ten has a severe disability. Within that group are people with visual, hearing, cognitive, or physical disabilities, so it becomes pretty obvious why it is important to create content that is accessible to everyone. Without accessibility, much of your audience would be unnecessarily denied access to valuable information.

Accessibility is important for many reasons:

■ Accessibility is the right thing to do.

■ It opens doors to information for individuals with disabilities.

■ It is the law and/or policy for many colleges, universities, and organizations.

■ Accessibility offers increased usability to ALL site visitors, not just those with disabilities.

Making a Flash Document Accessible

To make the animated billboard accessible to screen readers, you need to provide descriptive text for a screen reader to translate into a spoken description.

The Flash Accessibility panel lets you set accessibility options for individual Flash objects or for the entire movie.

Some Flash objects are not intended for screen readers. For example, when a screen reader encounters the animated billboard, the visitor does not need a spoken description of the animated countdown or the background effect. Instead, the screen reader should detect and read the most important information about the upcoming film festival. The way to handle this is to make child objects inaccessible to screen readers. A *child object* is any object stored within the movie, or within an individual movie clip symbol.

To make the entire animated billboard accessible, make sure nothing on the Stage is selected. With no objects selected, the Accessibility panel applies to the entire document.

Make the Animated Billboard Accessible to Screen Readers

1. Open the document you created in the previous lesson, or open the practice file named **FL_Project1_Lesson5.fla**. If you use the practice file, be sure to save it as **FL_Project1_YourName.fla**.

2. Click in the empty workspace to make sure no objects are selected.

3. Click the **Window** menu, point to **Other Panels**, and then click **Accessibility**.

The Accessibility panel opens for the entire document.

4. Make sure **Make movie accessible** is selected.

5. Uncheck **Make child objects accessible**. This prevents the screen reader from seeing individual objects within the document.

The most important information that needs to be communicated is the name and description of the festival, the location and time, and the phone number for purchasing tickets.

6. Click in the Name text box and key: **Digital Impact Film Festival. Ten short films with special guest Santosh Chopra. Lakeview Theater, Detroit. April 12 to 14 2007. For tickets call 313 123 4567.**

FIGURE 5-1
Accessibility panel for the entire document

This information will be read by the screen reader. You can add additional information for the screen reader in the Description box, if desired.

7. Close the Accessibility panel and save the document. If you are continuing with the next lesson, leave the project open. If you are not continuing at this time, close the file and close Flash.

The important information for the animated billboard is now exposed to screen readers.

PUBLISHING FLASH ELEMENTS FOR THE WEB

OBJECTIVES

Upon completion of this lesson, you will be able to:

- Preview a Flash document before publishing.

- Adjust publish settings for a Flash document.

- Publish a Flash document for the Web.

Estimated time to complete this lesson: 10 minutes

Introduction

Before adding the animated billboard to a Web site, it is a good idea to preview it in a Web browser. Previewing in a browser offers a better representation of what viewers will experience than simply testing the movie in the stand-alone Flash Player or playing the document on the Timeline.

Publish settings tell Flash which types of files to produce each time you publish the document.

In this lesson, you preview the animated billboard in a browser, adjust the publish settings, and publish the document for viewing on the Web.

Previewing a Flash Document

When you preview the animated billboard in a browser, Flash generates a new HTML file and plays the SWF file in a browser of your choosing (assuming you have a copy of the browser installed on your system).

 ### Preview the Animated Billboard as it Will Appear in a Browser

1. Open the document you created in the previous lesson, or open the practice file named **FL_Project1_Lesson6.fla**. If you use the data file, be sure to save it as **FL_Project1_YourName.fla**.

2. Open the **File** menu, point to **Publish Preview**, and then click **Default - (HTML)**.

   The SWF file is generated and opened in a new HTML file. This shows you how the movie will play in your default browser.

3. Close the browser and return to Flash.

Publishing a Flash Document

When you publish a Flash document, you have the option of producing a variety of file types, but to view Flash content on the Web, you must output the SWF file and add it to an HTML page.

 ### Select Publish Settings and Publish the Document

1. Open the **File** menu and then click **Publish Settings**.

   The Publish Settings dialog box opens. The dialog box is divided into three tabs: Formats, Flash, and HTML.

2. Click the **Formats** tab if necessary.

   The Formats tab is used to select the types of files that are generated when you publish the document.

FIGURE 6-1
Formats tab on the Publish Settings dialog box

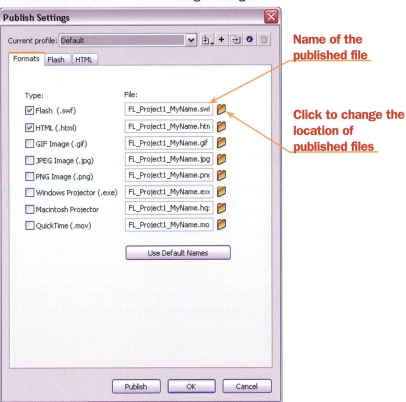

Name of the
published file

Click to change the
location of
published files

By default, Flash generates a SWF file and an HTML file each time you publish the document. The name of the FLA file is used for the files you publish. You can change these names on the Formats tab. To change the directory where the files are created, click the folder icon beside the filename and navigate to the new folder or directory.

3. Click the **Flash** tab.

Hot Tip

If you are publishing an HTML page that will be the home page of a Web site, you can name the file *index* or *default*. When placed at the root directory of a Web site, a file named index or default is opened automatically as the top-most page of a Web site.

The Flash tab allows you to modify the settings for the SWF file that is generated when publishing the document.

FIGURE 6-2
Flash tab on the Publish Settings dialog box

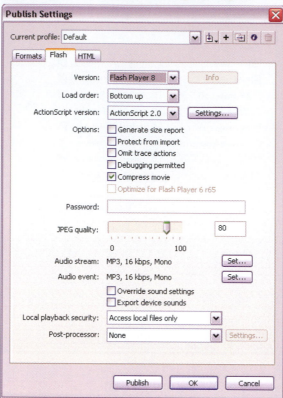

4. Click the **HTML** tab

The HTML tab includes options that affect the HTML file you generate when publishing the document. For example, you can insert code that automatically checks the visitor's computer for the most recent version of Flash Player.

FIGURE 6-3
HTML tab on the Publish Settings dialog box

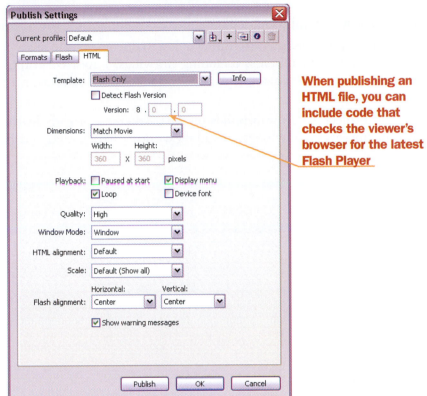

When publishing an HTML file, you can include code that checks the viewer's browser for the latest Flash Player

Because this document is going to be inserted on an existing HTML page, you only need to generate the SWF file.

5. Click the **Formats** tab and deselect the HTML option.

6. Click **Publish**.

The SWF file is created in the same directory as the FLA file.

7. Click **OK** to close the dialog box and save the changes to the Publish settings.

8. Save your document.

9. Close the file and close Flash.

Hot Tip

You can publish the document at any time by clicking the File menu and clicking Publish, or by pressing Shift+F12.

SUMMARY

You have successfully created an animated billboard for the upcoming film festival.

In this project, you learned to follow a design document and storyboard to produce and publish accessible Flash documents, including drawings, imported graphics, text, library symbols, and animation. These basic skills provide the necessary foundation for creating more complex Flash documents.

The next project in this unit builds on what you have already learned, reinforcing these skills and introducing several new ones, including working with sound and creating interactive buttons for navigation.

ON YOUR OWN – CREATING SHAPES, TEXT, ANIMATION, AND SYMBOLS

ACTIVITY 1: DRAWING AND MANIPULATING SHAPES

You have learned how to use the shape tools in Flash to draw simple shapes and then manipulate these shapes by using techniques such as:

- Using the drawing tools

- Pulling stroke lines with the Selection Tool to create curves

- Pasting shapes on top of other shapes to create cutouts

Apply these same techniques to create the drawings indicated here. You can review the techniques for this activity in Lessons 1 and 2.

Drawing a Leaf

1. Open a new document and change the name of *Layer 1* to **leaf**.

2. Click in the first frame of the *leaf* layer. Use the Rectangle Tool to draw a small rectangle. Make the fill color green **#00CC00** and the stroke color black **#000000**.

3. Select the rectangle (both the fill and stroke), and use the Free Transform Tool to rotate the shape about 45 degrees, so a corner is at the top of the shape.

4. Using the Selection Tool, drag the edges and corners of the rectangle until it resembles the shape of a leaf.

5. Using the Line Tool, draw segments to make veins inside the leaf and to draw its stem.

6. Using the Selection Tool, drag the stem line to add a slight curve to the stem of the leaf.

7. Save and name the document.

> **Hint**
>
> To move a corner of the rectangle, position the pointer over the corner and drag when you see a small corner attached to the pointer.

Drawing a Tree

The tree consists of two images brought together: a trunk and a tree top. If you draw these images on different layers, you will be able to manipulate the aspects of the tree top separately from the trunk.

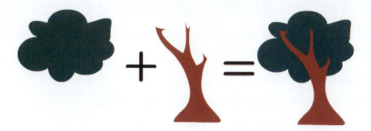

Tree trunk:

1. Open a new document. Use the Document Properties dialog box to change the width to **500** pixels and the height to **400** pixels. Select white (**#FFFFFF**) as the document background color. Add and name the following layers to create the tree drawing (listed from the top down): **tree trunk** and **tree top**.

2. Click in the first frame of the *tree trunk* layer. Use the Rectangle Tool to draw a rectangle that is tall and wide. Make the fill color brown (**#996600**) and set the stroke color to **None**. Be sure the Object Drawing option is turned off, to draw an ungrouped rectangle.

3. Using the cutout technique, cut rounded segments from each side of the rectangle to create a wide top and base, but a narrow middle.

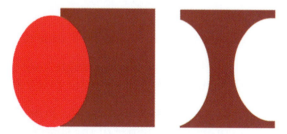

4. Using the cutout technique, cut two thin rectangles from the top of the image so you can manipulate the remaining parts into branches.

5. Using the Selection Tool, position the pointer over the edges and drag the edges of the rectangle to create curves for the trunk and branches, similar to the example shown. Lock the *tree trunk* layer.

Tree top:

1. Click in the first frame of the *tree top* layer. Select the **Oval Tool** and set the fill color to green (**#006600**) and the stroke color to **None**. Draw multiple overlapping circles to create the tree top.

2. If necessary, drag the edges of the circles to resemble a bushy tree top. Lock the *tree top* layer.

Hint
You may need to manipulate both the edges and the corners to create the branches. It may also help to turn off *Snap to Align* and *Snap to Objects* on the View menu.

Tree:

1. To assemble the tree, position the tree top behind the trunk such that all the branches fall within the tree top, similar to the example shown.

> **Hint**
>
> You may draw many circles of different sizes to generate a tree top large enough to sit behind all the branches. After drawing the tree trunk and tree top, you can use the Free Transform tool to manipulate the height and width of each element before combining them to form the tree.

You may choose to keep these images on separate layers if you plan to animate or manipulate either image separately (for example, changing the color of the tree top). Or, you can place them on one layer and make them one image, similar to the leaf.

2. Save and name the document.

ACTIVITY 2: CREATING AN ANIMATED TITLE CARD FOR A MOVIE

You have learned to create and format static text in a Flash document. You have also learned to use motion tween animation to animate text on the Stage. These techniques include:

- Entering and formatting text
- Using the Property inspector to apply text formatting
- Creating custom fills by using the Color Mixer
- Extending the Timeline by adding frames
- Inserting keyframes
- Using motion tween animation to animate text
- Using a *stop* action to prevent a movie from looping

Apply these same skills to create an animated title card for a movie. You can review the techniques for this activity in Lessons 1, 2, and 4.

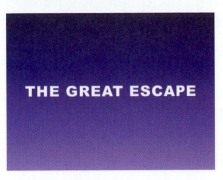

1.   Create a new Flash document and change the document size to **320** pixels wide and **240** pixels high. The background can be any color. Set the frame rate to **12** frames per second. Add and name the following layers for the title, background, and actions (listed from the top down): **actions, title text, background.**

2.   Click in the first frame of the *background* layer and use the Rectangle Tool to draw a rectangle with no stroke and any color fill. Make the rectangle the same size as the Stage (320 × 240). Use the Align panel to center the background rectangle on the Stage.

3.   Select the background rectangle and use the Color Mixer panel to apply a linear gradient fill that is dark blue (**#000033**) at the top and fades to light blue (**#9999FF**) at the bottom.

4.   Extend the Timeline to one second by adding frames to the *background* layer. Lock the *background* layer.

5.   Click in the first frame of the *title text* layer. Use the Text Tool to begin a new text block on the Stage. Key **THE GREAT ESCAPE**. Use the Property inspector to make the text **Static, Arial Black,** size **22,** white (**#FFFFFF**), center-aligned, and the letter spacing **1.**

6.   Use the Align panel to center the title both vertically and horizontally on the Stage.

7.   Use a motion tween to create a one-second animation in which the title text begins centered above the Stage in the workspace and moves into its final position, centered on the Stage. Lock the *title text* layer.

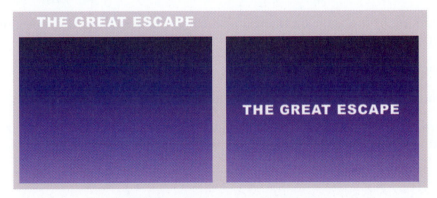

8.   Add a **stop** action to frame 13 (1 second) on the *actions* layer to prevent the movie from looping after it has played through once.

9.   Save and name the document. Test the movie by viewing the SWF in the Flash Player window.

ACTIVITY 3: WORKING WITH SYMBOLS, INSTANCES, AND THE LIBRARY

You have learned to convert graphic elements to symbols in the document library and then reuse instances of symbols to create interesting movies while maintaining smaller file sizes. These techniques include:

- Importing graphics

- Creating symbols

- Adding symbol instances from the Library panel

- Editing symbols

- Modifying the properties of a symbol instance

You can review the techniques for this activity in Lessons 1, 2, 3, and 4.

Use these same techniques to create the background for a document that features a coastal setting at night. Use graphic symbols to fill the night sky with stars.

1. Create a new document that is **500** pixels wide and **375** pixels high. The background color can be any color. Make the frame rate **12** frames per second. Add and name the following layers for the stars and image (listed from the top down): **stars** and **night**.

2. Import **night.jpg** to the Stage on frame 1 of the *night* layer. Center the image on the Stage, and then lock the *night* layer.

3. Import **black_star.swf** to the Stage on frame 1 of the *stars* layer.

4. Convert the black star to a graphic symbol named **star**.

5. Drag several copies of the star symbol from the Library panel to the Stage. Size, rotate, and manipulate the symbols to fill the night sky with a variety of stars.

6. Open the star symbol in editing mode and change the color of the star from black to blue (#0000FF).

7. Close the star symbol to return to Scene 1 and the main Timeline. Every instance of the star symbol on the Stage changes to the new color.

8. Select one instance of the star on the Stage, and then use the Color options on the Property inspector to change its Tint to a lighter shade of blue. This changes only the instance, not the original symbol in the library. Change the color properties for several other stars to different shades of blue.

9. Lock the *stars* layer. Save and name the document.

Hint

After you open the star symbol in editing mode, you need to ungroup the star graphic to change its color. You can double-click the star to temporarily ungroup the shape, or click **Modify** in the menu bar, and click **Ungroup** to permanently ungroup the shape. Once the shape is ungrouped, you can also manipulate the shape of the star symbol.

Hint

In addition to changing the tint color of each star, you can change the alpha transparency or brightness to create stars with a variety of appearances. To make additional copies of a modified symbol instance, select the instance, open the **Edit** menu, and then click **Duplicate**.

DIGITAL DOCUMENTARY

GOALS

- Follow a design document and storyboard to produce an online documentary.
- Use Flash to simulate film-style techniques and effects to tell a story.
- Create user-friendly navigation and features that provide ongoing feedback and put the audience in control of their online experience.
- Ensure that your online story is usable and accessible for the entire target audience.

TECHNICAL SKILLS

- Use guides and rulers for precise page layout.
- Import bitmap images.
- Convert a bitmap image to a vector drawing.
- Create film-style effects by using motion tweens.
- Add sound and adjust sound properties.
- Apply graphic filters.
- Create and modify buttons.
- Add ActionScript to buttons for navigation.
- Organize a Flash document by using folders.
- Test the performance and usability of a Flash document.
- Create and apply a mask.
- Make rich media content accessible.

Estimated time to complete this project: 6 hours

Summary

Digital storytelling uses film-style techniques to deliver compelling stories or messages directly to a viewer's desktop computer.

Regardless of whether the story is meant to inform, educate, inspire, sell something, or simply to entertain, the techniques for presenting online stories are similar to those used by professional filmmakers.

A common technique used by many online storytellers is to creatively blend still images, graphic art, titles, voice narration, music, and sound effects to produce the illusion of a motion picture.

Macromedia Flash is an ideal tool for producing digital stories. Much like a movie on DVD, online stories created with Macromedia Flash can include user controls for pausing, playing, rewinding, and locating chapters. Flash accessibility features expand the audience by making content accessible to people with hearing or vision disabilities.

The Assignment

In this project, you use Macromedia Flash to produce an accessible online documentary that tells a brief history of the Paradise Beach Boardwalk amusement park. The story features a collection of still photographs, voice narration, music, and sound effects that have been provided. You use the design document and storyboard to:

- Set the properties for your online documentary
- Set up an organizational scheme to keep the elements of the document organized
- Import and modify the photographs
- Create film-style camera moves and transitions
- Add the Paradise Beach Boardwalk logo and welcome title screen
- Create the elements and buttons used for navigation

Digital Documentary Design Document

Take a moment to review the project design document, shown in Figure 1, before starting a new Flash document. Note the elements that will help you set up your initial document.

FIGURE 1
Design document

> **Design Document – Digital Documentary**
>
> **Client: City of Oceanview – Paradise Beach Boardwalk Amusement Park**
>
> **Goals and Purpose**
>
> The online documentary will display on the Oceanview town website. Its goals are to:
> - Increase the number of new visitors to the Paradise Beach Boardwalk
> - Inform potential visitors and enthusiasts about the history of the Paradise Beach Boardwalk
> - Add interest to the Oceanview Web site.
>
> Key information in the story includes a brief history of the Paradise Beach Boardwalk.
>
> **Audience**
>
> Our target audience includes families, amusement park enthusiasts, and historians. Their age range is 8 and older. They can be frequent Internet users but don't need to be. Some adjectives to describe the audience are fun, curious, and adventurous.
>
> **Design Requirements**
>
> Colors: The Oceanview website includes deep shades of blue with orange and white accents. Colors for the documentary include Teal: #336699, Orange: #FFCC00, Navy: #000066, White: #FFFFFF, and Black: #000000.
>
> Navigation and Feedback: Visitors should be able to play, pause, rewind, or jump to segments within the story by using clearly identified buttons that are visible at all times. However, navigation elements should not be the focus of the screen and should not interfere with the photographs or caption text. The story should provide visual feedback indicating the visitor's current location in the story. Use button icons (Play, Pause, Rewind) provided to match the clients existing site navigation interface. Main navigation buttons should include keyboard equivalents.
>
> Accessibility: Accessible to screen readers. Include narration and onscreen text captions.
>
> Story duration: 45 seconds maximum
>
> Frame rate (FPS): 18
>
> Dimensions: 550 px by 340 px (no scrolling)
>
> Preloader: Yes
>
> **Delivery Requirements**
>
> The story will be built with Macromedia Flash and run with Macromedia Flash Player 8.
> - Internet Explorer, v6
> - Safari 2.0
> - AOL 8 or later
> - Mozilla Firefox 1.04 or later
>
> The story should run on
> - Macintosh OS10.3 or later
> - Windows XP Home or Professional
> - Internet connection speeds of 128Kbps or faster
>
> **Content**
>
> The story is told primarily by using voice narration and is supported by a series of photographs. Photographs include black and white and color images representing the Paradise Beach Boardwalk from 1845 to present.
>
> The following content should be included in the story:
> - *Welcome title*: The story begins on the welcome title. Visitors must click Play to begin the story.
> - *Logo*: The Paradise Beach Boardwalk logo will persist onscreen throughout the story.
> - *1845*: The boardwalk's origins.
> - *1902*: Introduction of the carousel.
> - *1924*: Introduction of the wooden roller coaster.
> - *Today*: The Paradise Beach Boardwalk includes history, rides, novelties, and entertainment for all ages.
>
> Paradise Beach Boardwalk Digital Documentary – Design Document   1

To view the design document for the Paradise Beach Boardwalk movie, open the file named *FL_Project2_Design.pdf*. This file is located in the Design folder in the Data files for this project.

Project Storyboards

Take a moment to review the storyboard, shown in Figure 2, before building the Paradise Beach Boardwalk movie. Note the elements that will help you set up your initial document.

FIGURE 2
Storyboard

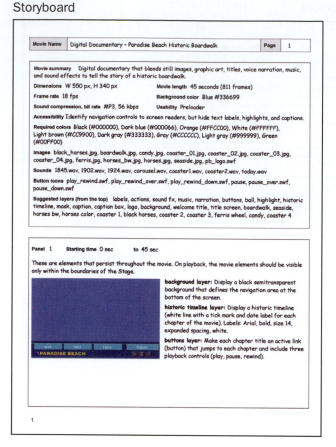

FIGURE 2
Storyboard

To view the storyboard for this project, open the file named *FL_Project2_Storyboard.pdf*. This file is located in the Design folder in the Data files for this project.

Preparing the Timeline and Stage for New Content

Introduction

The Paradise Beach Boardwalk story has requirements defined in the design document to ensure that it will play as intended when viewed on the client's Web site. From your review of the storyboards, you will see that there are photographs you will position on the Stage. A little planning for this up front can save time during the development process.

In this lesson, you prepare a new Flash document for the Paradise Beach Boardwalk movie by setting document properties, extending the Timeline, and using guidelines to maintain consistency and accuracy when placing content on the Stage. The storyboard, as shown in Figure 1-1, defines several document properties, including Stage size, frame rate, and estimated duration of the completed movie.

FIGURE 1-1
Storyboard

Movie summary   Digital documentary that blends still images, graphic art, titles, voice narration, music, and sound effects to tell the story of a historic boardwalk.

Dimensions W 550 px, H 340 px

Movie length 45 seconds (811 frames)

Frame rate 18 fps

Background color Blue #336699

Sound compression, bit rate MP3, 56 kbps

Usability Preloader

Accessibility Identify navigation controls to screen readers, but hide text labels, highlights, and captions.

Required colors Black (#000000), Dark blue (#000066), Orange (#FFCC00), White (#FFFFFF), Light brown (#CC9900), Dark gray (#333333), Gray (#CCCCCC), Light gray (#999999), Green (#00FF00)

Images black_horses.jpg, boardwalk.jpg, candy.jpg, coaster_01.jpg, coaster_02.jpg, coaster_03.jpg, coaster_04.jpg, ferris.jpg, horses_bw.jpg, horses.jpg, seaside.jpg, pb_logo.swf

Sounds 1845.wav, 1902.wav, 1924.wav, carousel.wav, coaster1.wav, coaster2.wav, today.wav

Button icons play_rewind.swf, play_rewind_over.swf, play_rewind_down.swf, pause, pause_over.swf, pause_down.swf

Suggested layers (from the top)   labels, actions, sound fx, music, narration, buttons, ball, highlight, historic timeline, mask, caption, caption box, logo, background, welcome title, title screen, boardwalk, seaside, horses bw, horses color, coaster 1, black horses, coaster 2, coaster 3, ferris wheel, candy, coaster 4

Opening a New Document and Setting Properties

The first step to creating a new Flash project is to open a new document and set document properties as they are defined in the design document and storyboard.

The design specification for the Paradise Beach Boardwalk movie requires it to play in a window that is 550 pixels wide and 340 pixels high.

The movie is going to include several film-style effects and transitions, which may not look smooth at the default 12 frames per second. When you increase the frame rate to 18, the file will still play well on most computer systems and will include smoother-looking animation and effects.

Open a New Document and Set Properties

1. Start the Flash program.

2. Click **Flash Document** in the Create New column.

   A new untitled Flash (FLA) document opens. The window shows whichever panels were open the last time Flash was used.

3. Open the **Modify** menu, and then click **Document**.

   The Document Properties dialog box opens.

Inside the Design

The designer chose the dimensions of this movie specifically to allow it to fit on a Web page while not invoking scrollbars. The frame rate controls how quickly each frame will show, which impacts the image's transitions. Sometimes the complexity of animation requires you to increase the intended frame rate. For example, the film-style transitions between images in this project will play more smoothly at a higher frame rate.

4. Make sure the Ruler units are set to Pixels. Set the width to **550 px** and the height to **340 px**.

5. Change the Background color to blue **(#336699)**.

6. Change the frame rate to **18** fps.

7. Click in the Title text box and key **Paradise Beach Boardwalk**.

8. Click in the Description box and key **A brief history of the amusement park**.

FIGURE 1-2
Storyboard

Document Properties

Title: Paradise Beach Boardwalk

Description: A brief history of the amusement park.

Dimensions: 550 px (width) x 340px (height)

Match: ○ Printer ○ Contents ◉ Default

Background color:

Frame rate: 18 fps

Ruler units: Pixels

Make Default   OK   Cancel

9. Click **OK**.

10. Select **Fit in Window** from the Magnification pop-up menu. (See Figure 1-3.) You can adjust the magnification as needed while you work.

FIGURE 1-3
Magnification pop-up menu

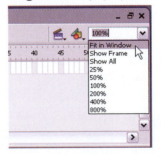

Viewing Rulers and Setting Guides

The Paradise Beach Boardwalk story includes several photographs that are larger than the Stage. As you add these images to the Stage, you need a visual indicator of where the Stage ends and the workspace begins.

An easy solution is to add guides that identify the Stage boundaries. Guides are also used for precise alignment of objects on the Stage and to maintain balance and symmetry. Guides do not appear in the published document.

 ## Set Guides That Identify Stage Boundaries

1. Open the **View** menu, and then click **Rulers** to display the rulers.

   Rulers are added above and to the left of the Stage. The upper left corner of the Stage represents the 0 (zero) position on the horizontal and vertical rulers as shown in Figure 1-4.

   FIGURE 1-4
   Rulers

   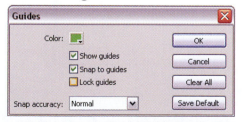

2. Open the **View** menu, point to **Guides**, and then click **Edit Guides**.

   The Guides dialog box opens.

3. Make sure the **Show guides** and **Snap to guides** check boxes are selected.

   As you drag objects near a guide, the object will snap into position and align with the guide.

4. Make sure the **Lock Guides** check box is not selected. Your dialog box should look like Figure 1-5. Click **OK**.

   With the guides unlocked, you can reposition a guide after adding it to the Stage.

   FIGURE 1-5
   Guides dialog box

5. Position the pointer anywhere on the horizontal (top) ruler, then click and drag a guide from the ruler onto the Stage. Drag the guide so it aligns with the top edge of the Stage, as shown in Figure 1-6.

FIGURE 1-6
A guide identifies the top edge of the Stage

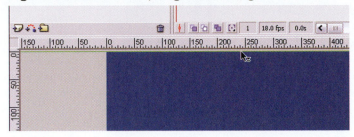

6. Position the pointer anywhere on the vertical (left) ruler and drag a guide from the ruler onto the Stage. Drag the guide so it aligns with the left edge of the Stage.

7. Add two additional guides that align with the bottom and right edges of the Stage, as shown in Figure 1-7.

FIGURE 1-7
Guides identify the top, bottom, left, and right edges of the Stage

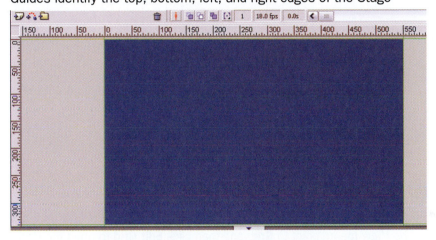

8. Open the **View** menu, point to **Guides**, and then click **Lock Guides**.

For additional information, see the Learn More feature "Viewing the Grid and Setting Snapping Options."

Learn More

VIEWING THE GRID AND SETTING SNAPPING OPTIONS

The grid divides the workspace into horizontal and vertical lines. Turn on the grid for precise alignment of objects and guides. By combining the power of the grid and guides, you can maintain structure and balance on the Stage.

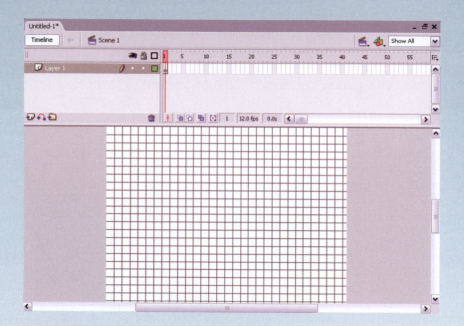

To Set Grid Properties

1. Open the **View** menu, point to **Grid**, and then click **Edit Grid** to open the Grid dialog box.

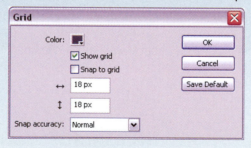

2. Select or deselect options, and then click **OK**.

The grid does not appear in the published document. You can also show or hide the grid by opening the View menu, pointing to Grid, and then clicking Show Grid.

As you draw or place objects on the Stage, you can make them snap to the nearest object, guide, grid, or pixel. Whether you enable snapping is a personal preference. Snapping makes aligning objects accurate but can also prevent you from aligning objects close to but not exactly on a guide or other object. *(Continued . . .)*

To Turn Snapping On or Off:

1. Open the **View** menu, point to **Snapping**, and then click **Edit Snapping** to open the Edit Snapping dialog box.

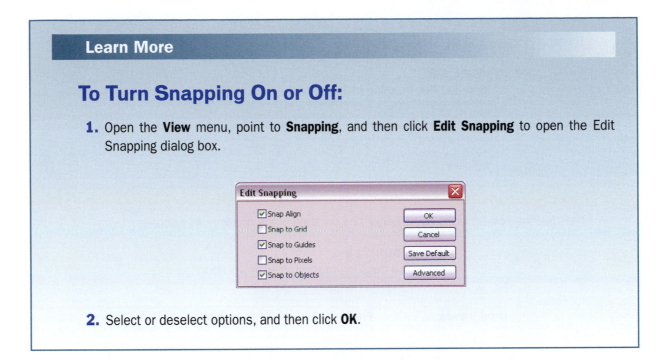

2. Select or deselect options, and then click **OK**.

Extending the Timeline

The Paradise Beach Boardwalk storyboard shows the duration of the movie to be approximately 45 seconds. You can save development time by adding the correct number of frames to the Timeline. This eliminates the need to repeatedly extend individual layers.

At 18 frames per second, the Timeline will play for 810 frames (45 seconds × 18 frames = 810). The playhead starts on frame 1, which is at zero seconds, so to make the movie 45 seconds long, extend the Timeline to frame 811.

 ## Extend the Timeline to Make the Movie Duration 45 Seconds

1. Scroll the Timeline to the right as far as it will go.

2. Click in the empty slot for the last frame on your Timeline.

3. Open the **Insert** menu, point to **Timeline**, and then click **Frame**.

> **Note**
>
> Flash does not let you scroll all the way to the empty slot for frame 811, so you will add a frame and then drag the new frame down the Timeline to 811 to extend the Timeline further.

4. Position the pointer over the frame you just added in step 3, and then drag the selected frame down the Timeline to frame **811**, as shown in Figure 1-8.

FIGURE 1-8
Extending the Timeline to frame 811

The Timeline now includes 811 frames. The duration of the movie is 45 seconds.

FIGURE 1-9
The duration of the movie is 45 seconds

Total frames   Frame rate   Duration

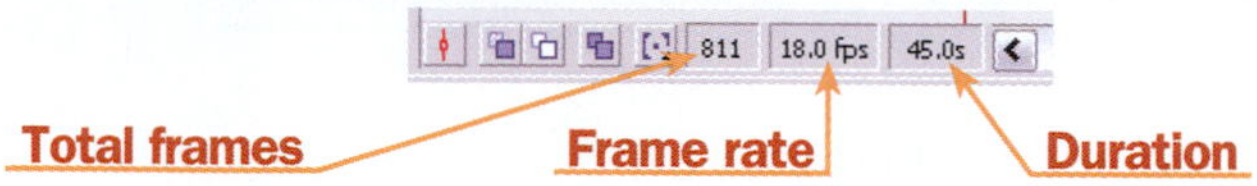

5. Save the document as **FL_Project2_YourName**. You may want to create a new folder (such as MyFiles) for storing your project files.

6. If you are continuing with the next lesson, leave this file open. If you are not continuing at this time, close the file and close Flash.

IMPORTING AND WORKING WITH BITMAP GRAPHICS

OBJECTIVES

Upon completion of this lesson, you will be able to:

- Import bitmap images.
- Add bitmap images to the Stage.
- Convert a bitmap to a vector by using Trace Bitmap.
- Organize the document by using folders.

Estimated time to complete this lesson: 15 minutes

Introduction

The Paradise Beach Boardwalk story is enhanced by a collection of photographs featuring the park's rides and attractions.

When importing bitmaps, such as photographs, it is best to manipulate, size, crop, and optimize the images before importing. This is done by using a graphics program such as Macromedia Fireworks. Proper optimization helps reduce the file size of the imported image, which improves performance of the completed Flash document.

Once a bitmap is added to Flash, you can size it, convert it to a symbol and change its color settings, break it apart and edit it by using the drawing tools, or convert the image to a vector drawing by using a feature called Trace Bitmap.

In this lesson, you begin by importing photographs for the Paradise Beach Boardwalk movie. You then create a background for the movie's opening title screen by tracing a copy of a photograph, as described in Figure 2-1.

FIGURE 2-1
Storyboard

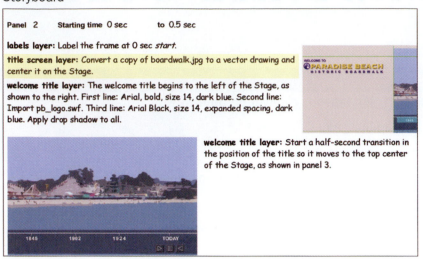

Importing Bitmap Images

The Paradise Beach Boardwalk movie includes a series of photographs that have already been sized, cropped, retouched, and optimized according to the project storyboard.

The next step is to import the images to the document library.

 ## Import Photographs of the Paradise Beach Boardwalk

1. If necessary, open the file you created in the previous lesson. Alternately, you can open the file named **FL_Project2_Lesson2.fla** which is found in the **Practice_files** folder in the data files for this lesson. If you use **FL_Project2_Lesson2.fla** be sure to save it as **FL_Project2_YourName.fla**.

2. Open the **File** menu, point to **Import**, and then click **Import to Library**.

3. Navigate to the Data files for this project and open the **Photos** folder.

4. Click the first file in the list, hold down **Shift**, and select the last file in the list to select every file. There are 11 files.

5. Click **Open** (Windows) or **Add to Library** (Macintosh) to add the photographs to the document library.

   The images are added to the Library panel, as shown in Figure 2-2.

FIGURE 2-2
Library panel

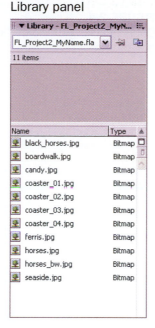

Organizing the Library Panel with Folders

Y̲ou can organize the document library by sorting objects into related folders.

For example, you may want to store bitmap images in the same folder to keep them separated from the symbols, buttons, sounds, and other content used in the project.

Step by Step **Add Folders to the Library Panel**

1. Click the **New Folder** button at the bottom of the Library panel.

FIGURE 2-3
New folder button at the bottom of the Library panel

New Folder button

2. Key **Bitmap Images** as the name of the new folder. Press **Enter** (Window) or **Return** (Macintosh) to name the folder.

3. Drag each of the bitmap photographs you imported into the Bitmap Images folder. They have the green bitmap icon beside them and include the .jpg filename extension.

4. Double-click the folder icon to expand the Bitmap Images folder.

FIGURE 2-4
Double-clicking the folder icon opens and closes the folder

Adding Bitmap Images to the Stage

The Paradise Beach Boardwalk movie begins with a long (distant) shot of the amusement park. Each photograph sits on a separate layer, so begin by renaming Layer 1, and then adding the first image of the Boardwalk to the Timeline.

> **Note**
>
> You will create additional folders as you add new content to the library.

 ## Add an Image From the Library Panel to the Stage

1. Double-click **Layer 1** on the Timeline and change the name to **boardwalk**.

2. Scroll back in the Timeline and click frame **1** on the *boardwalk* layer and drag a copy of the **boardwalk** bitmap from the Library panel to the Stage.

3. If it is not already open, open the Align panel and select the **To stage** option to turn it on, as shown in Figure 2-5.

> **Hot Tip**
>
> Some layer names may be too wide to fit in the available space. If this happens, drag the border to the right of the Layer names until you can see the entire name.

FIGURE 2-5
Align panel

Align vertical center

Align horizontal center

Align objects to the Stage

4. Use the Align panel to center the photo horizontally and vertically on the Stage.

FIGURE 2-6
The photo is centered horizontally and vertically to the Stage

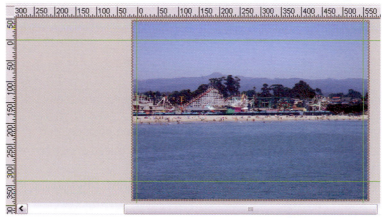

The green guides identify the boundary of the Stage. You may want to change the window magnification to Show All to see the entire image in relation to the Stage.

Converting a Bitmap to a Vector by Using Trace Bitmap

The background for the opening title screen is a traced version of the boardwalk image. Tracing the bitmap converts the image to a vector drawing, giving it the appearance of a painting. Following the opening title screen, the movie will transition from the traced version of the boardwalk image to the original photograph, so the traced bitmap is placed on a new layer above the photo.

Inside the Design

The Paradise Beach Boardwalk movie begins on a title screen with a traced bitmap as the background. The image is traced to look like a painting of the original photograph.

Convert a Bitmap Image to a Vector Drawing

1. With the photograph in frame 1 of the *boardwalk* layer selected, click the **Edit** menu and then click **Copy**.

2. Add a new layer above the boardwalk layer and name it **title screen**.

FIGURE 2-7
The title screen layer

3. Click on frame 1 of the *title screen* layer, open the **Edit** menu, and then click **Paste in Place**.

   A copy of the boardwalk photo is placed in the exact same position, but on the new layer. You apply the tracing to the top image and then transition from the traced image to the original photo.

4. Open the **Modify** menu, point to **Bitmap**, and then click **Trace Bitmap**.

   The Trace Bitmap dialog box opens.

5. Make sure the Color threshold is set to **100**, the Minimum area to **8** pixels, and the Curve fit and Corner threshold are both set to **Normal**, as shown in Figure 2-8.

FIGURE 2-8
Trace Bitmap dialog box

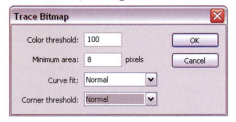

6. Click **OK**, and then click anywhere away from the image to deselect it.

   The image is traced and converted from a bitmap to a vector drawing. The image now appears as an abstract painting of the original photograph, as shown in Figure 2-9.

   For additional information, see the Learn More feature "Understanding Trace Bitmap Options."

FIGURE 2-9
Traced bitmap

Learn More

UNDERSTANDING TRACE BITMAP OPTIONS

The Trace Bitmap command converts a bitmap into a vector graphic with editable, discrete areas of color and produces an artistic rendering of the original bitmap image. An example of this can be seen in the figure below.

Bitmap   Vector

By combining various settings in the Trace Bitmap dialog box, you control the level of detail and the final look of the vector graphic. The settings that you can control are explained in the table below.

Color threshold	The amount of color each picture element can vary before it is considered another color. As the threshold value increases, the traced image has fewer colors. Color threshold ranges from 1–500.
Minimum area	The number of surrounding pixels taken into consideration when determining the color of each picture element. As the minimum area increases, the traced image looks more abstract, with less detail. The minimum area ranges from 1–1000.

(Continued . . .)

Learn More

Curve fit	Controls how smoothly each curve is drawn and how closely the vector matches the original bitmap image. A smoother selection results in a smaller file with less detail. A tighter selection results in a larger file with more detail.
Corner threshold	Fewer corners results in smoother edges and a smaller, more abstract-looking file. Many corners results in a larger file with more detail.

Converting a bitmap to a vector can either reduce or enlarge the file size of the published document, depending on the settings in the Trace Bitmap dialog box. The more detail and the lower the settings in the dialog box, the longer it takes to convert the bitmap to a vector, resulting in a larger file.

Tracing a bitmap only affects the image on the Stage and does not affect the original graphic stored in the document library. When you trace a bitmap, you break the link between the image and the graphic in the library.

Organizing the Timeline with Layer Folders

You can organize the Paradise Beach Boardwalk layers by placing the images and titles, sounds, and control elements in separate folders. Once you have placed items in a layer folder, you can collapse the folder, hiding its contents and reducing the amount of screen space it takes to view the Timeline.

 Add Layer Folders

1. Click the *title screen* layer on the Timeline. Open the **Insert** menu, point to **Timeline**, and then click **Layer Folder**.

   A layer folder, named Folder 1, is added to the Timeline above the *title screen* layer.

2. Double-click **Folder 1**, and then rename it **Images & Titles**.

FIGURE 2-10
Images & Titles layer folder

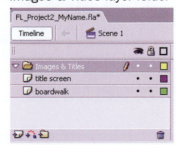

3. Click the *title screen* layer, hold down the Shift key, and then click the *boardwalk* layer. Both layers are selected.

4. Drag the selected layers onto the Images & Titles folder.

The layers are indented to show they are stored inside the folder.

FIGURE 2-11
The layers are indented to show they are inside the folder

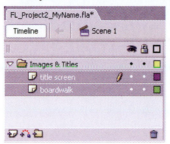

5. Save the document.

6. If you are continuing with the next lesson, leave this file open. If you are not continuing at this time, close the file and close Flash.

CREATING FILM-STYLE EFFECTS

OBJECTIVES

Upon completion of this lesson, you will be able to:

- Create a variety of film-style transitions between images.

- Simulate camera moves.

Estimated time to complete this lesson: 90 minutes

Introduction

The Paradise Beach Boardwalk story is enhanced by joining together a collection of still images using a variety of film-style transitions that help define the structure and pace of the story. Transitions are special effects used to change from one image to another.

The story also includes several camera techniques designed to add interest and create drama. Camera techniques are divided into two main categories:

1. Fixed Position: The camera appears to be in a fixed position, as if on a tripod, but it pans side to side or tilts up and down across an image or zooms in and out to reveal more or less of an image.

2. Moving Camera: The camera appears to move, simulating a hand-held camera or a camera attached to movable device such as a dolly, crane, or cable system.

The Paradise Beach Boardwalk movie includes both fixed position and moving camera techniques. In this lesson, you learn different transitions, such as dissolving between photographs, using color fades, creating wipe transitions, simulating a moving camera, fading to black, and using camera techniques such as panning, tilting, and zooming. You learn these transitions to generate specific effects such as setting the pace of a movie, indicating the passage of time, or indicating changes in the story.

Dissolving Between Images

A dissolve, sometimes called a cross fade, is a transition effect for moving from one image to another. This technique appears to fade in one image while another fades out.

123

The Paradise Beach Boardwalk story begins with the title screen (the traced bitmap) but quickly dissolves to the original photograph of the boardwalk, as described in Figure 3-1. This is the establishing shot that introduces Paradise Beach Boardwalk to the audience.

To dissolve between images in Flash, place the images in the same frames on separate layers. Use a motion tween to fade the upper image from opaque to transparent, slowly revealing the image below it.

Inside the Design

Fading from one image to another is a transition used to very simply and elegantly show a new image. The designer of the boardwalk uses the dissolve fade to change the "painting" of the boardwalk into the original image, bringing the boardwalk to life.

FIGURE 3-1
Storyboard

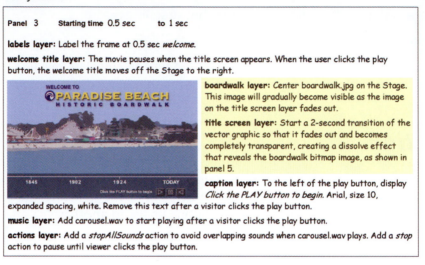

Panel 3   Starting time 0.5 sec   to 1 sec

labels layer: Label the frame at 0.5 sec *welcome*.

welcome title layer: The movie pauses when the title screen appears. When the user clicks the play button, the welcome title moves off the Stage to the right.

boardwalk layer: Center boardwalk.jpg on the Stage. This image will gradually become visible as the image on the title screen layer fades out.

title screen layer: Start a 2-second transition of the vector graphic so that it fades out and becomes completely transparent, creating a dissolve effect that reveals the boardwalk bitmap image, as shown in panel 5.

caption layer: To the left of the play button, display *Click the PLAY button to begin.* Arial, size 10, expanded spacing, white. Remove this text after a visitor clicks the play button.

music layer: Add carousel.wav to start playing after a visitor clicks the play button.

actions layer: Add a *stopAllSounds* action to avoid overlapping sounds when carousel.wav plays. Add a *stop* action to pause until viewer clicks the play button.

Dissolve Between Images

1. If necessary, open the document you created in the previous lesson. Alternately, you can open the file named **FL_Project2_Lesson3.fla** which is found in the **Practice_files** folder in the Data files for this lesson. If you use **FL_Project2_Lesson3.fla** be sure to save it as **FL_Project2_YourName.fla**.

2. Click frame **1** on the *title screen* layer to select the traced bitmap.

3. Convert the image into a Graphic symbol named **boardwalk_traced** as shown in Figure 3-2. (*Hint*: The Convert to Symbol dialog box is accessed through the Modify menu.)

FIGURE 3-2
Convert to Symbol dialog box

4. Insert keyframes at frames **10** and **46** on the *title screen* layer.

The traced photo will fade out between .5 and 2.5 seconds on the Timeline.

5. Click frame **46** on the *title screen* layer if necessary, and then (with the Selection Tool) click to select the instance of the traced photo on the Stage to activate the Property inspector.

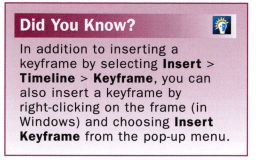

Did You Know?

In addition to inserting a keyframe by selecting **Insert > Timeline > Keyframe**, you can also insert a keyframe by right-clicking on the frame (in Windows) and choosing **Insert Keyframe** from the pop-up menu.

6. Select **Alpha** from the Color pop-up menu and set the Alpha to **0%**.

FIGURE 3-3
Setting the Alpha to 0% makes the symbol transparent

7. Create a motion tween between frames **10** and **46** on the *title screen* layer.

FIGURE 3-4
Motion tween that causes the title screen to become transparent

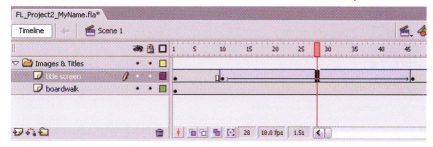

8. Insert a blank keyframe at frame **47** on the *title screen* layer.

Because the traced image becomes transparent in frame 46, you might as well remove it. The blank keyframe removes the image at frame 47.

9. Lock the *title screen* layer.

10. Click frame **1** on the *boardwalk* layer. Convert the photo to a Graphic symbol named **boardwalk**.

You convert the **boardwalk** image to a symbol so that you can dissolve to the next image by using a motion tween animation.

11. Drag the keyframe from frame **1** to frame **10** on the *boardwalk* layer, as shown in Figure 3-5.

The photo will begin to appear as the traced image fades out.

FIGURE 3-5
The boardwalk photo appears in frame 10 as the title screen begins to fade

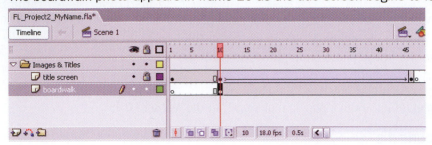

12. Position the playhead at frame **1** and press **Enter** (Windows) or **Return** (Macintosh) to preview the movie.

The movie begins on the traced image and slowly dissolves to the original photograph.

After the establishing shot of the boardwalk, the movie transitions to a black and white photograph of the seaside. The Boardwalk was founded in 1845 when visitors came to visit the area's seaside health spas. This image will reinforce the narration that describes the boardwalk in 1845, as described in Figure 3-6.

Did You Know?

Pressing **Enter** or Return starts and stops the playhead on the Timeline. So you can press **Enter/Return** once you pass frame 46 to stop the playhead rather than letting it play all the way through frame 811. You can also drag the playhead back and forth across the Timeline to preview the animation. This is called scrubbing.

FIGURE 3-6
Storyboard

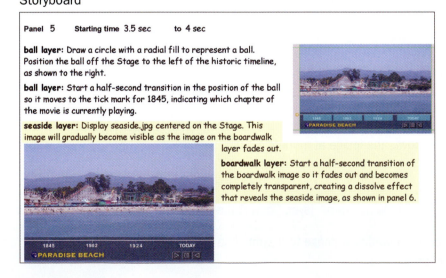

Dissolve Between the Introduction and the Seaside Photograph

1. Insert keyframes at frames **64** and **73** on the *boardwalk* layer (at 3.5 and 4 seconds).

2. Click frame **73** on the *boardwalk* layer if necessary, click the image on the Stage, and then use the Property inspector to change the Color to Alpha. The setting should already be **0%.** (This will be the default setting for Alpha until another setting is chosen.)

3. Create a motion tween between frames **64** and **73** on the *boardwalk* layer.

4. Insert a blank keyframe at frame **74** on the boardwalk layer.

   The boardwalk photo fades between 3.5 and 4 seconds on the Timeline.

FIGURE 3-7
The boardwalk photo fades between 3.5 and 4 seconds

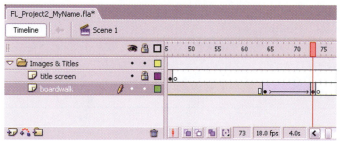

5. Lock the *boardwalk* layer.

6. Add a new layer named **seaside** and drag it below the *boardwalk* layer, being careful to keep it inside the Images & Titles folder.

FIGURE 3-8
The seaside layer is below the boardwalk layer and inside the Images & Titles folder

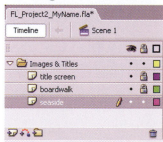

7. Insert a keyframe at frame **74** on the *seaside* layer.

8. Drag an instance of the seaside bitmap from the Library panel to the Stage. Use the Align panel to center the photograph horizontally and vertically to the Stage.

9. Convert the seaside bitmap to a Graphic symbol named **seaside**.

10. Click frame **74** on the *seaside* layer if necessary. Drag the keyframe to frame **64** on the same layer. The seaside photo will appear as the boardwalk begins to fade.

Note

The reason you created the keyframe in frame 74 and then dragged it back to its correct position is because in frame 64 the seaside image is hidden by the boardwalk layer, making it difficult to work with the seaside image. Another way to accomplish this is to temporarily hide the boardwalk layer while adding the seaside image. The danger of hiding layers is that you might forget to turn them back on.

FIGURE 3-9
The seaside photo appears in frame 64 as the boardwalk photo begins to fade

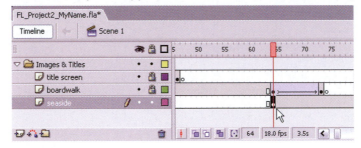

11. Fade the **seaside** image between frames **199** and **208**. Be sure to include the blank keyframe at frame **209**, as shown in Figure 3-10. (*Hint*: Reference steps 1–4 above if you need to review the process.)

FIGURE 3-10
The seaside layer becomes transparent between frames 199 and 208

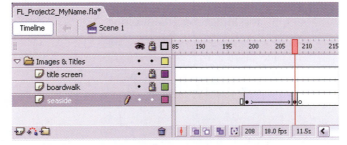

12. Lock the *seaside* layer.

13. Save the document.

Using a Color Fade to Indicate Passage of Time

A color fade is similar to a cross dissolve, but involves transitioning between two instances of the same image that have been colored or treated differently.

In the boardwalk, you dissolve between black and white and color versions of the carousel horses to show that time has passed, but the ride remains virtually unchanged, as described in Figure 3-11.

FIGURE 3-11
Storyboard

Step by Step   Use a Color Fade to Indicate Passage of Time

1. Create a new layer named **horses bw** and drag it below the *seaside* layer.

FIGURE 3-12
The horses bw layer

2. Insert a keyframe at frame **209** on the *horses bw* layer and drag a copy of the **horses_bw** image from the Library panel to the Stage.

3. Use the Align panel to center the photo horizontally and vertically to the Stage.

FIGURE 3-13
The horses_bw photo is centered on the Stage

4. Convert the **horses_bw** image to a Graphic symbol named **horses_bw**, and then drag the keyframe from frame **209** on the *horses bw* layer back to frame **199** on the same layer.

FIGURE 3-14
The horses_bw photo appears in frame 199 as the seaside layer begins to fade

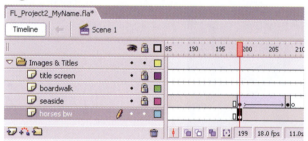

5. Fade the **horses_bw** image between frames **235** and **244**. Be sure to include the blank keyframe at frame **245**, as shown in Figure 3-15.

FIGURE 3-15
The horses_bw photo becomes transparent between frames 235 and 244

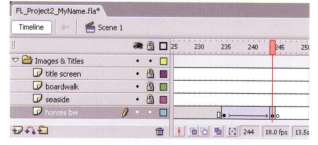

6. Lock the *horses bw* layer.

7. Create a new layer named **horses color** and drag it below the *horses bw* layer, as shown in Figure 3-16.

FIGURE 3-16
The horses color layer

8. Insert a keyframe at frame **245** on the *horses color* layer and drag a copy of the **horses** image from the Library panel to the Stage. Center the photo horizontally and vertically on the Stage.

FIGURE 3-17
The horses photo is centered on the Stage

9. Convert the **horses** image to a Graphic symbol named **horses**.

10. Click frame **245** on the *horses color* layer. Drag the keyframe to frame **235** on the same layer.

FIGURE 3-18
The horses photo appears at frame 235 as the horses_bw photo fades

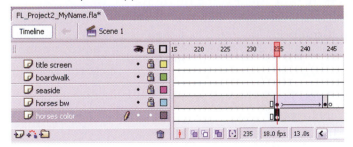

The colored horses will appear as the black and white horses fade.

11. Fade the colored horses between frames **271** and **281**. Be sure to include the blank keyframe at frame **282**, as shown in Figure 3-19.

FIGURE 3-19
The colored horses become transparent between frames 271 and 281

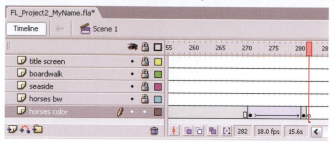

12. Lock the *horses color* layer and preview the movie.

Creating Camera Pans, Tilts, and Zooms

Unlike film edits, which are used to transition from one image to another, camera moves manipulate the view of the current image. For example, a filmmaker might begin on a close-up and then slowly pan from left to right to reveal more of the scene. Panning is often used to view a larger area while maintaining a close-up of the subjects. A similar move is to tilt the camera up or down vertically.

The most recognizable camera technique is the zoom. Filmmakers start wide and then zoom in to focus our attention. The opposite of a zoom is the reveal (or zoom out). The camera starts very close and then pulls away to reveal more information.

In the boardwalk, you will use the zoom-out technique by going from a close-up of a carousel horse to reveal more of the carousel, as described in Figure 3-20.

Camera moves are created in Flash by animating between two instances of the same image at different sizes, angles, and positions on the Stage.

FIGURE 3-20
Storyboard

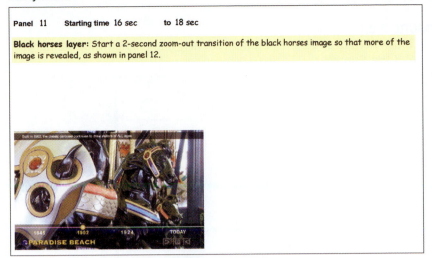

Panel 11   Starting time 16 sec   to 18 sec

Black horses layer: Start a 2-second zoom-out transition of the black horses image so that more of the image is revealed, as shown in panel 12.

 Use a Camera Move to Reveal More of an Image

1. Insert a new layer named **black horses** and drag it below the *horses color* layer.

FIGURE 3-21
The black horses layer

2. Insert a keyframe at frame **282** on the *black horses* layer and drag a copy of the **black_horses** image from the Library panel to the Stage.

   This image was made much larger than the others to allow for the close-up without distorting the image.

3. Use the Align panel to center the photograph vertically on the Stage and align the right edge of the photo with the right edge of the Stage.

FIGURE 3-22
The black horses photo is centered vertically and aligned with the right edge of the Stage

Align vertical center

Align to stage

Align right edge

4. Convert the image to a Graphic Symbol named **black_horses**.

5. Click frame **282** on the *black horses* layer. Drag the keyframe to frame **271** on the same layer.

   The black horses will appear in this position as soon as the previous image begins to fade. After the dissolve, the camera will begin to zoom out to reveal more of the image. This effect is created by reducing the image over time to fit more of the photograph within the borders of the Stage.

> **Did You Know?**
> You can combine these basic techniques to form more interesting moves, such as zooming out while panning and tilting at the same time.

6. Insert keyframes at frames **289** and **325** on the *black horses* layer. These are the beginning and end frames of the zoom.

7. Click frame **325** on the *black horses* layer if necessary, and click the photo to select it. On the Property Inspector, click on the constrain padlock to lock it. This will maintain the height-to-width ratio of the image. Then use the Property inspector to change the width of the photograph to **550 px**.

FIGURE 3-23
Constrain padlock on the Property inspector

Constrain padlock →

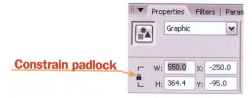

8. Center the photo both horizontally and vertically on the Stage, as shown in Figure 3-24.

FIGURE 3-24
The black horses photo is centered on the Stage

9. Create a motion tween between frames **289** and **325** on the *black horses* layer.

   After the camera pulls out, the image will remain onscreen for a moment before the next image appears.

10. Insert a blank keyframe at frame **352** on the **black horses** layer.

FIGURE 3-25
The black horses will disappear at frame 352

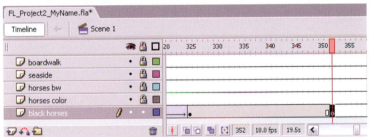

11. Lock the *black horses* layer and preview the movie.

Using Wipe Transitions to Indicate Change

A wipe is a transition in which a new scene or image wipes or slides into view, pushing aside or covering up the previous image. A wipe is an excellent way to indicate a change in location or time.

The Paradise Beach Boardwalk storyboard, described in Figure 3-26, identifies a wipe to transition from the carousel in 1845 to the introduction of the roller coaster in 1902. Although you could use a standard horizontal wipe to indicate the change, the story is transitioning from the carousel to the excitement and drama of the historic wooden roller coaster. One way to add impact to the transition is to vary the angle or entry of the wipe. Instead of simply sliding the image into view, you will rotate and drop the photo into place, as if it is falling from the sky and landing on the Stage.

Inside the Design

A wipe transition helps emphasize a change in location or time. The designer chose to use the wipe transition as a transition to the roller coaster and to emphasize the drama and excitement of the images to come.

FIGURE 3-26
Storyboard

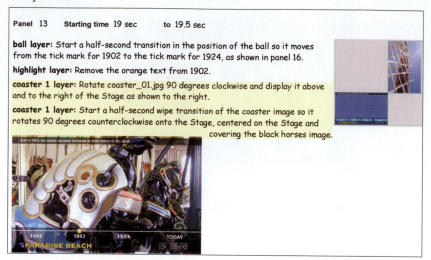

Panel 13   Starting time 19 sec   to 19.5 sec

ball layer: Start a half-second transition in the position of the ball so it moves from the tick mark for 1902 to the tick mark for 1924, as shown in panel 16.

highlight layer: Remove the orange text from 1902.

coaster 1 layer: Rotate coaster_01.jpg 90 degrees clockwise and display it above and to the right of the Stage as shown to the right.

coaster 1 layer: Start a half-second wipe transition of the coaster image so it rotates 90 degrees counterclockwise onto the Stage, centered on the Stage and covering the black horses image.

 Use a Wipe Transition to Indicate Change

1. Insert a new layer above the *black horses* layer and name it **coaster 1**. Be sure to leave the *coaster 1* layer above the black horses for the wipe transition.

FIGURE 3-27
The coaster 1 layer

2. Insert a keyframe at frame **343** on the *coaster 1* layer. This is the beginning of the wipe transition.

3. Drag a copy of the **coaster_01** image from the Library panel to the Stage. Use the Align panel to center the image horizontally and vertically to the Stage.

4. Convert the image to a Graphic symbol named **coaster_1**.

5. Insert a keyframe at frame **352** on the *coaster 1* layer. This is the end of the wipe transition.

6. Click frame **343** on the *coaster 1* layer and use the Free Transform Tool to rotate the photo 90 degrees clockwise.

7. Position the photo above and to the right of the Stage, as shown in Figure 3-28. You need to zoom out to see the workspace around the Stage to do this.

FIGURE 3-28
Starting position of the wipe transition

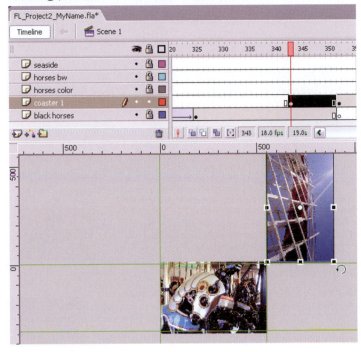

8. Create a motion tween between frames 343 and 352 on the *coaster 1* layer.

9. Insert a blank keyframe at frame **397** on the *coaster 1* layer.

10. Lock the *coaster 1* layer. Change the magnification back to **Fit in Window**, and then preview the movie.

Using Transitions to Set the Pace of the Story

Most films and television programs use a mix of transitions to vary the mood or pacing from scene to scene. For example, a car chase appears more exciting when edited together as a series of fast cuts.

In the Paradise Beach Boardwalk story, use cuts (instead of dissolves) to piece together the three images of the roller coaster, as described in Figure 3-29.

FIGURE 3-29
Storyboard

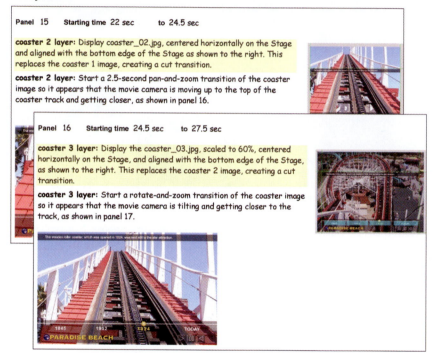

Add Cut Transitions to Change the Pace of the Story

1. Insert two new layers below the *black horses* layer and name them **coaster 2** and **coaster 3**, as shown in Figure 3-30.

FIGURE 3-30
The coaster 3 layer

2. Insert a keyframe at frame **397** on the *coaster 2* layer. This is where the coaster 1 image disappears.

3. Drag a copy of the **coaster_02** image from the Library panel to the Stage.

4. Use the Align panel to center the image horizontally to the Stage and align the bottom edge of the photo with the bottom edge of the Stage.

FIGURE 3-31
Using the Align panel to center the image horizontally and align the bottom edge to the Stage

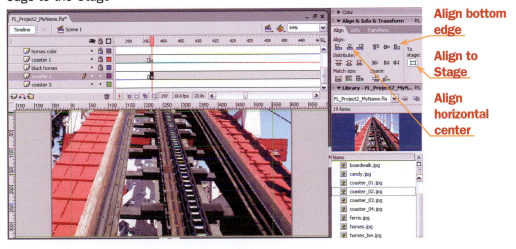

Align bottom edge

Align to Stage

Align horizontal center

5. Convert the image to a Graphic symbol named **coaster_2**.

6. Insert a blank keyframe at frame **443** on the *coaster 2* layer.

Frame 443 is where the movie will cut from coaster 2 to coaster 3.

7. Insert a keyframe at frame **443** on the *coaster 3* layer.

8. Drag a copy of the **coaster_03** image from the Library panel to the Stage.

9. Align the image horizontally to the Stage, and align the top edge of the photo with the top edge of the Stage, as shown in Figure 3-32.

FIGURE 3-32
Using the Align panel to center the image horizontally and align the top edge to the Stage

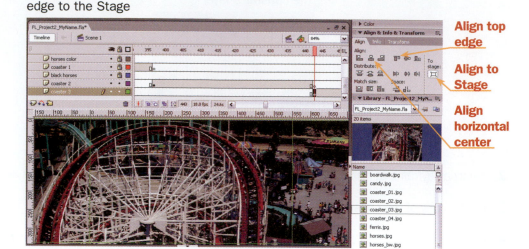

10. Convert the image to a Graphic symbol named **coaster_3**.

11. Preview the movie. Notice the differences between the dissolve and cut transitions. Think about how different transitions can be used to set the pace or vary the mood of a story.

Simulating a Moving Camera

Filmmakers sometimes mount a camera on a dolly, cable system, crane, or other device that allows them to physically move the camera during filming. A moving camera gives the audience a sense of realism, as if they are actually part of the scene.

In the Paradise Beach Boardwalk movie, you can take the viewer on a virtual roller coaster ride by simulating camera moves. You do this by animating between modified or repositioned copies of the roller coaster photos.

The first part of the roller coaster ride is to move the viewer up the big hill. Then take them for a soaring ride down and into the first turn of the tracks, as shown in Figure 3-33.

FIGURE 3-33
Storyboard

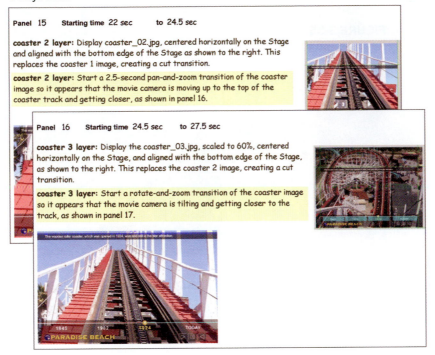

Panel 15   Starting time 22 sec   to 24.5 sec

coaster 2 layer: Display coaster_02.jpg, centered horizontally on the Stage and aligned with the bottom edge of the Stage as shown to the right. This replaces the coaster 1 image, creating a cut transition.

coaster 2 layer: Start a 2.5-second pan-and-zoom transition of the coaster image so it appears that the movie camera is moving up to the top of the coaster track and getting closer, as shown in panel 16.

Panel 16   Starting time 24.5 sec   to 27.5 sec

coaster 3 layer: Display the coaster_03.jpg, scaled to 60%, centered horizontally on the Stage, and aligned with the bottom edge of the Stage, as shown to the right. This replaces the coaster 2 image, creating a cut transition.

coaster 3 layer: Start a rotate-and-zoom transition of the coaster image so it appears that the movie camera is tilting and getting closer to the track, as shown in panel 17.

Simulate a Moving Camera

1. Insert a keyframe at frame **442** on the *coaster 2* layer. This will be the end of the first camera move (going up the hill).

2. Use the Align panel to align the top edge of the photo to the top edge of the Stage.

FIGURE 3-34
Using the Align panel to align the top edge of the photo in frame 442 to the top edge of the Stage

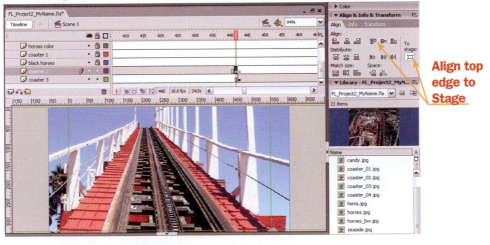

Align top edge to Stage

3. Use the right arrow key to nudge the photo to the right to keep the tracks centered on the Stage, similar to Figure 3-35.

FIGURE 3-35
Keeping the tracks centered on the Stage

4. Create a motion tween between frames **397** and **442** on the *coaster 2* layer.

The camera will begin at the bottom of the tracks in frame 397 and move to the top of the tracks at frame 442.

5. Lock the *coaster 2* layer.

6. Insert a keyframe at frame **496** on the *coaster 3* layer. This is the end of the second camera move (going down the hill).

7. Use the Free Transform Tool to rotate the image to the left slightly. If necessary, move the top edge of the photo so it still covers the Stage, as shown in Figure 3-36.

FIGURE 3-36
Using the Free Transform tool to rotate the image

8. Click frame **443** on the *coaster 3* layer. This is the beginning of the second camera move.

9. Use the Transform panel to change the photo's height and width to **60** percent of its original size.

FIGURE 3-37
Using the Transform panel to change the photos height
and width to 60%

10. Align the photo with the bottom edge of the Stage.

FIGURE 3-38
Using the Align panel to align the photo with the bottom edge of the Stage

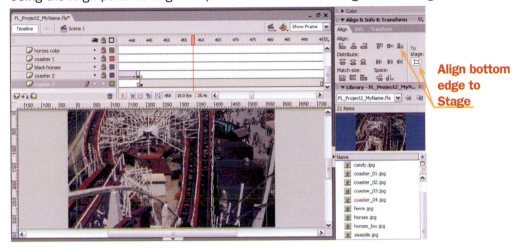

11. Create a motion tween between frames **443** and **496** on the *coaster 3* layer.

12. Preview the movie and make adjustments to the camera moves if needed.

Creating a Dip to Black Transition to Indicate Change

A simple dip to black is a very effective way to tell the audience one event or scene has ended and another is about to begin.

Use a dip to black to introduce the final chapter of the Paradise Beach Boardwalk story, as described in Figure 3-39.

FIGURE 3-39
Storyboard

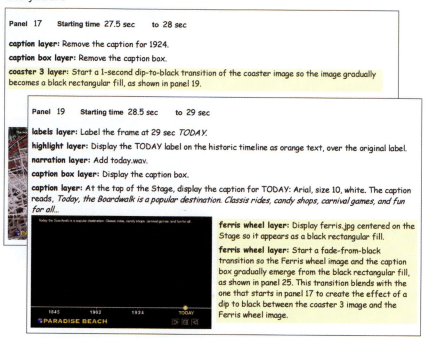

Panel 17   Starting time 27.5 sec   to 28 sec

caption layer: Remove the caption for 1924.

caption box layer: Remove the caption box.

coaster 3 layer: Start a 1-second dip-to-black transition of the coaster image so the image gradually becomes a black rectangular fill, as shown in panel 19.

Panel 19   Starting time 28.5 sec   to 29 sec

labels layer: Label the frame at 29 sec *TODAY*.

highlight layer: Display the TODAY label on the historic timeline as orange text, over the original label.

narration layer: Add today.wav.

caption box layer: Display the caption box.

caption layer: At the top of the Stage, display the caption for TODAY: Arial, size 10, white. The caption reads, *Today, the Boardwalk is a popular destination. Classis rides, candy shops, carnival games, and fun for all...*

ferris wheel layer: Display ferris.jpg centered on the Stage so it appears as a black rectangular fill.

ferris wheel layer: Start a fade-from-black transition so the Ferris wheel image and the caption box gradually emerge from the black rectangular fill, as shown in panel 25. This transition blends with the one that starts in panel 17 to create the effect of a dip to black between the coaster 3 image and the Ferris wheel image.

Use a Dip to Black Transition to Indicate Change

1. Insert a keyframe at frame **514** on the *coaster 3* layer.

2. Click the instance of the **coaster_3** symbol on the Stage to select it.

3. On the Property inspector, select **Brightness** from the Color pop-up menu, and then drag the slider to **–100%**, as shown in Figure 3-40.

FIGURE 3-40
Changing the brightness of a symbol

The image is completely dark.

4. Create a motion tween between frames **496** and **514** on the *coaster 3* layer. The image slowly fades to black.

5. Insert a blank keyframe at frame **515** on the *coaster 3* layer.

6. Lock the *coaster 3* layer.

7. Insert a new layer below the *coaster 3* layer and name it **ferris wheel**.

FIGURE 3-41
The ferris wheel layer

8. Insert a keyframe at frame **515** on the *ferris wheel* layer.

9. Drag a copy of the **ferris** image from the Library panel to the Stage. Use the Align panel to center the photo horizontally and vertically to the Stage.

10. Convert the **ferris** image to a Graphic symbol named **ferris**.

11. Insert a keyframe at frame **523** on the *ferris wheel* layer.

12. Click frame **515** on the *ferris wheel* layer, click on the Stage to select the instance of the ferris symbol, and then use the Property inspector to change its brightness to **–100%**.

13. Create a motion tween between frames **515** and **523** on the *ferris wheel* layer.

FIGURE 3-42
The ferris wheel will fade in from black between frames 515 and 523.

The movie will briefly dip to black between the roller coaster and the Ferris wheel, indicating a change to the viewer.

14. Preview the movie.

Creating the Conclusion

The Paradise Beach Boardwalk story begins with a traced bitmap of the amusement park. The movie tells a brief history of the park, and peaks with a ride on the wooden roller coaster. The dip to black signals the end of the movie.

Conclude the movie by using a series of dissolves describing the park as it is today. End the story as it began, on a traced bitmap of the amusement park, as described in Figure 3-43.

FIGURE 3-43
Storyboard

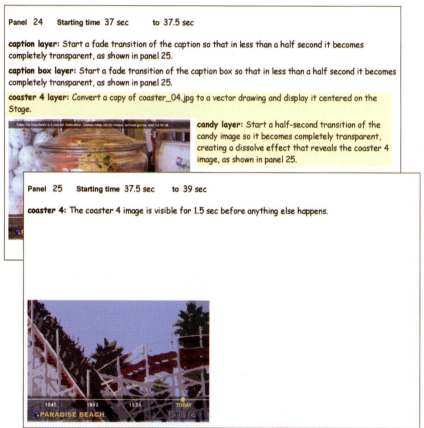

Build the Today Section of the Movie

1. Fade the **ferris wheel** image between frames **568** and **577** on the *ferris wheel* layer. Be sure to include the blank keyframe at frame **578**, as shown in Figure 3-44.

FIGURE 3-44
The ferris wheel image becomes transparent between frames 568 and 577

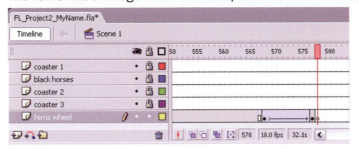

2. Lock the *ferris wheel* layer.

3. Insert two new layers below the *ferris wheel* layer and name them **candy** and **coaster 4**, as shown in Figure 3-45.

FIGURE 3-45
The candy and coaster 4 layers

4. Insert a keyframe at frame **578** on the *candy* layer. Drag a copy of the **candy** image from the Library panel to the Stage. Use the Align panel to center the image horizontally and vertically to the Stage.

5. Convert the **candy** image to a Graphic symbol named **candy**.

6. Click frame **578** on the *candy* layer. Drag the keyframe to frame **568** on the same layer. The candy will appear as the ferris wheel fades out.

FIGURE 3-46
The candy layer appears in frame 568 when the ferris wheel begins to fade

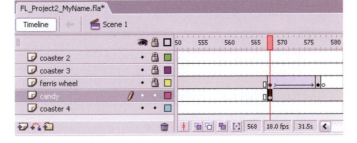

7. Fade the **candy** image between frames **667** and **676** on the *candy* layer. Be sure to include the blank keyframe at frame 677, as shown in Figure 3-47.

FIGURE 3-47
The candy image will become transparent between frames 667 and 676

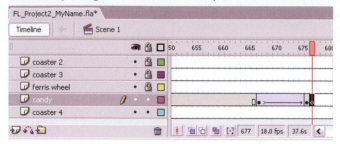

8. Lock the *candy* layer.

 ## End the Movie on a Traced Bitmap of the Roller Coaster

1. Insert a keyframe at frame **677** on the *coaster 4* layer. Drag a copy of the **coaster_04** image from the Library panel to the Stage and center the image horizontally and vertically to the Stage.

2. Open the **Modify** menu, point to **Bitmap**, and click **Trace Bitmap** to trace the coaster_04 image and convert it from a bitmap to a vector. Leave the most recent trace bitmap settings and click **OK**.

FIGURE 3-48
Traced bitmap version of the coaster_04 image

3. If necessary, click frame **677** on the *coaster 4* layer to select the entire vector image, and then convert the vector to a Graphic symbol named **coaster_4**.

4. Click frame **677** on the *coaster 4* layer. Drag the keyframe to frame **667** on the same layer, as shown in Figure 3-49.

FIGURE 3-49
The last roller coaster will appear as the candy begins to fade

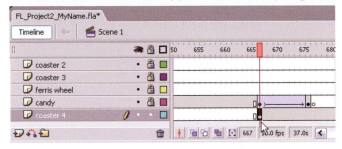

5. Insert keyframes at frames **721** and **757** on the *coaster 4* layer.

6. If necessary, click frame **757** on the *coaster 4* layer and click the instance of the symbol on the Stage to select it.

7. Use the Property inspector to change the symbol's brightness to **–100%**.

8. Create a motion tween between frames **721** and **757** on the *coaster 4* layer.

FIGURE 3-50
The last images will fade to black between 40 and 42 seconds

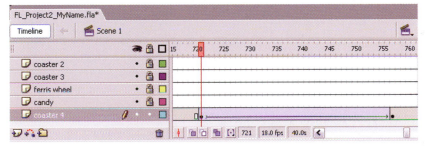

The last photo will slowly fade to black between 40 and 42 seconds on the Timeline.

9. Lock the *coaster 4* layer and preview the movie.

10. Collapse the **Bitmap Images** library folder. Create a new library folder named **Graphic Symbols** and place the graphic symbols you created in this lesson inside the new folder.

FIGURE 3-51
Creating a folder for storing graphic symbols in the library

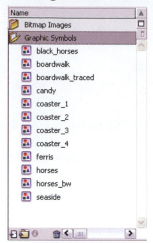

11. Save the document. If you are continuing with the next lesson, leave this file open. If you are not continuing at this time, close the file and close Flash.

WORKING WITH SOUND

Introduction

What you hear is sometimes as important as what you see. Imagine a scary movie without its haunting musical score and sound effects. Not so scary? How would you describe in text the sound of passengers descending the first hill of an old wooden roller coaster?

Sound adds drama, stirs emotions, and improves communication. In the Paradise Beach Boardwalk movie, sounds are used to narrate a story and re-create the sounds you might hear if you were actually there.

All types of sound can be added to Flash documents, including music, narration, and sound effects. Sound can be added to the main Timeline but is also sometimes attached to buttons, providing feedback to viewers.

In this lesson, you add sound to the Paradise Beach Boardwalk movie, including voice narration, carousel music, and sound effects.

Take a moment to review the storyboard to see where sounds are used to tell the story. An example of this is shown in Figure 4-1.

FIGURE 4-1
Storyboard

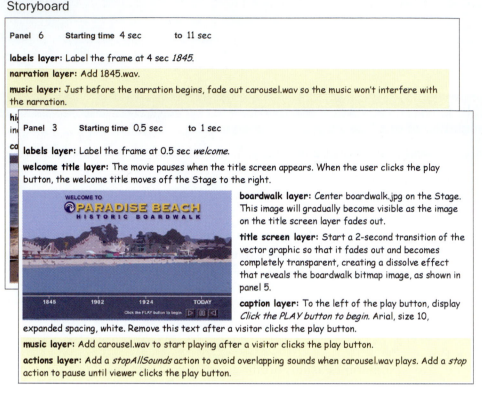

Panel 6   Starting time 4 sec   to 11 sec

labels layer: Label the frame at 4 sec *1845*.

narration layer: Add 1845.wav.

music layer: Just before the narration begins, fade out carousel.wav so the music won't interfere with the narration.

Panel 3   Starting time 0.5 sec   to 1 sec

labels layer: Label the frame at 0.5 sec *welcome*.

welcome title layer: The movie pauses when the title screen appears. When the user clicks the play button, the welcome title moves off the Stage to the right.

boardwalk layer: Center boardwalk.jpg on the Stage. This image will gradually become visible as the image on the title screen layer fades out.

title screen layer: Start a 2-second transition of the vector graphic so that it fades out and becomes completely transparent, creating a dissolve effect that reveals the boardwalk bitmap image, as shown in panel 5.

caption layer: To the left of the play button, display *Click the PLAY button to begin*. Arial, size 10, expanded spacing, white. Remove this text after a visitor clicks the play button.

music layer: Add carousel.wav to start playing after a visitor clicks the play button.

actions layer: Add a *stopAllSounds* action to avoid overlapping sounds when carousel.wav plays. Add a *stop* action to pause until viewer clicks the play button.

Importing Sound to the Document Library

Before adding sound to the Timeline, you must import the sound file to the document library. The sound file formats listed in Table 4-1 can be added to a Macromedia Flash document.

TABLE 4-1
Acceptable sound file formats

WITHOUT QUICKTIME INSTALLED	WITH QUICKTIME 4 OR LATER INSTALLED*
WAV (Windows Only)	**AIFF** (Windows or Macintosh)
AIFF (Macintosh Only)	Sound Designer II (Macintosh Only)
MP3 (Window or Macintosh) (Windows or Macintosh)	Sound Only QuickTime Movies
	Sun AU (Windows or Macintosh)
	System 7 Sounds (Macintosh Only)
	WAV (Windows or Macintosh)
* This project requires QuickTime 4 or later to be installed.	

Import Sound to the Document Library

1. If necessary, open the file you created in the previous lesson. Alternately, you can open the file named **FL_Project2_Lesson4.fla** which is found in the **Practice_files** folder in the Data files for this lesson. If you use **FL_Project2_Lesson4.fla** be sure to save it as **FL_Project2_YourName.fla**.

2. Open the **File** menu, point to **Import**, and then click **Import to Library**.

   The Import to Library dialog box opens.

3. Navigate to the data files for this project and open the **Sounds** folder. Select the following sound files: *1845.wav, 1902.wav, 1924.wav, carousel.wav, coaster1.wav, coaster2.wav,* and *today.wav.*

   FIGURE 4-2
   Import to Library dialog box

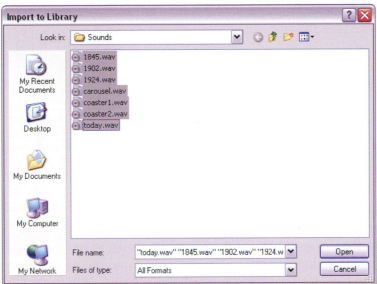

4. Click **Open** (Windows) or **Import to Library** (Macintosh) to import the selected files to the document library.

   The files are added to the Library panel.

5. Click to select the **1845.wav** file in the Library panel.

   The file is represented by an audio waveform at the top of the panel, as shown in Figure 4-3.

FIGURE 4-3
Sound file selected on the Library panel

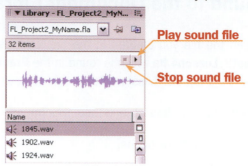

Play sound file

Stop sound file

6. Click the **Play** button on the Library panel to listen to the file.

7. Click the **Stop** button to stop listening to the file.

8. Create a new Library panel folder named **Sound**, and then drag the sounds you imported into the Sound folder. Expand the Sound folder if necessary so you can access the sounds on the Library panel.

Adding Narration to the Timeline

The Paradise Beach Boardwalk story is divided into four separate time periods: 1845, 1902, 1924, and Today. By providing you with four separate audio clips, you can easily divide the story into four distinct chapters where you can add narration.

You can add sound to the Timeline in two ways. You can select the keyframe where you want the sound to begin playing, and then drag a copy of the file from the Library panel to the Stage. Or, you can use the Sound pop-up menu on the Property inspector. You will use both methods in the following exercise.

Inside the Design

The designer wants the audience to see how the boardwalk has evolved from its roots in 1845 to the modern theme park it is today while maintaining its turn-of-the-century charm. To do this, the designer has chosen to divide the story into four segments that highlight changes to the boardwalk.

Add Sound From the Library Panel

1. Insert a new Layer Folder above the *Images & Titles* folder and name it **Sound**.

2. Insert a new layer named **narration** and drag it to place it inside the **Sound** folder, as shown in Figure 4-4.

FIGURE 4-4
The narration layer is inside the Sound folder

3. Insert a keyframe at frame **73** on the narration layer. The narration will begin at 4 seconds.

4. Drag the **1845.wav** file from the Library panel to the Stage.

When you release the mouse button, the sound file is added to the selected keyframe on the Timeline, as shown in Figure 4-5.

FIGURE 4-5
A sound file is represented by an audio waveform line

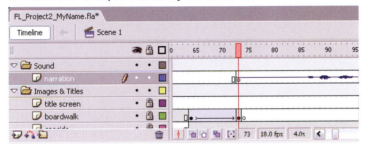

5. Click frame **73** on the narration layer, and then select **Stream** from the **Sync** pop-up menu on the Property inspector.

FIGURE 4-6
Sound properties

For additional information about sound, see the Tips & Techniques feature "Event and Streaming Sound Properties."

Add Sound From the Property Inspector

1. Insert a keyframe at frame **208** on the *narration* layer. This is the beginning of the images that represent the boardwalk in 1902.

2. Select **1902.wav** from the **Sound** pop-up menu on the Property inspector.

FIGURE 4-7
Adding a sound from the Property inspector

Flash automatically applies the most recently selected Sync option, which in this case is Stream.

3. Insert a keyframe at frame **352** on the *narration* layer and add the **1924.wav** file to the Timeline. Verify that the Sync option is set to **Stream**.

4. Insert a keyframe at frame **514** on the *narration* layer and add the **today.wav** file to the Timeline. Verify that the Sync option is set to **Stream**.

The Timeline now includes four separate streaming sound files.

5. Lock the *narration* layer and preview the movie.

Tips & Techniques

EVENT AND STREAMING SOUND PROPERTIES

Sound in Flash can be defined as an Event or set to Stream.

Event sounds play independent of the Timeline. The sound starts in the keyframe but can continue playing after the movie ends. When played over the Internet, event sounds do not begin until the entire sound file is downloaded. You can use event sounds repeatedly in a movie without increasing file size.

Streaming sounds are closely tied to the Timeline. Streaming sounds can begin to play as your computer downloads them. They stop playing at the end of the movie. Each time a streaming sound is added to the Timeline, the file size increases.

If you plan to use a sound repeatedly or to loop a sound, it is best to use an event sound. Streaming is best when you want the sound to sync with animation or images along the Timeline, as in the Paradise Beach Boardwalk movie.

Adding Music and Sound Effects

By combining moving images with sound, the designer hopes to achieve a sense of live motion and realism. Music and sound effects bring the boardwalk to life, offering the audience a rich and sensory experience of the actual boardwalk from the safety of their desktop.

Flash allows multiple audio tracks to be used in the same document. In the boardwalk movie, you will enhance the narration track with music (carousel) and ambient noise (screaming riders and roller coaster sounds).

Inside the Design

Sound effects, such as screaming riders on an old wooden roller coaster, add drama and excitement to the story. The designer chose to combine music with the ambient sound of screaming riders and a roller coaster to give the illusion of being at the boardwalk.

Add Music and Sound Effects

1. Add two new layers above the *narration* layer and name them **music** and **sound fx**. These two layers are also positioned inside the **Sound** folder.

FIGURE 4-8
The soundfx and music layers are inside the Sound folder

2. Insert a keyframe at frame **11** on the *music* layer. The music will begin following the welcome title.

3. Add the **carousel.wav** file to frame 11 on the *music* layer. Verify that the Sync option is set to **Stream** on the Property inspector.

4. Insert a keyframe at frame **352** on the *sound fx* layer. This is the introduction of the roller coaster.

5. Add the **coaster1.wav** file to frame 352 on the *sound fx* layer. Verify that the Sync option is set to **Stream**.

6. Insert a keyframe at frame **658** on the *sound fx* layer. This is about 1/2 second before the last roller coaster image appears.

7. Add the **coaster2.wav** file to frame 658 on the *sound fx* layer. Verify that the Sync option is set to **Stream**.

The sound of the roller coaster will begin to play before the last photo of the roller coaster appears.

Inside the Design

The designer wants the sound effect of the final roller coaster to begin playing before the last roller coaster image appears. This creates anticipation and signals the end of the story.

Adjusting Audio Levels and Fading Sound

Listen to the soundtrack of any motion picture and you will quickly hear the complexity and multitude of sounds blended together to tell the story in a way that would not be possible in silence. Yet somehow these sounds all work together without overpowering or interfering with the main dialog.

As the sound director of the Paradise Beach boardwalk movie, you can use Flash to balance overlapping sounds such as the voice narration, the music, and the roller coaster. For example, you can begin with the music at a higher level and then slowly fade the music down and under the voice narration without removing it entirely.

 Edit Sound Properties

1. Click frame **11** on the *music* layer. This is the keyframe where the music begins.

2. Click the **Edit** button on the Property inspector.

FIGURE 4-9
Edit button on the sound Property inspector

The Edit Envelope dialog box opens. It is divided into left and right sound channels. The top panel represents the left speaker and the bottom panel represents the right speaker.

3. Click the **Frames** button in the Edit Envelope dialog box to select it.

FIGURE 4-10
Frames button in the Edit Envelope dialog box

4. Scroll the Edit Envelope dialog box to view frame 65, and click anywhere below frame 65 to add a marker, as shown in Figure 4-11. This is just before the voice narration begins on the Timeline.

FIGURE 4-11
Adding a marker in the Edit Envelope dialog box

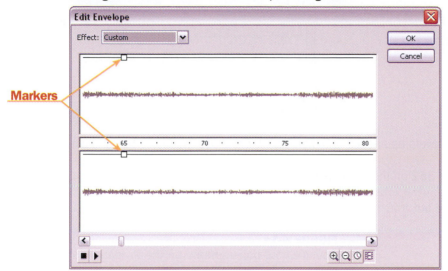

5. Add another marker to the right of frame 65 and then drag the markers for both the left and right channels so the levels begin to reduce when they reach frame 65 as shown in Figure 4-12. The farther apart you place the two sets of markers, the more gradually the music will fade.

FIGURE 4-12
Positioning markers in the Edit Envelope dialog box

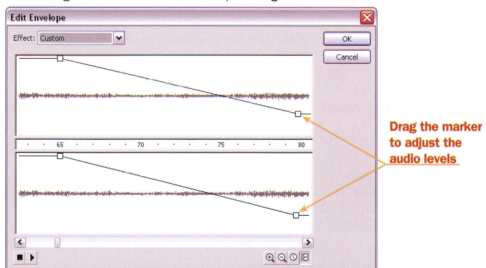

This prevents the music from interfering with the spoken narration.

6. Click the **Play** button in the Edit Envelope window to preview the edits, as shown in Figure 4-13.

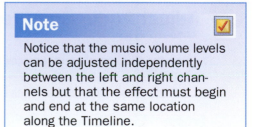

Note

Notice that the music volume levels can be adjusted independently between the left and right channels but that the effect must begin and end at the same location along the Timeline.

FIGURE 4-13
The Play buttons lets you preview sound edits in the
Edit Envelope dialog box

FIGURE 4-13
The Play buttons lets you preview sound edits in the
Edit Envelope dialog box

7. Adjust the levels as needed and then click **OK** to close the dialog box and confirm the changes.

8. Click frame **352** on the *sound fx* layer. This is the keyframe where the first roller coaster appears.

9. Select **Fade out** from the Effect pop-up menu on the Property inspector.

FIGURE 4-14
Sound Effect pop-up menu on the Property inspector

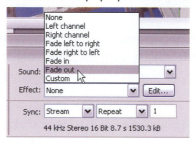

The roller coaster sound gradually fades as the image dips to black.

10. Lock the *music* and *sound fx* layers, and then preview the movie.

Adjusting Audio Compression Settings

The Paradise Beach Boardwalk story will be delivered over the Internet, so it is important to do whatever possible to reduce the size of the published movie while maintaining an acceptable level of quality. Sound files are notorious for increasing the size, and therefore the download times, of rich media Web content.

To control this balance between file size and sound quality, you can adjust the audio compression settings on the Flash tab of the Publish Settings dialog box.

 Adjust Audio Compression Settings

1. Open the **File** menu and then click **Publish Settings** to open the Publish Settings dialog box.

2. Click the **Flash** tab and then click the **Set** button next to *Audio stream*, as shown in Figure 4-15.

FIGURE 4-15
Set Stream button in the Publish Settings dialog box

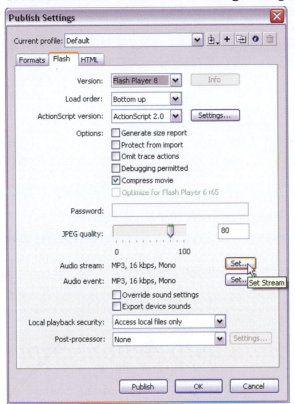

The Sound Settings dialog box appears.

3. Select **MP3** on the Compression pop-up menu.

4. Select **56 kbps** on the Bit rate pop-up menu.

Note

After testing the movie, if you find the download time to be unacceptable, you can compress the audio further and republish the document.

Inside the Design

According to the design document for this project, your target audience is expected to have at least 128Kbps or faster Internet connection speeds, so the designer is recommending a higher-quality sound selection.

5. Select **Best** on the Quality pop-up menu, as shown in Figure 4-16.

FIGURE 4-16
Sound Settings dialog box

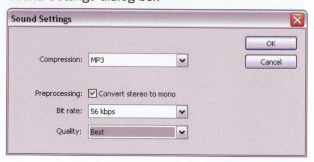

6. Click **OK** to close the Sound Settings dialog box and confirm the changes.

7. Click **OK** to close the Publish Settings dialog box and confirm the changes.

> **Note**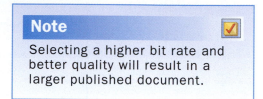
>
> Selecting a higher bit rate and better quality will result in a larger published document.

Controlling Sound with ActionScript

As your audience navigates from one segment of the boardwalk movie to the next, Flash Player could accidentally overlap an event sound that was previously playing from this or another movie. To prevent this from happening, add a stopAllSounds action at the beginning of the new sound clip.

 ## Prevent Sounds From Accidentally Overlapping

1. Add a new layer above the Sound layer folder and name it **actions**.

FIGURE 4-17
The actions layer

2. Insert a keyframe at frame **10** on the *actions* layer.

3. Expand the Actions panel and make sure the script pane is visible, as shown in Figure 4-18.

FIGURE 4-18
Actions panel

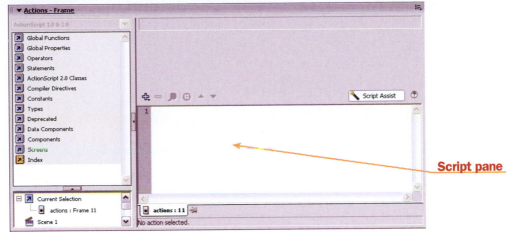

4. Expand the **Global Functions** and **Timeline Control** categories.

5. Double-click the **stopAllSounds** action to add it to the script pane.

FIGURE 4-19
The stopAllSounds action

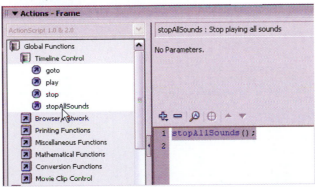

The *StopAllSounds* action is added to the script pane and to the keyframe in frame 10. When the playhead reaches frame 10, any sounds that are currently playing will be stopped before reaching the narration in frame 11. This will prevent sounds from overlapping accidentally.

6. Collapse the Actions panel and save the document. If you are continuing with the next lesson, leave this file open. If you are not continuing at this time, close the file and close Flash.

CREATING TITLES BY USING TEXT AND GRAPHIC FILTERS

OBJECTIVES

Upon completion of this lesson, you will be able to:

- Create and format titles.
- Apply graphic filters to text.
- Animate text with graphic filters.

Estimated time to complete this lesson: 20 minutes

Introduction

The Paradise Beach Boardwalk movie includes a welcome title that incorporates the Paradise Beach Boardwalk logo.

The storyboard shows the title and logo with drop shadows. You will create the welcome title as a movie clip symbol and then apply a drop shadow to the entire movie clip by using graphic filters.

By combining the text and logo into a single movie clip symbol, you can also animate the entire title as a single object, rather than animating the text and logo separately.

In this lesson, you will create the welcome title by combining the logo and text as a movie clip symbol, adding a drop shadow, and then animating the movie clip to create the welcome title, as shown in Figure 5-1. You will then add a second instance of the logo that will stay onscreen after the movie has advanced beyond the title screen.

FIGURE 5-1
Storyboard

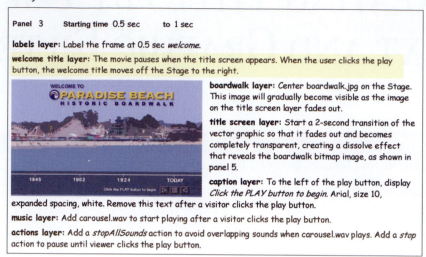

Panel 3   Starting time 0.5 sec   to 1 sec

labels layer: Label the frame at 0.5 sec *welcome*.

welcome title layer: The movie pauses when the title screen appears. When the user clicks the play button, the welcome title moves off the Stage to the right.

boardwalk layer: Center boardwalk.jpg on the Stage. This image will gradually become visible as the image on the title screen layer fades out.

title screen layer: Start a 2-second transition of the vector graphic so that it fades out and becomes completely transparent, creating a dissolve effect that reveals the boardwalk bitmap image, as shown in panel 5.

caption layer: To the left of the play button, display *Click the PLAY button to begin.* Arial, size 10, expanded spacing, white. Remove this text after a visitor clicks the play button.

music layer: Add carousel.wav to start playing after a visitor clicks the play button.

actions layer: Add a *stopAllSounds* action to avoid overlapping sounds when carousel.wav plays. Add a *stop* action to pause until viewer clicks the play button.

Creating and Formatting the Welcome Title

The Paradise Beach Boardwalk story begins when the welcome title appears over the traced bitmap image of the amusement park. The title includes descriptive text and the Paradise Beach Boardwalk logo.

Create the Welcome Title Movie Clip Symbol

1. If necessary, open the document you created in the previous lesson. Alternately, you can open the file named **FL_Project2_Lesson5.fla** which is found in the **Practice_files** folder in the Data files for this lesson. If you use **FL_Project2_Lesson5.fla** be sure to save it as **FL_Project2_YourName.fla**.

2. Open the **File** menu, point to **Import**, and then click **Import to Library**.

3. Open the data files for this project, open the **Graphics** folder, and double-click the file named **pb_logo.swf**.

   The logo is added to the Library panel.

4. Insert a new layer above the *title screen* layer and name it **welcome title**, as shown in Figure 5-2.

FIGURE 5-2
The welcome title layer

5. Open the **Insert** menu, and then click **New Symbol**. Name the new symbol **welcome_title**, select the **Movie clip** Type, and then click **OK**.

FIGURE 5-3
Create New Symbol dialog box

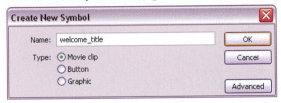

Movie clip symbols can have graphic filters applied to them. By selecting the movie clip behavior, you can apply a drop shadow to the entire welcome title.

6. Drag an instance of the **pb_logo.swf** from the Library panel to the Stage.

7. Add the text **WELCOME** above the logo, and the text **HISTORIC BOARDWALK** below the logo, as shown in Figure 5-4.

Inside the Design

By making the welcome title a movie clip symbol, you can apply a graphic filter, such as a drop shadow, to the entire movie clip. Because it is a movie clip, you can animate the title as a single object.

FIGURE 5-4
Welcome title

Arial, 14, bold, blue (#000066)

Arial Black, 14, blue (#000066), letter spacing 8.4

8. Click **Scene 1** on the Information bar to return to the main Timeline.

9. Click frame **1** on the *welcome title* layer and drag an instance of the **welcome_title** movie clip symbol from the Library panel to the Stage. Position the symbol as shown in Figure 5-5.

FIGURE 5-5
Welcome title positioned on the Stage

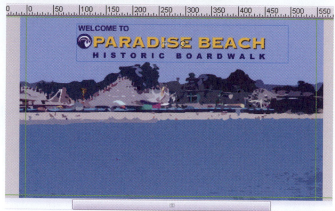

Applying Graphic Filters

Now that you have created the Paradise Beach Boardwalk title as a movie clip symbol, you can apply a drop shadow to the symbol and it will be applied to each element within the symbol, including the logo and the text. The drop shadow is one of many graphic filters available in Macromedia Flash.

Graphic filters can be applied to movie clip symbols, buttons, and text by using the Filters tab on the Property inspector. After you apply a filter, you can change its options any time. You can enable or disable filters or delete them in the Property inspector. When you remove a filter, the object returns to its previous appearance.

Inside the Design

Drop shadows appear to lift an object from the background and add dimensionality to a composition. The designer chose to add a drop shadow to the title and logo to create a sense of dimensionality for a two-dimensional work.

Step by Step

Apply a Drop Shadow to the Welcome Title

1. Click the welcome title on the Stage to select it.

2. Click the **Filters** tab on the Property inspector.

3. Click the **Add Filter** button (plus symbol), and then click **Drop Shadow**.

    The Filters tab shows properties for a drop shadow.

4. Set the properties, as shown in Figure 5-6. Make sure the Strength is set to 36%.

FIGURE 5-6
Drop Shadow filter

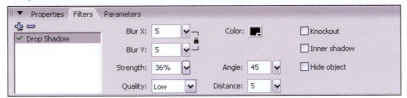

Animating the Welcome Title

When the movie first downloads, the Paradise Beach Boardwalk title animates into view from the left of the Stage and comes to a stop over the traced bitmap image. When the visitor plays the movie (by clicking a Play button), the title exits by moving off the Stage to the right.

You will use motion tweens to create the entry and exit animation for the welcome title.

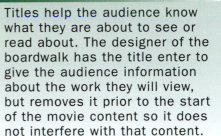

Inside the Design

Titles help the audience know what they are about to see or read about. The designer of the boardwalk has the title enter to give the audience information about the work they will view, but removes it prior to the start of the movie content so it does not interfere with that content.

 ## Animate the Welcome Title

1. Insert keyframes at frames **10** and **19** on the *welcome title* layer.

2. Insert a blank keyframe at frame **20** on the *welcome title* layer.

3. Click frame **1** on the *welcome title* layer and drag the title onto the workspace to the left of the Stage. You may need to change your window magnification to do this.

FIGURE 5-7
Start position of the welcome title animation

4. Click frame **19** on the *welcome title* layer and drag the title onto the workspace to the right of the Stage.

FIGURE 5-8
End position of the welcome title animation

5. Create a motion tween between frames **1** and **10** on the *welcome title* layer.

6. Create a motion tween between frames **10** and **19** on the *welcome title* layer.

7. Add a *stop* action to frame 10 on the *actions* layer. (*Hint*: From the Timeline Control category.)

   The welcome title will animate into view and stop on frame 10. In the next lesson, you will add a Play button for starting the movie after the title screen.

8. Lock the *welcome title* layer.

Adding the Logo

As soon as the viewer clicks the Play button, the movie begins and the welcome title moves out of view. To reinforce the Paradise Beach Boardwalk brand, the designer wants the logo to persist onscreen throughout the movie.

Add an instance of the logo to the lower left corner of the screen, immediately following the exit of the welcome title, as described in Figure 5-9.

FIGURE 5-9
Storyboard

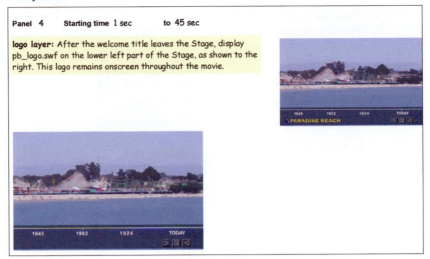

Step by Step Add the Logo So It Remains On the Screen

1. Insert a new layer above the *welcome title* layer and name it **logo**.

FIGURE 5-10
The logo layer

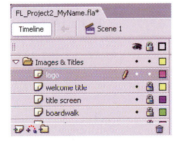

2. Insert a keyframe at frame **20** on the *logo* layer.

3. Drag an instance of the pb_logo.swf graphic from the Library panel to the Stage.

4. Use the Transform panel to change the height and width of the logo to 60% of actual size. (*Hint*: Remember to select the Constrain option.)

FIGURE 5-11
Transform panel

5. Position the logo in the lower left corner of the Stage (X:20 Y:312), as shown in Figure 5-12.

FIGURE 5-12
Positioning the logo by using the Property inspector

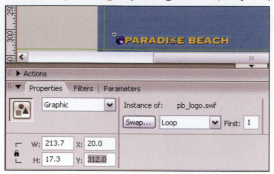

6. Lock the *logo* layer.

7. Open the **Control** menu, and then click **Test Movie** to preview the movie in Flash Player.

The title screen animates into view and then stops.

8. Press **Enter** (Windows) or **Return** (Macintosh) to continue previewing the movie.

The welcome title slides off screen and the smaller version of the logo appears in the lower left corner and remains onscreen until the end of the movie.

9. Close the Flash Player window and save the document.

10. If you are continuing with the next lesson, leave this file open. If you are not continuing at this time, close the file and close Flash.

Adding Navigation Elements

OBJECTIVES

Upon completion of this lesson, you will be able to:

- Draw control panel elements.

- Use animation to provide visual feedback to the viewer.

Estimated time to complete this lesson: 40 minutes

Introduction

Much like chapters on a DVD, the Paradise Beach Boardwalk story is separated into five parts for easy navigation. These include the welcome title, 1845, 1902, 1924, and Today.

As the movie plays, a historic timeline identifies which chapter of the movie is currently playing.

In this lesson, you create the historic timeline that identifies each chapter of the Paradise Beach Boardwalk story. The current chapter of the movie is always highlighted and a moving ball slides along the historic timeline to identify the transition between chapters, as described in Figure 6-1.

FIGURE 6-1
Storyboard

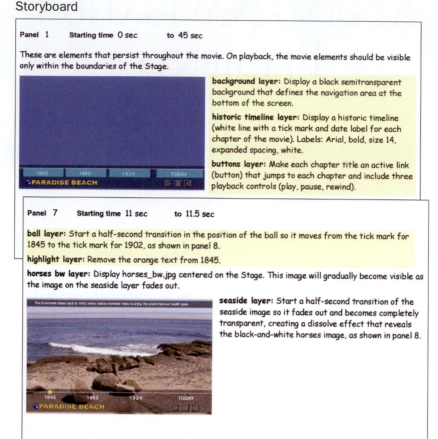

Panel 1   Starting time 0 sec   to 45 sec

These are elements that persist throughout the movie. On playback, the movie elements should be visible only within the boundaries of the Stage.

background layer: Display a black semitransparent background that defines the navigation area at the bottom of the screen.

historic timeline layer: Display a historic timeline (white line with a tick mark and date label for each chapter of the movie). Labels: Arial, bold, size 14, expanded spacing, white.

buttons layer: Make each chapter title an active link (button) that jumps to each chapter and include three playback controls (play, pause, rewind).

Panel 7   Starting time 11 sec   to 11.5 sec

ball layer: Start a half-second transition in the position of the ball so it moves from the tick mark for 1845 to the tick mark for 1902, as shown in panel 8.

highlight layer: Remove the orange text from 1845.

horses bw layer: Display horses_bw.jpg centered on the Stage. This image will gradually become visible as the image on the seaside layer fades out.

seaside layer: Start a half-second transition of the seaside image so it fades out and becomes completely transparent, creating a dissolve effect that reveals the black-and-white horses image, as shown in panel 8.

Creating a Background for the Navigation Bar

The design document for the Paradise Beach Boardwalk movie requires images, text, a graphic logo, and controls to fit within a relatively small amount of space. To allow the aesthetics of the boardwalk photographs to show, the navigation control panel is made semitransparent.

Inside the Design

The designer of this project was faced with a challenge of providing adequate navigation and feedback without diverting attention from the main focus of the story. To separate the logo and navigation from the photographs, the designer chose to use a semitransparent box. Because the control panel is partially transparent, viewers can see the entire photograph but still have access to important navigation and feedback controls.

Add a Semitransparent Control Panel for the Navigation Bar

1. If necessary, open the document you created in the previous lesson. Alternately, you can open the file named **FL_Project2_Lesson6.fla** which is found in the **Practice_files** folder in the Data files for this lesson. If you use **FL_Project2_Lesson6.fla** be sure to save it as **FL_Project2_YourName.fla**.

2. Add a new layer above the *welcome title* layer and name it **background**.

FIGURE 6-2
The background layer

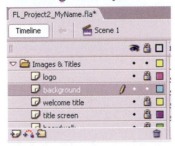

The background layer must go above the photographs and below the logo.

3. Click frame **1** on the *background* layer.

4. Select the Rectangle Tool and set the Stroke color to **No Stroke** and the Fill color to black (**#000000**).

5. Use the Color Mixer to change the Alpha setting for the fill color to **45%**.

FIGURE 6-3
Changing the Alpha transparency on the Color Mixer panel

6. Draw a rectangle on the Stage.

7. Select the rectangle and use the Property inspector to make the width **550** and the height **68**.

Note

You may need to unlock the Constrain option in order to set the width and height values in step 7.

8. Use the Property inspector to position the rectangle at the bottom of the Stage (X:**0** and Y: **268**), as shown in Figure 6-4.

FIGURE 6-4
Positioning the rectangle by using the Property inspector

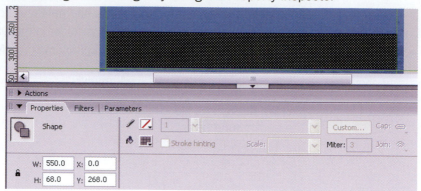

9. Lock the *background* layer.

Providing Visual Feedback for Navigation

The Paradise Beach Boardwalk movie includes three types of visual feedback designed to communicate the structure and flow of the story.

These include:

1. A historic timeline of events that identifies each chapter of the story. Each chapter represents a time period throughout the history of the amusement park.

2. As the story transitions from one chapter to the next, the current chapter title is highlighted in orange text.

3. A graphic image of a ball moves along the historic timeline, stopping at the current chapter of the story.

To create these elements in Flash, begin by drawing the historic timeline, and then add the highlights and animated ball.

 Draw the Historic Timeline and Add Chapter Titles

1. Add a new Layer Folder above the Images & Titles folder and name it **Controls**.

2. Insert a new layer named **historic timeline** and drag it inside the Controls folder, as shown in Figure 6-5.

FIGURE 6-5
The historic timeline layer is inside the Controls folder

3. Use the Line Tool with the Object Drawing option turned on to draw a horizontal white (**#FFFFFF**) line. Hold down the **Shift** key to draw a perfectly straight line. Make the Stroke height of **1.5**. Make the line width **549** and position it at X:**0** and Y:**277**, as shown in Figure 6-6.

FIGURE 6-6
Horizontal white line drawn with the Object Drawing option turned on

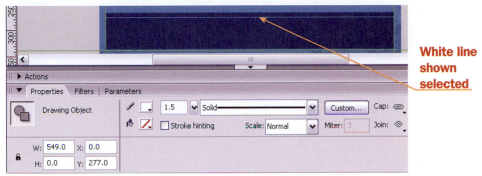

White line
shown
selected

4. Use the Line Tool to draw a vertical white line (tick mark) with a stroke height of **.75**. Make the line height **6** and position it just below the left end of the horizontal line at X:**70** Y: **278**.

FIGURE 6-7
Drawing the first white tick mark

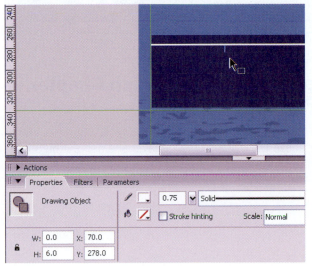

5. Select the small vertical line (tick mark), click **Edit** on the Menu bar, and then click **Duplicate** to create another small line.

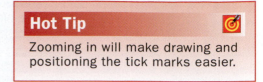

Hot Tip

Zooming in will make drawing and positioning the tick marks easier.

6. Duplicate the small line two more times to create a total of four tick marks, and position them as shown in Figure 6-8. Because the tick marks are so small, it might help to use the arrow keys or Property inspector to position the tick marks. (*Hint*: In the example, the tick marks are positioned at Y:**278** and X: **200**, **325**, and **470**.)

FIGURE 6-8
There are four white tick marks along the historic timeline

7. Use the Text Tool to add the chapter titles (**1845**, **1902**, **1924**, and **TODAY**) below each tick mark, as shown in Figure 6-9. The text is Static Text, Arial, size 14, bold, and white. The Letter spacing is **1**. Position the text close to the tick marks to leave room for the control buttons.

FIGURE 6-9
Chapter titles appear below each tick mark

Add Highlights to Identify Which Chapter is Currently Playing

1. Insert a new layer above the *historic timeline* layer and name it **highlight**, as shown in Figure 6-10.

FIGURE 6-10
The highlight layer

2. Click **1845** on the Stage to select it. Open the **Edit** menu, and then click **Copy**.

3. Insert a keyframe at frame **73** on the *highlight* layer.

4. Click the **Edit** menu, and then click **Paste in Place**.

   A copy of the 1845 text is placed on the *highlight* layer. It is positioned directly on top of the date in the *historic timeline* layer.

5. Click **1845** on the Stage to select it and use the Property inspector to change its color to yellow/orange **(#FFCC00)**.

FIGURE 6-11
Highlight for 1845

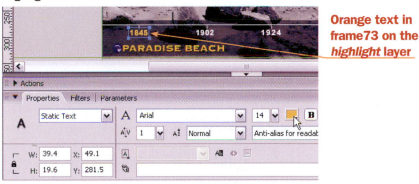

Orange text in frame73 on the *highlight* layer

When the Timeline reaches frame 73, the date changes color, identifying 1845 as the current chapter.

6. Insert blank keyframes at frames **199** and **208** on the *highlight* layer.

   The blank keyframe at frame 199 removes the highlight from 1845. The blank keyframe in 208 is where the next chapter title highlight will appear. You will add that next.

7. Click **1902** on the Stage to select it, click **Edit** on the Menu bar, and then click **Copy**. Click frame **208** on the *highlight* layer, click **Edit** on the Menu bar, and then click **Paste in Place**. Change the color of the 1902 text to yellow/orange **(#FFCC00)**.

   When the playhead reaches 208 (the beginning of the next chapter), 1902 becomes highlighted.

FIGURE 6-12
The highlight for 1902 appears in frame 208

8. Insert blank keyframes at frames **343** and **352** on the *highlight* layer.

   The blank keyframe at frame 343 removes the highlight from 1902. The blank keyframe at frame 352 is where the next chapter highlight will appear.

9. Click **1924** on the Stage to select it, click **Edit** on the Menu bar, and then click **Copy**. Click frame **352** on the *highlight* layer, click **Edit** on the Menu bar, and then click **Paste in Place**. Change the color of the 1924 text to yellow/orange **(#FFCC00)**.

   When the playhead reaches 352 (the beginning of the next chapter), 1924 becomes highlighted.

10. Insert blank keyframes at frames **505** and **514** on the *highlight* layer.

    The blank keyframe at frame 505 removes the highlight from 1924. The blank keyframe at frame 514 is where the next chapter title will appear.

11. Click **TODAY** on the Stage to select it, click **Edit** on the Menu bar, and then click **Copy**. Click frame **514** on the *highlight* layer, click **Edit** on the Menu bar, and then click **Paste in Place**. Change the color of the TODAY text to yellow/orange **(#FFCC00)**.

    When the playhead reaches 514 (the beginning of the next chapter), TODAY becomes highlighted.

12. Insert a blank keyframe at frame **703** on the *highlight* layer. This removes the highlight from TODAY when the Timeline reaches the conclusion of the story.

13. Lock the *historic timeline* and *highlight* layers.

 # Draw a Ball Used to Identify Chapter Transitions

1. Add a new layer above the *highlight* layer and name it **ball**, as shown in Figure 6-13.

FIGURE 6-13
The ball layer

2. Open the **Insert** menu and then click **New Symbol**. Name the symbol **ball**, select the **Graphic** behavior Type, and click **OK**.

3. Select the Oval Tool, hold down the **Shift** key, and draw a perfect circle with no stroke and any color fill.

FIGURE 6-14
Holding down the Shift key draws a perfect circle when using the Oval Tool

4. Select the circle, open the Color Mixer panel, verify that the Fill color box is selected (not the Stroke color box) and then select **Radial** from the **Type** pop-up menu, as shown in Figure 6-15.

FIGURE 6-15
Selecting a Radial gradient on the Color Mixer panel

5. Use the gradient definition bar to change the color of the left marker to white (**#FFFFFF**) and the right marker to light brown (**#CC9900**).

With a radial fill, the circle looks like a ball.

6. Use the Property inspector to change the width and height of the ball to **16**. (*Hint*: Turn the Constrain option on if necessary.)

7. Click **Scene 1** on the Information bar to return to the main Timeline.

Add a Moving Ball to Indicate When a New Chapter Is Beginning

1. Insert a keyframe at frame **64** on the *ball* layer. This is .5 seconds before the 1845 chapter. The ball will slide into position as the 1845 chapter begins.

2. Drag an instance of the **ball** symbol from the Library panel to the Stage and position it over the tick mark above 1845, as shown in Figure 6-17.

FIGURE 6-17
The moving ball identifies the current chapter

3. Insert a keyframe at frame **73** on the *ball* layer.

4. Click frame **64** on the *ball* layer and use the left arrow key to move the ball off the Stage, as shown in Figure 6-18.

FIGURE 6-18
The start position of the moving ball animation

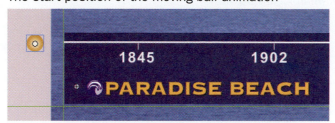

5. Create a motion tween between frames **64** and **73** on the *ball* layer.

    The ball slides along the timeline and comes to a stop above 1845.

6. Insert keyframes at frames **199** and **208** on the *ball* layer.

7. Click frame **208** on the *ball* layer and use the right arrow key to slide the ball to the right until it is over the tick mark above 1902.

8. Create a motion tween between frames **199** and **208** on the *ball* layer.

9. Insert keyframes at frames **343** and **352** on the *ball* layer.

10. Click frame **352** on the *ball* layer and use the right arrow key to slide the ball to the right until it is over the tick mark above 1924.

11. Create a motion tween between frames **343** and **352** on the *ball* layer.

12. Insert keyframes at frames **505** and **514** on the *ball* layer.

13. Click frame **514** on the *ball* layer and use the right arrow key to slide the ball to the right until it is over the tick mark above TODAY.

14. Create a motion tween between frames **505** and **514** on the *ball* layer.

15. Insert keyframes at frames **703** and **712** on the *ball* layer.

16. Click frame **712** on the *ball* layer and use the right arrow key to slide the ball to the right until it is off the Stage, as shown in Figure 6-19.

FIGURE 6-19
The ball moves off the Stage at the end of the movie

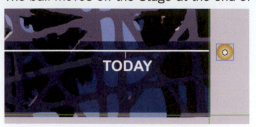

17. Create a motion tween between frames **703** and **712** on the *ball* layer.

18. Insert a blank keyframe at frame **713** on the *ball* layer.

19. Lock the *ball* layer and preview the movie.

20. Save the document.

21. If you are continuing with the next lesson, leave this file open. If you are not continuing at this time, close the file and close Flash.

ADDING BUTTONS FOR NAVIGATION

OBJECTIVES

Upon completion of this lesson, you will be able to:

- Create button symbols.

- Duplicate and modify button symbols.

- Add frame labels for navigation.

- Control buttons and the Timeline with ActionScript.

Estimated time to complete this lesson: 60 minutes

Introduction

Button symbols provide interactivity. When you click a button, an action occurs, such as to play or pause the Paradise Beach Boardwalk movie. Buttons can be used to jump to any frame along the Timeline, such as the beginning of a new chapter, or for rewinding to the start of the movie.

Any object you draw in Flash, including text, can be turned into a button symbol. Button symbols have four states: Up, Over, Down, and Hit. These states, described in Table 7-1, correspond to the use of the mouse and provide feedback to the visitor.

TABLE 7-1
Button states

STATE	DESCRIPTION
Up	The Up state represents how the button appears when the mouse pointer is not over it.
Over	The Over state represents how the button appears when the mouse pointer is over it.
Down	The Down state represents how the button appears when the button is being clicked.
Hit	The Hit state defines the area on or around the button that will respond to a click. The hit state is not visible. If the button is small, you can make a larger hit state, which makes the button easier to locate and click.

FIGURE 7-1
Sample button states

Up   **Over**   **Down**   **Hit**

The process for creating and testing a button is as follows:

1. Create a button by opening a new symbol and adding graphics or text to each state of the button.

2. Add an instance of the button by dragging the symbol from the Library panel to the Stage.

3. Preview the button on the Stage by selecting Enable Simple Buttons on the Control menu. Flash disables buttons by default so you can position and manipulate them on the Stage.

4. Assign ActionScript to the button that defines what happens when the button is clicked.

In this lesson, you will create two sets of navigation controls for the Paradise Beach Boardwalk movie. The main navigation buttons allow the audience to play, pause, and rewind the movie. A second set of buttons is used to skip between the four main chapters of the story by clicking along the historic timeline of events. These are described in Figure 7-2.

FIGURE 7-2
Storyboard

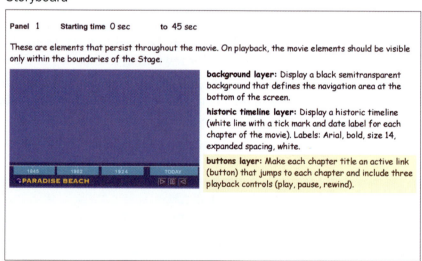

Creating Button Symbols

Y ou will create the Play button first, and then use it as a template for creating the Pause and Rewind buttons.

Create a Background For the Play Button

Inside the Design

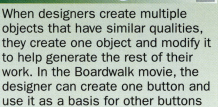

When designers create multiple objects that have similar qualities, they create one object and modify it to help generate the rest of their work. In the Boardwalk movie, the designer can create one button and use it as a basis for other buttons because they have a similar look and feel. The designer has to make only minimal changes to build the separate button and can maintain consistency of design and size by using this technique.

1. If necessary, open the document you created in the previous lesson. Alternately, you can open the file named **FL_Project2_Lesson7.fla** which is found in the **Practice_files** folder in the Data files for this lesson. If you use **FL_Project2_Lesson7.fla** be sure to save it as **FL_Project2_YourName.fla**.

2. Open the **Insert** menu and then click **New Symbol**. Name the symbol **play**, select the **Button** Type, and then click **OK**.

A new Timeline for the button opens. The button includes four frames representing the states: Up, Over, Down, and Hit.

FIGURE 7-3
Button timeline

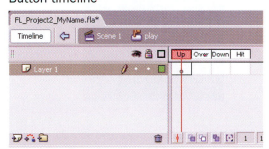

3. Rename Layer 1 **button background**.

4. Select the Rectangle Tool, turn off Object Drawing if necessary, and draw a rectangle with a black **(#000000)** stroke. Change the *Stroke height* to **1** if necessary.

5. Select the rectangle and use the Color Mixer to change the fill color to dark gray (**#333333**) and **50%** transparent.

FIGURE 7-4
Using the Color Mixer panel to set transparency

6. Select the top and left stroke lines and change their color to light gray (**#999999**). (*Hint*: Hold down the **Shift** key while selecting in order to select more than one object.)

FIGURE 7-5
The top and left stroke lines are light gray, giving the button depth

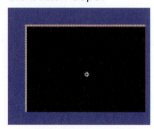

7. Double-click the rectangle to select both the stroke and fill. Use the Property inspector to make the width of the rectangle **24** and the height **20**. (*Hint*: You may have to turn off the Constrain option.)

FIGURE 7-6
Using the Property inspector to size the button

8. Use the Align panel to center the rectangle vertically and horizontally to the Stage.

9. Insert a keyframe in the Hit state for the *button background* layer.

FIGURE 7-7
The Hit stage defines the clickable area of the button

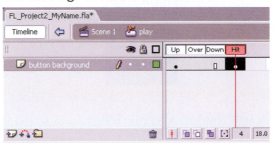

The Hit state defines the active area of the button. The contents of the Hit state are not visible.

10. Lock the *button background* layer.

 Add Icons to the Play Button

1. Open the **File** menu, point to **Import**, and then click **Import to Library**. Navigate to the Data files for this project, open the **Button_icons** folder, and import all six files.

> **Did You Know?**
>
> You can use the drawing tools to draw a hit state that is much larger than the visible button. When elements of a button are small, you can improve usability by increasing the hit state (clickable area) of the button.

FIGURE 7-8
Import to Library dialog box

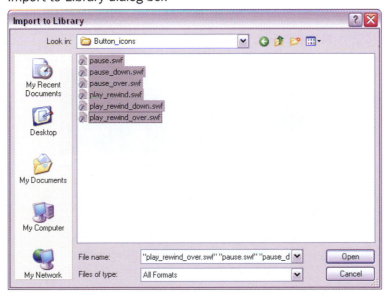

The button icons are added to the library.

2. Insert a new layer above the button background layer and name it **icon**.

3. Drag a copy of the **play_rewind.swf** graphic from the Library panel and place it on the button background.

4. Center the graphic horizontally and vertically to the Stage.

FIGURE 7-9

The Play icon is centered on the button

5. Insert a keyframe in the Over state on the *icon* layer.

FIGURE 7-10

The Over state defines what the button looks like when rolling over the button

When the viewer rolls over the button, the icon changes to indicate the button is active. Next you will replace the icon with the **play_rewind_over** icon you imported to the library.

6. Click the **play_rewind** icon on the button to select it, and then click **Swap** on the Property inspector.

FIGURE 7-11

Swap button on the Property inspector

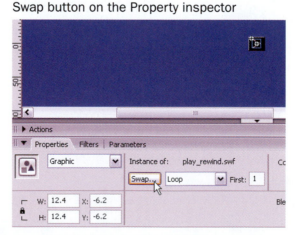

The Swap Symbol dialog box opens.

7. Select the symbol named **play_rewind_over.swf**, and then click **OK**.

The symbol is replaced with the orange icon for the over state.

8. Insert a keyframe in the Down state on the *icon* layer. Select the symbol and Swap it for the green **play_rewind_down.swf** symbol.

9. Add a new layer above the *icon* layer and name it **text**.

FIGURE 7-12
The text layer will include the name of the button

10. Insert a keyframe in the Over state on the *text* layer.

11. Use the Text Tool to add the text **PLAY** above the button. Make the text **Arial**, size **7**, bold, centered, and gray (**#CCCCCC**). Make the Letter spacing **1**. Position the text directly on top of the button, as shown in Figure 7-13.

> **Note** ☑
>
> The Up state of the text layer is empty, but when the viewer mouses over the button, text will appear to describe the function of the button.

FIGURE 7-13
The button text should be size 7 and as close to the button as possible

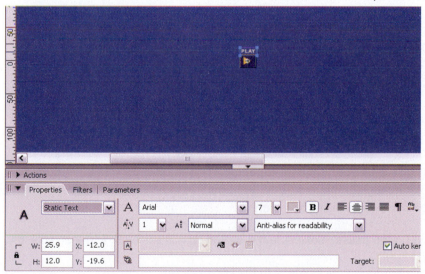

12. Click **Scene 1** on the Information bar to close the symbol and return to the main Timeline.

Duplicating and Modifying Button Symbols

Now that you have created the Play button, you can create the Rewind and Pause buttons by duplicating the Play button symbol and then replacing the icons and text.

 Create the Pause Button

1. Click the **play** button symbol on the Library panel.

FIGURE 7-14
The Play button symbol on the Library panel

2. Select **Duplicate** from the Library panel Options pop-up menu.

FIGURE 7-15
Duplicating a button

Library panel
Options button

The Duplicate Symbol dialog box opens.

3. Name the button **pause**, make sure the **Button** Type is selected, and then click **OK**.

The pause button symbol is added to the Library panel.

4. Double-click the icon beside the **pause** button symbol on the Library panel to edit the button.

5. Click the Over frame on the *text* layer. Using the Selection Tool, double-click the text to select it, highlight the text, and then key **PAUSE**. If necessary, widen the text box.

6. Click the Up frame on the *icon* layer, click the button icon on the Stage to select it, and swap it for the **pause.swf** icon. Center the icon on the Stage.

7. Use the Swap feature to replace the button's over and down state icons with the **pause_over.swf** and **pause_down.swf** icons. Center each of the icons on the Stage as you swap them.

8. Click **Scene 1** on the Information bar to return to the main Timeline.

 ## Create the Rewind Button

To create the Rewind button, you need to duplicate the Play button, replace the text label, and flip the icons so they face to the left.

1. Duplicate the play button symbol on the Library panel and name the new button **rewind**.

2. Double-click the icon beside the rewind button in the Library panel to edit the button.

3. Click the Over frame on the *text* layer, select the text, and then key **REWIND**. Resize the box if necessary and then center it above the button.

4. Click the Up frame on the *icon* layer and click the icon to select it. Open the **Modify** menu, point to **Transform**, and then click **Flip Horizontal**.

   The arrow points to the left, representing the rewind button.

5. Flip the icons in the Over and Down frames on the *icon* layer to complete the button.

6. Click **Scene 1** on the Information bar to return to the main Timeline.

Previewing Buttons on the Stage

By default, button symbols are disabled, which allows you to position and size them on the Stage. To see how each button will appear when you publish the movie, you can enable buttons, using the Control menu in Flash.

The storyboard for the Paradise Beach Boardwalk movie shows the Play, Pause, and Rewind buttons in the lower right corner of the control panel. In the next Step by Step you will add these buttons to the Stage and then enable buttons to preview the up, over, down, and hit states.

Add and Preview the Play, Pause, and Rewind Buttons

1. Insert a new layer above the ball layer and name it *buttons*.

FIGURE 7-16
The buttons layer

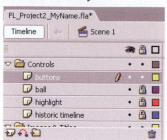

2. Click frame **1** on the *buttons* layer. Drag copies of the play, pause, and rewind buttons from the Library panel to the Stage and position them below the word TODAY, as shown in Figure 7-17.

FIGURE 7-17
Main control buttons positioned on the Stage

3. Open the **Control** menu, and then click **Enable Simple Buttons**.

4. Position the mouse pointer over the buttons on the Stage.

The mouse button changes to a hand, showing the Hit state, or active area, of the button. The icon changes color and the text labels appear above each button. This is the Over state.

5. Click a button to preview the Down state.

6. Click the **Control** menu and click **Enable Simple Buttons** to turn it off.

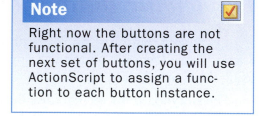

Note ☑

Right now the buttons are not functional. After creating the next set of buttons, you will use ActionScript to assign a function to each button instance.

7. If necessary, adjust the position of the buttons so the text labels do not interfere with the word TODAY, as shown in Figure 7-18. With the buttons selected, you can use the arrow keys to move them.

FIGURE 7-18
The button text does not overlap the chapter title, TODAY

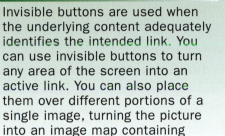

Creating Invisible Buttons

The buttons used to navigate between chapters of the Paradise Beach Boardwalk movie have invisible Up states but include underlines that appear when the mouse pointer gets near the chapter titles. This technique keeps the original design of the chapter titles intact while adding navigation capability.

You can also create buttons that are completely transparent by leaving the Up, Over, and Down states empty but including a graphic or text in the Hit state to indicate an active link.

Inside the Design

Invisible buttons are used when the underlying content adequately identifies the intended link. You can use invisible buttons to turn any area of the screen into an active link. You can also place them over different portions of a single image, turning the picture into an image map containing multiple links.

 ## Create Invisible Buttons for Navigating Between Chapters

1. Open the **Insert** menu, and then click **New Symbol**. Name the symbol **invisible**, select the **Button** Type, and then click **OK**.

2. Insert a keyframe in the Over state of the button.

FIGURE 7-19
The Up state of the invisible button is empty

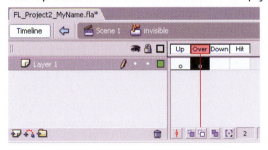

3. Select the Rectangle Tool from the Tools panel. Draw a rectangle with no stroke and a yellow/orange (**#FFCC00**) fill color. Use the Property inspector to change the width to **100** and the height to **25**.

4. Use the Align panel to center the rectangle horizontally and vertically to the Stage.

FIGURE 7-20
The large rectangle will define the Hit state of the button

5. Insert a keyframe in the Hit state. The rectangle represents the active area of the button.

6. Click the Over frame and use the Property inspector to change the width to **40** and the height to **2**.

The Over state is now a thin underline.

7. Use the Align panel to center the line horizontally to the Stage.

FIGURE 7-21
The small thin line will appear in the Over state of the button

8. Click the **Onion Skin Outlines** button on the Timeline.

FIGURE 7-22
Onion Skin Outlines button

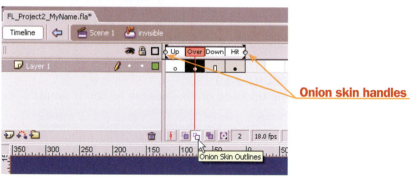

Onion skinning displays the contents of a range of frames. The selected frame is shown and the frames around it appear as outlines. You can use onion skinning to precisely align objects in different frames. You can adjust which frames are visible by dragging the onion skin handles on the Timeline.

9. Use the down arrow key to move the thin line so it aligns with the bottom edge of the rectangle in the hit frame, as shown in Figure 7-23.

FIGURE 7-23
The thin line in the Over state is positioned at the
bottom of the button

10. Click the **Onion Skin Outlines** button to turn off onion skinning.

The button has an invisible (or empty) Up state, a thin underline in the Over state, and a larger rectangle that defines the active area of the button in the Hit state.

11. Click **Scene 1** on the Information bar to close the button and return to the main Timeline.

12. Click frame **1** on the buttons layer. Drag four copies of the invisible button from the Library panel to the Stage and place them over the chapter titles, as shown in Figure 7-24.

FIGURE 7-24
Four instances of the invisible button appear over the chapter titles

Blue semi-transparent rectangles represent the Hit states of the buttons. When a viewer rolls over the button, the thin underline in the Over state will underline the text above it. You can preview the movie or enable simple buttons to view the position of the underline.

FIGURE 7-25
When the viewer rolls over a chapter title, a thin
underline appears

You may need to reposition the buttons so the underlines are centered directly below the text for each chapter of the movie.

Adding Frame Labels for Navigation

Frame labels work much like frame numbers in that they indicate locations on the Timeline. The advantage of using frame labels is that you mark the location and can change it when needed. You can use frame labels to identify the start, welcome title, and chapters of the Paradise Beach Boardwalk story.

By labeling the first frame for each segment, you can then program your navigation buttons to go to and play any part of the movie.

Add Frame Labels for Navigation

> **Inside the Design**
>
> Frame labels offer the flexibility to make changes to your Flash documents. When frame labels are used, the labels mark a location in the document. If the length of any segment of the movie changes, you can easily move the label in line with the change, thus keeping intact any navigation that points to the frame label.

1. Add a new layer above the *actions* layer and name it **labels**.

FIGURE 7-26
The labels layer

2. Click frame **1** on the *labels* layer, click in the Frame Label box on the Property inspector, and then key **start**. Press **Enter** (Windows) or **Return** (Macintosh).

FIGURE 7-27
Entering a frame label on the Property inspector

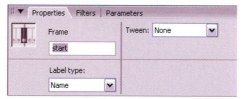

The name *start* and a red flag appear in frame 1 on the labels layer, as shown in Figure 7-28. This is the start of the movie, before the welcome title animates into view.

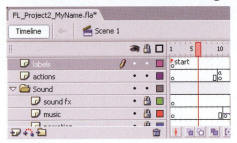

FIGURE 7-28
Frame labels include a small red flag and the label name

3. Insert a keyframe at frame **10** on the *labels* layer and label it **welcome**.

   This is the welcome title. When the movie ends or is rewound, the playhead will return to the welcome frame.

4. Insert a keyframe at frame **73** on the *labels* layer and label it **1845**. This is the beginning of the narration and photograph describing the boardwalk in 1845.

5. Insert a keyframe at frame **208** on the *labels* layer and label it **1902**.

6. Insert a keyframe at frame **352** on the *labels* layer and label it **1924**.

7. Insert a keyframe at frame **514** on the *labels* layer and label it **today**.

   With the Timeline divided into frame labels, you can easily program your navigation buttons to go to and play each part of the boardwalk movie.

8. Lock the *labels* layer.

   For additional information, see the Tips & Techniques feature "Benefits of Using Frame Labels."

Tips & Techniques

BENEFITS OF USING FRAME LABELS

Frame labels identify a specific frame or location along the Timeline by name, rather than using a frame number. As you add or delete frames in the movie, frame numbers change. If your movie includes ActionScript that points to a specific frame number, the entire movie can quickly become out of sync, causing broken links, navigation errors, and other problems. Frame labels remain constant so Flash can find the correct frame, even if the number changes. *(Continued . . .)*

Tips & Techniques

For example, in the Paradise Beach Boardwalk movie, the chapter buttons go to and play frames labeled *1845, 1902, 1924,* and *today*. Adding frames to the movie would cause each chapter to begin on a new frame number, but the buttons would still function properly because they reference frame labels, not numbers.

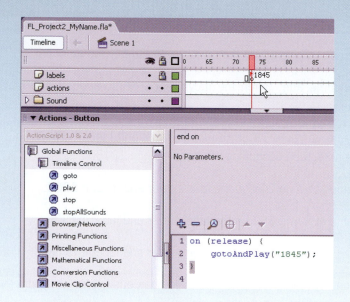

Frame labels are exported with the rest of the movie, so it is a good idea to keep the frame labels short. This also makes the name much easier to refer to in ActionScript.

Controlling Buttons and the Timeline with ActionScript

Now that you have created the control buttons for navigating the Paradise Beach Boardwalk movie, you can add ActionScript to tell each button what to do when the button is clicked. For example, the Play button starts the movie and resumes play if the movie has been paused. The Pause button stops the movie and holds the playhead in its current location. The Rewind button returns to the welcome title.

You can also program the invisible buttons to go to and play each chapter of the movie.

Actions can be added from the left pane on the Actions panel. You can also use the blue plus symbol (Add button) above the script pane labeled "Add a new item to the script." Clicking the blue plus symbol opens a menu tree for accessing all the available actions.

 Program the Play Button

1. With the Selection Tool, click the instance of the **Play** button on the Stage.

2. Expand the Actions panel, and make sure **Script Assist** is selected.

   Script Assist is a feature that simplifies the process of writing ActionScript by supplying options from which to choose rather than having to write all the code.

3. Click the plus symbol to add a new item to the script pane. Point to **Global Functions**, point to **Movie Clip Control**, and then click **on**.

FIGURE 7-29
Adding the on action to the script pane

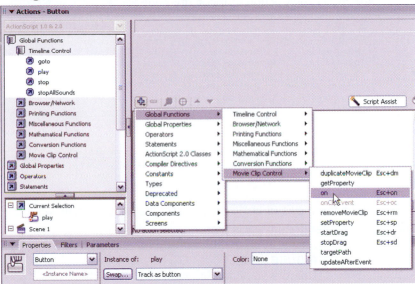

4. If it is not already selected, select the **Release** check box in the Script Assist pane.

5. Select the **Key Press** check box in the Script Assist pane, and then press **Enter** (Window) or **Return** (Macintosh) to associate the Enter or Return key with the Play button.

FIGURE 7-30
Pressing Enter or Return will activate the Play button

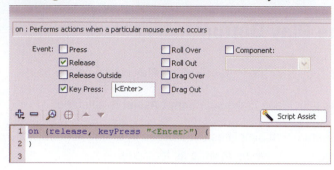

6. Click the plus symbol to add a new item to the script pane. Point to **Global Functions**, point to **Timeline Control**, and then click **play**.

FIGURE 7-31
Adding the *play* action to the script pane

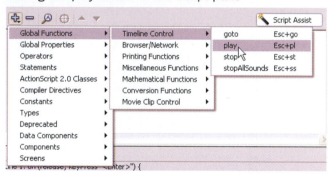

The ActionScript tells the movie to begin playing from the current frame when the mouse button is released or when the Enter/Return key is pressed.

FIGURE 7-32
Completed ActionScript for the Play button

Program the Pause Button

1. Collapse the Actions panel and then click the **Pause** button on the Stage.

2. Expand the Actions panel.

3. Click the plus symbol to add a new item to the script pane. Point to **Global Functions**, point to **Movie Clip Control**, and then click **on**.

4. Select the **Key Press** check box in the Script Assist pane, and then press the **Spacebar** to associate the Spacebar with the Pause button.

5. Click the plus symbol to add a new item to the script pane. Point to **Global Functions**, point to **Timeline Control**, and then click **stop**.

The ActionScript tells the movie to stop playing when the mouse button is released or the Spacebar is pressed.

FIGURE 7-33
Completed ActionScript for the Pause button

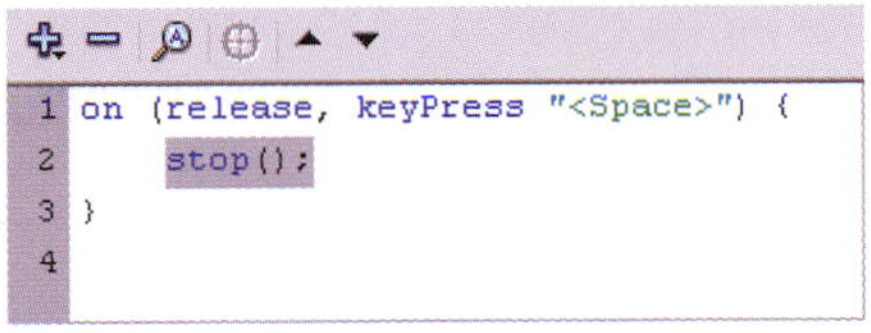

```
1 on (release, keyPress "<Space>") {
2     stop();
3 }
4
```

Program the Rewind Button

1. Collapse the Actions panel and then click the **Rewind** button on the Stage.

2. Expand the Actions panel.

3. Click the plus symbol to add a new item to the script pane. Point to **Global Functions**, point to **Movie Clip Control**, and then click **on**.

4. Select the **Key Press** check box in the Script Assist pane, and then press the **left arrow** key to associate the left arrow key with the Rewind button.

5. Click the plus symbol to add a new item to the script pane. Point to **Global Functions**, point to **Timeline Control**, and then click **goto**.

6. Select the **Go to and stop** option button in the Script Assist pane.

7. Select **Frame Label** from the Type pop-up menu in the Script Assist pane.

8. Select **welcome** from the Frame pop-up menu in the Script Assist pane.

The ActionScript tells the movie to go to and stop on the frame labeled "welcome" when the mouse button is released or the left arrow is pressed.

FIGURE 7-34
Completed ActionScript for the Rewind button

 Program the Invisible Chapter Buttons

1. Collapse the Actions panel and then click the instance of the invisible button for 1845.

2. Expand the Actions panel.

3. Click the plus symbol to add a new item to the script pane. Point to **Global Functions**, point to **Movie Clip Control**, and then click **on**.

4. Click the plus symbol to add a new item to the script pane. Point to **Global Functions**, point to **Timeline Control**, and then click **goto**.

5. Select the **Go to and play** option button in the Script Assist pane if necessary.

6. Select **Frame Label** from the Type pop-up menu in the Script Assist pane.

7. Select **1845** from the Frame pop-up menu in the Script Assist pane.

The ActionScript tells the movie to go to the frame labeled *1845* and play the movie.

FIGURE 7-35
Completed ActionScript for the 1845 instance of the invisible button

8. Add Action Script to the remaining invisible buttons that "go to and play" the movie from the frames labeled *1902*, *1924*, and *today*.

 Test the Navigation Buttons

1. Open the **Control** menu and click **Test Movie**.

   The SWF file opens in the Flash Player window.

2. Test the Play, Pause, Rewind, and invisible chapter title buttons.

3. Close the Flash Player window and return to the main Timeline.

4. Lock the *buttons* layer and save the document.

5. Create a new Library folder named **Buttons**. Use the Buttons folder to store the button icons you imported and the buttons you created in this lesson.

6. Save the document.

7. If you are continuing with the next lesson, leave this file open. If you are not continuing at this time, close the file and close Flash.

TESTING AND REVISING A FLASH DOCUMENT

OBJECTIVES

Upon completion of this lesson, you will be able to:

- Preview a Flash document in a Web browser.

- Test download performance of a Flash document.

- Create and apply a mask layer.

Estimated time to complete this lesson: 30 minutes

Introduction

The Paradise Beach Boardwalk movie will be available as a link on the client's Web site. The movie is intended to launch in its own window and play in the viewer's Web browser.

It is a good idea to test the movie as it will appear in a Web browser and evaluate the download performance based on expected Internet connection speeds.

When checking the completed Paradise Beach Boardwalk movie, compare the entire movie to the storyboard, checking both content and navigation. Refer to the design document to confirm that specifications are met and client goals have been addressed.

In this lesson, you preview the document and test the download performance. Based on the result of your test, you will make revisions that improve the playback of the finished document. An example of improving playback could be to create a simple mask that prevents the audience from seeing any images or text that extend beyond the boundary of the Stage. Using this technique to mask, or hide, content beyond the Stage produces a movie that is more aesthetically pleasing and true to the intended design.

Testing Playback in a Browser

To preview the Paradise Beach Boardwalk movie, you can use the Publish Preview command. This command exports the file and opens the preview in your default Web browser. It is a good idea to test the document in as many Web browsers as possible, but keep in mind that you must have the browsers installed on your computer system to test them.

When testing the movie, be sure to compare your final project against the design specifications and storyboard panels. Test all navigation buttons, timing, and transitions.

Preview the Document in a Web Browser

1. If necessary, open the document you created in the previous lesson. Alternately, you can open the file named **FL_Project2_Lesson8.fla** which is found in the **Practice_files** folder in the Data files for this lesson. If you use **FL_Project2_Lesson8.fla** be sure to save it as **FL_Project2_YourName.fla**.

2. Open the **File** menu, point to **Publish Preview**, and then click **Default - (HTML)**.

The SWF file is generated and opened in a new HTML file. This shows you how the movie will play in your default Web browser. Using your current Publish Settings, Flash creates the SWF and HTML files in the same location as the FLA file. These files remain in this location until you overwrite or delete them.

3. Compare the entire movie to the design specifications and storyboard, noting any necessary corrections.

4. Close the Web browser and return to Flash.

Testing Download Performance

The target audience for the Paradise Beach Boardwalk movie is expected to have Internet connection speeds of 128 Kilobytes per second (Kbps) or faster.

In simulating the download speed, Flash uses estimates of typical Internet performance, not the exact speed. For example, if you select to simulate a modem speed of 28.8 Kbps, Flash sets the actual rate to 2.3 Kbps to reflect typical Internet performance.

For testing the download performance of the Paradise Beach Boardwalk movie, you will use the DSL (32.6 KB/s) Internet connection setting. You want to test the movie by using a slower target connection speed than you expect most viewers will have, just to be safe.

Test Download Performance

1. Open the **Control** menu, and then click **Test Movie** to create a new SWF file.

2. In the Flash Player window, open the **View** menu, point to **Download Settings**, and then select **DSL (32.6 KB/s)**, as shown in Figure 8-1.

FIGURE 8-1
Selecting an Internet connection speed for the download test

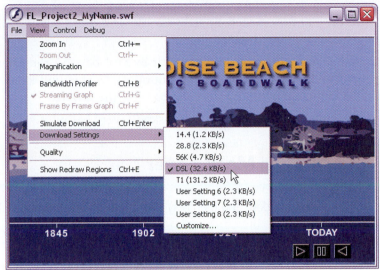

3. In the Flash Player window, open the **View** menu, and then click **Simulate Download** to turn it on.

The movie simulates a download at the Internet connection speed you selected.

4. In the Flash Player window, open the **View** menu, and then click **Bandwidth Profiler**.

The left side of the profiler displays information about the document, its settings, its state, and streams, if any are included in the document.

The right section of the profiler shows the Timeline header and graph. On the graph, each bar represents an individual frame of the document. The size of the bar corresponds to that frame's size in bytes. The red line beneath the Timeline header indicates whether a given frame streams in real time with the current modem speed set in the Control menu.

5. Adjust the view of the graph by taking one of the following actions:

Select **View > Streaming Graph** to show which frames cause pauses.

This default view displays alternating light and dark gray blocks that represent each frame. The size of each block indicates its relative byte size. The first frame stores a symbol's contents, so it is often larger than other frames.

Select **View > Frame by Frame Graph** to display the size of each frame.

This view helps you see which frames contribute to streaming delays. If any frame block extends above the red line in the graph, Flash Player stops playback until the entire frame downloads.

6. Press the Play button or use the scroll bar to move along the timeline so you can see which parts of the movie might take longer to download on some computers.

7. Open the **View** menu, and then click **Bandwidth Profiler** to turn it off.

8. Open the **View** menu, and then click **Simulate Download** to turn it off.

Creating and Applying a Mask Layer

Several images in the Paradise Beach Boardwalk movie extend beyond the Stage boundaries because of the film effects you have created.

To prevent the audience from seeing objects that extend beyond the Stage, you can apply a mask layer that crops the movie along the Stage boundaries. This will keep a clean view of the Stage in case viewers expand the window they use to view the movie.

A mask layer defines the visible area for the masked layers below it.

Create and Apply a Mask Layer

1. Maximize the Flash Player window, and then play the Paradise Beach Boardwalk movie.

   Many of the images and the title text extend beyond the Stage boundaries and they are seen when the window is maximized. To fix this, you will add a simple mask.

2. Close the Flash Player window.

3. Add a new layer above the *logo* layer and name it **mask**. This is the top layer in the Images & Titles folder.

FIGURE 8-2
The mask layer

4. Click frame **1** on the *mask* layer. Select the Rectangle Tool and draw a rectangle with no stroke and a bright color fill, such as green **(#00FF00)**. This rectangle is used for the mask and will not appear in the published document.

5. Use the Property inspector to make the rectangle's width **550** and height **340** (the same size as the Stage).

6. Use the Align panel to align the rectangle horizontally and vertically to the Stage, as shown in Figure 8-3.

FIGURE 8-3
Aligning the mask shape to the center of the Stage

7. Double-click the icon beside the mask layer to open the Layer Properties dialog box.

8. Select the **Mask** option and then click **OK**.

FIGURE 8-4
Layer Properties dialog box

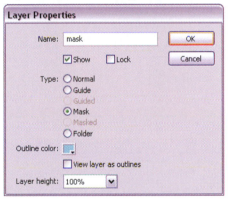

The icon beside the mask layer changes to indicate that it is a mask layer.

FIGURE 8-5
The mask layer

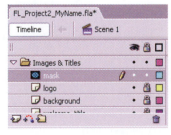

Next, you need to define which layers are masked.

9. Click to select the *logo* layer, scroll to the bottom of the layers, hold down **Shift**, and then click to select the *coaster 4* layer.

Every layer below the mask layer is selected.

10. Drag the selected layers above the mask layer, and then without releasing the mouse button, drag them back to their original position below the mask layer. When you release the mouse button, the layers are indented and their icons change to show they are masked, as shown in Figure 8-6. The mask defines the visible area, so anything beyond the rectangle (in the masked layer) will be invisible when the movie is published.

FIGURE 8-6
All layers in the Images & Titles folder are masked

11. Lock and hide the *mask* layer.

FIGURE 8-7
Hiding the mask layer

12. Open the **Control** menu, click **Test Movie**, and maximize the Flash Player window to see the results of the mask. Play the movie. Anything beyond the mask is invisible, cropping the images and text to fit within the boundaries of the Stage.

13. Close the Flash Player window and save the document.

14. If you are continuing with the next lesson, leave this file open. If you are not continuing at this time, close the file and close Flash.

For additional information, see the Learn More feature, "Creative Masks."

Learn More

CREATIVE MASKS

A mask is a special layer that defines what is visible on the layer or layers below it. In this lesson, you learn to mask the entire Stage, preventing objects from appearing beyond the boundary of the Stage. But you can also use masking to turn images into creative-looking cutouts or shapes.

For example, you place a shape or a block of text on a mask layer with an image masked on a layer below it.

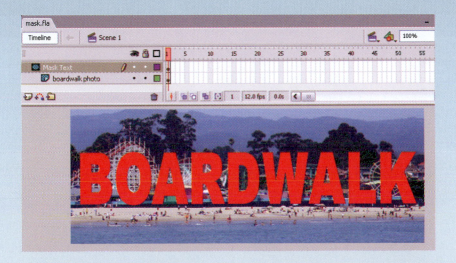

The mask layer defines which portion of the image is visible in the published document.

IMPROVING ACCESSIBILITY AND USABILITY

Introduction

The Paradise Beach Boardwalk online documentary needs to function with or without sound and be accessible to screen reader software. By making the movie accessible, you will make it available to the entire target audience, including people with vision and hearing disabilities and people using computers without sound.

The designer has included several accessibility and usability features, some of which you have already included in the document. Others still need to be added. Table 9-1 describes these features.

TABLE 9-1
Accessibility and usability features

FEATURE	DESCRIPTION
Voice Narration	With sound enabled, visitors sit back and enjoy a brief history of the Paradise Beach Boardwalk amusement park.
Captions	Onscreen text captions substitute for voice narration on computers without sound and for visitors with hearing disabilities.
Navigation Buttons	Navigation buttons give visitors complete control over their viewing experience, allowing visitors to pause, rewind, or jump to a specific chapter. The main navigation buttons also include keyboard equivalents.
Navigation Hints	As an aid to navigation, the Over state of the Play, Pause, and Rewind buttons includes text labels that identify the buttons' functions. When the movie begins, a brief message reminds visitors to click the Play button to begin.
Preloader	The Paradise Beach Boardwalk movie can take several seconds to download and play. The design document requires the movie to include a preloader that monitors the movie's download progress and informs visitors when the movie is ready for viewing.
Screen Reader Support	The design document requires the movie to include accessibility features that identify the navigation buttons and important content for screen readers.

In this lesson, you will add the onscreen text captions and instructions for playing the movie. These are described in the storyboard shown in Figure 9-1. You will also identify navigation and content for screen readers and create the preloader.

FIGURE 9-1
Storyboard

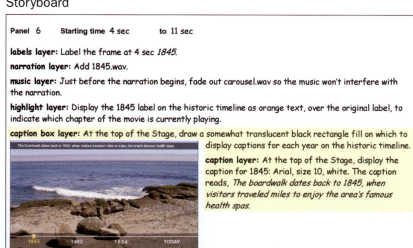

Adding Captions

The Paradise Beach Boardwalk movie could potentially be viewed on computers without sound or by people with hearing disabilities.

Using the storyboard as your guide, add captions for each chapter of the story.

Create a Background For the Captions

1. If necessary, open the document you created in the previous lesson. Alternately, you can open the file named **FL_Project2_Lesson9.fla** which is found in the **Practice_files** folder in the Data files for this lesson. If you use **FL_Project2_Lesson9.fla** be sure to save it as **FL_Project2_YourName.fla**.

2. Add two new layers above the *logo* layer and name them **caption box** and **caption**, as shown in Figure 9-2. Make sure the caption layer is on top.

   Notice that when you add a new layer above a masked layer, the new layer is also masked.

FIGURE 9-2
The caption box and caption layers are masked automatically

3. Insert a keyframe at frame **73** on the *caption box* layer.

4. Use the Rectangle Tool to draw a rectangle with no stroke and a black **(#000000)** fill.

5. Use the Property inspector to make the rectangle's width to **550** and the height **20**.

6. Position the rectangle at X: **0** and Y: **5**, as shown in Figure 9-3.

FIGURE 9-3
Background for the caption text

7. Convert the rectangle to a Graphic Symbol named **caption_box** and change its Alpha transparency to **65%** on the Property inspector.

 Add the Caption Text

1. Insert a keyframe at frame **73** on the *caption* layer. This is the beginning of the 1845 section of the story.

2. Select the Text Tool, click to start a new text block, and use the Property inspector to select **Arial**, size **10**, **white**, **left-aligned**, and Letter spacing **0**.

Inside the Design

The designer chose to make the background box for the captions black and semitransparent to maintain balance and offset the control panel at the bottom of the Stage. The caption box is made slightly less transparent than the control panel because the caption text will appear in a small white font and needs the extra contrast so it is easy to read.

3. Create a caption that reads: **The Boardwalk dates back to 1845, when visitors traveled miles to enjoy the area's famous health spas**.

4. Position the text as shown in Figure 9-4. The left end of the text box is aligned approximately with the left side of the logo at the bottom of the screen.

FIGURE 9-4
The caption text is left aligned

5. Insert a keyframe at frame **208** on the *caption* layer. This is the beginning of the 1902 section of the story.

6. Replace the caption text in frame 208 with the following: **Built in 1902, the classic carousel continues to draw visitors of ALL ages**.

7. Insert a keyframe at frame **352** on the *caption* layer. This is the beginning of the 1924 section of the story.

8. Replace the caption text in frame 352 with the following: **The wooden roller coaster, which was opened in 1924, was and still is the star attraction**.

9. Insert a keyframe at frame **514** on the *caption* layer. This is the beginning of the TODAY section of the story.

10. Replace the caption text in frame 514 with the following: **Today the Boardwalk is a popular destination. Classic rides, candy shops, carnival games, and fun for all...**

Fade the Captions at the End of the Movie

1. Insert a keyframe at frame **667** on the *caption* layer.

2. Convert the caption at frame 667 to a Graphic Symbol named **last_caption**.

3. Insert a keyframe at frame **672** on the *caption* layer.

4. Click frame **672** on the *caption* layer, click the instance of the last_caption symbol on the Stage. Make sure you select the caption and NOT the caption box. Use the Property inspector to change the **Alpha** to **0%**.

5. Create a motion tween between frames 667 and 672 on the *caption* layer.

6. Insert keyframes at frame **667** and **672** on the *caption box* layer.

7. Click frame **672** on the *caption box* layer, click the instance of the caption_box symbol on the Stage, and use the Property inspector to change its **Alpha** to **0%**.

8. Create a motion tween between frames 667 and 672 on the *caption box* layer.

9. Insert blank keyframes at frame **673** on the *caption box* and *caption* layers.

FIGURE 9-5
The caption and caption box fade at the end of the movie

There is one last adjustment to make to the captions. When the movie fades to black between the 1924 and the TODAY sections of the movie, the caption box and text should temporarily disappear so they do not interfere with the transition effect.

10. Insert a keyframe at frame **514** on the *caption box* layer.

11. Insert blank keyframes at frames **497** on the *caption box* and *caption* layers.

FIGURE 9-6
Turning the captions off during the dip to black

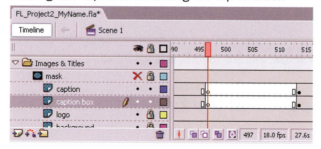

The caption box and text disappear at frame 497 and then reappear after the transition at frame 514. You can scrub (drag the playhead on the Timeline) to preview the transition.

Adding an Onscreen Hint for Navigation

When the Paradise Beach Boardwalk movie downloads, it begins to play and then pauses on the welcome screen. It may not be obvious to everyone how to continue playing the movie. To improve usability, you can add instructions to click the Play button.

Add Text Explaining How to Start the Movie

1. Insert a keyframe at frame **10** on the *caption* layer.

2. Add text to the left of the play button that reads: **Click the PLAY button to begin**.

3. Format text as **Arial**, **white**, size **10**, Letter spacing **.5** (point five). Position the text as shown in Figure 9-7.

FIGURE 9-7
Instructions to the viewer

4. Insert a blank keyframe at frame **11** on the *caption* layer.

    This text will disappear as soon as the movie begins to play.

5. Lock the *caption* and *caption box* layers.

Exposing Content to Screen Readers

The Paradise Beach Boardwalk movie includes a voice narration track making the story accessible to people with limited vision, but several other items, such as the Play, Pause, and Rewind buttons, need to be exposed to viewers who rely on screen reader software to identify objects and describe what occurs onscreen.

Expose the Navigation Buttons to Screen Readers

1. Open the **Window** menu, point to **Other Panels**, and then click **Accessibility**.

    The Accessibility panel opens.

2. Unlock the *buttons* layer (in the Controls folder). With the Selection Tool, click away from the Stage to deselect the buttons, and then click the **Play** button on the Stage to select it.

3. Click in the Name box on the Accessibility panel and key **Play**.

4. Click in the Description box and key: **This story includes narration and images of the Paradise Beach Boardwalk amusement park, featuring the carousel and the classic wooden roller coaster. Press Enter or Return to begin.**

FIGURE 9-8
Accessibility panel for the Play button

Screen reader software will read the name and description of the button. If you leave the name field blank, the screen reader will use the button symbol instance label (on the Property inspector) instead.

5. Click the Pause button on the Stage to select it, click in the Name box, and then key **Pause**. Click in the Description box and key **Press the Spacebar to pause the story**.

6. Click the Rewind button on the Stage to select it, click in the Name box, and then key **Rewind**. Click in the Description box and key **Press the left arrow key to rewind the story**.

Expose the Welcome Title to Screen Readers

1. Unlock the *welcome title* layer, and then click frame 10 on the *welcome title* layer.

2. Click in the Name box on the Accessibility panel, and key **Welcome to Paradise Beach Historic Boardwalk**.

3. Deselect the check box that reads *Make child objects accessible*.

FIGURE 9-9
Exposing the welcome title to screen readers

Screen readers will not see the individual objects that make up the title. The title will be read as a single object. The Timeline contains two additional instances of the welcome title, in frames 1 and 19. You will hide these from screen readers in the next exercise.

Hiding Objects from Screen Readers

Some Flash objects, when encountered by screen reader software, cause more confusion than support. For example, this movie includes three instances of the welcome title movie clip symbol to create the animation of the welcome title. You have exposed one instance to screen readers so you can hide the other two instances. Also, buttons with an empty Up state can present problems for some screen readers so you will hide the invisible chapter buttons, their text labels, and the chapter highlights. Also, the caption text, when read by screen readers, will interfere with the audio narration.

To prevent screen readers from reading text objects, you can convert them to movie clip symbols and then disable accessibility.

 ## Hide the Extra Instances of the Welcome Title Movie Clip Symbol

1. Click frame **1** on the *welcome title* layer and deselect **Make object accessible** on the Accessibility panel.

FIGURE 9-10
Hiding an instance of the welcome title from screen readers

2. Click frame **19** on the *welcome title* layer and deselect **Make object accessible** on the Accessibility panel.

3. Lock the *welcome title* layer.

The two extra instances of the welcome title movie clip symbol will be ignored by screen readers.

Hide the Invisible Buttons From Screen Reader Software

1. Click the instance of the invisble button symbol over 1845 and deselect **Make object accessible** on the Accessibility panel.

2. Click the instance of the invisible button symbol over 1902 and deselect **Make object accessible** on the Accessibility panel.

3. Click the instance of the invisible button symbol over 1924 and deselect **Make object accessible** on the Accessibility panel.

4. Click the instance of the invisible button symbol over TODAY and deselect **Make object accessible** on the Accessibility panel.

   The invisible button instances are now hidden from screen readers.

5. Lock the *buttons* layer.

Hide Text Objects From Screen Reader Software

1. Unlock the *historic timeline* layer.

2. Click **1845** on the Stage to select it. Hold down the **Shift** key and click **1902**, **1924**, and **TODAY** to select the remaining labels.

   All four text labels are selected. Notice that the Accessibility panel now reflects the fact that the selected labels can not have accessibility applied to them.

FIGURE 9-11
All four chapter titles selected

3. Open the **Modify** menu, and then click **Convert to Symbol**. Name the symbol **chapter_titles**, select the **Movie clip** Type, and then click **OK**. Notice that the Accessibilty panel immediately changes to make accessibility options available.

4. With the *chapter_titles* symbol still selected on the Stage, deselect **Make object accessible** on the Accessibility panel.

5. Lock the *historic timeline* layer and unlock the *highlight* layer.

6. Click frame **73** on the *highlight* layer. This is the highlight for 1845.

7. Convert the text to a Movie clip symbol named **1845_highlight**.

8. With the 1845 highlight selected on the Stage, deselect **Make object accessible** on the Accessibility panel.

9. Convert the other text highlights in frames 208, 352, and 514 to Movie clip symbols and disable accessibility.

10. Lock the *highlight* layer and unlock the *caption* layer.

11. Convert the caption text in frames 73, 208, 352, and 514 to separate Movie clip symbols, and disable accessibility.

12. Lock the *caption* layer, close the Accessibility panel, and save the document.

For additional information, see the Tips & Techniques feature, "Accessibility Strategies."

Tips & Techniques

ACCESSIBILITY STRATEGIES

The images in the Paradise Beach Boardwalk movie are intended to reinforce the spoken narration that tells a brief history of the amusement park. This creates an accessibility challenge. If you add accessibility descriptions for each image, a screen reader will attempt to read them while the narrator is speaking. Some of the images advance rapidly, creating an additional challenge for the screen reader. But even without these images, the Paradise Beach Boardwalk story is communicated effectively by using audio narration and sound effects.

If your document relies primarily on a sequence of images that are critical to the story and does not include voice narration, or if the document contains several images (a movie duration greater than one minute), you should pause the movie on each image, giving the screen reader enough time to describe the images in detail. To do this, place a *stop* action at the location of each image. Then add a button, such as Continue or Next, that contains a *play* action or a *gotoAndStop* action to advance viewers to the next image in the series. This allows viewers to step through the entire presentation, one image at a time, much like viewing a slide show.

Creating a Preloader

The Paradise Beach Boardwalk movie will take longer to download for some viewers than for others. If a viewer attempts to play the movie before it has completely downloaded, the movie might not run as intended. One way to prevent viewer frustration is to include a preloader.

A preloader monitors the download progress and informs the viewer when the movie has downloaded enough frames to play properly.

To create a preloader for the Paradise Beach Boardwalk movie, you will add a new scene and designate it as the first scene to play when the movie downloads. The preloader uses ActionScript that detects whether the SWF file has finished downloading. When the movie has downloaded, the movie will play.

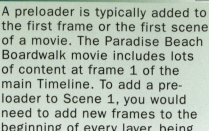

Inside the Design

A preloader is typically added to the first frame or the first scene of a movie. The Paradise Beach Boardwalk movie includes lots of content at frame 1 of the main Timeline. To add a preloader to Scene 1, you would need to add new frames to the beginning of every layer, being careful not to get the existing keyframes out of sync. By placing the preloader in a new scene, the main Timeline of Scene 1 is left intact.

 Add a New Scene to the Document

1. Open the **Window** menu, point to **Other Panels**, and then click **Scene**.

   The Paradise Beach Boardwalk movie includes one scene, named Scene 1.

FIGURE 9-12
Scene panel

2. Click the **Add scene** button.

   A new scene is added to the Scene panel and an empty Timeline opens for the new scene.

3. Double-click the name of the new scene and rename it **preloader**.

4. Drag the preloader scene and drop it above *Scene 1*, as shown in Figure 9-13.

FIGURE 9-13
The preloader scene will load first

The preloader will now load first, followed by Scene 1.

5. Close the Scene panel.

The scene name, preloader, appears on the Information bar.

 ## Create the Preloader Message

1. Double-click Layer 1 of the preloader scene, and change the name to **looping message**. This will be the layer that contains the feedback to viewers while the Paradise Beach Boardwalk movie downloads.

2. Use the Text Tool to key the message **loading . . .** Make the text **Arial**, size **16**, **white**, and **bold**. Select the ellipses (three dots) and adjust the letter spacing so they are spread further apart.

3. Position the loading message text in the center of the Stage.

FIGURE 9-14
Loading message

4. Insert keyframes at frames **10**, **19**, and **28** (every half second) on the looping message layer.

FIGURE 9-15
A new dot is added to the loading message every half second

5. Click in frame **19** and delete the last dot in the loading message.

FIGURE 9-16
Editing the loading message

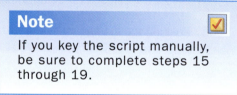

6. Click in frame **10** and delete the two last dots.

7. Click in frame **1** and delete all three dots.

As the loading message plays, a new dot is added every half second.

In the next Step by Step you will create the ActionScript for the preloader. The first frame of the preloader includes ActionScript that monitors the download process by using a conditional statement. The statement checks to see if the total number of bytes loaded is less than the total number of bytes in the movie. If this is true, the loader repeats itself by returning to frame 1 and checking again. If the total number of bytes loaded is equal to the total number of bytes in the movie, the movie goes to, and plays, the start frame of Scene 1.

 ## Create the ActionScript For the Preloader

1. Insert a new layer above the *looping message* layer and name it **actions**.

> **Note** ☑️
>
> If you key the script manually, be sure to complete steps 15 through 19.

2. Click frame **1** on the *actions* layer, expand the Actions panel, and make sure Script Assist is selected.

As you follow steps 3 through 14 below, you will create the script shown in Figure 9-17. Alternately, you could key the script in manually and skip to step 15 below.

FIGURE 9-17
Completed ActionScript for the preloader

```
1  if (_root.getBytesLoaded() != _root.getBytesTotal()) {
2      gotoAndPlay(1);
3  } else {
4      gotoAndPlay("Scene 1", "start");
5  }
6
```

3. Click the plus symbol to add a new item to the script. Point to **Statements**, point to **Conditions/Loops**, and then click **if**.

4. Click in the Condition text box in the Script Assist pane, click the plus symbol, point to **Global Properties**, point to **Identifiers**, and then click **_root**.

5. Click at the end of the script in the Condition box (after_root), click the plus symbol, point to **ActionScript 2.0 Classes**, point to **Client/Server and XML**, point to **LoadVars**, point to **Methods**, and click **getBytesLoaded**.

This script retrieves the value for the total number of bytes loaded.

6. Click at the end of the script in the Condition box, click the plus symbol, point to **Operators**, point to **Comparison Operators**, and then click **!=**.

This is the "not equal to" comparison operator.

7. Click at the end of the script in the Condition box, click the plus symbol, point to **Global Properties**, point to **Identifiers**, and click **_root**.

8. Click at the end of the script in the Condition box. Click the plus symbol, point to **ActionScript 2.0 Classes**, point to **Client/Server and XML**, point to **LoadVars**, point to **Methods**, and click **getBytesTotal**.

This script retrieves the value for the total number of bytes for the entire movie.

9. Click at the end of the script in the Condition box, click the plus symbol, point to **Global Functions**, **Timeline Control**, and then click **goto**.

By default the gotoAndPlay action is set to go to and play frame 1 of the current scene. If the total number of bytes loaded does not equal the total number of bytes in the movie, the movie will go to frame 1 of the preloader, play the loading message again, and continue checking.

10. Click the plus symbol to add a new item to the script. Point to **Statements**, point to **Conditions/Loops**, and then click **else**.

So if the total number of bytes loaded does equal the total number of bytes in the movie, then the movie will not go to frame 1 of the preloader but will follow this script path to the location specified in the following steps.

11. Click the plus symbol, point to **Global Functions**, **Timeline Control**, and then click **goto**.

12. Select **Scene 1** on the Scene pop-up menu of the Script Assist panel.

13. Select **Frame Label** on the Type pop-up menu of the Script Assist panel.

14. Select **start** on the Frame pop-up menu of the Script Assist panel.

The script in Figure 9-18 shows that when the entire movie is downloaded (the total number of bytes loaded is equal to the total number of bytes in the movie), the movie will go to and play the frame labeled start on the Scene 1 Timeline.

FIGURE 9-18
When the entire movie is loaded, the movie will go to and play the start frame of Scene 1

```
1  if (_root.getBytesLoaded() != _root.getBytesTotal()) {
2      gotoAndPlay(1);
3  } else {
4      gotoAndPlay("Scene 1", "start");
5  }
6
```

15. Collapse the Actions panel.

16. Click the **Edit Scene** button on the Information bar, and then click **Scene 1**.

FIGURE 9-19
Edit Scene menu

The preloader is replaced by the Timeline for Scene 1.

17. Open the **Control** menu, and then click **Test Movie** to view the preloader.

18. Close the Flash Player window, save and close the document, and then close Flash.

For additional information on improving usability, see the Tips & Techniques feature "Usability Testing."

Note

If the movie loads quickly, you may not be able to see the entire preloader message.

Hot Tip

After completing your movie, you may find it helpful to tidy up the Library panel by grouping files into related folders. For example, you may want to create additional Library panel folders for storing miscellaneous graphic symbols or movie clips.

Tips & Techniques

USABILITY TESTING

Usability is the extent to which the target audience or intended user can meet his or her goals using the system or product being tested.

Consider the following when testing a Flash document for usability:

- Does the product meet its intended goals?
- Can users locate important content?
- How do people interact with the system you are testing?
- Are navigation buttons and links easy to identify and use?
- Observe each user's experience. Are they enjoying themselves? What is exciting about it? Do they appear lost or frustrated?
- What changes would users like to see?

A usability test can be as simple as observing people using your product. Do the following when testing your Flash document for usability:

- Test the product with at least five users from your target audience.
- Publish the document to the Internet and have users test the product by using expected Internet connection speeds.
- Listen and observe. Write everything down.
- If possible, videotape each user during testing.
- Do not offer assistance if users become stuck or encounter a problem.
- Provide a means for feedback, such as a questionnaire or post-test interview.
- Don't take feedback personally.

Usability testing lets you study users to understand precisely what the audience expects compared to their actual experience with your product. The way subjects actually use your system may reveal issues that are invisible to you.

SUMMARY

You have successfully created a digital documentary to promote the Paradise Beach Historic Boardwalk amusement park.

In this project, you learned to follow a design document and storyboard to produce and publish accessible Flash documents. You learned to use Flash to simulate film-style techniques and effects to tell a story and to create user-friendly navigation that puts the audience in control of their online experience. You also learned to include features like captions and preloaders to ensure that your online story is usable and accessible for the entire target audience.

Some of the technical skills covered in this project include:

- Using guides and rulers for precise page layout
- Importing bitmap images
- Converting a bitmap image to a vector drawing
- Creating film-style effects by using motion tweens
- Adding sound and adjusting sound properties
- Applying graphic filters
- Creating and modifying buttons
- Adding ActionScript to buttons for navigation
- Organizing a Flash document by using folders
- Testing the performance and usability of a Flash document
- Creating and applying a mask
- Making rich media content accessible

The next project in this unit builds upon what you have already learned, reinforcing these skills and introducing several new ones, including working with Flash video and dynamic text objects.

ON YOUR OWN – CREATING FILM-STYLE TECHNIQUES

ACTIVITY 1: APPLYING FILM-STYLE TRANSITIONS

You have learned to combine image manipulation, such as tracing a bitmap, with motion animation to simulate film-style transitions and camera techniques including:

- Fading images in and out
- Dissolving and wiping between images
- Zooming, panning, tilting, and moving a camera

Apply these same skills to create a mini-movie that links together photographs of Hawaiian beaches. Bring in all the images, convert the first image to a vector graphic so it looks like a painting, and then apply film-style effects to transition between all the images. You can review the techniques for this activity in Lessons 1, 2, and 3.

1. Open a new document with a width of **460** pixels and a height of **345** pixels. Change the frame rate to 18fps. Extend the Timeline so the duration of the movie is approximately **20** seconds.

2. Import the following images to the document library: **hawaii_1.jpg, hawaii_2.jpg, hawaii_3.jpg,** and **hawaii_4.jpg**.

3. Add an instance of the hawaii_1 photo to the Timeline and convert the image to a vector graphic.

> **Note**
>
> If you don't like the results of the trace bitmap command, you can open the **Edit** menu, and then click **Undo Trace Bitmap** to cancel the command and start over with a new combination of settings.

4. Create a transition effect that fades in the vector graphic from black. Allow the vector image to remain visible for about three seconds.

5. Add another copy of the hawaii_1 photo to a new layer on the Timeline and create a dissolve transition between the vector graphic and the original copy of the hawaii_1 photo. Allow the hawaii_1.jpg image to remain visible for about three seconds.

6. Add the hawaii_2 photo to the Timeline and create a cut transition between the hawaii_1 and hawaii_2 photos. When the hawaii_2 photo appears, start with the photo the same size as the Stage (460 × 345). Create a three-second zoom that starts with the hawaii_2 photo the same size as the Stage and ends with the hawaii_2 photo 100% of its original size (600 × 450).

7. Add the hawaii_3 photo to the Timeline and create a horizontal wipe transition between the hawaii_2 and hawaii_3 photos. Allow the hawaii_3 photo to remain visible for about three seconds.

8. Add the hawaii_4 photo to the Timeline and create a transition of your choice between the hawaii_3 and hawaii_4 photos. Allow the hawaii_4 photo to remain visible for about three seconds.

9. End the movie by fading out the hawaii_4 photo to black. Save the file and test the movie.

10. Make the entire document accessible by adding a name and description for screen readers. Disable accessibility for child objects.

11. Save the final file and publish the final accessible document.

ACTIVITY 2: CREATING ANIMATED TITLES

You have learned to apply graphic filters to produce interesting-looking animated titles for digital documentaries and other Flash movies. Using graphic filters, you can apply:

- Drop shadows
- Blurs
- Glows
- Bevels
- Colors

You can review the techniques for this activity in Lesson 5.

Use Flash graphic filters to create the following animated title.

1. Create a new document that is 550 pixels wide, 300 pixels high, 12 fps, and change the background color to black (#000000). Create a text block for the title. Apply text properties by using the Property inspector (**Arial Black,** size **43,** blue (**#00FFFF**), letter spacing **6**).

2. Apply one or more graphic filters to the title text, such as a drop shadow and an inner bevel.

3. Animate the title so it begins in the workspace outside the right side of the Stage and moves across the Stage. When the title reaches the left Stage boundary, animate the text again so it moves to the center of the Stage, creating the effect of text moving in and then bouncing back from the side of the Stage and stopping in the center.

4. Use the Property inspector to apply easing to the animation (Ease in −30 and Ease out 60).

5. Save the file and test the movie.

6. Make the entire document accessible by adding a name and description for screen readers. Disable accessibility for child objects.

7. Save the final file and publish the accessible movie.

> **Extra Challenge**
>
> You can experiment with various filters and filter settings as well as the various Ease settings to see how they affect the animation.

ACTIVITY 3: CREATING A PHOTO SLIDE VIEWER

You have learned to create and program Flash button symbols that navigate to any location along the Flash Timeline. These skills include:

- Creating Up, Down, Over, and Hit states

- Programming buttons by using ActionScript

You can review the techniques for this activity in Lesson 7.

Use these same techniques to create a photo slide viewer that displays photographs of popular travel destinations. Include a navigation button that advances from one photo to the next when clicked.

1. Open a new document and set the width to **345** pixels and the height to **300** pixels. Change the background color to black (#000000). Add guides that will help you align the photographs and button on the Stage.

2. Import the following three photographs to the document library: **baja.jpg, colorado_river.jpg,** and **grand_canyon.jpg**.

3. Create and name layers for each of your images, a layer for the button, and a layer for actions.

4. When placing the photos on their respective layers, be sure to stagger their placement such that the first photo appears only in frame 1, the second photo appears only in frame 2, and the third photo appears only in frame 3. Use the guides to help you position the photos on the Stage.

5. Create a new button symbol named **Next**. Design and create Up, Over, Down, and Hit states for the Next button. Place an instance of the Next button on the button layer near the bottom right corner of the Stage. Make sure the button layer has enough frames that the button will always be visible.

6. Using Script Assist, program the Next button to go to and stop at the "next frame" on the Timeline. Assign the Right Arrow key as the keyboard equivalent.

7. Add an action at frame 1 that stops the show on the first photograph. The show begins paused.

8. Add an action in frame 4 (or one frame after the last image on the Timeline) that goes to and stops on frame 1. When visitors click Next after viewing the last photograph, the show automatically returns to the first photograph.

> **Note** ☑
>
> If you add a frame label to frame 1, you can reference the label when adding the *gotoAndStop* action at frame 3. If you add a frame label, place it on a new layer named *labels*.

9. Create a title **Likeable Places** on a new layer named **title**, and position the title in the lower-left corner of the Stage. Make sure the *title* layer has enough frames that the title will always be visible. Save and test the movie.

10. Make the document accessible by converting each photograph on the Stage to a movie clip symbol and adding a name and description for each symbol on the Accessibility panel. Assign a name and description to the Next button.

11. Save the file and publish the accessible movie.

ACTIVITY 4: WORKING WITH SOUND

You have learned how to use sound to enhance a Flash document. Techniques for working with sound include:

- Importing sound
- Previewing sound
- Adding sound to the Timeline
- Editing sound properties

Apply these techniques to create a simple language translation between English and Spanish. You can review the techniques for this activity in Lesson 4.

1. Open a new document and create layers named **text** and **buttons**.

2. Key the following text on the *text* layer:

   English

   "The Ball Bounces."

   Spanish

   "La Pelota Rebota."

3. Import the sound files **ball.wav** and **pelota.wav** to the Library panel.

4. Open the **Window** menu, point to **Common Libraries**, and click **Buttons** to open the common library for buttons. Open the **classic buttons** folder and then open the **Circle Buttons** subfolder.

5. Drag the **Play** button from the Library panel to the Stage on the *buttons* layer and position it next to the English text. Close the Library - Buttons panel. Notice that the Play button is added to the Library panel for your document. Rename the button **Play_English** on the Library panel.

6. Double-click the **Play_English** button to edit the symbol. Add a layer to the button and name it **sound**. Insert a keyframe in the Down state of the *sound* layer and add the sound file **ball.wav** to this keyframe. Set the sound to play as an **Event**.

7. Duplicate the Play_English button on the Library panel and name the new button **Play_Spanish**. Edit the Play_Spanish button by replacing the ball.wav sound file in the Down state with the pelota.wav sound file.

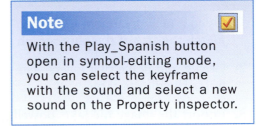

Note ☑️

With the Play_Spanish button open in symbol-editing mode, you can select the keyframe with the sound and select a new sound on the Property inspector.

8. Click **Scene 1** on the Information bar to close the button symbol and return to the main Timeline.

9. Drag a copy of the **Play_Spanish** symbol from the Library panel to the Stage and position it beside the Spanish text.

English
The Ball Bounces. play

Espanol
La Pelota Rebota. play

10. Save and test the movie.

11. Add accessibility names to identify the English and Spanish Play buttons to screen readers.

12. Save the file and publish the accessible movie.

ACTIVITY 5: CREATING A RADIAL WIPE TRANSITION BY USING A MASK

You have learned to create film-style transitions and to crop the Stage by applying a mask layer.

By combining these techniques, you can produce interesting film-style transitions, including a radial wipe. A *radial wipe*, sometimes called an *iris*, begins with a small hole in the center of the screen through which a small portion of an underlying image is visible. The hole grows in diameter until the entire image fills the screen.

Combine the following techniques to create a radial wipe transition.

- Drawing simple shapes
- Animating objects by using shape tweens

- Creating film-style wipe transitions
- Creating and applying a mask layer

You can review the techniques for this activity in Lessons 3 and 9.

1. Open a new document and set the width to **345** pixels and the height to **260** pixels to match the size of the photograph you will import.

2. Create and name two layers. The top layer holds the shape tween and the bottom layer holds the photograph.

3. Import the image file **lake_powell.jpg** to the Library panel and then add the photograph to the bottom layer, centered on the Stage.

4. Draw a perfect circle with no stroke and any color fill on the shape tween layer.

5. Create a three-second shape tween that begins with the circle centered on the Stage and very small (about 2 px by 2 px) and ends with the circle diameter large enough to cover the entire Stage. Extend the layer containing the photograph so that it displays for the same number of frames as the shape tween (three seconds).

> **Note**
>
> Make the fill color of the shape a bright color that is not the same color used for the document background so you can easily distinguish it from the rest of the image.

6. Convert the layer that contains the shape tween (the top layer) to a mask layer and apply the mask to the layer containing the photograph. Hide and lock the mask layer. Save the document and test the movie.

7. Use a *stop* action to prevent the movie from looping after it completes showing the entire image.

8. Make the entire document accessible. Add a name and description for the document and disable accessibility for all child objects.

9. Save the document and publish the accessible movie.

VIDEO GALLERY

GOALS

- Follow a design document and storyboard to produce an online gallery of video clips.
- Create Flash Video (FLV) files and prepare video for display on the Web.
- Learn methods for improving Flash performance by storing content outside the main FLA document.
- Learn techniques for improving accuracy and readability of text in Flash.
- Link to content stored on another Web site.
- Improve usability and accessibility of Flash documents.

TECHNICAL SKILLS

- Encode Flash Video (FLV) files for the Web.
- Use guides to create page structure and balance.
- Create thumbnail buttons.
- Format text.
- Check spelling of a Flash document.
- Create external links.
- Use ActionScript to load and display content stored outside the main Flash document.
- Use ActionScript to display text dynamically.
- Expose and hide content for screen readers.
- Perform a technical test of a Flash document.
- Select publish settings and publish a document.

Estimated time to complete this project: 4 hours

Summary

Flash Video has many useful applications on the Internet, the most obvious being entertainment. Many Web sites offer daily news and events from around the world, bringing sites to life with full motion video and sound. Other sites blend traditional Web marketing with television-style ads, making sites more interesting and effective. Flash Video is also an excellent teaching tool and is often used for education and business skills training. This project demonstrates how you can use video to enhance a traditional Web site, add interest, entertain, and promote e-commerce by allowing potential customers to preview short segments of a full-length video.

The Assignment

In this project, you use Macromedia Flash to produce a video gallery featuring short video clips from recent surfing events held at the world-famous surfing location known as Mavericks. The video clips are samples taken from a video that can be purchased on the client's Web site. The client, Blue Mountain Riders, will host the video gallery on their Web site designed for big wave surfers and other surfing enthusiasts, shown in Figure 1. You will use the design document and storyboard to:

- Create separate Flash Video files for each clip

- Publish a separate SWF file to open and play each video

- Create the main Flash document for the gallery

- Create thumbnail buttons for selecting a video clip to preview

- Add and format informative text

- Add a link to the Blue Mountain Riders online store

- Add onscreen directions and video captions

FIGURE 1
Blue Mountain Riders Web site example showing placement of the video gallery

Video Gallery Design Document

Take a moment to review the design document shown in Figure 2 before starting the project. Note the elements that will help you set up your documents.

FIGURE 2
Design document

Design Document – Interactive Video Gallery

Client: Blue Mountain Riders Surfing Association – A Resource for Big Wave Surfers and Big Wave Surfing Enthusiasts.

Goals and Purpose
The primary goals of the video gallery are to:
- Increase the number of new visitors to the Blue Mountain Riders Web site.
- Promote sales of videos and other products available in the Blue Mountain Riders online store.
- Promote travel to surfing destinations.
- Increase awareness of the featured big wave surfing events.
- Provide exposure to up-and-coming big wave surfers sponsored by Blue Mountain Riders.

Audience
Our target audience includes big wave surfers, big wave surfing enthusiasts, potential advertisers, and event sponsors. Their age range is 13 and older. Some adjectives to describe the audience are adventurous, risk-takers, environmentally aware, and cooperative.

Design Requirements

VIDEO ENCODING

Video file format: Flash Video (FLV)	**Deployment method:** Progressive download
Codec: On2 VP6	**Video frame rate:** Same as source video
Keyframes: Automatic	**Data rate:** video=400 audio=48Kbps-mono
Video Dimensions: 300x200	**Controls:** Play, Pause, Seek, Mute

VIDEO GALLERY DESIGN

Document dimensions: 500 pixels wide by 380 pixels high
Frame rate: 12 fps
Colors: The Blue Mountain Riders Web site includes rich shades of blue and yellow with black, gray, and white accents. Colors for the video gallery are Blue (#006699), Dark Gray (#333333), Gray (#999999), Light Gray (#CCCCCC), White (#FFFFFF), and Black (#000000).
Navigation and Feedback: Viewers select a video by clicking thumbnail images. The name of each video clip appears below the button. Buttons include an Over state that indicates the button is active. Onscreen directions tell the viewer to click a thumbnail button to preview the video. They also inform the viewer when a video is loading. Caption text appears below each video when loaded.
Accessibility: Buttons, links, directions to the viewer, and caption text should be exposed to screen readers. The videos can be hidden from screen readers so the background music does not interfere with the descriptive caption text.
Preloader: No. Because the videos are stored outside the video gallery, the video gallery is so small that a preloader isn't needed.

Delivery Requirements

The gallery will be built with Macromedia Flash and run with Macromedia Flash Player 8.
- Internet Explorer, v6
- Safari 2.0
- AOL 8 or later
- Mozilla Firefox 1.04 or later

The gallery should run on
- Macintosh OS 10.3 or later
- Windows XP Home or Professional
- Internet connection speeds of 128Kbps or faster

Content
The featured video gallery includes short clips from a recent video shot at the world-famous big wave surf spot called Mavericks. Additional galleries will be created in the future, featuring other surfing locations, events, travel destinations, accomplished surfers, and new-release surfing videos.

Blue Mountain Riders Video Gallery – Design Document   1

To view the design document for the video gallery, open the file named *FL_Project3_Design.pdf*. This file is located in the Design folder in the data files for this project.

Project Storyboard

Take a moment to review the storyboard before building the video gallery. Note the elements that will help you set up the Flash documents for the video gallery.

FIGURE 3
Storyboard

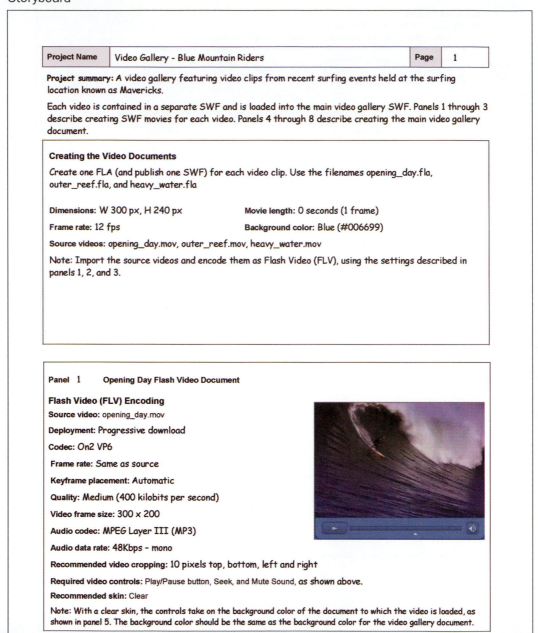

Project Name	Video Gallery - Blue Mountain Riders	Page	1

Project summary: A video gallery featuring video clips from recent surfing events held at the surfing location known as Mavericks.

Each video is contained in a separate SWF and is loaded into the main video gallery SWF. Panels 1 through 3 describe creating SWF movies for each video. Panels 4 through 8 describe creating the main video gallery document.

Creating the Video Documents

Create one FLA (and publish one SWF) for each video clip. Use the filenames opening_day.fla, outer_reef.fla, and heavy_water.fla

Dimensions: W 300 px, H 240 px   Movie length: 0 seconds (1 frame)

Frame rate: 12 fps   Background color: Blue (#006699)

Source videos: opening_day.mov, outer_reef.mov, heavy_water.mov

Note: Import the source videos and encode them as Flash Video (FLV), using the settings described in panels 1, 2, and 3.

Panel   1   Opening Day Flash Video Document

Flash Video (FLV) Encoding

Source video: opening_day.mov

Deployment: Progressive download

Codec: On2 VP6

Frame rate: Same as source

Keyframe placement: Automatic

Quality: Medium (400 kilobits per second)

Video frame size: 300 x 200

Audio codec: MPEG Layer III (MP3)

Audio data rate: 48Kbps – mono

Recommended video cropping: 10 pixels top, bottom, left and right

Required video controls: Play/Pause button, Seek, and Mute Sound, as shown above.

Recommended skin: Clear

Note: With a clear skin, the controls take on the background color of the document to which the video is loaded, as shown in panel 5. The background color should be the same as the background color for the video gallery document.

1

To view the complete storyboard for this project, open the file named *FL_Project3_Storyboard.pdf*. This file is located in the Design folder in the data files for this project.

PREPARING VIDEO FOR THE WEB

OBJECTIVES

Upon completion of this lesson, you will be able to:

■ Encode Flash (FLV) video files.

■ View the properties of the FLVPlayback component.

■ Publish videos as SWF files.

Estimated time to complete this lesson: 1 hour

Introduction

The video gallery for the Blue Mountain Riders Web site features three video clips. Visitors to the Web site will play the videos by selecting from one of three thumbnail images in the video gallery. In this lesson, you use Macromedia Flash to prepare the video files for the gallery. For additional information, see the Tips & Techniques feature "Web Video Production Tips."

Flash Video

Flash Video is based on the technology of Macromedia Flash Player, so it is easy to produce and even easier to play. With Flash Video, when the page loads, the video plays without requiring a third-party player. It is that simple. Flash Video offers several technological and creative benefits that allow designers to create a rich Web experience. Most computers already have the Flash Player installed. Flash Video integrates seamlessly into your Web site, and you can design custom sets of controls, called "skins," to match the look and feel of any Web site. You can also set the size and aspect ratio of your video, and the video can dynamically change based on a data source. Flash Video starts playing quickly, and provides immersive and interactive experiences. Because Flash treats Flash Video as simply another media type, you can view a video just like any other object in a SWF file.

Using Macromedia Flash, there are three ways to add Flash Video to the Blue Mountain Riders Web site. These include embedded video (bringing the video into the Flash document), progressive download (linking to the video to load it from outside the Flash document and then play), and streaming video (linking to video stored on Flash Communication Server to load it as it plays).

Progressive Download

In this project, you will use the progressive download method for delivering Flash Video. Progressive download stores the Flash Video (FLV) files outside the main document, keeping the size of the document small. For additional information, see the Learn More special feature "Embedding and Streaming Flash Video."

Learn More

EMBEDDING AND STREAMING FLASH VIDEO

Embedding Flash Video

Embedding video involves importing video and placing it on the Timeline of your Flash document. When the Flash movie is published, the video is fully contained in the SWF file.

As a result, the quality of the video is lower than with other methods, the file size of the published SWF file is large (causing longer download times), replacing the video is difficult, and the number of frames in a Flash document is limited, resulting in a limit to the length of the video.

Before Flash Video, videos were often embedded, and it is still an option, although not at all recommended.

Streaming Flash Video

Customers who want to deliver long videos (over 10 minutes) and want to deliver video to several hundred simultaneous viewers should consider the streaming video option.

As is the case with progressive download, FLV files for streaming video are kept external to the other Flash content and developers can use ActionScript commands to feed those external FLV files into a Flash movie and play them back on demand. But streaming video offers several advantages over progressive download, including:

- You can divide a long clip into separate "chunks" so viewers can view portions of a specific clip without requesting the entire video.
- You can automatically create "chapters" viewers can jump to by clicking a link without having to break up the video into shorter pieces.
- Videos can play seamlessly back to back, so you can break a long video into shorter clips and have it appear to play back as a single long video.
- You can deliver live or recorded events where everyone must see the same thing at the same time. With progressive download, viewers see prerecorded videos based on when they select them and cannot view streaming live or recorded video.

With so many advantages, you may be wondering why someone would ever use progressive download instead of streaming video. There are a couple reasons. First, progressive download can be added to any Web server, whereas streaming Flash Video requires your video (FLV) files to be hosted on a specialized video-streaming server. Second, for streaming Flash Video, you must use Flash Communication Server. It is the only software that can stream audio, video, and real-time data to Flash Player. So, you should use streaming video with Flash Communication Server when delivering long videos (over 10 minutes), when delivering to hundreds of simultaneous viewers, and when streaming live video and use progressive download video for other circumstances.

With progressive download, when the video is played, the video file is downloaded to the viewer's computer (hard drive) before playback. The file is served from a normal Web server just like a normal Web page or any other downloadable document. However, unlike traditional download-and-play methods of video delivery, the file starts playing before it has completely downloaded. This reduces the amount of time a viewer has to wait to see the video.

Keeping the Flash Video (FLV) files external and separate from the video gallery's main SWF document as shown in Figure 1-1 has a number of benefits, including the following:

- **Easy to update:** It is relatively easy to add or replace videos without the need to republish the gallery.

- **Small SWF file size:** Your SWF file can remain very small for fast page loads and the video can be delivered when a viewer selects it.

- **Better performance:** Because the FLV and SWF files are separate, the performance and results of your video playback typically will be better.

FIGURE 1-1
Progressive download stores the Flash Video (FLV) files outside the main document

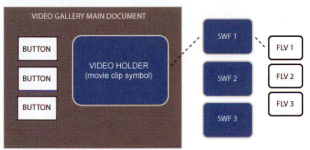

In this lesson, you will create and encode the given video (currently MOV files) into three Flash Video (FLV) files and then place them each in their own Flash documents to generate three movies—opening_day.swf, outer_reef.swf, and heavy_water.swf. These movies will link to their respective FLV files so that each video will be loaded progressively. You create these separate movies so you have more flexibility with building the overall structure of the Flash document that will hold the different video clips.

Encoding a Flash Video (FLV) File

The Blue Mountain Riders video gallery features three short videos from recent surfing events at the big wave surfing location called Mavericks, also knows as Mavs. The videos have been edited and provided to you as large QuickTime (MOV) files. To link the videos to the gallery and deliver them by using progressive download, you must first convert the MOV files to Flash Video (FLV) files.

Converting video to the FLV format creates smaller, more Web-friendly files and allows them to be played by using Macromedia Flash Player, which is installed automatically with most Web browsers.

To create the FLV files, you simply import the source video into a Flash document and select properties for the video, including a set of built-in video controls. The FLV files are created automatically and placed in the same directory as your Flash document. The Flash document contains an FLVPlayback component that downloads and plays the video.

According to the design document and storyboard, the videos must be 300 × 200 pixels and include a set of controls below the video that allows the viewer to play, pause, seek, and mute the audio. The built-in controls for Flash Videos are approximately 40 pixels high, so the SWF document that contains the FLVPlayback component must be 300 × 240 pixels.

 ## Set Document Properties for the Flash Video File

1. Open a new blank Flash document.

2. Click **Modify** on the Menu bar, and then click **Document**.

3. Make sure Ruler units is set to **Pixels**, and then change the width of the document to **300** pixels and the height to **240** pixels (300 × 200 for the video plus 40 for the video controls).

4. Change the background color to teal blue (**#006699**). This is the same color that will appear behind the video when it loads into the main video gallery file.

5. Key **Surfing Mavericks** as the title of the document.

6. Click **OK**.

7. Save the document as **opening_day.fla** in a new folder named **Video_gallery** on your computer. This folder is the directory for the collection of files that make up the gallery.

> **Note**
>
> You can make the background any color. It will not appear when the video is loaded into the main video gallery document, but selecting the same color helps you see how the video and controls will appear when loaded into the gallery.

 ## Import Video and Produce a Flash Video (FLV) File

1. Click **File** on the Menu bar, point to **Import**, and then click **Import Video**.

   The Import Video dialog box opens, as shown in Figure 1-2. The first step is to locate the source video file you want to encode as an FLV file. The default location for the source video is *On your computer*.

FIGURE 1-2
Import Video dialog box – selecting a source video

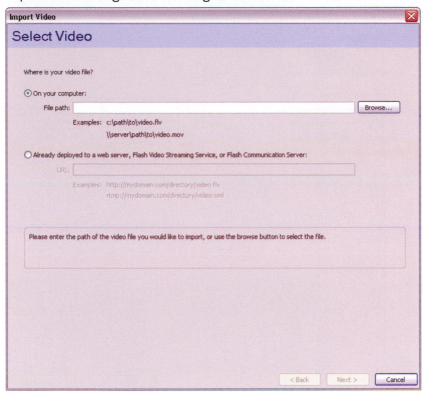

2. Click **Browse** (Windows) or **Choose** (Macintosh), navigate to the data files for this project, open the **Video_source** folder, select the **opening_day.mov** file, and then click **Open**.

3. Click **Next** (Windows) or **Continue** (Macintosh).

In this step you specify how you will deploy the video on the Web, as shown in Figure 1-3.

FIGURE 1-3
Import Video dialog box – selecting a deployment option

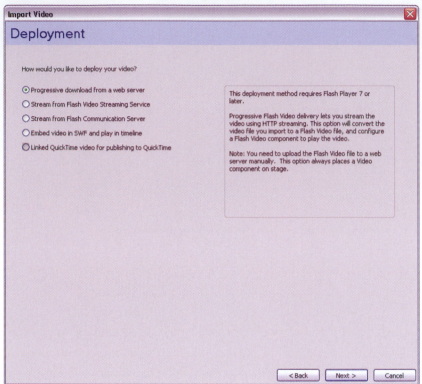

4. Select the **Progressive download from a web server** option, if it is not already selected.

5. Click **Next** (Windows) or **Continue** (Macintosh).

   In this step you specify how to encode the video. Many of these settings are identified on the project design document or storyboard.

6. Click **Show Advanced Settings**.

   The advanced settings are divided into three tabs; Encoding, Cue Points, and Crop and Trim.

7. For the Video codec, select **On2 VP6** if necessary.

8. For the Frame rate, select **Same as source** if necessary.

9. For the Key frame placement, select **Automatic** if necessary.

10. For the Quality, select **Medium** if necessary.

11. Select the **Resize video** check box if necessary. Set the width to **300** and the height to **200**. (Note that if the *Maintain aspect ratio* check box is selected, the height will fill in automatically with the correct number when you enter the width.)

12. Verify that the **Encode audio** check box is selected, and then select **48 kbps (mono)** on the Data rate pop-up menu.

Selecting a higher data rate will produce a larger file with higher quality sound. 48kbps (mono) matches the quality of the audio track on the source video, offers good quality sound, and will keep the file size small enough for delivery over the Web.

Your dialog box should look like Figure 1-4.

FIGURE 1-4
Import Video dialog box – selecting encoding options

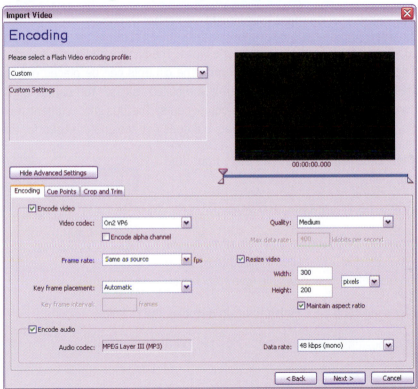

It is common for digitally produced video to display unwanted artifacts along the border of the video frame or uneven borders. To remove these, you can crop the video by using the Crop and Trim tab.

13. Click the **Crop and Trim** tab.

14. Change the top, bottom, left, and right crop settings to **10**, as shown in Figure 1-5. Crop marks appear around the edges of the video as you fill in these values. Note that you are cropping the entire video, not just the frame you are viewing.

FIGURE 1-5
Cropping the video by 10 pixels

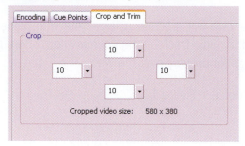

15. Click **Next** (Windows) or **Continue** (Macintosh).

In step 16, you select a control panel for the video. The control panel can include play, pause, stop, rewind, next, seek, volume, and mute buttons. The controls can be placed over or below the video frame. These pre-built collections of controls are called "skins." You can select from the available skins, or create your own by using Flash components. The design document requires the video to include play, pause, seek, and mute controls but does not designate a color for the controller.

16. Select **ClearExternalPlaySeekMute.swf** from the Skin pop-up menu.

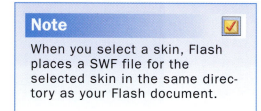

Note

When you select a skin, Flash places a SWF file for the selected skin in the same directory as your Flash document.

17. Click **Next** (Windows) or **Continue** (Macintosh).

You are reminded that your file must be saved before encoding the video and that you will need to host the FLV file and the selected skin.swf file on a Web server.

18. Read the message and click **Finish** to begin encoding the FLV file.

The encoding begins.

FIGURE 1-6
Encoding the video

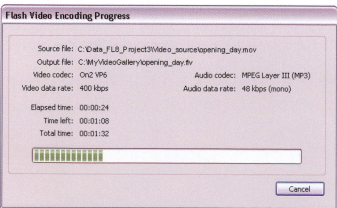

When the process is complete, a new FLVPlayback component is added to the Stage and the Library panel, as shown in Figure 1-7. The instance of the FLVPlayback component on the Stage is linked to the opening_day.flv video you just created. The FLV file is stored outside the document but will download and play when the Timeline encounters the FLVPlayback component.

FIGURE 1-7
FLVPlayback component added to the document

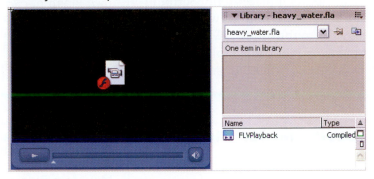

19. Using the Selection Tool, click the instance of the FLVPlayback component on the Stage to select it.

20. Position the FLVPlayback component at X: **0** and Y: **0** by using the Property inspector.

For information on changing the settings associated with the FLVPlayback component, see the Learn More feature "Viewing and Changing the Parameters of a Video Instance."

21. Save the document.

Learn More

VIEWING AND CHANGING THE PARAMETERS OF A VIDEO INSTANCE

When you import video for progressive download, Flash creates the FLV file and adds the FLVPlayback component to the document library. Each instance of the FLVPlayback component on the Stage includes a unique set of parameters such as which FLV file to download and play, whether the video window can be sized, which set of controls to use, and whether the video plays automatically when loaded.

To view the parameters for the FLVPlayback component that downloads and plays the opening_day.flv video, select the instance of the FLVPlayback component on the Stage and then select the Parameters tab on the Property inspector.

The contentPath points to the location of the FLV file.

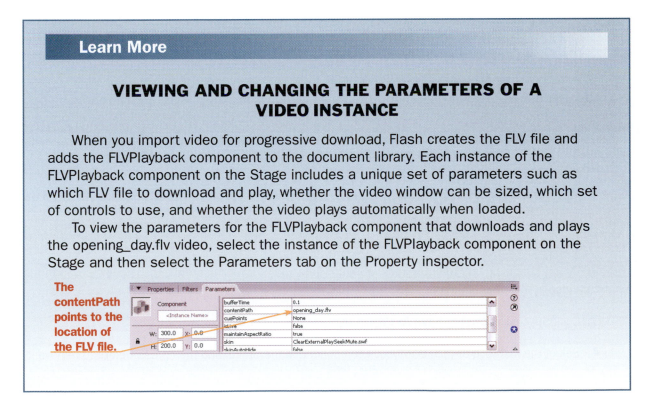

Publishing the Video as a SWF File

The Blue Mountain Riders video gallery includes three buttons that, when clicked, load and play the selected video. Because Flash SWF movies can load and play other SWF movies, you will generate a separate SWF for each video. You can then place ActionScript in the video gallery that tells each button which SWF movie to load and play. To publish the SWF file, you can publish the document or you can simply open the Control menu and select Test Movie to generate the SWF file.

Inside the Design

Designers can encode video files and place them in their own Flash documents so they can be easily loaded and displayed inside another SWF document by using a simple *loadMovie* action. The *loadMovie* action opens and plays a SWF, JPEG, GIF, or PNG file from a URL into a movie clip symbol. By storing the videos as separate SWF files, you can load them into any other SWF document, including the Blue Mountain Riders video gallery.

Create a SWF File for the Video Clip

1. Open the **Control** menu, and then click **Test Movie**.

   The video is exported as an SWF and then plays in the Flash Player window.

2. Test the **Play**, **Pause**, and **Mute** buttons.

3. Close the Flash Player window. Leave your document open for the next exercise.

   Check to be sure the opening_day.swf, opening_day.flv, and ClearExternalPlaySeekMute.swf files are stored together at the root of the Video_gallery folder you created.

Preparing Additional Video Clips

So far you have created the first of three surfing videos for the gallery. In the following two Step by Step exercises, you create two additional videos by creating SWF and FLV files for each additional clip. Be sure to create each video in the folder you created at the beginning of this lesson. All of your SWF and FLV files need to be in the same folder to function properly.

Create the outer_reef.swf and outer_reef.flv Files

1. Open the **File** menu, and then click **Save As**.

2. Change the file name to **outer_reef.fla** in the File name box. Make sure the file is being saved to the **Video_gallery** folder.

3. Click **Save** (Windows) or **Save As** (Macintosh).

4. Select the instance of the FLVPlayback component on the Stage, and then press **Delete** to remove it.

5. Import the video file named **outer_reef.mov** by using the same settings you applied to opening_day.mov. Select the skin named **ClearExternalPlaySeekMute.swf**.

   By default Flash applies the most recent settings you selected. Verify that the video size is **300 × 200** and crop the video by **10** pixels.

6. Position the video at X: **0** and Y: **0**.

7. Open the **Control** menu, and then click **Test Movie** to preview the movie and create the outer_reef.swf file. This file is created in the Video_gallery folder.

8. Close the Flash Player window.

9. Save the document.

 ## Create the heavy_water.swf and heavy_water.flv Files

1. Open the **File** menu, and then click **Save As** to save the new file in the Video_gallery folder.

2. Change the file name to **heavy_water.fla** in the File name box.

3. Click **Save** (Windows) or **Save As** (Macintosh).

4. Select the instance of the FLVPlayback component on the Stage, and then press **Delete** to remove it.

5. Import the video file named **heavy_water.mov** by using the same settings you applied to outer_reef.mov. Select the skin named **ClearExternalPlaySeekMute.swf**.

   By default, Flash applies the most recent settings you selected. Verify that the video size is **300 × 200** and crop the video by **10** pixels.

6. Position the video at X: **0** and Y: **0**.

7. Open the **Control** menu, and then click **Test Movie** to preview the movie and create the heavy_water.swf file.

8. Close the Flash Player window.

   There are now three separate SWF files for opening_day, outer_reef, and heavy_water. Each of these files points to a different Flash Video file, which is currently stored in the same directory. Check to be sure that all six files are stored in the Video_gallery folder.

9. Save and close the **heavy_water.fla** file. If you are continuing with the next lesson, leave the Flash program open. If not, close the Flash program.

Tips & Techniques

WEB VIDEO PRODUCTION TIPS

How you compress your video is largely determined by the content of the video. A video clip of a talking head with little action and only short bursts of moderate motion compresses differently from footage of surfing big waves at Mavericks. Follow the guidelines listed in Table 1-1 to deliver the best possible Flash Video:

TABLE 1-1
Tips for producing Web video

TIP	DESCRIPTION
Simplicity	Avoid elaborate transitions. Hard cuts or simple short fades are usually best. Elaborate moves or page turns can be eye-catching, but they usually do not compress well and should be used sparingly.
Data Rate	When you deliver video over the Internet, keep clips short and apply lower data rates. Viewers with fast Internet connections can view the files with little or no wait, but higher data rates present longer waits and playback issues for dial-up viewers.
Frame Size	Recommended frame size for Web video: - Modem: 160 × 120 (or smaller) - Dual ISDN: 192 × 144 (or smaller) - T1/DSL/cable: 320 × 240 (or smaller)
Source Video	The higher the quality of the original, the better the final result. The same considerations exist for audio production as for video production. To achieve good audio compression, you must begin with clean audio.

CREATING THE MAIN DOCUMENT FOR THE VIDEO GALLERY

OBJECTIVES:

Upon completion of this lesson, you will be able to:

- Use guides to create page structure and balance.

- Create background elements.

- Create thumbnail buttons for selecting a video clip.

- Duplicate and modify thumbnail buttons.

- Assign instance names to buttons.

Estimated time to complete this lesson: 45 minutes

Introduction

Now that you have created Flash Video files for the Blue Mountain Riders video gallery, you can develop the main document for the gallery. This document includes the background elements, descriptive text, attributions to the filmmaker and musicians, and thumbnail buttons for selecting each video, as the storyboard in Figure 2-1 shows. When the viewer selects a thumbnail button, the video gallery will load and play the video SWF files you published in Lesson 1.

In this lesson you begin to create the video gallery by setting guides, adding background elements, and creating the thumbnail buttons used to identify and select the surfing video clips.

FIGURE 2-1
Storyboard

Creating the Main Video Gallery Document

Dimensions: W 500 px, H 380 px

Movie length: 0 seconds (1 frame)

Frame rate: 12 fps

Background color: Dark gray #333333

Usability: Thumbnail buttons include a brighter Over state. When the gallery opens, a message instructs viewers to click an image on the left to preview a video. This message changes to "Video loading..." when the viewer makes a selection. Descriptive captions appear below each video when loaded.

Accessibility: Identify thumbnail buttons, onscreen directions, and video captions to screen readers, but hide the movie clip used to load and display selected video.

Required colors: Black (#000000), White (#FFFFFF), Dark gray (#333333), Gray, (#999999), Light gray (#CCCCCC), Blue (#006699)

Images: wave.jpg, opening_day.jpg, outer_reef.jpg, heavy_water.jpg

Suggested layers (from the top): actions, video, directions, captions top-bottom text, buttons, still image, background

Suggested guides: horizontal - 50, 60, 260, 350, vertical - 30, 45, 155, 455, 170

Note: These guides create a top margin of 50 pixels and bottom, left, and right margins of 30 pixels. This leaves an interior area for the gallery that is 440 x 300 pixels. The exterior margins are dark gray and the interior is blue. The guides also divide the Stage into a grid for placing text, buttons, and background.

Panel 4   Video Gallery Framework

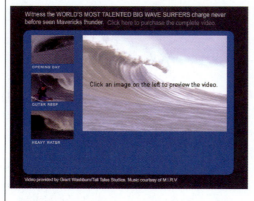

Document background: A dark gray background shows behind the blue background shape, creating the outer border (margins) of the video gallery window.

background layer: Blue rectangle with rounded corners. The rectangle is W:400 x H:300, creating a top margin of 50 pixels and left, right, and bottom margins of 30 pixels.

still image layer: The wave.jpg image is visible when the video gallery opens. This acts as a placeholder until the first video is selected. This image has a white filter applied (approx. 50% white) to make the image appear brighter, drawing attention to the directions text.

directions layer: Dynamic text (Arial, 13, centered, black) reads, "Click an image on the left to preview the video." This text changes to "Video Loading..." after a button is clicked.

Top-bottom text layer: Introductory static text appears in the top margin (Arial, 12, light gray) and attributions to the filmmaker and musician appear in the bottom margin (Arial, 9, light gray).

Introductory text: Witness the WORLD'S MOST TALENTED BIG WAVE SURFERS charge never before seen Mavericks thunder.

Attributions: Video provided by Grant Washburn/Tall Tales Studios. Music courtesy of M.I.R.V.

buttons layer:

Thumbnail buttons: Buttons display thumbnail images (opening_day.jpg, outer_reef.jpg, heavy_water.jpg) and static text labels (Arial, 7, light gray, left aligned, letter spacing 1). The buttons have a semitransparent dark gray filter (only in the Up state) to make the buttons appear dimmed until the viewer rolls over a button. Thumbnail buttons are 30% of the height and 30% of the width of the videos, making them 90 x 60 pixels.

Link to the online store: A gray text link with a white Over state reads, "Click here to purchase the complete video." This is created as a button to make the link accessible to screen readers, but appears to be an extension of the introductory text in the top margin.

Using Guides to Create Page Structure and Balance

The Blue Mountain Riders video gallery must fit within an area that is 500 pixels wide and 380 pixels high. This allows the gallery to fit in the designated space on the Blue Mountain Riders Web page, without scrolling needed to see the entire gallery.

You use guides to maintain page structure and balance when adding elements to the gallery. Guides create a grid for aligning objects accurately and adhering to the design specifications described in the design document and storyboard. By adding guides to the Stage, you can more easily position the background elements, text, buttons, video, and captions that come together to form the gallery.

 ## Open a New Document and Set Properties

1. Open a new blank Flash document.

2. Open the **Modify** menu, and then click **Document**.

3. Make sure Ruler units is set to **Pixels**, and then change the width of the document to **500** pixels and the height to **380** pixels.

4. Key **Video Gallery** as the title of the document.

5. Change the background color to dark gray (**#333333**).

6. Click **OK**.

7. Save the document in the Video_gallery folder where you created the opening_day.swf, outer_reef.swf, and heavy_water.swf files and the FLV files. Name the document **FL_Project3_YourName**.

Inside the Design

Designers will often set the color of their Flash documents to match the backgrounds of the Web sites on which their Flash movies will sit. For the Blue Mountain Riders site, the background of the Web page is dark gray, so the Flash document must be set to the same color to help it blend with the site.

Use Guides to Create Page Structure and Balance

1. If Rulers are not already visible, open the **View** menu, and then click **Rulers** to display the rulers.

2. Drag from the horizontal (top) ruler to place horizontal guides at **50** pixels, **60** pixels, **260** pixels, and **350** pixels as shown in Figure 2-2.

3. Drag from the vertical (left) ruler to place vertical guides at **30** pixels, **45** pixels, **155** pixels, **455** pixels, and **470** pixels as shown in Figure 2-2.

   This creates a top margin of 50 pixels and left, right, and bottom margins of 30 pixels. It also divides the page into a grid for aligning the thumbnail buttons, still image, and videos.

Inside the Design

By leaving more space at the top of the Stage, there is more room for the introductory text. The bottom margin includes a short attribution to the filmmaker and musician. Extra space in the top margin places importance on the top section of the document and also creates additional empty or "white" space, making the text easier to read.

FIGURE 2-2
Guides help maintain structure and balance when you are adding objects to the Stage

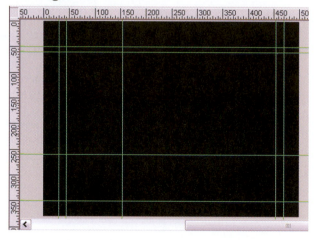

4. Open the **View** menu, point to **Guides**, and then click **Lock Guides**.

Creating Background Elements

As shown on the storyboard in Figure 2-1, the interior of the gallery is defined by a blue rectangle with rounded corners used to frame the buttons, video, and captions.

Inside the Design

Designers will use imagery to entice the expectation of viewers. In the Blue Mountain Riders site, a striking image of a wave creates a mood of excitement and anticipation until the video is selected and played.

The video clips do not appear until the viewer clicks a button, so you will add a still image of a wave to act as a placeholder until the viewer makes a selection.

FIGURE 2-3
Static background elements of the video gallery

Introductory text

Link to the store

Thumbnail buttons

Placeholder image

Blue background

Attribution text

Witness the WORLD'S MOST TALENTED BIG WAVE SURFERS charge never before seen Mavericks thunder. Click here to purchase the complete video.

OPENING DAY

OUTER REEF

HEAVY WATER

Video provided by Grant Washburn/Tall Tales Studios. Music Courtesy of M.I.R.V.

Step by Step Create a Background for the Video Gallery

1. Rename Layer 1 **background**.

FIGURE 2-4
The background layer

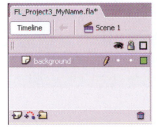

FL_Project3_MyName.fla*

Timeline   Scene 1

background

2. Select the **Rectangle Tool** and select the **Object Drawing** option to turn it on if necessary.

FIGURE 2-5
Rectangle Tool Options

Options

Object Drawing

Set Corner Radius

3. Click the **Set Corner Radius** button to open the Rectangle Settings dialog box, key **15** for the corner radius, and click **OK**.

4. Draw a rectangle with a blue (**#006699**) fill and no stroke.

5. Select the blue rectangle if necessary and use the Property inspector to change the width to **440** pixels and the height to **300** pixels. (Note that you may have to turn off the Constrain option in order to enter these values.)

6. Using your guides for reference, position the blue rectangle at X: **30** and Y: **50**.

Inside the Design

Designers choose colors not only to match the Web sites into which Flash elements will be displayed but also to help emphasize the content within the Flash movie. The designer for Blue Mountain Riders chose the color blue for the video gallery background to match the Blue Mountain Riders logo and Web site color scheme. This particular shade of blue was selected to contrast with the darker grayish blues and greens found in the waters off the Northern California coast that appear in the video clips.

FIGURE 2-6
Using guides to position the blue background

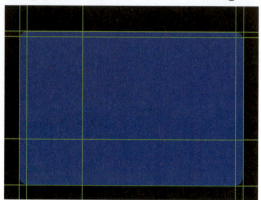

7. Lock the *background* layer.

8. Save the document.

Add a Still Image to the Background

1. Insert a new layer above the *background* layer and name it **still image**.

FIGURE 2-7
The still image layer

2. Open the **File** menu, point to **Import**, and then click **Import to Stage**.

3. Navigate to the data files for this project, open the **Stills** folder, and then double-click **wave.jpg** to import the file.

4. Use the guides and the Property inspector to position the wave image at X: **155** and Y: **60**.

   The wave image functions as a placeholder until the viewer selects a video clip.

FIGURE 2-8
The still image is a placeholder for the video clips

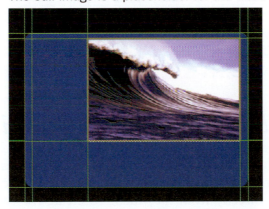

5. If necessary, select the wave image on the Stage, open the **Modify** menu, and then click **Convert to Symbol**. Name the symbol **wave**, select the **Graphic** type if necessary, and then click **OK**.

FIGURE 2-9
Convert to Symbol dialog box

6. On the Property inspector, change the Color option to **Tint**. Verify that white (**#FFFFFF**) is selected as the Tint color and that the tint is set to **50%.**

Inside the Design

By making the still image the brightest element on the page, you draw the viewer's eye to this space when the video gallery opens. This space will contain instructions for selecting a video clip.

FIGURE 2-10
Changing the tint to 50% white

7. Lock the *still image* layer.

8. Save the document.

Creating Thumbnail Buttons for Selecting Video Clips

The video gallery includes a separate thumbnail button representing each video clip. A thumbnail is a small image representing a larger image, which in this case is a video. Each button features a still image taken directly from the video. To create the thumbnail buttons, you will import the still images provided by the client, create the first thumbnail button, and then duplicate the button and swap the images to create the additional buttons. The name of the related video clip will appear below each button.

Create the First Thumbnail Button

1. Open the **File** menu, point to **Import**, and then click **Import to Library**. Navigate to the data files for this project, open the Stills folder, and then import the **opening_day.jpg**, **outer_reef.jpg**, and **heavy_water.jpg** images.

    The images are added to the Library panel.

2. Open the **Insert** menu, and then click **New Symbol**. Name the new symbol **opening_day**, select the **Button** type, and then click **OK**.

    The Timeline for the opening_day button symbol opens.

3. Rename Layer 1 **photo**.

FIGURE 2-11
The photo layer of the opening_day button symbol

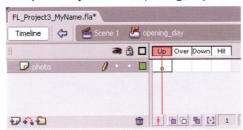

4. Drag a copy of the **opening_day.jpg** image from the Library panel to the Stage.

5. Use the Transform panel to change the height and width of the image to **30%**. Be sure the Constrain check box is selected.

FIGURE 2-12
Using the Transform panel to size the image

6. Use the Align panel to center the image both horizontally and vertically to the Stage.

FIGURE 2-13
Using the Align panel to center the image on the Stage

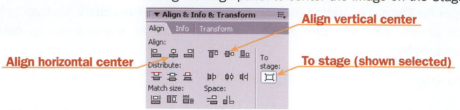

Align vertical center

Align horizontal center

To stage (shown selected)

7. Click in the **Hit** frame on the *photo* layer, open the **Insert** menu, point to **Timeline**, and then click **Keyframe**.

The photo defines the active area of the button.

8. Lock the *photo* layer.

9. Insert a new layer above the *photo* layer and name it **filter**.

FIGURE 2-14
The filter layer of the opening_day button symbol

10. Click in the **Up** frame on the *filter* layer. Select the **Rectangle Tool** and set the Fill color to dark gray (**#333333**) and the Stroke color to **No Stroke**. Set the corner radius to **0**.

11. Draw a rectangle on the Stage and use the Property inspector to change the width to **90** pixels and the height to **60** pixels.

> **Inside the Design**
>
> The filter color is the same color as the document background, which helps to maintain the current color scheme.

12. Use the Align panel to center the dark gray rectangle on the Stage.

The dark gray rectangle temporarily hides the *photo* layer.

13. Convert the rectangle to a Graphic symbol named **button_filter**.

14. Select the **button_filter** symbol on the Stage. On the Property inspector, change its color to **Alpha**, and set the alpha amount to **25%**.

15. Click in the Over frame on the *filter* layer, open the **Insert** menu, point to **Timeline**, and then click **Blank Keyframe**.

The filter only appears in the Up state of the button. The button will appear darker in the Up state and brighter when the viewer rolls over the thumbnail image, indicating the button is active.

FIGURE 2-15
The blank keyframe removes the filter from the Over and Down states of the button

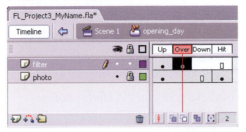

16. Lock the *filter* layer.

17. Insert a new layer above the *filter* layer and name it **text**.

18. Click in the **Up** state of the *text* layer. Select the **Text Tool** and use the Property inspector to set the text properties shown in Figure 2-16 (Static Text, Arial, size 7, light gray (#CCCCCC), left-aligned, Letter spacing 1).

> **Inside the Design**
>
> Because you place a filter in the Up state of the button, the button appears to illuminate when the mouse pointer is placed over the button. This communicates to the viewer that the button is turned on. It also causes the viewer to focus on the active area of the window which, in this case, is the button.

FIGURE 2-16
Text properties for the thumbnail button text

19. Click below the image and key **OPENING DAY**. Use the arrow keys to position the text as shown in Figure 2-17.

FIGURE 2-17
Position of thumbnail button text

20. Lock the *text* layer, and then click **Scene 1** on the Information bar to return to the main Timeline.

21. Save the document.

> **Hint**
>
> If you have trouble positioning the text, turn off snapping options. To do this, open the **View** menu, point to **Snapping**, and deselect snapping options.

Duplicating and Modifying Thumbnail Buttons

Now that you have created the first thumbnail button, you can quickly create additional buttons by duplicating the button, swapping the still image, and replacing the text label. Do this to create the second and third thumbnail buttons.

Duplicate and Modify the Thumbnail Button to Create Additional Buttons

1. Select the **opening_day** button symbol on the Library panel.

2. Select **Duplicate** from the Library panel Options pop-up menu.

FIGURE 2-18
Library panel Options pop-up menu

3. Name the symbol outer_reef, and then click **OK**.

FIGURE 2-19
Duplicate Symbol dialog box

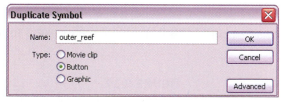

4. Double-click the **outer_reef** button symbol on the Library panel to open the button in editing mode.

5. Unlock the *text* layer. Double-click the text to select it and change the text to **OUTER REEF**.

6. Lock the *text* layer and unlock the *photo* layer.

7. Using the Selection Tool, click the photo on the Stage to select it. On the Property inspector, click **Swap** to open the Swap Bitmap dialog box, shown in Figure 2-20.

FIGURE 2-20
Swap Bitmap dialog box

8. Select **outer_reef.jpg**, and then click **OK**.

The still image on the photo layer is replaced.

FIGURE 2-21
The outer_reef button symbol

9. Lock the *photo* layer, and then click **Scene 1** to return to the main Timeline.

10. Duplicate the outer_reef button symbol to create a new button symbol named **heavy_water**.

11. Open the heavy_water button symbol in editing mode, change the text to **HEAVY WATER**, and swap the photo for the image named **heavy_water.jpg**.

FIGURE 2-22
The heavy_water button symbol

12. Return to Scene 1, and save the document.

Adding Thumbnail Buttons to the Gallery

Now you will complete the initial layout of the video gallery by placing a copy of each thumbnail button on the Stage, using the guides and Align panel for precise alignment.

 Add Thumbnail Buttons to the Gallery

1. Insert a new layer above the *still image* layer and name it **buttons**.

FIGURE 2-23
The buttons layer

2. Click frame **1** on the *buttons* layer. Drag the opening_day, outer_reef, and heavy_water button symbols from the Library panel to the Stage.

3. Position the thumbnail buttons in the empty space to the left of the wave image, as shown in Figure 2-24. (*Hint:* First align the opening_day button at X: 45 and Y: 60. Use the arrow keys to position the other two buttons. Select the top button, hold down the Shift key, select the other two buttons, and then use the Align panel without *To stage* selected to align the left edges and space evenly vertically.)

FIGURE 2-24
Thumbnail buttons positioned on the Stage

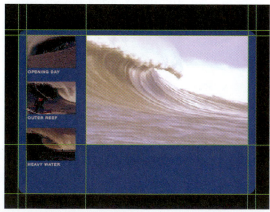

4. Open the **Control** menu, and then click **Enable Simple Buttons** to select it.

5. Roll over the buttons with the mouse pointer to preview the Over state of the buttons.

The buttons begin dimmed (because of the button filter) in the Up state. When you roll over the buttons, they appear brighter (because there is no filter). The photo defines the active area of the button.

6. Open the **Control** menu, and then click **Enable Simple Buttons** to deselect it.

Assigning Instance Names to Buttons

After placing buttons on the Stage, you can assign a unique name to each button instance. You do this by using the Instance name box on the Property inspector. Assigning unique names to each instance will help you when you want to associate particular actions with a specific button. You will refer to these unique names in Lesson 4 when you write the ActionScript that links the buttons to the videos.

 ## Assign Instance Names to Buttons

1. Using the Selection Tool, click the **opening_day** button symbol on the Stage to select it. (You may have to click away from the Stage to deselect all of the buttons first and then click to select just the one button symbol.)

2. Click in the **Instance Name** box on the Property inspector and key **opening_day_bt**.

FIGURE 2-25
Instance name box on the Property inspector

It is a good idea to add _bt to the button instance name so that when you reference the button in ActionScript, you will know you are referring to a button symbol.

3. Select the **outer_reef** symbol on the Stage.

4. Click in the **Instance Name** box and key **outer_reef_bt**.

5. Select the **heavy_water** symbol on the Stage

6. Click in the **Instance Name** box and key **heavy_water_bt**.

7. Lock the *buttons* layer.

8. Save the document.

9. If you are continuing with the next lesson, leave this file open. If you are not continuing at this time, close the file and close Flash.

> ### Hot Tip
>
> Be sure to spell the button instance names correctly. You will refer to these names when you write the ActionScript to control the buttons.

FORMATTING BLOCKS OF TEXT

OBJECTIVES:

Upon completion of this lesson, you will be able to:

- Create flexible- and fixed-width text.
- Format paragraphs.
- Check spelling.
- Create external links.

Estimated time to complete this lesson: 30 minutes

Introduction

In this lesson, you add text to the Blue Mountain Riders Web site, as shown in Figure 3-1. The text at the top of the gallery describes the contents of the gallery and includes a link to the Blue Mountain Riders online store. The video gallery also includes an attribution to the film-maker who provided the surfing video and to the musician who provided the soundtrack for the videos. This attribution appears in the margin at the bottom of the gallery window.

In this lesson, you learn to create flexible- and fixed-width text objects, apply paragraph formatting, check spelling of a Flash document, and link text to external Web content.

FIGURE 3-1
Storyboard

Panel 4   Video Gallery Framework

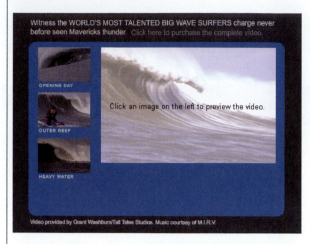

Document background: A dark gray background shows behind the blue background shape, creating the outer border (margins) of the video gallery window.

background layer: Blue rectangle with rounded corners. The rectangle is W:400 x H:300, creating a top margin of 50 pixels and left, right, and bottom margins of 30 pixels.

still image layer: The wave.jpg image is visible when the video gallery opens. This acts as a placeholder until the first video is selected. This image has a white filter applied (approx. 50% white) to make the image appear brighter, drawing attention to the directions text.

directions layer: Dynamic text (Arial, 13, centered, black) reads, "Click an image on the left to preview the video." This text changes to "Video Loading..." after a button is clicked.

Top-bottom text layer: Introductory static text appears in the top margin (Arial, 12, light gray) and attributions to the filmmaker and musician appear in the bottom margin (Arial, 9, light gray).

Introductory text: Witness the WORLD'S MOST TALENTED BIG WAVE SURFERS charge never before seen Mavericks thunder.

Attributions: Video provided by Grant Washburn/Tall Tales Studios. Music courtesy of M.I.R.V.

buttons layer:

Thumbnail buttons: Buttons display thumbnail images (opening_day.jpg, outer_reef.jpg, heavy_water.jpg) and static text labels (Arial, 7, light gray, left aligned, letter spacing 1). The buttons have a semitransparent dark gray filter (only in the Up state) to make the buttons appear dimmed until the viewer rolls over a button. Thumbnail buttons are 30% of the height and 30% of the width of the videos, making them 90 x 60 pixels.

Link to the online store: A gray text link with a white Over state reads, "Click here to purchase the complete video." This is created as a button to make the link accessible to screen readers, but appears to be an extension of the introductory text in the top margin.

Creating Flexible- and Fixed-Width Text

The descriptive text at the top of the Blue Mountain Riders video gallery must fit within left and right margins, marked by the guides at 30 and 470 pixels. This creates balance on the Stage because the text aligns evenly with the blue rectangle below it.

By default, when you enter text in Flash, the text continues to expand to accommodate the width of your text box. This is called flexible-width text. You can force a text object to wrap to a specific width by converting the text to fixed width and then dragging the text box to a desired width. This ensures that text stays within designated boundaries and maintains balance and page structure. Fixed-width text is also a perfect choice for creating side-by-side columns of text. Flexible-width text is represented by a round corner handle, and fixed-width text has a square corner handle.

It is important to size text by dragging the square handle instead of attempting to change its dimensions on the Property inspector. Changing the dimensions of a text box on the Property inspector will scale the text, distorting its size and shape.

 ## Create Flexible- and Fixed-Width Text

1. If necessary, open the file you created in the previous lesson. Alternately, you can open the file named **FL_Project3_Lesson3.fla**, which is found in the **Practice_files** folder in the data files for this lesson. If you use **FL_Project3_Lesson3.fla**, be sure to save it as **FL_Project3_YourName.fla** in the Video_gallery folder.

2. Insert a new layer above the *buttons* layer and name it **top-bottom text**.

3. Select the **Text Tool** and use the Property inspector to set the text properties shown in Figure 3-2 (Static Text, Arial, size 12, light gray (#CCCCCC), justified, letter spacing 0).

FIGURE 3-2
Text properties

4. Click in the gray space near the top of the gallery and key: **Witness the WORLD'S MOST TALENTED BIG WAVE SURFERS charge never before seen Mavericks thunder.**

   Notice that as you type, the text continues horizontally across the page. By default, the text block is set to flexible width, which means the text will continue to extend to the right until you press the Enter/Return key or force the text to wrap by sizing the text object. A flexible text box is identified by a small circle on the corner of the text block.

FIGURE 3-3
Flexible-width text

Indicates flexible text box

5. Position the mouse pointer over the circle on the corner of the text box, and then click and drag the circle to the left to resize the text box. The circle changes to a box, converting the text to fixed-width. A fixed-width text block forces text to wrap automatically and fit within a defined area.

6. Click and drag the text box until it fits within the vertical guides at 30 and 470 pixels, and position the text as shown in Figure 3-4.

FIGURE 3-4
Fixed-width text

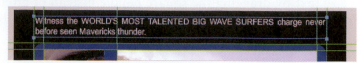

7. Add the following attribution text to the bottom of the Gallery, as shown in Figure 3-5: **Video provided by Grant Washburn/Tall Tales Studios. Music courtesy of M.I.R.V.**

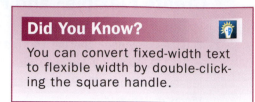

Did You Know?

You can convert fixed-width text to flexible width by double-clicking the square handle.

8. Select the text you have keyed and change the size of the attribution text to **9**.

9. Select the text box and position the text in the empty gray space at the bottom of the document, aligned with the guide at 30 pixels, as shown in Figure 3-5.

FIGURE 3-5
Attribution text

10. Save the document.

Formatting Paragraphs of Text

One way to make the text at the top of the video gallery easier to read is to add white space by increasing the space between lines of text.

In addition to character formatting, the text Property inspector includes options for formatting entire paragraphs. You have already applied paragraph formatting by selecting alignment options.

Using the Property inspector, you can also change the indent, line spacing, and margins for an entire text box or for individual paragraphs within a single text box. If you have the text selected (surrounded by a blue outline), your changes apply to the entire object. If you have an individual paragraph selected, the changes apply only to the current paragraph.

 ## Apply Paragraph Formatting

1. Select the **Selection Tool** and then click to select the text at the top of the gallery.

The text is surrounded by a blue outline.

2. Click the **Edit format options** button on the Property inspector. (It looks like a paragraph symbol.)

FIGURE 3-6
Edit format options button on the Property inspector

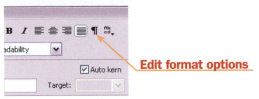

Edit format options

The Format Options dialog box opens. You can indent text, adjust line spacing, and increase the left or right margins.

FIGURE 3-7
Format Options dialog box

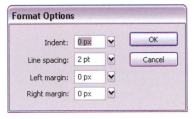

3. Verify that the Indent, Left margin, and Right margin boxes are set to 0. Change the Line spacing to **3 pt**, and then click **OK** (Windows) or **Done** (Macintosh) to close the dialog box.

The space between the two lines of text increases slightly. This creates additional white space, making the text easier to read.

4. Click away from the text to deselect it.

5. Lock the *top-bottom text* layer and save the document.

Checking Spelling

Spell-checking your document before publishing is always a good idea. Before you check spelling the first time, you must specify spelling options in the Spelling Setup dialog box to initialize the Check Spelling feature. You can then check the spelling in the entire document, including text on the Stage, text strings that appear in ActionScript, and frame labels.

When you check the spelling of a Flash document, the spelling checker looks for words it does not recognize. When it finds a word that is not in the selected dictionary, it stops and offers a suggested correction, similar to checking spelling in a word processor.

Many documents, including the Blue Mountain Riders video gallery, include words or phrases that are spelled correctly but are not recognized by the spelling checker. If your document includes an unfamiliar word that you use often, you might want to add it to your personal dictionary.

View Options for Checking Spelling

1. Open the **Text** menu, and then click **Spelling Setup**.

The Spelling Setup dialog box opens.

FIGURE 3-8
Spelling Setup dialog box

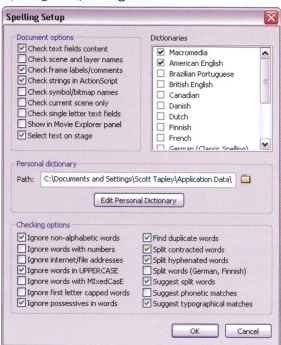

2. Verify that the **Macromedia** and **American English** dictionaries are selected.

3. Click **OK** to close the dialog box.

4. Click in the workspace away from the Stage to make sure no objects are selected. With no text selected, Flash will spell-check the entire document.

5. Open the **Text** menu, and then click **Check Spelling**.

6. If you receive a message telling you that Flash has reached the end of the document, click **Yes** to start checking again from the top of the document.

The Check Spelling dialog box opens, as shown in Figure 3-9. The spelling checker stops at the first word it does not recognize. If the word is spelled correctly, you can choose to ignore the word.

Note

By default, the spelling checker looks for spelling errors within text fields, frame labels and comments, strings in ActionScript, and text on the Stage. You can modify these settings in the Document options section of the Spelling Setup dialog box.
By default, Flash ignores non-alphabetic characters, words in ALL CAPS, and possessive forms of words. Flash identifies unfamiliar words, including duplicate words. Flash automatically splits contracted and hyphenated words and offers suggested corrections. You can modify these settings in the Checking options section of the Spelling Setup dialog box.

FIGURE 3-9
Check Spelling dialog box

7. When you have finished checking the document and making necessary changes, a message informs you that Flash has reached the end of the document and is finished checking. Click **OK** to close the message.

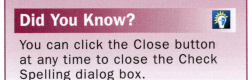

Did You Know?

You can click the Close button at any time to close the Check Spelling dialog box.

Creating External Links

One of the goals of the Blue Mountain Riders video gallery is to promote sales of several full-length videos featuring big wave surfing. These videos can be purchased by visiting the Blue Mountain Riders online store, so the video gallery needs to include a link to the store's Web page.

There are a few ways to link text to an external Web address. The simplest method is to select the text you want to link and then enter the Web address in the URL box at the bottom of the Property inspector. Unfortunately, when you do this, the text link is not accessible to screen reader software.

To make a text link accessible, you can create a separate text object, convert the object to a button symbol, and then apply a *getURL* action to the button. By turning the text into a button symbol, you can also add an Over state to the text, which helps identify the text as an active link.

Link Text to an External URL by Using a Button Symbol and the getURL Action

1. Unlock the *buttons* layer.

2. Click in an area off the Stage to deselect the items on the *button* layer.

3. Select the **Text Tool** and set the text Properties to those shown in Figure 3-10 (Static Text, Arial, size 12, gray (#999999), left aligned, Letter spacing 0).

FIGURE 3-10
Text properties for the store link button

4. Click the *buttons* layer to select it. Click to start a new text block after the last sentence at the top of the gallery, and then key **Click here to purchase the complete video.**

5. Use the Selection Tool to position the text so that it aligns with the second line of text at the top of the page, as shown in Figure 3-11. (*Hint*: You may want to zoom in temporarily to position the text. Use the arrow keys for precise alignment.)

FIGURE 3-11
Position of the store link text

6. With the text still selected, open the **Modify** menu, and then click **Convert to Symbol**. Name the symbol **store_link**, select the **Button** type, and then click **OK**.

7. Double-click the store_link button on the Stage to open the symbol in editing mode.

8. Insert a keyframe in the Over state of the button. Change the text in the Over state to white (**#FFFFFF**).

9. Insert a keyframe in the Hit state, select the **Rectangle Tool**, and then draw a rectangle that covers the text you want to link, as shown in Figure 3-12.

The rectangle creates a larger Hit state, which makes the button easier to click.

FIGURE 3-12
Drawing a larger Hit state for the button

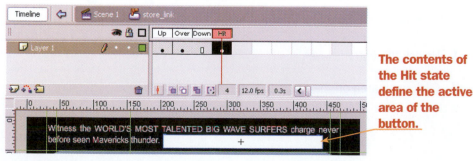

The contents of the Hit state define the active area of the button.

10. Click **Scene 1** on the Information bar to close the symbol and return to the main Timeline.

11. Using the Selection Tool, click the **store_link** button on the Stage to select it. Expand the Actions panel, and be sure that Script Assist is turned on. Macintosh users may need to open the Actions panel from the Window menu.

12. Click the plus symbol above the Script pane, point to **Global Functions**, point to **Browser/Network**, and then click **getURL**.

13. Click in the URL text box in the Script Assist pane and key **http://www.macromedia.com**.

14. Click the arrow beside the Window text box to open the pop-up menu, and then select **_blank**.

The _blank target tells Flash to open the linked Web page in a blank new browser window. When the viewer closes the Web page, the video gallery will remain open.

Hot Tip

To view the Over state of the store_link button, open the Control menu and select **Enable Simple Buttons**. After viewing the button, be sure to open the **Control** menu, and select **Enable Simple Buttons** to turn this feature off.

Note

Because the Web page for the Blue Mountain Riders online store is not yet developed, you are inserting a link to www.macromedia.com instead. This will allow you to test the link at the end of this project.

Did You Know?

To create a link to an e-mail address, use the mailto: URL. For example, you could enter **mailto:support@bluemountainridersstore.com** to create a link that automatically addresses an e-mail message to the support staff at the Blue Mountain Riders store.

FIGURE 3-13
Completed ActionScript linking the button to an external Web site

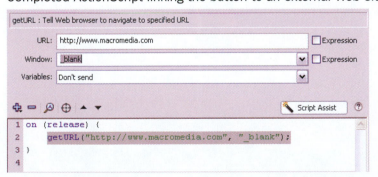

15. Collapse the Actions panel, lock the *buttons* layer, and then save the document. If you are continuing with the next lesson, leave this file open. If you are not continuing at this time, close the file and close Flash.

Note

You will make this button accessible to screen reader software in Lesson 5.

DISPLAYING VIDEO STORED OUTSIDE THE FLASH DOCUMENT

OBJECTIVES:

Upon completion of this lesson, you will be able to:

- Create a movie clip for loading and displaying video.

- Link buttons to external video by using ActionScript.

- Add comments to identify ActionScript.

Estimated time to complete this lesson: 30 minutes

Introduction

The Blue Mountain Riders video gallery document does not actually contain any video files. Instead, it loads the opening_day.swf, outer_reef.swf, or heavy_water.swf movie each time the viewer clicks a thumbnail button. Each SWF file includes an FLVPlayback component that downloads and plays one of the three Flash Video (FLV) files you created in Lesson 1. Using this method helps keep the file size of the main document small.

You control where the video displays in the gallery by creating a *holder* for the video. The video holder is simply a movie clip symbol positioned exactly where you want the video to appear, as shown in the storyboard panel in Figure 4-1.

By storing rich media content, such as large images or video, outside the main interface of the video gallery, you reduce the file size of the gallery, improve download times, increase performance, and make it easier to replace the content without making significant changes to the Flash document.

In this lesson, you first create the video holder movie clip symbol and then add the ActionScript that tells the document which videos to load when the thumbnail buttons are clicked.

FIGURE 4-1
Storyboard

Panel 5   When a viewer clicks the Opening Day thumbnail button

buttons layer: When the viewer rolls over the Opening Day button, the button appears brighter, indicating it is an active button.

directions layer: When the viewer clicks the Opening Day button, the directions dynamic text field changes to "Video loading..." as shown to the left.

video layer: When the viewer clicks the Opening Day button, the opening_day.swf movie is loaded over the still image of the wave and plays the opening_day.flv file, as shown to the right.

caption layer: When the viewer clicks the Opening Day button, the video caption appears below the video and controls, as shown to the right.

Caption for the opening_day video: "Opening Day at Mavericks. Watch as local legends pull into enormous barrels, leaving spectators breathless."

Creating a Movie Clip Used to Load and Display Video

In this exercise you create a movie clip symbol named vholder (for video holder). The vholder movie clip sits exactly where you want the videos to appear when someone clicks a thumbnail button.

Create the Video Holder Movie Clip Symbol

1. If necessary, open the file you created in the previous lesson. Alternately, you can open the file named **FL_Project3_Lesson4.fla**, which is found in the **Practice_files** folder in the data files for this lesson. If you use **FL_Project3_Lesson4.fla**, be sure to save it as **FL_Project3_YourName.fla** in the Video_gallery folder.

2. Insert a new layer above the *top-bottom text* layer and name it **video**.

FIGURE 4-2
The video layer

3. Open the **Insert** menu, and then click **New Symbol**.

4. Name the new symbol **vholder**, select the **Movie clip** type, and then click **OK**.

    A blank Timeline for the new movie clip opens. The vholder movie clip symbol is added to the Library panel. The movie clip is an empty holder for displaying video.

    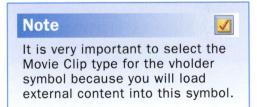

    > **Note** ✓
    >
    > It is very important to select the Movie Clip type for the vholder symbol because you will load external content into this symbol.

5. Click **Scene 1** on the Information bar to close the movie clip and return to the main Timeline.

6. Click frame **1** on the *video* layer, and then drag a copy of the vholder movie clip, as shown in Figure 4-3. symbol from the Library panel to the Stage.

    The movie clip is empty, but it is represented by a small circle with a crosshair, as shown in Figure 4-3.

FIGURE 4-3
The vholder movie clip symbol is represented by a small circle with a crosshair

Empty vholder movie clip symbol

7. Using the Property inspector, position the vholder movie clip symbol at X: **155** and Y: **60**. This is exactly the same position as the wave photo. The video clips will load directly on top of the still image of the wave.

8. With the instance of the vholder movie clip still selected on the Stage, click in the **Instance Name** box on the Property inspector and key **vholder_mc**.

Note

The size dimensions do not need to be set for this movie clip because the vholder is empty until a video loads. The contents of the movie clip will load from the top left corner and extend down and to the right. Because you placed the vholder movie clip in the top left corner of the wave image, and the wave image is the exact size of the video clips, you know the videos will load directly on top of the wave.

FIGURE 4-4
The instance of the vholder movie clip is named vholder_mc

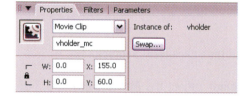

This is the name you will use when referring to the video holder in the ActionScript that loads the video clips. When you reference this symbol in your ActionScript, the _mc will identify this symbol as a movie clip.

9. Lock the *video* layer and save the document.

Linking Buttons to External Video by Using ActionScript

When viewers visit the Blue Mountain Riders video gallery, they can preview a video by clicking one of three thumbnail buttons. Each button is linked, using a loadMovie action, to a video clip stored outside the main document. The loadMovie action can be used to open and play a SWF, JPEG, GIF, or PNG file inside a movie clip symbol.

Although you can place ActionScript directly on a button, you can improve the performance of the document by placing your script in a single frame on the main Timeline. When you place ActionScript in the first frame of the Timeline, the document gets its instructions for all three buttons as soon as the document opens. By keeping the ActionScript separate from the buttons, it is also easier to replace button instances without rewriting script, making the document more reusable.

To prevent the movie from looping (and reading the same script over and over), you should start the script by adding a *stop* action in frame 1 of the movie.

 ## Add the ActionScript that Links Buttons to Video Clips

1. Insert a new layer above the *video* layer and name it **actions**.

FIGURE 4-5
The actions layer

2. Click frame **1** on the *actions* layer and expand the Actions panel. Verify that Script Assist is turned on by clicking the **Script Assist** button, if necessary.

3. Add a *stop* action to the Script pane. (*Hint*: To do this, click the plus symbol above the Script pane, point to **Global Functions**, point to **Timeline Control**, and then click **stop**.)

FIGURE 4-6
The Stop action prevents the movie from looping

4. Click the plus symbol above the Script pane on the Actions panel, point to **ActionScript 2.0 Classes**, point to **Movie**, point to **MovieClip**, point to **Event Handlers**, and then click **onRelease**.

FIGURE 4-7
Adding ActionScript by using the Script pane

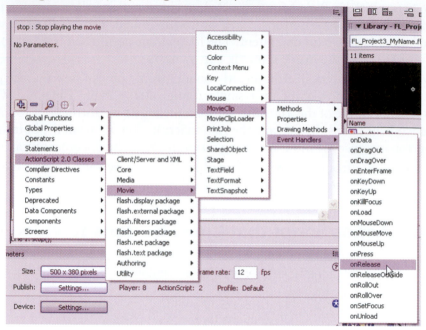

5. Click in the Object text box in the Script Assist pane and key **opening_day_bt**.

The object you want the action applied to is the thumbnail button with the instance name *opening_day_bt*. The method *onRelease* tells the action to occur when the mouse button is released (after clicking the opening_day_bt button). Then you need to define what action to take when this happens. The action is to load the movie named opening_day.swf into the vholder movie clip.

6. Click the onRelease action you just added for the opening_day_bt button, as shown in Figure 4-8.

The next script you add will go below the selected line of script.

FIGURE 4-8
New script is added below the selected line of script

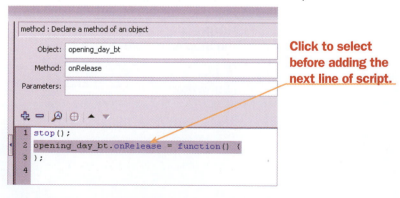

7. Click the plus symbol above the Script pane on the Actions panel, point to **ActionScript 2.0 Classes**, point to **Movie**, point to **MovieClip**, point to **Methods**, and then click **loadMovie**.

8. Click in the Object text box in the Script Assist pane and key **vholder_mc**.

The object you want the action applied to is the movie clip with the instance name *vholder_mc*. This tells Flash to load a movie into the vholder movie clip symbol.

9. Deselect the Expression check box beside the URL text box.

10. Click in the URL text box in the Script Assist pane and key **opening_day.swf**.

The URL appears in quotes in the Script Pane, as shown in Figure 4-9.

The script shown in Figure 4-9 now tells Flash, "Upon release of the opening_day_bt button, load the movie named opening_day.swf into the movie clip named vholder_mc." Keep in mind, the opening_day.swf movie includes an FLVPlayback component that loads and plays the opening_day.flv video file you created in Lesson 1. By clicking the opening_day_bt button, the viewer is asking the Flash document to load and play the opening_day.flv video in the position of the vholder_mc movie clip.

FIGURE 4-9
Completed ActionScript that tells the opening_day button to load the opening_day.swf movie

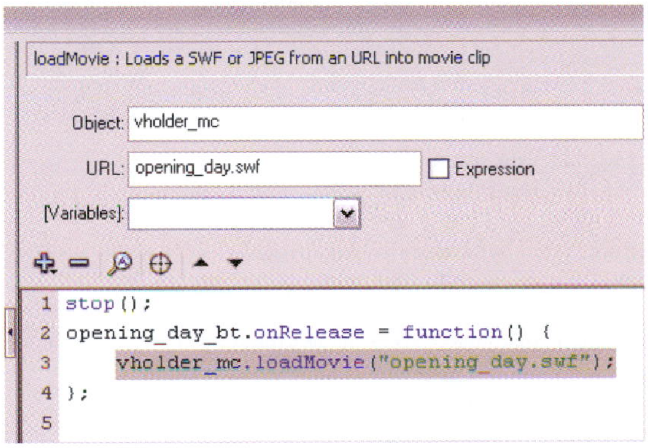

11. Click the last line of script, as shown in Figure 4-10. The next script you add will go below the selected line.

FIGURE 4-10
New script is always added below the selected line of script

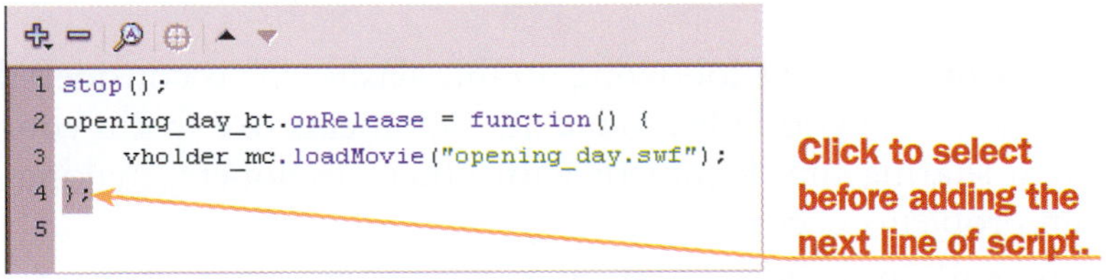

12. Click the plus symbol above the Script pane on the Actions panel, point to **ActionScript 2.0 Classes**, point to **Movie**, point to **MovieClip**, point to **Event Handlers**, and then click **onRelease**.

13. Click in the Object text box in the Script Assist pane and key **outer_reef_bt**.

14. Click the onRelease action you just added for the outer_reef_bt button.

15. Click the plus symbol above the Script pane on the Actions panel, point to **ActionScript 2.0 Classes**, point to **Movie**, point to **MovieClip**, point to **Methods**, and then click **loadMovie**.

16. Click in the Object text box in the Script Assist pane and key **vholder_mc**.

17. Deselect the Expression check box, click in the URL text box, and key **outer_reef.swf**.

18. Click the last line of script.

19. Repeat steps 12 through 17 to add the ActionScript for the third thumbnail button, as shown in Figure 4-11. Be sure to change the object name to **heavy_water_bt** in step 13 and the URL to **heavy_water.swf** in step 17.

FIGURE 4-11
Completed ActionScript for all three thumbnail buttons

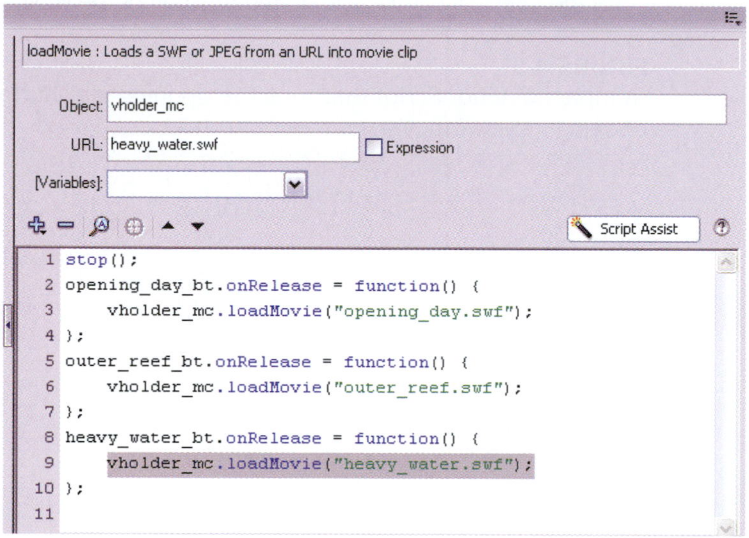

```
loadMovie : Loads a SWF or JPEG from an URL into movie clip

Object: vholder_mc
URL: heavy_water.swf          [ ] Expression
[Variables]:                  [v]

                                        Script Assist  (?)
 1  stop();
 2  opening_day_bt.onRelease = function() {
 3      vholder_mc.loadMovie("opening_day.swf");
 4  };
 5  outer_reef_bt.onRelease = function() {
 6      vholder_mc.loadMovie("outer_reef.swf");
 7  };
 8  heavy_water_bt.onRelease = function() {
 9      vholder_mc.loadMovie("heavy_water.swf");
10  };
11
```

20. Save the document.

Adding Comments to Identify ActionScript

In ActionScript, any text following double slashes (//) is considered a comment and is ignored by Flash Player. It is a good idea to include comments to explain your script. Comments are very helpful when sharing the document with other developers, making changes, or debugging the script when problems occur.

You can add comments by starting a line with two forward slashes or by selecting the *Comment* action and entering a comment in the Script Assist pane.

Add Comments to Identify ActionScript

1. Click the *stop* action at the top of the Script pane.

The comment will go before the ActionScript that controls the thumbnail buttons.

2. Click the plus symbol above the Script pane on the Actions panel, point to **Global Functions**, point to **Miscellaneous Functions**, and then click **comment**.

3. Click in the **Comment** text box in the Sript Assist pane and key **this loads a video each time a thumbnail button is clicked**.

Comments are represented by gray text preceded by two forward slashes. Flash ignores comments when running the script.

FIGURE 4-12
Comments are gray and begin with two forward slashes

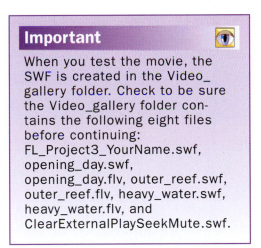

4. Collapse the Actions panel.

5. Open the **Control** menu, and then click **Test Movie**.

> **Important**
>
> When you test the movie, the SWF is created in the Video_gallery folder. Check to be sure the Video_gallery folder contains the following eight files before continuing: FL_Project3_YourName.swf, opening_day.swf, opening_day.flv, outer_reef.swf, outer_reef.flv, heavy_water.swf, heavy_water.flv, and ClearExternalPlaySeekMute.swf.

6. In the Flash Player window, click each thumbnail button to preview the videos in the video gallery.

FIGURE 4-13
This video plays when the opening day button is clicked

Notice the empty space below the video controls. This area is reserved for captions, which you will add in Lesson 5.

7. Close the Flash Player window and save the document.

8. If you are continuing with the next lesson, leave this file open. If you are not continuing at this time, close the file and close Flash.

IMPROVING ACCESSIBILITY AND USABILITY

Introduction

The Blue Mountain Riders video gallery is considered *usable* when the target audience can locate and view each video clip, learn more about the video, and access a link to the online store to purchase products. The target audience includes people with disabilities, so to make the gallery accessible to people with limited vision, you need to expose the movie to a special type of computer program called a screen reader. Visitors with screen reader software hear a spoken description of what appears on the screen.

In this lesson, you increase usability and accessibility by adding dynamic text to display onscreen directions and video captions. For example, when the gallery opens, directions tell the viewer to click on a thumbnail image to preview the video. When the viewer selects a video, a message informs the viewer that a video is loading. When the video loads, a descriptive caption appears, as shown in Figure 5-1.

Instead of creating several static text objects on separate frames (two sets of instructions and three captions), you can add two dynamic text objects on a single frame and then use ActionScript to display different text as needed.

FIGURE 5-1
Storyboard

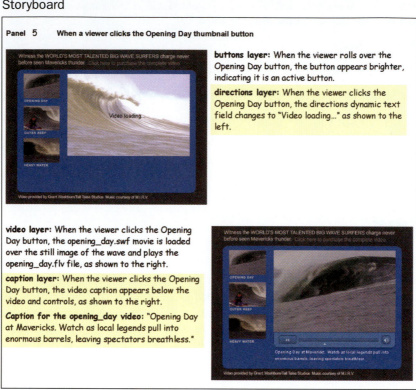

Creating Dynamic Text Fields

Dynamic text displays data from an outside source. The source of the data can be a separate text file, a database, or ActionScript within the same SWF document.

The Blue Mountain Riders video gallery displays two types of dynamic text: directions to the viewer and video captions. First you will create and name the dynamic text fields; then, in the next set of step-by-steps, you add ActionScript that tells the document which text to display and when and where to display it.

 Create Dynamic Text for Onscreen Directions

1. If necessary, open the file you created in the previous lesson. Alternately, you can open the file named **FL_Project3_Lesson5.fla**, which is found in the **Practice_files** folder in the data files for this lesson. If you use **FL_Project3_Lesson5.fla**, be sure to save it as **FL_Project3_YourName.fla** in the Video_gallery folder.

2. Insert two new layers above the *top-bottom text* layer and name them **directions** and **captions**.

FIGURE 5-2
The *directions* and *captions* layers are above the *top-bottom text* layer and below the *video* layer

3. Click frame **1** on the *directions* layer.

4. Select the **Text Tool**, click on the Stage to start a new text block, and key **Click an image on the left to preview the video.**

5. Use the Property inspector to apply the formatting shown in Figure 5-3 (Dynamic Text, Arial, size 13, black (#000000), left aligned, letter spacing 0).

FIGURE 5-3
Text properties for the directions dynamic text field

Dynamic Text

6. If necessary, widen the text block to fit on one line. Position the text over the still image of the wave at X: **170** and Y: **152**, as shown in Figure 5-4.

> **Important**
>
> Do not use the Property inspector or the small blue selection handles to resize a dynamic text block after drawing it. This will scale the size and shape of the characters, potentially causing the text to appear distorted or not fit over the wave image.

FIGURE 5-4
Position of the directions text

7. With the text block selected (surrounded by a blue outline), verify that Dynamic Text is selected as the Text type on the Property inspector.

8. Click in the **Instance Name** box on the Property inspector and key **directions_txt**.

This is the name you will use to refer to the dynamic text field in your ActionScript. The ActionScript will define which text to display when the gallery opens and when a video is loading.

> **Note**
>
> The directions text you placed on the Stage will be replaced with the instructions and loading message you define in your ActionScript on the main Timeline. Entering the text here helps you align and position the text on the Stage.

FIGURE 5-5
Naming the directions_txt dynamic text field

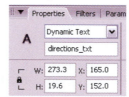

9. Click away from the Stage to deselect the text.

Dynamic text is identified by a thin, dashed border as shown in Figure 5-6.

FIGURE 5-6
Dynamic text is identified by a thin, dashed border

10. Lock the *directions* layer and save the document.

 ## Create Dynamic Text for Video Captions

1. Click frame **1** on the *captions* layer.

2. Select the **Text Tool**. Click and drag to draw a fixed-width text block in the space below the image of the wave, as shown in Figure 5-7. Use the square white selection handle to size the text block so that it fits between the vertical guides at 155 and 455.

FIGURE 5-7
Drawing the text field for the video captions

3. Select the **Selection Tool** and use the Property inspector to set the text properties, as shown in Figure 5-8 (Dynamic Text, Arial, size 10, white (#FFFFFF), left aligned, Multiline). Be sure to select the Multiline type so the captions can flow onto two lines.

> **Important**
>
> Do not use the Property inspector or the small blue selection handles to resize a dynamic text block after drawing it. This will scale the size and shape of the characters, potentially causing the captions to appear distorted and expand beyond two lines of text.

FIGURE 5-8
Text properties for the captions text

Dynamic
Text
Multiline

4. Use the Property inspector to position the text object at Y:**300**. It is okay if the text block extends into the bottom margin.

Note

When creating the dynamic text field for the captions, you need to leave the text field empty so it remains empty until a viewer selects a video clip.

Inside the Design

Designers will specify character amounts to provide the developer with guidelines on how large to make text boxes that will hold text. The designer specified a character limit of 100 characters for captions. At 10 points, this forces each caption to fit on two lines of text.

FIGURE 5-9
Position of the dynamic text field that displays video captions

5. With the caption text field still selected, click in the **Instance Name** box on the Property inspector and key **captions_txt**.

This is the name you will use to refer to the dynamic text box in your ActionScript. The ActionScript will define which caption to display when a video loads.

6. Lock the *captions* layer and save the document.

Using ActionScript to Display Onscreen Directions

When the video gallery opens, directions tell the viewer to select a thumbnail image to preview the video. When a viewer clicks a button, the directions change to inform the viewer that a video is loading. Both messages appear in the dynamic text field named directions_txt.

There are two steps to defining the dynamic text in ActionScript. First you must add two text *strings* that define the different text options. A string in ActionScript is a text value and is enclosed in quotation marks. You will call the first string of text "instructions." This is what viewers see when they open the gallery. The second string of text will be called "loading." This is the message that appears when a viewer clicks a thumbnail button.

In the following exercise, you will create the two strings of text. Then you will add ActionScript that tells the document when to display each text string inside the dynamic text field named directions_txt.

 ## Define the Directions Text

1. Click frame **1** on the *actions* layer and expand the Actions panel.

   This frame already contains script for loading each video clip. You will place the ActionScript that defines the directions text between the *stop* action and the script that controls the buttons.

2. Click the *stop* action at the top of the Script pane.

3. Click the plus symbol above the Script pane on the Actions panel, point to **Global Functions**, point to **Miscellaneous Functions**, and then click **comment**.

4. Click in the Comment text box in the Script Assist pane and key **this defines the instructions and loading video messages**.

   A new comment is placed below the *stop* action.

5. Click the plus symbol above the Script pane on the Actions panel, point to **Statements**, point to **Variables**, and then click **var**.

6. Click in the Variables text box in the Script Assist pane and key **instructions_str = "Click an image on the left to preview the video."**

   A variable in ActionScript is a container that holds information, such as a name or number. In this case, the container is named **instructions_str** and the information is "Click an image on the left to preview the video."

FIGURE 5-10
Variable for the instructions text

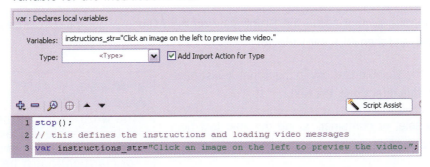

This creates a string of text named "instructions" that is noted by the _str that displays the text "Click an image to preview the video."

7. Click the plus symbol above the Script pane on the Actions panel, point to **Statements**, point to **Variables**, and then click **var**.

8. Click in the Variables text box in the Script Assist pane and key **loading_str = "Video loading…"**.

This creates a string of text named "loading" that is noted by the _str that displays the text "Video loading…"

FIGURE 5-11
Completed ActionScript that defines the instructions and loading text messages

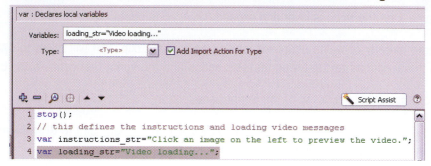

var : Declares local variables

Variables: loading_str="Video loading…"

Type: <Type> ☑ Add Import Action for Type

```
1  stop();
2  // this defines the instructions and loading video messages
3  var instructions_str="Click an image on the left to preview the video.";
4  var loading_str="Video loading...";
```

 Create the ActionScript that Tells the Document When to Display Directions Text

1. Make sure you have selected the line of script that reads *var loading_str = "Video loading…";* in the Script pane, as shown in Figure 5-11.

The new script will be added below the selected line of script.

2. Click the plus symbol above the Script pane on the Actions panel, point to **Global Functions**, point to **Miscellaneous Functions**, and then click **comment**.

3. Click in the Comment text box in the Script Assist pane and key **this displays instructions in the directions text field**.

A new comment is added to the Script pane.

4. Click the plus symbol above the Script pane on the Actions panel, point to **Statements**, point to **Variables**, and then click **set variable**.

5. Click in the Variable text box in the Script Assist pane and key **this.directions_txt.text**

The variable, or container, is the dynamic text field named *directions_txt*.

6. Click in the Value text box in the Script Assist pane and key **instructions_str**.

7. Examine the script in the Script pane.

> **Note**
>
> The word "this" at the beginning of the variable you entered in step 5 is optional and is added for clarification. It helps explain what you are targeting, which in this case is the directions dynamic text field.

As it appears now, the script will literally display the text "instructions_str" in the directions_txt dynamic text field, but what you really want is to display the *string* of text *named* instructions_str. To fix this, you must select the Expression check box.

8. Select the **Expression** check box next to the Value text box.

Now the script refers to the expression *instructions_str="Click an image on the left to preview the video."* when determining what to display in the *directions_txt* dynamic text field.

FIGURE 5-12
Variable and Value

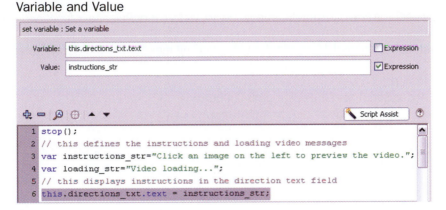

When the viewer clicks a thumbnail button, the directions text should display the Video loading message.

9. Click to select the line of script that reads, *opening_day_bt.onRelease = function()* in the Script pane.

10. Click the plus symbol above the Script pane on the Actions panel, point to **Statements**, point to **Variables**, and then click **set variable**.

11. Click in the Variable text box in the Script Assist pane and key **directions_txt.text**

12. Click in the Value text box in the Script Assist pane and key **loading_str**.

13. Select the **Expression** check box next to the Value text box.

When the opening_day_bt button is clicked, Flash will display the string of text named loading_str in the directions_txt dynamic text field and then load the opening_day.swf movie.

FIGURE 5-13
ActionScript for the opening_day_bt button symbol

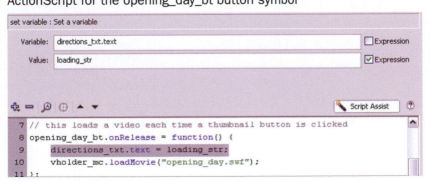

14. Click to select the line of script that reads, *outer_reef_bt.onRelease = function()* in the Script pane.

15. Click the plus symbol above the Script pane on the Actions panel, point to **Statements**, point to **Variables**, and then click **set variable**.

16. Click in the Variable text box in the Script Assist pane and key **directions_txt.text**.

17. Click in the Value text box in the Script Assist pane and key **loading_str**.

18. Select the **Expression** check box next to the Value text box.

19. Click to select the line of script that reads, *heavy_water_bt.onRelease = function()* in the Script pane.

20. Repeat steps 15 through 18 to add the Video loading message to the heavy_water button.

FIGURE 5-14
ActionScript for all three thumbnail buttons

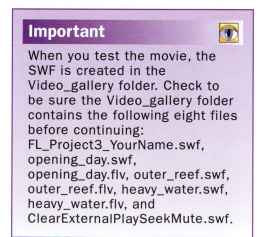

21. Collapse the Actions panel and save the document.

22. Open the **Control** menu, and then click **Test Movie**.

When the gallery loads, directions tell the viewer to click an image on the left to preview the video.

23. Click each thumbnail button to test the ActionScript that displays the *Video loading* message.

Clicking any button briefly displays the text "Video loading...". This text is hidden by a video clip when the selected movie loads because the video layer is placed above the directions layer on the Timeline.

24. Close the Flash Player window.

> **Important**
>
> When you test the movie, the SWF is created in the Video_gallery folder. Check to be sure the Video_gallery folder contains the following eight files before continuing: FL_Project3_YourName.swf, opening_day.swf, opening_day.flv, outer_reef.swf, outer_reef.flv, heavy_water.swf, heavy_water.flv, and ClearExternalPlaySeekMute.swf.

Using ActionScript to Display Video Captions

Adding video captions improves usability and accessibility by providing important information about each video and by adding a description of the videos for screen readers.

To define the captions that appear when a video loads, first create an *array*. An array is really just a list of items—in this case, captions. Then add ActionScript to each button that tells Flash which caption to display when the button is clicked.

Create an Array that Defines the Caption Text

1. Click frame **1** on the *actions* layer and expand the Actions panel.

   You will place the array directly above the ActionScript that controls the buttons.

2. Click to select the line of script that reads *this.directions_txt.text = instructions_str* in the Script pane.

3. Click the plus symbol above the Script pane on the Actions panel, point to **Global Functions**, point to **Miscellaneous Functions**, and then click **comment**.

4. Click in the Comment text box in the Script Assist pane and key **this array contains the captions for each video**.

   A new comment is added to the Script pane.

5. Click the plus symbol above the Script pane on the Actions panel, point to **Statements**, point to **Variables**, and then click **var**.

6. Click in the Variables text box in the Script Assist pane and key **captions_arr:Array = ["Opening Day at Mavericks. Watch as local legends pull into enormous barrels, leaving spectators breathless.", "When it's too big to paddle, PWCs turn dreams into reality for those brave enough to challenge the outer reef of Mavericks.", "From rookie to legend in ten seconds... 30 feet of heavy water places this local ripper in big wave surfing's hall of fame."]**

> **Note**
>
> The captions for the videos are included on the project storyboard if you would like to copy and paste this text rather than keying it.

   The entire array is placed in brackets. Each caption is placed in quotation marks and separated by a comma. The first item in an array is referred to by the number 0, the second item is number 1, and so on.

Add ActionScript that Defines When to Display Caption Text

1. Click to select the line of script that reads, *opening_day_bt.onRelease = function()* in the Script pane.

2. Click the plus symbol above the Script pane on the Actions panel, point to **Statements**, point to **Variables**, and then click **set variable**.

3. Click in the Variable text box in the Script Assist pane and key **captions_txt.text**

4. Click in the Value text box in the Script Assist pane and key **captions_arr[0]**.

The number 0 refers to the first caption in the array.

5. Select the **Expression** check box next to the Value text box.

When the opening_day_bt button is clicked, Flash will display the first caption [0] from the captions_arr array in the captions_txt dynamic text field. It will also display the *Video loading...* message in the directions_txt dynamic text field and load the opening_day.swf movie.

FIGURE 5-15
Completed ActionScript for the opening_day_bt button symbol

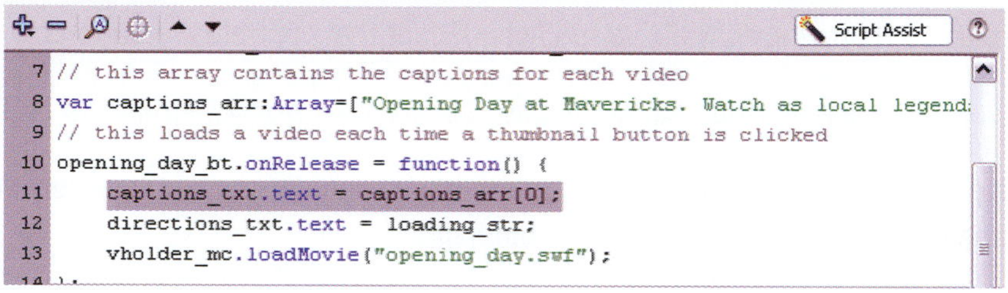

```
 7  // this array contains the captions for each video
 8  var captions_arr:Array=["Opening Day at Mavericks. Watch as local legend:
 9  // this loads a video each time a thumbnail button is clicked
10  opening_day_bt.onRelease = function() {
11      captions_txt.text = captions_arr[0];
12      directions_txt.text = loading_str;
13      vholder_mc.loadMovie("opening_day.swf");
14  }
```

6. Click to select the line of script that reads, outer_reef_bt.onRelease = function() in the Script pane.

7. Click the plus symbol above the Script pane on the Actions panel, point to **Statements**, point to **Variables**, and then click **set variable**.

8. Click in the Variable text box in the Script Assist pane and key **captions_txt.text**.

9. Click in the Value text box in the Script Assist pane and key **captions_arr[1]**.

The number 1 refers to the second caption in the array.

10. Select the **Expression** check box next to the Value text box.

11. Click to select the line of script that reads, *heavy_water_bt.onRelease = function()* in the Script pane.

12. Repeat steps 7 through 10 to link the third video caption to the heavy_water button. Be sure to change the array number to **[2]** in step 9. Compare your document to the script shown in Figure 5-16.

FIGURE 5-16
Completed ActionScript for all three thumbnail buttons

```
10 opening_day_bt.onRelease = function() {
11     captions_txt.text = captions_arr[0];
12     directions_txt.text = loading_str;
13     vholder_mc.loadMovie("opening_day.swf");
14 };
15 outer_reef_bt.onRelease = function() {
16     captions_txt.text = captions_arr[1];
17     directions_txt.text = loading_str;
18     vholder_mc.loadMovie("outer_reef.swf");
19 };
20 heavy_water_bt.onRelease = function() {
21     captions_txt.text = captions_arr[2];
22     directions_txt.text = loading_str;
23     vholder_mc.loadMovie("heavy_water.swf");
```

13. Collapse the Actions panel and save the document.

14. Open the **Control** menu, and then click **Test Movie**.

15. Click each thumbnail button to test the ActionScript that displays the video captions.

16. Close the Flash Player window, save the document, and lock the *actions* layer.

Exposing the Video Gallery to Screen Readers

To make the Blue Mountain Riders video gallery accessible to screen readers, you need to provide descriptive text for a screen reader to translate into spoken descriptions.

The screen reader should identify the most important elements of the gallery, including buttons and text. Screen reader software recognizes dynamic text, so the directions and captions are exposed to screen readers automatically. You use the Accessibility panel to identify the thumbnail buttons.

 Expose the Video Gallery to Screen Readers

1. Open the **Window** menu, point to **Other Panels**, and then click **Accessibility**.

The Accessibility panel opens.

2. Click anywhere away from the Stage to be sure no objects are selected.

The Accessibility panel displays the accessibility settings for the entire document. Be sure the *Make movie accessible* and *Make child objects accessible* check boxes are both selected.

3. Click in the Name box on the Accessibilty panel and key **Big Wave Surfing at Mavericks**.

FIGURE 5-17
Accessibility panel

4. Unlock the *buttons* layer.

5. Click the **opening_day_bt** instance on the Stage (the top thumbnail button).

The Accessibility panel changes to show settings for the selected button symbol.

6. Click in the Name text box on the Accessibility panel and key **Opening Day**.

FIGURE 5-18
Accessibility panel for the opening_day_bt symbol

7. Click the **outer_reef_bt** instance on the Stage (the second thumbnail button).

8. Click in the Name text box on the Accessibility panel and key **Outer Reef**.

9. Click the **heavy_water_bt** instance on the Stage (the bottom thumbnail button).

10. Click in the Name text box on the Accessibility panel and key **Heavy Water**.

11. Click the **store_link** text button at the top of the gallery (*Click here to purchase the complete video*).

12. Click in the Name text box on the Accessibility panel and key **Click to purchase the complete video**.

13. Lock the *buttons* layer and save the document.

Hiding Objects from Screen Readers

Some Flash objects are not intended for screen readers. For example, the *vholder* movie clip symbol is used to load and play the video clip but should remain hidden from screen reader software. The visitor does not need a spoken description of the video container.

Use the Accessibility panel to hide the *vholder* movie clip symbol from screen readers.

 Hide the Video Holder from Screen Readers

1. Unlock the *video* layer.

2. Click frame **1** on the *video* layer to select the **vholder** movie clip symbol.

3. Deselect the **Make object accessible** check box on the Accessibility panel.

FIGURE 5-19
Accessibility panel for the vholder movie clip symbol

4. Lock the *video* layer.

5. Close the Accessibility panel and save the document. If you are continuing with the next lesson, leave this file open. If you are not continuing at this time, close the file and close Flash.

TESTING AND PUBLISHING THE VIDEO GALLERY

OBJECTIVES:

Upon completion of this lesson, you will be able to:

- Perform a content review.
- Perform a technical test.
- Publish the video gallery.

Estimated time to complete this lesson: 15 minutes

Introduction

The design document and storyboard provide specific instructions for building the Blue Mountain Riders video gallery. To ensure that the document meets specified design requirements, perform a content review before submitting the gallery to the client for review. To complete the content review, test the gallery and compare the finished document to the design specification and storyboard. Look for any discrepancies in design, color, layout, content, and functionality.

After confirming that the video gallery meets the required design specifications and matches the development storyboard, check the document for technical accuracy. Verify that every button functions properly, the correct dynamic text displays, and the videos load. If possible, check the document for accessibility by using one or more screen reader applications.

When the document is complete, publish the finished gallery and prepare the files for hosting on the client's Web site.

Performing a Content Review

In the following exercise, you will print a copy of the design specification and storyboard, open the document in the Flash Player window, and perform a thorough content review.

 Perform a Content Review

1. If necessary, open the file you created in the previous lesson. Alternately, you can open the file named **FL_Project3_Lesson6.fla**, which is found in the **Practice_files** folder in the data files for this lesson. If you use **FL_Project3_Lesson6.fla**, be sure to save it as **FL_Project3_YourName.fla** in the Video_gallery folder.

2. Be sure you have a printed copy of the design document and storyboard for this project.

3. Open the **Control** menu, and then click **Test Movie**.

The video gallery opens in the Flash Player window.

4. Use the checklist in Table 6-1 to compare the finished video gallery to the design document and storyboard for the project.

TABLE 6-1
Comparing the finished document to the design document and storyboard

FEATURE	DESIGN REQUIREMENT
Layout	Compare the design and placement of content, including the background elements, thumbnail buttons, wave.jpg image, video clips, video controls, descriptive text, attribution, directions text, and captions.
Video	Confirm that the videos reflect the correct content as described in the storyboard.
Thumbnail buttons	Confirm that each thumbnail button displays the correct still image and text label in the Up state of the button. Confirm that each button has a dim Up state that gets brighter when the pointer rolls over the button.
Text	Proofread the descriptive text at the top of the gallery and the attribution at the bottom of the gallery. Compare the text to the required text described in the storyboard.
Captions	Load each video and check to make sure the correct caption loads below the video. Proofread each caption and compare against the captions described in the storyboard. Check to make sure each caption fits on one or two lines of text.

5. Close the Flash Player window and make any necessary corrections to the document.

Performing a Technical Test

To test the video gallery locally (on your computer), open the document in the Flash Player window and test each button and link. Check to be sure the Video_gallery folder contains the following eight files: FL_Project3_YourName.swf, opening_day.swf, opening_day.flv, outer_reef.swf, outer_reef.flv, heavy_water.swf, heavy_water.flv, and ClearExternalPlaySeekMute.swf.

 Perform a Technical Test

1. Open the **Control** menu, and then click **Test Movie**.

The video gallery opens in the Flash Player window.

2. Use the checklist in Table 6-2 to test the technical features of the video gallery.

> **Note**
>
> To test the accessibility of the document by using a screen reader, you must first publish SWF and HTML files and test the document from within the HTML file in a Web browser.

TABLE 6-2
Performing a technical test

FEATURE	TECHNICAL TEST
Directions text	When the video gallery opens, check to be sure the directions text that reads "Click an image on the left to preview the video" appears over the still image of the wave.
Thumbnail buttons	Position the mouse pointer over each image. Be sure the Up and Over states are functioning properly, as described in the storyboard. Be sure the entire area of the button represents the Hit (active) state of the button.
Loading video message	Click each thumbnail button and be sure the message "Video loading…" appears before each video loads.
Video	Click each thumbnail button and be sure the correct video loads into the designated space on the video gallery. Confirm that you have selected the correct video controls (skin), as described in the storyboard and design document.
Captions	Click each thumbnail button and ensure that the correct caption loads in the designated space below the video controls.
Text link	Click the text link that reads "Click here to purchase the complete video." Confirm that the link opens a Web page in a new browser window.
Screen reader support	The design document requires the gallery to include accessibility features that identify the navigation buttons and important content for screen readers. If possible, test the video gallery with a screen reader application running. (Note: This requires you to first publish the SWF and HTML files and test the document by opening the HTML file in a Web browser.)

3. Close the browser window and/or the Flash Player window.

4. Make any necessary corrections to the document and save your changes.

> **Note** ☑️
>
> To make changes to the size of the video window or the video controls (skin), you will need to open the Video FLA files you created in Lesson 1.

Publishing the Video Gallery

The video gallery is going to be added to an existing HTML page on the Blue Mountain Riders Web site. When you publish the document, you only need to generate the video_gallery.swf file.

The following files must be published to the same directory for the video gallery to function properly:

- Video Gallery: video_gallery.swf (currently named FL_Project3_YourName)
- Video Movies: opening_day.swf, outer_reef.swf, heavy_water.swf

- Flash (FLV) Videos: opening_day.flv, outer_reef.flv, heavy_water.flv
- Video Controller (skin): ClearExternalPlaySeekMute.swf

Refer to Table 6-3 for a description of these files.

TABLE 6-3
These files must be in the same directory or folder when publishing the video gallery

FILE	DESCRIPTION
Video gallery	This is the main interface for the video gallery. You created this file in Lessons 2 through 5. This is the SWF file that will be added to the Blue Mountain Riders HTML page. You can provide a final name for this file in the Publish Settings dialog box.
Video SWF movies	The video gallery for this project loads each video into the main gallery by loading individual SWF movie files (opening_day.swf, outer_reef.swf, and heavy_water.swf). Each SWF contains a Flash component that loads and plays the correct FLV file.
Flash Videos (FLV)	The Flash Video files were created automatically when you imported the videos in Lesson 1. The Flash Videos for this project are opening_day.flv, outer_reef.flv, and heavy_water.flv.
Video controller (skin)	When you created the Flash Videos in Lesson 1, you selected a video controller (skin). Flash generated a copy of the selected skin and placed it in the same directory as your FLV files. The skin you selected for the Blue Mountain Riders video gallery is ClearExternalPlaySeekMute.swf.

 Publishing the Video Gallery

1. Open the **File** menu, and then click **Publish Settings**.

The Publish Settings dialog box opens with the Formats tab selected, as shown in Figure 6-1.

FIGURE 6-1
Publish Settings dialog box

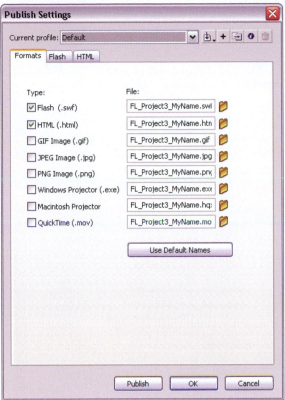

2. Deselect the **HTML** check box.

The video gallery will be added to an existing HTML page on the Blue Mountain Riders Web site.

3. Double-click in the File text box to select the filename for the published SWF file. Key **video_gallery.swf.**

Now, when you publish the document or select Test Movie from the Control menu, Flash will create a SWF file named video_gallery.swf. This is the file to be added to the Blue Mountain Riders HTML Web page.

4. Click the **Flash** tab to select it.

5. Click and drag the JPEG Quality slider to **60**, as shown in Figure 6-2.

FIGURE 6-2
Adjusting the JPEG quality

The JPEG quality controls the amount of compression that is applied to bitmap images when you publish the document. A higher quality setting means less compression is applied, but the file size of the published document will be larger. A lower setting reduces the document file size, but will also reduce the quality of JPEG images in the document. The JPEG images in this document include the still images used on the thumbnail buttons and the still image of the wave.

6. Click **Publish** to publish the document with the new settings.

7. Click **OK** to close the dialog box.

8. Save and close the document and then close Flash.

> **Note**
>
> If you choose to store Flash Videos in a directory outside the root folder where your video_gallery.swf file is stored, you will need to edit the FLVPlayback component parameters to point to the new location of the video. Refer to Lesson 1 for how to change the parameters for an instance of the FLVPlayback component.

SUMMARY

You have successfully created a video gallery for previewing video clips on the Blue Mountain Riders Web site.

In this project, you learned to follow a design document and storyboard to produce and publish accessible Flash documents. You learned to create Flash Video (FLV) files by using the Import Video feature and to reduce the size of a Flash document by storing larger video and image files outside the main document and then using ActionScript to load and play the files on demand. You learned to control button instances and dynamic text by using ActionScript on the main Timeline, and you were introduced to advanced features for working with text.

Some of the technical skills covered in this project include:

- Encoding Flash Video (FLV) files for the Web
- Using guides to create page structure and balance
- Creating thumbnail buttons
- Using Advanced text formatting
- Checking spelling of a Flash document
- Creating external links
- Using ActionScript to load and display content stored outside the Flash document
- Using ActionScript to display text dynamically
- Exposing and hiding content for screen readers
- Performing a technical test
- Selecting publish settings and publishing a document

ON YOUR OWN – CREATING VIDEO, LOADING EXTERNAL CONTENT, AND DISPAYING DYNAMIC TEXT

ACTIVITY 1: CREATING A VIDEO ADVERTISEMENT

You have learned to enhance a Web page by importing Flash Video and creating external links. These techniques include:

- Importing and encoding Flash Video
- Creating background elements
- Converting text to buttons and linking to external Web pages

Apply these same skills to create a short advertisement promoting San Francisco as a tourist destination. Set up the document, background elements, and text for the advertisement. Create an e-mail link and import a short Flash Video of the Golden Gate Bridge. Publish the movie as an accessible document. You can review the techniques for this activity in Lessons 1, 2, 3, and 5.

1. Open a new document with a width of **380** pixels and a height of **380** pixels. Select red (**#990000**) as the document background color.

2. Because your advertisement will contain video, text, and a link, add and name the following layers (listed from the top down): **actions**, **button** (for the link), **text**, **video**, **background**. Save and name the document. FL_Project3_Activity1_YourName.fla

3. Click in the first frame of the *text* layer and create a flexible-width, static text block that reads, **VISIT SAN FRANCISCO**. Make the text **Arial Black**, size **18**, white (**#FFFFFF**), center-aligned, and spread the letters across the top using letter spacing **3**. Position the text at Y:**12** and centered horizontally at the top of the page. Lock the *text* layer.

4. Click in the first frame of the *button* layer and create a static text block that reads, **Click here to request a brochure**. Make the text **Arial**, size **12**, white (**#FFFFFF**), bold, center-aligned, and spread the letters across the bottom using letter spacing **2**. Position the text at Y: **355** and centered horizontally at the bottom of the page.

5. Convert the text in the bottom margin to a button symbol named **link**. Edit the button to have black (**#FFFFFF**) text in the Over state and an enlarged Hit state (such as a rectangle shape over the entire button). Close the button and return to the main Timeline.

6. Apply a *getURL* action to the *link* button that links to the e-mail address **mailto:moreinfo@letsvisitsf.com**.

7. Click the first frame of the *background* layer and draw a white (**#FFFFFF**) rectangle with size **15** rounded corners. Make the rectangle **340** pixels wide and **300** pixels high. Position the rectangle at X: **20** and Y: **50**. Lock the *background* layer. This will serve as the background for the Flash video file.

8. Click in the first frame of the *video* layer and import the video source file named **san_francisco.mov**. Select **Progressive download from a web server** as the deployment option. Use the following settings when importing the video:
   - Video codec: **On2 VP6**
   - Frame rate: **Same as source**
   - Key frame placement: **Automatic**
   - Quality: **Medium**
   - Check **Resize video** option
   - Video width: **300**
   - Video height: **225**
   - Encode audio data rate: **48Kbps (mono)**
   - Crop: No cropping
   - Skin: **SteelExternalPlayMute.swf**

9. Position the FLVPlayback component that is generated at X: **40** and Y: **73**.

10. Click in the first frame of the *actions* layer. Add a *stop* action to prevent the movie from looping.

11. Add an accessibility name and description for the entire movie. Make child objects accessible. Select the link button in the bottom margin and add the accessibility name **Click here to request a brochure**. Disable accessibility for the FLVPlayback component (the video). Lock the *actions*, *button*, and *video* layers.

12. Save and test the movie.

ACTIVITY 2: CREATING A PHOTO VIEWER BY LOADING EXTERNAL CONTENT ON DEMAND

You have learned to load and display content, such as video, images, or other SWF documents, stored outside the Flash document. These techniques include:

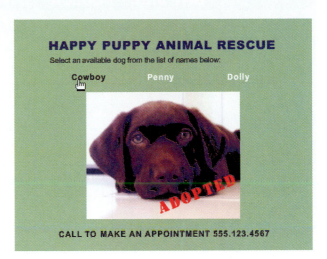

- Creating buttons from text and assigning instance names to buttons
- Using a movie clip symbol as a container for displaying external content
- Using ActionScript on the main Timeline to control buttons and to load external content
- Making buttons accessible to screen readers

Apply these same skills to create a photo viewer for an animal adoption Web site. You can review the techniques for this activity in Lessons 2, 3, 4, and 5.

The photo viewer features three puppies that are available for adoption. The photo viewer includes the name of each available dog. When a dog's name is selected, an image of the dog appears. The movie opens with an image of a recently adopted pet (as a placeholder).

1. Create a new folder for the photo viewer and name it **PhotoViewer**. Place the **cooper.jpg**, **cowboy.jpg**, **penny.jpg**, and **dolly.jpg** image files in the new folder. These files are located in the data files for this project. Create a new Flash document named **PhotoViewer_YourName.fla** and save it in the PhotoViewer folder.

2. Change the document size to **450** pixels wide and **350** pixels high. Change the background color to sage green (**#99CC99**). Add and name the following layers for the pictures, buttons, and text content (listed from the top down): **actions**, **pictures**, **buttons**, and **text**.

3. Click in the first frame of the *text* layer and create the following text blocks, and then lock the *text* layer:

TEXT	FONT/ FONT SIZE	FONT COLOR	ALIGNMENT	LETTER SPACING	POSITION
HAPPY PUPPY ANIMAL RESCUE	Arial Black, size 18	navy (#000066)	left-aligned	letter spacing 1	X: 50 and Y: 25
Select an available dog from the list below.	Arial, size 11	black (#000000)	left-aligned	letter spacing 0	X:52 and Y: 55
Call to make an appointment 555.123. 4567.	Arial, size 12, bold	black (#000000)	center-aligned	letter spacing 1	X: 64 and Y: 315

4. Click in the first frame of the *buttons* layer. Create a separate static text block for each dog that needs adopting. The dogs' names are *Cowboy*, *Penny*, and *Dolly*. Make each text block **Arial**, size **12**, white (**#FFFFFF**), bold, left-aligned, and letter spacing **1**. Position Cowboy at X: **80** and Y: **80**. Position Penny at X: **202** and Y: **80**. Position Dolly at X: **314** and Y: **80**.

5. Convert each dog's name (text block) into a button symbol. Change the text color in the Over and Down States to black. Use a rectangle shape to enlarge the Hit state so that it completely covers the text. Use the Property inspector to assign an instance name to each button. Use the following instance names: **cowboy_bt**, **penny_bt**, and **dolly_bt**. Lock the *buttons* layer.

6. Click in the first frame of the *pictures* layer. Create an empty movie clip symbol named **iholder** (for image holder). Return to the main Timeline of Scene 1 and position an instance of the iholder movie clip symbol on the Stage at X: **110** and Y: **110**. This is the top left corner where each image will load. Using the Property inspector, name the instance of the iholder movie clip symbol **iholder_mc**. Lock the *pictures* layer.

7. Click in the first frame of the **actions** layer. Add a **stop** action to prevent the movie from looping. Add a **loadMovie** action that loads the image file cooper.jpg into the iholder_mc movie clip when the movie loads. You can also add comments to describe your ActionScript.

> **Hint**
>
> The cooper image is not tied to a button, but is just the placeholder image. You can add the **loadMovie** action from the *Global Functions* group under *Browser/Network*. The URL is "cooper.jpg." Be sure to set the Location as **Target** and key **iholder_mc**.

8. For each button, add ActionScript that loads the corresponding JPEG image into the iholder_mc movie clip when the button is clicked. Clicking **cowboy_bt** loads the cowboy.jpg image; clicking **penny_bt** loads the penny.jpg image; and clicking **dolly_bt** loads the dolly.jpg image.

> ### Hint
>
> Loading objects requires an event handler such as OnRelease for the picture to load when the button is released. This can be found in the ActionScript 2.0 Classes group under **Movie** and then **MovieClip**. For the Object, use the button's instance name, such as cowboy_bt. Use a loadMovie action to indicate what should be loaded and where to load the image. You'll find this action under the **ActionScript 2.0 Classes** group, under **Movie**, then **MovieClip**, and then **Methods**. The Object (where to load the image) is iholder_mc and the URL (what to load) is the name of the still image.

```
1  stop();
2  // this loads a placeholder image when the movie opens
3  loadMovie("cooper.jpg", "iholder_mc");
4  // this loads still images when the viewer clicks a button.
5  cowboy_bt.onRelease = function() {
6      iholder_mc.loadMovie("cowboy.jpg");
7  };
8  penny_bt.onRelease = function() {
9      iholder_mc.loadMovie("penny.jpg");
10 };
11 dolly_bt.onRelease = function() {
12     iholder_mc.loadMovie("dolly.jpg");
13 };
```

9. Close the Actions panel and lock the *actions* layer.

10. Make the buttons accessible. Use each dog's name as the accessibility name and enter a short description for each puppy by using the Description box on the Accessibility panel. Disable accessibility for the iholder_mc movie clip symbol.

11. Save and test the movie.

ACTIVITY 3: CREATING VOCABULARY FLASH CARDS

You have learned to display text dynamically, based on the way a viewer interacts with the document. These techniques include:

- Creating dynamic text fields
- Creating buttons and assigning instance names to buttons
- Using ActionScript to control buttons
- Using ActionScript to define the contents of a dynamic text field

Use these same techniques to create a document that displays a list of vocabulary words and displays a definition when the viewer rolls over a word in the list.

VOCABULARY FLASH CARDS

Point to a word to see its definition.

WORD	DEFINITION
appease	to bring to a state of peace or contentment
exemplify	
suffrage	

You can review the techniques for this activity in Lessons 2, 3, and 5.

1. Open a new document and set the width to **550** pixels and the height to **400** pixels. Change the background color to white (**#FFFFFF**). Add and name the following layers (listed from the top down): **actions**, **buttons**, **definitions**, and **text**. Save and name the document.

2. Click the first frame of the *text* layer and create the following text blocks, and then lock the *text* layer:

TEXT	FONT/ FONT SIZE	FONT COLOR	ALIGNMENT	LETTER SPACING	POSITION
VOCABU-LARY FLASH CARDS	Arial Black, size 14	black (#000000)	left-aligned	letter spacing 1	X: 26 and Y: 24
Point to a word to see its definition.	Arial, size 12	black (#000000)	left-aligned	letter spacing 0	X: 26 and Y: 52
WORDS	Arial Black, size 12	blue (#0000FF)	left-aligned	letter spacing 1	X: 28 and Y: 90
DEFINITIONS	Arial Black, size 12	blue (#0000FF)	left-aligned	letter spacing 1	X: 211 and Y: 90

3. Click in the first frame of the *buttons* layer and add the following vocabulary words. Create each word as a separate text block as follows:

TEXT	FONT / FONT SIZE	FONT COLOR	ALIGNMENT	LETTER SPACING	POSITION
appease	Arial Black, size 14	blue (#000033)	left-aligned	letter spacing 1	X: 28 and Y: 110
exemplify	Arial Black, size 14	blue (#000033)	left-aligned	letter spacing 1	X: 28 and Y: 140
suffrage	Arial Black, size 14	blue (#000033)	left-aligned	letter spacing 1	X: 28 and Y: 170

4. Convert each vocabulary word into a separate button symbol. Change the color of the Over state for each button and enlarge the Hit state.

5. Use the Property inspector to assign an instance name to each vocabulary word button. Name the buttons **appease_bt**, **exemplify_bt**, and **suffrage_bt**. Lock the *buttons* layer.

6. Click the first frame on the *definitions* layer. Select the **Text Tool** and change the *Text type* to **Dynamic Text**. Drag to draw a text block to the right of the vocabulary words and under the Definitions label. Make the text block approximately **300** pixels wide and **75** pixels high.

> **Hint**
>
> To change the size of the text block, be sure to use the square corner handle, and not the small blue sizing handles or the Property inspector. Resizing the text field after it is drawn can distort the text.

Select the dynamic text field and use the Property inspector to set the following properties: **Arial**, size 12, green (#006600), left-aligned, letter spacing 0, and **Multiline**. Use the Property inspector to name the instance of the dynamic text field **definitions_txt**. Lock the *definitions* layer.

7. Click in the first frame of the *actions* layer. Add a *stop* action to prevent the movie from looping. Add an array that holds the definitions for each vocabulary word. Then add ActionScript for each button that displays the correct definition from the array in the definitions_txt dynamic text field. Use the following definitions in the array:

appease: **to bring to a state of peace or contentment**
exemplify: **to show or illustrate by example**
suffrage: **the right to vote**

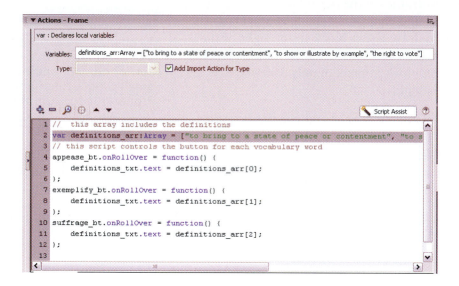

8. Close the Actions panel, lock the *actions* layer, and make each button accessible. Use the vocabulary word as the accessibility name. Leave the Description box empty.

9. Check the spelling of the document.

10. Save and test the movie.

MACROMEDIA CONTRIBUTE 3

MACROMEDIA CONTRIBUTE 3

IN THIS UNIT YOU LEARN TO:

- Explore the Contribute interface and workflow process.
- Understand Web site connections.
- Edit existing content on a page.
- Add content and images to a page.
- Organize content on a page using tables and lists.
- Link content to pages inside and outside the site.
- Build on a Web site by adding new pages and FlashPaper documents.
- Review and publish content.

Summary

Macromedia Contribute 3 makes Web publishing simple without in-depth knowledge of HTML. You can easily update content on Web sites, add images, and create links using familiar word-processing techniques. Many site designers use templates to design their Web sites, thereby allowing you to focus on the content that needs to be updated without having to worry about compromising the design or structure of a site.

In this unit, you complete two projects that help you build the skills you need to use Contribute to maintain a Web site. You will edit and update a course Web site and an electronic portfolio Web site. Both Web sites are template based and are designed to maintain a consistent look and feel. Pages based on templates offer editable regions where you can add and edit content. You will also learn to easily browse to the Web page you want to change, edit that page, and publish it.

To begin work on these projects, you first need to become familiar with Contribute 3.

Getting to Know Contribute 3

The Contribute interface consists of the windows, toolbars, panels, and other elements you use to browse to pages, edit pages, publish pages, and send drafts for review. You can access Contribute commands and features by using menus or by selecting options from the toolbar. The Contribute interface operates in two modes:

■ The Contribute browser allows you to browse to pages in your Web site. It functions much like a regular Web browser.

■ The Contribute editor allows you to edit, publish, and send drafts for review. It functions much like a word processor or like Macromedia Dreamweaver 8.

You switch from the Contribute browser (the default view) to the Contribute editor when you click the Edit Page button to edit an existing page, or the New Page button to create a new page. In addition, the Contribute Draft Console allows you to track the status of drafts that you are currently editing, drafts that others have sent you to review, and drafts that you have sent to others for review.

Finding Your Way Around the Contribute Interface

Figure 1 shows the components of the Contribute interface and Table 1 provides a brief description.

FIGURE 1
The Contribute interface

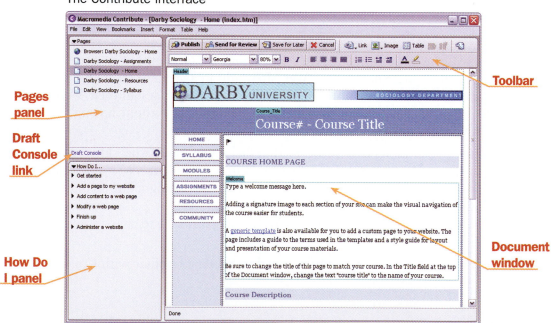

The Contribute interface components and description

Document window	Displays pages as you view and edit them.
Toolbar	Changes depending on whether you are in the Contribute browser or the Contribute editor.
Pages panel	Lists current drafts and provides a link to the Draft Console.
How Do I panel	Provides information on how to complete tasks in Contribute.

Contribute Browser

You use the Contribute browser to browse to Web site pages to view or edit them. The buttons in the browser toolbar, shown in Figure 2, function much like those in Microsoft Internet Explorer and Netscape Navigator. Table 2 provides a short description of each of the tools in the browser toolbar.

You stay in the Contribute browser until you click the Edit Page button to edit an existing page, or the New Page button to create a new page.

FIGURE 2
Toolbar in the Contribute browser

TABLE 2
The Contribute toolbar components and description

Edit Page	Opens a page as a draft in the Contribute editor.
New Page	Creates a new page from a blank page or template.
Back/Forward	Browses through recently viewed pages.
Stop	Stops a page from loading.
Refresh	Refreshes the current page.
Home	Returns to the Web site home page.
Return to Contribute Start	Opens the Contribute start page.
Address text box	Use to enter location for a Web page. You can browse to pages that are part of your Web site and to any page on the Internet.
Go	Opens the page entered in the Address text box.
Choose	Opens the Choose File on Web site dialog box, which allows you to select a page from a Web site.

Contribute Editor

You open the Contribute editor by clicking the Edit button in the Contribute browser. The toolbar in the Contribute editor enables you to edit drafts, publish drafts, send drafts for review, save drafts for later, and cancel drafts. For example, you can add text to a draft, change the text font, and publish the draft to the Web site with the changes.

The buttons in the editor toolbar, as you can see in Figure 3, are similar to those found in word-processing programs and in Macromedia Dreamweaver 8. Table 3 provides a brief description of each of the tools in the editor toolbar.

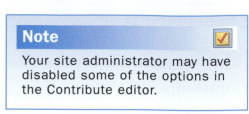

Note ☑️
You cannot edit a page that is not part of your Web site.

Note ☑️
Your site administrator may have disabled some of the options in the Contribute editor.

FIGURE 3
Toolbar in the Contribute browser

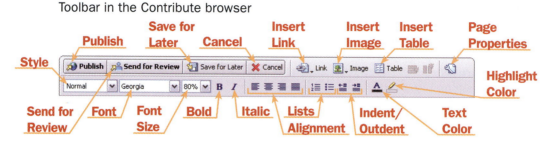

TABLE 3
Description of tools in the Contribute editor toolbar

Publish	Publishes a draft to a Web site, making it live for your users.
Send for Review	Sends a draft to another user to review.
Save for Later	Saves changes to the draft for later editing.
Cancel	Cancels all changes to a draft. Deletes the current draft on your computer.
Insert Link	Inserts a hyperlink.
Insert Image	Inserts an image from a file, a Web site, or another application.
Insert Table	Inserts a table.
Page Properties	Opens the Page Properties dialog box for the current draft.
Style	Changes the text style.
Font	Changes the text font.
Font Size	Changes the text size.
Bold	Makes text bold.
Italic	Makes text italic.
Alignment	Sets the text alignment as left, right, centered, or justified.

TABLE 3 Continued
Description of tools in the Contribute editor toolbar

Lists	Adds numerical or bulleted list formatting.
Indent/Outdent	Changes the text indenting/outdenting.
Text Color	Changes the text color.
Highlight Color	Adds or changes the highlighting applied to text.

Draft Console

The Contribute Draft Console, shown in Figure 4, allows you to track the status of all your drafts. It lists drafts that you are currently editing, drafts that other users have sent you to review, and drafts that you have sent other users to review, as summarized in Table 4. You open the draft console by clicking the Draft Console link in the Pages panel. To view a draft, click its link.

FIGURE 4
Contribute Draft Console

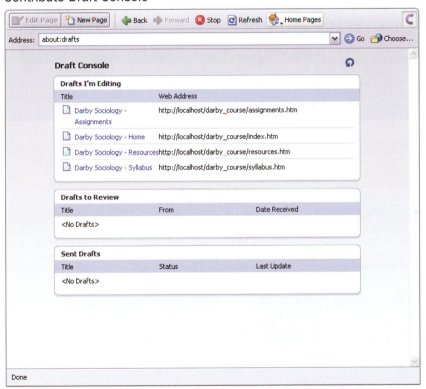

TABLE 4
Draft console headings description

Drafts I'm Editing	Current drafts that are you are editing.
Drafts to Review	Drafts that other Contribute users have sent you to review.
Sent Drafts	Drafts that you have sent to other Contribute users to review.

Working in Contribute

Step by Step Web page editing is accomplished in an easy three-step process. Using a browse-edit-publish workflow, you locate pages on a Web site, update them, and then publish the changes with a click of a button.

Here's how the process works:

1. Start Contribute.

2. **Browse:** In the Contribute browser, locate the page you want to edit, as shown in Figure 5.

FIGURE 5
The Contribute browser

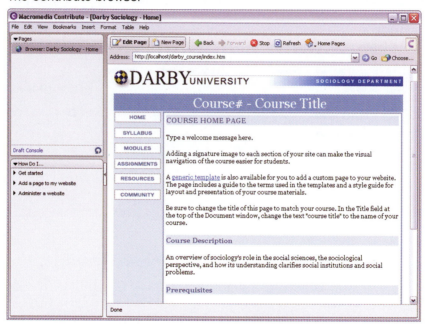

3. **Edit:** Click the Edit Page button in the toolbar to begin editing. Contribute automatically opens a draft copy of the page, as shown in Figure 6. You can add a variety of content, such as text, images, tables, lists, and Web-ready, portable FlashPaper and PDF documents, to your draft page.

FIGURE 6
The Contribute Editor

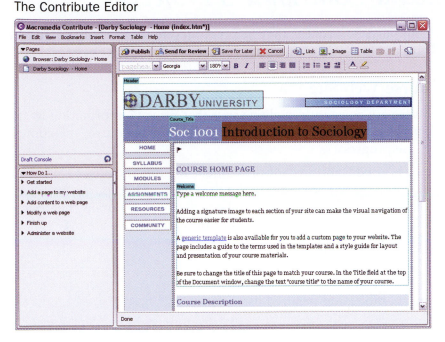

4. Publish: After you finish editing the draft, click Publish to save your work and make the new information available at the Web site, as shown in Figure 7.

FIGURE 7
Your edits are now available on the Internet

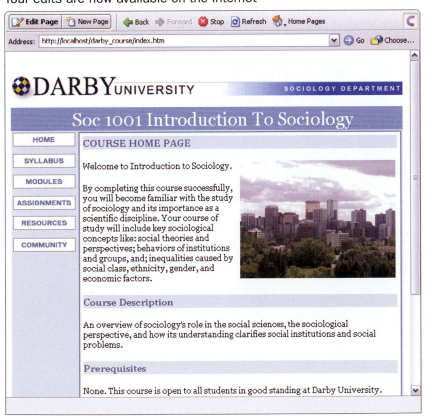

Macromedia Contribute 3 Projects

This unit contains two projects that help you develop your skills in adding and updating content on a Web site.

Project 1: Course Web Site

Course Web sites are constantly evolving sites that provide information to students, parents, and faculty. Since these sites reflect the current status of the course, the content is edited and revised as the course progresses.

In this project, you edit and update the content for the Sociology Department Web site at Darby University based on requirements set by the faculty. This course Web site was built using an existing set of Sociology Department templates that will maintain the design consistency of the site. Your task will be to update four pages of the course Web site by:

- Setting up a Web site connection
- Modifying text on the page
- Adding an image, table, and itemized list

Project 2: Electronic Portfolio

A program portfolio for a preservice teacher is a deliberate, carefully designed and integrated selection of artifacts and reflections representing the teacher candidate's professional experiences, competencies, and growth over a period of time.

In this project, you perform more advanced site building tasks while adding and creating content for an electronic portfolio for a preservice teacher. This electronic portfolio Web site is based on a prebuilt set of portfolio templates that will maintain the design consistency of the site. Your task will be to continue adding content to the Web site by:

- Creating links to internal and external Web pages
- Creating new pages and FlashPaper documents
- Sending for review and tracking drafts

COURSE WEB SITE

GOALS

- Understand Web site connections.
- Edit existing content on a page.
- Add content to a page.
- Organize content on a page using tables and lists.

TECHNICAL SKILLS

- Set up a connection to a Web site.
- Add bookmarks.
- Browse to, open, and edit Web pages.
- Modify a Web page title.
- Insert and edit images.
- Insert and modify tables and lists.
- Publish pages.

Estimated time to complete this project: 2 hours and 15 minutes

Summary

Course Web sites are constantly evolving sites that provide information to students, parents, and faculty. Since these sites reflect the current status of the course, the content is edited and revised as the course progresses.

The Assignment

In this project, you edit and update the content for the Sociology Department Web site at Darby University based on requirements set by the faculty. This sociology course Web site was built using an existing set of Sociology Department templates that will maintain the design consistency of the site. Your task will be to update four pages of the Sociology Department course Web site by:

■ Setting up a Web site connection

■ Modifying text on the page

■ Adding an image, table, and itemized list

Figure 1 shows the home page for the course site you will be building.

FIGURE 1
Darby University sociology course home page

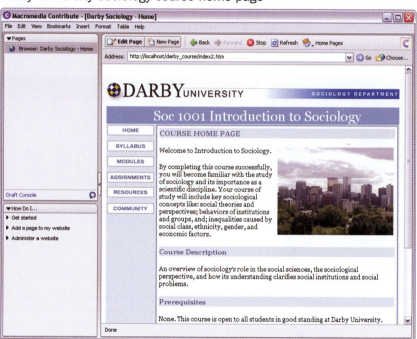

The flowchart in Figure 2 shows the layout and page relationships of the sociology course Web site you will be working on. Shaded blocks indicate those Web pages that you will be updating in this project.

FIGURE 2
Darby sociology course Web site map

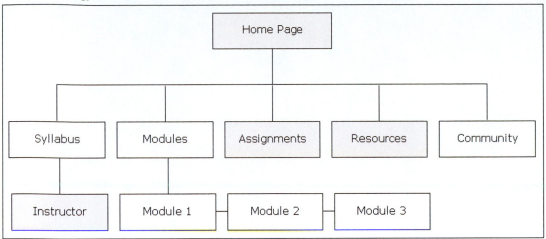

SETTING UP A WEB SITE CONNECTION

OBJECTIVES:

Upon completion of this lesson, you will be able to:

- Create a connection to a Web site using a Contribute connection key.

- Add a bookmark.

Estimated Time: 15 minutes

Introduction

Before you can begin editing the Darby Sociology Department Web site using Contribute, you need a connection key (a file with an .stc extension) and a password to establish a connection to the Web site. A connection key contains the technical information to give you access to particular pages on a Web site. Once you've established a connection to the Web site, you can create bookmarks to quickly and easily locate pages that you are working on or other pages of interest that may be outside your site.

In this lesson, you connect to the sociology course Web site you will be working on and bookmark the instructor's curriculum vitae page in the site.

Setting Up a Connection

To begin editing content, you first need to set up your connection to the Darby sociology Web site. A connection key is included in the Darby Course assets, along with other documents you will use in the project. The connection key contains all of the network information Contribute needs to connect to the Web site.

Note

There are other ways to obtain connection keys. Your site administrator or instructor may send you an e-mail with the key attached or give you the network location where you can download the key. The site administrator should also communicate the connection key password to you.

Set Up a Connection

1. Locate the connection key, shown in Figure 1-1, by browsing to the **darby_documents** folder located in the **darby_course** folder.

The network path for Windows is C:\Inetpub\ wwwroot\darby_course\darby_documents.

FIGURE 1-1
Connection key icon

DarbySociology-
Home-Administrator

2. Double-click the connection key.

Contribute starts (if it is not already running), and the Import Connection Key dialog box appears as shown in Figure 1-2.

FIGURE 1-2
Import Connection Key dialog box

3. Enter your name, your e-mail address, and the password for the connection key. The password for this connection key is **ConnKey**.

4. Click **OK**.

The Web site's home page appears in the Contribute browser as shown in Figure 1-3.

Important

Check with your site administrator or instructor to verify the location of the key.

Note

The connection key in the darby_documents folder is Windows compatible only. For Macintosh machines, your instructor will provide an alternate connection key. The network path for Macintosh is Library:WebServer:Documents: darby_course.

Note

You can also click Edit in the menu bar, and click My Connections. Then click the Import button to navigate to the connection key.

FIGURE 1-3
Darby course home page in the Contribute browser

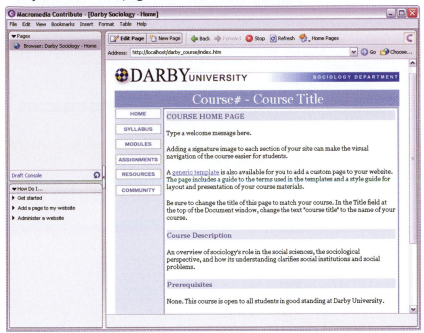

Adding a Bookmark

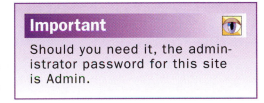

You will be making some changes to the instructor curriculum vitae page of the Darby sociology course Web site. Since you will access this page often, adding a bookmark for the page will help you quickly locate that page. Contribute lets you keep a list of bookmarks for pages that you visit frequently. You can add a bookmark for any page—not just pages in Web sites you are connected to.

When you add a page as a bookmark in Contribute, it appears in your list of bookmarks. You can have up to 1,000 bookmarks. In Windows, Contribute also includes your Internet Explorer bookmarks (up to 2,000 bookmarks) in the Other Bookmarks list under your Contribute bookmarks.

In this next Step-by-Step exercise, you add a bookmark for the curriculum vitae page to help you quickly locate it for your work in the following lesson.

 ## Add a Bookmark

1. Use the Contribute browser to navigate to the **SYLLABUS** page.

2. Click the link under **Instructor's Name** to go to the instructor's curriculum vitae page.

3. Click **Bookmarks** on the menu bar, and click **Add Bookmark**, as shown in Figure 1-4.

FIGURE 1-4
Bookmarks menu

The Add Bookmark dialog box opens. In the Name field, replace the default filename with Darby Sociology - Instructor, as shown in Figure 1-5.

FIGURE 1-5
Add Bookmark dialog box

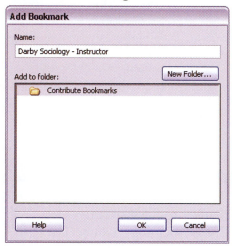

4. Click **OK**.

Contribute adds the page to your bookmarks list on the Bookmarks menu as shown in Figure 1-6.

FIGURE 1-6
Bookmarks list with the instructor curriculum vitae page added

> **Note** ☑️
>
> You can change the name of the bookmark by entering a new name in the Name text box. This is the name that appears in your bookmarks list.

MODIFYING TEXT ON A PAGE

Introduction

The sociology course Web site is based on templates that its site administrator created to maintain a consistent layout, look, and feel for all course Web sites at Darby University. Although the design and layout have been determined, the content has not. Now that you have a connection to the Web site, you can add and edit the content needed to build the site. Macromedia Contribute 3 enables you to add and format text, much like a word processor. You can make changes to the font, size, and color, and you can also apply premade styles.

In this lesson, you add content to the home page of the sociology course Web site and the instructor curriculum vitae page of the Web site.

Inside the Design

The site administrator can make any number of styles available to allow you to create pages with a consistent look. In the Darby site, certain styles and colors have been chosen for the Sociology Department site so that it will be consistent with the look and feel of other department's course Web sites.

Adding and Editing Text

Since the layout, look, and feel of the sociology course Web site are controlled by the templates, you can focus on the content. The home page of the site needs a course title, welcome message, course description, list of prerequisites, and How to Get Started content. Contribute provides three easy ways to add text to a page:

■ Place the insertion point in the draft where you want to add the content and simply start typing.

■ Copy and paste content from another application into your Web page.

■ Drag and drop content from another application into your Web page.

In this Step-by-Step exercise, you work on a draft copy of the Web site home page. The template for this page contains several fixed editable areas for you to add content.

 ## Add and Edit Text

1. Using Contribute, browse to the Darby course **HOME** page, **index.htm**, if you are not already there.

2. Click the **Edit Page** button.

   The browser window transforms into the editor window.

3. Select the **Course# - Course Title** placeholder text and delete it.

4. Place the insertion point in the editable space and then key **Soc 1001 Introduction to Sociology**, as shown in Figure 2-1.

FIGURE 2-1
Adding a title to the course home page

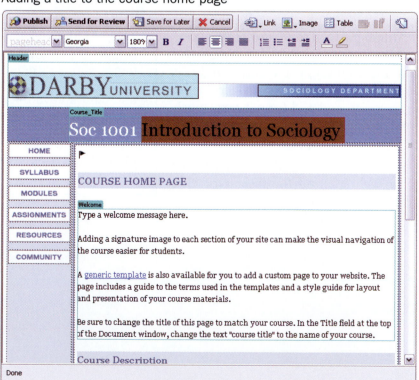

5. Use a text editor or word processor to open the file **welcome_message.txt**. This text file is in the **darby_documents** folder, the same folder that contains the connection key.

6. Click **Edit** on the menu bar, and click **Select All**. Then click **Edit**, and click **Copy** to save the text contents of the file to the Clipboard. Close the **welcome_message.txt**. document.

7. Return to the Darby Sociology **HOME** page in Contribute and select the placeholder text in the **Welcome** editable space and delete it.

8. In Contribute, click **Edit** on the menu bar, and click **Paste** to insert the contents of the Clipboard, as shown in Figure 2-2.

FIGURE 2-2
Pasting content into an editable region

The welcome message appears on the page.

9. Continue to populate the remaining areas of the home page by repeating the cut-and-paste action for the balance of the editable regions, as shown in Figure 2-3. Use the corresponding text file documents to add text content to the **Course_Description**, **Prerequisites**, and **How_to_Get_Started** editable regions.

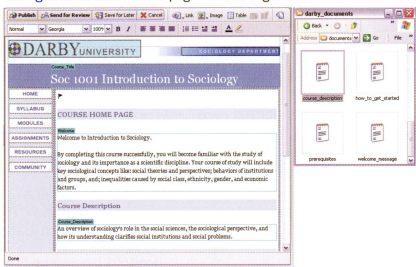

FIGURE 2-3
Adding content to the home page editable regions

10. When you have finished, click the **Publish** button.
A dialog box may appear confirming that the updates
have been published to your Web site. If so, click **OK**.
Your changes to the Darby course home page are
now live.

Hot Tip

Repetitive tasks like cutting and
pasting can be more quickly
accomplished by using keyboard
shortcuts instead of menu commands. You will want to remember the keyboard shortcuts for
cut and paste:
Cut: Ctrl + C (Windows) and
Command + C (Macintosh)
Paste: Ctrl + V (Windows) and
Command + V (Macintosh)

Inserting Contents of Word Documents

Next you build the instructor curriculum vitae
page of the sociology course Web site. Since the instruc-
tor information is contained in a Microsoft Word document, you can add this content without
having to re-create it. With Macromedia Contribute 3, you can easily add Microsoft Word documents to a site. There are two ways to add Word or Excel content to a site:

- Insert the contents of a Word document into a new or existing Web page (Windows only;
  recommended for smaller documents, under 300K when converted to HTML).

- Insert a link to a Word or Excel document on an existing Web page (recommended for
  larger documents, over 300K when converted to HTML).

Adding Word Content to a Page

The instructor for the sociology course has curriculum vitae she would like included at the sociology
course Web site. She has provided the vitae in a Word
document for you to put on the site. You can easily add
the contents of a Word or Excel document to an existing Web page. When you add content to a page,
Contribute converts the content to HTML and copies it

Note

The Insert Microsoft Office
Document feature is available
only in Windows.

to your Web page. You can then edit the content in Contribute. Any changes you make to the
original file on your computer will not appear on your Web site unless you add the file again.

Add Content from a Word Document

1. In Contribute, browse to the **INSTRUCTOR** curriculum vitae page (or use the bookmark that you created in Lesson 1).

2. Click the **Edit Page** button.

   The browser window transforms into the editor window.

3. Select the placeholder text in the **Course# - Course Title** editable space and delete it.

4. Place the insertion point in the editable space and key **Soc 1001 Introduction to Sociology**.

5. Select the placeholder text in the **Page_Contents** area and delete it.

6. Add the contents of **vitae_wright.doc** to the instructor curriculum vitae page.

If you are using a Windows machine, follow these instructions:

a. Click **Insert** on the menu bar, and click **Microsoft Office Document**.

b. In the Open dialog box, browse to the **darby_documents** folder, select the **vitae_wright.doc** Word document, and then click **Open**.

c. When the Insert Microsoft Office Document dialog box appears, as shown in Figure 2-4, select the option **Insert the Contents of the Document into this Page** and then click **OK**.

FIGURE 2-4
Insert Microsoft Office Document dialog box

If you are using a Macintosh, follow these instructions:

a. Launch Microsoft Word or other word processing program. Locate the **darby_documents** folder and open the file **vitae_wright.doc**.

b. Select all of the text in the document. Click the **Edit** menu and then click **Copy**.

c. Return to Contribute. In the **INSTRUCTOR** curriculum vitae page, place the insertion point in the editable region of the page. Then click the **Edit** menu and click **Paste**.

The content of the Marion Wright curriculum vitae appears on the draft instructor curriculum vitae Web page.

Next you refine the formatting of the curriculum vitae.

 **Format Content**

1. Select the instructor's name, **Marion Wright**, and click the **Indent** button in the editor toolbar as shown in Figure 2-5.

FIGURE 2-5
Indent button in the editor toolbar

indent

2. Repeat the indent step for the text that appears under the **Email**, **Address**, and **Telephone** headings.

3. Click the **Publish** button.

Your changes to the Darby course instructor curriculum vitae page, as shown in Figure 2-6, are now live.

FIGURE 2-6
The published instructor curriculum vitae page

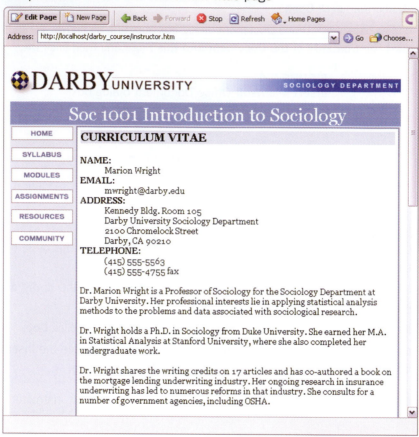

Editing Page Properties

Since the sociology course Web site is being built for the first time, the pages do not yet have titles. The title you give to the page appears in the browser title bar when a visitor views the page. Normally, the best time to add a Web page title is when you create a new Web page. However, in this Step-By-Step exercise, the page already exists, so you must supply it with the correct title.

Hot Tip

In Windows, another way to import Word content into your page is to drag a file from its current location to your Contribute draft where you want the content to appear. The Insert Microsoft Office Document dialog box will appear. Select the option Insert the Contents of the Document into This Page and then click OK.

Edit the Web Page Title

1. In Contribute, browse to the **INSTRUCTOR** curriculum vitae page (if you're not already there).

2. Click the **Edit Page** button.

The browser window transforms into the editor window.

3. Click the **Page Properties** button on the editor tool-bar, as shown in Figure 2-7.

Hot Tip

Proper page titles are an impor-tant part of a Web page design. Browsers display the title in the title bar at the top of the docu-ment window. It is a good prac-tice to provide a title for your Web page documents. If you don't, then the document file name will be used instead.

FIGURE 2-7
Page Properties button in the editor toolbar

page properties

4. In the Title text box of the Page Properties dialog box delete the filename then key in **Darby Sociology – Instructor Curriculum Vitae**, as shown in Figure 2-8, to match the other page titles in the Darby sociology course Web site.

FIGURE 2-8
Page Properties dialog box

5. Click **OK** to save the new page title.

6. Click the **Publish** button.

Your changes to the Darby course home page are now live.

Hot Tip

Using the page properties, you can specify layout and formatting properties, including the default font family and font size, back-ground color, margins, link styles, and many other aspects of page design. However, if you are editing a draft based on a template, then the page properties options that you can change may be limited.

ADDING IMAGES, TABLES AND LISTS

OBJECTIVES:

Upon completion of this lesson, you will be able to:

- Insert an image.
- Create alternative descriptive text for an image.
- Set image properties.
- Create a new table.
- Insert a table from a Microsoft Excel document.
- Set table properties.
- Create an unordered list.
- Set the bullet style for a list.

Estimated time: 1 hour

Introduction

Adding images, tables, and lists to the Darby sociology course Web site is an effective way to add visual interest and distinguish information on a Web page. In this lesson, you will add an image to the course home page, add a data table to the assignments page, and add a bulleted list to the resources page.

With Macromedia Contribute, you can add images to a Web page from several sources, including your computer, Web sites, e-mail, the Microsoft Internet Explorer Web browser, and other applications, and you can then edit the images. To learn more images and Web pages, see the Special Feature, "Image Types and Optimizing for the Web." Tables and lists are also easy to add and modify in the word processor-like environment of Contribute.

Adding Images

The sociology course home page needs an image to break up the text and to create interest on the page. The image needs to be aligned with the text so that it is easier to read the content. If your image is too large or needs enhancement, you can make these changes within Contribute. When you add an image to a page, it is

Note

Site administrators can enforce the image accessibility option so that a dialog box prompts you for an image description whenever you add an image.

good practice to also add descriptive text about the image so that the image is accessible to people with disabilities who use screen readers to access Web page content.

When you insert an image from your computer, Contribute copies the image to an images folder on your Web site when you publish the draft. You cannot edit the image in Contribute until you publish the draft. If the image is from your Web site, you can edit the image in Contribute before you publish.

There are three ways to add an image:

- Use the Insert menu or the Image button to add an image from your computer or Web site.

- Drag an image from another application (Windows only).

- Copy and paste an image from another application (Windows only).

> **Note**
>
> Images that you add to your page should be in a Web-ready format: JPG, GIF, or PNG (16). If necessary, you can use an image-editing tool, such as Macromedia Fireworks, to convert the image to a Web-ready format.

Tips & Techniques

Image Types and Optimizing for the Web

There are two main types of images that are used for publishing graphics and photographs to the web. These formats are GIF (Graphic Interchange Format) and JPEG (Joint Photographic Experts Group).

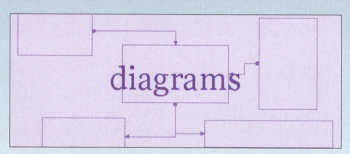

GIF images are generally used for line art, simple graphics, images with solid colors, or cartoon images. GIF images can contain transparent areas and can be used for animation. The disadvantage of GIF images is that they are restricted to 256 colors.

Images that feature solid areas of color with little blending are appropriate for a GIF

JPEG images are generally used for photographic images, images with many colors, or images with color tone changes or continuous color changes. JPEG images cannot contain transparent areas or be used for animation.

Photographic images or images with a large tonal range are best produced as a JPEG

(Continued . . .)

Tips & Techniques

Optimizing images for a Web page is the process of converting an image to a suitable format and making sure the file size is as small as possible. Small image file sizes help decrease the download time for a Web page. The goal of optimizing images for the Web is to strike a balance between finding the smallest file size that retains an acceptable level of quality.

If you have an image editing program, such as Macromedia Fireworks, installed on your machine, you can launch it directly from within Contribute. Fireworks allows you to fine-tune the settings of image files and preview the results of various optimization settings side-by-side. Fireworks provides several methods for creating high quality GIF and JPEG images with the smallest file size. The different options available vary based on image type. Because JPEG images have more color gradation, they require more fine tuning and cannot be reduced in size as much as GIF images.

Export Preview dialog box with optimizing options for a JPEG image

Add an Image

1. In Contribute, browse to the Darby sociology **HOME** page.

2. Click **Edit Page**.

3. Place the insertion point on the page just before the word "Welcome" in the first paragraph.

4. Click the **Image** menu on the toolbar and then click the **From My Computer** option, as shown in Figure 3-1.

FIGURE 3-1
Selecting From My Computer from the Image menu

5. Browse to the **darby_documents** folder, select the **city.jpg** image file, and then click **Select** (Windows) or **Choose** (Macintosh) to place the image on the draft page.

The image appears on the Darby course home page.

You will notice that the image is quite large and needs to be resized and balanced on the page. This can be accomplished using Image Properties. The Images Properties dialog box also allows you to add descriptive alternate text for users with disabilities.

6. Select the image on the page and click the **Image Properties** button on the toolbar, as shown in Figure 3-2.

FIGURE 3-2
Image Properties button in the toolbar.

The Image Properties dialog box opens.

7. To reset the size of the image, change the the Display Width setting to **250**. Ensure that the **Constrain Proportions** check box is selected to maintain the proper aspect ratio.

8. Click the **Alignment** menu and then click **Right**, as shown in Figure 3-3.

FIGURE 3-3
Image Properties dialog box

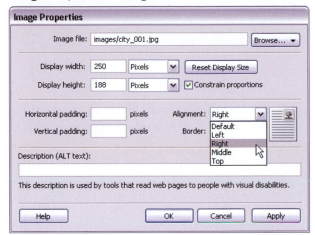

Contribute aligns the image in relation to surrounding elements, such as text.

9. In the Description (ALT text) field, key **City skyline** to add descriptive text to the image.

10. Click **OK**.

Contribute applies your settings to the image as shown in Figure 3-4.

Inside the Design

Aligning images with respect to text helps break up the text so that the eye can easily read the shorter lines. In the sociology course Web site, you right align the image to enhance visual balance on the page.

FIGURE 3-4
The course home page with image inserted with alternative text available

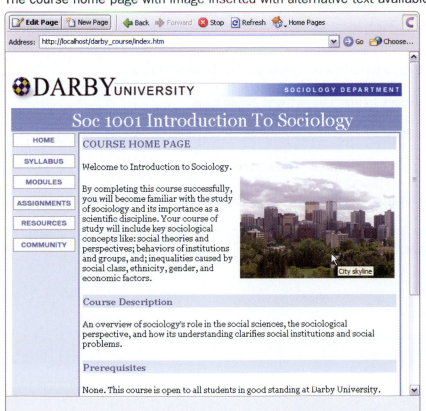

11. Click the **Publish** button.

Your changes to the Darby course home page are now live.

Using Tables

The assignments page of the sociology course Web site needs to show the semester's assignments organized so that students can clearly see when certain materials are due. You can use a table to organize the assignments. In Contribute, you can create tables in multiple ways, either by inserting a table as you would do in Microsoft Word, or by importing a spreadsheet. Once you have the table in the Web site, you can add text and images to table cells the same way that you add text and images to a page, and you can easily modify the table's appearance and structure.

Inserting a Table on a Page

When editing a page, you can insert a table anywhere in a page. You can quickly insert a standard table with three rows and three columns, or you can modify options to insert a custom table.

Since the assignments for the sociology course have already been prepared in a spreadsheet, you can easily add this content to the page. When you insert a table, it's a good idea to set the header property for a row or column if you use that row or column to provide labels for the information in the table. A header makes the table more accessible to people with visual impairments, since screen readers recognize that headers contain labels. (Note that you must set a header row or column to provide such accessibility. It is not sufficient to use bold or centered text entries.)

For this Step-By-Step exercise, you create a data table to summarize the Darby sociology course assignments. Then you modify the table properties to make the table more appealing and more accessible to users with disabilities.

 **Insert a Table**

1. In Contribute, browse to the Darby course **ASSIGNMENTS** page.

This is the page to which you will add a data table.

2. Click **Edit Page**.

3. Select the placeholder text in the **Course# - Course Title** editable space and delete it.

4. Place the insertion point in the editable space and then key **Soc 1001 Introduction to Sociology**.

5. Select the first sentence on the page, which reads **Add a table here to summarize the assignments for the year**, and delete this text.

6. Click the **Insert Table** button on the editor toolbar as shown in Figure 3-5.

FIGURE 3-5
Insert Table button

Insert table

The Insert Table dialog box opens as shown in Figure 3-6.

FIGURE 3-6
Insert Table dialog box

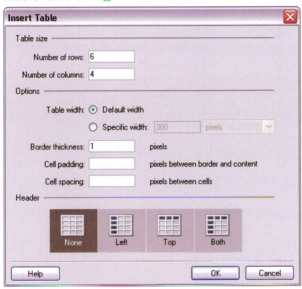

7. In the Number of Rows text field, enter **6**, and in the Number of Columns text field, enter **4**. Click **OK** to insert the table into the page.

8. In the table, key the following information:

NUMBER	ASSIGNMENT	DUE DATE	% GRADE
1	Midterm Exam: Module 1–6	March 1,2006	20%
2	Group Case Study	March 15,2006	20%
3	Term Paper	April 1, 2006	20%
4	Final Exam: Module 7–12	April 15, 2006	20%
5	Class Participation	Ongoing	20%

Now you modify the table properties by centering and applying padding and spacing.

Modify Table Properties

1. To modify the alignment of the table, click the table to select it.

Selection handles appear on the selected table's lower and right edges as shown in Figure 3-7.

FIGURE 3-7
Selected table with selection handles

Number	Assignment	Due Date	% Grade
1	Midterm Exam: Module 1-6	March 1,2006	20%
2	Group Case Study	March 15,2006	20%
3	Term Paper	April 1, 2006	20%
4	Final Exam: Module 7-12	April 15, 2006	20%
5	Class Participation	Ongoing	20%

2. Click **Table** on the menu bar, and then click **Table Properties**.

The Table Properties dialog box appears with the Table tab open.

3. Click the **Table Alignment** menu and then click **Center**, as shown in Figure 3-8.

FIGURE 3-8
Table Properties dialog box with the Table tab open

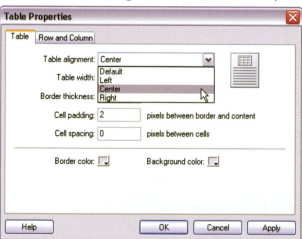

4. For Cell Padding, key **2** pixels.

5. For Cell Spacing, key **0** pixels.

6. Click **OK** to apply these changes

Finally, you make the table accessible to a screen reader by adding column headers to the table.

Make a Table Accessible

1. To create an accessible header row for the data table, select the topmost row of the table.

2. Click **Table** on the menu bar, and click **Table Cell Properties**.

The Table Properties dialog box appears with the Row tab open, as shown in Figure 3-9.

FIGURE 3-9
Table Properties dialog box with the Row tab open and the Header Row option selected

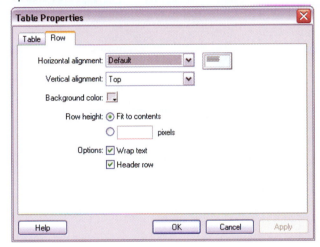

3. Select the **Header Row** option check box to make the top row of the table a header row.

4. Click **OK**.

As shown in Figure 3-10, the top row of the table now contains bold, center-aligned header text.

FIGURE 3-10
Bold, center-aligned header row

Assignments

Number	Assignment	Due Date	% Grade
1	Midterm Exam: Module 1-6	March 1,2006	20%
2	Group Case Study	March 15,2006	20%
3	Term Paper	April 1, 2006	20%
4	Final Exam: Module 7-12	April 15, 2006	20%
5	Class Participation	Ongoing	20%

5. Click the **Publish** button.

Your changes to the Darby course assignments page, as shown in Figure 3-11, are now live.

FIGURE 3-11
The completed assignments page

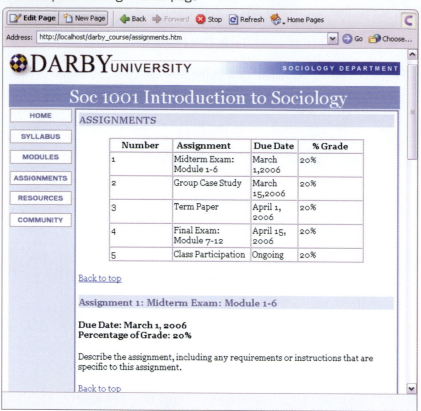

Creating Lists

The resources page of the Web site needs a bibliography of the books students can use to help them with the course. You will create a list to indicate the available resources. You can create numbered and bulleted lists with Contribute. Numbered lists are used for information that needs to be in order, such as a list of steps. Bulleted lists are used for information that does not need to be in any certain order.

Creating Bulleted Lists

With Contribute, you can apply bullets to a list as it is created, or add bullets to an existing list.

Create a Bulleted List

1. In Contribute, browse to the Darby course **RESOURCES** page.

   This is the page to which you will add a numbered list.

2. Click **Edit Page**.

3. Select the placeholder text in the **Course# - Course Title** editable space and delete it.

4. Place the insertion point in the editable space and key **Soc 1001 Introduction to Sociology**.

5. Select the first sentence in the Bibliography editable region, which reads **Use this area to provide a bibliography for the course**, and delete this text.

6. Click the **Bulleted List** button in the editor toolbar, as shown in Figure 3-12.

FIGURE 3-12
Bulleted List button in the editor toolbar

7. Key the following information to create your first bibliography item: **Andersen, Margaret L. Sociology: The Essentials. 2nd Ed. Boston: Wadsworth Thomson Learning, 2002.** Then press **Enter** (Windows) or **Return** (Macintosh) to go to the next line.

8. To create the second item, key **Outline of Lecture Notes: Introduction to Sociology. Copyright 2003 by Marion Wright, Ph.D. Printed copies available in campus bookstore.** Press **Enter** (Windows) or **Return** (Macintosh) to go to the next line.

9. To create the third item, key **Thompson, W.E. Society in Focus: Introduction to Sociology. 3rd Ed. New York: Addison, Wesley, Longman, 1999.**

10. Click the **Publish** button.

Your changes to the Darby course resources page, as shown in Figure 3-13, are now live.

FIGURE 3-13
Published bulleted list in the resources page

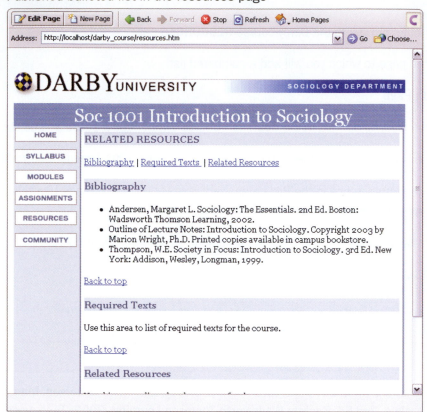

SUMMARY

You have successfully made edits and published your changes to the sociology course Web site.

In this project, you learned to use Contribute to modify Web sites without having to know HTML. You gained the fundamental skills and knowledge you need to connect to a site, add site bookmarks, browse to and edit pages, insert and edit images, organize content in data tables, and create lists.

These skills provide the necessary foundation for advanced Contribute tasks. The next project in this unit builds on what you have learned, reinforcing these skills and introducing more challenging ones. Tasks you will accomplish include adding links to pages, creating new pages and inserting content, and reviewing and publishing pages in your site.

ON YOUR OWN – COURSE WEB SITE

ACTIVITY 1: MODIFY TEXT ON A PAGE

You learned how to change existing text on a Web page using techniques similar to those you use in word processing. Apply the same techniques to update the course title and course information areas of the syllabus page.

To review techniques for modifying text on a page, see Lesson 2.

1. Browse to the **SYLLABUS** page of the sociology course Web site and switch to editing mode.

2. Key the following text, as shown in Figure 1:
    A. Course title:
        Soc 1001 Introduction to Sociology
    B. Course information:
        1001 - Introduction to Sociology
        Fall 2006
        Murphren Hall 337
        M W F 7:30–8:40
    C. Instructor information:
        Instructor's Name and link to CV: **Marion Wright**
        Office address: **Kennedy Bldg. Room 101**
        Office hours: **1:00–3:00 p.m., Monday through Friday or by appointment**
        Phone: **(415) 555-5563**
        Fax: **(415) 555-4755**
        E-mail: **mwright@darby.edu**

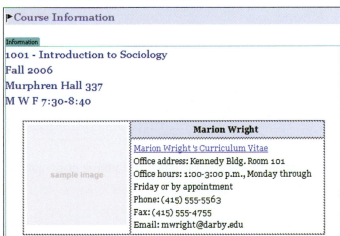

FIGURE 1
The course information area filled in

D. Teaching assistant information:
    T/A's Name: **Kelva Grant**
    Office address: **Kennedy Bldg. Room 304**
    Office hours: **3:30–4:30 Mon–Fri or by appt.**
    Phone: **(415) 555-5571**

Fax: (415) 555-4758
E-mail: **kgrant@darby.edu**

3. Publish the page.

ACTIVITY 2: ADD AN IMAGE TO A PAGE

You learned how to add an image to a page. Often, when adding images to a Web page, you may need to resize or enhance an image so that it is fits perfectly. Apply the techniques you learned to insert an image on the **SYLLABUS** page. Use the toolbar in the Contribute editor to add this image, add alternative text, and modify the image's properties.

To review techniques for modifying text on a page, see Lesson 3.

1. Browse to the **SYLLABUS** page of the sociology course Web site and switch to editing mode.

2. In the instructor information table, select the sample image and delete it. Insert the **marion_wright.jpg** image from the **darby_documents** folder included in the data files.

3. Open the image properties and make the following changes, as shown in Figure 2:
   A. Change the image size so that the image is **150 pixels** wide.
   B. Key **Portrait of Marion Wright** as the alternative text for the image (in the Description text box).

FIGURE 2
The Image Properties dialog box

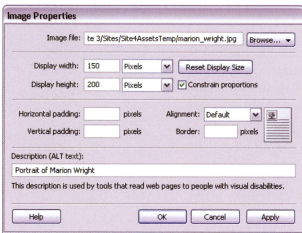

C. Use the Image properties toolbar to enhance the image contrast by **+5**.

The image now appears next to the instructor information, as shown in Figure 3.

4. Publish the page.

ACTIVITY 3: INSERT MICROSOFT WORD CONTENT

You learned how to insert the contents of a Word document onto a page using two methods:

- Copy and paste
- Insert Microsoft Office Document (Windows only)

Apply these techniques to insert Microsoft Word content for the Prerequisites and Course Structure of the syllabus page.

To review techniques for modifying text on a page, see Lesson 2.

> **Note** ☑
>
> The Insert Microsoft Office Document feature is available only in Windows. Mac users should use the copy-and-paste method to import Word content into the editable areas.

Copy and Paste Method

1. Browse to the **SYLLABUS** page of the sociology course Web site and switch to editing mode.

2. Browse to and open the **prerequisites** Microsoft Word document in the **darby_documents** folder.

3. Copy and then paste the contents of the text file into the **Prerequisites** editable area on the page.

4. Adjust fonts and font sizes to match the rest of the text on the page.

5. Publish the page.

Insert Microsoft Office Document Method

1. Browse to the **SYLLABUS** page of the sociology course Web site and switch to editing mode.

2. Delete the existing text in the Course Structure section of the page, then select **Insert > Microsoft Office Document**. Browse to the **course_structure** Microsoft Word document in the **darby_documents** folder, and insert the contents in the Course Structure section of the page (see Figure 4). For Macintosh, copy and paste the course_structure content to the appropriate location on the page.

FIGURE 4
The Insert Microsoft Office Document dialog box

3. Adjust fonts and sizes to match the rest of the text on the page.

4. Publish the page.

ACTIVITY 4: CREATE A BULLETED LIST

You learned to build both numbered and bulleted lists. Apply the techniques you learned to create a bulleted list of objectives on the syllabus page.

To review techniques for modifying text on a page, see Lesson 3.

1. Browse to the **SYLLABUS** page of the sociology course Web site and switch to editing mode.

2. Key the following text into the Course Objectives section of the page, adding bullets where needed, as shown in Figure 5:

   By completing this course successfully, you will:
   - **Become familiar with the study of sociology and its importance as a scientific discipline**
   - **Become familiar with a variety of social theories and perspectives**
   - **Recognize the qualities of a culture that distinguish it from other cultures**
   - **Identify factors which influence social behaviors of institutions and groups**
   - **Identify issues related to inequalities caused by social class, ethnicity, gender, and economic factors**
   - **Apply reasonable criteria for the acceptability of historical evidence and social research**

FIGURE 5
The completed course objectives bulleted list

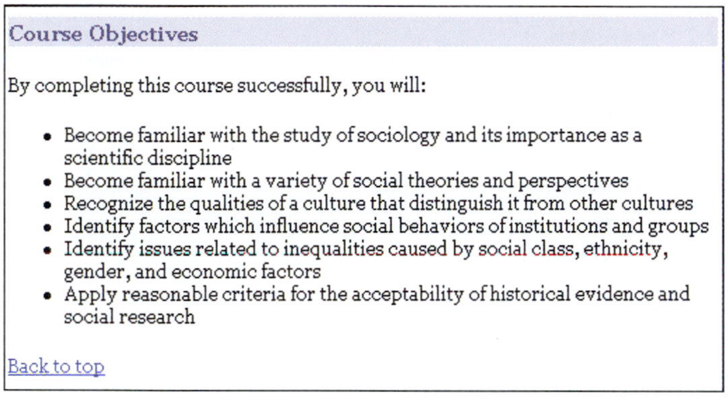

3. Publish the page.

ACTIVITY 5: INSERT A DATA TABLE

You learned how to use data tables to effectively organize information on a page. Apply the techniques you learned to insert an evaluation table on the syllabus page, modify the table, and make the table accessible.

To review techniques for modifying text on a page, see Lesson 3.

1. Browse to the **SYLLABUS** page of the sociology course Web site and switch to editing mode.

2. Insert a table in the Evaluation area with the settings shown in Figure 6:
   A. Number of Rows: **6**
   B. Number of Columns: **4**
   C. Border Thickness: **1**
   D. Cell Padding: **2**
   E. Cell Spacing: **0**
   F. Header: **Top**

FIGURE 6
The Insert Table dialog box

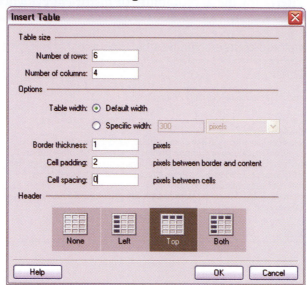

3. Key the following information in the table that you created:

NUMBER	ASSIGNMENT	DUE DATE	% GRADE
1	Midterm Exam: Module 1–6	March 1, 2006	20%
2	Group Case Study	March 15, 2006	20%
3	Term Paper	April 1, 2006	20%
4	Final Exam: Module 7–12	April 15, 2006	20%
5	Class Participation	Ongoing	20%

4. Center-align the table in the section. Change the table background color to light gray (#CCCCCC), as shown in Figure 7.

FIGURE 7
Select the background color

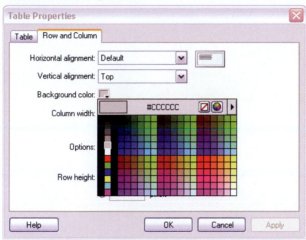

FIGURE 7
Select the background color

5. Publish the page.

ELECTRONIC PORTFOLIOS

GOALS

- Link content to pages inside and outside the site.
- Build upon a Web site by adding new pages.
- Review and publish content.

TECHNICAL SKILLS

- Create links to existing pages.
- Create e-mail links.
- Create links to outside pages.
- Copy existing pages to create new pages.
- Create new pages from templates.
- Produce and insert FlashPaper documents.
- Send pages for review.
- Track drafts with the Draft Console.

Summary

Portfolios are often used to communicate accomplishments, works in progress, or personal history. Many people use portfolios to showcase their previous work when applying for a job. Traditionally, a portfolio is a large book or leather case containing work samples. With the Internet, portfolios can be electronic, allowing them to be shared easily and quickly with anyone in the world.

The Assignment

In this project, you help a preservice teacher, Anastasia Hernandez, edit and add new content to an electronic portfolio Web site. The site is her program portfolio, and she is completing it after completing her teacher-education program. This electronic portfolio was built using templates that will maintain a consistent look, feel, and navigation across the site.

Your task will be to update the pages of the electronic portfolio Web site by:

- Creating links
- Creating new pages
- Controlling your drafts, reviewed pages, and published pages

Figure 1 shows the home page for the electronic portfolio site for which you will be updating content.

FIGURE 1
Anastasia Hernandez electronic portfolio home page

The flowchart in Figure 2 shows the layout and page relationships of the electronic portfolio site you will be working on. Shaded blocks indicate those Web pages that you will be updating in this project.

FIGURE 2
Anastasia Hernandez electronic portfolio site map

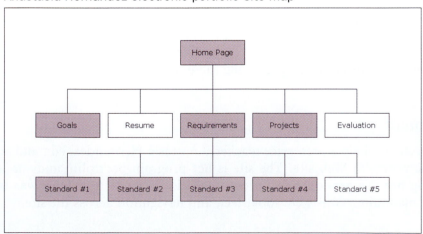

ADDING LINKS

OBJECTIVES

Upon completion of this lesson, you will be able to:

- Create a link to a page within the electronic portfolio Web site.

- Create a link to a page on an external Web site.

- Add an e-mail link.

Estimated Time: 1 hour, 30 minutes

Introduction

A hyperlink, often called a link, connects one Web page to another Web page, a file, an e-mail address, or information within a Web page. Links typically are a different color than the surrounding text and may be underlined. When a visitor to your Web site clicks a link, the browser takes the visitor to another Web page within your site, downloads a file, takes the visitor to a page on another Web site, or starts the visitor's e-mail application. The portfolio for Anastasia has pages documenting her achievements and highlighting what she has learned. You will be helping her complete some of the content for her site, first by using Contribute to link pages that include standards she has met and sample work she has completed.

In this lesson, you create the following links:

- A link from a page in the portfolio site to a new page created for the portfolio site that is not yet linked

- A link to a page on another Web site

- A link to an e-mail address

- Links within a page

- A link to a file on your computer

Creating a Link to a Page Within Your Site

The portfolio site has a Requirements page that needs to contain the list of standards Anastasia achieved during her program. Each standard listed should link to its own page, which contains information documenting the way she has achieved the standard.

You can create a link from a page to a current draft or to a recently published page. In the Insert Link dialog box, Contribute provides a complete list of current drafts and stores a list of the last 10 pages you published. To create a link, you need to provide Contribute with a draft or recently published page from which to select. You then proceed with creating the link to the published page. Prior to creating this link, you must connect to the site.

> **Note**
>
> When you add a link in a draft, the link is not live until you publish the draft. Before you publish a draft with a link, you can use the *Preview in Browser* feature to test the link.

Set Up a Connection to the Portfolio Site

1. Locate the connection key placed on your computer by browsing to the documents folder located in the **eportfolio_documents** folder.

   For Windows, the network path is **C:\Inetpub\www-root\ePortfolio\ePortfolio_documents**.

   Figure 1-1 shows the connection key icon.

> **Note**
>
> The connection key in the ePortfolio_documents folder is Windows compatible only. For Macintosh machines, your instructor will provide an alternate connetion key. The network path for Macintosh is Library: WebServer:Documents: ePortfolio.

FIGURE 1-1
Connection key icon

A.Hernandez-Program
Portfolio Administrator

2. Double-click the connection key. Then enter your name, your e-mail address, and the password for the connection key. (The password for this connection key is **ConnKey2**.)

3. Click **OK**.

> **Important**
>
> Check with your site administrator or instructor to verify the location of the key.

The Web site's home page appears in the Contribute browser.

Create a Link to a Recently Published Page Within Your Site

1. Locate the page to which you will create a link by keying the following address in the Contribute browser:

For Windows, key **http://localhost/ePortfolio/standard_1.htm** and press **Enter**.

For a Macintosh, key **http://localhost/ePortfolio/standard_1.htm** and press **Return**.

2. Click the **Edit Page** button.

The browser window transforms into the editor window.

3. Select the text **Requirement Title** in the Standard_Number editable area and delete this text.

4. In the Standard_Number editable area, key **1. Mastery of Subject Matter**.

5. Click the **Publish** button on the editor toolbar.

6. Use the Contribute browser to navigate to the **requirements.htm** page.

This is the page on which you will add the link to the **Standard 1** page.

7. Click the **Edit Page** button.

The browser window transforms into the editor window.

8. Select the **Mastery of Subject Matter** text in the draft to create the link as shown in Figure 1-2.

FIGURE 1-2
Select text to create the link

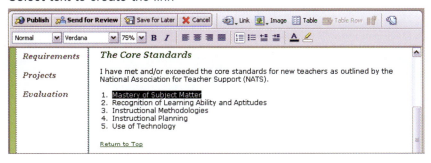

9. Click the **Link** button on the editor toolbar and then click the **Drafts and Recent Pages** option, as shown in Figure 1-3.

FIGURE 1-3
Link button with Drafts and Recent Pages option selected

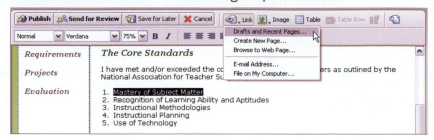

The Insert Link dialog box appears.

10. In the **Select a Page to Link To** section, select the **Standard 1** Web page from the list of drafts and recently published pages.

The Insert Link dialog box displays a preview of the page you selected, as shown in Figure 1-4.

FIGURE 1-4
Insert Link dialog box open to the Drafts and Recent Pages tab with the Standard 1 page selected

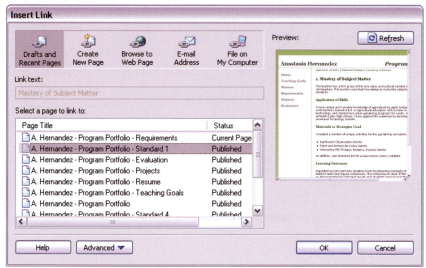

11. Click **OK**.

The link appears in your draft.

12. Click the **Publish** button.

Your changes to the electronic portfolio Requirements page are now available, as shown in Figure 1-5.

FIGURE 1-5
The Requirements page with an active link to the Standard 1 page

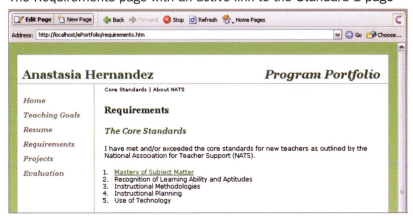

Creating a Link to an External Web Page

Anastasia Hernandez would like to include a link to Macromedia, the software company that creates the program that she used to build her electronic portfolio Web site. You can link to another Web page, either on the same site or on another site.

 ## Create a Link to a Page on Another Web Site

1. Use the Contribute browser to navigate to the **teaching_goals.htm** page.

2. Click the **Edit Page** button.

The browser window transforms into the editor window.

3. In the draft, under the Skills heading, select the text **Incorporate technology into the curriculum** to create the link.

4. Click the **Link** button on the editor toolbar and then click the **Browse to Web Page** option. For Macintosh, the Insert Link tabs in the dialog box are labelled Drafts, New Page, Browse, E-mail and File.; clcik the Browse option.

The Insert Link dialog box opens, as shown in Figure 1-6, with the Browse to Web Page tab selected.

FIGURE 1-6
Insert Link dialog box with the Browse to Web Page tab selected

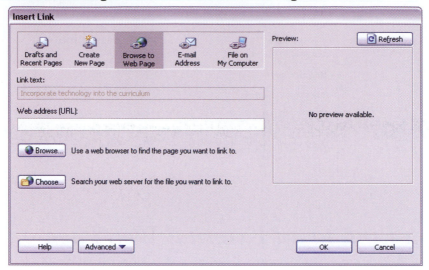

5. In the **Web address (URL)** text field, key **http://www.macromedia.com/resources/education/k12/** to create the link.

6. In the **Insert Link** dialog box, click the **Advanced** tab, if the tab is not already open, to view more linking options. For Macintosh, look for Advanced Options to view more linking options. Click the **Target Frame** menu and then click **New Window**, as shown in Figure 1-7, to display the linked page in a new window.

> **Note**
>
> You can also use the *Browse* button to find the page you want to link, or you can copy the Web address from another source and paste it in the text box. When you select a page using these options, a preview appears in the dialog box so that you can confirm that this is the page you want to link to.

FIGURE 1-7
Insert Link dialog box with Target frame, New Window option selected

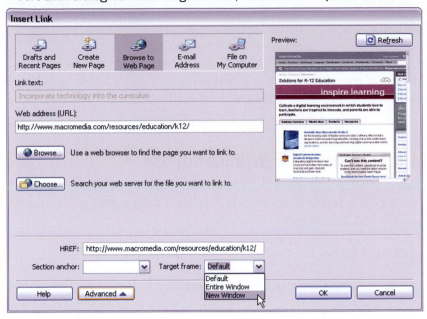

7. Click **OK**.

Contribute adds the link to your draft.

8. Click the **Publish** button.

Your changes to the Teaching Goals page are now available, as shown in Figure 1-8.

FIGURE 1-8
The Teaching Goals page with an active link to an external Web site

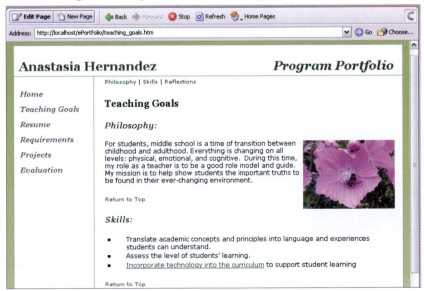

Creating an E-Mail Link

T he portfolio needs a link to Anastasia's e-mail address. With Contribute, you can easily add a link to an e-mail address. When a Web site visitor clicks the link, the browser begins a new message, with the e-mail address you specified, in the visitor's default e-mail application.

Note

You can also use the *Browse to Web Page* option to create a link to a page on your site that is neither a draft nor a recently published page.

 Create a Link to an E-Mail Address

1. Use the Contribute browser to navigate to Anastasia's Program Portfolio home page, **index.htm**, where you will insert the e-mail link.

2. Click the **Edit Page** button.

 The browser window transforms into the editor window.

3. In the draft page, in the Contact information, select the text **ahernandez@darby.edu** to create the e-mail link.

4. Click the **Link** button on the editor toolbar and then click the **E-mail address** option.

 The Insert Link dialog box opens, as shown in Figure 1-9, with the E-mail address tab selected.

FIGURE 1-9
Insert Link dialog box with the E-mail address tab selected

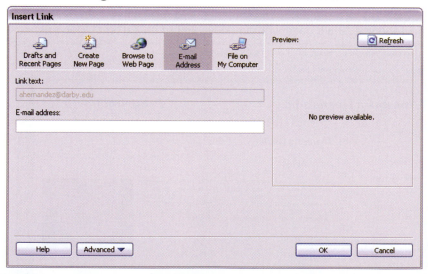

5. Enter Anastasia's e-mail address in the E-mail address text box by keying **ahernandez@darby.edu**.

6. Click **OK**.

 Contribute adds the link to the page.

7. Click the **Publish** button.

Your changes to the home page are now available, as shown in Figure 1-10.

FIGURE 1-10
The home page with an active e-mail link

Contact:	
Address:	456 Ocean View Road, Apt 203 Darby, CA 99999
Phone:	(555) 555-8956 home (555) 555-6512 mobile
Email:	ahernandez@darby.edu

Return to Top

Creating an Anchor Link

The Requirements page of the portfolio has the potential to become a long page that will require quite a bit of scrolling. To make this page easier for site visitors to access, you will add anchor links to the top of the page so that visitors can easily jump to main content areas.

Anchor links can be an effective way to provide navigation within long Web pages. When a Web site visitor clicks an anchor link, typically placed at the top of the page, the visitor is directed to the linked anchor point within that same page.

Create an Anchor Link Within a Page

1. Use the Contribute browser to navigate to the **requirements.htm** page, where you will insert the anchor link.

2. Click the **Edit Page** button.

The browser window transforms into the editor window.

3. Place the insertion point in the Secondary_Navigation editable area and key the text **Core Standards | About NATS** to echo the main headings on the page.

4. In the Requirements_Content editable area, place the insertion point before the heading The Core Standards. Click **Insert** on the menu bar and then click **Section Anchor.**

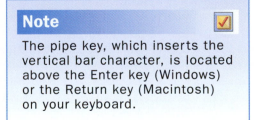

Note ✅

The pipe key, which inserts the vertical bar character, is located above the Enter key (Windows) or the Return key (Macintosh) on your keyboard.

The Section Anchor dialog box opens, as shown in Figure 1-11.

FIGURE 1-11
Section Anchor link dialog box

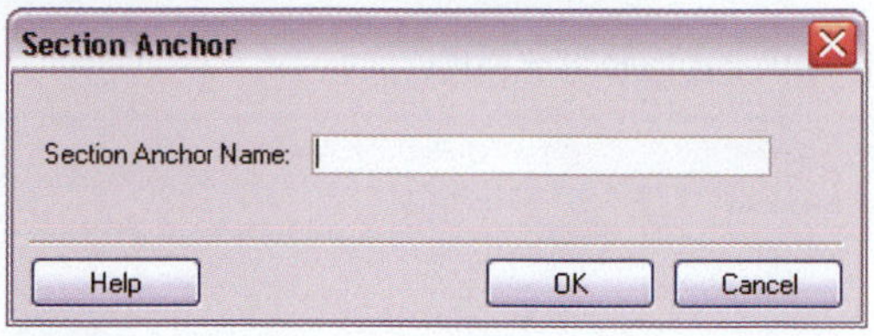

Section Anchor	☒
Section Anchor Name:	
Help	OK Cancel

5. In the **Section Anchor Name** text box, key **standards** and then click **OK**.

   Contribute adds the anchor to the page.

6. Insert another anchor in the page by placing the insertion point before the heading About NATS. Click **Insert** on the menu bar and then click **Section Anchor.**

7. In the **Section Anchor Name** text box, key **about** and then click **OK**.

   Contribute adds the anchor to the page.

8. Return to the Secondary_Navigation editable area and select the text **Core Standards**.

9. Click the **Link** button and then click the **Browse to Web Page** option**.**

   The Insert Link dialog box opens.

10. Click the **Browse** button.

The Browse to Link dialog box opens. This mini-browser allows you to browse to the page you want to link to, without having to key the URL. The browser opens to the site to which you have an active connection, as shown in Figure 1-12.

FIGURE 1-12
Browse to Link mini-browser

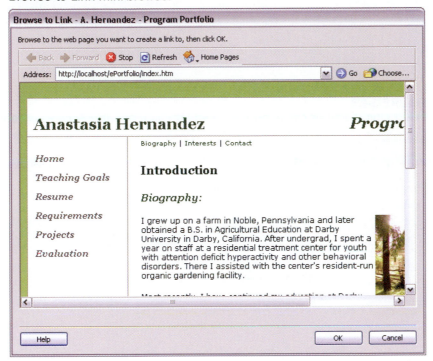

11. Use the Browse to Link dialog box to navigate to the **requirements.htm** page. Then click **OK**.

12. Contribute returns to the Insert Link dialog box. Click the **Advanced** tab, if the tab is not already open, to view more linking options. Click the **Section Anchor** menu and then click **standards**, as shown in Figure 1-13.

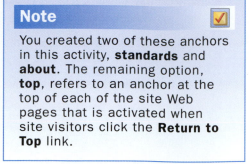

Note ✅

You created two of these anchors in this activity, **standards** and **about**. The remaining option, **top**, refers to an anchor at the top of each of the site Web pages that is activated when site visitors click the **Return to Top** link.

FIGURE 1-13
Insert Link dialog box with the Advanced tab open and the Section anchor menu open

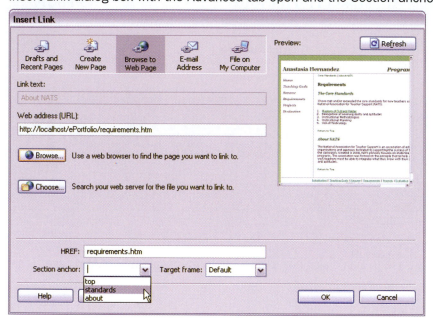

13. Click **OK**.

Contribute adds the link to the page.

14. To insert the other link, return to the **the Secondary_Navigation** editable area and select the text **About NATS**.

15. Click the **Link** button and then click **Browse to Web Page.**

The Insert Link dialog box opens.

16. Click the **Browse** button.

The Browse to Link dialog box opens.

17. Browse to the **requirements.htm** page and click **OK**.

18. In the **Insert Link** dialog box, on the **Advanced** tab, click the **Section Anchor** menu and then click **about**. Click **OK**.

Contribute adds the link to the page.

19. Click **Publish.**

Your changes to the Requirements page are now live.

Linking to a File on Your Computer

To show an example of her work, Anastasia wants to include her sample assessment rubric. While sharing this rubric, she wants to leave it open for her changes, so she needs it in a format that will allow her to use Contribute to update it, as well as allow site visitors to access the original document.

You can also link to files currently saved on your computer, such as Microsoft Word files or PDF documents. When you publish the page with the link, Contribute copies the file to the site and then links to that copy—not to the file on your computer. If you make any changes to the original file on your machine, you will need to upload the file again to the Web server so site visitors can see the changes. (The files on the Web site and the files on your computer are in separate locations.) You will create a link on the Project page to the Microsoft Word file that contains the assessment rubric.

> **Note**
>
> When you publish the page with the link to a file, Contribute creates a special documents folder, copies the document to the folder, and then links to that copy (not to the original file on your computer).

 ## Create a Link to a File on Your Computer

1. Use the Contribute browser to navigate to the **projects.htm** page, where you will insert the link to a document file.

2. Click the **Edit Page** button.

The browser window transforms into the editor window.

3. In the second paragraph beneath the heading Sample Lesson Plan and Rubric, select the text **assessment rubric** to create the link.

4. Click the **Link** button on the editor toolbar and then click the **File on My Computer** option.

The Insert Link dialog box opens, as shown in Figure 1-14, with the File on My Computer tab selected.

FIGURE 1-14
Insert Link dialog box with the File on My Computer tab selected

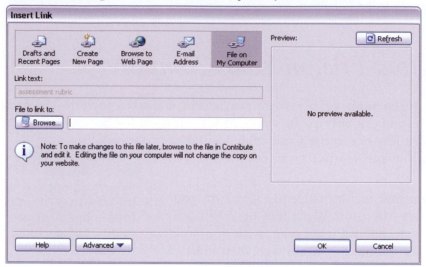

5. In the **File to Link To** section, click the **Browse** button and browse to **assessment_rubric.doc** in the **ePortfolio_documents** folder on your machine. Then click the **Select** (Windows) or **Choose** (Macintosh) button to close the Find File dialog box.

6. In the **Insert Link** dialog box, click **OK**. Contribute may warn you that if you need to make changes to this file later you should browse to the file in Contribute and edit it. Editing the file on my computer would not change the copy on the website. Click **OK** to continue.

A link to the new uploaded assessment rubric document appears in your draft.

7. Click the **Publish** button.

Your changes to the Project page are now available.

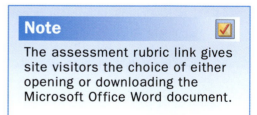

Note

The assessment rubric link gives site visitors the choice of either opening or downloading the Microsoft Office Word document.

CREATING NEW PAGES

OBJECTIVES

Upon completion of this lesson, you will be able to:

- Create a new page by copying an existing page.
- Create a new page from a template.
- Create a new page by publishing a page as a new page.
- Produce and insert a FlashPaper document.

Estimated Time: 1 hour, 30 minutes

Introduction

New pages can be added to a portfolio to update it with new work and to include additional evidence that highlights achievement. To add pages to a site using Macromedia Contribute 3, you can create a copy of a page, create a blank page, create a copy of your current page, or create a page based on a template. After you create a page, you can change its properties, and you can add keywords and a description so that visitors can find the page with a search engine.

The best way to create a new page is to create the page while also adding a link to it from another page. This ensures that the new page will be linked to an existing page. If you create a page without linking it first, you must remember to link it from another page so that site visitors can navigate to it. Contribute makes the new page live on the site when you publish it.

In this lesson, you create new pages for the Requirements section of the portfolio using four methods: copying an existing page, creating a new page from a template, publishing a page as a new page, and creating a blank page on which you insert a FlashPaper document—a document type typically much smaller than other document types and which can be displayed on a Web page.

Creating a New Page by Copying an Existing Page

The portfolio contains a Requirements page on which you already linked an existing page documenting the first standard achieved by Anastasia. The other pages for the standards have not yet been created. When you are producing pages that are similar in structure, it is easy to make new pages by copying and editing an existing page. But remember that you need to link to the new page afterwards; otherwise, visitors to your site will not be able to find the page. You create the second standard page using a copy of the first standard page.

Create a New Page and a Link

1. Browse to the **standard_1.htm** page and click the **New Page** button on the browser toolbar.

   The New Page dialog box opens

2. In the **Create New Page For** section, select the **Copy of Current Page** option to create a new page identical to the current page.

   A preview and a description appear in the dialog box, as shown in Figure 2-1.

FIGURE 2-1
New Page dialog box with the Copy of Current Page option selected

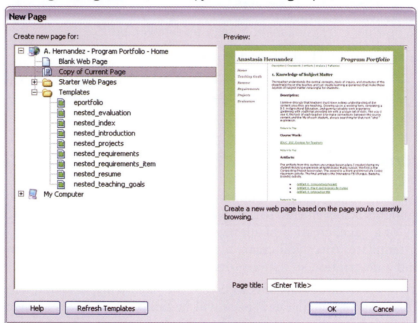

3. In the **Page title** text box, enter **A. Hernandez - Program Portfolio - Standard 2** and then click **OK**.

   Contribute opens the new page in the Contribute editor.

4. In the Standard_Number editable text field, remove the existing text and key **2. Recognition of Learning Ability and Aptitudes**.

   You now need to remove the existing text for Standard 1 and replace it with the text for Standard 2.

5. Select all of the text contained in the Standard_Item_Content editable area and delete it.

6. Add the contents of **standard_2.doc** to the Standard 2 page.

If you are using Windows, follow these instructions:

a. Click **Insert** on the menu bar and then click **Microsoft Office Document**.

b. In the Open dialog box, browse to the **ePortfolio_documents** folder, select the **standard_2.doc** Word document, and then click **Open**.

c. When the **Insert Microsoft Office Document** dialog box appears, select the **Insert the Contents of the Document into This Page** option, as shown in Figure 2-2. Then click **OK**.

FIGURE 2-2
Insert Microsoft Office Document dialog box

If you are using a Macintosh, follow these instructions:

a. Launch Microsoft Word. Locate the **ePortfolio_documents** folder and open the file **standard_2.doc**.

b. Select all of the text in the document. Click the **Edit** menu and then click **Copy**.

c. Return to Contribute. On the Standard 2 page, place the insertion point in the **Standard_Item_Content** editable region of the page. Then click the **Edit** menu and click **Paste**.

The content of the standard_2 document appears on the draft Web page.

7. Click the **Publish** button.

8. Contribute may remind you that you have not yet created a link to this page. Click **Yes** to publish the page without linking to it.

The Publish New Page dialog box opens.

9. In the **Filename** text box, change the supplied filename to the shorter version **standard_2.htm** and then click **Publish**.

10. Using the Contribute browser, navigate to the **requirements.htm** page and enter editing mode.

The browser window transforms into the editor window.

11. Select the text **Recognition of Learning Ability and Aptitudes** and use the **Link** button and the **Drafts and Recent Pages** tab to create a link to the Standard 2 page. Then click the **Publish** button.

Your changes to the Requirements page are now available.

Creating a New Page Using Templates

You need to add a third standard page to the site. To add this page, you will use a different method, using a pre-existing template. Templates provide a structured means of controlling the look, feel, and navigation across a Web site. Templates contain the structure of the page and enable the creation of multiple pages from a single design. Contribute supports the building of Web sites using templates.

 ## Create a New Page Using a Template

1. Use the Contribute browser to navigate to the **requirements.htm** page and enter editing mode.

The browser window transforms into the editor window.

2. Select the text **Instructional Methodologies**.

3. Click the **Link** button on the editor toolbar and click the **Create New Page** option.

The Insert Link dialog box opens.

4. In the **Create New Page From** section, expand the **Templates** folder so that you see the full range of templates available in the electronic portfolio site.

5. Click the **nested_requirements_item** template.

A preview and description appear, as shown in Figure 2-3.

FIGURE 2-3
Insert Link dialog box with Create New Page and a template selected

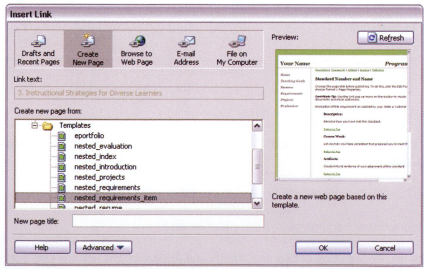

6. In the **New Page Title** text box, key **A. Hernandez - Program Portfolio - Standard 3**. Click **OK** to continue.

7. In the Name editable field at the top of the page, remove the existing text and key **Anastasia Hernandez**.

8. In the Standard_Number editable field, key **3. Instructional Methodologies**.

9. Select the placeholder text in the Standard_Item_Content editable area and delete it.

10. Add the contents of **standard_3.doc** to the Standard 3 page.

If you are using Windows, follow these instructions:

a. Click **Insert** on the menu bar and then click **Microsoft Office Document**.

b. In the Open dialog box, browse to the **ePortfolio_documents** folder, select the **standard_3.doc** Word document, and then click **Open**.

c. When the **Insert Microsoft Office Document** dialog box appears, select the option **Insert the Contents of the Document into This Page** and then click **OK**.

Learn More

USING STARTER WEB PAGES

Contribute comes with a wide range of professionally designed, built-in starter Web pages and templates. You can use any of the over 200 pages as a starting point for a Web site project. These pages offer a pre-made look and feel, and provide a complete design for a site, leaving only the content up to you. These pages are thematic, with options for many different types of sites.

To access these pages, click the **New Page** button to open the New Page dialog box. Expand the Starter Web Pages folder to see the range of sites sorted into categories—Basic Pages, Business, Community, Personal, Wedding, and more.

New Page dialog box with a list of starter Web page designs and a preview

If you are using a Macintosh, follow these instructions:

a. Launch Microsoft Word. Locate the **ePortfolio_documents** folder and open the file **standard_3.doc**.

b. Select all of the text in the document. Click the **Edit** menu and then click **Copy**.

c. Return to Contribute. On the Standard 3 page, place the insertion point in the Standard_Item_Content editable region of the page. Then click the **Edit** menu and click **Paste**.

The content of the standard_3 document appears on the draft Web page.

11. Click the **Publish** button.

12. Contribute may remind you that you have not yet created a link to this page. Click **Yes** to publish the page without linking to it. You will return and link to it later in this lesson.

The Publish New Page dialog box opens.

13. In the **Filename** text box, change the supplied filename to the shorter version **standard_3.htm**. Then click **Publish**.

Your changes to the Standard 3 page are published.

14. In the Contribute **Pages** panel, click the draft **requirements.htm** page and click the **Publish** button to make the link to the Standard 3 page live.

Publishing Pages as New Pages

Another way to create new pages is to publish a page as a new page. You can update an existing Web page and then publish it as a new page without overwriting the original page. This feature is similar to the Save As feature in other applications. As long as you do not click Publish, the original page is unchanged. The Publish as New Page feature publishes the modified page as a new page on the Web site.

You will create a fourth standard page using this method.

 ## Publish an Existing Page as a New Page

1. Use the Contribute browser to navigate to the **standard_3.htm** page and enter editing mode.

The browser window transforms into the editor window.

2. In the Standard_Number editable field, key **4. Instructional Planning**.

3. Remove the existing text for Standard 3 and replace it with the text for Standard 4 by first selecting all of the text contained in the **Standard_Item_Content** editable area and deleting it.

4. Add the contents of **standard_4.doc** to the Standard 4 page.

If you are using Windows, follow these instructions:

a. Click **Insert** on the menu bar and click **Microsoft Office Document**.

b. In the Open dialog box, browse to the **ePortfolio_documents** folder, select the **standard_4.doc** Word document, and then click **Open**.

c. When the **Insert Microsoft Office Document** dialog box appears, select the **Insert the Contents of the Document into This Page** option and then click **OK**.

If you are using a Macintosh, follow these instructions:

a. Launch Microsoft Word. Locate the **ePortfolio_documents** folder and open the file **standard_4.doc**.

b. Select all of the text in the document. Click the **Edit** menu and then click **Copy**.

c. Return to Contribute. On the **Standard 4** page, place the insertion point in the Standard_Item_Content editable region of the page. Then click the **Edit** menu and click **Paste**.

The content of the Standard 4 page appears on the draft Web page.

5. Click **File** on the menu bar, point to **Actions**, and then click **Publish as New Page**.

Contribute warns you that the new page is not linked. You will link the page later.

6. Click **Yes** in the warning box.

The Publish as New Page dialog box appears

7. In the **Page Title** text box, change the page title for the draft to **A. Hernandez – Program Portfolio – Standard 4**.

The page title appears in the title bar of the browser when a visitor views the page, not on the page itself.

8. In the **Filename** text box, change the name to **standard_4.htm**, as shown in Figure 2-4, and then click **Publish**.

FIGURE 2-4
Publish as New Page dialog box

9. Use the Contribute browser to navigate to the **requirements.htm** page and enter editing mode.

The browser window transforms into the editor window.

10. Select the text **Instructional Planning** and use the **Link** button and the **Drafts and Recent Pages** tab to create a link to the new Standard 4 page. Then click **Publish**.

Your changes to the Requirements page are now available.

Note

If you do not change the file-name, Contribute automatically changes it for you, so that you do not overwrite the existing page when you publish.

Did You Know?

If you want to save this page in another location, click *Choose Folder* beside the filename and navigate to the folder in which to save it. The current folder location appears in the Web address under the filename.

Learn More

ROLLING BACK TO A PREVIOUS VERSION OF A PAGE

Rollback to a Previous Version of a Page is a useful feature available to Contribute site users. Rollback pages are backup versions of each Web page published with Contribute. To provide an extra degree of safety in publishing, Contribute enables you to undo any page you publish and roll back to a previously published version of that Web page. If a mistake is found in a published page, users with site administrator– level permissions can undo a published page and reset it to a previous version.

Here are some important points to remember about the rollback feature:

- You can change the number of rollback versions, up to a maximum of 99 versions.
- Contribute automatically creates a folder in the site called _baks to store older versions of a page.
- The rollback feature is available only if your Contribute administrator has enabled it.

Administer Website dialog box with rollback enabled

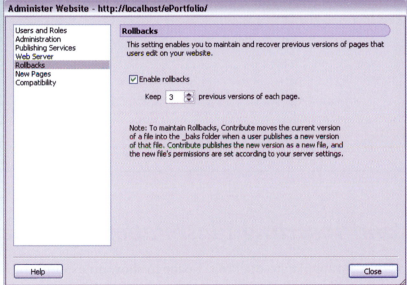

(Continued . . .)

Learn More

To access the rollback feature on a page you are working on, click **File** on the menu bar and click **Actions**. Then click **Roll Back to Previous Version**. The Roll Back Page dialog box opens. It contains a record of when the page was published and by whom. A preview pane allows you to compare changes from previous versions and to choose the version you want to roll back to.

Roll Back Page dialog box with version options and preview pane

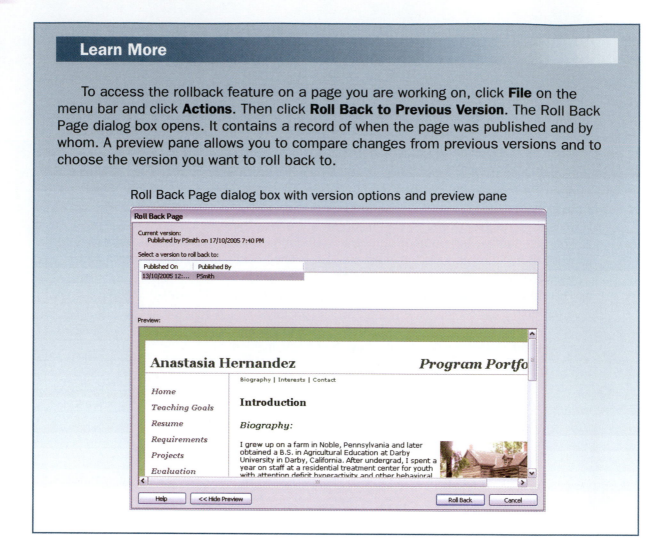

Creating and Inserting FlashPaper Documents

Y ou need to add a lesson plan to the Project page to show an example of Anastasia's work. Since this document is in Microsoft Word, you can add it to the site using many different methods, some of which were explored in the previous exercises. Another method you can employ is to convert the lesson plan to FlashPaper. By using FlashPaper, you can quickly convert a Microsoft PowerPoint, Word, or Excel document to a Macromedia Flash movie file so it can be viewed in a browser. Flash files are typically much smaller than other documents and load faster when viewed in a browser. Content in your FlashPaper documents is also better protected because the content cannot be selected and copied.

You process the lesson plan using FlashPaper and insert the document as a link in a new blank page you create.

Create and Insert a FlashPaper Document

1. Use the Contribute browser to navigate to the **projects.htm** page and enter editing mode.

The browser window transforms into the editor window.

2. In the first paragraph beneath the heading Sample Lesson Plan and Rubric, select the text **sample lesson plan**.

3. Click the **Link** button on the editor toolbar and click the **Create New Page** option.

The Insert Link dialog box opens.

4. In the **Create New Page From** section, select the **Blank Web Page** option.

5. In the **New Page Title** text box, key **Sample Lesson Plan** and click **OK.**

You now have a blank Web page.

6. Insert the sample_lesson_plan FlashPaper document into the blank Web page and publish the file.

> ### Inside the Design
>
> To maintain consistency, designers tend to prefer that contributors use pre-existing templates or pages on the site when creating new pages, except when contributors plan to link site visitors to specific files that are not part of the actual Web site. In this portfolio, the lesson plans, like the assessment rubric, are examples of work and not directly pages in the portfolio.

Windows users can convert a document to Flash directly in Contribute, and then insert it into a Web Page. If you are using a Windows machine, follow these instructions:

a. Click **Insert** on the menu bar and click **Document with FlashPaper**.

b. In the dialog box that appears, browse to and select **sample_lesson_plan.doc** in the **ePortfolio_documents** folder on your computer and then click **Open**.

The FlashPaper Options dialog box appears, as shown in Figure 2-5.

FIGURE 2-5
FlashPaper Options dialog box

c. In the FlashPaper Options dialog box, select the **Portrait** page orientation and **Standard Letter** paper size and click **OK**. Then click **Publish**.

Contribute carefully converts the document to FlashPaper and inserts it in your draft, and the Publish New Page dialog box opens.

> **Note**
>
> To delete a FlashPaper document from a draft, click the FlashPaper document to select it. Then press Delete.

d. In the **Filename** text box, change the supplied filename to include underscores; for example, key **sample_lesson_plan.htm**. Then click **Publish**.

Macintosh users must create a Flash document in another application, then use Contribute to insert it into a Web page. If you are using a Macintosh, follow these instructions to use another application to convert a document to a Flash document:

a. Browse to the **ePortfolio_documents** folder on your computer locate the **sample_lesson_plan.doc**. Open the document in the word processing application of your choice.

b. In Word, click **File** on the menu bar and click **Print**.

c. The Print dialog box appears.

For the printer name, select **FlashPaper**.

d. Click **Print**.

e. In the Save dialog box that appears, change the supplied filename, for example, key **sample_lesson_plan.swf** and save the document to your desktop.

f. In your blank Contribute draft, place the insertion point where you want the Flash document to appear, and then click **Insert** on the menu bar, point to **Flash**, and click **From My Computer**.

g. In the Open dialog box, navigate to the recently created SWF file and click **Choose**. You may choose to resize the SWF file to better fit onto the blank Web page. Then click **Publish**.

h. In the **Filename** text box, change the supplied filename to include underscores; for example, key **sample_lesson_plan.htm**. Then click **Publish**

Your changes to the FlashPaper document page are published.

7. In the Contribute Pages panel, click the draft **projects.htm** page. Then click the **Publish** button to make the link to the Sample Lesson Plan FlashPaper page live.

Learn More

CREATING FLASHPAPER DOCUMENTS

When you install Contribute on a Windows machine, FlashPaper is automatically installed. FlashPaper lets you create portable Flash documents from any type of printable document.

A FlashPaper document retains the look and feel of the original source document

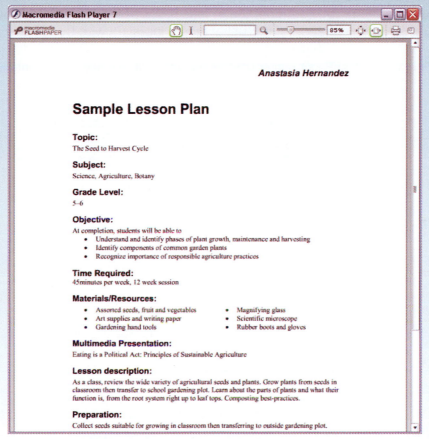

(Continued . . .)

Learn More

The benefits of using FlashPaper documents are many. Flash files are typically much smaller than other documents and can be viewed in any browser that supports Flash. These Flash files can be viewed across different platforms while maintaining the original look and feel of the source documents. FlashPaper documents can be printed but cannot be copied, which allows Web content contributors to protect their original content while allowing site visitors to benefit from the information.

Windows users can produce FlashPaper documents from within any Microsoft Office document or directly from Contribute. Macintosh users can create Flash documents by using the FlashPaper Printer utility that is installed with Contribute.

The FlashPaper printer utility is automatically installed with Contribute

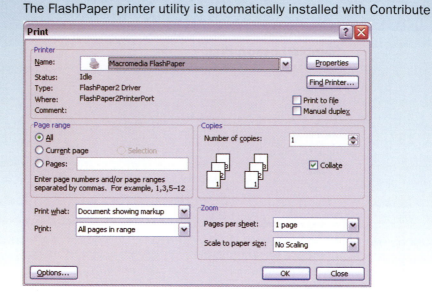

REVIEWING CONTENT

OBJECTIVES

Upon completion of this lesson, you will be able to:

■ Send a page for review.

■ Track sent drafts.

Estimated Time: 30 minutes

Introduction

Collaboration is an important aspect of Web site development, whether it involves having multiple people update content or having someone review your work. In the portfolio site, documents that are being developed could benefit from review. Contribute 3 enables contributors to send drafts to others for review and feedback. Reviewers who have Contribute can use it to provide feedback directly on the page, and users without Contribute can provide feedback via e-mail.

In this lesson, you send pages in the portfolio to be reviewed, and you track the drafts created for these pages.

Sending a Page for Review

Feedback is an important tool for improving a portfolio. Often, you may want to get a page reviewed before it is published. Contribute allows you to send drafts for review to other Contribute users, as well as to nonusers.

Sending drafts to other people in your organization is a good way to ensure that mistakes in a Web site are not missed. You send the Evaluation page for review.

 Send a Page for Review by E-Mail

1. Use the Contribute browser to navigate to the **evaluation.htm** page and enter editing mode.

   The browser window transforms into the editor window.

2. Under the Recognition heading, change the text **Secretary-Treasurer** to **President**.

3. Click the **Send for Review** button on the editor toolbar.

4. Contribute copies the draft to a temporary folder on the Web site and notifies you that a temporary copy of the draft has been placed in a temporary folder. Click **OK** to accept this notice.

Contribute creates an e-mail message with a link to a temporary location, using your default e-mail application, such as Microsoft Outlook or Eudora, as shown in Figure 3-1.

FIGURE 3-1
Send for Review e-mail request

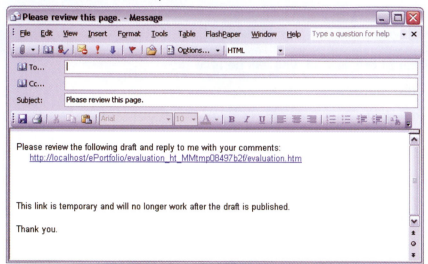

5. Address the e-mail message to your reviewer and send the e-mail.

Contribute puts a message at the top of the open draft reminding you that you have sent the draft for review, as shown in Figure 3-2. You can work with other drafts until you receive feedback from the reviewer. After you receive feedback, you can incorporate necessary changes and then publish the draft, send it to another user for review, or cancel the draft.

Note

If Contribute does not find a default e-mail application or cannot start your e-mail application, you can create the e-mail message by clicking the Click Here link in the message area under the toolbar. Copy the link for the draft and paste the link in an e-mail message to send to reviewers.

FIGURE 3-2
Editor toolbar with an e-mailed review reminder

When you cancel or publish the draft, Contribute removes the temporary copy that it placed on the Web server.

Tracking Drafts

The Draft Console helps you keep track of drafts that you are editing, drafts you are reviewing, and drafts that were previously sent.

Because Anastasia is using her electronic portfolio to show a progression of skills and abilities over time, she must occasionally have her faculty supervisor review her site.

Track Drafts Using the Draft Console

1. To see the **Draft Console**, click the **View** button on the menu bar and click **Draft Console**.

2. Since the Evaluation page has been sent for review, it is available in the **Drafts I'm Editing** space. To review the draft you are editing, click the **A. Hernandez – Program Portfolio – Evaluation** link.

The draft version of the Evaluation page appears.

3. To review the posted version of this page, click the link in the reminder message on the editor toolbar.

Contribute opens a browser window using your default browser application, such as Microsoft Internet Explorer or Netscape. The browser window shows the temporary file that you previously posted, as shown in Figure 3-3.

FIGURE 3-3
Contribute opens your default browser to display the temporary page

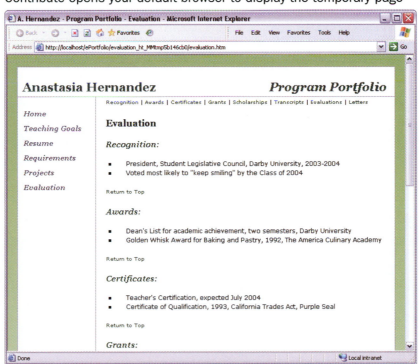

SUMMARY

You have successfully made edits and published your changes to the Anastasia Hernandez electronic portfolio Web site.

In this project, you continued learning to use Contribute to modify Web sites without having to know HTML. You gained advanced skills and knowledge needed to connect to a site, add links to pages, create new pages and insert content, and review and publish pages in your site.

ON YOUR OWN – ELECTRONIC PORTFOLIO

ACTIVITY 1: CREATE NEW PAGE FROM TEMPLATE AND SEND FOR REVIEW

You have learned how to create a new page from a template while at the same time linking to it. You also learned how to send a document for review to get it approved before you publish it. Apply the same techniques to add a final standards page to Anastasia Hernandez's electronic portfolio and send this new page for review.

To review techniques for creating a new page from a template, see Lesson 2. To review how to send a draft for review, see Lesson 3.

1. Browse to the **requirements.htm** page of the electronic portfolio Web site and switch to editing mode.

2. Select the text for the **Standard 5** page and use the Link button to create a new page.

3. Use the **nested_requirements_item** template to provide the structure for the new Standard 5 page.

FIGURE 1
Select the nested_requirements_item in the New Page dialog box

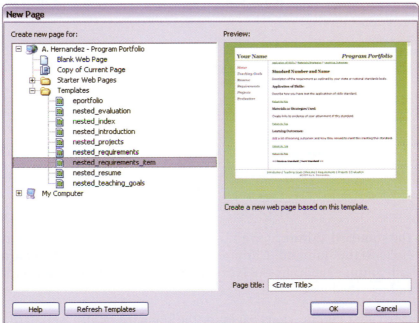

4. Change the following content areas:
   A. New Page Title: **A. Hernandez - Program Portfolio - Standard 5**
   B. Name placeholder text: **Anastasia Hernandez**
   C. Standard number placeholder text: **5. Use of Technology**
   D. Standard_Item_Content editable field: Insert the **standard_5.doc** content from the **ePortfolio_documents** folder included in the Data files.

5. Click the **Publish** button. In the Publish New Page dialog box, rename the file **standard_5.htm**.

6. Select the newly published page **standard_5.htm** and send it for review using an e-mail link to the page.

ACTIVITY 2: ADD LINKS TO PAGES WITHIN A SITE

You have learned how to create different types of hyperlinks, including how to create links to a page on your site.

Use the linking techniques to connect all of the standards pages within the electronic portfolio Web site.

To review techniques for adding links to a page on your site, see Lesson 1.

1. Browse to the **standard_1.htm** page of the electronic portfolio Web site and enter editing mode.

2. Scroll to the bottom of the page. In the **previous_next_page** editable field, select **<< Previous Standard** | and delete it.

3. Select the **Next Standard** text and use the **Link** button, as shown in Figure 2, to locate and select the **standard_2.htm** page. Publish the page when it is complete. Test the link in the Contribute browser.

FIGURE 2
Click the Link button and click Drafts and Recent Pages to link to the next page

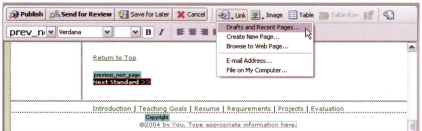

4. Navigate to the **standard_2.htm** page and switch to editing mode. At the bottom of the page, create links to the **standard_1.htm** page using the **<< Previous Standard** text link, and to the **Standard_3.htm** page using the **Next Standard >>** text link. Publish the page when it is complete and test the links.

5. Repeat linking to next and previous pages for the **standard_3.htm**, **standard_4.htm**, and **standard_5.htm** pages. Remember to delete | **Next Standard >>** on the final, **standard_5.htm**, page. Publish each page as it is completed. Test all the new links in the Contribute browser.

ACTIVITY 3: ADD ANCHOR LINKS TO PAGES

You created new content in the Standard pages by adding the contents of Microsoft Word documents. The pages, however, are fairly long and require anchors from the headings at the top of the page to each section on the page. Add section anchors to the headings within each of the Standard pages of the electronic portfolio Web site.

To review techniques for adding section anchor links to a page on your site, see Lesson 1.

1. Browse to the **standard_1.htm** page of the electronic portfolio Web site and enter editing mode.

2. Place the insertion point before the heading Application of Skills, click **Insert** on the menu bar, and then click **Section Anchor**. In the text box, key **application**, as shown in Figure 3.

FIGURE 3
Section Anchor dialog box with name added

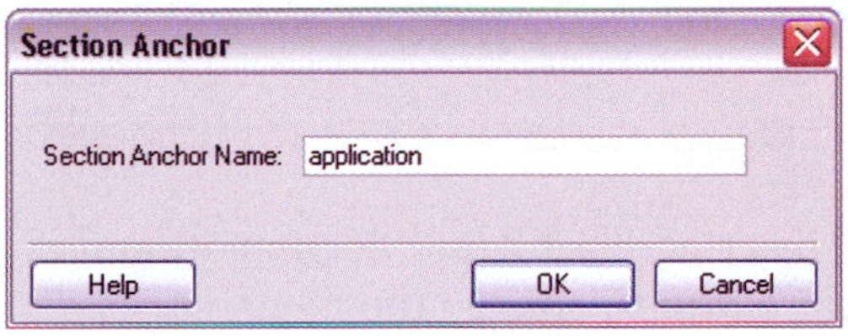

3. Place the insertion point before the heading Materials and Stategies Used, click **Insert** on the menu bar, and then click **Section Anchor**. In the text box, key **matstrat**.

4. Place the insertion point before the heading Learning Outcomes, click **Insert** on the menu bar, and then click **Section Anchor**. In the text box, key **learning**.

5. Publish the page. Test the links in the Contribute browser.

6. Repeat adding section anchors to the **standard_2.htm, standard_3.htm, standard_4.htm,** and **standard_5.htm** pages. Publish each page as it is completed. Test all new anchor links in the Contribute browser.

ACTIVITY 4: CREATE AND INSERT A FLASHPAPER DOCUMENT

You have learned how to create and insert a FlashPaper document into a Web page. Apply the same techniques to process and publish a letter of recommendation for Anastasia Hernandez to the Evaluation page on the electronic portfolio site.

To review techniques for creating and inserting a FlashPaper document, see Lesson 2.

1. Browse to the **evaluation.htm** page of the electronic portfolio Web site and switch to editing mode.

2. Scroll to the bottom of the page and select the text **Anna Williamson** under the Letters of Recommendation heading. Use the **Link** button to create a new page.

3. Create the new page by using **Blank Web Page**. Provide a page title in the **New Page Title** text box by keying **A. Hernandez - Program Portfolio - Letter of Recommendation**.

4. Insert a FlashPaper document into the blank Web page by processing the **letter_of_ recommendation_1.doc** content from the **ePortfolio_documents** folder included in the data files. Figure 4 shows FlashPaper options for inserting documents into a Web page.

FIGURE 4
The FlashPaper Options dialog box

5. Publish the page with the inserted FlashPaper document, and in the **Filename** text box, key **letter_of_recommendation_1.htm** to change the filename.

6. In the **Pages** panel, select the draft **evaluation.htm** page and then publish this page.

GLOSSARY

A

Absolute path Path that provides the complete URL of a linked document, including the protocol. You must use an absolute path to link to a document on another server. You should not use absolute paths for local links.

ActionScript In Macromedia Flash, a scripting language used to control the Timeline, buttons, movie clips, or other content within a Flash document. ActionScript is also used by those with programming expertise to create sophisticated Web applications.

B

Behaviors Prewritten JavaScript codes used to add interactivity to Web pages, enabling users to change or control the information they see. A behavior combines a user event (for example, moving the pointer over a graphic button) with an action or series of actions that take place as result of that event.

Bitmap Bitmap graphics are composed of dots, called pixels, arranged in a grid. When you modify a bitmap, you modify each dot and how it displays. The display of pixels varies with screen resolution.

Button An object that performs some action when you click it.

C

Cascading Style Sheets Cascading Style Sheets, or CSS, are a collection of formatting rules that control the appearance of content in a web page.

Cloning In Fireworks, the process of painting a copy of some area of a bitmap object onto another area of the bitmap object.

Components In Macromedia Flash, prebuilt objects that you can use in your own Flash documents. Most components are user interface elements such as buttons, menus, and so on. Some

are not meant to be seen on the Stage and are used instead to perform data-handling functions.

Connection Key Contribute lets you share website connections by embedding information in an encrypted connection key file. The connection key file uses the filename extension .stc. Double-clicking the file launches Contribute and imports the website connection information.

D

Declaration The part of a CSS rule that tells what the rule does. It consists of a property and a value for that property. A collection of declarations is called a *declaration block*.

Design Document A document that encompasses the goals, purpose, audience, technical, and accessibility requirements for the overall graphic, Web site, or rich media element.

Document-relative path, Document-relative referencing Path that identifies a Web file by omitting the part of the absolute URL that is the same for both the current document and the linked document, providing only the portion of the path that differs. This is the best choice for most local links.

Draft Console Contribute automatically saves a copy of a draft when you switch to the browser, switch to another draft, publish the draft, or exit Contribute. The Draft Console keeps track of current drafts, sent drafts, and drafts to review.

F

Fill Color applied to a closed path or text.

FlashPaper Lets you create portable documents from any type of printable document. FlashPaper files are typically much smaller than other document types. FlashPaper files can be viewed in any browser that supports Flash, or directly in Flash Player.

Flash Player A program that needs to be installed on a computer to view a Flash movie.

Frames Individual cells that make up the Timeline in Flash.

G

Gamma setting Setting on a computer that affects the apparent brightness and contrast of the monitor display.

Gradient fill A region of several colors or shades that gradually blend into each other.

H

Hotspot Area associated with a URL that when clicked, triggers an action.

Hypertext link Creates a connection from one page to another page. In a Web page, links are typically underlined and differentiated by color from the surrounding text. Links may also be created to email addresses, other file types like Microsoft Word, or to specific places within a Web page.

I

Instance In Flash, an instance is a copy of a symbol or graphic object that has been added to the Stage or workspace. The original symbol or graphic remains unchanged in the document library.

Interlacing A method of defining the way an image is displayed in a Web browser; it displays every other pixel on every other line and then goes back and repeats the process, filling in areas not already displayed.

K

Kerning Refers to the amount of space between letters.

Keyframe In Macromedia Flash, you use keyframes to mark a change in what appears on the Timeline.

L

Layers In a Macromedia Flash document, you use layers to help organize the artwork, animation, and other elements in your document.

Leading Refers to the amount of space between lines of text.

Library In Macromedia Flash and Fireworks, the library stores symbols created in these programs. In Flash, the library also stores imported files such as video clips, sound clips, bitmaps, and imported vector artwork.

Live Filters In Fireworks, Live Filters are enhancements (such as drop shadows or blurs) you can apply to vector, bitmap, and text objects.

M

Mask In Fireworks and in Macromedia Flash, it is a window to something underneath. You can think of the mask as a mat within a picture frame: only the area inside the mat is visible. In Flash, a mask layer is used to create a mask.

Morphing In Macromedia Flash, the process of changing one object into another. This can be done in Flash by using shape tweening.

Motion tweening The process used in Macromedia Flash to automatically fill in the frames between keyframes in an animation that changes the properties of an object such as the position, size, or color.

Movie A Flash document which has been exported in the SWF format.

N

Named anchor A link, normally created in a document that is long or has many sections, that jumps the user to a specific place in the document.

Navigation bar A group of buttons that provide links to different areas of a Web site.

Nested grouping Combination of groups of objects that have already been grouped. Groups and nested groups can be manipulated as a single unit.

O

Optimizing The process of converting images to the proper format and making sure they are as small as possible, resulting in faster downloads.

P

Paths In Fireworks, the lines you draw to form basic shapes.

Pixels Colored picture elements that are grouped to form a bitmap graphic.

Playhead An indicator specifying which frame is playing in the Timeline of a Flash movie.

Projector A standalone executable version of a Macromedia Flash movie.

R

Raster images Also called bitmaps, these graphics are created with pixels. When you create a raster image, you map out the placement and color of each pixel, and the resulting bitmap is what you see on the screen.

Rollback A rollback lets you revert to a previous version of a Web page published with Contribute. You do not have to roll back to the last published version; you can select any version that is saved as a rollback file.

Rollover An image that changes when the user moves the pointer over the image.

S

Scenes Smaller, more manageable segments in a Macromedia Flash movie.

Selector The part of a CSS rule that identifies the formatted element. A tag selector is one that uses an HTML tag to identify the formatted element. A class selector is used for rules that can be applied to a variety of document elements.

Shape tweening In Macromedia Flash, the process of animating between two different shapes.

Site flowchart Visual representation of a Web site and all its linked pages.

Site-root-relative path, Site-root-relative referencing The path from the site's root folder to a linked document. Useful for large Web sites that use several servers.

Slicing Dividing graphics into separate sections in order to keep the file size of images as small as possible.

Spacer image Used to control the spacing in a Web page layout but is not visible in the browser window.

Stage In Macromedia Flash, the area where the artwork you build is visible in the browser or movie.

Storyboard A collection of frames or panels encompassing an entire animation, Web site pages, or movie.

Stroke Refers to the width, color, and style of lines, as well as the lines that border the shapes you create.

Symbol In Macromedia Flash, a graphic, button, or movie clip that you create once and can reuse throughout a document.

T

Templates Provide a structured means of controlling the look, feel, and navigation across a Web site. Templates define which areas of a page can be edited, and which areas are locked.

Timeline In Macromedia Flash, the Timeline includes the elements used to organize and control the contents of a movie over time, by specifying when each object appears on the Stage.

Tweening A method by which Macromedia Flash automatically creates "in-between" frames to complete an animation.

U

URL (uniform resource locator) A link containing information about where a file is located on the Web.

V

Vector graphics Graphics created with lines and curves and descriptions of their properties. Commands within the vector graphic tell your computer how to display the lines and shapes, what colors to use, how wide to make the lines, and so on.

W

Workspace In Macromedia Flash, the space outside the Stage that is not visible in the browser or movie.

INDEX